ORGANIZING & ORGANIZATIONS

FOURTH EDITION

STEPHEN FINEMAN, YIANNIS GABRIEL & DAVID SIMS

Los Angeles | London | New Delhi
Singapore | Washington DC

First edition published 1993
Second edition published 2000
Third edition published 2005, reprinted 2006, 2007
This edition published 2010
Reprinted 2012

SAGE Publications Ltd
1 Oliver's Yard
55 City Road
London EC1Y 1SP

SAGE Publications Inc.
2455 Teller Road
Thousand Oaks, California 91320

SAGE Publications India Pvt Ltd
B 1/I 1 Mohan Cooperative Industrial Area
Mathura Road
New Delhi 110 044

SAGE Publications Asia-Pacific Pte Ltd
3 Church Street
#10-04 Samsung Hub
Singapore 049483

Library of Congress Control Number: 2009924357

British Library Cataloguing in Publication data

A catalogue record for this book is available from the British
Library

ISBN 978-1-84860-085-0
ISBN 978-1-84860-086-7 (pbk)

Typeset by C&M Digitals (P) Ltd, Chennai, India
Printed and bound in Great Britain by CPI Group (UK) Ltd, Croydon, CR0 4YY
Printed on paper from sustainable resources

MIX
Paper from
responsible sources
FSC
www.fsc.org   FSC® C013604

CONTENTS

1 Introduction: Organization and Organizing   1

Where we argue that organizing is a set of social activities through which we
try to make our lives more predictable, effective and stress-free. Yet, organizing is
itself far from an orderly process, usually involving conflicts and compromises with
others and a constant attempt to make sense of what is going on around us.

2 Entering and Leaving   13

Where we explore the realities of joining an organization, becoming socialized and
eventually moving on. Entering and leaving highlight the important role of
organizational rituals. They also concern the politics of managing personal and organizational appearances, especially in recruitment and selection. Often the 'brochure'
picture of an organization is a very partial, if not misleading, one.

3 Lifelong Learning   28

Where we look at different kinds of knowledge and different learning styles, including
narrative learning, learning from stories and exeriences. We look at what stops people
from learning, and the way that communities of practice may enhance the learning
for their members. We talk about learning that seems to reside in the organization,
and about learning which goes beyond the intellectual level; we also consider the
possibilities of learning unhelpful lessons and of finding that some organizations may
not allow you to learn in order to maintain existing power relations.

4 Motives and Motivating   49

Where we examine why the idea of motivation has become so popular in
organizations and whose interests it serves. We refer to some traditional
psychologicial theories of motivation at work, but argue that searching for a motive
is full of pitfalls; often many possible motives are at play. But more than that, the
language or discourse of 'motivation' often owes more to cultural and social factors
than to the existence of 'deep' psychological needs.

Where we examine the formal, bureaucratic rules of organizations and ask whether these are rational or not. Rules are part of the political process aimed at controlling what people do and how. Yet, the interpretation and enforcement of rules is itself part of the political processes of organizations whereby rules may be bent, ignored or violated.

Where we look at what physical buildings do for the process of organizing and what they tell us about the organizations they house. We argue that an organization's physical environment is far-reaching and that changes in this environment can generate resistance, both political and emotional.

Where we ask why we seem to know so little that is definite about leadership, despite many years of work on it. We look at some of the different ways in which leadership has been studied, and then at some of the different roles acted out in leadership relations.

Where we reveal politics as core to the very essence of organizational life. Political behaviour stems from inevitable differences in outlook, in resources, in personalities, in interests, in power and in organizational position or role. Some politics can be benign in effect, others beneficial or creative, and still others conflictual or destructive.

Where we explore what constitutes power and influence in organizations; where power is used or abused, constructive or disruptive. Power is closely linked to politics. It is not only about how high one is in the organizational pyramid, but concerns the networks fostered, the rarity of one's knowledge or skills, and the crafting of appearances and language.

Where we look closely at groups, teams and teamwork in organizations. We try to establish the conditions under which groups can add value to organizations generating synergies and unleashing creativity and examine why groups lapse into dysfunctional behaviour.

for family life. We also address how today's fragmented careers may make it difficult for people to develop a coherent story of either their working or their family life.

23   Learning and Organizing in Uncertain Times

Where we consider how the learning with this book can be taken forward. We argue that life in and out of organizations is too complex, calling for lifelong learning rather than rigid theories and formulas. Success, both at the individual and organizational levels, comes to those who are not prisoners of their earlier achievements, but those who can engage the situations facing them with flexibility and practical acumen. We give a range of specific suggestions on how to take this subject further.

CREDITS

PREFACE TO THE CURRENT EDITION

This fourth edition of *Organizing & Organizations* follows firmly in the footsteps of its predecessors. It retains an informal style, grounded in illustrations from actual organizational events and experiences. The chapters continue to eschew many of the neat, but artificial, divisions to be found in more traditional organizational behaviour textbooks, reflecting our conviction that organizational life rarely follows such tidy segmentalization. Typically, an amalgam of different concepts and frameworks need to be brought to bear if we are to make sense of the oddities, crises and regularities of organizational life.

We are mindful, however, that the student of organizations needs guidance, so we have added still further study aids to this revision. Each chapter is now enlivened with pictorial illustrations and concludes with a summary of key theoretical strands, review questions and downloadable readings. We have not deserted the Thesaurus – a mine of up-to-date information at the end of this book. And should you wish quickly to find a traditional organization behaviour topic, we have expanded the matrix at the start of the book to help you locate it.

All chapters in this edition have been updated, but we have added two new ones: 'Influence and Power', and 'Innovation and Change,' reflecting the ascendance of these issues over recent years.

Stephen Fineman, Yiannis Gabriel and David Sims, 2009

HOW TO USE THIS BOOK

Readers familiar with conventional textbooks on organizations will find this book rather different in structure. Instead of the usual sequence of analytic levels – the individual, the group and the organization – all three are embedded in each chapter, befitting the topics discussed. So we invite you to move from section to section as your fancy takes you – but please read the introduction, Chapter 1, first. If you do not find what you are looking for there, go to the index.

Each chapter offers you a guideline on how to go into further depth on a subject if you wish. The latter is achieved via the user-friendly information at the end of each chapter. This is in four parts:

1. **Key points** — a brief listing of the major points or arguments in the chapter
2. **Theoretical signposts** which identify the key theoretical strands that inform the chapter's contents
3. **Review questions** to test and apply your understanding of the ideas in the chapter
4. **Reading on** — downloadable articles from especially pertinent journals, all obtainable from the companion website to this book: www.sagepub.co.uk/fineman.

The Matrix

To help you quickly identify where a popular organizational topic is located (e.g. change, leadership, communication), we have, apart from the contents and index pages, included a matrix on pages xiii–xv. This shows you, at a glance, the most appropriate chapters to turn to if you want to track down a traditionally popular topic in organizational behaviour.

The Thesaurus

Throughout the book, you will notice highlighted words in the text. These provide a short-cut route to more detailed knowledge as you go along – via the Thesaurus at the end of the book. The Thesaurus covers much of the material you will find in other textbooks.

For example, should you wish to know more about **rituals**, **empowerment** or **emotions**, terms highlighted in a number of chapters, turn to the alphabetically ordered Thesaurus where you will find a cogent summary of each and some key academic references (which are cited in full in the book's bibliography).

The Thesaurus, the Matrix and the end-of-chapter information will, together, help you thoroughly explore significant phenomena of organizing – their meanings, their real-time experiences, conceptual foundations and applications. Alongside the illustrations and stories in the book, these resources should help you in your essay writing and exam revision. We hope you enjoy this multi-layered approach to our subject.

The Companion Website

Be sure to visit the book's companion website at http://www.sagepub.co.uk/fineman for a range of teaching and learning material for both lecturers and students, including full texts of key journal articles, comprehensive study skills guides, and personal tips from the authors on using the book as a teaching resource.

WHERE TO FIND A POPULAR ORGANIZATIONAL TOPIC

WHERE TO FIND A POPULAR ORGANIZATIONAL TOPIC

Popular Topic	Chapter
Ethics	Ch. 12: The moral foundations of businesses and how they are shaped and challenged by personal agendas and politics.
	Ch. 13: Protecting the planet as an ethical concern. Organizations that proclaim their social responsibilities and organizations that evade or suppress them.
	Ch. 17: The ethics of 'using' sex at work; the ambiguities and oppressions of sexual harassment and sexual politics.
Gender	Ch. 11: How gendered language, stereotypes and prejudices divide people at work. The effects on individuals and organizations.
	Ch. 17: The way notions of femininity and masculinity infuse organizational cultures and workplace practices.
Group	Ch. 10: The history and evolution of groups in the workplace. Intra- and inter-group dynamics.
Innovation	Ch. 15: Innovation as a process, often linked to entrepreneurship. Innovation is hard to plan and fickle in realization. Why some innovations fail while others succeed. Fashion and innovation.
Leadership	Ch. 7: Contrasting conceptualizations of leadership and leading. The importance of followership and the deployment of power.
	Ch. 9: How different forms of power underpin a leader's influence. How such power is used.
Learning	Ch. 2: Learning about an organization from a job applicant's perspective and as a regular employee.
	Ch. 3: Different forms of knowledge. Learning styles and developing skills. The politics of learning.
	Ch. 5: Learning the overt and tacit rules of the organization.
	Ch. 23: Active learning; ways of learning about organizing and organizations in changing times.
Motivation	Ch. 4: Motivation – a cultural resource or personal need? Critique of motivation theories. Attempts to 'manage' motivation at work.
Organizational Structure	Ch. 5: The role of a bureaucratic structure; its functions and dysfunctions.
	Ch. 20: The increasing flexibility of organizational structures. Invisible structures on which advancement and promotion depend.

WHERE TO FIND A POPULAR ORGANIZATIONAL TOPIC

Popular Topic	Chapter
Perception (Social)	Ch. 4: Perceptions of fairness and of others' intentions and trustworthiness. Ch. 1: Shaping perceptions through marketing and image making.
Personality	Ch. 1: Measuring personality; pitfalls and politics.
Power and Politics	Ch. 8: The 'games' played in organizations; their sources, rewards and social costs. Ch. 9: Bases of power; links between knowledge, power and politics. Sources of powerlessness.
Technology	Ch. 14: The effects of technologies on the meaning and feeling of work. Machines as sources of liberation or powerlessness and enslavement.

1

INTRODUCTION: ORGANIZATION AND ORGANIZING

What is an organization? Everyone knows: universities, airlines, chemical plants, supermarkets, government departments. These are all organizations. Some have been around for a long time, employing numerous people across many continents – Microsoft, Shell, McDonald's, Toyota. Others are smaller, locally based – a school, a family-owned restaurant, a small consulting firm, a pottery.

Organizations enter our lives in different ways: we **work** for them, we consume their products, we see buildings which house their offices, we read about them in the newspapers and absorb their advertisements. When we look at organizations, especially the larger, older, famous ones, they seem solid, they seem permanent, they seem orderly. This is, after all, why we call them organizations. Images of organizations as solid, permanent, orderly entities run through many textbooks. But, in our view, these books tell only half the story. They obscure the other half: the life and activity that buzzes behind the apparent order. Sometimes this bursts into view, revealing chaos even – such as when computer systems break down, when there is delay or accident on an airline, when products are sent to the wrong destinations or when bookings are made for the wrong dates. They also obscure the immense human efforts and energies that go into keeping organizations more or less orderly.

In this book, our focus is not on 'organization' but 'organizing' – the activities and processes of doing things in organizations. We do not take organization for granted; after all, many large and well-known organizations have faded or died for one reason or another. Instead, we focus on the *processes* of organizing and being organized. We highlight the *activities* which go on in organizations. We look at our **emotions**, the **stories** and gossip which we trade, the deals we strike, the games we play and the **moral** dilemmas we face when in organizations.

Organizations get likened to many things – machines, armies, garbage cans, theatrical plays, the human body, and so on. We find the analogy of a river helpful. Like a river, an organization may appear static and calm if viewed on a map or from a helicopter. But this says little about those who are actually on or in the moving river, whether swimming, drowning or safely ensconced in boats. Our aim in this book is to highlight the experiences of those people who actually know and understand the river well, to present their stories and learn from their adventures. We are hoping that the images of organization which we generate have more in common with the moving, changing, living river than with the tidy lines of a map.

WHAT DO YOU KNOW ALREADY ABOUT ORGANIZING?

You probably know far more than you think. If you have been formally employed, you have already peeped behind the organizational screen; felt what it is like to be told what to do or to tell others what to do; to do boring or exciting work; to sink into mundane routine or cope with unexpected crises and problems; to interact with a wide range of people; to daydream; to see inefficiency around you; to try and meet deadlines; to feel **stress**; to experience elation and excitement; to see how differently different managers do their work; to give and receive help from others … If you have not had a job, you have been part of organizing in project groups at school, sports meetings, family holidays, Christmas dinners, pub crawls, cinema outings with friends, trips to clubs and so forth. You do not have to have had a **leadership role** in these to be part of organizing, and already to know, through experience, what seems to operate successfully and what seems to fail. Trust these experiences; they are very important. Use them actively as you read this book; build on them with the concepts, stories and studies that we relate to you.

ORGANIZING – KEEPING THINGS IN ORDER

In this book, organizing is treated as a continuous set of activities. We all have different perceptions of, and tolerances for, disorder – revealed classically in the contrast between a teenager's view of a 'tidy' bedroom and that of his/her parents. In work settings, 'getting organized' means different things to different people. Some people seem to operate effectively for years in offices with papers and files strewn all over the place, using their memory as a diary. When challenged about the apparent chaos, they will usually retort that it is fine for them, as long as no one else moves things around.

But not all of us find organizing easy or agreeable. This is how Bill, a manager, described his 'typical day':

Real-Life Example

REAL-LIFE EXAMPLE

Getting organized is something that I don't find easy. I have in front of me a book called *Get Yourself Organized* offered by a friend, who was perhaps trying to give me a hint. It looks appealing; it looks sensible. It is written in clear type, with a bold 'key message' printed on every other page:

- Decide on your major priorities.
- Put a timescale and deadline on each priority.
- If you can do it today, do it!
- Who do you need to contact to make things happen?

- Interruptions – avoid them!
- At the end of the day, leave your desk clear.

Well, I kept a diary of some of the things that happened to me the other day. Here are some snippets:

It's 7.30 in the morning and I'm driving to work, the loose ends of yesterday still in my head. I've got a 9.30 meeting with the strategy committee and I'm not looking forward to it. I need to get my ideas straight on how we market the new truck, or I know John will screw me and get the cash for his new project … Mobile rings. It's my secretary, Alice – have I remembered the lunch meeting with Dr Hosikkii from our Japanese subsidiary? I'd totally forgotten about it.

At my desk and a screen full of emails. I'll answer the important-looking ones first. Bill phones; he urgently wants to see me before the 9.30 meeting … He comes in, looks awful. He tells me he needs a few days off because his son's very ill. Of course, he must go home, but how am I going to manage with him away?

I'm ten minutes late for the meeting; I feel embarrassed and the Chief Executive looks disapproving … It's a tense meeting but I seem to have at least one ally – Jean from Sales. I can trust her, but it's Alan from Production who I can't figure out. Sometimes he's with me, sometimes he's really obstructive. I must take him out for a drink and have a bit of a chat…

The meeting breaks up and I take the opportunity to walk back with the Chief Executive. I explain my lateness and manage to get him to hear my plans for shifting the staff around in my section and the problem of overload. At least he didn't say a new appointment was out of the question…

Back to my office and Alice looks tense. The main computer is down and we need the financial forecasts for the annual report. I phone Helen in Accounts – she's helped me in the past. Meanwhile a call-waiting from Germany on the spec for the new truck. They need to go to press on it this week. I'm really angry with the agency who were supposed to coordinate this. I phone them and lay it on the line. They cost us a small fortune; I'm going to have to look around for a new agency…

A good lunch with Hosikkii; I realize now that I'm going to have to visit him in Tokyo much sooner than I thought. It's an exhausting journey and I can't stay away more than three days. I'm away from my kids yet again…

2.15 pm. The Chief Executive calls me – I've won! Great! Not only will I get what I wanted for marketing the truck, but I can also hire a new assistant. Sometimes I love this job … I tell Alice to pass the news around. I dash over to Mark's office and congratulate him. He persuaded me in the first place to increase our bid.

I stop at Brenda's desk in the big, open-plan office. 'I know you want something from me', she says, 'that's the only reason you ever visit me'. 'How can you say that!', I reply, sounding offended. She's right, of course. I ask her if she has any advance news on the customer survey we conducted last month. She feigns ignorance, and then slips me a computer print-out from her draw. 'I need this back today, please; it's red hot.'

I find a quiet corner to hide and read the report. Wow! Two of our products have done disastrously. We are going to need a completely revised PR plan. Is that why the Chief Executive's been so accommodating? More work for me?

Alice bleeps me. Says I need to call Eric. I call right away. Never keep your Director waiting. He wants me to stand in for him at an executive meeting tomorrow because 'something's come up'. I dutifully agree; I bet it's the customer survey stuff. But it also means cancelling the appraisal interview I'm doing on Marcus. He'll get even more stressed now. I'll get Alice to make my excuses.

Two more meetings. The first is terminally tedious: a presentation from a consultant on a computer information system. He couldn't sell me a washing machine. Fortunately, I'm interrupted, with a query over the copy on our new trade brochures – are we being sexist? The second was an hour with a research student from a university who was looking at marketing in the automotives sector. She actually had some thought-provoking questions; it's a shame I couldn't give her more time. And it was hardly quality time – my phone rang four times, each time with someone wanting an instant decision or opinion.

4.00 pm already. Grab a coffee. Meet Jane at the machine. Had I heard that Martin was leaving? No, I hadn't. It's rumoured that he's got a plum job in Wales with one of our competitors. 'More re-organization for us', I quipped. The rest of the afternoon I found I couldn't get Martin's leaving out of my head. Maybe that's just what I should do…

It's 6.15 pm and things, at last, have quietened down. I'll see what's left of the emails and what new messages there are. Oh yes, I must get the agenda for tomorrow's executive meeting, otherwise I'll look a prat. 'Alice, are you still there …?'

AT THE END OF THE DAY, LEAVE YOUR DESK CLEAR, says the book.

They must be joking!

Organizing, in this account, involves tensions, preferences, interruptions, politics, power and personalities. Maybe Bill could have been a better organizer, but his account chimes with what we know about the experienced realities of managing. It is often a whirl of activity; quick switches from one issue to another; gossip and speculation; people dependent on each other; bargaining and compromise; developing contacts and friends; reconciling work pressures with domestic demands; time is always precious. The picture of the cool, **rational** thinker, quietly planning the day, is a myth.

FRONT STAGE, BACK STAGE

The process of organizing defies tidy, universal, categories. As consumers (customers, students, passengers and so on), we take for granted that things will get done. Lectures, meetings, examinations, happen. Individual and group effort come together to create the hard product – the car, mobile phone, DVD player, pen, paper; or the service – delivering a meal, cutting hair, preaching a sermon, policing a city, running a train. We hardly bother with the organizing processes behind these events. The struggles, **politics**, negotiations, anguish and joys of actual organizing remain, for the most part, invisible to the consumer: they are back stage. When they are inadvertently revealed, showing how precarious organization can be, it can come as something of a shock – as the following tale from of one us reveals:

REAL-LIFE EXAMPLE

Once I was booking tickets for a family holiday at a local, family-run, travel agent. They were busy, and I queued for a long time. Eventually, I was served by an elderly gentleman who was having difficulty matching the glossy brochure packages with the figures on his computer screen. He got very confused – neither the dates nor the prices seemed to match the published details. The queues behind me were growing ever longer. The staff were getting hopelessly overloaded and stressed. The tension was growing, but, like good British customers, no one in the queue complained. The breaking point came with a loud, sharp, whisper from a younger, female, member of staff to the man who was serving me:

'For Christ's sake, give it up, Dad! He only wants a flight reservation; it's not worth our trouble.'

The man turned on her immediately and retorted, through clenched teeth:

'How dare you! A customer is a customer; that's what we're here for!'

He then proceeded to tell me that 'they only tolerated him in the shop at weekends now' and they had their 'differences of opinion'.

Some of the entrails of the organization had suddenly been revealed. I had seen something I should not have seen, and I was uncomfortable. I did not want to witness a row or receive a confession – I wanted a family holiday! I now mistrusted the service. I could not play my customer role properly if they did not play out their role as 'travel agents'.

I decided to go elsewhere.

ORGANIZING AS A MEANING-CREATING PROCESS

When we get close to the experience of people organizing, there is the impression of a lot of personal and interpersonal work going on. In the above exchange, the protagonists were not just observing or responding to each other's actions; they were also making judgements and creating meanings for themselves.

Seen through the eyes of different individuals, what happened may have seemed very different. Each may have told a different story about what 'really' happened. For example:

- the elderly gentleman's story: 'customers were happy to queue for personal, caring service'
- his daughter's: 'customers were in a hurry, dear old dad all at sea'
- the story-teller's: 'customer pressure reveals cracks in the organization'
- other customers': 'incompetent travel agents'; 'rude young people'; 'poorly organized office'.

The *meaning* of the incident is not obvious. Even the meaning of particular words or sentences may be ambiguous. 'It's not worth our trouble' could be interpreted as a personal insult, or as an expression of frustration with dad – or with customers in general.

'A customer is a customer' could be taken as a brave assertion of good old-fashioned service. But in this case, what about all the customers waiting? Does their inconvenience count for nothing? Alternatively, it may have been a dig at the way young people conducted business, just for the money. We are continuously creating meanings for ourselves; a better understanding of organizing can help improve our understanding of others' meanings.

While most of us in organizations seem to be 'doing a job', listening to someone talking, tapping keyboards, talking into telephones or soldering electronic components, we are also making and exchanging meanings – a fundamental human/social process. Organizing, as we are presenting it in this book, is intimately concerned with the way that people create meaning for themselves, with others, during their working lives. As we interact with others at work, we bring our personal histories and our past experiences with us – finding common ground, compromising, disagreeing, **negotiating**, coercing. This is a vibrant, mobile process, often full of tensions, frustrations and possibilities.

Some portraits of organizations present a bleak picture: the isolation of the individual, lost in an impersonal **bureaucracy**. Some employment is indeed experienced in this way. But this is only part of the picture. People at work also create their own **realities**, an ever-rich **symbolic** life providing a sense of who we are and where we belong. Among other things, this involves swapping rumours, stories, gossip, **jokes** and laughter. We pick up and contribute to the chat about the organization's heroes, villains and fools. In this way, 'the organization' takes on a special, personal meaning. The organization may then be seen as a caring employer, an impersonal machine, a nest of vipers, a pressure cooker, a castle under siege or any of many different symbolic entities.

ORGANIZING AS A SOCIAL PROCESS

For much of the time, organizing is a social as well as a personal process, involving groups working together – part of the raw material of meaning-making. This is well illustrated when organizing something from scratch. Imagine yourself as a newly appointed area manager in the sales department of a large publishing organization. You and your four fellow area heads, Sunil, Barbara, Robyn and Nick (each representing different geographical regions) have had some informal discussions and one of the ideas that you came up with was to reward the top performers in the department with a range of awards. You feel that this will provide a boost for morale and enhance the motivation of the salespeople; you want to give it a try before maybe turning it into an annual event. This has been a good year for sales. There is some money in the system and you are confident that your budget can absorb a lively ceremony.

You and your fellow area heads decide to hold a meeting to discuss the ceremony. A host of initial questions arise: what exactly do you want to organize? What is the real purpose of the function? What kind of function is it going to be: 'Serious'? 'Light-hearted'? A mixture of both? What exactly is the budget? What are the possible dates and venues for the event? What events may compete or clash with yours? How are you going to decide whom to award? What awards are you going to offer? It is beginning to look rather complicated – so it is comforting to know that there are others there to help out.

Yet early discussion with your fellow area heads seems to make things worse – more disorganized. They each seem to have different ideas, opinions and interests. Robyn and Nick seem very concerned about the budget – in the past, they have been accused of wasting money on social events when the organization could ill-afford them. They argue for a modest ceremony on company premises, modest catering (tea and biscuits) and modest awards (music tokens and the like). Sunil, on the other hand, wants 'more style' – an expensive hotel, lavish entertainment, an after-dinner speaker and big prizes: weekend breaks in posh hotels, expensive pieces of electronic gadgetry. He always likes doing things with a flourish and his budget is certainly larger than any of the others. You and Barbara appear to occupy the middle ground. During the discussions, the stress level rises and sometimes the five of you seem to be speaking different languages – and getting quite angry with each other. And this is just about organizing an award ceremony! It is impossible to move forward without making some compromises – and you feel you have made lots. The meeting ends up without a decision.

For a week or so, nothing happens and you are beginning to suspect that the awards ceremony will be yet another good idea that came to nothing. Then, quite by chance, Linda, a management student from the local university, arrives to start a six-month internship in your section. You had quite forgotten about her. Linda seems a very competent and assertive person, she has masses of energy and her laughter is infectious. The idea dawns on you that maybe she is the person who could run the event. This gives you enough impetus to call another meeting of the area heads, re-opening discussion on the awards' ceremony – they seem interested, especially when you offer to 'resource' the planning and organizing of the event with a dynamic new member of your staff.

The second meeting is far more effective. Things are starting to shift. The five area heads are now listening more to each other – maybe they feel that they have already invested enough in the idea of the awards ceremony not to let it stall again; besides, the young intern seems full of energy and ideas which inspire confidence and trust. While few firm decisions are made, a tentative budget is agreed and many positions on many issues draw closer – the venue, the number of awards, the size of the prizes and so on. In the next few days, Linda sets up an email discussion list for the area heads called 'Prize Ideas' which generates some good thoughts – as well as some outrageous ones!

Over the next few weeks, a plan of action was agreed and things started to fall into place. As Linda assumes more and more responsibility for the event, you are happy to delegate decisions to her. She seems to have an eye for detail, keeps meticulous records of decisions and has a knack of anticipating difficulties before they emerge. She is certainly an excellent planner. At crucial moments in the process, she will ask for advice or guidance, and you occasionally consult with your fellow area heads. You have each decided to award the top three performers in your areas and have used a rather rough measure – the size of sales – to decide whom to award. This seems to be fair and equitable. It is Linda, however, who points out that the top performer of one area has generated less revenue than some lesser performers from other areas. After prolonged discussions, all five area managers decide to stick with the original plan, but not to announce publicly during the ceremony the size of each prize-winner's sales. A big difficulty emerges on who should receive the top prize – this becomes a major bone of contention and threatens to derail the entire plan. Each area manager can think of very good reasons why his or her top performer should win the overall prize. Many strange and fanciful ideas are proposed on how to break the deadlock. Eventually, a compromise is reached: there will be no overall winner this year. Instead, each area will have a gold, a silver and a bronze prize winner.

As the key day approaches, up pop the snags. The grand plan has to be re-negotiated several times – usually when someone fails to deliver on what they promised or the group has neglected an important item. Linda continues to be excellent – gently nagging, independent and persuading. Some people in the office (not you) find her too bossy, too controlling; they get sulky or irritated. But they hang in there nevertheless as the time pressures are enormous and the whole group now wants the event to succeed. **Communication** and coordination are essential – which are often easier said than done.

ORGANIZING AND IMPROVISING

Things, it seems, rarely go entirely according to plan; even the best laid plans occasionally come to grief. On the day of the event, you face near calamity: the food and wine for the reception fail to be delivered at the agreed time; there is a bus strike in the city; and your after-dinner speaker, a local literary celebrity, informs you by text message that she is stranded by fog at Milan airport and will be unable to attend. Rapidly, you, your fellow area managers and the excellent Linda start making urgent contingency plans. Some of them are a waste of time – the food and wine arrive, if a little late. At the last minute, Linda resolves the after-dinner problem. Her favourite uncle, it turns out, is none other than the former CEO of the country's largest chemical company, someone well-known as the television presenter of a popular programme in which he grills the directors of large multinationals. Sir Eric will be delighted to be the guest of honour at the awards, even if his name does not feature on the official programme.

What have you learned? Successful organizing may depend on a sound plan but **planning** alone is no guarantee of success. Planning ahead provides a needed sense of security and direction, but a rigidly planned event can fail because it does not allow people sufficient opportunity to improvise when things are not working out. When crisis strikes, the group responsible for the organizing may fall apart. Those who had expressed reservations about the plan may say: 'we told you so, you insisted on doing things your way, now you sort out this mess.' Being able to work effectively as a team, thinking on your feet, maintaining your cool and the goodwill of those involved under pressure, are all important in ensuring the success of your project.

There are, of course, individual differences here. Some people are quite happy improvising and managing crises. They can live with uncertainty and chaos, placing their faith in 'muddling through'. They believe that 'it will be alright on the night', and they are frequently proven right – to the intense annoyance of others. These others seek to **control** uncertainty. They are serious, methodical people; they like order, planning, routine and do not generally like 'fooling around'. They mistrust improvisation, chance and spontaneity, but what they really abhor is unpredictability.

SUCCESS OR FAILURE?

Some of the causes of **success** and failure in organizing are common, no matter what the specific organizing at hand seeks to achieve. Placing excessive reliance on a machine, an animal, a person or the weather, on anything over which you have limited control may undermine your plan. Poor **communication**, inadequate budgets, irreconcilable differences, personality clashes, unanticipated events and low motivation can frustrate any organizing.

However, even if things run smoothly, it does not make an event a success. In fact, success and failure are themselves **meanings** which we attribute to events, meanings which we usually develop as we **talk**, **joke** and **gossip** with others. Imagine if, a few days after the awards ceremony which you organized and which everyone enjoyed, you come under criticism from the head of your sales department for 'misspending the department's money on extravagant functions, like that farce of a drunken party organized recently'. Imagine too if rumours start to reach you of salespeople who grumble about the awards, claiming that they all went to the 'yes men' in the department, those same ones with the cosy routes and easy sales.

You may be surprised at such a development. Instead of receiving thanks for organizing what seemed a much enjoyed event, you come in for criticism. This may be one of the best lessons that the example teaches us: just when we think that we are free to organize others, we may ourselves be part of someone else's organizing activities. Your event may have been a success in terms of your objectives and values, but a resounding failure in terms of theirs – and they have the power to make their judgement stick.

Under such circumstances, it may be helpful to present to the departmental head some arguments and evidence, showing that most of those participating in the function found the event not just enjoyable but also extremely useful, that morale has soared since the event and that sales have taken off. This type of evaluation and assessment is itself an important aspect of organizing. Would you do things differently, if you were organizing the same function all over again? Are there any short cuts that you have learned? Might you have opted for a different event? Would you like to work with the same people again?

Some major events are organized on a one-off basis, as in the example above. A military campaign, the staging of the Olympic Games, a business take-over, a wedding – such events seem to call for their own unique organization. Most events, however, are not organized like this. They are part of ongoing processes of organizing. Admitting a new class of undergraduates to a degree, preparing a company's accounts, taking in new stock, recruiting new staff, purchasing new equipment, and many other activities, are like painting the Golden Gate bridge in San Francisco: by the time you have finished, it is time to start all over again. The awards ceremony may itself become an annual event – with new experience, the earlier mistakes are avoided, the difficulties are ironed out and the ceremony becomes a ritual about which people grumble, gossip and joke, but which they ultimately respect and value.

ORGANIZING AND MANAGING

Most organizations designate certain types of employees as managers. This is an important part of their **identity**, something that differentiates them from mere foremen, supervisors, clerks or workers. Yet, the example suggests that managing is not something that only designated managers do. Everyone involved in a collective project is involved in managing – managing budgets, managing information, managing timetables and so forth. Managing his boss's diary can be a consuming activity for a personal assistant, someone *not* designated as a manager. The personal assistant may also have to manage his boss's moods, his public appearances and even his family crises.

IN CONCLUSION

We have argued for a shift from the notion of organization to organizing. Organizing is to be seen as a social, meaning-making process where order and disorder are in constant tension with one another, and where unpredictability is shaped and 'managed'. The raw materials of organizing – people, their beliefs, **actions** and shared **meanings** – are in constant motion, like the waters of a river. And, like a river, they look quite different depending on how close you are to it. In the chapters that follow, we attempt to communicate the feel of this flow; to portray something of the richness, variety and surprise of life in organizations.

KEY POINTS

o Unlike other textbooks that start with organizations as 'facts' and then examine what goes on 'inside them', this textbook starts with organizing as a set of actions, before moving on to examine organizations.

o Unlike many other areas of study, students already know a great deal about organizing and organizations from their personal experiences as employees, consumers or observers; hence, this book invites you to build on this experience as the basis of your learning.

o Organizing seeks to maintain order in order to make our lives more predictable, efficient and stress-free; however, organizing is not always 'orderly', involving tensions, preferences, interruptions, politics, deals and personalities.

o Organizing is a social process, involving interactions of different people with different interests, priorities and needs.

o Sense-making is crucial for organizing; any kind of organizing requires that participants make sense of the task facing them, of their needs and priorities, and of each other's words and actions.

o Organizing involves strong emotions, both positive and negative, generated by the task as well as by the relations between those who collaborate; these include hope, frustration, anxiety, excitement, satisfaction and disappointment.

o Organizing frequently encounters unexpected situations and events; plans are rarely implemented in every detail; hence, improvising, taking action which has not been planned, frequently must come to the aid of organizing.

o Management is not something done by people designated as 'managers', but is distributed and shared among all those involved in organizing a collective project.

>>>>>>>>>> THEORETICAL SIGNPOSTS >>>>>>>>>>>

The major themes in this chapter lie in the areas of learning, organizing and sense-making. How do we learn to organize? How do we learn to act effectively in organizations? How do we learn to be successful managers? These are questions that have generated much scholarship and will be addressed in several of the chapters of this book where you will find references to relevant literature. The importance of sense-making as a dimension to all organizing was demonstrated by Weick (1979), while Fineman (2006b) has explored the emotions of organizing. Czarniawska (1999) is one of many theorists who have highlighted the importance of language for all organizing, while Gabriel (2008b) has provided a systematic account of 240 keywords that help us organize our thinking and our actions.

REVIEW QUESTIONS

1. Reflect on the organizing that you undertook before joining the academic programme that you are currently engaged in. What organizing was necessary before you could join the course? Who helped you? What technology helped you in your organizing? Were there any times when you had to rely on improvising?

2. What exactly is meant by 'sense-making'? How do you make sense of the following events:

   (a) your manager offers promotion to one of your junior colleagues, who will become senior to you

   (b) your employer announces a merger with one of your organization's main competitors

   (c) your academic performance has taken a sudden change for the worse; having become accustomed to getting high marks, you now find yourself consistently earning middle and low marks.

companion
website
ww.sagepub.co.uk/fineman

Reading On

The articles below are available for free to readers of the fourth edition of *Organizing & Organizations* via the book's companion website at www.sagepub.co.uk/fineman

Currie, G. and Brown, A.D. (2003) 'A narratological approach to understanding processes of organizing in a UK hospital', *Human Relations*, 56 (5): 563–86.
This article outlines a narratological approach to understanding how middle managers and senior managers in an NHS hospital made sense of the introduction of a series of interventions led by senior managers, illustrating the role of individual and group narratives in processes of collective sensemaking.

Gherardi, S. (1999) 'Learning as problem-driven or learning in the face of mystery?', *Organizational Studies*, 20 (1): 101–23.
This paper explores, from the perspective of the sociology of knowledge, the implicit assumptions underlying the Organizational Learning literature, and looks for alternative ways of conceptualizing learning-working-innovating as non-distinct activities. The term

'learning-in-organizing' is proposed as a replacement for 'organizational learning', so that it's distributed and provisional nature can be considered when interpreted as a practical accomplishment.

Hatch, M.J. (1999) 'Exploring the empty spaces of organizing: How improvisational jazz helps redescribe organizational structure', *Organizational Studies*, 20 (1): 75–100.
This paper uses jazz as a metaphoric vehicle for redescribing the concept of organizational structure in ways that fit within the emerging vocabulary of organization studies. It begins with a description of some basic elements of jazz performance – soloing, comping, trading fours, listening and responding, groove and feel – and builds on these to redescribe organizational structure as ambiguous, emotional and temporal.

Vince, R. (2002) 'Organizing reflection', *Management Learning*, 33 (1): 63–78.
This article considers what is involved in the practice of reflection for organizational learning and change, with emphasis on reflection as an organizing process rather than on the individual, 'reflective practitioner'. The author describes a way of 'organizing reflection' that can create and sustain opportunities for organizational learning, exploring some of the literature on reflection and describing four reflective practices. Collectively, these four reflective practices constitute an approach to reflection that represents one way of organizing for learning and change.

2

ENTERING AND LEAVING

This chapter explores the realties of joining a new organization, becoming socialized and part of the culture, and then exiting or moving on. Each of these interlinked areas highlights specific organizational processes and procedures – such as recruitment, selection, redundancy programmes, downsizing and retirement. But, also, in their different ways, each is shaped and experienced through individual and organizational politics, values and emotions. How do we learn to survive or thrive in an organization? When does this work well and when does it fail?

Joining a new organization is usually a memorable experience, because of its mix of emotions – apprehension, excitement, tension, confusion. Each new encounter, each new person introduced, adds to the impression of what the place is like. It is the first of many steps through which we become part of something called 'the organization'. But while we gradually fuse with the organization, we also help make it what it is – we confirm and reproduce its culture and, maybe, change it.

Our initial experiences set some of the psychological and physical boundaries to the place that we call **work**. We cautiously experiment with what we say or do. What is the reaction? Is it acceptable? We are learning our way around, finding where we fit in. In social science terminology, we are seeking clues to the culture, **norms** and **values** of the community we are entering. None of this appears in the organization's recruitment literature. There may be a hint of things to come from rumours and stories about the organization. Mostly, however, we have to find out as we go along.

Leaving the organization changes the scene. It may occur smoothly and comfortably at the statutory end of a working lifetime. Traditionally, this has been celebrated in eulogies and the presentation of gifts, often for long, loyal service. But this picture is becoming rarer. Fewer organizations nowadays have permanent employees, signed up for a lifetime **career**. There is a flow of short and medium-term appointments, a coming and going. Entering and leaving can often be a fairly anonymous affair, neither particularly celebrated nor mourned. Aaron, an engineering manager, makes the point:

You know, in this place it's hard to keep track of who's joining and who's away. People are moving around all the time. I'm now on my third assistant in 18 months! I keep getting emails from my boss about who's arriving and who's going – would I like to sign a farewell card? Often I haven't a clue who they are! Working in project teams doesn't help. When the project ends, people move on – sometimes here, sometimes to another company, sometimes unemployed. It's a peculiar atmosphere, but I take it for granted now.

While Aaron has accepted the rapid changes, those seeking stability and security at work can feel unsettled by the shifting patterns. The temporariness, the faces that come and go, reduce feelings of belonging and commitment to the organization – 'I obviously have to look after myself here; I'm on my own'.

Retrenchment and downsizing sharpen the picture. Layoffs and redundancies are commonplace in our times of boom and bust. They mark a pragmatic approach by companies: when times are tough, people will lose their jobs; they are costly 'extras'. They may also be victims of a **management** fashion to create a 'leaner', 'fitter', or 're-engineered' organization. But redundancy, for whatever reason, is typically a harsh way of separating a person from an organization and can leave psychological – as well as organizational – scars. Like most separations or drastic changes, it quickly exposes the raw elements of the relationship between the individual and the organization.

GETTING IN – FIRST IMPRESSIONS

Why Join Shell?

The top five reasons to join us:

- We're committed to securing a responsible future.
- We offer huge diversity.
- We're at the forefront of technology.
- We offer great training and development.
- We're truly global.

Shell lets you choose. What you do and where your career goes depends entirely on how curious you are. There are no limitations. Shell invests in its people and recognises them as its most valuable asset. (Amir)

The Shell emblem is reproduced with permission of Shell Brands International AG.

I have great opportunities to make a difference by influencing the content of policies that are being developed for all Shell businesses in the UK and across the EPE businesses. I love working in an environment where I have real responsibilities, where I continue to be challenged and where I can add real value to the development of others – that's what's important to me. (Joanne)

Glossy brochures and company websites, like Shell's, contain enticing descriptions of corporate life.[1] They are skilled exercises in public relations, designed to extol the benefits and delights of joining the organization. Collectors of recruitment brochures will detect common images. They suggest, for example:

- multi-ethnicity
- advancement
- training
- internationalization
- equal opportunities
- serious work
- the latest technologies
- excitement.

In these ways, the organization parades its best costume, carefully tailored to influence the newcomer. The business of self-presentation has begun, exposing the surface symbols of the organization's **culture**. Shell includes a statement of corporate values that suggests care for the environment and contribution to community development. McDonald's vision is to 'put people at the centre of everything we do – and that goes for our employees as much as our customers'. And the British Army promises that 'Army life is always full of challenges and no two days will ever be the same'.

The formal apparatus of the organization has swung into action – and there is more to come. Wooing new, desirable-looking, employees means presenting an attractive organizational image. Blemishes are heavily camouflaged or simply left out of the picture. It is assumed, not unreasonably, that when people have to make a difficult decision on what job to choose, relatively unambiguous information is helpful. Given that the organization wants your skills, they gain little by revealing that, actually, there are controversies over its environmental record, that its employment practices are sometimes exploitative, that very few black people or women get to the top, that you might be bullied, that international travel is reserved for senior managers, that the computer system is in desperate need of renewal, or that the training budget has just been substantially cut. Moreover, it is likely that many potential applicants will want to believe the organization is glamorous, socially responsible, international, aggressive, or whatever, because that represents some ideal image they hold of themselves. They are therefore content to collude in the **myth** of the exemplary organization – especially if jobs are in short supply. The business of selection has begun; both parties – candidate and organization – are exchanging the **impressions** they want to present to one another.

Typically, interested job candidates will groom themselves for the part. 'Respectable' suits and shirts – 'power dressing' – replace casual wear for males and females alike.

Men's Interview Attire

- Suit (solid color – navy or dark grey)
- Long-sleeved shirt (white or coordinated with the suit)
- Belt
- Tie
- Dark socks, conservative leather shoes
- Little or no jewellery
- Neat, professional hairstyle
- Limited aftershave
- Neatly trimmed nails
- Portfolio or briefcase

Women's Interview Attire

- Suit (navy, black or dark grey)
- The suit skirt should be long enough so you can sit down comfortably
- Coordinated blouse
- Conservative shoes
- Limited jewelry (no dangling earrings or arms full of bracelets)
- No jewellery is better than cheap jewellery
- Professional hairstyle
- Neutral-coloured tights
- Light make-up and perfume
- Neatly manicured and clean nails
- Portfolio or briefcase

Figure 2.1 How to dress for an interview?

There are recruitment consultants keen to advise on such matters, such as About.com. Figure 2.1 shows some of their suggestions.

To deviate too far from expected, conservative dress risks being stereotyped, labelled as 'unreliable', 'radical', or 'will not fit in'. First appearances are notoriously poor guides to character; nevertheless, we use them all the time in our interpersonal judgements. Street-wise job applicants know this, and learn to adjust their résumés to the requirements of the job – accentuating some features and playing down others. They also research the organization in advance to demonstrate the seriousness of their intent to an interviewer. Some will have topped off their armoury of **skills** with special training on being an effective interviewee, to create the right impression or **perception** (countered, ironically, by interviewers trained to see beneath a feigned presentation).

CONVINCING PERFORMANCES

The initial coming together of company and candidate involves careful make-up and posturing. At first sight, this may appear irritatingly trivial: 'what's it got to do with the real me, and the actual job?' But the way we present ourselves to others, through a rich array of social protocols – language, dress, gestures, rhetoric – constitutes an essential part of social reality. From an early age, we learn certain social conventions through which we can interact – with a fair amount of shared meaning. There is much

Figure 2.2   The vagaries of impression management.

Source: www.cartoonstock.com

'impression management'. We are constantly managing how we come over to others, wanting to look 'right' in their eyes.

At certain points in time, getting our **performance**, appearance or act right – doing what is socially correct within extant conventions – is vitally important. This holds as much for a first romantic date as a selection **interview**. The moment is all. If we fail in our judgement or act, we risk rejection. This sometimes means a strange 'double take', of the sort: 'I need to give that person interviewing me a strong impression of my strengths and enthusiasm for the job. But I'm sure she knows I'm doing that, so will she believe what I say?' If we extend this analysis, it is possible to view life as a stream of public performances, a dramaturgy, accompanied by private, in-the-head, commentaries.

Selection

The time and effort a company wishes to devote to selecting its employees can vary enormously. A selection decision may be made on the basis of a letter or web-based application and a short interview. In the now global recruitment market, the face-to-face interview can be dispensed with in favour of a virtual interview via video conference, web cam, or the services of a recruitment consultant to screen candidates.

Many large companies subject candidates for managerial and professional jobs to a sequence of interviews, **psychological tests**, group discussions and exercises. Assessors will record their observations and candidates will be judged against a set of previously agreed criteria of competence. This is the questionable arena of selection. Questionable, because there are many studies which reveal that devices such as selection interviews and **personality** tests have variable reliability and predictability. Judging people's competence in areas such as leadership, interpersonal relationships, working under pressure and so forth is notoriously difficult, not least because, as suggested earlier, a candidate's performance in a selection procedure can reveal as much, if not more, about that procedure as the candidate's actual work behaviour. But an elaborate selection process offers the apparent reassurance that a poor decision will be unlikely and it will be possible to control entry to the organization. It is also a **ritual** through which difficult decisions can be made to appear possible. With tools that promise objectivity, selector and candidate alike can feel that a thorough and fair job is being done.

Sometimes the **ritual** of selection can border on the absurd or reckless when some of the common methods are omitted, or treated too casually. In 2003, for example, officials at Buckingham Palace, the London residence of the British monarch, failed to do a basic web search which could instantly have revealed details about a particular applicant for a footman's job. They also failed to follow up a brief telephone conversation they had had with the applicant's referee. The man, nevertheless, got the job. He happened to be an investigative journalist for a major newspaper. He was given access to some of the most sensitive areas of the Palace in a time of very high concern about security and terrorism. Moreover, the Palace was supposedly ringed by foolproof security. Events such as these show selection in a different light: how it is done provides a clue to how the organization appears to care for its staff and how professional it is in some of its judgements and procedures.

Politics and Cultures

Yet the elegance, or professionalism, of a selection procedure does not insulate it from political influences. **Politics** focuses attention on the personal interests and idiosyncrasies of the selectors and their power to make their own particular judgements prevail. They also demonstrate that we often need to turn our attention to *informal* mechanisms in the organization for a more complete understanding of what is happening.

An associate of ours failed to win a top appointment with a London-based publishing company. She was one of two shortlisted candidates and she had attended four separate interviews, the last one being with a panel of directors in the company. To all outward intents and purpose, the job should have been hers. She had a fine reputation in her field – she outshone the other candidate in her qualifications and experience. Furthermore, the night before the final interview, she heard, from an 'inside source', that the job was hers. So what went wrong?

It was hard to find out – details of the proceedings were secret, as they often are. But the insider, now much embarrassed, was determined to uncover the reason. It transpired that, in the final interview, our colleague had mentioned that if she were offered the job, she would have to commute to work for a time. Her family were well settled in their home town out of London where her children went to school. She would consider setting up a second home if necessary, but first she would like to take the commuting route. The point was well taken, with apparent sympathy, during the interview. Her honesty, however, proved to be a tactical error. After the interview, the Managing Director, who was chairing the selection panel, declared firmly that this was not his idea of commitment or loyalty to the job; it was not what he would do if he were in the applicant's position. He would not permit the appointment of someone who did not move to the job right away. **Prejudices** and dubious practices meld in the informal practices that underpin some selection decisions.

Job applicants who dutifully respond to advertised vacancies can unwittingly fall foul of invisible political structures. Personal contacts and friendship networks bring some people, but not others, to the special attention of employers. In close communities, informal channels (rumour, casual chat) can keep many available jobs filled – especially in times when work is scarce. It is not unknown for an applicant to be processed right through a selection procedure, ignorant of the fact that the job has already been offered to someone else – secretly. Sometimes, when various people are involved in an appointment (such as a specially convened interview panel), not all of them know that there is already a favoured candidate – something that is revealed in the discussions and **political** squabbles following the interview.

This is a clear example of 'homosocial reproduction', rather inelegant shorthand for the phenomenon of hiring people who are similar to influential people already in place. Put another way, people feel less **anxious** about working with others who are like them, so they will consciously or unconsciously veer toward people who seem, on first impressions, like them in social values and **attitudes**. This is the psychological explanation for the 'old school tie' phenomenon – feeling warmer towards people who share one's own educational background, especially a specific school or university. It also accounts for why certain, 'strong', organizational cultures perpetuate themselves: that 'Shell', 'Disney', 'Hewlett Packard' or 'Marks and Spencer' way.

A strong **organizational culture**, where everyone shares a common vision and purpose (often influenced by a charismatic chief executive), can be a recipe for corporate success. It is an idea that gained prominence in the 1970s to account for the considerable success of Japanese organizations. Japanese organizations and Japanese society, it was argued, foster values of cooperation, loyalty, innovation, flexibility and sheer hard work, which account for their success. Above all, Japanese companies have strong cultures, which bond their members into highly cohesive and effective teams (although under fairly paternalistic management). In sharp contrast to many Western companies, they are part of a bigger 'us'. People are inspired to great feats of productivity, seeing themselves as heroes. A British, an American and a Japanese car worker, runs the story, were asked by a researcher what they do: 'I'm fitting hub-caps' says the British worker; 'I'm making profits for Henry Ford', says the American; 'I'm a member of a team who make the best cars in the world', says the Japanese worker.

The Japanese success story has faded in recent years, as have many of the Western corporations that have followed their lead. This is because strong cultures have been found to work well in stable social and economic times, but when they need to respond to rapid economic or social **changes**, to transform themselves to survive, they are often slow and ponderous. Indeed, it almost spelled the demise of an inward-looking Marks and Spencer in the 1990s. The company had failed to acknowledge and respond to radically changing consumer tastes.

SETTLING IN AND SOCIALIZATION

The period of settling in can be a confusing time. The cultural messages from the recruitment literature and selection process do not always match the actualities of being in the organization. The first hint about organizational *sub-cultures* begin to emerge – the sales department is cynical about the production unit; both despair about the poor service from the human resources department; no one speaks to quality control.

Sub-culture is an important concept in that it describes the special understandings, bondings, shared backgrounds and beliefs of particular groups within an organization. They are *sub*-cultures because they exist beneath the wider organizational culture. While the *overall* culture of an organization may be shared by everyone, significant sub-cultures will bind, say, just all women within the organization, all the older staff, all the black employees or all the smokers who meet outside the building for a cigarette break. These people may feel that, irrespective of rank or department, they are emotionally bonded through their particular common experience, background or heritage. Different departments may develop their own sub-cultures and end up seeing other departments as 'them'.

Some of these organizational sub-cultures may challenge the **values** promoted by management. For example, one of our students worked for a large accounting firm, the product of a recent merger. The merged company produced an attractive brochure extolling its 'core values' – the fundamental beliefs which supposedly underpinned its whole way of working: 'excellence, dedication, team work, decisiveness and integrity'. But these values, according to our student, carried little credibility with the staff. In her own words:

> The merger had produced a company in which people refer to themselves as ex-A or ex-B; different paperwork and different procedures are still in operation. As far as decisiveness is concerned, after nine months of negotiation, no decision has been made by the two rival camps about which computer system should be used. As for integrity, who can forget that the man who masterminded the merger, and who now stands behind the 'values campaign', had told the financial world that there would be no merger, just three months before the event?

In these instances, we can talk of the emergence of 'counter cultures', which define themselves through their opposition to the dominant value system – or at least to the values of those who dominate. Newcomers are exposed to such cultural nuances, sometimes in surprising ways. For example:

> Christine started working at a branch of an elite jewellers which was based in the duty-free area of Manchester airport in the UK. 'I had a short training in which the company's main values were drummed into me. Customer service – doing anything to please the customer and effect a sale. It didn't take me long to realize that this was not how the employees saw it. I was surprised to see that the unspoken rule among employees was to be as difficult and unpleasant to the customers as possible. If a customer was in a hurry to catch a plane, staff would prolong the procedure to the point where the customer was red with impatience. If a customer appeared not very well off and asked for a price, staff would say: "this is outside your price range, Sir." In fact, I soon realized that there was a kind of league table – the more unpleasant and difficult you were to the customers, the more you rose up the scale.'
>
> Hassan discovered he had made a mistake and mentioned it to his boss. 'Listen', retorted the boss, '**you** haven't made a mistake. The system has. Whenever something is wrong, you must come and tell me the accounts system has screwed up. Then we can look at the problem and try to improve the system. The system will lose prestige, whereas you'll have gained recognition because you spotted the error. You see, this company likes winners'.

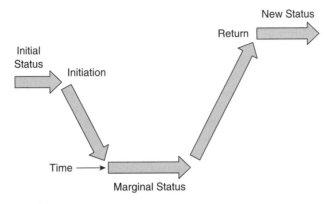

Figure 2.3   Rite of passage

These events are **rites of passage**, ways by which established organizational members initiate and socialize new people into the actual working customs of the organization. Rites of passage appear in all communities and have long fascinated anthropologists. They are key processes or events that affirm or deny a worker full status amongst their colleagues. Figure 2.3 tracks the way one's status shifts during a rite of passage, from entering the initiation process to successful accomplishment.

Rites of passage can sometimes be gentle and full of light but pointed humour. At other times, they can be harsh, even humiliating. Indeed, groups as diverse as military personnel, prisoners, chefs, the police and fire-fighters will use degradation as a way of socializing the newcomer. Others are mixed in their methods. For instance, wait-resses can confront some **stressful** challenges in order to 'make the grade' with their colleagues:

> I remember my cousin who was hazed [initiated] in a job. It was her first night as a cocktail waitress in a bar. Her manager and colleagues told her, about 20 minutes into the job (so she was already set up for stress), that a key part of her job was count-ing how many straws and napkins she was distributing to customers that evening. It was a Friday night in a college town bar. You can imagine how crazy the place got. Well, needless to say, she lost count, and things got dicey. Some convincing drama by the manager and colleagues reduced her to tears by 2:30 am. Then she was let in on the joke. All night, her colleagues had been observing her frantic efforts to comply with the napkin/straw inventorying, and it must have given them all that warm fuzzy sense of re-commitment to the team. But I can tell you it bonded her instantly to the organization and she got a lot of mileage out of the story over the years.[2]

Rites of passage are part of the unwritten socialization procedures of organizational life; they are not to be found neatly listed in a job description. They are akin to a second selection system, but are every bit as important as the first one. Surviving them connects the individual to the work group, an emotional bonding that is crucial for group cohe-sion and is at the core of an organization's sub-culture. Rites of passage reveal them-selves most clearly and consistently in strong-culture companies. For example, some present new employees with a series of specific hurdles to jump – surviving punishing working hours; performing very basic work to remind them of their humble status in the face of all they will have to learn; complete immersion in one part of the company's core business until they have full mastery of it; sacrificing domestic and leisure time for the company. McDonald's, the pervasive hamburger chain, is meticulous in ceremonially rewarding its staff with badges and certificates as they move from one hurdle to the next. In this way, one's progress is visibly delayed until one conforms to the company's expectations. Such is the potency of this form of conditioning that it can take a remarkably short time for people to fall into line. They soon speak the corporate language and perform according to the rules: socialization is complete. This often involves a change in self-identity where our self gets fused, to a lesser or greater extent, with those with whom we now feel we belong. The tell-tale signs of this are when people start making statements about what 'we' are doing at work; 'our' latest project; the way government fails to understand 'our' way of working and so forth. 'I' is not used; it has become part of a greater whole.

... AND LEAVING

Some people leave organizations quietly, unnoticed. This can be because it is the way they want it: they are uncomfortable about public attention on themselves. Alternatively, they may be part of a floating population of temporary workers who have no deep, or sustained, attachment to the organization. As we have mentioned, such impermanence is becoming much more prevalent in today's organizations. For longer-term employees, however, the farewell party is perhaps the most common organizational ritual, an exit rite of passage. There are the complimentary farewell speeches tinged with nostalgia and humour and the presentation of a gift. A mix of alcohol and bonhomie helps transcend political frictions which may have existed and the leaver should feel able to quit gracefully, with a sense of completion to his or her endeavours. A brief period of mourning may follow, with people talking about how things used to be when the leaver was around. If the person strongly influenced the direction of the organization (for good or ill), his or her memory may be enshrined in stories which are passed on to future employees.

As well as marking an end to someone's organizational efforts, the farewell celebration legitimates vacating the job for someone else. It is problematic if this point is misread, or misunderstood. To illustrate: many a leaver will exit to the sentiment, 'it will be great to see you around here any time.' Those who respond literally to such an invitation may be disappointed, as the following tale from a human resources manager reveals:

> Brian was a production executive. He loved his work with us; I guess he was a workaholic. He's been retired about a year now. We gave him a lavish send-off, a huge party. He was a popular man, you see. About a month after he left, he popped in to see us. Of course, it was great to see him and to exchange stories. I got the feeling then that he wasn't adjusting too well to retirement. He said he'd keep in touch with us, and that he did! It seemed like every week he'd be in – trying, really, to be where he thought he belonged. Eventually, one of his old colleagues came to see me, in despair. 'He's driving us mad,' he said. 'He's a nice guy, but we don't want him any more. He wants to do our job for us; he can't let go.'

The emotional bonds of organizing are very real, but they are often temporary and heavily entwined with daily work routines. The leaving ritual effectively marks an end to a person's organizational membership and disenfranchisement can be rapid. Only special friendships survive. Without the everyday sharing of work, old interpersonal attachments are left without roots, or a proper context for expression. This can come as quite a shock to people who quickly find their old workmates relative strangers once they have left the organization. More cynically, one can regard many organizational relationships as a means to an end. We try to get on with people because we have to – to get the job done, to get through the day, to earn a living.

Recently, exiting organizations and employment has become complicated by an additional factor: the longer active lifespan of many workers and a trend away from a mandatory retirement age. Changing demographic patterns have challenged traditional notions of retirement. There is an increasing number of people wanting to work beyond 60 or 65 years of age and many are supported by legislation that outlaws age discrimination at work. Furthermore, as both the state and employers begin to withdraw from pension provision, many workers need to supplement their existing pensions with further paid work.

These changes have opened the door to more flexible retirement policies: some employees choose to continue to work full-time into their senior years, deferring the exit process, while others will complete the retirement ritual, only to return to their previous jobs on a part-time basis. For employers, such arrangements challenge any overt or covert ageism in their employment policies, while offering the benefits of retaining important knowledge, skills and social capital.

Yet there is another image of leaving, which is far removed from the canapés and congratulations. This is the world of redundancy, restructuring and **downsizing**. People have to leave because their jobs are no more. The vagaries of the market economy can sometimes, seemingly overnight, turn a 'caring, family' organization into a beast which consumes its own children – in order to survive commercially. 'Our most important asset, people', rarely endures a severe downturn in trade, a world recession, or new mechanization; other interests take precedence. Yet when people invest fair parts of themselves and their security in their employing organizations, job loss comes as a very upsetting event. A person's identity is at stake. For the first-time **unemployed**, the loss of income, status and routine activity can feel like a collapse of **meaning** at the centre of their lives. Those who have been made redundant more than once tread warily through the world of work, cautious about their commitment to any one company and with a sense of detachment – 'it's just a job'.

Organizations approach the management of redundancy in different ways. The closest one finds to a supportive ritual is in attempts to soften the blow through generous redundancy payments and 'outplacement' support – to help people find new jobs or other activity. Otherwise, there is a mishmash of responses. Some senior managers cannot face the task of announcing redundancies themselves, so they delegate it to an internal, or external, 'hatchet person', some of whom are well practised at that kind of work. Then there are people who find out about their own redundancy from internal rumours or what they read in their local newspaper. Others hear by letter, or return from a break to find that their job is no more. The UK Accident Group has added a new dimension to this process. The company employed a large number of staff to advise clients on how to recover damages due to accidents they had suffered.

In 2003, without warning, all staff received a mobile phone text message that they were not being paid and were redundant, forthwith. The company had gone out of business. The message came as a huge shock. But the technology that carried the message added insult to the injury.

In sum, we cannot but wonder at the apparent courtesy and charm which can bring a person into an organization, and the acrimony and disarray which, sometimes, can mark the leaving. Perhaps, most of all, it reminds us of the curious fragility of social orders and of organizing.

KEY POINTS

○ Entering and leaving organizations are critical transitions in our work lives.

○ Most organizations wish to present a glossy image to the outside world, but once inside an organization, one often gets a different picture.

○ The rational procedures of recruitment and selection are often overlaid with political interests – which may not give the candidate a 'fair' hearing or decision.

○ Entering and leaving is marked by both formal and informal social rituals, exposing the deeper aspect of the organization's culture and sub-cultures.

○ There is a gradual process of getting to know one's place in an organization – learning its customs and practices, becoming socialized. This is crucial to survival, and can sometimes be testing.

○ An organization can soon become part of our self-image and identity, complicating departures, especially forced departures.

○ We can insulate ourselves from the stresses of job change by reducing our commitment to an employer.

> > > > > > > > > > > THEORETICAL SIGNPOSTS > > > > > > > > > > > >

The major ideas in this chapter can be found in three main areas:

> career theory
> dramaturgy and impression management
> socialization and rites of passage.

Career Theory

Entering an organization has traditionally been associated with a step on the career ladder, a notion that can be traced to the seminal writings of Max Weber and his ideal type bureaucracy (Weber, 1946). Workers can gradually ascend the hierarchical ladder as they acquire more qualifications and experience; and their personal identity is much determined by their work role, their position and their organization. While this picture has not vanished, career theorists are now more concerned with 'post-bureaucratic' organizations, where structures are more fluid and people are in and out of different types of work, refining their 'employability' through training and education (see Hall, 1996; Osterman and Arthur, 1998). Theorists, such as Arthur and Rousseau (1996) and Hall (1996) have described the 'boundaryless career' where people criss-cross different employment sectors. Others talk of 'portfolio careers' (Handy, 1996) where several mini-careers or contrasting jobs are pursued with no exclusive commitment to any one or to any single employer. Flexibility is the key. Post-modern theorists, such as Fournier (1997) and Grey (1994) have argued that such shifts are marked by more fragmented personal identities, assisted by 'disciplinary technologies', such as frequently re-crafted CVs and advice on new ways of presenting who you are.

Dramaturgy and Impression Management

These are rooted in the seminal work of sociologist Erving Goffman (1959). He speaks of the Presentation of Self in Everyday Life – how we don particular 'masks' and use role 'scripts' to give the right social impressions to others. In his turn, Goffman was inspired by role theory, a cornerstone of social psychology (Biddle, 1986). Dramaturgy, as the label suggests, takes the theatre as analogy for social life and the importance of pulling off a good performance – as befits formal interviews for jobs and other social encounters where we are being evaluated or judged. For dramaturgists, appearances are everything and rehearsals are vital: we are managing the impressions we give off to others and adjusting them to particular contexts. These can sometimes be subtle processes as we adjust to the feedback we receive from others. Following such ideas, writers such as Mangham and Overington (1987), Rosen (1985) and Giacalone and Rosenfeld (1991) have looked at the nature of impression formation in a variety of organizational events or settings.

Socialization and Rites of Passage

Socialization theory aims to explain how we become part of a social unit, gradually adopting some of its ways: norms, values and beliefs. Schein (1968) argues that socialization in the organization's process varies in its consistency. Some individuals may accept socialization and conform, while others will rebel or even adapt the organizational norms to their own needs. In other words, it can often involve conflict and struggles. Nonaka and Takeuchi (1995) focus on the importance of organizational learning in a dynamic model of socialization, where tacit knowledge – such as stories and gossip – is in constant interplay with formal knowledge – the sort found in rule books, reference manuals and job descriptions. The two different sorts of knowledge inform each other while sharing tacit knowledge is fundamental to the process of socialization.

Rites of passage are often intrinsic to organizational socialization, defining the passage from one status to another. Its academic origins attest to the early twentieth century work of anthropologist Arnold Van Gennep (2004). He noted how particular rites, or ceremonies – such as baptism, marriage and funerals – were key to a major change in one's position in society. He argued that all rites of passage are marked by a phase when the individual is separate from their social group; a phase when they are in 'liminality', between the old and new groups; and a final phase when then have passed successfully into their new group. Formal rites of passage can be found in the swearing-in ceremony that marks a foreigner's passage to full citizenship of a nation, and an employee's need to complete the 'rites' of their company training programme in order to move from probation to full-employee status. Informally, organizational folklore abounds with stories of ritual fun or humiliation that the novice must bear in order to become fully accepted. Indeed, some writers, such as Nuwer (1999), see rites of passage as an important way of deciphering the key values and constraints of an organization how micro changes occur (see also Ashforth et al., 2000; Trice and Beyer, 1984).

REVIEW QUESTIONS

1. In what way is impression management part of the recruitment and selection process? How have you managed your part in such circumstances?

2. What are the roles of dramaturgy and organizational culture in explaining how we become socialized in the workplace?

3. What is the function of rites of passage when entering and finally leaving an organization? Could we do without them? Relate to ones you have personally experienced.

NOTES

1. See http://www.shell.com/home/content/uk-en
2. See http//www.hrpost.com/forums/teamwork/9910/msg00017.html

companion
website
www.sagepub.co.uk/fineman

Reading On

The articles below are available for free to readers of the fourth edition of *Organizing & Organizations* via the book's companion website at www.sagepub.co.uk/fineman

Bozionelos, N. (2005) 'When the inferior candidate is offered the job: the selection interview as a political and power game', *Human Relations*, 58 (12): 1605–31.
The article advances the view that the selection interview frequently serves as a political arena for various power networks in the organization whose interests may be conflicting. Members of the interview panel try to advance the interests of the power networks to which they belong by lobbying for the candidates whose background and values concur most with

those interests. The notion of the interview as a political and power game is illustrated with a case from the academic environment.

Feldman, D.C. and Ng, T.W.H. (2007) 'Careers: mobility, embeddedness, and success', *Journal of Management*, 33 (3): 350–77.
This article proposes refinements of the constructs of career mobility and career embeddedness and reviews the array of factors that have been found to energize (discourage) employees to change jobs, organizations, and/or occupations. The article also reviews the literature on career success and identifies which types of mobility (and embeddedness) are most likely to lead to objective career success (e.g., promotions) and subjective career success (e.g., career satisfaction).

Schein, E.H. (2004) 'Learning when and how to lie: a neglected aspect of organizational and occupational socialization (Introduction by Hugh Gunz and Paul Willman)', *Human Relations*, 57 (3): 259–73.
This article is based on the lecture delivered by Professor Schein at the Academy of Management meeting in Toronto, 2000. The article builds on Professor Schein's widely cited work on career anchors, examining the various kinds of socialization that individuals undergo in a typical organizational career, focusing in particular on the norms learned about information management in the different functions that the career occupant will encounter.

Sullivan, S.E., Martin, D.F., Carden, W.A. and Mainero, L.A. (2003) 'The road less traveled: how to manage the recycling career stage', *Journal of Leadership and Organizational Studies*, 10 (2): 34–42.
This article examines how organizations can better respond to the needs of individuals who are reexamining and changing their chosen career paths. The term, 'career recycling', reflects a segment of the workforce describing individuals who are reexamining and changing their career paths. Through exploratory interviews, the authors find that recylers were dissatisfied with their careers and willing to accept the risks associated with changing career direction.

3

LIFELONG LEARNING

Much is written on learning, a topic with far-reaching organizational, educational and political implications. We spend a large part of our lives learning – in our families, at school, in the streets, at college, in organizations. Massive resources are spent on education, training and development. Is this money well spent? How do we learn? What stands in the way of learning? Are there right and wrong ways of teaching? Right and wrong lessons?

And what about learning management? How do managers learn to do their job? What is it about management that can be learned? How is management knowledge diffused? And why are management students spending much time and money attending different types of courses to make use of the knowledge they acquire? How does knowledge translate into practice?

In this chapter, we consider some of the ways in which we learn. We go on to look at different learning styles and different types of learning. We then look at certain types of learning and knowing that go beyond the individual, becoming parts of **organizations**. Can we talk of **group** or organizational learning as processes involving something more than the learning undertaken by their members? Is it true that some organizations, like some individuals, are good learners and others not? We conclude this chapter by considering the relationship between knowledge and **power**.

SOME TYPES OF KNOWLEDGE

One of the difficulties with the word 'learning' is that there are many different things which we learn, many different ways of learning and many obstacles which stand in the way of learning. Some learning, like learning a football result, takes place almost instantaneously; learning to use a piece of software may take several days or months; learning to play the violin can take many years. Learning to practise as a professional, a consultant or a leader can take an entire lifetime.

Some of the things we learn are information (e.g. 'there are five divisions in this organization'); some are **skills** (e.g. learning how to drive a car or how to send an email) and academic disciplines (e.g. medicine or engineering); some are stories, like the story of how a particular product ensured the survival of our organization. Learning is something that takes place in the head (knowledge, information, stories), but also in the rest of the body. Juggling, skiing and playing the drums are skills which are located in the limbs at least as much as in the head.

COMMON SENSE

Sometimes we are aware that we know something. Sometimes it seems so obvious that we do not even think of it as knowing. This is referred to as common sense or a taken-for-granted view of the world. Until recently, it was assumed that the earth's resources were effectively limitless as was the earth's capacity to absorb pollution. Today, such views are no longer taken for granted. Instead, what seems common-sensical is the view that we cannot go on indefinitely using the earth's resources without jeopardizing the welfare of future generations.

One of the fascinations of coming into contact with different organizations is realizing that things which we consider absolutely unavoidable are in fact conventions which other organizations do without. We consider it inconceivable that an organization could function without a human resources department until we encounter an organization where 'personnel matters' are routinely handled by other departments, without the need for a special department.

We are bound to take some things for granted. We cannot be checking everything the whole time. So some learning is about distinguishing what is worth focusing on and learning about, as opposed to what should be taken for granted. Within organizations, we constantly make assumptions about the behaviour of other people, about the functioning of machines and equipment, about the operation of different types of systems. It is for this reason that we can easily find ourselves thrown off course if suddenly one or more of our assumptions fail – for example, if our colleague is so depressed that he only wants to talk about his divorce, if the electricity supply fails or if we discover that our boss has been sacked. Tacit knowing is both inevitable and useful – yet, there are times when it stands in the way of learning. We can rely on existing routines and assumptions which served us well in the past, not realizing that the world is changing and that the time has come for new ideas, new **skills** and new ways of engaging with others.

ACQUAINTANCE AND DESCRIPTION

One of the distinctions that has proved helpful for thinking about knowing in **organizations** is between 'knowing by acquaintance' and 'knowing by description'. A shopkeeper knows his or her shop by acquaintance. So too does a manager. By contrast, a management theorist knows his or her subject matter by description, that is through scientific theories or records and observations made by other people.

Most of us know about trench warfare by description, while war veterans who lived through it have a very different type of knowledge of its meaning.

I have read many books, I have seen films, I have been to lectures. Nothing but nothing can capture what it was like to be there. The horror of it. (Joe Laskem, World War I veteran, 'Today Programme', BBC Radio 4, 11 November 1998)

It is for this reason that those who 'know by acquaintance' often believe that nobody who has not lived through their experience can appreciate its meaning, no matter how many books, television programmes or films they are exposed to.

Knowing by description is sometimes referred to as *propositional knowledge,* while knowledge by acquaintance is known as *experiential knowledge.* Propositional knowledge is generally open to traditional forms of testing and proof – by testing the validity of the propositions through experiments, observations or arguments. Experiential knowledge, on the other hand, can be more difficult to test or even to talk about. As Louis Armstrong said about jazz, 'man, if you gotta ask what it is, you ain't never gonna get to know'.

The knowledge that people have of their own organizations is mostly experiential. When we join a new organization, we may be given a description of it – for example, through company prospectuses or corporate videos. These are unlikely to take us very far (see Chapter 2, 'Entering and Leaving'). As we become used to the place, we gain knowing by acquaintance – knowing individuals, knowing procedures, knowing past examples and likely outcomes, and we act with more confidence. Organizing is carried out on both bases, and could not be done on the basis of either one alone. This book, on the other hand, like all books, can only offer you knowing by description – this enhances and speeds up your learning from acquaintance with actual organizations. The two kinds of knowing are not totally distinct; a really good autobiography is a description, but the reader may come away from it feeling almost acquainted with the subject of the book. Knowing by description can be a help in gaining knowing by acquaintance.

SKILLS AND COMPETENCES

Much of our learning involves 'knowing how' to do things rather than 'knowing that' certain things are true. Often, we find ourselves doing things perfectly competently, without knowing the principles which underpin them. We can speak a language without knowing its rules of grammar and syntax; we can ride a bicycle and play billiards without knowing or understanding the physics. Many successful entrepreneurs may know how to set up and run profitable businesses without being able to articulate the underlying principles. Knowing how ('know-how') is often tacit knowledge. This sometimes passes unnoticed and unrewarded. Alternatively, tacit knowledge may be highly rewarded – some chief executives and football managers, for instance, receive large salaries for their supposed knowledge of how to turn around a failing company or football team.

Much of the knowledge in organizations is knowledge by acquaintance and knowing how. This is the knowledge on which much organizing is based. It often amounts to a range of **skills** and competences rather than the application of scientific concepts and theories. Rules of thumb, intuitions, past experiences, organizational folklore and tacit understanding can be more helpful than the latest scientific discoveries. One of our students wrote a dissertation in which he tried to show that, if only small businesses followed formal appointment procedures for their managers, they would make far fewer mistakes and be better able to compete with larger businesses. He investigated firms where an owner had started a business, and later recruited a manager as an employee. He was surprised to find that recruitment decisions which seemed to be intuitive, where the owner had followed 'gut feelings', were more successful than the ones where more formality and rationality had been attempted. It seemed that such owners knew how to choose a good manager for their business; the more they considered the 'knowing that', the factors they 'ought' to consider, the less likely they were to make a **decision** which turned out well.

One particular type of knowing how is knowing how to get things to happen. A lot of knowledge in organizations can go untapped, simply because people who possess it do not know how to make it work for themselves or the organization. An information systems manager said:

> I have been trying to get the board to take an interest in IT for years now. We are way behind most of the rest of the industry. But every time we get near to talking about it properly, the conversation slips off to somewhere else. I just cannot get them to focus on it.

What he was expressing is a common frustration. He has an area of expertise. It is almost self-evident to him that the company would do well to pay attention to that area, but he cannot get it onto senior people's agenda. Many managers are in a perpetual state of hurry, of trying to do more things at once than is really possible, and many issues compete for their attention. However well you know what you are talking about, getting something you care about on the organizational agenda requires a different kind of knowing – knowing how to time your attempt, knowing who to talk to in which order, and knowing how to get them interested. This requires a mixture of **communication** and **political** and interpersonal **skills** without which technical know-how can remain untapped.

LEARNING STYLES

Different people learn in different ways. In a classroom, a teacher may give pupils a question and then suggest that they carry out an experiment to find out the answer. Alternatively, the teacher may give them the answer directly. Is it a waste of time and resources to have students carry out the experiment, given that the experiment has already been done many times? Likewise, if pupils know how to solve a problem, is it necessary for them to know the abstract mathematical principles which underpin the solution?

Learning styles is a concept which seeks to capture the ways different individuals learn. Some people are referred to as 'pragmatic learners' – they prefer to learn how to get things to work, relying on a mixture of intuition, instruction and trial and error. They are interested in results, not theories. Others are known as 'discovery learners', approaching learning as an adventure and learning best from the satisfaction of solving problems themselves. For them, learning comes mostly from experience. Yet others are referred to as 'critical inquirers', approaching their subject in a systematic inquiring way, using analysis, reasoning and criticism as a means of reaching the deeper principles.

Learning by instruction and learning by experience are both active processes. Learning by instruction requires active engagement with what the instructor says, asking questions, raising criticisms, exploring new applications, trying out different examples. Learning from experience can involve hard work. It can be mental work, reflecting on experiences and trying to understand the reasons for mistakes or disappointments. It can also involve physical work, as in the following example:

> Once upon a time, an old man saw that his days were coming to an end. He called his three sons, blessed them and told them that he had hidden a treasure in the field. When he died, they should go and dig the treasure out - it would stand them in good stead for the rest of their lives, he said. The old man died. His sons mourned him and then started to dig the field. They dug every part of the field thoroughly but could find no treasure. Had the old man made a mistake? This is what they thought. Until harvest time came, when they reaped many times the usual crop, for they had dug the field so well. It is then that they realized that the old man had not lied to them.

The old man of the story wanted to teach his sons a lesson by experience rather than by instruction. Had he said: 'work hard, my sons, to earn your living', the message could easily have been lost. Hard work, the frustration of not finding the treasure and the final realization of what the treasure is are likely to leave a much deeper mark on the sons. You can see now why some of your best teachers were those who refused to spoon-feed you easily digestible pieces of knowledge, which are just as easily forgotten. Instead, they demanded hard work from you. Hard lessons can be harder to forget.

Experience does not necessarily lead different people to the same types of knowledge. Two people can go through what outwardly appears to be the same experience and end up knowing quite different things as a result. Even the three sons of our story could draw different lessons from their experience. The first one, for instance, might have learned that hard work on the fields is the secret of a happy life; the second son might have learned that his father wanted them all three to work together; the third son, for his part, might have learned that hard physical work was not for him and that becoming a watch-repair man was a better way of earning a living. Thus, our individual way of knowing, or **construing** the world, gives a particular spin on what we see happening, and therefore what experience we gain from events. People know things in very different ways. A painter and a policeman would look at a riot in quite different ways and could be expected to draw different kinds of knowing from their observations. A poet and a botanist bring different kinds of knowing to the observation of a flower, and they take different kinds of knowing from it.

If we now relate this to narrative knowing, we would expect people to differ considerably in terms of the kind of story they made out of what they had just seen.

Suppose that you miss an important meeting in your organization. You ask two or three of your friends who were present what happened. You are then likely to get different narratives or stories through which they make sense of what went on, and in which they cast themselves as characters. One may present the meeting as an arena of political and intellectual jousting, where he managed to outsmart an awkward adversary. A second one may report that the meeting was a complete waste of time, with two or three individuals on ego trips being intent to argue about the most trivial points. A third one may report that while much argument took place over trivial matters, the really important **decision** went through 'on the nod', right at the end of the meeting when most people were too tired to notice. These accounts may or may not be incompatible – they each seek to turn the experience of the meeting into a story from which the listener can extract the essence of the meeting.

Knowledge and meaning change as they travel from person to person through stories or information. Even seemingly hard statistics, like unemployment or profit figures, can lead to different conclusions being drawn, as different people read different meanings into them. One form of knowledge that we do not expect to change as it travels from person to person is scientific theory. After all, in the natural sciences, we expect a theory to hold across time, space and **culture**. Yet, in the human sciences, theories are constantly confronted with new and unpredictable realities which demand constant re-evaluation and rethinking.

OBSTACLES TO LEARNING

What stops us from learning? Why is it that sometimes we seem entirely unable to understand something or find ourselves repeating the same mistakes over and over again? It is sometimes said that some individuals can have 25 years' experience, while others merely have one year's experience repeated 25 times. Some people are better learners than others or better able to adapt, update and fine-tune their knowledge to changing circumstances. Learning itself involves a range of skills, which some of us can master better than others.

Many factors can conspire to inhibit learning – poor teaching, a lack of **motivation**, an absence of resources and the apparent lack of relevance can all prevent us from learning. A very important obstacle to learning is old learning, especially when it has assumed the form of habit. Habits that were once valuable can be difficult to shake off when they become counter-productive. One may learn to smoke as a way of being socially acceptable and successful; it is very difficult to quit later. Having learned to pass exams by simply memorizing pieces of information, it is hard to abandon this approach, even when it is no longer adequate or appropriate. Likewise, having learned that success is the product of hard work, we may be unable to stop and think whether the work we are currently engaged in is the right work or not.

Sometimes, old knowledge becomes an object of great emotional attachment. We can almost fall in love with our theories. This is especially the case with primitive theories, like stereotypes or theories which have served us well in the past. We are then quite reluctant to abandon them and replace them with new knowledge, just as an organization may be reluctant to abandon a tried-and-tested product that has brought it much success in the past, when the time for its replacement is ripe.

Maybe the most important obstacle to learning is the fear of failure, a fear that may itself be the product of earlier failures and disappointments. Learning is not nearly as comforting or as reassuring as habit. It can be exciting, enjoyable and life-enhancing but it inevitably draws us outside the comfort zone of what we already know. It can be a disorganized and unpredictable business. It generates many anxieties: are we on the right track? Are we wasting our time and money? Are we going to get the answers we want? Are we going to survive the tests and trials lying ahead? Shall we be branded failures? Are we perhaps stupid or intellectually incompetent? Faced with such anxieties, it is often tempting to fall back on old habits and routines, 'stick to the knitting' and continue doing what we already know how to do.

The teacher's skill lies in keeping these anxieties in check, never neutralizing them completely, but stopping them short of disabling the learning process. A good teacher can help us cope with the disappointment of failure, not by denying it or preventing it, but by turning it into a valuable lesson in its own right. A great teacher can inspire us with a genuine thirst for learning, maintaining our sense of adventure which combines danger with achievement. We can then develop a wide repertoire of learning styles and approaches which enable us to benefit and learn from subsequent experiences, both positive and negative ones.

NARRATIVE KNOWING

This type of knowledge has attracted much attention in recent years. Many statements in organizations may sound factual, but imply a story. Consider, for example, the statement 'since Jeff joined us, model 312 has really started to take off'. Such a proposition can go beyond a mere statement of causal connection between two facts. Instead, it may amount to a story, a very short one to be sure, since the teller of the story can assume that the listeners have the tacit knowledge to make sense of it. They may know, for example, that Jeff was lured from working for the customers' trade association with a big salary offer, and that he is a very personable character; they know the success of model 312 has been at the expense of model 314 which has declined; and they also know that the director who brought Jeff in reduced the chances of his **decision** being shown to be wrong by arranging a healthy price cut and a big advertising campaign for the 312 at the crucial moment.

It may be that narratives are central to learning. Making sense of the world around us, understanding what is going on, is achieved through turning 'facts' into 'stories'. After a football match or an interview, we prepare ourselves to tell a story of how that match or that interview went. In presenting ourselves to others, we invite them to share our stories, to get to know us through the stories we tell them and to form their own stories out of meeting us. When we go for an interview, for instance, we do not only offer a list of our achievements and experiences – rather, we weave them into a narrative, and usually one that will cast us in the best possible light. At the same time, we listen carefully to the stories told by others. A word or phrase can reveal that they see themselves as a hero struggling against enormous odds, or as a victim of circumstances. Narrative knowing consists of being able to spot the plots of such stories and make sense of them.

AN EXAMPLE

Consider the following story set in a naval camp. The story was often told before the inspection which preceded the handing out of furloughs – the permits to leave the barracks. This was a tense period, when the recruits could be denied exit leaves if their appearance was not up to standard. One particular officer, the story went, liked to torment the sailors by denying them their exit leaves on the most absurd grounds. On one such occasion, he had asked recruits to lower their trousers while standing to be inspected. He then proceeded to cancel everyone's leave. The navy, he had explained, went to great trouble and incurred substantial cost in providing each recruit with three full sets of underwear as part of the military uniform. But, he observed, the recruits had seen fit to discard the regulation white boxer shorts stamped with their serial number, in favour of a motley assembly of briefs. This he regarded as a violation of the military code with disciplinary consequences. The recruits needed a reminder that a sailor was to be a sailor through and through, for instance, by spending some more time in the barracks.

This story had an unsettling effect on new recruits, although more seasoned sailors appeared to find it amusing. As a piece of organizational lore, the story acted as a depository of important knowledge, though the precise nature of this knowledge would vary from person to person. Unlike a moral tale which has a simple message and a straigthforward moral, this story could be read in many different ways. Its meanings existed in many different layers. In one sense, the story cast the recruits in the role of victims of sadistic officers. They could take some comfort from feeling proud for surviving such ordeals. In another way, the story suggested that underneath the blinding uniformity of army clothes, each individual could maintain a part of their individuality, symbolized by their underwear. In yet another way, the story acted as a warning for new recruits. Navy life, it seems to announce, is full of unexpected troubles and dangers. Surviving requires more than just compliance to rules – it requires fortitude and, even, a sense of the absurd. As such, it makes its point in a far more telling way than would a mere admonishment: 'be prepared for the worst!' In this way, narrative knowing offers us both a way of making sense of our experiences and a way of coping with difficulties and problems which we face.

COMMUNITIES OF PRACTICE

One of the important functions of narrative knowledge is to inform people not what the main rules are but how they should be applied. Some rules are applied strictly, others are only applied in certain situations and yet others are routinely ignored. Another function is to inform people how to handle exceptional or difficult situations or to offer tips or good ideas. One of the authors was once delayed at the airport in Denver, Colorado, due to bad weather. As he sat at a café, waiting for his flight to be announced, he overheard the conversation of four pilots sitting at a table next to his. The conversation made uncomfortable hearing, as the pilots recounted some of the most terrifying experiences of their careers – near collisions, failure of equipment, freak weather phenomena, dangerous passengers and so forth. What the author gradually realized was that the pilots were not just trying to impress each other with evermore scary stories, but they were also passing on very useful information of the sort that may not be found in their flight manuals to their colleagues – they were *sharing knowledge*, in other words, giving tips, comparing experiences, making judgements, drawing very fine distinctions and so forth. They were, in effect, acting as a knowledge network or members of a 'community of practice'.

The importance of communities of practice has been known since some early studies of organizations. It was clear, in other words, that in order for people to do their work effectively, they often rely on knowledge that they have obtained not as part of a formal curriculum but through informal conversations with their peers. For a time, it appeared as though information available on digital networks might undermine the importance of informally shared local knowledge. But, if anything, the opposite has been the case. The ubiquity of information far from supplanting local knowledge networks makes them more important. Why? Because such networks shield their members from the masses of irrelevant noise or surplus information, communicating instantly on the right wavelength, sharing the same assumptions.

Many authors have argued that this is one of the reasons for the success of localized communities, epitomized in Silicon Valley. As Brown and Duguid have argued:

> The Valley persists as a densely interconnected innovative region, though its inhabitants loudly proclaim that the information technology they develop renders distance dead and place insignificant. It persists ... because of the local character of innovative knowledge, which flows in social rather than digital networks. The locality of innovative knowledge highlights the challenge of developing other regions for the modern economy. (2002: 427)

Communities of practice cut across organizational boundaries. A company's research scientists, maintenance engineers, software developers, accountants, purchasing staff and sales people may well belong to different communities of practice. They may well be able to communicate better with their fellow practitioners than with people within their own organization. Are managers a community of practice in their own right? Undoubtedly, in many ways, managers act as if they belong to a community of practice. It may well be that part of the success of the MBA (Masters of Business Administration) is that it represents an internationally recognizable badge which enables members to join such a community. The nature of managerial work itself, with its ad hoc, unpredictable, improvisatory qualities, would further support the emergence of managers as a community of people bound together by common practices and common concerns.

MANAGERS AS A COMMUNITY OF PRACTICE

Much of the research on communities of practice has been done on groups of skilled professionals and craftspeople. But how well does the concept of community of practice apply to management? Can there ever be a 'community' of managers within which learning can take place, where knowledge is shared? And does their 'practice' have enough in common with each other for the concept to be useful?

A group of managers may not look much like a community. The nature of managerial work tends to place them in competition with each other for resources, promotion or survival. Yet, managers also form alliances with others to produce particular organizational results (see Chapter 8, 'Politics and Deals'), as when the operations manager and the marketing manager of an organization start to look to each other regularly for support, not just on an issue-by-issue basis. Managers can even have friends. So it may be that managers are not so very different from other types of employee in their capacity to form a community in which to share practice. Photocopier repair technicians and flute makers (subjects of extensive studies on 'communities of practice') also have their career aspirations and competitive urges, and a tendency not to respect all their colleagues equally.

Does managerial practice have the right ingredients to be learned communally? It is often seen to be quite different from other kinds of skill, and there are three aspects in which this might make it unpromising for learning through a community of practice. First, it is prone to continuous interruption. Second, it is closer to improvisation than to following any particular script or programme. Third, it involves a kind of game playing where the manager is continually trying to anticipate and often outsmart the moves of other managers (who are trying to do exactly the same).

Managerial work is interrupted to such an extent that most activities are conducted in very short time spans. Managers rarely spend more than a few minutes doing anything before they are interrupted to deal with something else. This is so prevalent that we have to think of handling interruptions as a normal and defining quality of managerial work, rather than simply as a nuisance. Every interruption is different and unpredictable, and does not conform to any formula; that is what makes it an interruption. So how do managers learn to handle interruptions? Much of the learning may pre-date their time as managers. It is probably well enough known that being a manager means being able to live with constant interruptions so that only those who enjoy or are able to handle interruptions will be drawn to work as managers. Some of the learning comes from modelling, as managers observe their seniors during their formative years. But within organizations, there are also discussions on how to handle interruptions that follow the community of practice pattern. For example, we recently observed a number of managers from the same organization discussing, during a training day, the time that they normally arrived in the morning. Several of them made a practice of arriving about an hour before the start of their official working day, in order to spend time on tasks that needed to be done without interruption. Others had not thought of this strategy, and thought they might give it a try. This was a community of practice in action. It is interesting to note the trust shown between the discussants; if someone else knows that you are usually in early, they could always call you if they wanted to, which would defeat the purpose. So the managers in the discussion were prepared to trust each other not to abuse this information.

Much has been written about the improvisatory aspects of management. This does not of course mean that managers make it all up as they go along, but rather that, like skilled jazz musicians, they leave some important aspects of their practice open to being influenced by what they see and hear at the time. Improvisation sounds wonderfully relaxed – except to people who have done it. It takes years of practice to be able to improvise well, at least as long as it takes to be able to follow a more prescribed course of action. We worked with one manager who was well known for his improvisations and many people drew the wrong conclusions about him. They thought that he was simply brilliant, and could function effectively with no preparation; that is how it often appeared in meetings. Those who knew him better, however, knew that if you visited him at home in the evening before a meeting you would find his notes and ideas laid out all over the floor of his study. His improvisation was based on intense preparation. So those who modelled themselves on what they observed of his 'performance' often drew a misleading lesson, while those in his community of practice were much more likely to understand how his results were achieved.

Managers often make moves that rely on timing and the outsmarting of others in order to achieve their effects. A particular stratagem will only produce the desired result in the context of what others have recently done or are currently busy doing, and if the timing is right. A few hours or even minutes can make a vital difference as to whether a particular decision leads to the desired results or not. Going too early can be as self-defeating as going too late. As a member of a network or community of practice, a manager has information that may enable him/her to make well-timed interventions, at the expense of those who may be less well informed or less well networked. Yet, timing does not seem to us to be the kind of thing that is directly learned through a community of practice, though it may be learned from observation of other people. Rather like timing in a sport, it can be seen and felt, but not talked about in any systematic way. Intuition may be as important here as learned behaviour.

ORGANIZATIONAL KNOWING AND LEARNING

The last few years have seen a huge growth in the number of books and articles on organizational learning, the learning organization, knowledge management and similar topics. It has become increasingly common to link these rather academic-sounding concepts with competitive advantage and profit margins. Recently too, there has been an emphasis on understanding intellectual capital as one of the most important resources that an organization can deploy. In addition to physical, financial and human capital, organizations possess a type of capital which includes ideas, memories, recipes, timetables, forms, systems, routines, tacit knowledge and lore – all such forms of knowledge are so valuable that they should be understood and valued as capital. An organization starting from scratch would have to invent them afresh, and this would cost much time and money. There are already reasonably well established procedures for calculating the commercial value that should be put on such intellectual capital.

Does it make sense to speak of organizational learning or indeed of a learning organization? In one sense, **organizations** do not know anything. They do not have brains or memories in any conventional sense, even if it has become commonplace to view computers as the organization's brains and accounting systems and databases as its memories. Words like 'knowing', 'learning' or 'memory' have to be applied with caution to any subjects that are not people. Yet, both practising managers and academic writers find them quite useful in thinking about what is happening in their organizations.

Organizations are attributed with capacities to learn (or fail to learn) and to develop (or fail to develop) in their own right, over and above the knowledge and learning of their members. How is this possible?

KNOWLEDGE SURVIVES STAFF CHANGES

One reason for believing that organizations learn over and above what their members learn is that a certain kind of know-how or lore survives changes in staff. Certain orchestras are famous for the unique quality of the sound they produce over many decades, irrespective of the conductor who happens to direct them or the musicians who happen to be playing in a particular concert. In a similar way, organizations are known to have 'ways of doing things' which are inherently right and proper, irrespective of their staff at any particular moment in time.

How is such knowledge maintained within organizations even when the personnel changes? Some of it assumes the form of folklore, which passes down through generations. Some of the knowledge becomes embedded in routines, procedures and ways of working which are never questioned. Some of the knowledge becomes embedded in the ways that buildings, equipment and materials are arranged. In the same way, certain orchestras are reputed to produce a particular type of brass or string sound because of the musical instruments which they possess, because of the positions the players occupy in a particular hall or indeed because of the acoustics of the hall itself.

As a new entrant to an **organization,** you are likely to face a special situation. Your job description may say that you are to prepare spreadsheets which forecast the cash flow for the coming year, a job which you have already done in another company, a job in which you are already well trained. There will still be much that you need to learn in order to be able to do it right for your new organization. How do you know the things that are and are not taken into account in your new organization? Some of this knowledge will come from the other people you work with, who will fill you in on what is needed in the spreadsheet, thereby conveying to you some of the collective organizational learning. Some of it will come from the shape of the spreadsheet itself, its design being the result of past learning. Some of it will come from the feedback you will receive when you present your first set of figures.

Of course, changes of personnel may lead to some new ideas, but it is surprising how much stays the same. Bringing in 'fresh blood' to a situation, trying to produce organizational **change** by introducing new staff, can work, but it is surprising how often the new staff find themselves drawn back into doing things the way they were done before. In effect, their attempt at bringing a new way of thinking about things is absorbed by the organization. The stock of organizational knowledge can sometimes overpower the individual attempt to influence it.

KNOWLEDGE IS NOT JUST IN THE HEAD

One of the recent developments in **cognitive** social psychology has been to understand that knowing and thinking are processes much more widely distributed in the body. We do not only know the ideas that are represented in our brain. We also know things because we know where to find them or how to generate them; for example, because they are in our diaries, or because we have set up a regular meeting to talk about them. **Skills** and competences may be 'remembered' as much through other parts of the body as through the brain. Tennis players learn their sport in many ways, including watching it and vividly imagining what it would feel like to produce that particular shot. Such learning and imagination seem to happen in the nerves and muscles of the arms, legs and back. A flute player's skill may be embedded in the dexterity of her fingers, the sensitivity of her mouth or the speed with which her eyes can move along the score. Similarly, the skills of conducting a good meeting or inspiring colleagues to greater efforts may be based in physical movements, in facial expressions, in tone of voice rather than conscious ideas.

Similar phenomena can be observed at an organizational level, with knowledge becoming embedded in different parts of the organizational structure. The departments of the American government were once described as 'monuments to past problems' (Schon, 1971). Most organizations show something of their accumulated knowing in their structures; each department indicates the existence of an old problem which was addressed by assigning it to a specific department. The spatial layout, the location of different offices, the structure of different forms, the timetables, the procedures and regulations and many of the other features of an organization, similarly, reflect acquired knowledge and learning. The head office is imposing because they once found that a simple building was interpreted by customers as meaning that the organization was insubstantial. The consumer credit department is there because it was once found that sales could be boosted by offering favourable credit terms. The overseas relations department dates from the time when it was realized that the names and features of different models had to be adjusted for foreign sales.

LEARNING FROM MISTAKES

A large part of learning theory is dedicated to understanding how individuals and organizations learn from their mistakes. Recognizing a mistake is a first step involving the detection of a mismatch between the intentions behind an **action** and its actual outcomes. This recognition can be a difficult and painful process, since all kinds of excuses may be used to deny failure or to offload responsibility onto someone else. Recognizing a mistake by itself is no guarantee that the mistake will not be repeated. In order to ensure that the same mistake does not occur in the future, we must change behaviour, habits or procedures. This is known as *single-loop learning*. It can be observed easily in animals which can learn different skills by a combination of punishment and reward. Avoidance is a typical form of single-loop learning: being close to fire is painful, so stay clear of it. (Notice how this 'lesson' can actually disable learning: 'learning is painful, so avoid it.')

A deeper form of learning takes place when we assess not only the **action** which led to a mistake, but also the strategy for avoiding the same mistake in the future. *Double-loop learning* does not merely aim at fixing or resolving a problem but actually establishing why the problem arose and why it was constructed as a problem in the first place.

Avoiding fire may be an adequate strategy to stop oneself getting burnt, but rather obliterates any possible constructive uses to which fire may be put. Double-loop learning enables us not only to avoid errors and problems but to take better advantage of the opportunities in our environment by exploring our own learning capacities. In this sense, it involves not merely learning but also learning how to learn.

Organizations too can be seen as engaged in single- or double-loop learning. Single-loop learning may be said to take place if repeated failure to launch a new product leads to a **decision** not to attempt it again. Double-loop learning would involve an effort to understand why such attempts were unsuccessful in the past, the conditions under which they may be successful in the future and the reasons why they have taken place at all.

RIGHT AND WRONG LESSONS

Organizations, like other social phenomena, are complex. Relations of cause and effect are rarely direct. Failures and successes are rarely the result of a single factor. Profits might rise in the same year that the corridors were painted purple, without there being any necessary link. In the same year, there may have been an advertising campaign, a relocation of the warehouse, a **change** in the reporting relationships in production, a new accounting system, and a Total Quality Management effort. The managers behind each of these initiatives may do their best to suggest their **action** alone is responsible for the profit rise. With so many factors at play, how can an organization learn the right lesson? Indeed, is there a right lesson at all?

After the Second World War, there was a widespread belief in the USA that victory had been the result of American technical superiority. This was the 'lesson' the war had taught American politicians, military and the wider public. In the years of the Cold War which followed, the USA acted on this lesson by concentrating on further technological advance. This strategy was, of course, bolstered by the vast economic and political interests at stake in ever-expanding military expenditure. Recent historians have argued convincingly that America was not ahead of Germany in technology in the early 1940s, and that victory came through superior logistics, not technology. The lesson learned from the Second World War may have been at odds with evidence produced by historians. Yet the strategy which was adopted subsequently was not necessarily inappropriate – escalating military expenditure may have brought American success in the Cold War, not by ensuring victory on the battle front, but by bankrupting the Soviet Union which tried to keep pace with American military technology (Locke, 1996).

Under such circumstances, it is hard to know what is the right and what is the wrong lesson. At times, the 'right lesson' may lead to undesirable consequences, just as the 'wrong lesson' may lead to desirable results for entirely unpredictable reasons. The lessons which our organizations learn from past experiences often owe more to wishful thinking or **political** manoeuvring than to dispassionate analysis. Yet, such lessons are very difficult to alter. They become inscribed in collective memories in very stable ways, through symbols, stories and social structures.

Organizational learning is a matter of maintaining these symbols, stories and social structures by ensuring that new recruits become thoroughly attuned to their meanings.

New learning becomes encoded in fresh symbols, stories and structures, which modify, displace or complement older ones.

BUYING KNOWLEDGE AS A SUBSTITUTE FOR LEARNING

Learning, both at the individual and at the organizational level, is a slow process; it can also be an inefficient one. It involves the exploration of ideas which may turn out not to be good, costly mistakes, blind alleys, testing, implementation and practice. Calling a plumber, someone who already has the required knowledge and **skills**, prevents the need to learn how to fix one's leaking taps. Learning to play the piano in order to enjoy Beethoven's piano sonatas can be a lifelong project. How much quicker simply to listen to them performed by a great virtuoso at the concert hall or on CD.

For an organization, developing its own information system or even producing its own mission statement can be a costly and time-consuming process, involving many individuals, much argument and political posturing. It is not surprising that, increasingly, organizations seek to 'buy knowledge', making use of specialists and experts. The burgeoning of MBA education and the **consultancy** profession bears ample testimony to the fact that organizations seek to supplement their own learning with knowledge acquired from outside. Academic theories and techniques, concepts and buzz-words, fads and fashions have colonized organizations, at times co-existing but often subverting traditional forms of knowledge. Buying knowledge very often means buying the latest fashion to come out of a business school or out of a management guru's head.

THE LEAN, FLAT, AGILE, RIGHT-FIRST-TIME LEARNING ORGANIZATION

One recent management fashion was the idea of the lean, flat and agile organization. There must be enough people to fulfil the required functions and no extras, and there must be as few layers in the hierarchy as possible. The organization must be capable of very rapid **change** to meet new circumstances and must be able to get things right first time. Another current management fashion extols organizational learning as the key to competitive advantage and lasting success.

There is an inconsistency here. We argued earlier that organizational learning resides in part in the stories that members tell each other. Middle managers have been the most important repositories of such stories in the past, and they told these stories over lunch and at social times when story-telling was an appropriate activity. The tendency to right-sizing, producing a lean organization, means that the pressure to do the immediate work becomes too great to permit such stories to be told. The flattening of organizational hierarchies has particularly reduced the ranks of middle managers, thereby excising much of the organization's memory. Agility in an organization means that it responds very immediately to circumstances. To achieve this, it should be lean and flat. 'Right first time' means that there is no room for experimentation and error, but learning requires

Figure 3.1

that you allow for the possibility that you might be wrong. The requirement to be right first time discourages originality, risky experimentation and learning.

THE POWER OF KNOWING, AND OF NOT KNOWING

'Knowledge is power', runs the old cliché.

There is a very obvious sense in which knowledge is **power**. Like money, many kinds of knowledge are a currency that can be traded. This is especially true of one type of knowledge – information – which can be traded either directly (for instance, by selling entire databases or banks of information) or as **gossip**, rumour and innuendo. A single piece of information (such as knowing where a 'millennium bug' is located in a piece of software) can sometimes command enormous value. This is also evidenced by the world of military and industrial espionage, as well as by the practice of blackmail. More generally, intelligence gathering by companies represents an important investment, aimed at giving them competitive advantage or denying this advantage to their rivals.

Within organizations, possessing the right piece of information on an adversary gives one a valuable advantage. For example, if I know more about the context of a **decision** than you do, I can ask questions in a meeting which will make your proposals look silly. 'Have you considered the implications for your proposal of the … (and then comes something obscure)?' This can undo all the hard work you have been doing in presenting your case. Information then becomes a valuable resource. The dissemination of inadequate or deceptive information becomes itself part of organizational **politics**. Subterfuge, lies and disinformation, i.e. information which, though not inaccurate, is designed to mislead through omissions of vital elements, are features of the political life of many organizations, in which individuals and groups compete for power by affecting to know more than they do.

But information is not the only form of knowledge which accords **power**. Knowing by acquaintance, knowing by description, knowing that and knowing how can all also translate into power. Knowing an important politician, a manager from a rival company or a supplier can enhance a person's **political** standing within an organization, as can their technical or political expertise, their social and **communication skills** or the procedural know-how. The value of knowledge increases in times of crisis or rapid **change**, when particular information or expertise acquires great value. Mental and manual skills enhance the market power of their holders and usually translate into better pay, job security and working conditions. A skilled craftsman no less than a lawyer may be able to convert their skills into earning capacity, so long as these skills are in limited supply.

There are times, however, when lack of knowledge – ignorance – can be a source of power. Consider a new manager who arrives in a company with very little direct knowledge of what has happened in the past. Such a manager may, of course, be easily outmanoeuvred by her scheming rivals who already know the ropes. Alternatively, however, she may be able to use her ignorance to her advantage. She has, after all, no axe to grind. She is not burdened by past failures and past successes. She is not tied to a particular brand or strategy. She is not disabled by the past as her predecessors were. She may also be given a 'honeymoon' period by her colleagues and subordinates, a period in which to prove herself. Under such circumstances, she may be able to succeed in initiating policies which would be doomed had they been initiated by someone with inside knowledge. We know an organization which appointed a new chief executive two years ago. He was brought in from outside, and from the start made a virtue of the fact that he did not know all the history of the company. He got away with a lot of actions which he could not have taken if he had been around for longer, and he would occasionally let slip a boast: 'they won't try to stop me, because they think I don't know my way around yet!'

IN CONCLUSION

In this chapter, we have introduced a number of important distinctions regarding the nature of individual and organizational knowledge and have examined how knowledge within organizations is transferred through stories, symbols and structures. In this way, knowledge can be said to exist independently of the people who make up an organization and survives staff changes.

We also examined how individuals and organizations learn and some of the obstacles which they must overcome in order to learn. We raised some reservations on current views which regard organizational learning as the key to competitive advantage and corporate success; we noted that in the area of organizations, it is hard to speak of right and wrong lessons, since such lessons are strongly influenced by wishful thinking and organizational **politics**.

Finally, we examined the view that **power** is knowledge, and vice versa, and identified certain ways in which different types of knowledge can enhance an individual's or an organization's position. Information is a particularly useful prop for power, though other types of knowledge may readily translate into power. There are instances, however, when ignorance can free an individual from the burden of the past, enabling them and/or their organization to attempt **actions** that would have otherwise been inhibited.

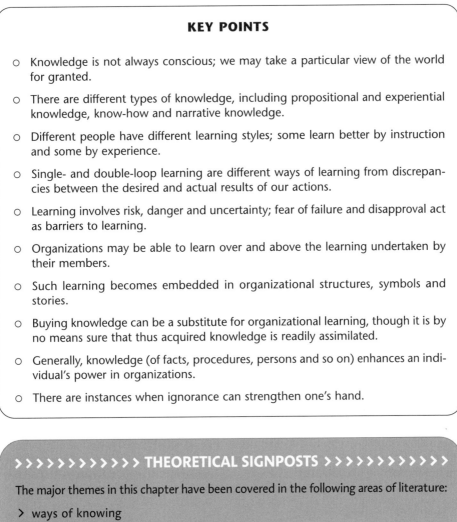

KEY POINTS

o Knowledge is not always conscious; we may take a particular view of the world for granted.

o There are different types of knowledge, including propositional and experiential knowledge, know-how and narrative knowledge.

o Different people have different learning styles; some learn better by instruction and some by experience.

o Single- and double-loop learning are different ways of learning from discrepancies between the desired and actual results of our actions.

o Learning involves risk, danger and uncertainty; fear of failure and disapproval act as barriers to learning.

o Organizations may be able to learn over and above the learning undertaken by their members.

o Such learning becomes embedded in organizational structures, symbols and stories.

o Buying knowledge can be a substitute for organizational learning, though it is by no means sure that thus acquired knowledge is readily assimilated.

o Generally, knowledge (of facts, procedures, persons and so on) enhances an individual's power in organizations.

o There are instances when ignorance can strengthen one's hand.

> > > > > > > > > > > **THEORETICAL SIGNPOSTS** > > > > > > > > > > >

The major themes in this chapter have been covered in the following areas of literature:

> ways of knowing
> communities of practice
> organizational learning.

Ways of Knowing

Ways of knowing takes us into the philosophical discipline of epistemology, which has been studied since ancient times and is still a matter of lively debate. How do we know when we know something? What would assure us that we really do know it, and that we are not being deceived? Knowledge can usefully be distinguished from belief, which is often used to mean an untested form of knowledge, and truth; believing something (e.g. that the stock market will rise over the next few weeks) does not necessarily make it true. The distinction between 'knowing by acquaintance' and 'knowing by description' goes back to the work of Russell (1946), whereas Polanyi (1964) distinguished between 'knowing that' and 'knowing how'. Narrative knowledge as a key to understanding human learning and remembering was discussed among others by Bruner (1990); Weick (1985) has examined how story-telling functions as a means of sense-making; Gabriel (1991b; 2000) has examined how we turn facts into stories and stories into facts. The view that everyday knowing is not unlike scientific knowledge and that we should look at people as if they were scientists – developing theories, anticipating events, and trying to understand the world they are living in – goes back to Kelly (1955).

Management learning is a relatively recent discipline which developed out of the writings of, among others, Argyris and Schön (1978) (who proposed the distinction between single- and double-loop learning), Mintzberg (1973) (who identified the competences deployed by actual managers in their work), Senge (1990) (who codified the features of a learning organization) and Pedler, Burgoyne and Boydell (1997) (who identified different types of learning). Learning, under conditions of complexity and unpredictability, has been studied by Stacey (1992, 1995) who brings together insights from chaos theory and psychoanalysis. On interruptions as a key feature of management work, Mintzberg's (1973) work remains seminal.

Communities of Practice

Communities of practice have come into the literature in the late twentieth century. One of the most significant early contributions came from Lave and Wenger (1991) whose research showed that much learning did not come from identifiable individuals, but from a number of people interacting in a situation. Elmes and Kasouf (1995) took the theme further, showing that much learning takes place in informal settings, often by people working in similar fields telling stories to each other as a way of passing on knowledge. Debate has continued about the managerial significance of these studies; for example, Wenger has argued that if someone tells him that they are trying to implement communities of practice, he knows that they have not understood the point, because they are not something which are amenable to such conscious managerial choice and action.

Organizational Learning

Organizational learning was brought to prominence by Argyris and Schön (1978) with their work which showed some of the practical and theoretical significance of the concept. It gained great popularity as a concept over the next few years, as well as receiving considerable further refinement and elaboration (Kim, 1993). Cook and Yanow (1993) offer a convincing image of organizational learning as something over and above the learning of their individual members. Based on a study of high quality flute-making firms in Boston, Massachusetts, they argued that the specialist expertise which made each firm unique did not reside in individual members of staff. When craftspeople moved from one company to another, even doing apparently the same job, there was a whole lot they had to learn about how that job was done in their new company.

Interest in the topic was further enhanced with a book which put more practical flesh on to the idea (Nonaka and Takeuchi, 1995). The concept of organizational learning as a key to competitive advantage has been explored, among others, by Moingeon and Edmondson (1996) and Probst and Buchel (1997). Interest in the field has been paralleled by interest in Knowledge Management, which is a concept which has often been used in a very similar way.

REVIEW QUESTIONS

1. People have very different ways of learning. What implications does this have for organizations that you have seen working? What is your own preferred way of learning, and can you learn in other ways if you need to?

2. Finding a community of practice in which you can develop is one of the most important features of learning for both the individual and the organization. What can be done to enable effective communities of practice to come about?

3. We do not learn much if we are too anxious about making mistakes, but it may take only one big mistake to kill our organization. How can this dilemma be resolved?

companion
website
.sagepub.co.uk/fineman

Reading On

The articles below are available for free to readers of the fourth edition of *Organizing & Organizations* via the book's companion website at www.sagepub.co.uk/fineman

Brookfield, S.D., Kalliath, T. and Laiken, M. (2006) 'Exploring the connections between adult and management education', *Journal of Management Education,* 30: 828–39.
In this interview, Stephen Brookfield, a four-time recipient of the World Award for Literature in Adult Education, responds to questions from Thomas Kalliath and Marilyn Laiken on a range of topics, including connections between adult education and management education, lifelong learning, team learning, organizational and workplace learning, and corporate social responsibility.

Cortese, C.G. (2005) 'Learning through teaching', *Management Learning,* 36: 87–115.
This work is the result of a study undertaken aimed at providing an insight into the way individuals learn through their work in an organization. The results of this study confirm certain evolutionary trends which are to be found in the current method of planning managerial training: the utilization of internal resources, the use of a dialogic style, the search for a link between work and training, and the use of small groups.

Gray, D.E. (2007) 'Facilitating management learning: developing critical reflection through reflective tools', *Management Learning,* 38: 495–517.

Critical reflection is not a process that comes naturally to many managers and may have to be learned or facilitated, either in formal classroom contexts, or through learning processes such as coaching, mentoring and action learning. This article discusses some of the tools available to learning facilitators, in helping a group or client towards a more critically reflective understanding of their situation and organization.

Tight, M. (2000) 'Critical perspectives on management learning: a view from adult/continuing/lifelong education', *Management Learning.* 31: 103–19.

This article focuses on the beliefs and understandings of adult/continuing/lifelong education, and considers what it might have to say to, and share with, management learning. Five particular areas of research are selected for discussion, and it is argued that what adult/continuing/lifelong education may have to offer is a more radical and political perspective, and one which is always concerned to look beyond the organization and below the management level.

4

MOTIVES AND MOTIVATING

Motivation is one of the most used – and abused – concepts in management. Is it a really helpful notion that explains important driving forces within individuals in organizations, or is it a concept that has been stretched beyond breaking point? This chapter puts motivation into perspective, examining some of the strengths and weaknesses of popular approaches and theories. Simplistic, one-dimensional, motivational accounts are critiqued. Attention is drawn particularly to how motivation is not so much rooted inside people, but is a learned discourse or vocabulary. As such, it is very much culture-bound and embedded in an organization's politics and managerial agendas.

REAL-LIFE EXAMPLE

Martin's Story

'Martin, please explain exactly why you did it!'

Martin was sitting nervously in front of Alex, his stern-looking boss. The previous day, he had flown in from the New York office for a crucial meeting in London with a client, concerning a two-million-pound contract. But Martin didn't show up. And he had left no word that he would not attend.

He knew his job was on the line. There was an uncomfortable silence while he struggled to say something. At heart, he was very confused ...

'Well ... Alex, I, er, can't really say how sorry I am. It's terrible. I feel awful about it. As you know, I've always been on top of things and that's very important to me. But yesterday I somehow lost track of time, and when I realized what had happened, I felt so ashamed that I didn't know what to do. My doctor says I've got a stress problem. It's been an awful year at work, what with all the organizational changes and losing three key people from the New York office – still not replaced. I guess the pressure has finally got to me; I'm so sorry.'

Alex listened intently: 'Oh dear. Are you sure that's the main problem, Martin? Your level of stress does bother me though – but I'm puzzled why you haven't said more about that to me.'

There were lots of things that Martin didn't tell Alex. On the way over on the plane, he found himself sitting next to a woman he once knew. They had attended the same MBA programme some seven years ago. Martin was what you might call a high achiever. The MBA had meant a rapid acceleration in his career and he was constantly looking for the next big break. Indeed, he had already started conversations about a new, better paid, job in New York and he felt confident he would get it.

After a couple of glasses of wine, they both started reminiscing and sharing the ups and downs of their lives. She was recently divorced and he was going through a bad patch with his partner. On landing, she invited him to dinner at her apartment and they ended up sleeping together. In the morning, he felt confused and jet lagged, and was running late for the meeting. He jumped into a taxi which immediately hit a huge traffic jam. He tried to relax, while feeling pangs of guilt about the night before. He liked to see himself as a loyal, trustworthy person, so why did he do that, he asked himself.

He picked up his mobile and rang to say hi to his elderly mother who lived in London. As ever, she was pleased to hear from him, but had some devastating news. His younger sister had just been admitted to hospital with suspected cancer. He was very close to his sister.

The taxi was making painfully slow progress and he was now 10 minutes late. He thought it better to walk so he hurriedly left the taxi and dashed towards the office where they were to meet. He arrived at the building some 20 minutes late, but not too late, he thought, to make his apologies. Then he noticed that he'd left a crucial file in the taxi. It contained all the details of his presentation. He felt a surge of panic, turned away and walked in daze towards the nearby park.

What motivated Martin to walk away? His shame at not being able to deliver? His fear of looking incompetent? His lack of commitment to the job – with a new one on the horizon? His confusion about his love life? His distress about his sister's illness? Or, perhaps, a mix of all of these. Like much of life, seeking *a* motive for something is often what we feel compelled to do; yet, in doing so, we often simplify situations which, on closer examination, could be full of possible motives and directions. Some will be self-evident, a consequence of immediate happenings; others will be echoes of past experiences.

But why even raise the issue of motive? The idea of 'motive' has become a key one for explaining social action – at least in Western societies. Organizations are seen to function with purpose when certain actions can be explained or justified, to self or to others. For managers especially, these explanations are often regarded as a clue to how to persuade or encourage people to work differently – longer, harder, or more rewardingly. They offer a hint at the right 'button' to press, a clichéd image peddled by some 'motivation consultants'.

But are there really such buttons? In essence, motives are accounts, or explanations, that give the impression that (a) human actions have reason and purpose behind them, and (b) there is meaning and cause to what we do. Often, there are many internally conflicting feelings about why we do something, but we experience pressures to present them as single and simple. Martin was struggling to explain to himself his one-night fling. With a motive located, he could, at least, convince himself that he now knew what he was dealing with, as unpalatable as it might be (e.g. 'loneliness', 'insecurity' or 'sheer lust'). Should Martin's partner discover his infidelity, it is unlikely that any of these justifications would be acceptable to her. To his boss, however, Martin could give an explanation of 'work stress' to excuse his failure to make the meeting, knowing that it could help his boss make sense of the event in acceptable management language. In these ways, **motivation** is not necessarily a mysterious, absolute, inner force, but a subtle social process of accepted justifications for present, future or past acts.

Some of these justifications are implicit. Much of what we do simply feels right or simply goes ahead smoothly without deliberation. We do not stop to analyse everything we do to identify a motive or reason for doing it. Often, when we do, we can struggle to find reasons. This may be because they seem complex and confusing, hard to pin down as Martin experiences; there really is no straightforward account that makes sense. Or it may be, as psychoanalysts claim, that much of what we do arises from unconscious motives – we are simply unaware of what impels us. Generally, however, motivation becomes an issue when an explanation is required to sustain, repair or restore a social relationship; or, as we will discuss, when there is intention to influence others' behaviours.

VOCABULARIES OF MOTIVES

We learn a vocabulary of motives from early on in life. For instance, a young child will happily eat whenever and whatever it wants until checked or regulated by a parent. However, it soon learns that uttering the words 'I'm hungry' is one acceptable way of explaining the reason for wanting more food, regardless of any inner physical pangs for food. On the other hand, 'I'm feeling greedy' is not so socially acceptable. Motives are very much social products, **social constructions** that are often post hoc in their application. In other words, we try and make sense of our own and others' feelings, **decisions** or actions by slotting them into one or more social–motivational categories: 'she did it because she needed recognition'; 'I guess I loved her so much that I couldn't help what I did'; 'he's ruthless because of his feelings of inferiority'. We draw on the kind of explanations that have social currency or worth in our social circles. When unusual behaviour is tagged with an accepted motive or motives, it can then be worked on as an issue to be addressed at its apparent source and 'managed'.

But vocabularies of motive vary. Different social circles and **cultures** give different priorities to the motives they consider relevant, good or bad. A manager undertaking performance appraisal, for example, can explain her action as motivated by her concern for increased organizational performance. The person being appraised, however, can see it as a means of manipulation. It is commonplace for trade union leaders to say they are calling for strike action in order to improve safety at work, or the standard of living of their members. The bosses affected by the strike can retort: 'it's nothing to do with safety or living standards, that's a rationalization; they just want to get more control over the company'. The parties bring different frames of reference, or values, to how they account for the event. One person's motivation is another's rationalization. It is a phenomenon evident in the apparent motives for large pay rises and bonuses for some senior executives. Contrast the union perspective with that of the bosses:

> Union: 'With such excessive pay packages for company directors, it is becoming clear to staff that "there's one rule for us and one rule for them". Indeed, the obscene pay-offs for directors leaving failing companies is more like throwing "good money after bad"'. (General Secretary, Trade Union Congress)

> Bosses: 'There will always be a significant difference between shopfloor and boardroom pay. Those individuals with the responsibility of running multinational companies and securing the jobs of thousands of employees worldwide rightly command large salaries'. (Deputy Director-General, Confederation of British Industry)

Here we see the motive of 'status and greed', pitched against 'reward for responsibility'. Both have strong resonance among the different parties and their constituencies. The point here is less a matter of the 'true' motive for each party (one could construct many possible motives for each group). The reality is to **negotiate** a balance or compromise, a vocabulary of motive that both groups can accept or live with, at least for the time being. Attributed motives are highly **politicized** in such contexts (and, to an extent, in all contexts), and the power of each party to sway the other is a crucial part of the process. Where the **power** balance is heavily skewed, the motive attributed by the more powerful person often prevails. When a 'tough' boss says to her junior assistant, recently out of college: 'Jennie, the more I see of your work style, and all the errors you make, the more I'm convinced that you are not a committed person and that you don't really want to progress here…', it asserts a motivational picture that Jennie can find hard to contest openly. She may well have a different account of her own motives ('I've felt so confused and have been wanting support') but feels too intimidated by her boss's style and position to say so.

What an organization's elite (usually managers and executives) view as 'proper' motivation will often hold sway over how people's performances are judged (such as their level of ambition, compliance, cooperativeness, perseverance). For instance, in the 1960s, Douglas McGregor spoke of managers tending to split in their views about human nature. Some managers were Theory X people, with others Theory Y. Theory X managers believed that workers generally disliked responsibility, were resistant to change and needed to be led. Theory Y managers, on the other hand, regarded workers as keen to work towards organizational **goals**, receptive to managerial initiatives and able to take personal responsibility for their actions (see Figure 4.1).

Once employees become labelled in these ways, certain 'motivational' approaches follow. Under Theory X, workers required direction, rewards and punishments, while, from a Theory Y perspective, workers would perform better under a more liberal regime, with opportunities to learn and develop.

The catch in this logic is plain to see: the more people are treated in a particular way, the more they become like that. It is a self-fulfilling prophecy as employees respond to the reality created for them. Crude motivational categories, however misguided, can be

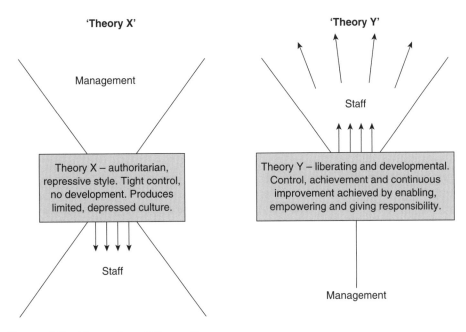

Figure 4.1   Theory X and Theory Y.

powerfully influential in the hands of those who are able to enforce them. Moreover, they tend to survive because the complexity of many real-life motivational circumstances (such as in our opening story) is difficult to handle in actual managerial practice.

Some motivational assumptions are **institutionalized**, deeply embedded in the way an organization is constituted. In courts of law, for instance, much effort goes into determining the specific motive for a crime. A motiveless crime is a contradiction in terms in the legal arena. Yet even casual reflection on accounts of crimes and the personal history of offenders, often reveals a hugely complex set of conditions which shaped the criminal and the crime.

But if the legal system requires a motive to be found in order to properly perform its role, then a legally appropriate motive will be identified (e.g. a crime of 'passion', 'jealousy', 'greed', 'malice', 'mental instability' and so on). Powerful groups, such as the police, barristers and judges, make this possible. A similar dynamic occurs with other professional groups. To account for others' intentions, they draw on a vocabulary of motives from their particular professional training. Teachers, psychiatrists, psychologists, management **consultants**, counsellors, psychoanalysts and medical practitioners all use their specific perspectives, ways of looking at things, to account for why a person does what he or she does. For instance, consider a 'workaholic' manager, someone who rarely seems to stop, whether at work or at home. What motivates such behaviour? A psychoanalyst can point to the manager's failures early in life which are constantly, and unconsciously, reworked in the present as a compulsive desire to feel in control. The workaholic, moreover, has created a 'good' excuse to avoid uncomfortable relationships at home. A workplace stress counsellor, on the other hand, may emphasize the person's over-concern with too many small details and a reluctance to delegate. The manager's boss, however (who is very pleased with the person's performance) says he's 'a man fired with ambition'. The attributed motives are true only insofar as the affected parties believe them to be true and feel they are helpful. And whether they are believed to be true, or false, they will always affect the way people treat each other. Motives, therefore, are useful props to meaning and action, but they are also the products of different '**discourses**', or vocabularies of motive, that different experts bring.

NEEDING NEEDS?

In seeking reasons for behaviour, the notion of 'needs' has been influential in popular accounts of motivation. The belief is that the secret to motivation lies, not in the way accounts are constructed or in the relationships between people, but in our biological drives and innate dispositions. They are honed through struggles to survive over many millennia. So we have innate *needs* for warmth, sex, water, food, oxygen and shelter, essential to our continued existence. To some extent, these approaches state the obvious (we will die if we do not eat, drink or breathe). But they also set an unfortunate precedent for other theories that suggest all our motives start with internal 'needs' that impel our behaviour. Unfortunate because it is tautological to say that, for example, we are ambitious because we have a need to achieve, or we are sociable because we have a need for contact. The approach tells us more about the ethos in Westernized, **achievement**-based which societies see the springs of behaviour 'inside' people and charge them with exclusive responsibility for their own actions.

The 'needs' thinking is starkly evident in the much regurgitated 'hierarchy of needs' of American Abraham Maslow. In the 1940s, Maslow proposed a 'general theory of motivation' that outlined various levels, or stages, of need. As one stage is relatively satisfied, allegedly the next one becomes dominant – the prime motivator. His hierarchy starts with physiological needs (e.g. food, air, water, sleep). The more these needs are met, he suggests, the more the person becomes preoccupied with the next level – finding safety, stability and security. On feeling safe, the desire to avoid loneliness then comes into view – through contact with friends, peers and other affectionate relationships. After this, self-esteem is more important – respect from others, status, achievement and appreciation. We may move up and down these different need-states, especially as we hit life crises. Losing one's job, for instance, soon triggers the need for safety and security. At the pinnacle of the hierarchy is self-actualization, a special state that represents the desire continuously to self-improve, to 'be all that you can be'. It is a need that gets stronger the more it is fed, but cannot prosper unless the 'lower' needs are relatively satisfied.

Maslow's ideas were not formulated for work situations, but they have been extensively applied there in terms of the circumstances that can facilitate or block motivational development. Specifically, they have been taken as a way of offering incentives to workers to move onwards and upwards. To an extent, the theory states truisms: workers, once feeling that they are able to feed and house themselves, may well require other incentives to ensure their cooperation or compliance, such as having the sociability of colleagues and opportunities for achievement. Additionally, the freedom continually to self-develop sounds attractive, if not highly idealistic. Maslow's formulations were published in an era when work under capitalism was feared to be dehumanizing and **alienating**, so they provided a refreshing contrast – and a convenient camouflage – for deeper questions concerning life's purpose and satisfactions. They gave management the opportunity, backed up by the authority of social science, to assert that alienating work was not so meaningless after all, if it was thought of as meeting particular human needs in a systematic, but progressive, way. It was a view that appealed particularly to white, adult, middle-class Americans, people who were doing well in life and aspired to do even better. But, black and ethnic **sub-cultures** and teenagers can promote their own, distinctive, value systems which do not correspond to Maslow's neat hierarchy. There are also national variations. Scandinavians, for example, tend to place more emphasis on social needs than individual self-actualization, while the Chinese put considerable priority on safety and security. Lastly, there are some stark individual exceptions to Maslow's logic – such as clergy who are prepared to live a life of sexual abstinence, and highly creative actors and artists who are constantly economically insecure.

Such exceptions draw attention to the naïvety of seeing motivation in simple, linear terms. While it is undeniable that we are born with predispositions to survive, in that our bodies require food and water, beyond this there is a huge influence of **culture** on how and when we express, address or account for these and other 'needs'. For example, eating is as much a social occasion as a desire for food. Even the desire to go to the toilet can be postponed if it seems rude or embarrassing to leave another's company. Our motives, and the stories we tell about them, are patterned by our work identities, group **norms** and social backgrounds. We learn to **desire**, more or less, whatever incentives the workplace has to offer, but workplaces are designed primarily for the economic movement of goods and services, not for the 'needs' of workers. Similarly, as consumers, we learn to 'need' new products because of the desires and **fantasies** they create for us, fostered by skilful advertising and marketing. Such needs are socially constructed.

What is managerially manipulable in such settings becomes the basis of workplace desires and incentives, such as money, status, pensions, social groupings, responsibility and power. Some such incentives will be more personally attractive, more motivating, than others, depending on the way we construct our **identities** at work, and how these intersect with other aspects of our lives. Our life positions as parents, elderly, carers, men, women, black, white, recently married, leisure lovers, ambitious professionals, new graduates, and so forth will shape what is desirable, or merely tolerable, in the workplace.

MOTIVES AND FAIRNESS

Perceptions of unfairness often nag people at work. They are at the root of how content, or otherwise, they feel, and are behind their judgements of what is right or wrong with the way they are treated. Ideas about fairness place motives firmly in the social arena. They provide a different vocabulary of motive, of the sort 'I did it because I felt I was treated unfairly'. They are based on the view that, in competitive societies, people are always making comparisons with others, consciously and unconsciously. In social

> **Good Day Stealing at the Office Dear?**
>
> Small-scale pilfering and expense fraud is costing the UK £831 million per year according to a survey of UK office workers.
>
> 43 per cent of UK workers think expense fraud is dishonest, many workers feel justified in making long-distance telephone calls from work.
>
> Some dishonest employees have even sent out their wedding invitations at the expense of the company.
>
> According to the survey results, 78 per cent of office workers have taken home stationery over the past year and 59 per cent have put personal post through the company mail.
>
> One in five has added £10 or more to an expenses claim while 15 per cent admit to having inflated their travel expenses.
>
> More seriously, two per cent say they took a friend out for a meal and charged their employer, while three per cent say they falsely claimed back £50 or more on an expenses claim.
>
> Many office workers feel that they are simply getting back a little of what their employers take from them.
>
> Two-thirds (67 per cent) say taking home stationery is justified due to having to make work calls from their personal mobile phone.
>
> 29 per cent say getting 'a little back' on expenses is OK as bosses very often ask for extras such as having to work beyond normal working hours.

Figure 4.2   Fair theft?

psychology, fairness is the principle underlying 'equity theory'. We set our aspirations and goals in relation to what we see others do or have, and we compare the rewards we get with what others get – a common basis for deciding what feels right, or equitable – on pay, for example. We seek fair exchanges. What happens next depends on how strongly we feel about those comparisons. We may choose to live with any unfairness, to rationalize it ('oh, I guess they do deserve more than me'). Or we may act to rectify discrepancies to achieve what we feel we rightly deserve, such as through petty larceny – stealing small items from the workplace because 'they owe it to me' – or making unauthorized telephone calls. A 2008 survey in the UK, summarized in Figure 4.2, reveals just how such 'dishonesty' is seen.

Fairness and unfairness are, of course, in the eye of the beholder. In organizations, they sit alongside different beliefs about what is or is not fair, as well as different reasons for grievances. Unresolved, however, unfairness can fester like a wound, and infect others – sometimes with cataclysmic results.

For example, on the afternoon of 24 August 1992, mechanical engineering professor Valery Fabrikant of Concordia University in Montreal, shot five of his colleagues, killing three of them. For two years, he had been engaged in a running battle with his department and the university over what he considered to be unfair treatment. He contended that the decision to deny him promotion, and then lay him off, was malicious and unfair.

'Good Day Stealing at the Office Dear?', *Swinton Advertiser*, Thursday 8 January 2004.

We do not normally murder our colleagues, however unfairly we feel treated. In Fabrikant's case, there were various social exchanges that fuelled his grievance and distress. Fabrikant, a highly prolific researcher, had been insistent that there had been academic fraud in his department, which made him very unpopular (despite the fact that his allegations were later upheld by the university). His actions had attracted the attention of an administrator who found 'minor discrepancies' in his personnel file, and asked Fabrikant for proof of his academic qualifications. As the **conflict** with his immediate colleagues escalated, he was 'disciplined' with an increase in teaching load, which, he asserted, was in an area beyond his expertise. His reputation as a 'difficult person' was growing. He was condemned by a senior member of the university as 'lacking compassion about, or concern for, or even interest in the well-being of any other adult human being'. Then, to compound matters, a former student appeared, accusing Fabrikant of rape, at which point the media began to take an interest in his story. At his trial, a psychiatrist described him as having a serious **personality** disorder, including paranoia and **narcissism**. He was found guilty of murder and jailed for life (where he still continued with his academic writings).

Fabrikant's devastating actions may well be those of a 'deranged' individual. But his case also illustrates how notions of fairness and grievance are deeply embedded in the **politics** and **prejudices** of organizations, where there are reputations to protect and social **norms** to respect. Our personal turmoils, whatever they be, are stoked and made meaningful within the social relationships of work.

WHOSE GOALS? WHOSE MOTIVES?

In **consultancy** and management development work, we often hear managers complain that 'my workers are not motivated' and a stock response has become: 'no, only dead people aren't motivated, they're just not motivated to do what you want them to do' (Thompson and McHugh, 2002: 314).

Experts in human resource management sometimes talk blithely about getting workers to 'buy in' to what management wants, getting them to embrace management's goals. It is fanciful, however, to assume that any prescribed goal can necessarily be a source of another's sustained motivation and **commitment**. If that **goal** (e.g. higher production targets, reduced manpower, new waste targets) is perceived as obviously belonging to management, in their exclusive interest, then its motivational edge is blunt. There is no buy-in. It does not provide a psychological hook whereby employees can say to themselves: 'this is meaningful to me, it is something I want and asked for' – what we earlier called an agreeable justification. They may comply, especially if bribed or forced, but often in an atmosphere of antagonism or resentment.

In the vast majority of work organizations, the final say rests with management, slanting the power relationship between employer and employee. In a culture of mutual **trust,** this may still work out reasonably effectively, in circumstances where motivation's vocabularies are shared or well negotiated. The boundaries between 'them' and 'us' are soft, or amicably drawn. Where such groundwork is shaky, mistrust is fomented, and even well-meaning motivational schemes can fail. Some approaches to '**empowerment**' and 'job enrichment' have floundered in this manner. These projects are normally presented as offering workers more autonomy, recognition and satisfaction in their jobs,

"Congratulations! You're now
empowered to accept all the blame!"

Figure 4.3   The myth of empowerment.

but can end up being received as trivial or, even, oppressive. One management cartoon (see Figure 4.3) satirically catches the mood.

Traditionally, empowerment has been a way of providing natural communities with resources – education, skills and technologies – to develop the kind of society that they want, in their own terms. In the workplace, however, empowerment rarely gives workers the freedom to improve their jobs in any way they choose. Rather, and ironically, someone in power determines what one is 'empowered' to do. The energy and ownership, the meaning of the initiative, can be seen to be second-hand. So some employees feel resentful that being 'empowered' involves having to take on, for instance, extra responsibilities, without commensurate pay, responsibilities that their managers or supervisors once had. It is seen as a cost-cutting exercise. Suspicion is further fuelled when managers appear to be using empowerment as way of offloading obligations which should, properly, be theirs. So the check-in clerk for Budget Airlines becomes 'empowered' to supervise passengers as they enter the aircraft, to help load the luggage and meals and to assist in the supervision of cabin-cleaning between departures – but his or her remuneration remains unchanged.

Empowerment, therefore, risks being seen as in no one's interests but the instigating directors'. The issue of the 'true' motive here is clearly debatable. More to the point, however, is that once such different **perceptions** are set, they become difficult to bridge. Empowerment's potential as a source of liberation and new meaning can only be fully realized if its subjects are not taken for granted and can **participate** fully, and willingly, in its shaping and rewards.

Job enrichment can be similarly viewed. Particularly popular in the 1970s, job enrichment has meant giving workers, who typically perform a limited task, the opportunity to do several different tasks, often collaboratively. It is assumed that this will enhance their motivation towards organizational goals (because of greater achievement and social contact). It also offers management indirect **control** over worker output and quality. It capitalizes on the power of the group to bring any 'slackers' into line, and optimizes its performance and financial rewards. For example, the car worker who routinely installs windscreens on a car production line now joins other workers around a work station, and together they assemble a section of the whole car, working out their own schedule, but within managerially set boundaries.

The extent to which this is, in fact, a psychologically richer, motivating, experience for the worker is questionable. Do the individuals have any choice in determining how their job is to be 'enriched'? Do they want it enriched? Is management offering discussions and discretion on the *context* of the job (e.g. pay, supervision, general working conditions), or is it confined just to the details of the *content* (who does what, quality standards, specific task requirements)? If workers are content to see themselves as recipients of such initiatives, and the rewards are indeed rewarding to them, then they may well respond positively.

IN CONCLUSION

Motivation is a loaded, significant term in organizational behaviour. This chapter draws attention to the important ways in which motivation is used, or deployed, in understanding the different ways that people in organizations account for their actions. This is a much more sophisticated process than the impulses of internal needs. Vocabularies of motives, who defines, who 'owns' them, are important in how we seek and create meaning and influence in organizations. We learn motivational scripts and apply them to ourselves, or impose them on others. In many respects, managers and other professionals are in powerful positions to 'create' others' motives, in ways that can be helpful, or restrictive and manipulative. There is often a tendency to try and understand complex situations or behaviours by reducing them to *a* motive, which then makes them more manageable. But it can also over-simplify, in that there are often several different, and plausible, accounts of 'why'.

KEY POINTS

o   There are many possible motives that can explain behaviour in organizations.

o   Ascribing a motive is itself a social phenomenon, learned and shaped within a particular culture.

o   Often, motives are contested and politicized during organizational conflicts and negotiations.

o   Motivation from internal biological needs explains only a small sub-set of organizational behaviours. Beyond this, there are few universal patterns of needs – culture being a powerful determinant.

o   Perceptions of fairness are central to how well people feel treated and what they will do to alter their circumstances.

o   In programmes of employee empowerment and commitment, management can often abuse, as well as constructively harness, principles and beliefs about motivation.

> > > > > > > > > > > > **THEORETICAL SIGNPOSTS** > > > > > > > > > > > >

Motivation theories, mostly psychological in origin, are part and parcel of almost all organizational behaviour textbooks, although their actual practicality is much argued over. The key motivation themes covered in this chapter can be found in three bodies of literature:

> critiques of the concept of motivation
> classical theories of motivation
> applications of motivation theories to the workplace.

Critiques of the Concept of Motivation

The idea that motives are specially learned vocabularies, socially constructed and culturally nuanced, rather than embedded 'inside' us, is explained in classic writings by Burke (1950) and Duncan (1962). A very readable introduction can be found in Watson (2008). Watson (1996) has argued that formal motivation theories serve more to prop up certain cultural values in the workplace, such as achievement and hard work, rather than to explain the roots of human action, and that few managers actually see them as directly useful. This line is also reflected in the critical writings of Thompson and McHugh (2002).

Classical Theories of Motivation

Classic, psychological, theories of motivation are summarized in traditional introductory textbooks on organizational behavior, such as Buchanan and Huczynski (2006) and Mullins (2007). In these works, Abraham Maslow's theory of a need hierarchy (Maslow, 1954), Frederick Herzberg's two-factor theory (Herzberg et al., 1959), Douglas McGregor's Theory X and Y (McGregor, 1960), Stacy Adams' Equity Theory (Adams, et al., 1976) and Victor Vroom's Expectancy Theory (Vroom, 1964) are discussed and critiqued. These theories in particular have shaped our common understanding about the nature of motivation but are often over-simplified representations of what are complex motivational issues. A further important influence is David McClelland's (1961) theory of achievement motivation featured in his book *The Achieving Society*. It illustrates the way the 'need to achieve' has been developed in entrepreneurial economies and how it may be triggered and enhanced in children and adults.

Psychoanalytic theories of motivation provide a rather different perspective, stressing the unconscious motives that drive behavior, rooted in our early family experiences and encounters with authority figures. Based on the extensive work of Sigmund Freud (1953), psychoanalysis suggests that we are often unaware of what impels us and we easily deceive ourselves and others as to our true intentions. Psychoanalysis challenges the picture of a rational organization where decision makers are in full control of themselves and others (see Elliott, 2002).

Applications of Motivation Theories to the Workplace

Psychoanalysis has been applied by Kets de Vries and Miller (1984) to 'the neurotic organization' to expose the hidden, inconsistent or irrational motivations of key decision makers. It is a theme further developed by de Board (1978), Carr (1998) and Gabriel (1999b). They explain how psychoanalysis can illuminate some of the tensions, rigidities and formation of individual identities in organizations. The other motivational approaches have been used to explain how specific management styles, reward systems and organizational structures can be more or less motivating to employees. Each tap into differing levels of need satisfaction (Maslow); the absence or otherwise of intrinsic work incentives or 'motivators' (Herzberg); and individual expectations about work goals and their attractiveness or 'valence' (Vroom, Adams). Overviews of these approaches can be found in Green (1992), Pinder (2008) and Steers et al. (2003).

REVIEW QUESTIONS

1. Consider what you have been doing over the past hour. How would the notion of 'vocabularies of motive' account for why you did what you did?

2. What are the shortcomings of some of the mainstream theories of work motivation?

3. In what ways should we consider the management of motivation in organizations as a politicized phenomenon?

---

companion website
w.sagepub.co.uk/fineman

Reading On

The articles below are available for free to readers of the fourth edition of *Organizing & Organizations* via the book's companion website at www.sagepub.co.uk/fineman

Ambrose, M.L. and Kulik, C. T. (1999) 'Old friends, new faces: motivation research in the 1990s', *Journal of Management*, 25 (3): 231–92.
This article reports the principal findings of over 200 studies of work motivation published between January 1990 and December 1997, examining research relevant to traditional motivational theories as well as emerging topic areas. For each area, the article summarizes the research, identify trends and issues that deserve further research attention.

Carlisle, Y.M. and Manning, D. J. (1994) 'The concept of ideology and work motivation', *Organization Studies*, 15 (5): 683–703.
Shamir noted that 'current reviews of work-motivation theories are unanimous in their dissatisfaction with the state-of-the-art'. He concluded that existing theories offer an inadequate account of the impetus of employment and should be 'supplemented by a self-concept based theory of work motivation'. This paper suggests that the concept of ideology can provide a foundation for this kind of theory.

Neher, A. (1991) 'Maslow's theory of motivation: a critique', *Journal of Humanistic Psychology*, 31 (3): 89–112.
This critique of Maslow's theory of motivation examines all of its major components. The theory is summarized and its basic propositions are analysed in the light of internal logic, other relevant theories, and related research, pointing up many deficiencies in Maslow's theory, which enjoys wide acceptance especially among humanistic psychologists.

Watson, T.J. (1996) 'Motivation: that's Maslow, isn't it?', *Management Learning*, 27 (4): 447–64.
This article focuses on students' reactions to their earlier study of motivation theories and on how they react to challenges put to them about their uncritical reception of material they now begin to see as lacking. The author suggests that the problems shown to exist may relate to ones of surface and deep learning in higher education more generally, as well as the symbolic and comforting role of material like Maslow's hierarchy of needs in management teaching and learning.

5

RULES ARE RULES

This chapter looks at the formal, bureaucratic rules that seek to control people's behaviour in most organizations, ensuring that they act in line with organizational objectives. Rules give organizations some of their impersonal, formal qualities – they affect people equally, without consideration of their personal needs and concerns. We examine whether such rules are 'rational' – whether, in other words, they enhance organizational functioning or whether, conversely, they place hurdles in the way of people trying to do their work efficiently and sensibly. In particular, we investigate why there are times when it is more rational to bend or disregard certain rules than to follow them. Rules in organizations, we argue, are closely related to relations of authority, authorizing certain individuals to give particular kinds of orders and ensuring that others will obey them. Yet, the interpretation and enforcement of rules is itself part of the political processes of organizations – different individuals and groups seek to mould and twist rules to their interests and use them to their advantage. Bending rules may lead to increasing violations and eventual anarchy, yet a degree of rule-bending and ignoring is normal practice in most organizations.

REAL-LIFE EXAMPLE

Mike's Story

'Password!'

I applied to Securecops on the off-chance. I attended an interview in their fortress-like headquarters on the Thames Embankment. It lasted all of five minutes. I would get my first job the following week. What I had to remember, at all times, was

SECURITY, they said. I would be given a secret password, which would be changed each night. In all communications with HQ, and with any caller to the place I was guarding, I had to use the password.

I left HQ with my free kit under my arm: an ill-fitting blue uniform, a cap with a peak, a whistle, a torch and a truncheon.

A week later, I turned up to my first job. It was a US navy stores depot in an isolated spot in north London. As far I could tell, it contained things like Coca-Cola, soap and paper towels. I could not figure out why the US navy should have such a place in London. I felt self-conscious – a bit of a nerd in my new uniform. A Securecops supervisor met me to show me around. The rules the supervisor told me were this:

- Keep everything locked.
- Patrol the building and the perimeter wire once an hour.
- Ring in and report to HQ after each patrol. They'll chase you if you don't call.
- Get the password from HQ at the start of each shift, and use it in all calls.
- *Don't* smoke on patrol.
- *Don't* let anyone in unless they give the password.
- *Don't* fall asleep on the job, or you will be sacked.

The supervisor left. The guard I was replacing packed up his stuff. As he was leaving, he winked at me and said: 'Listen … skip a patrol or two and get all the sleep you can'. I was puzzled.

I got through the first night, exhausted. It was really scary going around the dark buildings. The very thought of using my truncheon on a human being filled me with horror. I decided the best thing to do was to run it against the wire fence and along doors as I patrolled. It made a hell of a racket but that should deter an intruder – I hoped.

Night two. I realized that I could easily skip a few patrols – as long as I rang HQ on time. Also, I found myself plotting other ways of bucking the system. Surely, you could do a deal with another guard, elsewhere, to ring HQ on your behalf? You'd then get more sleep some nights, and he could sleep while you're doing it for him. I later learned that such a dodge was well known, but no one had prevented it.

I found myself falling asleep between patrols, so I kept an alarm clock to wake me on time to report to HQ. In the middle of such a slumber, at about four in the morning, I was jolted awake by the loud, persistent hooting of a car horn. I scrambled for my uniform jacket, and grabbed my truncheon. I dashed outside, my heart racing.

I was facing the headlights of a van, shining through the wire mesh of the locked main gate. In front of the lights was the silhouette of a tall man.

'Christ, where the hell have you been? Let me in!'

I got a bit closer and saw the guy was wearing a Securecops uniform. I plucked up courage and shined my torch in his face. I recognized the supervisor. What a relief! I fumbled for my keys – and then hesitated. Hell, this could be a trick, I thought. To test me out. I'd better watch it.

'Oh, hi', I said, 'could you tell me the password, please?'

The man looked confused. Then he shouted at me: 'Like hell I can! Open these bloody doors and let me in. Just stop fooling around!'

I fingered the keys nervously. What on earth should I do? I was sure he was OK, but I was breaking a cardinal rule if I let him in. And he still might be tricking me. I tried very hard to sound authoritative:

'I can't let you in unless you tell me the password. *Rules are rules.*'

'I don't know the bloody password for tonight', he retorted getting more and more wound up.

Fearing for my physical safety, I eventually phoned HQ who were not in the slightest bit interested in the man's identification. I should let him in. He marched passed me, saying not a word. He left the same way after a very cursory check.

RULES IN ORGANIZATIONS

Mike did not last long in this job. But the incident raises important issues. Entering the organization is entering a world of formal rules and procedures. They govern every aspect of work, and seem to leave little room for discussion. 'No smoking' meant precisely 'No smoking', no matter who you were, how badly you wished to smoke or what it was that you would choose to smoke. Yet, after a few days at Securecops, Mike learned that rules were sometimes disregarded, broken or bent, occasionally with the consent of **management**.

Train drivers found out long ago that if every rule and every procedure of starting their locomotives were followed, the trains would never leave the stations or reach their destinations on time. 'Work to rule', sticking to every small rule and regulation in the book, was recognized as a very effective way of paralysing organizational performance. Sometimes, it takes a major accident before it is realized that official procedures have been flouted for so long.

Organizational rules can be usefully distinguished from social **norms**. Norms are the 'unwritten rules'. Employees of many companies, for example, go to work wearing casual clothes on Fridays, even though this is not enshrined in any formal rule. Nor is it a rule of the road that truck drivers should flash their headlights to indicate to an overtaking truck that it is safe to pull back, or for the overtaking truck to flash their indicator, as a sign of appreciation. Social norms guide many of our **actions**, both inside and outside organizations. Some of the other chapters highlight their importance and implications. This chapter focuses instead on the formal written rules and regulations which seem to set modern organizations apart from other types of human **groups**, like families or truck drivers on highways.

Rules and Factory Despotism

Formal rules and regulations are not a new phenomenon. Medieval monasteries had rules banning different types of behaviour and specified detailed penalties for different offences. For instance, a monk guilty of sexual intercourse with an unmarried person was required to fast for one year on bread and water, a nun guilty of the same offence between three and seven years (depending on the circumstances), a bishop for twelve years (see Morgan, 1986: 208). However, the proliferation of rules at the workplace coincides with the rise of the factory system and especially of large bureaucratic organizations. Consider the following extracts from the rules of a nineteenth century mill in Lancashire.

RULES

TO BE OBSERVED AND KEPT BY THE PEOPLE EMPLOYED IN THIS FACTORY

1. Each person employed in this factory engages to serve THOMAS AINSWORTH AND SONS, and to give one month's notice, in writing, previous to leaving his or her employment, such notice to be given in on a Saturday, and on no other day. But the Masters have full power to discharge any person employed therein without any previous notice whatsoever.
2. The hours of attendance are from Six o'clock in the morning until half-past Seven at Night, excepting Saturday when work shall cease at half-past Four. ...
5. Each spinner shall keep his or her wheels and wheelhouse clean, swept and fluked, or in default thereof, shall forfeit One Shilling. ...
10. Any person smoking tobacco, or having a pipe for that purpose, in any part of the Factory, shall forfeit Five Shillings.
11. Any person introducing a Stranger into the Factory without leave of one of the Proprietors, shall forfeit Two Shillings and Sixpence. ...
17. Any Workman coming into the Factory, or any other part of these Premises, drunk, shall pay Five Shillings.
18. Any Person employed in this Factory, engages not to be a member of, or directly or indirectly a subscriber to, or a supporter of, any Trades Union, or other Association whatsoever.
19. Any Person destroying or damaging this Paper, shall pay Five Shillings. ...

Such rules may shock us and be considered unfair and one-sided. Imposed unilaterally by the employer, they make no secret of whose interest they seek to protect. Their aim was control. Like political dictators, Messrs Ainsworth and Sons and other early capitalists sought to bolster their **power**. They made little pretence that the rules served anyone's welfare other than their own.

Rules and Modern Organizations

There are still organizations in some countries with rules not unlike those above. Most Western organizations today, however, shy away from such brutal rules, especially when they emphasize the potential for **conflict** between employers and employees. Nevertheless, when we join an organization, we usually undertake, through a written contract, to obey its rules and procedures. These are impersonal, they apply to all, and are laid down in company manuals and ordinances, dictating, sometimes in minuscule detail, what we can and what we cannot do, our rights and our obligations. Not all organizational rules are written down; each organization has many tacit rules, rules which are part of a psychological contract between itself and its members. Such tacit rules may include working after hours or refraining from talking to reporters about matters that may embarrass the organization. In exchange, organizations are perceived by individuals to offer reciprocal favours and rewards to their members, such as promotion and training opportunities.

What has changed since the days of Messrs Ainsworth and Sons is not the nature of the rules but our perception of their rationale. Instead of 'Do A, B and C because I say so', rules in modern organizations proclaim 'Do A, B and C because it is sensible to do so'. Unlike the exploitative rules of the illustration, the rules of modern organizations appear rational. In this sense, they resemble the rules of the road. Most of us will stop at a red traffic light, not because we are afraid of the policeman or because of our sense of moral duty, but because we recognize that stopping at red lights is a rational means of regulating traffic. At times, a red light will cause us great frustration, especially if we are in a great hurry, it is late at night and there is no other traffic on the road. Nevertheless, this does not make us argue that stopping at red lights is silly, senseless or unfair.

In a similar way, we recognize most of the organizational rules we obey as rational. To appreciate the exact sense of 'rational', consider a rational rule next to a patently irrational one. Most colleges and universities have formal rules requesting that students write essays when asked to do so by lecturers. They have no rules requiring students to wash their lecturers' cars, much as some lecturers might appreciate it. Is this accidental? Hardly. What formal *educational* or *organizational* purpose could possibly be served by rules authorizing superiors to order their subordinates to carry out personal favours? Such rules would not merely be immoral, but also irrational. Of course, the fact that there is no car-washing rule does not imply that no personal favours are ever requested. Favours, bribes and backhanders can all be part and parcel of doing business, embedded in the **norms** of some organizations. But they are not in any of the rule books (see Chapter 8, 'Politics and Deals' and Chapter 12, 'Morals').

Organizational rules are rational in as much as they are seen to be a means of enhancing the achievement of organizational ends. This type of rationality is often referred to as instrumental or means–end rationality. Information regarding alternatives and technical **knowledge** is an indispensable ingredient of this type of rationality. Ideally, rational rules would be the result of a methodical comparison and analysis of alternatives and the choice of those alternatives which are best suited to the organization's **goals**. In practice, this is not always the case. While most members of an organization may agree that the organization has goals, there is often disagreement about the nature of these goals or the order of priority in which they are placed. For instance, a doctor, a hospital porter, a secretary, a personnel manager, a nurse and a patient may have very different notions of what a hospital's goals are. Is the hospital's goal to cure patients, to relieve pain, to improve the health standards of people, to carry out large numbers of operations, to offer a very high quality of medical care, to carry out world-class research, to make patients feel happy or to make profit?

Formal technical rules, therefore, underpin the single-minded pursuit of efficiency that characterizes the official position of many organizations. The frying and serving of potatoes becomes the object of extensive 'scientific' study for a fast-food organization. This determines specific types of potatoes, fat and fryers, the design of a new wide-mouthed scoop and other hardware and the drafting of 26 different rules on 'how to fry chips'. All this is aimed to ensure that even a person who has never cooked at home could produce, after a minimum of training, a standardized 'market-winning product' without accidents or waste.

REAL-LIFE EXAMPLE

Rough landing

'The offence'

Narasinha Gopal's flight was delayed. He arrived at Heathrow airport at 10:35 pm. The airport, normally a hive of activity, was virtually empty. Worse, there was no one there to meet him. This was not a good start to what had promised to be an exciting year abroad. Narasinha, a second-year Indian student, had won a prestigious scholarship that allowed him to spend the second year of his studies in a well-known British university; it was his first visit to a European country. Tired after the long flight, Narasinha approached the 'Information' desk to find that it had already closed. He felt anxious and upset; as a last resort, he called his parents who advised him to get a taxi to the university, no matter what the expense might be and subsequently try to reclaim the cost. Three hours later, Narasinha found himself in a bed, in a hall of residence, a long way away from home. He was exhausted but could not sleep. An intermittent noise, bleeping and persistent, seemed to wake him every time he came close to sleep. Narasinha turned the light on. He could see where the noise came from – a strange device attached to the wall with a red light flashing every ten seconds. Relieved, he covered it up with one of his socks and soon he was asleep.

He did not sleep long, however. Following a knock on the door, the hall warden entered his room, a little after 7:30 am. Before he could inquire who she was, the warden looked at Narasinha accusingly and said, 'Young man, have you not been told that covering the smoke detector in this room is a grave offence?' She left the room of a confused and anxious young man, returning two minutes later with a camera with which she took several pictures of the 'offence'. When asked what the consequences of the offence were, the warden advised Narasinha to consult the students' guidebook on his desk. On consulting the document, Narasinha reached page 17 where he found the ominous lines: 'Covering or tampering with smoke or heat detectors carries an automatic penalty of eviction from the halls of residence'. Four days later, he received a letter giving him one month's notice to vacate his room.

'The appeal'

Two weeks prior to Narasinha's eviction, an appeal hearing is held. His mother has come from India to support him; he is in a bad state. The appeal is heard by the University's Head of Support and Advisory Services who also happens to be the Head of Student Counselling, flanked by two elderly professors. The student is supported by a representative from the Student Welfare office. The charges against the student are put by the Chief Warden who offers photographic evidence of the offence and insists that students, prior to being issued with a key, have to sign a document confirming that they have read the rules and regulations and agree to observe them. Narasinha reads a carefully prepared document in which he reiterates what is already known, emphasizing the adverse effects that eviction from the halls of residence will have on his health, his studies and his reputation 'back home'; he insists that he had never seen a smoke detection device prior to his arrival in the UK, so he was not aware that he was committing an offence in covering it up; he concludes his statement with a 'prayer' in which he begs the panel to give him another chance.

'Do you understand the severity of the offence?' asks the chair. 'Are you aware that the buildings of this university are many centuries old and that by covering the smoke detection equipment, you are placing your health and safety and the health and safety of other students in serious jeopardy?' Narasinha nods.

'Are you a smoker?' asks the chair.

'Very occasionally, when I am with friends', says Narasinha.

'Did you smoke in your room on the night in question?'

'No, sir, I did not. Even if I had wanted to smoke, I would have gone outside to smoke. It was I who had requested a non-smoker's room in the hall of residence.'

'Are you aware that the smoke detector was checked carefully and it was found to be perfectly silent?'

'Yes, sir.'

'Has it made any noises subsequently?'

'No, sir.'

Following some closing formalities, the panel adjourns. There is a lively argument. The chair and one of the professors see absolutely no reason to reverse the decision to evict the student. He has done wrong, and what is worse is that he has come up with a story that is full of inconsistencies and contradictions. The other professor disagrees. It comes to a vote. Two against one. Narasinha breaks into tears when he hears that his eviction stands.

'The minority report'

I understand that what Mr Gopal did in covering a smoke detector with a sock is a serious offence and that students are generally warned that this offence carries the penalty of eviction. Yet, I am strongly of the opinion that there were strong mitigating factors in the case of Mr Gopal that would call for a display of a certain degree of leniency and flexibility in enforcing the penalty. In particular, I was persuaded by Mr Gopal's argument that he had arrived to the UK from India late in the evening when the offence occurred; that he had been through a long and tiring journey; that he was upset and disoriented by not being met at the airport as he had expected; that he had taken a tablet, on the advice of his parents, to help him calm down; that he found himself alone in a strange environment for the first time; that, under these circumstances, he heard or thought he heard disturbing noises, and that he attributed these noises to a device, the like of which he had not seen before. Furthermore, I accepted Mr Gopal's explanation that although he had been issued with a booklet of the regulations, he had neither attended the induction session (through no fault of his own) nor had the time to assimilate the numerous rules and regulations in the guidebook to the students. Since the hearing, I have tested a class of my students to see how many may be able to identify the nature of this device; I discovered that 4 out of 16 had no idea what the device was, and, maybe even more alarmingly, only TWO were aware that covering this device carried with it the penalty of automatic eviction from college accommodation.

Furthermore, I must say that in my experience as an academic over 30 years, I have never witnessed such inflexible enforcement of a penalty, even in cases of offences that carry a profound moral stigma (such as plagiarism and cheating in examinations). It has been invariably the practice to give students the benefit of the doubt, to treat them with care and consideration and, almost invariably, offer them a second chance. I was greatly alarmed to hear that 'many' students have been evicted for the same offence that Mr Gopal was guilty of. It seems to me that this represents a serious failure on the part of our system. Surely students would not commit offences if they knew they carried such severe penalties, unless either the rules or the rationale of the rules have not been made clear to them.

There is one further alarming feature regarding Mr Gopal's eviction. Mr Gopal, as a foreign student, should be expected to accept the customs and regulations of this country where he is pursuing his studies. All the same, some leniency should surely be shown about the fact that he is not aware (and probably does not share) the specifically British sensitivity to issues of health and safety, and the institution's understandable apprehension of fire hazards in an organization housed in old and valuable buildings. It is my firm belief that by showing some leniency to erring students, far from giving a message that infractions are tolerated provided a suitable story is concocted after the events, the institution displays its care and understanding towards students who may take a little time before assimilating its diverse regulations and customs.

All in all, I must say that I have found the outcome of this hearing very distressing. As an employee of this college, I always trusted that I worked for an institution that sincerely cares for its students, that shows maturity in enforcing its regulations and, where necessary, applies penalties commensurate with the severity of offences, taking into consideration any mitigating circumstances. The handling of this case has cast severe doubts in my mind about this trust.

I appreciate that the outcome of the appeal cannot be altered and that the decision made about Mr Gopal's eviction cannot be reversed. I will, however, be seeking an urgent review of the regulations that can lead to such undesirable outcomes.

Some questions

- How rational is the regulation that led to Narasinha's eviction?
- How rational was the strict enforcement of this regulation?
- Do you observe any disturbing features in the handling of Narasinha?

BUREAUCRACY

Formal rules do not only affect employees of an organization. The next time that you visit a park, have a look at the 'by-laws' stating what you are and what you are not allowed to do. Or consider the regulations governing behaviour in a swimming pool:

No eating	*No drinking*	*No running*	*No smoking*
No bombing	*No kissing*	*No shouting*	*No spitting*
No swearing	*No singing*	*No ducking*	*No jewellery*
No verrucas	*No pushing*	*No diving*	*No petting*

During a conference in Copenhagen, someone brought to the attention of the delegates a set of regulations issued by the Fire Brigade:

In the event of a fire:

1. *Stay calm;*
2. *Locate the fire;*
3. *Call the fire brigade;*
4. *Close windows and doors;*
5. *When the fire brigade arrives, introduce yourself;*
6. *If possible, put out the fire.*

We all had a good laugh at these regulations. Fortunately, no fire disrupted the proceedings. Had there been one, however, it is unlikely that anyone would have remembered the regulations or acted according to them, as people would hurry to the nearest fire escapes.

Seen through the eyes of delegates, rules like those above are the products of bureaucrats, who have little sense of the chaos and confusion that a fire would cause (see Chapter 1, 'Organization and Organizing'). They treat an event like a fire as something which can be controlled or at least contained through neat and orderly procedures. Their concern for organizing, order and planning blinds them to the forces of disorder that a fire would unleash. Seen through the eyes of those who devised them, both the fire regulations and the swimming pool regulations are not daft at all. They are quite rational, seeking to minimize damage, injuries, insurance liabilities and to contain the disorder. They also help satisfy certain political requirements – such as reassuring Head Office and the Safety Committee that 'there is a policy in place'.

Managers and administrators spend a lot of time fine-tuning rules and procedures; they are always on the look-out for new rules which will do what old rules did, only better. They believe that this is very important. What they sometimes fail to do is to question the objectives served by these rules and procedures. Are the objectives themselves appropriate? Have they become outdated? Are all the different objectives in harmony? Are there any other objectives which should be served? Whose interests do these objectives serve? Is it realistic to expect people to follow rules like those above?

Organizations vary in their emphasis on rules. Some offer a considerable margin of freedom to their members, allowing them to use their judgement and discretion in making **decisions**. Here is 'the rulebook' of Nordstrom, a North-American retailing company.

WELCOME TO NORDSTROM

We are glad to have you with our company.

Our number one goal is to provide outstanding customer service.

Set both personal and professional goals high. We have great confidence in your ability to achieve them.

Nordstrom Rules:

Rule #1: Use your good judgement in all situations.

There will be no additional rules.

Please feel free to ask your department manager any question at any time.

Other organizations, like Securecops in our opening example, appear to be strict and regimented, but insiders soon realize that their bark is worse than their bite. Most of their rules are routinely side-stepped. Yet other organizations seek to **control** everything through precise prescriptions and procedures. Employees are expected to 'do everything by the book', without asking questions. In such organizations, the rules become ends in themselves, rather than a means of achieving organizational objectives. In a French hospital, a rule stipulated that receptionists in the Accident and Emergency Unit were to only admit patients arriving by ambulance. The aim of the rule was to ensure that only genuine emergencies were given priority. Once, a seriously ill patient brought to the Unit by taxi was refused admission and sent to the Outpatients department; he died while waiting to be admitted.

Organizations in which rules are inflexibly applied, with no regard for the particulars of each individual case, are frequently referred to as bureaucracies. Such organizations remind us of machines. Order, predictability and reliability are the qualities towards which they strive. udgement, improvisation and fun are dismissed as the enemies of order. Standardization, **hierarchy** and **structure** are of the essence. By contrast, the term 'adhocracy' is sometimes applied to organizations which treat each case on its individual merits, and have few general rules and procedures to guide behaviour. Such organizations must rely on training, trust and strong shared **values** to ensure coordination and control. Adhocracies are never particularly orderly or predictable, but they appeal to individuals with artistic or anarchic temperaments. Adhocracies may have few rules, or may apply rules in a flexible way, relying on individuals' judgements and discretion. Even in such organizations, however, when things go badly wrong (accidents, financial crises, missed deadlines and so on), the search is likely to be for 'flaunted regulations' or 'inadequate procedures'. Individuals who used to be praised for their judgements and skills may then have the finger pointed at them for failing to observe procedures that were routinely bent in the past.

HOW RATIONAL ARE BUREAUCRATIC RULES?

> What is important is that you should understand why your work has to be done in a certain way and that you do it properly, to the best of your ability. Not because you have to, but because you want to. In the end this is the BEST WAY. (Handbook of fast-food company)

But is 'the book's way' always the best way? Most of the time, we assume that if a rule is there, it is there for a reason. The rules governing behaviour in the swimming pool may displease us, but most of us would not really question whether they are rational or not. We take on trust that 'experts', who have studied the situation, have developed these rules for everybody's benefit. We assume, for example, that 'no running' is there to stop people from slipping and injuring themselves, 'no bombing' to stop people intimidating or injuring others and so on. We take the rationality of many organizational rules and procedures for granted and do not question their legitimacy. We rarely complain about them and tend to disregard the inconvenience in which they result. Some of these rules are eventually observed mechanically; they become part of us. Life without them becomes inconceivable.

Yet, no rule can anticipate all contingencies. If every situation involved an appropriate set of rules, the odds are that paralysis would follow; there would be so many rules that few employees would be able to remember them all or be able to apply them appropriately. The risk of rule overload is one that administrators often overlook. Adding ever-increasing numbers of rules can be as counter-productive as failing to have a suitable rule when an unusual situation arises. The ambulance rule at the hospital was rational until the arrival of the fated patient; until then, it had served what most would regard as a useful purpose. However, one would have to suffer from bureaucratic blindness to argue that when it led to loss of life, it was still rational. Whether a rule is rational or not depends largely on circumstances. No rule can be rational at all times. There comes a time, usually under exceptional or unforeseen circumstances, when it is rational *not* to apply a particular rule. Some organizations recognize the constitutional inability of rules to be rational at all times. They also trust their employees. They allow them to use their discretion.

This, however, may lead to a different kind of difficulty. Imagine if the hospital allowed receptionists to exercise 'discretion' as to whom to admit directly and whom to refer to the Outpatients department. This is likely to put great pressure on the receptionists; how can they judge after all who is an 'emergency' and who is not? Besides, patients may complain that they are not treated fairly: why should a drunkard with a broken jawbone be admitted and the child with a fever referred?

DEPENDENCE ON RULES AND IMPERSONALITY

Officials become dependent on rules to guide and justify their **actions**. They sometimes feel that any rule, even a non-rational one, is better than no rule. Rules save one the trouble of having to make awkward **decisions** and then having to explain and defend them. **Impersonality** means that each decision is unaffected by the specific circumstances of individuals. No amount of begging, pleading or arguing will alter the decision. Some of the decisions people make in organizations are very unpleasant. Sacking an employee, putting a patient on a long waiting list or failing a student are not easy or agreeable decisions. Impersonality cushions us from the suffering and misery of others. 'It was nothing personal, Mrs Jameson, but rules are rules!' But impersonality can also have advantages for those affected by decisions. If everyone is treated according to the rule, everyone is treated the same; there is no cause for complaints.

Rules can become the opiate of bureaucratic officials. Without the rules, they are lost, paralysed. With the support of the rules, they are persons with **authority**. Without rules, chaos. With rules, order and organization. Unlike the authority of the father or mother in a family or of the founder of a movement, the officials' authority is legal – it rests on the rules which define their rights and responsibilities. Their authority lies not in who they are but in the hats they wear, i.e. the positions they occupy.

Impersonality, underwritten by rules, seeks to ensure that a task will be performed in a uniform way, no matter who is performing it. Officials will discharge their duties unaffected by erratic factors like their mood, their passions and their idiosyncrasies. Finally, it means that staff in organizations are replaceable, since they are appointed not for who they are but for what they can do.

IMPERSONALITY, ITS COSTS AND 'PERSONAL SERVICE'

As the size and power of organizations has increased, impersonality has become a dominant feature of Western societies. Constrained by countless rules, stripped of initiative and discretion, increasingly the players of **roles**, we frequently relate to others not as full human beings but as names on forms, numbers on computer terminals, voices at the end of telephone lines or distorted faces behind counters. Many of us feel that we know the characters of television soap operas better than we do our co-workers. Our decisions frequently affect people whom we scarcely know: a mastectomy may be a life-shattering ordeal for a woman and her family, but for the hospital administrator, it is an extra demand on hospital beds; for the medical secretary, a mere tick in box 6B.

We are all aware of the frustrations that impersonality causes. Generally, we do not like being treated as numbers and many organizations will try hard to create the impression of a personal service. The air stewardess will address business-class passengers by their names and the waiter in certain restaurants may introduce himself by saying, 'Hello, I am Pierre, your host for the evening'. Some of us feel uncomfortable or embarrassed about such personal touches which smack of premeditation and artifice. We may also suspect that they will increase the figure at the end of our bill. A fast-food employee said:

> It's all artificial. Pretending to offer personal service with a smile when in reality no one means it. We know this, management know this, even the customers know this,

but we keep pretending. All they want to do is take the customer's money as soon as possible. This is what it's all designed to achieve.

The irony, of course, lies in the fact that the 'personal service' is itself often the result of carefully planned rules. As if offering an efficient service were not enough, the rule books of some organizations seek to **control** our **emotions** and our thoughts. Thus, in addition to the physical and intellectual work that they do, many employees find themselves performing emotional labour – having to display a caring and friendly attitude, always ready to smile or to exchange some personal words with the customer (see Chapter 16, 'Feelings').

Faced with mock personal service, many prefer the no-nonsense anonymity of the machine. When cash-dispensing machines were first introduced by banks, it was thought that people would prefer the personal touch of the bank clerk over the fully impersonal transaction with the machine. It did not take long to find that most people, given a choice, prefer the latter. For anonymity and impersonality have advantages not only for the organization but also for the customer. For one thing, they remove the need to reciprocate false smiles and other unfelt pleasantries.

BENDING THE RULES

We have seen that the rigidity with which organizations enforce their rules varies. The more bureaucratic organizations are fastidious in the application of rules while others take a more relaxed attitude and allow their members a measure of discretion. We sometimes laugh at bureaucracies and their ridiculous regulations, like those of the Danish Fire Brigade. Rules which seem to serve no useful purpose are derided as 'red tape'. Bending such rules appears more rational than enforcing them.

But bending rules has its own difficulties. For one, it undermines one of the most important functions of rules, their guarantee of equal and consistent treatment. Some may fear that once a rule has been bent or violated once, a *precedent* is created for future bigger violations. The rule may then lose all credibility. In most British universities, students must get 50% in order to pass courses at Master's level. Student A has obtained 49.5%. Should he/she pass or not? Common sense and tolerant judgement may argue for lenience. What should then happen to Student B on 49%? Or Student C on 48.5%? Bureaucratic rationality would suggest that a line has already been drawn at 50% and should be observed.

Bureaucratic rationality often rules in organizations. The student on 49.5% may be failed. But then again, he/she may not. If every organizational rule was rigidly applied, life could grind to a halt. The fear of creating a precedent, frequently referred to in emotive terms like 'opening the floodgates' or 'the thin end of the wedge', is often based on imaginary dangers; most precedents are quickly forgotten or brushed aside with suitable excuses. Other 'precedents' may be entirely fictitious – having no foundation in an organization's history, yet being regularly invoked to stop change. What seems to happen in the majority of organizations is the establishment of a range of permissible deviations from rules. To new recruits, all rules and procedures may seem unbreakable. Nevertheless, as our opening example illustrated, individuals quickly realize that not all rules and regulations are equally sacrosanct. Some of them (like stopping at red lights) are fairly inflexible, but most of them contain loopholes or can be dodged in different ways. Many rules are highly circumstantial, applying only in specific situations, for instance during visits by inspectors. Others have fallen into total neglect. Yet others are the topic of constant **conflict** and negotiation, a continuous give and take between different organizational members.

Even in fast-food restaurants, rules are routinely bent. At peak times, more than four pieces of fish may be fried simultaneously, or chips may be kept for more than seven minutes. Such practices are against the regulations but essential in meeting the demand. What is more, managers themselves are seen bending the rules or turning a blind eye when others violate them. Side-stepping a rule is often essential to meet the demands of a job, but equally individual workers may earn exemptions in the form of privileges. A particularly hard-working employee who turns up to work on a busy day wearing an earring ('not allowed') or having forgotten to wear his deodorant (an 'essential' requirement) is unlikely to be disciplined or turned away.

It is important, then, to emphasize that rules do not blindly control our behaviour in organizations. They permit different interpretations and their enforcement becomes tied in with the **culture** as well as the **power relations** of organizations. The same rule may have very different **meanings** in different organizations or even to different individuals within the same organization. Contesting the meaning, the interpretations and the implications or rules is one of the central activities contributing to the instability, unpredictability and richness of organizational life.

IN CONCLUSION: CHANGING FASHIONS IN THINKING ABOUT RULES

In general, where there are rules, people will look for ways of getting more elbow room. Even in the strictest organizations, they are likely to get some, with or without the collusion of their superiors. Studying the behaviour of people in organizations, therefore, must involve examining both the rules that guide behaviour and the ways in which the rules are interpreted and challenged. It would be short-sighted then to reduce all behaviour in organizations to a passive following of rules; yet, it would also be short-sighted to disregard the profound and far-reaching implications of rules in our lives.

Management thinking about rules and procedures is changing. At one time, the fine-tuning of rules and procedures was regarded as the secret of organizational success. Flexibility and initiative, embodied in the Nordstrom rules illustrated earlier, are the current fashion. In the past, the frictionless machine represented the managerial ideal of an organization. The lean, highly responsive organism lies more closely to current thinking. It is increasingly argued that rules and procedures, however carefully designed, cannot cope with a highly complex and changing organizational **environment** or with massive **technological changes** (see Chapter 14, 'Machines and Routines').

In the past, some bureaucratic organizations prospered because of their predictability and order. Inflexibility and sluggishness were not problems in a stable, friendly **environment**. After all, dinosaurs ruled the earth for over 200 million years, inflexible and sluggish though many of them were. No one knows for sure why dinosaurs died away, but we all assume that it had something to do with their inability to adapt to new environmental conditions, whether these were brought about by a colliding asteroid or some other cause. The same, argue modern management theorists, is the fate of rigid bureaucratic **structures**. They stifle innovation, discourage new ideas, fail to capitalize on advantages conferred by modern **technologies** and are generally too slow and cumbersome to meet **competition**. It is for these reasons that they are already giving way to quicker, smaller, more adaptable, more enterprising organizations.

Such organizations seek to unleash human potential and creativity rather than constrain them through rules and regulations. 'Empowerment' has replaced control as a management buzz-word. This does not mean that control has faded away or that organizational rules and discipline have been replaced by trust and autonomy. It does mean, however, that many organizations seek to complement bureaucratic regulations with subtler forms of organizational control. Selection procedures aimed at ensuring highly committed staff, organizational **values**, reward structures and **corporate culture** are currently much favoured mechanisms of control; their importance will become clearer in some of the other chapters in this book.

KEY POINTS

○ Most organizations have formal, impersonal and highly specific rules.

○ Rules can be seen as 'rational' if they are carefully chosen to serve generally agreed organizational goals.

○ Rules are an important means of achieving control over individuals' behaviour in organizations.

○ Organizations differ in their reliance on rules and on the rigidity with which they apply them.

○ At times, it becomes more rational to bend or disregard a rule than to enforce it.

○ Bending rules may lead to ever-increasing violations and eventual anarchy, but in most organizations, a degree of rule bending is accepted as normal and necessary.

○ Officials often become dependent on rules to justify their actions and decisions and to bolster their authority.

○ Rules give organizations an impersonal quality; they reduce the influence of emotions on the way people do their job, and control the way emotions are displayed.

○ People in organizations frequently contest the meaning of rules and try to interpret them or change them to their advantage.

> > > > > > > > > > > THEORETICAL SIGNPOSTS > > > > > > > > > > > >

The major themes in this chapter lie in the following areas of literature:

> bureaucracy and formal organizational structure and procedures
> power, control and resistance in organizations
> the relevance of bureaucratic organizations in an information or network society.

Bureaucracy and Formal Organizational Structure and Procedures

Bureaucracy is one of the most popular subjects in the study of organizations. The theory of bureaucracy was initially put forward by German sociologist Max Weber. Weber (1946) argued that organizations increasingly rely on a type of authority based on a rational system of rules (rational–legal authority). He constructed an ideal type of bureaucracy or a model of organization in which rational–legal authority reigns supreme, suggesting that such an organization is highly predictable, reliable and efficient. Many theorists have taken issue with Weber's theory of bureaucracy. Gouldner (1954), for example, sought to distinguish between rational rules, punitive rules and mock rules. Theorists like Jaques (1976) and Drucker (1989) have defended Weber, elaborating and refining arguments of how organizational efficiency can be enhanced through planning, procedures, rules and control.

Peters and Waterman (1982) and numerous other writers, on the other hand, have attacked bureaucracy as the cause of virtually every organizational ill and have advocated more loosely structured organizations, coupled with strong organizational values and a heavy reliance on individual initiative as the recipe for success. Numerous writings by successful businesspeople have attacked bureaucracy along similar lines, notably Carlzon (1987), Morita (1987) and Roddick (1991). Charles Handy (1976) has argued that bureaucracy is itself a feature of the culture of certain organizations, which he terms 'role cultures', whereas other cultures (including power cultures, task cultures and support cultures) lay far less emphasis on standardized procedures and regulations. More recently, Paul du Gay (2000) has defended bureaucracy against the anarchy of the markets and entrepreneurialism, emphasizing those Weberian qualities of impersonality, fairness and equality of all in face of the rules.

Power, Control and Resistance in Organizations

The material presented in this chapter also addresses issues of power and control in organizations. Rules in organizations, like the laws of wider society, are not merely a means for the achievements of agreed-upon goals, but are also mechanisms of control, safeguarding the interests of those in positions of power. Robert Michels (1949), arguing against Weber's view of rational bureaucracy, envisaged bureaucracy as a smokescreen behind which a ruthless power game goes on, a game through which the few rule the many. This is what he described as the 'Iron Law of Oligarchy'. Two chapters in Morgan's (1986) *Images of Organization* discuss organizations as political systems and as instruments of domination – both are of considerable use to the reader who wishes to further explore the political dimension of the stories introduced in this chapter.

In a series of pioneering studies focusing on the mental asylum, the prison, the clinic, the army and the school, Michel Foucault (1961/1965, 1963/1973, 1977, 1978) has argued that these institutions signal the arrival of a new type of control over the masses, a form of control pervasive enough as to be absorbed in each and every individual's subjectivity.

Rules and bureaucratic procedures of observation, classification and punishment are, according to this view, powerful instruments of control not because of their tangible, visible effects, but because they create a pliant, self-controlled, disciplined population of people who are unable to envisage themselves outside of these procedures. Our society becomes saturated with ever-vigilant watchdogs.

A number of neo-Marxist theorists have developed theories of resistance, sometimes drawing on Foucault's work, according to which organizational subordinates can find more or less indirect ways of contesting, undermining or evading control mechanisms, such as those embodied in rules and regulations (see Jermier et al., 1994; Knights and Willmott, 1990). According to these arguments, there are instances when organizational red tape (such as that discussed in this chapter) is neither a dysfunction of bureaucracy nor a smokescreen for management control but rather an attempt by subordinates to reclaim some control through excessive or ritualistic adherence to rules and procedures.

The Relevance of Bureaucratic Organizations in an Information or Network Society

Some authors argue that as capitalism moves to an information age, new forms of organization emerge quite distinct from the bureaucratic model delineated by Weber. Organizations, it is argued, increasingly move away from hierarchies of control and rigid rules and regulations; instead they become networks of activities that are loosely coupled and capable of constantly revising their boundaries and their interrelationships. The benefits of networks have now been well established in the literature (e.g. Castells, 1996, 1998; Clegg, 1990; Sennett, 1998). Where bureaucracies are rigid, slow and centralized, networks are decentralized, flexible and adaptable. Where bureaucracies are based on routines, networks are creative and inventive. Where bureaucracies concentrate responsibility, networks disperse it.

REVIEW QUESTIONS

1. Bureaucratic organization has been likened to a machine. Identify some of the key similarities between machines and organizations and indicate some limitations to this metaphor. Can you think of some other metaphors that capture some of the other essential qualities of organizations?

2. What are the differences between bureaucratic rules and organizational norms? Describe *three* rules and *three* norms in an organization that you are familiar with and discuss the extent to which they control people's behaviour. Finally, try to assess whether these rules and norms can claim to be 'rational'.

3. Some authors like Paul du Gay have argued that bureaucracy represents a defence against organizational corruption and abuses of power. Discuss this view critically.

Reading On

The articles below are available for free to readers of the fourth edition of *Organizing & Organizations* via the book's companion website at www.sagepub.co.uk/fineman

Courpasson, D. and Reed, M. (2004) 'Introduction: bureaucracy in the age of enterprise', *Organization*, 11 (1): 5–12.
This paper is an introduction to a special issue of the journal *Organization* on the crisis of bureaucracy in the age of enterprise, and builds a picture of the recurring theme: the need to develop a more realistic and grounded appreciation of the inherent flexibility and durability of contemporary bureaucratic organization.

Du Gay, P. (2008) '"Without affection or enthusiasm" problems of involvement and attachment in "responsive" public management', *Organization*, 15 (3): 335–53.
The paper focuses on the changing ethical template that programmes of 'responsive' or 'entre-preneurial' managerial reform require of civil servants. Contemporary demands for responsive public management contain emotional injunctions to public bureaucrats, deemed to be more in tune with democratic principles and the currents of contemporary ethical culture ('diversity' or 'human rights', for example) than what is represented as the unlamented Weberian world of rule-bound hierarchy. The paper seeks to question this assessment.

Korczynski, M. (2004) 'Back-office service work: bureaucracy challenged?', *Work Employment and Society*, 18 (1): 97–114.
Much of the current literature on service work has focused on front-line, customer-facing jobs. This article reports on case studies of two types of back-office work – staff in the back office to a call centre in an insurance firm, and staff in the back office to a mobile sales force in two financial service firms, finding that to a significant degree back-office work in the three firms is organized according to bureaucratic principles.

Menzies, I. (1960) 'A case study in functioning of social systems as a defence against anxiety', *Human Relations*, 13: 95–121.
This study of a general teaching hospital in London is based on observational studies and interviews with 70 nurses and senior staff, using the relationship between social systems and anxiety to make the proposition that the success and viability of a social institution is intimately connected with the techniques it uses to contain anxiety.

6

BUILDINGS AND ORGANIZING

Buildings are physical structures where organizing takes place; buildings are also carriers of important public and private meanings – about the nature of an organization; its values and its priorities. In this chapter, we examine how an organization's physical layout and buildings influence its structure and control mechanisms as well as its culture and meaning systems. We argue that in all of these ways, the influence of an organization's physical environment is far-reaching and that changes in this environment can generate resistance, both political and emotional. In particular, we highlight that a building represents a certain arrangement of boundaries, some of which may be crossed and others not. Boundaries, we argue, are important for defending us and protecting us from outsiders; they allow us to operate with a degree of comfort and security. At the same time, however, boundaries may impede communication and understanding and may create invisible barriers that stand in the way of trust and produce insecurities of their own. The absence or removal of boundaries by itself does not guarantee effective communication and trust.

Until the advent of **virtual organizations**, one of the most visible expressions of organizations was the physical premises they occupied: the buildings, factories, warehouses, land and so forth. Those studying organizations were rather late in taking an interest in their physical presence. Gradually, however, we have started to appreciate the importance of physical location, layout and appearance. Buildings may facilitate or inhibit different activities, including the flows of information and material goods, opportunities for socializing and talking, the closeness of inspections and supervision, the conditions under which employees do their work and the ease with which people move in and out of the organization or across different departments.

In addition to these functional considerations, however, physical buildings are vital **symbols** of what an organization stands for, of what its chief corporate **values** are. Like the old cathedrals, organizational buildings can be viewed as statements about their organization's **identity**. An open-plan, glass building, like the one housing the Danish Bang and Olufsen corporation, one in which you can see the CEO working in his office from outside the building, gives quite a different impression from a concrete tower pyramid, where directors rule invisibly from the top floor or a Kafkaesque castle of dark corridors and oak-panelled offices where individuals work in their single cells. In addition to such overall symbolic effects, organizational buildings create symbolic divisions and classifications. The size and siting of each office, its accessories and furnishings, act as significant **status** and **power** symbols of its occupants. These are some of the issues that we shall introduce in this chapter.

Figure 6.1   a) Saltaire textile mill mid-19th century. b) Bang & Olufsen Denmark, Denmark. c) Kodak Headquarters, Rochester USA.

In Figure 6.1, there are three different organizational buildings: each one expresses a distinct set of meanings and images about the organization it houses.

'MODERN' BUILDINGS

The last 20 or 30 years have seen many organizations move their offices from traditional 'brick and mortar' buildings with long dark corridors to open-plan offices often housed in glass buildings. By knocking down walls, they have sought to create an atmosphere of openness, lightness and togetherness. Employees can mill around irrespective of their status, interacting with others and having quick, informal conversations, instead of spending long hours in the isolation of traditional offices with their thick walls. The ubiquity of open-plan offices today is eloquent testimony of changing corporate philosophies. Where the buildings of the past communicated authority, hierarchy and solidity, the new glass buildings, with their strangely fragile glass surfaces, appear to some to radiate equality, friendliness and trust.

Moving to a new building can undoubtedly be a liberating and life-enhancing experience. It can literally blow away the dust, removing barriers and unleashing forces of organizational **change** and renewal. One of the most interesting developments in the design of offices has been the erosion of personal or group territories. One extreme form of this is 'hot-desking' which does away with walls, offices and desks altogether, replacing them with sets of computer terminals, where employees can carry out their work, without forming personal attachments to a particular post or location. Each day, employees meet new people with different outlooks. They also create informal networks over the web, without being permanently stuck with a particular neighbour.

Many people adapt themselves and enjoy such working environments, which create no attachments and emphasize continuous movement and flexibility. A young management trainee spent six months working at the headquarters of an international airline, near a major airport. A new building, entirely encased in glass with wide, open-plan offices and completely interchangeable workstations, he found this environment both convenient and stimulating:

> From any point of the office you could see the entire floor, no clutter, no walls, no partitions. It was not so different from the university library really. You could sit wherever you wanted, access all the information you needed, without ever needing to look for a piece of paper or any material object. I liked it, it made me feel free. On occasions, I flew to some of the company's other offices and just as easily I could do my work anywhere in the world. Of course, there were special areas for drinking coffee or tea, it all came free, as well as glass-partitioned offices for meetings. Otherwise it was all open, no barriers and no boundaries.

The removal of boundaries can have several positive consequences: it makes people mobile, flexible, less attached to particular tasks or roles, less fixed by the conventions of an office and a desk. It also creates opportunities to be spotted, to be 'discovered', to impress those that matter. Instead of being buried in the photocopying room or a filing office, the employee can circulate, be seen and be recognized. This sense of freedom is strengthened in the quote above by the offer of 'free' coffee and tea, which suggests that everything in the open office is to be shared, as if property rights cease to exist.

Visibility, however, can be a mixed blessing. When everyone else in the office dresses in a particular way or looks or talks in a particular way, it is hard for one person to act differently. When everyone stays working late, leaving promptly at six o'clock marks one as a less committed worker. Yet, many people appear to get a thrill out of being constantly visible, constantly exposed. Like members of a cast in a theatrical play, they get a high out of being on show, attracting admiring looks and playing an important part in 'keeping the show on the road'. In this way, they are part of the organization's image, reflecting its style, values and **identity** (see Chapter 16, 'Feelings').

MOVING TO A MODERN BUILDING

Like moving to a new house, moving to a new office building can be an exciting experience. As we enter the new building, we may feel pride and elation on looking at the shining surfaces, pristine carpets and uncluttered surroundings. We may delight in the space, the size and the comfort it affords us. We may dream of a new chapter in the organization's life, a happier, stronger and more prosperous one than ever before.

Yet, in reality, moves to new premises are rarely without difficulties. It is common to speak of 'teething problems', machines that don't work, security problems, disruption of work patterns and so forth. Every move inevitably disturbs many of our familiar routines, forcing us to re-organize ourselves in a new physical location. Documents, objects and even people must be sought out in new places. Moving to a new building forces us to recognize how much of organizing lies in the tacit knowledge of being able to find things, information and people in places where we expect them to be. The expression 'teething problems' suggests that inconvenience and disruption are inevitable and that sooner or later the organization will grow out of them. It also suggests that such problems are justified by the subsequent advantages that the new building confers upon the organization, its customers and members.

But disruption can sometimes reach deeper, upsetting some of our social habits. Pleasures that were taken for granted, like small talk around the waterfountain or cigarette smoking outside the building's auxiliary entry, suddenly become impossible or awkward. Casual encounters with important colleagues, ones we took for granted and yet which were so important both for work and for company, get undermined or destroyed. Unfortunately, it is not uncommon for moves to new buildings to create long-lasting difficulties and grievances which reinforce each other. We may, for instance, become irritated or upset because we are stuck with fixed glazing and air-conditioning or because our telephone conversations can be overheard by others in close proximity. We, in turn, may get annoyed at having to listen to a particularly loud colleague or smell his overpowering after-shave. Gradually, we may start to worry about the size of our office, the distance from the photocopier, the quality of the furniture, the lighting and all sorts of other issues raised by the relocation, and before we know it, we may start looking nostalgically back at the old building, with its creaky floors, its dirty wallpaper, its slow lifts and its stiff but yielding windows.

This is very much what happened when a chemical multinational decided to radically refurbish its corporate headquarters. For two years, the staff had decamped to a nearby building while the headquarters were overhauled – the architects went about busily creating impressive new spaces with little consultation with the staff or even the managers. Little thought was given to the employees' work patterns or social habits. Kevin Michaels, the company's Communications Director, describes the rationale for the new building and the upheaval it brought about:

> The old building was like a gentlemen's club, long dark corridors, heavy oak doors, but during the recession we had lost a lot of staff and the rest were rattling like peas in a pod. When we moved out, I found people I didn't even know existed and I'm supposed to know everyone in the building. Everyone at that time worked in their distinct little cells, and the idea was to make the culture of the organization much more open; we would have an all-glazed environment, so that it would appear more open. I have my own personal views on whether this happened, but I'd rather not

Figure 6.2   Atriums: a current obsession?

> risk them ... As for my staff, a lot of them don't like the modern architecture, can't
> open the windows, we have a high incidence of sickness, headaches and so forth.
> Don't know if this is psychological, psychosomatic or the 'sick-building syndrome',
> but the staff personalize their work environment a lot more than they did in the old
> building. They didn't use to have all these fluffy toys around.

The new building, modern, largely open-plan, full of glass and wide-open spaces
had been designed to portray the company very differently from the gentlemen's
club image of the old building. It was meant to be open and egalitarian, but above
all cutting-edge – in short, 'modern'. Yet, in talking to many of the staff about the
building, we realized that, for many, it generated strong ambivalent or hostile
feelings. Pat, a Registry Supervisor who had worked for 30 years at the company,
recollected:

> When we went to the other building over the road, we had the most appalling loos,
> absolutely appalling, it had been a government building and while we were in there
> the government occupied some of the floors. It was depressing, I couldn't believe that
> people could work in such an environment. What people say now is that they would
> prefer to go back to that building as it was, with all the grotty loos. I've never had
> such a nice office as I have now, but I still prefer the old building, where we were for
> two years. It was friendlier, it's hard to say why. I hate [this building], I loathe it. It's
> a lovely building to come in and walk around and say: 'isn't it wonderful!' To work in

it it's hell, nothing goes right ... The idea was that there should be an atrium, where there used to be just a light well, sort of white lavatory tiles on it, an unused space, just open. They decided to turn it into usable space, originally they were going to have trees, then they said it was going to be too noisy. So they carpet it, it's quite stunning if you look from the eighth floor, but from the working point of view it's no good. The idea was that we'd all feel part of a whole, you could see everybody, but you don't. All you can see is the people in the corridors, or you look at the fish-tanks, the offices that line up the atrium, half of the time they are empty, so that's depressing!

It is fascinating what an **ambivalent** response the new building created – stunning, spacious and light, and yet unfriendly, forbidding and depressing. Such ambivalence was expressed by many others, including Sue, a Personnel Clerk, with 20 years' service:

I liked the look of the new building when I first walked in – very impressive. But the offices, the way that they are organized, you don't see an awful lot of people. From where we are, you may not see anyone all day. It is quiet. Conducive to work, but not conducive to gatherings or anything like that. The old building, well it was antiquated, but it had character, while this has no char-acter, and this is also how I feel about people. There used to be birthday parties in our offices, Christmas parties, whereas now, they don't have impromptu get-togethers any more.

For such employees, the move to the new building marked a watershed separating the old company from the new. The old one had been bureaucratic and hierarchical but also friendly, full of character and in a strange way 'family-like'. People cared for each other and supported each other. The organization was full of characters. The leaders themselves were characters. By contrast, the new organization was experienced as unfriendly, cold and character-less. It was almost as if the vast hol-low space created by the architects in the centre of the building, the magnificent atrium, symbolically came to stand for a hole in the heart of the organization. At the same time, the removal of the walls and their replacement with glass, created a sense of vulnerability and exposure, reducing socializing, gossiping and time-wasting. Finally, the problems of regulating the temperature were regularly invested with symbolic significance. Cold was experienced as emotional coldness; hot was experi-enced as pressure and stress.

This example illustrates how out-of-touch architecture can backfire. In short:

- The new architecture was meant to reflect the company's new values, to be seen as transparent, open and egalitarian but also glamorous, powerful and 'modern'.
- Yet the new building was viewed by some staff (especially the older ones) as unfriendly and impersonal (prompting employees to try and personalize their personal space).
- The new building disrupted informal social exchanges, in spite or because of its wide-open and exposed spaces.

- The new building reduced the amount of control that most people had over their personal space (with prohibitions about sticking posters on walls, the impossibility of controlling the temperature and so on).
- In spite of such prohibitions, people sought to personalize their personal spaces, by placing their own photographs, posters and mascots on their desks.
- In spite of the wonder inspired by the architecture, many features of the new building were invested with negative symbolic meanings.

IT MAKES ME ILL

One important consequence of the move was the increase in illness and labour turnover, noted by Kevin Michaels above. Even among those who liked the new building, the incidence of physical illness or discomfort increased. Nicky, like Pat a Supervisor, said:

> I like the building concept but I find it difficult to work in, because of the physical environment. It troubles me when I have a draft in the back of my neck and my shoulders are stiffening up. The fact that I can't open the windows doesn't particularly bother me, because as long as I am warm and comfortable my surroundings don't exist for me, but I know that it bothers other people not being able to open windows.

And one of her subordinates, Sally, said:

> In many respects I like the design, but I don't like the lighting, it's quite cold too, it's hopeless, it's hopeless. We all suffer from the usual symptoms; they've started looking into it because sickness has gone up, and it's silly things like coughs, cold, sore throats, generally feeling miserable. And eyes, I find that at the end of each day I have eye strain.

Many of the employees we interviewed mentioned the 'sick-building syndrome' and referred to symptoms like the above. It was certainly a regular topic of conversation in the organization. It is also one of the great puzzles for corporate architects and planners. Some of the causes of the sick-building syndrome may be technical and may allow for technical fixes: control over temperature, lighting, ventilation, sound and so forth. There is evidence, however, that some new 'modern' buildings, like the one here, can create a deeper malaise for those working inside them. Open-plan offices aimed at symbolizing openness, equality and informality, end up being experienced as oppressive and unfriendly. In this way, the glass building can end up being experienced by some of those working in it as a glass cage, glistening, alluring and even beautiful, but suffocating and entrapping. For others, it may represent a glass palace, whose grandeur and glamour washes off on all who inhabit it.

BUILDINGS, BOUNDARIES AND CONTROL

The physical layout of buildings defines visible and invisible **boundaries** – some of these boundaries can be crossed only if one carries the appropriate authorization (see Chapter 5, 'Rules are Rules'), some may not be crossed at all, and some may be so

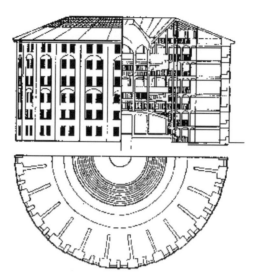

Figure 6.3   The Panopticon.

awkwardly placed that they discourage anyone from even seeking to cross them. Crossing a boundary imposes certain obligations on people to behave in particular ways – entering the Chief Executive's suite may require speaking or dressing in a partic- ular manner (not too loudly, not too casually). The location of boundaries controls our behaviour, but also our thoughts and outlooks in many overt and covert ways. For example, a very tangible barrier, a border or a limit encourages the desire to break it or overcome it in order to discover what lies behind it. A more subtle boundary, such as the location of an office or the ease with which others can overhear conversations, may be taken for granted, ending up acting as an obstacle without ever appearing to do so.

   Buildings are full of boundaries, such as walls, perimeter fences, corridors and so forth. Points of crossing such boundaries are controlled – for example, by guards and security devices (such as swipe-cards and 'No Entry' signs) to ensure that there are no clandestine crossings and violations. In the nineteenth century, the philosopher Jeremy Bentham designed a model for a special type of prison, the Panopticon (see Figure 6.3), in such a way that the location of its boundaries would reduce the chances of rebellions and breakouts. Within a cylindrical structure, a single guard, located at the centre, could survey every single one of the prisoners located on the periphery, thus minimizing costs and disobedience. As in the case of invisible security cameras, prisoners would never be sure whether the guard's gaze was trained on them. In this manner, a form of **control** is made possible, one that does not rely on bullying, shout- ing and beatings but on the spatial layout of the building itself.

   In the twentieth century, the philosopher Michel Foucault viewed the Panopticon (which was never actually built) as the model upon which a society of organizations watches, disciplines and punishes with a minimum of intrusion and fuss, through discreet and seemingly 'neutral' devices. In this way, many physical features of organizations can be seen as aiming at control: the placement of boundaries and security posts, the development of open-plan offices where every employee is exposed, the use of glass, a substance that simultaneously separates and exposes to controlling gaze, the elimination of 'dead spaces' which people may 'make their own' in different ways.

Exposure to the ever-present 'eye' becomes the basis of self-discipline, a discipline imposed on oneself for fear of being caught misbehaving. In addition to being exposed to their managers and to each other, many employees nowadays find themselves constantly exposed to the organization's customers, who are always eager to make comparisons or to criticize (see Chapter 16, 'Feelings'). Those working in the service sector as flight attendants, waiters or bar tenders, shop assistants and so forth are continuously on show in this way. Even employees working in call centres, answering telephone calls throughout their shifts, find themselves continuously assessed and judged. Thus, many of today's architects manage to combine a rhetoric of openness, equality and accessibility with subtle but pervasive surveillance and control.

CHALLENGING BOUNDARIES

How effective are such mechanisms of **control**? Are there any challenges to their discipline? There are some who argue that wherever there are boundaries, there will be attempts to cross them clandestinely, to test them, to shift them or to redefine them. There are wide cultural differences in the extent to which people conform, but, in most cultures, prohibitions create some desire to trespass. Even the harshest of all boundaries, like those of prisons, can be tested and violated, as in escape attempts or, less spectacularly, the illegal trafficking of banned objects. When the boundaries cannot be violated, they may be disfigured, as graffiti on walls and vandalism of every sort testify.

Another attempt to challenge boundaries happens when people in and out of organizations seek to appropriate particular areas for their own use. They convert 'organizational spaces' into their own 'places' where they can tell stories and jokes, escape from the intrusive monitoring of their behaviour, have a laugh or a cry and generally 'feel at home'. In a hospital which one of us investigated, we were invited by the porters to visit their 'den', a small, windowless room, decorated by paintings painted by a departed colleague, where they played cards, listened to the radio and kept a respectable supply of food and drink. This is where many of the interviews with these workers were conducted, out of management earshot, in a space that was strictly out of bounds for outsiders, a space that they had turned into their place. Boundaries in this way can make us feel safe and comfortable, protected from prying eyes and ears. Some theorists have argued that people are territorial animals, always seeking to secure a living space, which they then appropriate, personalize and defend against intruders.

To what extent can the design of buildings eliminate such territoriality, stopping people appropriating places and turning them into their own, by personalizing them, disfiguring them or using them for purposes other than those for which they were conceived? Undoubtedly, part of this disciplinary function can be absorbed in the way buildings are designed and constructed. They can be designed and constructed with a view to limiting or eliminating violations, by 'designing away' opportunities for spontaneous, unpredictable and recalcitrant behaviour. The physical **environment** may then be designed in such a way as to deter violations or even make them impossible, by preventing the turning of spaces into places – if a security camera deters graffiti writers, designing a graffiti-proof wall engineers the problem away (until some determined graffiti writer discovers a way of disfiguring such a wall); removing the wall eliminates the graffiti problem altogether. In such ways, architects of contemporary buildings may play their part in seeking to create a regime of invisible controls that silence recalcitrant or troublesome voices and ensure compliance and acquiescence. The open-plan office can then become the Panopticon of our times – its wide-open space offers no shelters or hiding places for the unruly and no surfaces to be disfigured by the discontent, while its closely monitored, transparent boundaries offer no opportunities for illegal crossings.

The concept of the Panopticon fills some people with instant gloom, easily lapsing into a Panoptic paranoia, with images borrowed from George Orwell's *Nineteen Eighty-four* and other dystopic novels. People in such visions are fully manipulated and controlled: nothing can escape the attention of 'Big Brother'. This is certainly not the impression we wish to create here. First, as we noted earlier, even the strictest disciplines and controls are often challenged, evaded and side-stepped. Second, it must be acknowledged that some discipline and control is necessary in every organization as well as in wider society. Without prison guards, even a prison disintegrates into complete anarchy, with the settling of accounts being done by force and terror. Even the original Panopticon – the prison – sought to ensure that prisoners did not assault each other and that the level of violence was checked, by maintaining discreet controls. The problem then is not control but excessive control.

BUILDINGS, MODERNITY AND POSTMODERNITY

The move from concrete office blocks to open-plan glass buildings is sometimes seen as part of the transition from modernity to a new historical period, which some call postmodernity. In fact, the term 'postmodern' was first used in connection with a new approach to architecture, whose main feature was a playful attitude towards juxtapositions of styles and traditions. The term 'pastiche' is sometimes used to describe postmodern architecture's willingness to 'borrow' from different traditions and schools indiscriminately and place incongruous features side by side. Another interesting quality of postmodern architecture was the transformation of older buildings for uses entirely different from those of their creators. Banks were thus converted into pubs, factories into shopping malls and warehouses into art museums.

Much debate has gone on as to whether **postmodernity** is a new historical period or if it represents a different way of looking at things, a new range of sensibilities and a new set of anxieties. If concrete symbolically stood as the signature material of modernity, glass can be viewed as the signature building material of our times. Concrete evokes structure and stability, whereas glass is a substance which generates changing images, a substance whose presence pleases the eye.

It can be argued that the transition from concrete to glass as the defining building material coincides with a transition undergone by Western society from a society of massive, concrete buildings and massive, concrete organizations to one of flexible but fragile work arrangements and flexible but fragile organizations. Modernity is then seen as a society driven by mechanism and Fordist production whereas postmodernity is a society preoccupied with spectacle, style and consumption. Within such a society, much of the value generated by organizations does not reside in tangible material products, but in intangible services, in the trading of information, comfort and, above all, meaning. Order, stability and well-honed routines are no longer what gives organizations a competitive advantage. Instead, an ability to tempt consumers with new ideas, to ride the ever-changing currents of fads and fashions, to capitalize on image and style become vitally important. Flexibility rather than mechanical efficiency becomes the key to success. Flexibility implies being on the lookout for new opportunities and never settling into comfortable routines, being able to operate on many different levels at the same time rather than doing one thing well.

Whether we accept that postmodernity is a radical break from the past or not, there is no denying that the buildings that fill our urban landscapes carry powerful messages about the organizations that they house and the values of the society which they represent. We read meaning into buildings just as we read meaning into stories, photographs and objects. It is to this symbolism of buildings that we now turn.

BUILDINGS AND WHAT THEY STAND FOR

Our experiences of different buildings are conditioned by earlier buildings that we know, but also our tastes, needs and desires. Sarah, a middle manager in a predominantly male government department, describes the organization's new building:

> The new building is a constant source of pleasure for me. The old building was all angular, full of corridors and straight lines, hard colours and hard surfaces. The new building is full of curves, soft colours and carpeted floors. Instead of hard metallic sounds you hear a constant hum of humanity at work. The new building is a feminine environment, much more attuned to my tastes and my moods than the old one.

Sarah's response to the building is an emotional, **aesthetic** and symbolic one. At times, we will all put up with discomfort and inconvenience and relish the sheer beauty, fantasy and spirit of a building. Buildings thus are easily endowed with symbolic **meanings**, which often extended to entire organizations. They can stimulate powerful **emotions** of solidarity, pride, envy, disgust, hope and so forth. Thus, particular types of buildings can act as **metaphors** used to encapsulate the nature of an organization itself. An organization, for example, can be seen or experienced as:

- a home – a sanctuary which creates unity and solidarity
- a prison – a space constricting and confining people
- a castle – a solid wall protecting people from outside forces
- a tower (of Babel) – the product of human arrogance, ambition and folly
- a bunker – from which people are unable to see what is going on outside
- a pyramid – where higher echelons dominate lower ones
- a cathedral – where certain values are proclaimed and celebrated or, alternatively, a building whose founders never expect to see its completion

Figure 6.4   Taj Mahal, Cathedral of Rouen, Eiffel Tower, Swiss Re.

- Camelot – a fabled place with mythical and superhuman meanings
- Valhalla – a centre of enormous power, built on unpaid labour.

As metaphors, the perceived qualities of buildings are easily transferred onto an organization. But buildings also function as *metonymies*, acting as labels which capture everything that is connoted by particular organizations–the palace, for instance, acts as a label for all things royal. Notice how often governments are referred to metonymically through the buildings in which they are housed: the Kremlin, the White House, Number 10 Downing Street, the Elysée Palace and so forth. Individual leaders, presidents and prime ministers may come and go, but a government's or an organization's buildings stay. The leaders may engage in all kinds of invisible manoeuvres and deals while the buildings remain visible and tangible.

As we saw earlier, an organization's building can easily be seen as making a statement about its long-lasting values, its character and its uniqueness. In this sense, buildings are organizational symbols. Yet, the symbolism of a building may go deeper than this. Buildings are vital entities in many **myths** (the tower of Babel; 'a little pig built his house of mud …'), and they are common features in dreams and proverbs. Consider the proverb 'an Englishman's home his castle' – that suggests that the home defends the Englishman against the outside world, that he takes the same pride in his home as a lord takes in his castle, but also that within his home, an Englishman is lord. The house then stands for an inviolable boundary that separates the self from the outside world, one that defines the self.

Most people spend a lot of time thinking about their house, working on it or planning how to improve it. Some of this is to secure their home against thieves (and also against the wear and tear of time and even the ravages of the property market), while some of this may be aimed rationally at enhancing their property's value. Yet, many home improvements are meant to communicate the owners' prestige, their good taste or rising fortunes. On buying a house, new owners may scrap a perfectly functional and attractive kitchen and replace it with a new one. Equally, on assuming office, an executive may expend much money on refurnishing and redecorating her office or her entire executive suite or indeed the entire building. We know of a senior manager who regularly changed office in order to get new furniture and a new computer. He rarely used his computer, but, like the furniture, it served as a status symbol announcing the owner's importance. In all these ways, it has pointed out that buildings and their contents are 'both bulletin boards for internal messages and billboards for external ones' (McCracken, 1988). Buildings continuously emit messages about their owners and their inhabitants directed both towards those inside and towards those outside.

One of the reasons why buildings carry such powerful symbolism lies in the fact that, like cars and clothes, they are highly visible. But as with cars and clothes, the symbolism they carry for people can go much deeper. Just as scratches and bumps on a car's surface may be experienced by its owner as physical injuries to himself, or a stain on a new jacket as a scar on the wearer's body, the ailments of a building can be experienced as personal afflictions by their owner. For example, dry rot and wet rot, subsidence or even the erosion of the property's value by the building of a nearby reception centre for refugees can be experienced as highly threatening conditions by their owners. It is for this reason that some authors have argued that the buildings we inhabit, like the jewels or the clothes that we wear, are part of an 'extended self', a self that extends beyond the boundaries of our body to boundaries that lie further out but which become just as significant. Losing a valued ring, a scratch on an automobile of which we are proud and the dry rot on the roof can all then be experienced as psychological injuries affecting the whole self.

IN CONCLUSION

This chapter has examined the importance of buildings and physical structures for organizing. Buildings, we argued, control many aspects of behaviour in organizations, but also carry important public and private meanings – buildings are powerful symbolic entities. An open-plan office, for example, proclaims values of openness, clarity and equality; however, it also ensures that each employee is constantly exposed to the critical gaze of fellow employees and managers. We examined how physical arrangements become part of people's way of living and working, and changes can generate **resistance**, both political and emotional. In particular, we highlighted how a building represents a certain arrangement of **boundaries**, some of which may be crossed and others not. Boundaries, we have seen, are important for defending us and protecting us from outsiders; they allow us to operate with a degree of comfort and security. At the same time, however, boundaries may impede communication and understanding, and may create invisible barriers that stand in the way of trust and proudce insecurities of their own.

KEY POINTS

○ Buildings are a fundamental, though often taken-for-granted, feature of organizations.

○ Buildings involve the location of boundaries that affect the flow of people, materials and information.

○ The physical layout of buildings controls people's behaviour, though it also creates opportunities evading or side-stepping such controls.

○ Traditional buildings sought to control the movements and behaviours of people through visible barriers and walls.

○ Contemporary buildings, with open-plan layouts and glass partitions, involve different types of control, relying on exposure and visibility.

○ Buildings also carry powerful symbolic significance, expressing an organization's values and status.

○ Sometimes a building's symbolic significance for those living and working in it is not what the building's architects or planners envisaged.

⟩⟩⟩⟩⟩⟩⟩⟩⟩⟩⟩⟩ THEORETICAL SIGNPOSTS ⟩⟩⟩⟩⟩⟩⟩⟩⟩⟩⟩⟩

The major themes in this chapter have covered the following areas of literature:

⟩ the influence and control exercised by buildings on human behaviour
⟩ the symbolic importance of organizational buildings as expressions of its culture and values
⟩ literature on boundaries which may be physical, but may also be emotional, moral, cognitive and so forth.

The Influence and Control Exercised by Buildings on Human Behaviour

Gutman (1972) has offered an imaginative and influential account of the relation between people and the buildings they inhabit. Guillen (1998) has explored the relationship between architecture and the functions of control in modern organizations. Foucault (1977) discussed the Panopticon as the basis of modern disciplinary surveillance in *Discipline and Punish*. Numerous authors have examined and extended this idea, including Bauman, 1988; Deetz, 1998; Fox, 1989; Gandy, 1993; Kornberger and Clegg, 2004; McKinlay and Starkey, 1998; Reed, 1999; and Sewell and Wilkinson, 1992a. Marx (1999) has offered us one of the most far-reaching accounts of new forms of surveillance and discipline in and out of work, while de Certeau (1984) has qualified Foucault's argument by proposing a distinction between official spaces and unofficial places, where the disciplinary gaze can be side-stepped. Fayard and Weeks (2007) have examined how the physical layout of organizations facilitates or inhibits informal interactions. Gabriel (2004a) has developed the idea of the 'glass cage' replacing the Weberian 'iron cage' and replacing an older set of controls with different ones.

The Symbolic Importance of Organizational Buildings as Expressions of its Culture and Values

Gagliardi's (1990b) anthology contains several interesting articles on the symbolic significance of an organization's buildings and other artefacts. Olins (1991) has discussed organizations' attempts to convey their values through their buildings. Hatch's (1997) is one of the relatively few textbooks on organizations to have taken an interest in the buildings and physical layout of organizations. The ability of architecture to create social identities is skilfully explored by Jones (2006) in relation to the difficulties afflicting the rebuilding of the Ground Zero site by architect Daniel Libeskind, while Barnstone (2005) has examined how the renovation of the German Reichstag by architect Norman Foster was meant to celebrate the transparency of a democratic culture.

Literature on Boundaries Which may be Physical, but may also be Emotional, Moral, Cognitive and so forth

Boundaries have always been seen as crucial qualities of human societies, groups and organizations, especially when studied as social systems (Katz and Kahn, 1978; Miller and Rice, 1967). One of the fundamental qualities of systems is having a boundary which separates them from their environments. Some organizational boundaries are physical (such as perimeter fences, patrolled by guards and security cameras, walls of a building or areas requiring security passes and keys to enter), but also legal, social, psychological, informational and moral ones. One of the foremost boundaries that individuals encounter in organizations is denoted by the idea of a position or role. This is both the way an organization defines a person's obligations and rights, and also the way a person experiences them. When using the expression 'my job', we usually refer to those things that we feel obliged to do as part of our psychological contract with our employer. In this way, we draw a boundary beyond which we are unwilling to act. Feelings (such as anger, remorse, shame and embarrassment) are especially important in defining where different boundaries are drawn (Sandelands and Boudens, 2000). If working late makes us feel resentful and angry, we become aware that our employer is expecting us to draw a work/leisure boundary which we find unacceptable. Boundaries are also currently debated in connection with 'boundaryless' organizations. Cross et al. (2000) argue that the need for boundaries does not disappear as organizations become 'boundaryless'. Rather, boundary activities increase in significance and migrate to lower organizational levels.

REVIEW QUESTIONS

1. It has been claimed that the buildings we inhabit control our behaviour in discreet, invisible ways. Identify some ways in which architecture controls people's behaviour at the workplace. Are there any ways in which individuals in organizations can sidestep or avoid these controls?

2. People working in open-plan offices sometimes complain of a lack of privacy. Are such complains justified, in your view?

3. 'Physical boundaries turn into mental boundaries' – discuss, offering some examples from your own personal experience of organizations.

---

companion website
www.sagepub.co.uk/fineman

Reading On

The articles below are available for free to readers of the fourth edition of *Organizing & Organizations* via the book's companion website at www.sagepub.co.uk/fineman

Baldry, C. (1999) 'Space – the final frontier', *Sociology – The Journal of the British Sociological Association*, 33 (3): 535-53.
This article contends that for too long the built working environment has been excluded from the analysis of work organizations. Buildings, like other cultural artefacts, encapsulate social and economic priorities and values, and represent prevailing power structures. Human resource management and information technology are currently combining to encourage a reappraisal of the working environment, but one that is not without its own contradictions.

Gabriel, Y. (2005) 'Glass cages and glass palaces: images of organizations in image-conscious times', *Organization*, 12 (1): 9–27.
Max Weber's metaphor of 'the iron cage' has provided an abiding image of organizations during the high noon of modernity. But these organizations – rigid, rational and bureaucratic – may no longer be sustainable in our times. This article contends that the new experiences of work and consumption allow for greater ambivalence and nuance, offering the twin metaphors of glass cages and glass palaces.

Jones, P.R. (2006) 'The sociology of architecture and the politics of building: the discursive construction of ground zero', *Sociology – The Journal of the British Sociological Association*, 40 (3): 549–65.
The capacity of architects to position their buildings in the face of competing identity claims provides the focus of this article, which argues that architects' discourses frequently reveal

many tensions between culture, politics, power, and identity. The symbolic nationalization of the architecture at the Ground Zero site has, in part, been achieved by the narrative, highly symbolic links between the buildings there and an 'American' collective identity.

Kornberger, M. and Clegg, S.R. (2004), 'Bringing space back in: organizing the generative building', *Organization Studies*, 25 (7): 1095–114.

In the past, management has been largely undergirded by a Cartesian rationality, one seen most clearly in the argument that structure follows strategy. Architecturally, this Cartesianism is present in the injunction that form follows function. Criticizing this point of view, this article argues that organizations should be thought of as material, spatial ensembles – not just cognitive abstractions writ large. Linking space and organization in this way, the article reflects on the power that every spatial organization necessarily implies, both in negative and positive terms.

7

LEADING

Leading is an activity that plays an important part in organizational life, and which is often talked about in terms of the roles and qualities involved as leadership. Leadership is a subject that has suffered from its own popularity, as well as from the ambiguity of the very word 'leadership'. For many years now, the view has prevailed that many other activities are not being performed as well as they could be because of a lack of leadership, and that lack of leadership is the cause of many of our most widespread social and economic ills. That is why we prefer the word 'leading', which emphasizes activities rather than a role in the organization. In this chapter, we consider first what leading is, and we talk more about some of the activities which comprise it, including the fact that not all these activities can be performed by the same person. We then consider the relationship between leading and following; you cannot have one without the other, and both are important in their own right.

REAL-LIFE EXAMPLE

The Gamma project team felt that they lacked leadership, and so Mike, a consultant working with them, asked them exactly what it was that they were lacking.

'Well', said Alan, 'what we really need is someone charismatic so that everybody else wants to gather round and work with them'.

'That's not the main problem, though', added Gurprit, 'our boss Chris means well, but we can't send him in to do battle for us when we need more resources from the board'.

'I think we need someone to make sure that all the bits that we are doing fit together', said Sarah.

'That's not a leader', said Alan, 'that's a manager'.

'I don't care what you call it', replied Sarah, 'that's what we need to take us forward'.

'But it's not the same as having someone who can see a clear image of where we are going, and then help us to get there', said Julia, 'and that's what other teams have got and we have always lacked'.

What is **leadership**? The conversation above went on a lot longer, because all sorts of dissatisfactions are currently laid at the door of 'a lack of leadership'. Leadership needs clear definition because it is a very fashionable modern solution to all organizational ills. Training **consultants** everywhere are being asked for courses in it. Universities are featuring it in their business programmes, and quite often claiming that it is a transferable skill for other students too. Newspaper articles and political commentators seem to take it as read that leadership is crucial. But what is it? We will use the following definition:

> Leadership is imagining, willing and driving, and thereby making something happen which was not going to happen otherwise. It is not following instructions on pieces of paper or the latest theory pronounced by a leadership guru.

It is possible to spend a long time debating definitions and discussing whether leading is the same as managing. We are going to take them as being different. Leaders make something happen which was not going to happen otherwise. Like managers, they also make something happen by working through other people. Sometimes these two activities are not distinguishable, but leadership implies originating something, which **management** does not. Managing implies a position which gives you the legitimate right to work through others, which leading does not. However, leading is often only possible if someone (often someone else) is contributing some effective managing, and so that managing makes as important a contribution to the act of leadership as any of the activities usually labelled 'leadership'.

In this chapter, we shall look at some of the activities involved in leading, and at the relationship between leading and following. We are not going to say that any one of these activities or relationships is the 'best' or 'most effective' way to lead, nor that any of them is a complete mistake. All of them are worth being aware of for those who want to understand their own and others' ways of leading.

ACTIVITIES OF LEADERSHIP

What do we know about what leaders actually do? We shall look at the activities of leadership under the following headings:

- Leadership as a Set of Qualities
- Leadership as Power Holding
- Leadership as Politics
- Leadership as Vision
- Leadership as Managing Meanings
- Leadership as Display
- Leadership as a Set of Arts.

Leadership as a Set of Qualities

Will you make an effective leader? Have you got what it takes? There are many lists of desirable personal qualities reeled out by recruitment specialists and psychologists which can make even a saint look suspect. Some can be found in job advertisements: 'reliable', 'takes initiative', 'self-starter', 'effective in groups', 'firm under pressure', 'good communicator' and so forth. Despite many studies which show there are no such things as universal qualities of leadership, many of us cling to the firm belief that we can spot a leader when we see one.

The trouble is that, despite years of attempting to say what the qualities of a good leader are, no consistency has emerged, and the number of **skills**, **competences** and other special qualities that might make people into good leaders has just gone on growing. One study, admittedly not a very serious one, suggested that many of the most successful leaders were significantly above or below the average height. Everyone can think of examples to support this theory and then of examples to argue against it.

One recent example of this search for the essential qualities of leaders has been the suggestion that leadership is a matter of **emotional intelligence**, and of being able to empathize with others. Indeed, our definition above was criticized in one investment bank in which we were working for not including the word 'caring'. The idea is attractive; most of us can think of examples of people using their empathetic abilities to influence others, and we can think even more easily of leadership that has been marred by not having enough understanding of the feelings of others. But there is another side to this. From our definition above, the activity of leading is essentially about making something happen, through others, which was not going to happen otherwise, something that would not have happened in the normal run of events. We are all held to this run of events by our understanding of the **culture** in which we are working, and by our understandings of what those around us will see as normal, reasonable behaviour on our part. It might be that those who are most aware of the culture and of the feelings of others are going to be less inclined to act as leaders, because they have a better understanding of the way things are normally done and why. So even this 'quality' of leaders is as likely to work in the opposite direction as in the one that has been recently proposed.

Despite the disappointing results from this approach to leadership, many people still seem to hope that they can discover the qualities of a great leader, and a lot of energy still goes into examining successful political, military and business leaders in the hope of discovering the quality, skill or competence that makes the difference.

Leadership as Power Holding

If leadership cannot be reduced to a set of qualities, let us look at the opposite approach; leadership is what is done by people who hold the **power** to make something happen through others which was not going to happen otherwise. This is not the whole of leadership, nor necessarily its most important part, but this exercise of wielding power is one of the commonest everyday views of leadership – that leadership is whatever is done by powerful people.

So there is a boss, sitting in a comfortable chair, in a fine office, telling others what they should do. He (occasionally she, in which case the stereotypes are even more extreme) is impatient, gets frustrated and stressed, and shouts a lot at people – because they often do silly things. This is a favoured, but predictable, image of organizational leadership among writers of television soap operas. It makes good drama. It is saturated with coercive power – the wielding of decisive influence over peoples' lives. Many of the early industrial barons were well practised at such leadership, as are some of their late twentieth century descendants. Lee Iacocca (1984), reflecting on his executive career in the Ford Motor Company, tells us that 'each time Henry (Ford) walked into a meeting, the atmosphere changed abruptly. He held the power of life and death over all of us. He could suddenly say "off with his head" – and he often did. Without fair hearing, one more promising career at Ford would bite the dust.'

Pushing people hard, with threats, can certainly get them moving; but in what direction? It has not proved a very successful strategy for engendering commitment and creativity, or reducing **conflict**, being based on a very crude **psychological contract** between boss and subordinate. The boss is doing just that: bossing. This style of leadership still exists, although coercion today is usually presented with a more friendly face; it has been called 'tough love'.

The written word is almost as prolific as the spoken one in the daily business of organizing. Some managers manage by email or memo. Each morning there can be a new flow of directives and suggestions for staff to read, collate and consider. The actual flow can symbolize something about the manager's style (intentional or otherwise). A constant stream suggests a possibly nervous individual, desiring to exert control over affairs: it is as if to say 'don't forget I'm here and I'm in contact with all key affairs'. On the other hand, the rarity or unusualness of a written **communication** can signify the importance of the message – 'if the chief executive has taken the trouble to write, it must be something crucial'. Increasingly, though, employees believe that emails from the Chief Executive really come from his or her PA, or from the corporate communications department. Employees of a major British computer company told us of their special version of such missives: Stanograms. The label was coined whimsically from the name of the Managing Director, and they were yellow pieces of paper containing his cryptic thoughts or key messages. No one could miss them.

The style and tone of correspondence from a leader can be manipulated to set the psychological distance preferred. Does William Draycot receive messages from his boss addressed 'Dear Bill', 'Dear William', 'Dear Mr Draycot' or even 'Draycot'? Does the boss always feel impelled to write out his or her title in full – as if to reinforce the **status** of the position? Or is the boss perhaps the only person not to do so, which ends up having a similar effect. Does the message invite a reply, and will that reply be acknowledged? Is it only the bad news and personal criticism which get put in writing? Dismissal or redundancy is a case in point. Rather than face directly the shock or discomfort it can cause, a manager might choose to do it all in writing, regardless of the effects on the receiver of the news. For example, we know of a senior manager from an engineering company who received his dismissal notice by personal delivery at his home. What made the event particularly poignant was that the letter was carried by his boss's secretary in the very early hours of the morning; and up until that moment the man had felt perfectly secure in a job he had held continuously for 11 years (see also Chapters 2 and 12, 'Entering and Leaving' and 'Morals').

In a high profile case recently in the UK, most of the employees of a company were sacked by text message. What does this say to the recipients of the message about whether their managers care about them? For some leaders, maintaining (or switching to) formal, impersonal relationships, helps them cope with issues which otherwise would get swamped by feelings. Hiding behind the written word, or using others to deliver unpleasant messages, provides the leader with a protective screen. In one company, the Chief Executive sent an email to his board reminding them of their 'collective responsibility' for board decisions, and how they should all support those decisions in all their discussions, whether or not they agreed with them in the first place. A few days later, he was confronted by one of the board members about the importance of open discussion of options. The Chief Executive said: 'yes, I'm sorry, I was in a terrible temper at the time'. In other words, he had used the power that he held, but could see that it might be a damaging and expensive strategy, so he was apologizing for it.

These various manifestations of the written word are normally taken for granted in the daily melée of organizational life. To the student of organizations, they are significant clues to the texture and health of the leadership process.

Leadership as Politics

Perhaps leadership is not simply about the power that you hold in your position, but your **competence** in making that power work for you in the **politics** of the organization.

> The good thing about being in Supply and Development is that John Chartres will always make sure that we have a strong voice with the board. He's really got the ear of everybody who matters. The previous director was a nice guy, but you just knew that everybody else walked all over him.

Organizations are political systems. People are doing deals with each other (see Chapter 8, 'Politics and Deals'), making fixes and trading, and leaders have the role of doing this on behalf of their subordinates. Leaders are often judged by their subordinates according to their skills as a player within the politics of the organization.

Some people find a political model of organizations particularly convincing. If we take this view, the key to leading is skill within the political system of the organization. Many people have a fascination with the power that politicians hold, and both those who are senior in organizations and those who aspire to succeed them take quite readily to a political view of leadership. It makes the leader rather like a gladiator, where he or she is quite well looked after, but in return is expected to go out and fight for his or her life, watched by excited onlookers.

This view became less dominant after a study of Chief Executives in top US corporations (Bennis and Nanus, 1985), which found that hardly any of them had any interest in, or real understanding of, the politics of their corporations. Instead, their focus was mostly on building a vision. This may be a false dichotomy; even if the CEO is not interested in politics, they may have a friend who is. Perhaps they had close allies who enabled them to focus on vision by looking after the political side? Either way, this leads us on to thinking about visionary leadership.

Leadership as Vision

A leader may be able to create a vision which others can identify with and carry forward. Such 'envisioning' – the offering of a major creative idea – has been the trademark of many high-profile executives, such as Jan Carlzon of SAS, Anita Roddick of The Body Shop, Richard Branson of the Virgin Corporation, Stelios Haji-Ioannou of easyJet and Lee Iacocca of the Chrysler Corporation. Each, in their own way, offered a vision of the shape and style of the company they wanted, presented in a form which aims to tap into the desires and values of the people who work for them, or simply to catch the mood of the moment. Anita Roddick, for example, attempted to demonstrate – by personal example, by her products, and by her whole business policy – that ecologically sound principles should govern all aspects of her enterprise. Contrast this with a television interview with a senior director of ICI who, when challenged about his company's publicly declared 'green' credentials, stumbled when asked for his target for waste reduction. After an embarrassing silence, he stated a generous-sounding figure, which later turned out to be untrue: no specific target existed. In contrast, the later Jan Carlzon spoke of an ailing airline business and a demoralized workforce. He has talked of the difficulties in maintaining the 'big idea' and in finding a new one. Clearly, leadership credibility means that grand words have to be matched by grand deeds – and both can decay in plausibility and attractiveness as time goes by.

Some leaders will catch the different moods of the time and create new images accordingly. Rupert Murdoch, the owner of an international newspaper, publishing and broadcasting empire, has gained both fame and notoriety for his flexibility in this respect. In the 1970s, he presented himself as a sensationalist, advocating journalism that focused on sex, crime and sport. In the 1980s, he decided to shift his interests to bastions of respectability – he purchased *The Times* and the *Sunday Times* newspapers – to apply, many believed, a disguise to his more coarse and opportunist values and ambitions. This may have given him the respectability which has enabled him to continue acquiring newspapers and television channels worldwide. Even fierce critics are inclined to forgive him everything as the person who brought us the well-known cartoon show, *The Simpsons*. But even this tells us something about his vision. *The Simpsons* has a tradition of guest appearances by powerful people, and in one of them Rupert Murdoch appeared as 'ruthless media tyrant, Rupert Murdoch'. To appear under that label on a show made by his own company and transmitted by his own TV channel suggests a more interesting and complex view of the vision he is pursuing than many of his critics have given him credit for, even if others regard it as a cynical camouflage.

Figure 7.1

Leadership as Managing Meanings

Creating and sharing a vision is just one of the ways in which people try to **manage meanings** for each other. The visionary leader gives meaning to a situation by giving a vision for how it might develop. We now turn to look at other ways in which leaders manage meanings. Organizations comprise different **groups** of people with different beliefs and interests (even if it is just the different perspective of the marketing, production and finance departments, each of whom think that the latest success was primarily down to them). People vie with each other for influence and power. In this environment, few leaders can expect automatic compliance with what they personally think is important. Leaders need to know what is important and meaningful to the people they work with, and somehow shape their beliefs, or 'meanings', in a direction which makes organizational sense. In other words, the leader has to appreciate the world as seen through the follower's eyes, if only in order to try to influence it.

Power is often exercised through the **management of meanings**. It has been suggested (Lukes, 1975) that there is a relatively straightforward form of power where one person can force another to do something (*first dimension power*), like the power a guard has over a prisoner. There is a more subtle form of power where one person persuades another to do something by limiting their thoughts to harmless areas (*second dimension power*). For example, this is the form of power exercised by teenagers over their parents when they distract them from asking questions which they do not want to have to answer. Then there is power which is exercised by influencing someone else's view of what is in their own interest (*third dimension power*). This is the power that is exercised by managing the other person's meanings, so that they come to believe that something which is in the leader's interest is actually in their own. If a manager tries to get an employee to do an unpleasant job on the grounds that 'it will be wonderful experience for you', and the employee comes to believe it, that may be leadership by management of meanings. This is not necessarily manipulative; the skilled leader may have been able to bring new meanings to what was going on so that the new meanings are compelling, believable and persuasive to those involved. The fact that the employee may not have needed much persuasion that it was in their interest means that it is difficult to be certain when we are seeing this form of leadership; who is to say whether someone else's view of what is in their own interest is false, or whether a leader has influenced a situation in such a way that they have managed their own meanings just as much as those of the employee?

Leadership as Display

Monarchs and dictators have long **symbolized** their authority by grand physical props: a palace, a throne, lavish furniture and decor, luxurious transport, expensive clothes – the physical setting speaks for itself. The corporate manager has followed suit. Sometimes the whole building does the job, becoming more luxurious as one moves up the floors (see Chapter 6, 'Buildings and Organizing'). One company chose to construct its headquarters to resemble a vast set of steps, like a stairway. No visitor, or employee, could fail to know who was more important than whom. Divisions of corporate status have long been marked by what and where people eat, from work canteens to plush dining rooms. The very occupancy of a four-walled office amidst an open-plan layout can immediately mark out who has power. Gradations among those leaders are shown by the degree of opacity of the glass walls: the higher the manager, the more privacy they get.

All offices say something about their occupants; some ooze authority and **power**: the huge desk, the thick carpet, the original paintings, the dark wood panelling, the carefully placed fresh flowers and the throne-like chair behind the desk where the manager sits. All of this says: 'I am important, I deserve more space than other people, and I deserve to have people serving me'. Contrast this with the room which has light, bright colours, easy chairs and a coffee table in the centre; the desk is tucked away in a corner – all suggestive of someone who is comfortable with a relaxed, consultative style of management.

The acquisition of material symbols of power and status can turn into something of an obsession. The floor area of the room, the engine size of the company car, personalized car-parking space, access to privileged dining areas, first-class air travel: these are just a few of the outward signs of having 'arrived'. They are often jealously guarded by their owners, and envied by those who lack them. In some companies, they are seen as part of the way that people can be motivated to strive for promotion. Likewise, they are carefully dispensed by the organization. In some organizations, carpet is reserved for employees above a certain status, even though it is cheaper than the hard floor coverings in the offices of their juniors. The carpet, of course, not only speaks of the person's status, but also of those who fall into order above and below. We have a professorial colleague who was keen to remove the large executive desk from his office in order to create a more informal feel to the room. He asked his secretary to arrange this. The weeks turned into months, but nothing happened. His secretary offered all manner of administrative excuses, until, one day, the true reason dawned on him. She was very proud of his senior **role**, especially because it offered her reflected glory and a certain authority. The 'important' desk symbolized this. To remove it meant diminishing her role, as well as that of her boss.

The symbols of leadership have to be carefully managed to convey the meanings they intend. A slip, an over-usage or a misuse can render them invalid. For example, we know of one company director who ends memos to his staff with the statement: 'if you have any problems or queries about this, do not hesitate to contact me'. At first, this sentiment was well received; it was an indication of a person who would listen. After a time, though, staff realized that it was presented ritualistically on all correspondence, on virtually every issue. It lost its impact. Some began to see it as a cover for the director's lack of consultation with them in the first place. This reaction runs close to the 'I've heard it all before' one. The leader makes a bold speech, full of fine sentiments and imagery but fails to stir hearts and minds. The imagery fails to connect, because the previous fine speeches were seen to have come to nothing. 'It's all words', mumble people as they leave the conference room. Those much-prized physical symbols of power can also backfire. How, for example, can the director whose office is lavished with fine objects and whose expensive car sits in the courtyard, preach on the virtues of austerity and economy to the workforce?

A very reflective company chairman uses the word 'leadering' to describe a kind of leadership which is all display and no substance. This is where people have watched others leading, or possibly dramatic presentations on stage or television of leadership, and then tried to make themselves look like leaders by imitation. They do things which they believe will give them the aura of leadership, but they are not actually leading anyone anywhere. One journalist characterized the Clinton era in the United States as 'leadership without direction'. It all looks like effective leadership until you ask: 'where was he leading people to?' This is where the displays that can go with leadership activity have been mistaken for the substance. This is where '**narcissism**', i.e. exaggerated concern with appearances conceals the absence of true leadership, but locks leaders and followers into a mutual admiration society.

Leadership as a Set of Arts

Much of the research on leadership has focused on trying to make a science of it. If we can work out the variables, then we can measure how they are correlated. After that we will know when we have to add a little more of a particular ingredient in order to produce the result we want. In contrast to this, several writers have emphasized the importance of thinking of leadership as an art, and one author has gone further by suggesting that it is better to think of a set of arts (Grint, 2000). He suggests that you can divide leadership into philosophical, fine, martial and performing arts.

Philosophical art is about **identity**: who are we who are trying to achieve this outcome? A leader may give a group or an organization a sense that they all belong together, that they have something in common which means that they should stay together and work together. We see a leadership attempt of this kind when we hear the American President address 'my fellow Americans'; the speaker and audience know that this may be a group of people with almost nothing in common. Some of them did not want that person to be their President. But the President is attempting to exercise the philosophical art of leadership through identity. Where we see a collective loyalty to an organization we can expect that we are witnessing a philosophical leader developing an identity. Stelios Haji-Ioannou, the founder of the pioneering low-cost airline, easyJet, has created a sense of delight among many of his employees at being part of what is widely seen as a 'clever' and exciting company.

Fine art is about the design of vision, which we discussed earlier. Most leaders act through the imagination rather than the body. The fine art is about imagining a possible future that people can move towards. What is being imagined is a journey, and for this reason it is about the past as well as the future, as a leader can tell people about where they have come from as well as where they are going. This way of leading involves creating a **story** for an organization. A few years ago, a once well-respected British retailer, Marks & Spencer, went through a series of changes in its top leadership. Each new CEO came in with a new story about where the company had come from, how it had been developing, and thus where would be a good place for it to go next. For several years, each of them has had difficulty getting their story to stick. Then came one, Stuart Rose, who gave a clear focus to the company. His efforts were widely admired, he became chairman as well as chief executive, and then once again things turned sour. He had designed a vision, but perhaps missed out on the continuous refreshing and redesign that a good vision needs.

Martial art is the **planning** and tactical work involved in leading; sometimes the biggest leadership contribution may be to get things well organized and make sure the photocopiers are working. During the Second World War, Winston Churchill said: 'give us the tools, and we will finish the job'. Leadership may consist in enabling someone else to do something, which we will come back to when we consider empowerment. This is the form of leadership which comes closest to management. It is leading by sheer good organization. Amazon, the on-line bookseller, has achieved a dominant market position largely through excellent organization, through a fine application of the martial art of leadership.

Performance art is what people often think of as leadership, the **charismatic** activity of persuading others to do something. The shaping of what other people think and feel is central to the leadership process. It is accomplished through the skilful use of **symbols**: talk, stories, visual images, ceremonies, writings and **rituals**. These are the essential tools of the leader's trade. They are used variously to represent the leader's aspirations, visions and beliefs.

Some organization leaders appear to spend an inordinate amount of time talking. In meetings, in corridors, over lunches, at conferences, in cars, on trains, in planes, and on telephones – they talk. **Talk**, and its words, is a basic symbolic process through which leaders define and re-define their ideas, and those of others. For some leaders, all this talk *is* their action, and their action *is* the talking. This can be particularly effective if a leader is able to combine listening and talking in a way which gently shapes a direction which offers mileage to both leader and led. We can eavesdrop on a (fictitious) conversation between a Managing Director and her Marketing Manager to see the process at work:

REAL-LIFE EXAMPLE

MD: So what you are saying Joan is that you would like a marketing strategy for our magazine which extends the age range of readers.

Joan: Exactly! I've been feeling for a long time that we need to take into account the shifting attitudes of youngsters. Today's 15-year-olds think like 18-year-olds did when we launched this magazine in the 1980s. Their attitudes to sex, drugs, personal relationships, work, education, the family and so forth are nothing like ours were!

MD: Mmm. That's a good point.

Joan: And I really would love to have a go at re-framing our advertisements and feature articles with a younger market in mind.

MD: Joan. I really think you could be on to a winner. But first of all I need to get straight the financial implications. Our parent company is unhappy about our turnover and profit this year, and I'm keen to find a new image. Your idea could be the answer. I wonder if there's a way in which you could do a trial run to test the water first?

Joan: I hadn't thought of that. I suppose we could do a supplement to our November issue – say, one special feature with ads.

MD: Fine. Go ahead. Meanwhile, I need a long-term financial estimate to prepare my case for the Board – as soon as possible. Why don't I arrange a meeting between you, me, and Mark from Financial Planning? He can help us put the financial flesh on your idea.

In this exchange, we witness the Managing Director building on an idea suggested by her Marketing Manager in a way which (a) supports the marketing manager's initiative and (b) re-channels it in a form which meets the MD's own objectives. Notice that the MD shifts Joan's initial expectations to a rather more cautious position, while also setting up a structure to keep *her* involved in the development of *her* idea. It is easy to identify all four arts of leadership here.

LEADING AND FOLLOWING

How does leadership fit in with other roles that can be played in an organization, and especially with the complementary activity of 'following'? We shall consider this question under the following headings:

- Leadership as a Two-way Process
- Leadership as Empowerment of Others
- Leadership as Distributed
- Leadership as a Panacea
- Leadership as a Way of Placing Blame
- Leadership as Responsibility.

Leadership as a Two-way Process

As the image of the omnipotent boss fades, we sometimes have to search harder in the organization for the leader. The following is an exchange that took place between one of us and a junior employee we interviewed:

REAL-LIFE EXAMPLE

Neil's Story

Interviewer: Who do you report to here?
Employee: Well, no one really. I suppose Bill, officially.
Interviewer: Yes, but who guides your work?
Employee: Oh. Quite a few people. We all help each other.
Interviewer: But the project you're on. Who's in charge of it?
Employee: It depends what you mean by 'in charge'. As we work in a mixed team, there are several different managers who are looking after different bits – one on design, one on production, and one on marketing.
Interviewer: OK, then, how do you get your instructions on what to do?
Employee: It comes from several sources: I usually have to go and ask, and then make my own work.
Interviewer: What happens if you can't do the work?
Employee: I just say so. We then work out something between us.

What this employee was trying to convey was something about the quality of working in an organization which had little of the traditional **hierarchy** of **control**. She worked in a project team. Leadership was not the prerogative of a single boss; it was distributed across managers and team members. She went on to describe how, in meetings, senior managers seemed to 'just chat' with them, after a lot of listening to their issues and **problems**. She could not remember many times when she was actually told what to do: 'it feels as if I'm being given space to draw my own conclusions and work schedule, which is nice. Sometimes I can even help others'.

Not everyone would feel as comfortable as this person with the kind of direction she was receiving, but she illustrates an important feature of organizational leadership: it is a two-way process of mutual influence. What happens, as we saw under 'Leadership as Managing Meanings' is often a subtle shaping of another's world. A major theorist on organizational behaviour made the important point that 'executives are essentially powerless until the time comes when followers grant their leaders the authority to lead'. In other words, if everyone refused to be led, then there is often nothing the leader can do about it. A supervisor in a large chemical corporation told us of her shock when she first discovered this simple principle early in her career: 'I said: "do this" and "do that" to someone and he simply said "no". I was stumped. I could have said: "Well,

I'll go to Personnel" or something like that, but what kind of atmosphere would that have created?'

Leadership as Empowerment of Others

Leading may be a matter of giving others the right and the self confidence to do what they believe needs doing. The psychological logic here is fairly straightforward. We are likely to be more committed to actions which have been crafted and steered subtly by a leader than to ones that have been thrust down our throats; and the shaping starts with what we, not the leader, think is crucial. This involves an interesting reversal of the old maxim that power can corrupt; **powerlessness** too can corrupt, in that it leaves people weak, and out of control of their own destinies. Powerlessness can be corrosive, and its effects can be observed in many organizations. Powerless people feel insecure, and one response is to cling to whatever fragment of control they can acquire. It is as if they are saying: 'well, if I'm valued as no more than a cog in a machine, someone to be ordered around, then I'll show you how valuable I really am'. The janitor will make himself very hard to find when someone wants his services. The secretary will point to the backlog of work on her desk when asked to do an urgent job. Quite often the power of seemingly powerless people to be destructive is enormous.

   The paradox of leadership as empowerment is the very idea of the leader turning his or her so-called followers into leaders; to 'empower' them to use their talents to serve themselves and their organization. It is a bit like being ordered to 'be independent'; if you obey the order, you are not showing independence, so you are still not obeying the order. Similarly, a leader who wants to empower followers is trying to influence people to be less easily influenced in future. The notion of **empowerment** is appealing, and it is a fashionable one in current leadership thought. However, it should be borne in mind that in re-setting the power balance the leader's hand is still firmly on the steering wheel, which leaves empowerment open to the accusation that it is just a subtle form of manipulation where some people remain 'more equal' than others.

Leadership as Distributed

Leadership, in some form or another, is an essential ingredient of social organization – but you do not have to be a designated leader to lead. Working relationships involve many different leading–following interactions, often aimed at meeting different needs: **emotional**, task, organizational. Within groups or teams different people can play different leadership roles at different times – leadership is 'distributed'. Some recent researchers have suggested the idea of a 'leaderful' organization (Raelin, 2003), that is, an organization where there are many leaders, indeed in which potentially everyone is a leader, but on different occasions, for different activities and at different times. For example, in one organization we were told:

> Who's the leader? Well, it is hard to say, but if I had to pick just one, I would probably say Dorothy, the cleaning lady, because she knows everyone, knows everything that goes on, and always has a word with someone if things are going wrong. And she can really make things happen.

We may not have believed that Dorothy was really the leader; however, it does sound as if she certainly sometimes feels that it is her place to give a lead. It is hard to imagine a social situation where there are no attempts at organization through leadership, but let us try:

> You are asked to attend a managerial training meeting. Around the table are six people you have not seen before, but you know that they work for your organization. A trainer (whom you have not met) is sitting there, the obvious leader you think. But he does nothing, says nothing. There is silence; an extremely long silence. You feel uncomfortable. Others look uncomfortable too. Where is the agenda? What are you supposed to do?

This scenario is not fictitious – it happens in 't-groups', ('t' stands for training) once popular in **management** training. They are events specially stage-managed to be free of obvious **structure**; free from formal leadership. They create a social vacuum, but this, like its physical counterpart, is very soon filled. Leadership soon arises. People begin to talk, laugh nervously, get angry – anything to produce some structure and meaning out of the highly ambiguous situation. In doing so they reveal something of their own style and anxieties. Some will specifically try to influence the direction of affairs; others will gratefully fall into line. A few may protest, offering their own ideas about what everyone should do. As is often the case, the absence of something tells us something important about the thing that is absent.

The effect of a leadership vacuum on people's desire for leadership is pervasive. Populations in countries which experience long periods without stable leadership will often look appreciatively – for a time – on anyone who is willing to pick up the mess (a fact not missed by opportunistic dictators). Even in organizations as casual as groups of friends, the person who is prepared to offer some leadership at the level of suggesting which movie or which pub the group might go to is often thoroughly appreciated and rewarded for their efforts. This is why leadership can become a panacea.

Leadership as a Panacea

If an organization is not doing as well as it should, and especially if it is underperforming compared with similar organizations in other places, what is wrong with it? A current fashionable answer to that question is to suggest that there is a lack of leadership. This can be resolved either by changing the leadership or by developing it.

What does a 'lack of leadership' mean? We can tell that the phrase is not very precise when we look at the places that are alleged to suffer from such a lack. They may have nothing at all in common except that things are not going well. It is easily assumed that lack of leadership is always a problem. Plenty of people in organizations have complained about a 'lack of leadership', been rewarded with a new, strong leader, and have lived to regret this. A bad leader, which could mean one who lacks skill in just one of the leadership arts we discussed earlier, can neutralize or demoralize an organization very quickly. In some places, staff look back on the days when they lacked leadership as a golden era when comparing it with a time when they are offered leadership they do not want.

If there are attempts to develop leadership in places where it is seen as lacking, these may not be welcome. As soon as leadership is seen it is rejected. So 'lack of leadership' may mean lack of willingness to accept leadership, or at least the leadership that is being offered. Sometimes leadership is only wanted as a way of placing blame for everything that is irritating about the present.

Leadership as a Way of Placing Blame

Again, we return to **attributions** – what people choose to ascribe to the leader, and how fickle a process it can be. As part of this, one burden for the leader is to carry the projected disaffections and inadequacies of organizational members. This means he or she is a visible focus for blame, as well as a source of balm. Organizational leaders will often find that they inherit a history of problems in working relationships, which they are expected to shoulder. In this manner we can dump our most intractable problems on the leader and pretend they are his, or hers, to fix. But they are rarely solved in this manner, because the difficulties lie within us, not with the leader. Many an energetic, but naïve, company director has enthusiastically re-structured the organization to improve its effectiveness, while old hands quietly look on. Sure enough, after a short period of time, the old patterns re-emerge. Sometimes this is because people gain a vicarious pleasure and power from helping them to re-appear; at other times, it is because shifting the organizational pieces around does not touch underlying **cultural** beliefs and tensions. The power of the **institution** to replicate itself in the future overcomes the attempts to change the way it operates.

Audiences can, on one day, praise the leader and on the next castigate the person, branding him or her as fool or villain. Indeed they do not need to wait until the following day; feelings towards leaders are often ambivalent, with people often wanting simultaneously to admire their leader and to reassure themselves that the leader has feet of clay. Timing is everything in leadership. Politicians who say the wrong thing at the wrong time (or the right thing at the wrong time) can quickly be eased out of prominent positions. National heroes, whose words, wisdom and faces become immortalized in books and stone, can face sudden obliteration when their message is no longer seen to be appropriate: tumbled effigies of Lenin now litter the junk yards of Eastern Europe, where the effigies of Stalin had been some years earlier. Winston Churchill was voted out of office within weeks of having led his country to victory in the Second World War. Western political leaders are simultaneously admired, re-elected, and mocked by television satirists. The same happens with business leaders. Successive CEOs in companies that are in difficulties can pass through a very quick cycle in which they are seen as the potential saviour, hero, and false god in very quick succession, as the next incumbent is lined up as a potential saviour.

Leadership as Responsibility

The notion of responsibility is coming increasingly to the fore as another way of thinking about leadership. If you are asking someone to take a role in which they will need to look beyond the obvious, in which they will need to take ownership of problems which may not appear on anyone's job description, and to look to the future for possible threats and opportunities, what do you call this? The answer may be: leadership if the person is officially a leader, or responsibility otherwise. When we talked earlier about leaderful organizations, it may be that 'responsible' might be a better word for what we are talking about. Modern notions of leadership are very close to responsibility, so long as responsibility goes further than just 'feeling responsible and therefore guilty' and becomes 'feeling responsible and ensuring that action gets taken'. Responsibility ends up very similar to our original definition of leadership, as '*imagining, willing* and *driving*, and thereby making something happen which was not going to happen otherwise'.

We asked Anna, a Research Nurse we were interviewing, what influence she had on the issues that were being talked about in her organization. 'None', she said, 'I am not senior enough for that'. 'Tell us about the combined clinic project', we persisted. She went on to explain how a particular clinic had been set up because, 'obviously', the patients needed a combined clinic so that several related conditions could be treated at the same time. She had set the clinic up, but as far as she was concerned, she had just done what needed doing. Was this leadership or responsibility? She thought it was responsibility, but it sounded to us like leadership. Perhaps responsibility is the new leadership for a less **authoritarian** era in organizations.

The fact that a leader can wield influence does not necessarily make that leader effective, or his or her actions **ethical**. Somewhere along the line a judgement of quality has to made. Effective by what criteria and in whose terms? A leader may be regarded by his or her staff as delightful to work with and attentive to their needs. However, the leader's manager may see things differently: 'a nice person, but perhaps too nice; a low productivity section'. Different people can look for different qualities in a leader, according to what *they* think is important. Leadership is a **moral** activity, and is never value-neutral. Leaders are responsible for the direction in which they take the organization, and for the consequences, positive and negative, for all those affected, of 'making something happen, through other people, which was not going to happen otherwise'.

Leaders are responsible not only for the strategic direction in which they take their organization, but also for the cultural direction and the interpersonal climate. There is not much point in leading your organization in such a way that it cannot survive, but nor is there ultimately much point in mere survival, or even in profitability for its own sake. The idea that business leaders are interested solely in profit is one of the strangest fantasies to afflict the study of management; almost all the evidence is against it.

Instead, leaders often find themselves taking a moral stance on what sort of organizations they want to be part of. Followers can only make this choice by moving from one organization to another, but leaders can make it by leading the culture and climate in a particular direction. A leader can influence an organization so that its members and its customers are treated as ends and not just as means. A leader can raise the standards of integrity and quality within an organization. Equally, a leader can set standards of cynicism and indifference to others and to the organization which can infect the whole of the organization.

Leadership is as prominent in organizations as ever, but its nature seems to have changed. Leaders now have to rely less on hierarchical power; there are other ways to manage people.

KEY POINTS

○ There has been little progress on discovering the qualities, skills and competencies required for leadership.

○ Leadership involves exercising power.

○ Leadership may focus on managing the politics of an organization or building a vision.

○ Leaders often manage meanings of events and symbols for their followers.

○ There can be a display of leadership which is not necessarily closely related to the activity.

○ Leadership can be thought of as a set of philosophical, fine, martial and performing arts.

○ Leadership is always a two-way process.

○ Leadership may consist of empowering others to lead.

○ Leadership can be distributed widely in an organization.

○ Leadership may be seized upon as a panacea, or as a way of placing blame.

○ Leadership is very much the same as taking responsibility.

○ Leadership is always a moral, values-based activity.

〉〉〉〉〉〉〉〉〉〉〉〉 **THEORETICAL SIGNPOSTS** 〉〉〉〉〉〉〉〉〉〉〉〉

The major themes in this chapter have been covered in the following areas of literature:

〉 leadership as qualities or traits
〉 leadership as performance
〉 leadership in context.

Leadership as Qualities or Traits

This implies that some people are better leaders than others because of qualities that they themselves possess. Although many years of leadership research have failed to show us what these traits might be, new forms of trait theory keep emerging. Good summaries of the research in this area can be found in Northouse (1997), Yukl (2002) and Heifetz (1994). It is striking that even writers such as Grint (2000) find themselves using a kind of trait theory of leadership, even if those traits are subtler than earlier versions. Leadership, and to a lesser extent followership, has captivated organizational researchers for decades, symbolizing the importance placed on the role of the leader in many societies. Burns' (1978) classic study explores the 'transactions' between leader and follower – a two-way influence process – but distinguishes this from leadership which focuses on major 'transformations' in organizations. He argues that transactional and transformational leadership essentially require different leader characteristics. There has been an interesting take on the notion of transformational leadership by Tourish and Pinnington (2002), who talk about it as cultism. Just as it is very hard to state a critical or uncommitted point of view in a cult, it can be equally difficult in an organization which is undergoing transformational leadership. The consequences too can be similar, that alternative view points are not heard, and ideas are therefore insufficiently tested.

Leadership as Performance

This suggests that there are particular ways of leading that are impressive because of the quality with which they are performed. For example, Bass (1985) develops the work of Burns (1978) to suggest that leadership can be both transformational and transactional, and suggests that leadership performance can be distinguished by including, first, charisma, second, inspirational motivation, third, intellectual stimulation and fourth, individualized consideration. The psychodynamics of leadership – such as the way subordinates use leaders as parental figures and become dependent upon them, as well as disappointed with them, feature in the writings of Bion (1961), Hirschhorn (1988) and Kets de Vries (1990a). The charisma of some leaders is an intriguing issue: is it to do with the leaders themselves, their followers, or both? (See Bryman, 1992). Grint (2000) has explored the arts of leadership thoroughly, and Heifetz (1994) is a valuable source for a comprehensive account of where the field of leadership studies has got to so far.

Leadership in Context

This emphasizes the situational character of leadership, with a lot of emphasis on what is going on in the place and at the time that leadership is happening. This way of thinking has led to an emphasis on leadership as being quite widely distributed in an organization, where many different people may make a contribution to the activity of leadership and to its effectiveness (Kets de Vries, 1990a; Raelin, 2003). Some writers (Bennis, 1989; Zaleznik, 1977) regard leaders as separate from managers, the former doing 'right things' and the latter 'doing things right'.

REVIEW QUESTIONS

1. Leadership studies have been likened to the drunk looking under the lamppost for his keys; this is not where he dropped them, but at least the light is good. Where would you look for the key to understanding how good leadership comes about?

(Continued)

(Continued)

2. Do you think that all the arts of leadership could be exercised by the same person? If not, how can people who are experts in the different arts be brought together to enable leadership?

3. Some have argued that we are not short of leadership so much as follower-ship. What do you think can be done to encourage effective followership in organizations?

companion
website
www.sagepub.co.uk/fineman

Reading On

The articles below are available for free to readers of the fourth edition of *Organizing & Organizations* via the book's companion website at www.sagepub.co.uk/fineman

Buchanan, D.A., Addicott, R., Fitzgerald, L., Ferlie, E. and Baeza, J.I. (2007) 'Nobody in charge: distributed change agency in healthcare', *Human Relations*, 60: 1065–90.
This article illustrates how distributed change agency can implement complex organizational changes in the absence of formal management plans, roles and structures. Distributed change agency typically involves small teams and senior groups. In this qualitative study of service improvements in the treatment of prostate cancer at an acute hospital, Grange, change roles were distributed more widely, with responsibilities migrating among a large informal cast supporting four central characters.

Bell, B.S. and Kozlowski, S.W.J. (2002) 'A typology of virtual teams: implications for effective leadership', *Group Organization Management*, 27: 14–49.
As the nature of work in today's organizations becomes more complex, dynamic and global, there has been increasing emphasis on distributed, 'virtual' teams as organizing units of work. The authors focus on delineating the dimensions of a typology to characterize different types of virtual teams, while discussing propositions addressing leadership implications for the effective management of virtual teams.

Clarke, M. (2006) 'A study of the role of "representative" leadership in stimulating organization democracy', *Leadership,* 2: 427–50.
This article explores how models of distributed leadership appear at odds with the dominant bureaucratic and unitary model of organizing. It offers a model of Representative Leadership (RL) derived from a political institutional discourse and suggests that in settings of contested plurality, constituencies, by a wide range of individuals, is central to effective organizing.

James, K.T., Mann, J. and Creasy, J. (2007) 'Leaders as lead learners: a case example of facili-tating collaborative leadership learning for school leaders', *Management Learning*, 38: 79–94.
Distributed leadership is increasingly desired in traditionally top-down organizations. This article bridges a gap between theory about distributed leadership, which addresses not only *how* leader-ship is exercised through collaborative practices, but also *where* and by *whom* it is undertaken. The idea of distributed leadership highlights the need for new and congruent development methodologies, without which calls for distributed leadership will flounder.

8

POLITICS AND DEALS

'Politics is everywhere' is the major theme of this chapter – and to appreciate and harness it is a key feature of organizing. Politics can be damaging or constructive, secret or open, for good or for ill, but is part of the lifeblood of the organization. The politically skilled manager will be attuned to the interests and agendas of those she or he manages and the serious games that are played in order to influence outcomes: game theory offers us some insights here. A political perspective highlights how differences between people or departments can turn into destructive or creative conflict. Conflict management rarely follows a single recipe and needs to reflect the wider culture of the organization.

REAL-LIFE EXAMPLE

Real-Life Example

Neil's Story

I love selling. It's what I'm really good at – not in a nasty way, but in the way that I reckon we've got some really good products in CLEMCO, and I like getting those products out to good customers. And I really like our customers – if I don't like them, that means I've just got to get to know them better. I'm one of the top salesmen in CLEMCO, and the group of us working for Simon are the top group, and that's where we want to stay.

When we get a new salesman, I try to look after them; I owe so much to Simon for helping me build my sales career, and I want to do the same for others. When Greg joined us last year, I could see he was a natural salesman, even though he came straight from university. We meet up in the pub at the end of every week to talk about how it's going. He is full of ideas and very ambitious; he wants to work in corporate HQ as soon as possible. He's always going on courses to get himself better known, so I tease him about that.

A couple of weeks ago, Greg was really pleased because he had heard that one of his stores had written to CLEMCO's HQ to say how well one of his merchandising ideas had worked. He thought it might help him to get known at corporate level, which is always what he has wanted. Then, last week, Simon asked him if he would take over Jack's patch; Jack has been in and out of hospital, and his patch was falling to pieces. Greg told Simon it would take six months to sort out, but he was sure he could do it, and would be delighted to take the opportunity. It meant taking on Go-Lo stores, which have been a mess, but we talked it through in the pub and even I was convinced that Greg could do it.

And then today I was getting the stuff out of the filing cabinet to check on one of my accounts, and I heard Ian, Vice President of CLEMCO, down from HQ, talking to Simon. We have open-plan offices with screens, and they obviously didn't realize I was there. Ian was asking Simon about Greg, saying that they had heard good things about him, but he couldn't believe how bad the Go-Lo stores merchandising was, with no sign of the account being run properly, no sign of creative merchandising ideas and so on. Well, I was thinking, come on, Simon, explain to him that Greg only took that account a week ago, and has had no chance to sort it out yet. But Simon just said that he and I were working hard on Greg, that the Store Manager who had written to head office was probably a bit over the top in Greg's favour because Greg was going out with his daughter, and that Greg had good potential but still needed a lot more development. I couldn't believe my ears. I know that Greg is now Simon's best salesman, and he does not want to lose him too soon, but surely he would not stoop so low? Anyhow, Ian went away with no idea as to why Go-Lo had not improved yet, with the impression that Greg was much less good than he actually is, and that Simon was the guy he should listen to in future to know how people were doing. It made me feel sick. (Adapted from Frantzve, 1983)

This story shows **politics** at work: people talking about others behind their backs; rumours and alliances among powerful people; pub chat that makes (or breaks) opportunities; overheard conversations; attempts to impress powerful people. Indeed, it is hard to think of organizing without politics. Differences of opinion, **values** and interests, clashes of **personality**, limited resources and personal ambition add to the tension, as well as the buzz and excitement, of organizing. People sometimes describe their organization as 'all politics' to suggest a devious, conflict-ridden atmosphere where intrigue, gossip and whispering are endemic. They appear to be 'looking over their shoulders' much of the time and the language of politics – what secret deals are happening; who is abusing the system; who is the boss's favourite – permeates the corridors and the area around the water coolers. At its most extreme, politics can be harsh, vindictive and vicious, where power is used and abused. It can also bring about strange alliances and strange enmities. In a **conflict** situation, such as the one above, it is clear that **power** is not always simply a matter of the boss being able to do what they want. The information that people have about what other people are doing and how well they are doing it is always limited, partial and often presented with a bias by someone who wants them to see it in a particular way.

Secret deals and plotting behind closed doors are fascinating. As Henry Kissinger, former American Secretary of State, said of his time serving President Kennedy: 'before I served as a consultant to Kennedy, I had believed, like most academics, that the process of decision-making was largely intellectual and all one had to do was to walk into the President's office and convince him of the correctness of one's view. This perspective, I soon realised, is as dangerously immature as it is widely held'. But just as fascinating are those organizations where such events seem rare, or non-existent. These may be happier (or duller, depending on your perspective) organizations to work in, but does that mean there are no politics? Far from it. Politics are both the expression and resolution of inevitable differences between people and their preferences. But these do not have to be expressed and tackled through devious means: some organizations handle their differences in a more open manner, without rancour or distrust. Let us examine this a little further.

GAMES WITHIN GAMES

Sometimes people in organizations say that someone else is 'just playing games'. This may mean that they seem to be engaging in politics for the fun of it, as a virtuoso activity, or a way of showing off their skills in confusing or manipulating people. For example, someone will start a rumour just to see if they can get away with it. But the idea of **games** in organizations has gone much deeper than this. Referring to politics and dealings as 'games' does not mean that they do not have serious intentions, nor that they may not have serious consequences. The idea of a 'game' has been used for a long time as a metaphor for the way that people attempt to influence or score 'points' off one another. However serious the players are, it is a point-scoring activity played out within a set of rules, just like other games. Indeed, Berne (1964) has suggested that many of our conflicts can be unravelled by seeing them in terms of the games we play, where the rules are sometimes so taken for granted that we cannot see how they operate. The games can be complex and intertwined; they can be multiple games each with rather different rules and different outcomes, and all going on simultaneously. Games can be played coolly and calculatively, or aggressively and passionately.

Another helpful conceptual notion is the *metagame*. This is a kind of game where, each time it is a player's turn to play, they may do something which influences the rules of the game. This is similar to the way in which, in some board games, there is the choice of making a move or playing a token which changes the rules for the next round. An organizational example follows:

Gordon was getting heartily sick of the way that James seemed to be forever attacking his department. James had lost no opportunities in the past to tell everyone that he thought Gordon's people were a 'waste of space', and as if to make this point even more clearly, he had even started encroaching on Gordon's open-plan office space with some of his team. Gordon could either oppose the loss of space directly, and argue that he needed that space for his next expansion (which would be a move within the game as it stands), or he could spend his time trying to suggest to the Chief Executive that James was an empire-building schemer (which would be a move in the metagame, trying to change the rules on which their power struggles were played out for the future). Gordon chose the second, and everyone's opinion of his wisdom as a manager went up as a result.

In organizations, we often have a sense of some of the rules of play, the turns, the refereeing and so on. We learn about their intricacies, such as that it is OK to criticize John when you are talking to your friend Sue, but not when you are talking to Mary (who is John's boss). If such niceties are misunderstood or ignored, there can be a price to pay (e.g. personal embarrassment, a lost friendship or working relationship, even your job). Neil, in the story at the beginning of the chapter, had a 'rule' that a boss should stick up for his staff unless there was some good reason not to. Another **'rule'** might be that new product ideas must always be taken to the development committee before the production department is asked to comment on them.

Organizations abound in such tacit rules of the game – rules that do not appear in writing or a rule book (see Chapter 5, 'Rules are Rules'). Many organizational games are of the someone-wins-someone-loses sort. For example, in the 'game' of appointments and promotions, if there is only one vacancy, and one person gets it, another does not – he or she loses. However, there are organizational games where one person's gain is not necessarily another person's loss. If someone gives an excellent presentation to a client, there may be a sneaking envy from others, but still everyone in the department gains. There are also organizational situations that are like the games at a children's party: if one person or **group** wins too convincingly or too often, the others will not want to play with them any more. So the art is to learn just where to cooperate sufficiently to make sure that opponents are doing well enough not to quit, and also so that it does not look as if the person not cooperating is being childish and selfish. While this is not a win–win situation, it is sufficiently promising for everyone so that they stay in the game.

Negotiators skilled in making inter-company deals know this well. A complete loser is likely to feel de-motivated and refuse to deal on another occasion, or worse still, to find a way of unpicking or sabotaging the deal later. They may find other ways of scoring off an opponent, such as wrecking the efforts of others through poor workmanship, blocking initiatives, spreading rumours, **sabotage** or sheer bloody-mindedness. This reminds us that winning and losing can have different meanings to different participants, to the extent that one person's 'obvious' win may not feel that way to her, and another person's 'clear' loss is regarded by him or her as a personal victory. Behind this lies a range of social and psychological processes, such as perceptions of fairness, defensiveness and the kind of audience to whom the success or failure is presented. We see such variety of meanings in, for example, the way football supporters handle their team's losses, and how heads of state, who have lost a war, claim a 'moral victory'. We see it in organizations where the manager who introduced a re-organization which looks like a disaster to everyone else explains how valuable it was for organizational learning. The careful use of language and **rhetoric** is crucial to this process.

Some organizational activities resemble a constellation of agendas and games such that winning at one level allows you to proceed to the next level. For example, competing successfully for a budget is used as entry to bidding for a larger contract, and then for entry to competing for promotion. It may also be that succeeding in one game, against a particular set of rules, excludes you from another game. A typical example here is 'rate busting'. Exceeding the work rate – how much and how long to work – that immediate colleagues informally agree is appropriate, may win praise from senior management (for more production, more profit) but at the cost of being snubbed or excluded by colleagues. The same can often be found with groups of students who together set a **norm** for the standards that can be expected in their group projects, and ostracize any person or group who tries to go beyond that norm.

There are occasions where the principle at stake for both parties is so high that nothing but an all-out win will do, yet that win seems unattainable. It is not uncommon to observe the sad and destructive spectre of two-loser games in organizations: a strike which leaves the workers unemployed and the company in ruins; an interdepartmental rivalry in which each department effectively blocks the other's efforts; a price war between two firms driving both of them to bankruptcy. But, interestingly, even such losses can be described by the warring parties as victories of a sort. They become so focused on defeating one particular enemy that they hardly concern themselves with whether they are better off as a result. Organizational history is littered with examples of Pyrrhic victories.

The sixteenth-century political theorist, Machiavelli, made the point that sometimes it was crueller not to take a conflict through to its conclusion than it was to attempt a compromise. He suggested that, if someone is going to engage in a conflict, they should make sure that it concludes, and they should make sure that the opposition has been thoroughly and visibly defeated. Only such steps, even if they appear vicious, will prevent the conflict lingering and re-asserting itself later.

Machiavelli is often misrepresented in discussions of organizational politics as someone for whom power and might were everything. In fact, he argued that glory was equally important. Only if people are prepared to accept what someone is doing, and believe it to be more than an exercise in power for its own sake, will they achieve the glory which can go with it. If Mark destroys Alan's argument in a meeting, and appears to be doing it to prevent the company setting up a project which is likely to fail, he will be admired for it. If he appears to be doing it to get himself promoted, he might gain himself some short-term power, but he will get no glory in the eyes of his colleagues, and will be despised as a scheming careerist. That is one of the reasons why Neil felt so angry with Simon in our story at the beginning of the chapter; he was making Greg look incompetent in the eyes of Ian for Simon's own personal benefit. If Neil had believed that Simon might have been somehow acting for Greg's long-term benefit, he would still have been angry, but might have felt a little more ambivalent.

If some organizational games disintegrate into apparently no-win situations, others generate multiple winners. Situations that appear stubbornly win–lose can suddenly be unlocked through the creative art of politics and diplomacy. There is the delightful tale of two pharmaceutical companies after the same resource – ugli oranges – which contained the essential raw ingredients for their products. The oranges were in very short supply so they were both prepared to pay 'any price' to obtain them. Two senior executives from each of the two companies had a meeting to see if they could reach a compromise. But they soon discovered that they were both in an all-or-nothing situation; they both needed the full supply of oranges to fulfil their demand. Their agendas appeared irreconcilable.

Just as they were preparing to part and 'fight to the death', it occurred to one of them to ask the other *how* they were going to use the oranges:

'Exactly which part of the orange do you need?'
'Why, the juice, of course!'
'Good grief, let's celebrate ... we only need the rind!'

"The meeting's at 10. I'll send you a copy of the agenda, the hidden agenda and your personal agenda."

Figure 8.1   Many agendas.

Source: http://www.cartoonstock.com

ABOVE AND BELOW THE TABLE

Some conflict or competition in organizations is built into the structure. So the members of the board of directors have roles which invite them to fight for different interests within the company. The Marketing Director, the Production Director and the Finance Director are appointed to represent different interests. Although they need to collaborate for the good of the company, they are also expected to do the best deals they can for their department and to see the special importance of their own department's contribution. As is said of the members of the US Congress, 'where you stand depends on where you sit'. This is a way of formalizing conflict, containing it by establishing rules and formulae within which it takes place. In many commercial organizations, some conflict is legitimized as competition, a force for profit, growth and constructive contest.

Competition has its rules, such as there being a 'level playing field', undistorted by monopoly power or special privileges. Organizations which engage in international trade can often be seen to be in dispute or conflict because the tax, legal or employment conditions in one country give organizations there a competitive edge; this is a little like a runner in a race starting from a point ahead of all the rest of the field. The rules of international trade are seen by many of the players as unfair, and one of the fastest-growing retail sectors in many Western countries recently has been the 'fair trade' sector, where consumers voluntarily pay more than they otherwise would for goods (mostly foodstuffs) in order to compensate producers for this unfairness.

Once certain rules and formulae are recognized as the sensible way of doing business, they acquire special significance; they become institutions. **Institutions** shape our expectations and generate a sense of fairness. Consider the democratic institution

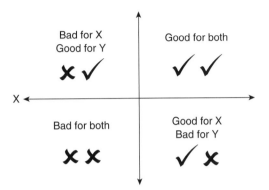

Figure 8.2   Outcomes of wins and losses.

of general elections through which much political conflict is channelled. One party loses the elections; its supporters may not be happy about this, but they accept it. People do not like some of the laws which the government passes, but they observe them. The party in opposition is not pleased, but they do not try to mobilize the army to gain power by force. In this way, institutions, rarely perfect, can work. The various outcomes of wins and losses can be seen below.

The 'good for both' or win–win situation is laudable (see Figure 8.2), but often difficult to achieve in organizations. This is because the meanings that people attach to their own and others' wins and losses varies, and people often have to engage in a fair degree of rationalization and emotion work to feel comfortable with their position. However, well-institutionalized procedures can help. For example, someone can fail to gain promotion. They are not happy about this. But they are able to live with it if (a) it is the result of a clearly stated procedure, and (b) the colleague who got promoted instead was noticeably better on the stated criteria. In other words, the decision appears fair and to have been made according to the rules. This does not mean that people always accept the rules as they find them. In organizations, the referees are often themselves players. Trying to change the rules, twist them, re-interpret them, is itself a major part of organizational, politics, as well as the metagaming we referred to earlier. Nevertheless, having some rules which give all sides a 'winning chance' is necessary if people are going to accept the outcomes as fair.

Is it better for conflict to come out into the open? There are no hard and fast answers. Sometimes we feel better if a conflict that has been bubbling away for some time becomes open and acknowledged. A middle manager in a high-volume factory producing biscuits, told of his own experiences:

It's funny. You can be supervising a bloke who has been cheerful for weeks on end, and then suddenly he turns on you – for no apparent reason. This has happened to me a number of times. I'm always caught unprepared, and I'm always baffled by it. It has worried me a lot. I've now started to talk about it more with the people involved. I've noticed that their anger is nearly always about something that happened weeks ago, maybe at work, maybe outside. The blokes have been sitting on it until it becomes just too much to hold.

A big storm can sometimes clear the air. At other times, small quarrels can escalate into major disputes. Sometimes the very act of declaring a conflict institutionalizes it. If Neil had confronted Ian and Simon about their conversation, they would have had to defend it to him, and might easily have become harsher in their view of Greg (and Neil) as a result. As soon as there are two sides in a dispute, it becomes difficult for people not to join up with one side or the other, and for either of them to back down. The theatre of conflict is enlarged, making a resolution tougher to achieve. So, recognizing conflict may or may not be a wise thing to do.

This creates some dilemmas. For example, the advantages of cohesive, strife-free, work groups are extolled by many managers. The groups instil a positive team spirit in their members, they are pleasant to work in, and they are not split by differences of opinion. The downside is that, in their desire to remain cohesive, the group members suppress internal conflicts and disagreement which could lead to more creative actions or solutions and, worse, they become blind and deaf to disturbing information. This phenomenon has been called *groupthink*, and it has been used to explain events as calamitous as the unpreparedness of the USA for the invasion of Pearl Harbor in the Second World War and, more recently, the collective groupthink of the CIA and British intelligence in the lead up to the 2003 Iraq war, where they collectively came to believe in a level of threat from 'weapons of mass destruction' which later turned out not to have been there. Less dramatically, many organizations have failed as the result of their members collectively reassuring themselves so that they did not see critical changes in the demand for their product. The moral, it seems, is to be suspicious of conflict-free zones in organizations.

GLITTERING PRIZES

An oft-cited source of conflict in organizations – where politics, haggling, dealing and double-dealing flourish – is the getting and giving of resources. Resources are the people, money, buildings and equipment that a manager requires to run and develop his or her part of the business. They are funded from a budget allocated from the total monies available to the organization. Given that the cake is rarely large enough to meet the appetites of all managers, its division is almost bound to disappoint some.

The fact that the vast majority of organizations have to function with less resources than they would ideally like (and considerably less in times of recession), means that there is potential for serious conflict at least once a year, perhaps every quarter, when budgets are decided. The legacy of such allocations, with its winners and losers, can rumble on for a long time, setting the tone of working relationships both within and between working groups. The rehearsals for the next round of allocations and the jockeying for position as the budget period is approached means that this can be a year-round preoccupation.

The players in the conflict are already in place. As mentioned, the various directors – marketing, production, finance, sales, human resources, training, quality control, research and development – each have their own interests to fight for and protect, and they are in continuous **communication** with one another. Their interests will include their personal careers as well as the size, prestige and effectiveness of their particular department or function. It is also likely that they each sincerely believe that what is best for their department is best for the whole company too. Given the centrality of budget-setting in an organization's functioning, one would expect it to be well institutionalized, with clear, rational and fair rules to play by. In practice, it is institutionalized, but the rules are not all that apparent or clear. They are much contested and negotiated. We have a glimpse of just how from a production director of a medium-sized clothing manufacturer:

REAL-LIFE EXAMPLE

We were about three months off the new financial year, and things had been tough for the company. I knew I could do much better with a special new cutting machine – made only in Germany. The Chief Executive knew of the problem, but said that the £175,000 was just too much; it was cheaper to keep repairing the old one. I disagreed, but I couldn't shift him. I knew that Bob from sales was after a new fleet of trucks, and Alan was determined to increase his marketing staff and get them all into a decent office. They each had a strong case, so I had to do something. Firstly, I found an excuse to get the Chief Executive down on the shop floor on the next breakdown to see the waste and chaos. It happened three times; some people think I actually fixed the breakdowns! Next, I had a long chat on the phone with the German supplier. I got them to knock 15% off the price and give us one-year interest-free credit, and install the machine. A brilliant deal, I thought. Finally, I got their sales representative to call by with a sample of the cutter's work at a time when I knew I'd be with the Chief Executive. The Chief Executive was non-committal, but that was better than a refusal. Then, on 3rd April, I received my new budget – with an allowance for a new machine! Bob and Al didn't get half of what they wanted, and they aren't too happy. Bob says he's now looking for a new job, and Al seems to avoid me and the Chief Executive.

We see here the reality of lobbying, politicking and creating alliances. The Chief Executive, for his part, was faced with a number of competing, but plausible, claims for extra resources. He also had to try and make a wise budget distribution for the overall survival, and ultimate success, of the organization. In such difficult and ambiguous conditions, he is likely to find it hard to ignore special pleading, particularly if it is handled skilfully and seems to link with his own aims and plans. In this particular case, however, his decision was costly in certain non-financial ways: the disaffection of two of his senior managers. In the longer term, that could translate into financial costs from the poorer effectiveness of the managers, and from their possible replacement. There are no simple recipes for **decision making** in these sorts of circumstances. Skilled managers will need to acknowledge the political and **emotional** features that underlie such resource allocations, and, as shrewdly as possible, steer a path between the various interests involved.

There are a number of variations on the theme of this case. Returning to Neil, could it have been that Simon did not want to quarrel with Ian about Greg's performance because there were still some budget negotiations going on? In some organizations, groups will fight hard, and bitterly, with each other over available resources. Others will do secret deals with colleagues to their mutual advantage. Less furtively, senior managers may sit around a table in a private room and not emerge until they have thrashed out a budget allocation with which they can all live, accepting that not everyone can get all they want. Many would argue that this is the best way of making the most of a seemingly impossible situation. On the other hand, some executive teams are so divided from the outset that nothing short of a directive from their superiors will sort it out.

PLACING THE GOAL POSTS

Closely related to the resource allocation are the **goals** and criteria by which individuals and groups are judged. The idea that there can be a set of rationally determined organizational goals, agreed and understood in the same way by all, probably only exists in some of the more unrealistic management textbooks. In practice, different members of an organization have different views as to what the goals of their organization should be, and which of the goals they consider most important. This may be done for the best of motives; as we said earlier, each department will retain its commitment by sincerely believing that what it is doing is essential for the long-term health and wealth of the company. Because each department believes this, its members will be willing to play the political game hard and if need be dirty, but for the best of motives: they know that what they are doing is for the good of the company. As one observer puts it:

> . . . many would not be able to act with such passionate intensity if they did not also sincerely believe that they were fuelled on altruism. But the fact remains that even such people will encounter others whom they perceive as motivated by self-interest, who advocate opposing policies, and who therefore must be tripped up, knifed in the back, or in some other way disposed of so that the general good may be served. (Bailey, 1977)

But people are not always so concerned about the good of the company. Each group wishes to have overall organizational goals adopted that will make them look as if they are crucial to, and are achieving well for, the organization. Within oil companies, for example, there may be goals that are officially stated for the organization, including, for example, profitability and growth. However, the members of the shipping department will be particularly interested in how their performance measures up to that of their competitors. Is their company showing the most competitive shipping costs? The more storage tanks their company has at refineries, the fewer ships have to wait outside a port to load or unload oil, so this makes the shipping department look good. In the refineries department, there will be a similar goal of trying to show competitive costings for the refineries; the fewer storage tanks their company has at refineries, the lower their capital costs at refineries, and this makes the refineries department look good. These two goals are clearly in conflict with each other. How do you compare the contribution of each to reaching the goals of the company? The more expensive shipping department may have contributed more, by storing oil outside a port and thus reducing the tankage costs for the refinery. But in so doing, they are likely to look worse than their opposite numbers in competitor companies.

The contention that surrounds such questions leads to all sorts of anxiety, and much political behaviour: partisan negotiations, lobbying the board to have the criteria changed, and 'creative' declarations of costings. At worst, it produces an air of divisiveness and mistrust. More whimsically, it serves as an opportunity for those who wish to mock the system (see Chapter 18, 'Serious Joking'). For example, one of us once worked in an organization with a colleague who used to telephone the human resources department about once a month to ask them for an update on how much pension she would get. She had no plans to retire within the next 25 years, but, as she put it, 'it keeps them on their toes'.

RESOLVING CONFLICT?

It is not possible to live organizational life without politics, even if it were desirable. Furthermore, as we have illustrated, there are ways in which conflict can contribute to the richness of organizational life. We are not always – or even usually – talking about major conflicts here. Everyday organizational politics has more to do with **negotiating** the use of a room on behalf of your department than with some grand battle between good and evil.

There have been a number of studies on how to resolve conflicts, although we need to bear in mind that the resolution is never final. One of the early, but still intriguing, experimental studies is by Muzafer Sherif (1966). Sherif examined conflicts between groups in an American boys' summer camp. After deliberately creating conflict between two groups (such as by giving one group more attractive rewards), various strategies were tried for resolving the conflict. Religious services stressing togetherness had no effect. Talks on the importance of collaboration had no effect. Providing new, 'helpful' information rarely worked because the conflicting parties would interpret it in such different ways. It then became the fuel for further conflict. Detailed negotiations between the leaders of two conflicting groups were not usually successful because, even if they reached agreement, the negotiators were then seen as traitors by the other members of their groups. Voting for a solution simply left those who voted for the losing solution feeling disenfranchised.

Finding a common enemy for the two conflicting groups could be effective – by transferring the problem to a new location. There was still conflict, but this time between the now non-warring groups and the common enemy. However, if a constructive common objective could be created for the two groups, this was much more effective in producing a longer-term resolution. This is a good outcome, but can be less conclusive than it appears. As we have seen in our discussion above, various hues of conflict are not just rather annoying blips in the sweet harmony of organizational life; they are endemic. At the same time, we do not wish to create the impression that organizational life is one long conflict. While some conflicts go on for a very long time, embedded in the organization's culture, others fade because people get tired of them, forget about them, or get distracted by another issue or conflict.

Conflict management needs to be sympathetic to, or in tune with, the prevailing political **culture** of the organization. An organization that 'thrives' on deals and double-deals is unlikely to respond well to consensus seeking. In an organization that prides itself on its strong culture, people will be puzzled if asked to vote. And an open, confrontational style would be hard to implement in a company predominated by power and **status** divisions.

IN CONCLUSION

People will bring their interests, attitudes, prejudices and allegiances into the making of organizational life. In order to achieve the best they can, they will engage in organizational politics and the making of deals, and neither of these is necessarily negative. This can end up with a very complex set of options and possible moves that they can make. Whom they meet, whom they work with, and whom they are controlled by, will influence how people 'present' themselves, and what they choose to do. This is organizational politics. So 'dealing', tacitly or openly, nicely or nastily, with or without open conflict, is part of organizational life. How much, though, and in what form, depends on the issues faced and the political culture of the organization – and we have offered a framework to indicate the range of possibilities.

KEY POINTS

- ○ Politics are a normal feature of organizational life.
- ○ Politics are as much about trust and loyalty as about deception and corruption.
- ○ Organizational politics do not have to be conducted in a destructive way.
- ○ Conflict in organizations is often regarded as acceptable and even good if it is kept within bounds.
- ○ Many of the deals and games within organizations are about resource allocation.
- ○ People often engage in politics and deals sincerely believing that what they are doing is for the good of the organization.
- ○ The criteria by which departments and proposals are evaluated are a key issue in organizational politics.
- ○ Different ways of handling conflict may be appropriate in different organizational cultures.

> > > > > > > > > > > THEORETICAL SIGNPOSTS > > > > > > > > > > > >

The foundations of this chapter can be found in three major areas:

- > organizations as political systems
- > conflict and conflict management
- > game theory.

Organizations as Political Systems

This viewpoint reflects the belief that all human beings are political animals who seek to promote and defend their own interests by using power – formally and/or informally (see also Chapter 9). Therefore, the very lifeblood of organizations is political. Political activity is normal but can vary in intensity, constructiveness or destructiveness. Feminist theorists since the 1960s have been strident about 'identity politics', that the 'personal is political' (see Alcoff, 2006; Walter, 1999). They have argued strongly that political forces shape our personal lives and individual identities to the relative disadvantage of women in the workforce. This has encouraged a vibrant stream of feminist organizational theory (e.g. Flax, 1990; Griffiths, 1995; Laws, 1978) as well as wider studies on the politics of gender in organization (Tancred-Sheriff, 1989; Wilson, 2003).

An organization's political behavior is evident in alliances, deals, coalitions and interpersonal rivalries, described well in a landmark text by Morgan (2006). Other writers, such as Zaleznik (1970) and Pettigrew (1973), have focused on the politics of managerial decision making and strategy formation. Labour process theorists look somewhat wider to the structural features of employment, especially the imbalances of power between workers, managers and owners. These divisions are seen to foster political activity in the shape of resistance, negotiation, deception and, more generally, tussles for control (Edwards, 1990; Jermier, 1995; Knights, 1990).

Conflict and Conflict Management

The study of conflict is dominated by two distinct views – unitarist and pluralist (Burrell and Morgan, 1979). Unitarists focus on the ways that individuals 'misbehave' to subvert the formal goals of the organization. Conflict, therefore, is destructive and something that managers have to address through tighter controls and clearer instructions. Pluralists, in contrast, argue that conflict is inevitable in the ebb and flow of interests and status differences, and that conflict is a necessary and healthy expression of such differences (Dunlop, 1958; Salaman, 1981). We therefore have a picture of dysfunctional or disruptive conflict set against creative or functional conflict – where individuals and the organization develop and grow. Charles Handy (1976) notes the former is divisive and destructive of morale, while the latter are all part of desirable 'argument' and 'competition' in the workplace.

The extent to which conflict should be actively managed depends on where one stands in the unitarist–pluralist debate. There is certainly no shortage of advice books for managers on how to manage conflict (e.g. McConnon and McConnon, 2008). Thomas (1976) speaks of different classes of management responses to conflict – from avoidance to collaboration or mixes of wins and losses. It is a perspective developed by De Dreu and Van Vianen (2001) who stress how compromise is sometimes possible where all parties win a little and lose a little.

Game Theory

Game theory was originally outlined by mathematicians Von Neumann and Morgenstern in their book *Theory of Games and Economic Behavior* (1943). Their thesis is that in economic, business and major societal decisions (such as on wars), competing players will wish to maximize the pay-offs from their available choices. Game theory has become an important vehicle for understanding business strategies involving uncertainty, risk, competition and cooperation, as well as for appreciating the limits of rationality in such settings (see Garciano, 1999; Martin, 1978; Smith, 1996). It has also been used to analyse conflict in business (Gardner, 1995; Radford, 1986).

The language and metaphor of games is central to Eric Berne's popular *Games People Play* (1964) in which interpersonal conflicts are regarded as games that people regularly play out, characterized by habitual patterns of behavior – words and body language – all aimed at achieving a specific pay-off or goal. Berne suggests that much of this goes on unconsciously and becoming aware of one's games is a first step towards change and conflict resolution. The art of gaming has been extolled by Maccoby in his study of corporate managers. In *The Gamesman* (1976), he identifies 'the gamesman' as a distinctive, successful kind of manager who loves the glory of winning – for its own sake. Gamesmen revel in the corporate game and pitching their wits and strategies against others. They want to win through their political skills; they are not into power or prestige for its own stake. Mangham's (1986) lively perspective links political games with dramaturgy – the way game players, such as corporate executives, finely tune their public images, scripts and postures in order to gain advantage or avoid undue disadvantage.

REVIEW QUESTIONS

1. Consider a recent meeting with your friends or at your workplace. What do you think were the personal agendas and how did they affect the outcome?

2. How would you apply the notion of 'gaming' to (a) formal negotiations and (b) you trying to get a friend of colleague to do you a favour?

3. What might be meant by 'constructive conflict'?

Reading On

The articles below are available for free to readers of the fourth edition of *Organizing & Organizations* via the book's companion website at www.sagepub.co.uk/fineman

Ferris, G.R., Fedor, D.B., Chachere, J.G. and Pondy, L.R. (1989) 'Myths and politics in organizational contexts', *Group Organization Management*, 14 (1): 83–103.
Myth systems and politics help to establish the internal context of organizational settings, and thus are quite important processes contributing to more meaningful interpretations of events and phenomena in organizations. Both processes have been studied, albeit, independently. In this article, the argument is made that the integration of these two processes provides a potentially richer understanding of the dynamic processes of intraorganizational contexts, which is critical to effective organizational change.

McNary, L.D. (2003) 'The term "win-win" in conflict management: a classic case of misuse and overuse', *Journal of Business Communication*, 40 (2): 144–59.

Words evolve in their usage and meaning over time, but few words in the business language have changed as much as the term 'win-win'. Once confined to the literature on conflict management, the term has been co-opted in the trade press and often used incorrectly in place of the term 'compromise'. This article describes these interpretative errors and the effects of these errors on the meaning of the term.

Wall, J.A., Jr. and Callister, R.R. (1995) 'Conflict and its management', *Journal of Management*, 21 (3): 515–58.

This article reviews the conflict literature, first examining the causes of conflict, its core process, and its effects, then subsequently probing into conflict escalation (and de-escalation), contexts, and conflict management. When examining this last topic, the authors note that conflict can be managed by the disputants themselves, by managers, or by other third parties.

West, C. (1982) 'Why can't a woman be more like a man?: an interactional note on organizational game-playing for managerial women', *Work and Occupations*, 9 (1): 5–29.

Literature in the 1980s suggested that women's success in 'a man's world' is partially contingent on learning the rules of men's 'games', with aspiring women advised to 'dress for success', attend the subtleties of 'power desking', and, of special interest here, 'speak up' in order to be heard. Research reviewed in this article suggests that the significance of actions changes according to the gender of the actors and that women conversing with men may have special difficulties being heard even when they do 'speak up'.

9

INFLUENCE AND POWER

Power and influence pervade all forms of interactions in organizations, usually affected by one's level in the hierarchy. But power is more complex than this: it is embedded in ideological and gender patterns; it accrues to people we are attracted to, to those with specialized knowledge and to individuals who can determine the agenda, regardless of hierarchical level. How and why power can be misused or abused is examined, as well as different forms of resistance to that misuse. The fine details of performing power are explored, such as in the use of words and body language.

REAL-LIFE EXAMPLE

Real-Life
Example

Ed's story

Alan, our CEO, called me at home last night. It was 10:00 pm. I was just settling down to watch the news on television. What on earth could he want at this hour?

'Ed, I need to see you at 8:30 prompt in the morning. We've got to decide immediately on who we're going to appoint to the marketing director job. I thought we could wait a bit but I really want to get this out of the way before I fly off to China on Wednesday. I'll make sure the others come along.'

I was irritated. Alan knew I was travelling to our Newport office in the morning and I'd have to cancel my appointments at the last moment. But Alan wasn't the sort of guy you'd say 'no' to. The only good thing was that it was going to be a short meeting. Me from Finance and the three other departmental directors: Carina from HR, Bruno from Production and Arieti from Sales. We'd all interviewed the candidates for the job and agreed that one candidate, Aaron Bernstein, who works for one of our competitors, stood out as the clear winner.
We turned up dutifully in the morning at Alan's huge, lavishly furnished office (certainly compared with ours!) – but Alan wasn't there. So we sat there waiting.

He arrived over twenty minutes late and said not a word of greeting, but just sat down and got down to business:

> 'Well, let's make this as brief as possible' (I was relieved to hear that!). 'As I told you, we need to make a decision about the marketing job and get it moving fast. It's pretty clear to me that Marietta should get the job.'

There was a deathly silence. This was totally unexpected and simply crazy. Marietta had been with us just little under a year. She had only very recently completed her MBA, was inexperienced and still a long way off a major directorship. Indeed, she had confided to me that she was only 'trying it on' in making an application and was amazed to have even been shortlisted.

We all glanced at each other and then back to Alan. You could cut the atmosphere with a knife. Only Alan looked relaxed, frequently gazing at his BlackBerry as if 'that was that'. What could I say? Well, I said it – it stumbled out:

> 'Er, Alan ... that's a bit of a surprise. We really felt, well, erm ... that Aaron Bernstein had an outstanding CV and interviewed very well. Marietta's great ... but, well ... she's still very new in the job ...'

Alan glared at me – a long hard stare. I looked round the room for support, but none came. Then Arieti chipped in, amazingly saying 'I guess you could be right about Marietta, Alan – you've probably seen her in situations we haven't'. And the others nodded.

> 'Fine', said Alan with a quick smile. 'Marietta it is then. I need to go now'.

As we filed out, no one made eye contact. I felt deflated. What on earth was behind this? What kind of deal had Alan made with Marietta? I remember he was dead keen to get her here in the first place. What was going on? And what's the point of meetings if Alan had already made up his mind?

A POWER TRIP

The use and abuse of **power** is central to Ed's tale. At its centre is the **hierarchical** nature of power in many organizations where those at the top wield direct influence over those beneath them. That Alan 'wasn't the sort of guy you'd say "no" to' suggests that those who had refused Alan in the past had suffered the consequences. Power, at its crudest, resides in the capacity to punish and reward, something long known to dictators and tyrants. Alan trades on this, demanding a meeting ('I'll make sure the others come along') of his senior colleagues at the last moment with little concern about the intrusion or inconvenience to them.

The meeting becomes a stage for Alan's power performance: coming late; no attempt at excuse or apology; a curt announcement of who he wants to appoint with every indication that dissenters will not be tolerated (the 'long hard stare'). His preoccupation with his BlackBerry shuts off communication. The 'huge, lavishly furnished' physical setting itself creates an image of the power and importance of its occupier, held in awe and possibly envy by others. Arieti's ready acquiescence is noteworthy: could it be that she might expect some later reward for supporting her boss? (See Chapter 8, 'Politics and Deals'.)

In forcing compliance, Alan gets his way but leaves a legacy of bitterness and suspicion. And so it is when power becomes highly centralized and is used by its holder to bolster their position and ego. Robert Maxwell, the late newspaper tycoon, a larger-than-life character, reputedly kept his staff in a state of constant terror, either through his impulsive actions or the ambiguity of his humour. The tale is told of one journalist who was working at his desk when he felt a sharp blow to the back of his head. Turning round, he was dismayed to see Maxwell looming over him. Maxwell peered at his victim. 'Oh', he said, before walking away. 'Mistaken identity.'[1] Another example, in a different industry, is provided by Lee Iacocca, once CEO of Chrysler. Reminiscing about his earlier career at the Ford Motor Company in the USA, he recalls:

> Each time [Henry Ford II] walked into a meeting, the atmosphere changed abruptly. He held the power of life and death over all of us. He could suddenly say 'off with his head' – and he often did. Without fair hearing, one more promising career at Ford would bite the dust ... This arbitrary use of power wasn't merely a character flaw. It was something Henry actually *believed* in. (Iacocca, 1984: 103)

These accounts reveal that power, when it is tightly held by a top or senior member of an organization, can achieve fast results – but simultaneously stifle dissent and breed fear and disaffection. Such naked use of power is often a source of fascination to outside observers, rich fodder for journalists and satirists and frequently parodied in films and TV programmes. For example, the British business entrepreneur, Sir Alan Sugar, has headed up his own prime-time television programme where he summarily dismisses unworthy candidates for jobs with a robust 'You're fired!' This caricatured view of power resonates more with early twentieth-century baron industrialists than with today's more positive philosophy.

Nevertheless, business still has its autocrats who will use their power to justify personally desired results by any means, creating fertile territory for bullying and corruption. As the adage goes, 'power corrupts, absolute power corrupts absolutely'. Returning to Robert Maxwell, he became entangled in a labyrinthine web of his own making: secret deals and alliances culminating in his mysterious death in 1991. It transpired that he had robbed his company's pension fund to boost the company's share price and keep it afloat.

Maxwell's behaviour verged on megalomania, a self-obsession that some put down to his early life experiences. He suffered extreme childhood poverty in his native Czechoslovakia, losing his parents to Nazi persecution. He escaped to Britain in 1940 fired with a compulsion to get to the top. His story points to two things: firstly, the personal histories of power-holders give us clues as to how they perceive the world and what makes them feel secure or insecure – however unsavoury their behaviour may appear; secondly, some people will obsessively seek power and wealth in market economies where such behaviour is minimally regulated and, indeed, often celebrated. For example, it is only recently that city financial traders' million-dollar bonuses and high-risk decisions have been seen as a form of institution-alized greed that has played a significant part in undermining the world's financial stability.

Figure 9.1   Robert Maxwell.
Source: www.cartoonstock.com

POWER AND THE LESS POWERFUL

Those who are in top positions enjoy a power boost by virtue of their position; they are structurally advantaged in their command over significant resources and decisions – such as on organizational strategy, promotion and rewards. But power is not just concentrated at the top, nor simply coercive. It has many different guises, located and diffused throughout the organization. The following brief tales make the point. The first account is from Joan, secretary to the marketing director of a soft drinks company. The second is from Pete, a computer technician in a large government department.

Joan

You know, I get really angry when people say I'm just a lackey to my boss – his 'little wifey' serving his needs. It's nothing like that! Of course I'm here to help John in his work as director – that's what I'm paid for. But how I do it is up to me. So I don't run around making cups of coffee for him all the time or doing his shopping. In fact, I set that out right at the beginning so he certainly knows where I stand. What's really great (though don't tell anyone I said this) is that I can find out a load about what's going on from people who want to see John. They know that I control his diary and that it's up to me to find a suitable date. Now, I won't be very helpful to them if they are rude or abrupt to me or don't want to tell me exactly why they want a meeting. Do you see what I'm getting at? And you know what, John often tests out many of his ideas on me before he goes public, so that must mean something, don't you think?

Pete

I've been here nearly nine years – I guess I'm beginning to look like a typical civil servant. But there's not much that I don't know about the Department's IT system. I designed it,

I got it installed and I maintain it. That might look a bit dependent, a bit risky, from the Department's point of view, but it's great as far as I'm concerned. They really need me! It's amazing how even the directors will pop in here, right down in the basement, for a chat or to buy me coffee – if they want something fixed or installed. You see, they need me and if I say – very politely of course – that I'm just overwhelmed with work at the moment, there's absolutely nothing they can do but wait.

Neither Joan nor Pete was high in the organization, but they were far from powerless. Both, in their own way, had acquired influence that was key to keeping the organization running. And they were partial or particular in how they used it, underscoring the close connection between power and **politics**. Joan was a gatekeeper to her boss and controlled whom she let pass. She filtered who could have access to her boss – when and for how long. In the meantime, she would gain valuable insider knowledge about the organization, social knowledge that was itself a source of power and influence. Moreover, as her boss's confidante, her potential authority belied her relatively subordinate position in the organization. Joan linked and shaped requests for assistance and access. She sat at a key intersection point, a node in the social network of her organization. And her power was additionally enhanced *by proxy*. In acting for her powerful boss, she embodied and enjoyed some of his influence.

Pete's role is squarely in the knowledge economy where, for him, technical expertise is a source of power. Wherever there is a shortage of skill or expertise in an organization, this instantly confers more power, more potential influence, on the holder of such skills. Like Joan, Pete is calculative in his use of his expert knowledge. He knows that he can use it to his advantage in scheduling his load and in temporarily establishing an alternative power hierarchy.

Underpinning both Pete and Joan's roles is the dependency of others on them and their unique resources; it is hard or impossible for others to get their work done without the help of the Joans and Petes of the world. Dependency can extend to whole departments or companies, where little can progress without their actions or authorization. In this manner, monopolies or oligopolies, such as rail and telecommunications services, can exert considerable control over their consumers, as can government departments such as the Inland Revenue and Immigration. Dependency of this sort places much responsibility in the hands of the power holder, a responsibility that can readily be misused or abused.

KNOWLEDGE AND POWER

Pete is a prime example of how specialist knowledge can be deployed as a source of influence and power. But his circumstances are a little more complex. Pete's specialist knowledge also creates a *regime of* **control** – in the way that knowledge is used or deployed. In other words, how he expresses and applies his knowledge will affect how and what the IT users in his organization come to believe about their IT facilities, what they can do with their machines and how helpless they feel when this system goes down – all of which Pete oversees. Here, power and knowledge are intimately connected; they are co-determinate. This was one of Michel Foucault's principle insights: power through knowledge and knowledge through power produce reality. For instance, information gained via Google on the web is significantly determined by the way information is added to it in the first place, and then how the search engine records, sifts, orders and describes things. But we rarely reflect on or question these matters in our web searches: all power to Google. This point was made poignantly during the 2008 Beijing Olympic Games when it was noticed by visiting journalists that web pages that were critical of the Chinese regime had been censored. While the journalists were indignant, it appeared that few Chinese residents were particularly bothered.

We can see organizational practices such as Human Resource Management (HRM) in a similar light – as a powerful *disciplining **discourse*** that underpins the power of HRM professionals. Through the **language** and practices of HRM, people, 'human resources', can be *divided* (by selection procedures), *ranked* (through appraisal mechanisms), *allocated* (via job descriptions and psychometric tests), *changed* (through training) and *rewarded* or *punished* (following performance measurement). Power resides in the way these technologies and their discourses are used to categorize and define the status, reality and management of those affected – such as being a 'star' in the organization, a 'poor performer', a 'salary band 2', a 'high flier', 'unskilled', 'at risk' or 'highly stressed'.

A Way with Words

Language itself is central to such analyses; language operates to create a microtechnology of power. For instance, terms such as 'hospital', 'asylum', 'special school', 'university' or 'prison' carry with them a set of connotations and assumptions about what can be done with and to those who receive their services. And they simultaneously condition how their users ('inmates', 'patients', 'students') come to see themselves – such as bright, sick, bad, inadequate, flawed, invisible or marginalized. In other words, the power of **institutional** labels lies in producing the very conditions they describe.

Ken Kesey's iconic book, *One Flew Over the Cuckoo's Nest*, graphically illustrates such dynamics as the authoritarian regime of a psychiatric hospital which bears down on a ward's 'voluntary patients', medicalizing and drugging their worries and eccentricities and ultimately stifling their sparks of humanity. The popularization of the notion of **stress** at work has been subject to similar observation. We now give the label 'stress' to all manner of commonplace pressures or worries and so pathologize what are often fairly normal, workday emotions. Likewise, the apparent authority of a 'low IQ' or 'EI' (emotional intelligence) score can trap individuals in the belief that they are 'like that' and 'nothing can be done'. The label or category colonizes their **identity**.

The significance of language to propagate a particular organizational viewpoint, while shutting out or silencing an alternative, can be seen in some commonplace euphemisms:

- 'Personnel' departments have now given way to 'Human Resource' departments. It follows that, as a resource, employees are on a par with other, non-human, resources (such as machines and materials). It also implies that they can be used and discarded.
- 'Our most important asset is our people' is a wise-sounding, even comforting, message, but one that often collapses in times of economic turmoil or recession.
- Trimming the 'fat', or 'downsizing' a 'too bureaucratic' organization to create a 'slim, agile' one, creates a picture of economically prudent management, eclipsing an alternative image: sacking, job losses, personal distress, redundancy.

Figure 9.2   Redundant.

Organizational euphemisms can be seen as a way to enhance the appearance and attractiveness (to both applicants and incumbents) of a job by re-labelling it – while leaving the actual content untouched. There are many examples, such as rat catchers becoming rodent officers, dustmen re-termed refuse collectors, postroom helpers transformed into despatch room facilitators, railway train guards redefined as customer operations leaders and – as appeared in an advertisement for a major supermarket – shelf-stackers described as ambient replenishment assistants (Rees, 2008). The number of bank employees who now find themselves labelled 'vice-president' may not be so different from this. In power terms, it is a 'way with words' that gives a professional or marketing gloss to jobs that essentially remain, and feel, the same to those who perform them.

THE POWER TO DISRUPT

Power can be used to all sorts of ends, not all of them helpful to the formal aims and objectives of the organization but certainly in the interests of the wielders of that power. The power deliberately to disrupt one's own or others' work is one of these instances. From a strictly **managerialist** perspective, such actions are at best a nuisance to steer through, at worst a major obstruction that requires a firm response. But this reveals little about the different forms and meanings of disruption – and its contribution to the lifeblood of organizing and organizations.

At an individual level, for instance, the desire to disrupt can stem from feeling oppressed, unfairly rewarded, angry with 'the system', in conflict with another person, or simply overburdened with demands. Some form of disruption appears (rightly or wrongly) the only way of garnering influence and control over one's circumstances. This may be subtle – such as by delaying responses to, or 'losing', certain emails; being 'sick' and unable to attend a key meeting; 'accidentally' failing to schedule a particular work task; or promising to meet a deadline that one has no intention of honouring. Less subtle is deliberately underperforming as a protest against the way work has been allocated. There are salutary tales of university lecturers who intentionally alienate their students by poor teaching. Their aim (which is sometimes achieved) is to be transferred to a more acceptable programme or be removed altogether from teaching duties to pursue a preferred activity – such as research.

Collective Disruption

In unionized organizations, 'working to rule', to the literal letter of one's job specification, or striking, are ways of destabilizing or disabling the organization (see Chapter 5, 'Rules are Rules'). The power of the collective is mobilized to improve working conditions or to right a perceived wrong. There is strength in numbers. Working to rule is a way that lower-echelon employees, especially, can demonstrate their importance to the organization, while still remaining at work. They do no more than what is contractually required and do it pedantically. They operate literally to the formal rules in ways which can paralyse the organization. In a recent work-to-rule by train drivers in the UK, the drivers followed the rule book precisely to 'Always ensure your windscreen is clean and clear of all obstructions'. They left their cab at every station stop, fetched a bucket of hot water and very carefully cleaned every bit of the windscreen. This, of course, played havoc with the train timetable.

In some occupations, industrial action is illegal because of the dangers that the withdrawal of labour poses to society. In the UK, for example, police and prison officers cannot strike so any grievances have to be handled informally, bureaucratically or simply suppressed. However, now and again, frustration boils over, as it did for prison officers in August 2007. They went on strike – unofficially. One newspaper reported the event as follows:[2]

Prison Officers' Unofficial Strike Rattles Government

Some 20,000 prison officers in England and Wales took illegal unofficial action on Wednesday 29 August against [Prime Minister's] Gordon Brown's public sector wage cuts and the disastrous overcrowding in prisons.

However the action has forced … Gordon Brown to the negotiating table.

Brian Caton, general secretary of the Prison Officers Association, disputed that the action was illegal. 'I believe every officer has human rights, and they include the right to withdraw their labour,' he said.

Traditionally prison officers – like their colleagues in the police – have been accommodated at the first sign of trouble. This is the Prison Officers Association's first strike in 68 years.

In this commentary, we see glimpses of a possible resolution, but also a **narrative** crafted to give the impression that the prison officers, although technically illegal in their action, could claim the moral high ground by exercising their 'human rights' for 'the first time in 68 years'. Crucially, power lies in the **rhetorical** structure of the language as much as the actual action, an important weapon in the postures of bargaining.

Some employers have tried to minimize work disruptions by prohibiting union membership as a condition of employment. Or, less radically, they will attempt to inhibit organized action or 'excessive' claims by pointing to their futility: 'they put the very viability of our business and your jobs in jeopardy'. Such a **discourse** is a classic form of power posturing aimed at disarming or neutralizing the other party and keeping them in line. Of course, there may be some truth in an employer's claim; organizations have indeed collapsed under the weight of sustained industrial action. On the other hand, it can be a bluff to be challenged. Where opportunities to do so are limited, some employees have resorted to organized 'grievance' websites. There, openly or anonymously, they can express their concerns, in sometimes forceful terms. In doing so, they attempt to influence public opinion and embarrass the company into action. An example is WakeUpWalMart.com where, amongst extensive critical reports on the organization, there is a section in which 'Wal-Mart Workers Speak Out'. An example is from Mona Curtis:

> My name is Mona Curtis. I have been a door greeter at Wal-Mart in Hillsboro, OH ever since it opened in 2002. When I first started working at Wal-Mart I thought it was a great place to work. My co-workers were very friendly and my managers were willing to work with me on my schedule. Prior to being hired, I explained to Wal-Mart I could only work four days a week. I'm a foster parent, and I have to attend trainings every Saturday. On Fridays, I volunteer at the local soup kitchen and I attend church every Sunday.
>
> Recently, I noticed a change in culture when a new manager came in. A few of my co-workers have been terminated, and schedules have been changed without notice. I believe Wal-Mart is making these changes in order to push out the older associates in favor of younger associates as a way of phasing us older associates out in order to hire younger associates.
>
> Once I realized what was happening, I wrote a letter to the Bentonville office to address my concerns. The letter was supposed to be confidential and I thought I would be protected under Wal-Mart's confidentiality and open door policy. After being informed of my letter, my store manager began to harass me. She told me if I was not able to work on any day they scheduled me, she would cut my hours ... To this day, management continues to harass me and pressure me to quit.

Desperate Measures

There are occasions where a lone, aggrieved individual goes outside their organization to allege a major corporate wrongdoing. Power resides in 'blowing the whistle', loudly and very publicly (see Chapter 12, 'Morals'). Whistleblowers rarely disguise their identity, so risk their personal reputation, retaliation and certainly their job, in speaking out. Typically, their attempts to be heard inside their organization have failed and rather than let it pass, they feel morally impelled to act. These are often David and Goliath occasions where a corporate giant can be

Figure 9.3   Blowing the whistle.

chastened, if not severely damaged, by a well-aimed shot. Jeffery Wigand's experiences illustrate this:

> In 1996, Jeffey Wigand was interviewed on the prime-time US television programme '60 Minutes'. In it, he revealed that, as President of Research and Development for the major tobacco corporation Brown and Williamson, he had become increasingly concerned about a cover-up of evidence linking tobacco to health; carcinogenic material was knowingly being added to cigarettes in what was a 'nicotine delivery business'. Initiatives to develop a safer cigarette were blocked. Wigand was constantly frustrated in his attempts to raise his concerns internally, so he resigned. The company was very nervous about his insider knowledge so they forced him to sign a confidentiality agreement – which he decided to break. Wigand was publicly praised for his courage and revelations (dramatized in the film 'The Insider'), but he bore severe personal costs, including anonymous death threats requiring 24-hour bodyguard protection.

In revealing a major organizational misdeed, whistle-blowers act from conscience, hoping that others outside the organization will share their concern. But the practical and emotional consequences for many whistle-blowers can be dire. The odds are stacked against them when the **authority** and **ideology** of those in power are challenged. Goliath can still seek revenge as Wigand discovered, fearing for his personal safety following his revelations. Typically, whistle-blowers can be hailed as public heroes yet also be branded as corporate traitors and can find it very difficult to get work. Many suffer prolonged **stress** and depression. But as Rothschild and Miethe point out, whistle-blowing is essentially about 'the struggle for dignity and integrity in work organizations' (1994: 267). We are diminished without it.

Sabotage

Sabotage represents an extreme form of disruptive power. It can be a malicious act of vengeance or self-promotion, but more often it is a reaction to difficult or intolerable conditions that a person feels they cannot address by any other means – such as insufficient resources to do the job, chronically boring work, a burning sense of injustice at being treated unfairly, or a lack of freedom and control. The sabotage may be planned or unplanned, individual or group, subtle or obvious. It cuts across organizational levels – there are managers as well as workers who sabotage. In all cases, the saboteur's power emanates from knowing exactly what to do to disrupt or halt organizational processes. A recent, and particularly potent form of sabotage, is cyber sabotage where an organization's computer systems can be skilfully disabled or infected, often with dramatic consequences.

Sabotage – originally a French term – is said to reach back some 100 years to the 1910 French railway strike when the sabots, or wooden shoes, that fastened the rails were deliberately shattered by rail workers to prevent normal use of the line. This kind of disruption can put considerable pressure on employers to accede to strikers' demands. But sabotage can be more covert and disguised – such as temporarily sabotaging a production line to give operators some relief from relentlessly paced work. Lance, a pineapple packer, describes how this worked for him:

> I worked at the Janacka machine, which cuts the hides and skins off the pineapple. We usually worked a straight ten-hour shift, so a lot of people would just burn out. To combat that, people would try to get more breaks – we were only allowed two breaks per shift. To do this, they would send a pineapple down the wrong direction, or send a glove down, and it would break the whole machine. If the Janacka machine shuts down you can't cut the pineapple, the line can't go on. The whole production line shuts down. It takes at least three hours to fix, so you're getting paid for three hours at least for just sitting around. (Sprouse, 1992: 18)

Both sabotage and whistle-blowing have been described as mischief making – suggesting that the cause lies in the 'mischievous' or 'troublemaking' qualities of the person. While this might sometimes be the case, in practice very different sorts of people feel impelled to such actions. Typically, the saboteur or whistle-blower do what they do because they feel unable, powerless, to shape their own destinies and exert sufficient control over their work. We need initially to seek explanations for their behaviour in the conditions and management of the workplace, not in their personality.

POWER'S DRAMA AND MICROPOLITICS

In our opening story, Alan, the CEO, expressed his power dramaturgically, that is, in his verbal and body language. Interpersonally, power is expressed through scripts and mannerisms – standard arguments, ideas, postures and emotions – that are socially understood as influential. Power is 'performed' on a particular 'stage' (e.g. in the office, over lunch, across the negotiation table, on a conference platform) where the use of rhetoric, **body language**, tone of voice, dress and **emotion**, are brought together in a more or less persuasive manner. This extends to the minutiae of **communication**, such as a raised voice or eyebrow, a wink, a brief smile, a sigh, a pointed joke, a dismissive remark, a touch on the shoulder, a long silence and so forth. The meanings of these are often culturally specific, which can be problematic for strangers in cross-cultural business settings, such as negotiations. For example, we find US negotiators' keenness to be rapidly focused and to-the-point contrasts with their Chinese counterparts who prefer more 'soft time' devoted to building trust and liking.

The dramaturgy of power is often fine-tuned in interpersonal interactions. Take the mundane matter of employees submitting expense claims to their organization. Marek, a middle manager in a computer sales firm, explains how this works for him:

> Once a month it's expenses time, and I put in my expenses claim. I do loads of travelling and entertaining and it's sometimes hard to be precise on the form. And I don't always have receipts. So what do I do? Well, there's no point in just putting in the form – I know it will get bounced back by Accounts; they have the real power in this place! So I sidle up to Janet, our accounts supervisor, over coffee – all friendly like. We've known each other for ages and we laugh and joke about life here and its absurdities. She's great. Anyhow, I tell her that I'm having some problems filling out my form and explain why. Could she possibly help me out? She usually gives me a knowing sort of smile but says nothing. My expenses are always met. And I always make sure that I pay for the coffees!

Marek has a clear view of the key gatekeeper he has to charm. He trades on the history of his relationship with Janet and their mutual liking to cut across the formal constraints of power. A mini drama unfolds at which they are both well rehearsed. Such informal *power work* typically flows throughout organizations, cultivated by familiarity and experience.

Uneven Playing Fields

In organizations, interactions rarely occur on a power-even playing field, as our earlier examples show. The power scripts and permissible deviations are greater for some people than others because of their formal **status**, their age, their **ethnicity**, their tenure in the organization, how much they are liked, their networking, their **gender**, their physical attractiveness, their gatekeeping, their scarce skills, or their command over key resources. As theorist Steven Lukes (1975) notes, these factors can shape power in different ways – some more visibly than others. Ed, in our opening tale, was able to make and implement crucial decisions directly – Lukes' 'first dimension' of power. His senior status prevailed. Others, who are not at the top of the organization, can exercise power differently, such as by setting or limiting agendas – Lukes' 'second dimension' of power. Their particular role, perhaps departmental accountant or safety officer, can be used to grab the attention of others. As one junior manager in the food-additives industry claimed: 'I can always get people's attention by saying, "if this goes wrong I'm the one who goes to prison"'.

Lukes was particularly concerned with a third dimension to power: the power to shape, sometimes insidiously, other peoples' needs and wants; to persuade them to accept or believe in things that may or may not actually benefit them. Strong societal **ideologies** can generate these conditions, such as an unquestioned belief in the superiority of the free market, of a particular religion, of the subordinate role of women, or the superiority of a particular race or class. Carefully engineered, these values can soon become part of what people take as natural – potent features of how they define themselves and others.

Italian political writer Antonio Gramsci articulated this view in some depth through the concept of *hegemony* (a term derived from the Greek *hegemon*, 'leader'). Hegemony occurs when a socially constructed ideology is transmitted and reinforced by a dominant group, striving to attain the agreement of subordinate groups to its leadership. Gramsci was imprisoned in Italy for a lengthy period in the 1920s for his outspoken opposition to Mussolini's fascist ideology. He died in prison but his writings survived. His work is significant in exposing the way hegemony operates to condition people to a set of particular beliefs, or a world view, that places them at a seemingly unquestionable advantage or disadvantage, while the disadvantaged come to believe that they 'deserve' their oppressions.

IN CONCLUSION

This chapter reveals that influence and power are at the very core of organizing processes. While the formal structure of the organization exposes broadly how power is likely to be distributed, it is only part of the story, often the lesser part. Influence is exercised and power cultivated through specialist knowledge, by being a gatekeeper and networker, by the dependency of others, by the capacity to with-hold labour or disrupt the work processes, and by being able to set the agendas that others have to work to. Control of language and staged performance are major features of many of these processes, making power one of the most intriguing areas of organizational life.

KEY POINTS

○ The crudest form of power lies in the capacity to punish or reward subordinates; it is also potentially corrupting.

○ The roots of power abuse can be found partly in the personal background of the power holder and partly in the cultural ethos that tolerates or sanctions such conduct.

○ Hierarchical power is counterbalanced by other bases of power, such as being a gatekeeper or having specialized knowledge.

○ Language can sanitize intentions or policies – a subtle form of influence.

○ Those with less formal power can influence events by collective action, disruption or sabotage.

○ Organizational whistle-blowers act as moral signposts, but with possible high costs to themselves.

○ Micro expressions of power are expressed in body language and the engineering of physical settings.

○ Ideologies and dominant agendas create realties for others – that may not be in their best interest.

> > > > > > > > > > > > **THEORETICAL SIGNPOSTS** > > > > > > > > > > > > >

This chapter draws on the following main, interlocking areas:

> theories of power
> language and discourse
> dramaturgy and impression management.

Theories of Power

Theories about the nature and processes of power range from the macro political to the micro psychological. Of the former, Karl Marx classically viewed power as embedded in the economic order of society, essentially in terms of who had control over the means of production and capital – the land, the factories, the technology, the raw materials, the information and the know-how. Workers' labour power was in constant tension with power capital. For Marx, employees' resistance was inevitable in this unequal contest (Marx, 1975). Max Weber (Weber, 1981) was cognizant of such divisions but was more interested in the evolution of power in the proliferation of bureaucratic organizations, where the pyramidal structure (now rapidly fading) vests power and authority according to hierarchical position. Subordinates, 'ideally', take their place in such arrangements with equanimity. In practice, though, it often seeds both active and passive resistance, motivating different forms of political behaviour.

Lukes' *Power: A Radical View* (Lukes, 1975) is more nuanced (see the description in the current chapter), revealing that power in one or more of three prototypical forms acts both to constrain behaviour as well as to facilitate it, within certain boundaries. The broadest, and most insidious, is the power of dominant ideologs and ideologies in society, something that preoccupied Gramsci's theorizing on hegemony (Gramsci et al., 1971; also see the current chapter). Alvin Toffler, in his book *Powershift* (1990), envisioned the end of traditional bureaucracies. Their ponderous ordering is no match for the speed and change of knowledge in late modern economies, a key source of muscle for wealth creation. Flexibility and power conjoin in this formulation. An organization that is agile in the transmission, control and creation of knowledge accrues wealth and power, power that is 'totally dependent on the instant communication and dissemination of data, ideas, symbols, and symbolism'.

A micro, social-psychological perspective can be found in the work of French and Raven on the 'bases of social power' (1959). They identified five key bases, or resources, that an individual can draw upon – more or less, in their influence attempts. These are 'legitimate' power, which comes from their formal position in the organization; 'referent power' based on mutual liking, charisma and loyalty; the 'expertise' on which others' depend; 'coercive power', the power to force someone to do something against their will; and 'reward power' – the provision or withholding of what others desire or value, such as money, praise, comfort, security or information.

Language and Discourse

These are interrelated approaches to power, characteristic of postmodern theorizing. They constitute what Rorty (1967) has called a 'linguistic turn' in our understanding of organizing processes. In its more radical form, this perspective regards language as not simply a representation of what people think and feel, but actually constituting our realities. That is, there is nothing beyond language (see Alvesson and Kärreman, 2000a; Derrida, 1973). It follows that how language is adopted, circulated and impressed on others constitutes a significant medium of power. It establishes and perpetuates power relations and inequalities – such as the use of 'junior', 'senior', and 'executive' in organizations; or in referring to people as 'redundant', 'low achievers' or 'emotional'; or where male pronouns are persistently used, thus silencing or obscuring women (Speer, 2005). All such labels ascribe a particular value and status.

Discourse is typically taken to be more than just a single word, but extended speech or written expression: sentences, written communication, formal documents, debates, discussions, arguments. Discourse is pivotal to Foucault's influential view of power (Foucault, 1980). As we talk about and symbolize our world and the things/relations in it we are reproducing categories that can eventually be taken as indisputable, truth, marking off right from wrong, the good from the bad. When certain discourses – systems of belief or points of view – become commonly accepted, power and knowledge coalesce, as does the authority of those who lead those discourses (Hardy et al., 1998).

We see this, for example, with medical, religious and political discourses and the respective statuses of doctors, priests and presidents. Some of these discourses are, of course, more stable and normalised than others. Power through discourse is always mobile and subject to counter-discourses – contention or resistance (Deetz and Mumby, 1990). In this manner, for instance, we can view hospitals as organizations where the discourse of patient care and public service clashes with a that of financial performance and efficiency; or universities where the discourse of teaching excellence is at odds with that of a world class research institution; and bosses who assert that a salary award for employees is impossible while trade unions claim precisely the opposite (O'Leary, 2003). In the wider public domain we witness collisions of 'grand' discourses, such as between Creationists and Darwinians, between major religious, between political parties, and between those who believe in the human contribution to global warming and those who do not.

Dramaturgy and Impression Management

This perspective is outlined in the theoretical signposts to Chapter 2, 'Entering and Leaving'. Power through a dramaturgical lens focuses on the organizational actor's 'staged' performance The dramaturgical metaphor takes seriously life as 'acted', with its rehearsals, scripts, improvisation, costumes, stages and audiences (Mangham, 1986). Building on Erving Goffman's insights, power resides in influencing others through self presentation (Goffman, 1967). This can include: the use of persuasive rhetoric and evocative metaphors; dressing 'powerfully'; and using wel-practised negotiation stances (as in management–union bargaining); deliberately arranging a physical setting with 'props' to create a particular atmosphere – such as tranquillity, awe, strict formality or intimidation (contrast a yoga studio, an Olympic stadium, a court of law and a police interrogation room). Power relations can be dramaturgically sustained through any or all of these means, but also by employing cultural and sub-cultural scripts that favour one individual, party or group over another. For instance, by asserting 'well known' prejudices or stereotypes as if they were incontrovertible facts. These can diminish or stigmatize a particular person, department, occupation, gender, age or religion. Such utterances can be especially powerful when they are orchestrated by opinion leaders, those with position power. The potency of such attempts is increased when they are crafted to disarm or neutralize dissent. One approach is to offer a serious debate, but where, in fact, the outcome is already pre-ordained.

REVIEW QUESTIONS

1. When we talk about 'powerful people', what exactly does that mean?

2. In what ways can language shape and determine influence?

3. 'Much power is invisible'. What do you understand by this statement?

NOTES

1. See http://news.bbc.co.uk/1/hi/magazine/6620291.stm
2. See http://www.socialistworker.co.uk/art.php?id=12919

Reading On

The articles below are available for free to readers of the fourth edition of *Organizing & Organizations* via the book's companion website at www.sagepub.co.uk/fineman

Ailon, G. (2006) 'What B would otherwise do: a critique of conceptualizations of "power" in organizational theory', *Organization*, 13 (6): 771–800.
The paper presents a critique of organizational theories that is based upon Robert Dahl's famous definition: 'A has power over B to the extent that he can get B to do something that B would not otherwise do'. This definition highlights the fact that appreciating 'power' often demands knowledge not only about what B does but also about what B would otherwise do. Reviewing major conceptualizations of power in organizational theory, the paper unravels and categorizes underlying assumptions of this sort, instead promoting an alternative strategy for dealing with this issue.

Greve, H.R. and Mitsuhashi, H. (2007) 'Power and glory: concentrated power in top management teams', *Organization Studies*, 28 (8): 1197–221.

Strategic change is one of the most critical decisions that organizations make. This article focuses on the role of groups at the upper echelon of hierarchies, proposing that concentrated power either in the CEO or the top management team is prone to be exercised, leading to a high rate of strategic change. The findings suggest that power concentration strongly affects decision making.

Hajer, M.A. (2005) 'Setting the stage: a dramaturgy of policy deliberation', *Administration Society*, 36 (6): 624–47.

This article aims to shed light on the performative dimension of participation in policy making. Portraying political processes as sequences of staged performances of conflict and conflict resolution, the author analyses how the design of the setting affects what is said, what can be said, and what can be said with influence.

Rosen, M. (1985) 'Breakfast at Spiro's: dramaturgy and dominance', *Journal of Management*, 11 (2): 31–48.

This article presents an approach for analysing the relationship between cultural and social action in bureaucracy, showing symbols and power as the primary variables of sociocultural study. Through their interrelationship the organizational conditions of production are reproduced or transformed. Social drama is the processual unit through which power relations, symbolic action, and their interaction are played out, and through which social structure is made evident. This perspective is applied to data from an ethnographic study of an advertising agency.

10

US AND THEM

Working in an organization a lot of the time means working with groups of people. We work in project groups, teams, committees, panels and so forth. We also find ourselves sometimes competing against other groups, departments and organizations. How are feelings of cohesion and togetherness built in such groups? How do we sense who is one of us and who is not? This chapter explores in depth how groups fit within organizations, why they can be instrumental in organizational success, but also why sometimes they generate dysfunctions, conflicts and waste. Groups, we argue, can generate synergies, stimulate motivation and enhance performance; they account for some of the most interesting and enjoyable experiences in people's working lives. But they can also lead to painful and traumatic experiences, in which personal rivalries and intense negative feelings make collaboration difficult or impossible. Being a member of a group can be an anxiety-provoking experience and, unless the anxiety can be adequately contained, it may feed other negative emotions. Then, group members are liable to display a tendency to conform with group decisions, to take more risky decisions or to reach unanimity without considering alternatives in adequate detail, for fear of being ostracized. The containment of anxiety is therefore an important priority for many groups and their leadership.

REAL-LIFE EXAMPLE

The director of an engineering firm attended a 'team-building' course and came back to his office fired up with new ideas. **Teamwork**, he had heard, is the key to success; everyone within the organization must be made to feel that they are a member of a winning team. From senior executives to part-time clerical staff, everyone has a contribution to make, everyone counts. The director decided to start by holding a Christmas dinner for his staff to strengthen team spirit. Unfortunately, he was embarrassed when all the workers crowded around one table, while he, his wife and the managers had the second table all to themselves. He commented, with irony, on how successful he'd been in fostering team spirit among his workers, only to be stuck in the opposite team!

Figure 10.1   Who is working harder?

Social divisions in organizations, as this director found, can run deep. The idea, or ideal, of bringing everyone together, unified in purpose, is often bedevilled by two social factors. Firstly, people often feel more comfortable in one social **group** than in another. Secondly, they will resist attempts to bind them with groups to which they feel no particular affinity. From an organizational point of view, this is important. People will behave in tune with those with whom they identify most and this can shift according to place and time. So you might feel one of 'us' when in a committee meeting with colleagues, but a different 'us' when having coffee with your immediate team members. You may see management as 'them' – except when you are invited to a working party which has a mix of managers and other employees.

Some of the groupings we identify with are large social ones: class, religious, professional, political and so on. Others are small groups or teams which are assigned particular tasks or responsibilities. Such teams have assumed greater importance in organizations. We spend much of our time in meetings and discussions with other people, brainstorming, taking decisions, making plans and interacting with others. Teamwork is sometimes extolled as one of the secrets of organizational success, and for good reasons too. Teams often draw the best out of their members: they stimulate, energize and inspire them. For example, in Figure 10.1, who is working harder? The team member or the single rower?

Effective teams can generate synergies and perform at a much higher level than as just the sum of their parts. It is not accidental then that educational programmes rely increasingly on group learning and group assessments. Amy, an American MBA student studying in England, had looked forward to this aspect of her course:

> Working as a member of a syndicate group was one of the main attractions of an MBA programme, especially in an international group, where different students can bring their different cultural experiences and ways of looking at things. The group I was assigned to included another American student with great entrepreneurial experience, two British students, a Biology PhD and an IT consultant, an Egyptian PR expert and a Greek engineer. The group's energy during the first few meetings was amazing – everybody was committed, ideas flowed and the work got done with the minimum of fuss.

Unfortunately, however, things did not continue to run smoothly. After about a month, the group had hit the rocks. Nobody is sure about the cause, but everybody agreed that a particular strategy assignment had gone badly wrong. The group had to write a report and make a presentation on a particular company and views had divided as to which company to choose. Three members of the group, led by Amy, had wanted to focus on a US-based IT company; the other three, led by Mike, the Biology PhD, had opted for a large UK-based pharmaceutical company. Both sub-groups had much expertise and useful data on their chosen company, but were unable to convince the other. Amy said:

> After several meetings in which we failed to reach an agreement and with the deadline fast approaching, we had an almighty fallout. The three of us decided to go ahead with our chosen company, while the other three claimed that they would do the project on the other company. We kind of agreed that we would eventually go with the better one of the two projects. Eventually one of the other group's members came over to our side. The Biology PhD, however, and the Egyptian student continued working on the other project on their own.

Frustrations built up. The two sub-groups separately approached the lecturer asking her to mediate between them. She told them that learning to work as a group was part of the assignment - it was up to them to resolve their dispute. She also mentioned that she would accept an assignment based on two separate cases, provided they offered a good justification for doing so. Two weeks later and with only a couple of days to go, the group approached their personal tutor, who had supported them since the start of the course, and asked for help. The tutor was very surprised – every time he had previously talked to any member of this group, he had been assured that things were going extremely well and that that group was making good progress and enjoying the course enormously.

The scene he encountered when he met the group suggested no enjoyment – long, tired faces and no eye contact between the members of the group. Tensions soon broke into recriminations, anger and tears. Amy's sub-group was accusing Mike, the Biology PhD, of having sabotaged this project 'just as he had done the previous one', that he always wanted to get his own way and could not be a team player. Mike, for his part, argued that Amy and her sidekicks, the other American and the Greek students, had been unwilling to listen, that they had continuously disregarded his suggestions and had marginalized the other two students. He refused to have anything more to do with Amy and her supporters and proposed to submit a separate project on behalf of himself and Lubna, the Egyptian student. At this point, everybody was talking animatedly together, except for Lubna who was sitting quietly, looking miserable. Repeatedly, Aaron, the second American student tried to intervene and come up with some compromise, but every time his voice was lost among the shouting. Eventually, he suggested that the project prepared by Amy and her sub-group would be the core of the group's submission with an appendix which included the work of Mike and his sub-group. But then it turned out that the quality of this project was far from satisfactory. Nick, the Greek student, was accused of having failed to write the literature review he had promised, having merely reproduced some files he had found on the internet. Suddenly, Nick found himself at the centre of much group aggression – 'a group has no place for free-riders' was a comment addressed to him. Lubna looked more and more depressed.

The tutor was watching the group tear itself apart. 'How is it possible that six intelligent human beings, who have paid huge amounts of money to be on the course and who only a month ago were working together so well, have ended up like this?', he was musing. 'And what is the point of teaching students in groups, when some groups become so dysfunctional?' Realizing that the meeting was going nowhere, that passions were rising and that the risk of one or more dropouts from the course was escalating, the tutor asked for a break.

GROUPS AND ORGANIZATIONS

Working as a member of a group is something that all of us experience. For some of us, all our work is done as parts of groups. The importance of groups for organizations was first recognized by the **Human Relations** School of Management Thinking. This approach emerged in a famous study conducted in the Hawthorne works of Western Electric, a company producing telephone equipment in the outskirts of Chicago. The study, known as the **'Hawthorne Experiments'**, started in the mid-1920s and continued over many years. Its main finding was that when workers work in small groups, strong group bonds (feelings of '*us*ness') are established, morale rises and **motivation** thrives. People work hard, argued Elton Mayo, one of the study's chief authors, not for instrumental reasons (money, career, job security) but because they identify strongly with cohesive work groups (see Chapter 4, 'Motives and Motivating'). Mayo made it his life's ambition to counter the impersonality and bureaucracy of modern organizations with vibrant groups in which people care for each other as people. He argued that management should promote informal relations in groups in order to increase output.

Another important discovery of the study was a recognition of the importance of group **norms** in determining output. Mayo and his co-workers observed that informal groups established norms of output or, in other words, standards of a 'fair day's work', which were distinct from management targets. These norms then ensured that each worker's output was roughly in line with that of the group, with no one working too hard or too slackly. Deviant behaviour was discouraged, initially through hints and whispers, and later on through ridicule and ostracism. In this way, groups controlled the behaviour of their members (see Chapter 18, 'Serious Joking'). Mayo concluded that productivity depends on the motivation of the social unit, not on the motivation of individual workers. People are social beings, not just individual economic ones.

Since the Hawthorne studies, the importance of cohesive groups and teamwork has become an accepted feature of management ideology. While in no way displacing Taylorism (see Chapter 13, 'Machines and Routines') as the bedrock on which much of production was organized, the Human Relations School has influenced the way managers think. In particular, groups are seen as doing wonders for motivation, pooling resources, generating cross-fertilization of ideas and unleashing creativity. For many complex tasks and complex decisions that organizations are required to carry out today, the view that 'many heads are better than one' appears self-recommending.

Groups, teams and committees are now ever-present in organizations. You will find them, for example:

- delivering a service, such as running a restaurant, an aeroplane or a health unit
- operating a campaign, such as a new fund-raising scheme or a change of management initiative
- administering any of a huge number of projects, such as implementing a new IT system, testing a new product or planning an advertising campaign
- drafting strategy, including examining potential mergers and acquisitions, exploring new business opportunities or revising HR policies
- dealing with a wide range of perceived problems, such as a lack of integration among departments, sexual harassment and discrimination or poor utilization of resources
- gathering around a water cooler to discuss the latest management announcement or the activities of other groups.

SOME DIFFERENCES BETWEEN GROUPS

Not all groups are the same. Committees, for example, are special types of groups where people get together, each representing a department or a particular interest; each individual's primary allegiance is to their department rather than to the committee. In teams, on the other hand, allegiance to the team is paramount. There is a sense that in order for the team to succeed, everyone must play their part. While committees tend to be constrained by procedures and regulations, teams tend to have to work out their own norms as they go along. Teams are also groups with far more specific tasks to accomplish. A football team will seek to win the next match, a medical team will try to operate successfully on a patient, a theatrical team will seek to put up a good show. Even Amy's project group has the task of preparing a successful presentation and a report on a particular company. If you consider an orchestra as typical of a team, we notice that each member has an indispensable part to play, that each one can spoil the good work of the others by playing the wrong notes or missing their entry and that good performance from each member is not enough to ensure a good overall performance. Unless all the musicians play well together, i.e. in a coordinated, harmonious and musically matched manner, the performance of the task, the musical score, will suffer. Even if all the musicians play well and in a well coordinated way, there is no guarantee of a successful, let alone a great, performance, if the overall conception of the work, its rhythm, timing and architecture are flawed. In this case, we could say that one member of the orchestra, the conductor, has not played well.

One of the first difficulties that groups can encounter is over different conceptions of the task. In fact, talking about 'a task' may be misleading since it is more common for different people to envisage the task differently, at least in the early stages. Amy's group may have agreed that their task was a successful project, but different members saw 'success' differently. Amy herself looked for a company about which she knew a great deal, thinking that this would enable her to get top marks for the project. She was determined to get a distinction on her MBA. Mike too was ambitious; he too wanted to get a distinction on his MBA – he knew a lot about the pharmaceutical company he proposed for the project; he had worked there for three years as a scientist after all. This made him particularly keen to spend some time researching it. Besides, he did not like what he viewed as American students' automatic assumption that all roads lead to the front door of an American multinational.

Other students in the group viewed the task differently. For some of them, the task became less important than the painful experiences they were having. Lubna later said:

> My experience in the syndicate group was one of the most painful ones I had since returning to Higher Education. Listening to Amy and Mike shout at each other – this was something I had never witnessed before. They were both very strong personalities, eager to lead the group, yet never listening to the views of others. I lack some confidence in my ability to express myself; I never felt respected or that others wanted to listen to me and this made me feel even more uncertain about myself. As the deadline came closer, my levels of anxiety and panic rose. I was overwhelmed by feelings of frustration, anger and guilt. Everyone in the group seemed paralysed and even the smallest decisions could not be made. Eventually, I would have settled for anything that ensured we would get a pass for the assignment. Or, even, for anyone who could have restored trust and cooperation among the members of the group. We ended up having continuous arguments and never getting anything done.

Lubna's experience is that of a member of a 'dysfunctional group' – a group that has ended up preoccupied by personal conflicts and tensions, sucked into a whirlpool of resentment and recrimination and unable to focus on the task. As a member of such a group, maintaining one's self-respect becomes a lot more important than any formal task facing the group. Anger, despair and vulnerability significantly shape the thoughts and attitudes of their members:

- 'She wants to usurp the group for her own purposes.'
- 'He has never done any work at all – he is a free-rider.'
- 'They want to kick me out of the group.'
- 'We have been assigned an impossible task.'
- 'We will be destroyed.'
- 'Someone ought to get a grip over this one.'
- 'Our tutor will step in at the last minute to save us from disaster.'

GROUP TROUBLES

Few groups may inflict on their members the depth of despair that Lubna experienced. Yet, we are now aware of the difficulties that beset groups and of the effort that must be dedicated in preventing groups from imploding. For all the trumpeted virtues of groups, synergies, cross-fertilization of ideas, motivational boosters and so forth, group process can easily be derailed. Groups may then end up performing far less well than any single individual. It is common to refer to such groups as dysfunctional. This label can, however, be misleading. We can all too easily think of inefficient groups as dysfunctional and efficient ones as 'functional'. Yet, the opposite can also be true. A group that appears to be functioning well, such as Amy's group in its early phases, may be storing up troubles for itself. Equally, a group whose members experience much pain and anxiety may, in fact, be performing important tasks (for instance, tasks that are highly unpleasant and dangerous) or even helping its members heal from previous ordeals and distress. Instead of talking of group dysfunctions, therefore, it is more profitable to look at how different group processes may affect the group's performance as well as the feelings and attitudes of the members towards each other.

What are the major effects that groups have on their members? A well-known tendency of groups is their ability to instil **conformity**, even among opinionated, independent-thinking people. There is a wealth of experimental data suggesting that people will rarely disagree with an opinion or a view they perceive other members of the group to be holding. Imagine yourself being the fifth person having to answer the question: 'should we go ahead with Project X?' (where Project X could be a marketing campaign, the building of a nuclear power station or the invasion of a foreign country). And imagine that the previous four have all answered firmly and decisively in the affirmative (or, for that matter, in the negative). How do you feel? How likely are you to disagree with them, especially if you hold them in high esteem and want to maintain good group relations, since the success of a project depends on them?

Conformity is frequently associated with a clouding of judgement. In their desire not to stick out from the group, individuals often agree with ideas which in the cold light of day are full of difficulties. One well-known tendency is for groups to opt for more risky choices ('should we develop this new product?'; 'should we go ahead with the spaceship launch?'; 'should we carry out these potentially damaging experiments?') than people making decisions individually. The dilution of responsibility accounts for a phenomenon known as **risky shift**, the tendency of groups to play down hazards and opt for more dangerous or even unsafe actions.

A related and even more pervasive group process has been given the name *groupthink* by the psychologist Irving Janis. His theory is based on the infamous decision of President Kennedy's administration to support the invasion of Cuba at the Bay of Pigs by a group of Cuban exiles in 1961. The plan for the invasion and subsequent overthrow of Fidel Castro was so flawed that the invasion ended up in a fiasco – virtually all those exiles were killed or captured in a matter of hours without posing the slightest threat to the Cuban government. Yet, a group of the brightest stars from Kennedy's administration had agreed to endorse it. Janis argued that cohesive groups lapse into a collective mode of thinking (hence group*think*) where striving for unanimity supersedes a systematic and careful consideration of alternative courses of action. Under the sway of groupthink, groups develop illusions of invulnerability (e.g. 'our technology is superior to anyone else's, so no one can stand in our way') while diminishing the threats posed by their adversaries through negative stereotypes (e.g. 'they have never been able to come up with any really original ideas'). Strong censorship is exercised in such groups, preventing the voicing of opposing ideas and closing up debate. Finally, such groups adopt an unquestioned assumption of their own morality ('we stand for the forces of freedom, innovation, decency and so on') and tend to view their adversaries (or anyone who disagrees with them) as standing for the forces of evil and darkness.

What is important to recognize is that these processes do not affect groups of weak-willed or easily influenced individuals. Putting together a group made up of highly motivated, intelligent and dedicated individuals does not preclude these processes and sometimes may exacerbate them. The term 'Apollo syndrome' has been used by

Belbin to describe teams of highly capable individuals with sharp analytical minds which, collectively, perform badly. Belbin argued that the dynamics of groups made up of similar 'bright' people make them less effective than more balanced, more heterogeneous groups. Members of Apollo groups tend to be excessively competitive among themselves, they find it hard to reach agreement and tend to neglect important but routine tasks – a situation not dissimilar to that of 'too many cooks spoiling the broth' or 'too many chiefs and not enough Indians' or 'one head is better than two'.

Given the seriousness of these processes, it is not surprising that organizations try hard to reduce their effect. There are some measures that can help. Organizations should generally avoid assigning like-minded, like-talented people to the same team. Balancing the qualities and personalities of different team members is an important management skill. But often we find ourselves in groups that we have not chosen, with others who we may not immediately like. Groups will work together better if they can follow some simple procedures. Members, for example, should not interrupt each other, until trust and cooperation has been established. Individuals should not monopolize the discussion. At times, groups may pause and ask each member to explicitly state their view on a particular topic. One particularly effective device is for each member of the group to write down their preferred course of action, before declaring it in public. In this way, people cannot simply change their mind because a particular view has been advocated by one or two highly assertive individuals. Under certain circumstances (when agreement seems to be reached too easily), groups may appoint individuals to play devil's advocate, before a particular decision is taken. Another important measure is for groups to agree on certain deadlines for making decisions or achieving some objectives. This reduces endless, and often fruitless, discussion. Finally, appointing an outside consultant is another way of stopping a group from lapsing into constant bickering, ready agreement, groupthink or conformity. This outsider, however, may all too easily be sucked into a group's own dynamics.

GROUPS AND ANXIETY

In order to understand better the reasons why some groups are both happy and effective and others are almost like nightmares, we need to examine some of the deeper emotional experiences that people have in groups. One **emotion** that has attracted considerable attention in groups is **anxiety**. Anxiety is an emotion we experience in many situations, especially those engendering uncertainty or danger. Before a stage performance or a job interview, we may experience excitement and nervousness, as the adrenalin flows, our senses are sharpened and we concentrate on the task. Meeting an important person, starting a new job, finding ourselves in a city where people speak a language we do not understand may all cause us anxiety. Anxiety can range from anticipation and nervousness to paralysing fear and panic. We all learn how to manage our anxieties and, sometimes, we help others manage theirs. Seeking advice and reassurance, talking about our problems, making plans, developing routines, analysing our situations and seeking diversion in things that give us pleasure and take our mind away from our troubles are some of the ways we use to handle anxiety. Giving our feelings a name, for instance, such as panic, nervousness, anticipation, worry or apprehension is itself part of the process of learning to live with them.

Now our experiences of being members of groups trigger all kinds of different anxieties. Some of these anxieties are related to the task:

- What actually is the task?
- Can we achieve it?
- Can we meet deadlines?
- Have we been set up?
- Can we keep up being the winning team? How 'good' is good enough?

Other anxieties relate to our own position or role in the group:

- Will I fit in without losing my individuality?
- Will they kick me out?
- Will they squash me?
- Will they respect my views?
- Will I be scapegoated?
- Will I be stereotyped?
- Will I be able to manage in the company of such outstanding individuals?

Yet other anxieties arise from the group itself:

- Can we handle disagreements/conflict?
- Will we be able to communicate with each other?
- Will we break down into cliques and sub-groups?
- Will everyone pull their weight?
- Will other groups stand in our way? Can we compete against them?

Leadership is a particularly acute cause of anxiety:

- Should we have a leader?
- Who should be our leader?
- Why not me?
- Is the leader competent?
- Does he/she know what he/she is doing?

For much of the time, such anxieties remain under the surface. If the group begins to perform well and its members get on well with each other, the anxieties are 'contained'. This containment is not necessarily a good thing. Groupthink may be a very effective way of containing anxiety and feeling happy with each other, yet one that leads to very poor decisions. Equally, however, if a group encounters difficulties and the containment of anxiety fails, anxiety can start feeding various other negative emotions: fear, jealousy, mistrust, anger, disappointment and so forth. These, in turn, assume greater and greater importance, often inhibiting a group's ability to function effectively and to carry out its objectives. It is then that a group, like Amy's, can lose itself in internal squabbling and acrimony.

When faced with such turmoil, some groups may seek the solution to their problems in accepting unquestioningly the authority of one person (the leader) whom they idolize and consider infallible. Alternatively, they may focus their attention on a target, internal or external, who is seen as posing a grave danger to the group and being responsible for all its troubles, and then proceed to attack the target or to run away from it in blind panic. This target can be one of the group's own members or another group or person. Amy's syndicate group, for example, may well have become just such a group in which individuals were continuously scapegoated for the group's difficulties – Amy and Mike with their leadership ambitions, Lubna with her lack of assertiveness, Nick with his skiving and plagiarizing and so forth. In such a group, there is a continuous shifting of alliances as people desperately seek to scapegoat others and avoid being scapegoated themselves.

THE MANAGEMENT OF ANXIETY

How then can groups manage their anxieties, contain them and channel them towards accomplishing their objectives? Experience suggests that talking about dangers and worries is important. Discussing disagreements and conflicts is better than allowing taboo subjects to emerge which may temporarily quell fears but may be storing up trouble for the future. The use of some agreed procedures and boundaries is another way of containing anxieties. These may involve plans, deadlines, timetables which, however, should not become sources of further anxiety by being too strictly enforced. A flexible approach to planning is usually a good thing.

Diversions are also important for handling anxiety. Socializing, doing things outside the task, having some fun, exchanging some good jokes can do wonders for keeping worries in perspective. **Leaders** are especially important in helping groups contain their anxieties, by taking some of the burden of responsibility and also offering guidance and direction when there is uncertainty. Some leaders are so effective at containing anxieties that they have been likened to toxic sponges, removing toxins from the group dynamics (see Chapter 7, 'Leading'). Other leaders seem to generate excessive anxieties by being unpredictable, intimidating or setting targets that are seen as unrealistic. On the other hand, a leadership vacuum may exacerbate anxieties as small tasks are endlessly discussed and a group finds it difficult to reach agreement.

Apart from collective ways of handling anxieties, individuals have their own individual ways. These may include relaxation techniques, yoga, meditation, sport and so forth. Some people rely on private rituals, superstitions and routines. Others may resort to drugs or self-destructive compulsive behaviour which starts off as a coping strategy but backfires. Respect for these individual coping strategies is important, though at times members of a group may find them irrational, childish or counter-productive.

AMY'S SYNDICATE GROUP – THE END OF THE STORY

It would be gratifying to report that Amy's syndicate members were eventually able to overcome their difficulties and that they re-discovered their ability to work together as a group. Sadly, this was not the case. With the deadline for the presentation and the submission of the report fast arriving, a token effort at collaboration was made. The task was barely accomplished and the group was soon disbanded amidst recrimination, anger and guilt. Reflecting some months later, Nick expressed the following view to his personal tutor:

The syndicate group experience came as a shock. I didn't know what the problem was, the people's personalities or the mix. Normally if I have a problem I try to identify the fault, the things that make me annoyed, the things that make me happy, the priorities I need to have. I was happy in many of the other groups I worked – I felt that the others wanted to listen to my views, I was respected and I respected the other members of the group. There was trust. But within this group I found myself lost, unable to think, cornered. I ended up hardly going to any of the meetings, they upset me so much. When I went to a meeting, I would say nothing. Since they didn't see anything good in anything I said, then it was better not to say anything. It was a hard time, but I have now put it all behind me. Let sleeping dogs lie.

With the experience of the group behind him, Nick's recollection focuses on his own experience of victimization, ostracism and exclusion. The dynamics of the group, the split over leadership, the disagreements over the choice of project and other significant episodes in the group's development have all been obliterated. All that is left is a scar, and a determination not to allow himself to be in the same situation again. If this experience were typical, it would be a grave indictment of the current emphasis on group learning and syndicate work. Fortunately, most students' experiences in their groups are much less traumatic. However, the unhappy experiences of groups like this serve as a reminder of the fragility of group relations and the care, energy and effort that must be put into sustaining them.

KEY POINTS

o   Much of the work in organizations is done in groups.

o   There are different types of groups, including teams and committees.

o   Many complicated processes in organizations require team effort and cannot be split into individual tasks.

o   Groups can generate synergies, stimulate motivation and enhance performance; they account for some of the most interesting and enjoyable experiences in people's working lives.

o   … but they can also lead to painful and traumatic experiences, in which personal rivalries and intense negative feelings make collaboration difficult or impossible.

o   People working in groups are liable to display a tendency to conform with group decisions, to take more risky decisions or to reach unanimity without considering alternatives in adequate detail.

o   They are also liable to develop a morality in which they see themselves as superior to others.

o   Being a member of a group can be an anxiety-provoking experience and, unless the anxiety can be adequately contained, it may feed other negative emotions.

o   The containment of anxiety is therefore an important priority for many groups.

> > > > > > > > > > > > **THEORETICAL SIGNPOSTS** > > > > > > > > > > > >

There are several overlapping areas in the study of groups – these include:

> groups and the effectiveness of organizations
> groups and their effects on individual behaviour, thinking and emotion
> group development and dynamics
> group decision making
> dysfunctional groups
> groups and learning
> group composition.

Groups have been the focus of extensive studies from many different perspectives in the social sciences (Brown, 2000). Early theories, inspired by observations of crowds, emphasized the loss of individuality that occurs in groups. The view that when people find themselves in a group, the group 'mind' dislodges their own individual judgements, values and personalities still surfaces in the work of social psychologists. The now classic 1920s and 1930s Hawthorne experiments in the USA first revealed the importance of group dynamics for organizational effectiveness and success (Mayo, 1949/1975; Roethlisberger et al., 1939). The experiments showed how workers' informal allegiances, friendships, norms and pressures to conform outweighed managerial attempts to manipulate productivity. The desire to be accepted by a group seemed more fundamental than the need to maximize earnings or enhance careers. The experiments also highlighted that by being members of cohesive groups, members showed enhanced motivation and quality of work. 'Group dynamics' is the academic discipline examining the formation and subsequent development of groups, the nature of interactions between their members and their relations to other groups and organizations.

Since then, it has been recognized that informal groupings meet the social, emotional and security needs of individuals which cannot be addressed in the formal organization. Group dynamics developed subsequently through the work of Kurt Lewin (Lewin and Lewin, 1948) and others in the United States and the Tavistock Institute in Great Britain. There is an extensive literature on the characteristics of effective groups. These include a shared understanding and commitment to the group's goals, a high degree of mutual trust, effective leadership and the means of resolving conflicts without avoiding them. Why it is so difficult for many groups to attain these characteristics is not so well established. While it is easy to blame poor leadership, the inability to deal with conflict or a lack of mutual respect as causes of group troubles, these may very well represent the consequences rather than the causes of group dysfunctions (Anzieu, 1984). Psychoanalyst Wilfred Bion (1961) argued that the failure to tame and contain potentially destructive emotions, especially anxiety, leads groups to lose sight of the tasks they seek to accomplish and tips them into what he termed 'basic assumption' functioning. By this, he meant that groups start to behave *as if* they held certain shared assumptions about each other, about the leader and about the task they seek to accomplish. These assumptions are products of fantasy, collective delusions that severely distort their sense of proportion and reality. The casual observer may have the impression that a group is working smoothly and even efficiently, yet, in reality, the group may have lost its ability to interact with the outside world, to test its ideas against the evidence and to act rationally.

An influential theory of group dysfunctions centres on the term 'groupthink', first used by psychologist Irving Janis (1972) to describe a situation where members of a group facing an important decision lapse into a form of collective wishful thinking and fantasy. They imagine themselves invulnerable, they dismiss opposing ideas and take wild risks. There is a strong tendency to stereotype all opponents and to censor even the slightest dissenting voices. Conflict within the group is avoided, but at a serious cost to the quality of decision making. Groupthink can be seductive as each individual shares the group's sense of superiority and power. It can also have devastating results. Groupthink has been blamed for a number of major disasters at national and international levels, such as the Bay of Pigs military fiasco (the original case study in Janis's book), the space shuttle *Challenger* disaster, Britain's do-nothing policy towards Hitler prior to the Second World War, and the unpreparedness of US forces on the eve of Pearl Harbor.

A different way of explaining group dynamics was proposed in a much-cited article by Bruce Tuckman (1965). Tuckman argued that groups pass through several stages as they develop, all of which are inevitable. Groups start by going through forming, a stage when they acquire a collective identity and begin to discuss the nature of their task and objectives; then groups move on to storming, a stage characterized by tensions and disagreements, which, when handled effectively lead to norming, the third stage, when the group acquires set assumptions and work routines. Finally, groups move to the fourth stage, performing, where members know how to approach their task but also know how to handle disagreements and conflicts.

More recently, a number of authors have examined the importance of groups for the purposes of learning or sharing knowledge. An important concept is that of a 'community of practice', a loosely connected group or network of people, who share knowledge by trading experiences and stories (Brown and Duguid, 1991; Wenger, 2000). Such communities may include computer analysts facing similar problems, patients suffering from uncommon medical conditions or professionals facing similar uncertainties. They are able to communicate quickly and effectively; their members cut through information overload by learning from each other's direct experiences. Learning groups have also been studied in connection with classroom learning, for instance MBA syndicate groups. Different authors have developed theories of appropriate styles of instruction to facilitate group learning (De Vita, 2001; Simpson et al., 2000) and also of other factors that may affect the ability of such groups to work effectively together (Gabriel and Griffiths, 2008).

REVIEW QUESTIONS

1. Is it true that groups are more than the sum of their parts?

2. Are organizations groups?

3. In what ways are emotions experienced by people in group situations different from those in the rest of their lives?

Reading On

The articles below are available for free to readers of the fourth edition of *Organizing & Organizations* via the book's companion website at www.sagepub.co.uk/fineman

Brown, J.S. and Duguid, P. (2002) 'Local knowledge – innovation in the networked age', *Management Learning*, 33 (4): 427–37.
The ubiquity of information makes it easy to overlook the local character of innovative knowledge. It persists, the authors argue, because the local character of innovative knowledge flows in social rather than digital networks. The authors argue that developing regions should develop new technologies in service of their existing competencies and needs, finding new ways to address indigenous problems.

Wenger, E. (2000) 'Communities of practice and social learning systems.', *Organization*, 7 (2): 225–46.
This essay argues that the success of organizations depends on their ability to design themselves as social learning systems and also to participate in broader learning systems such as an industry, a region, or a consortium. It explores the structure of these social learning systems and proposes a social definition of learning, distinguishing between three 'modes of belonging' by which we participate in social learning systems.

Simpson, R., French, R. and Vince, R. (2000) 'The upside of the downside – how utilizing defensive dynamics can support learning in groups', *Management Learning*, 31 (4): 457–70.
This paper suggests that it is important in management education to work with the defensive dynamics in learning groups. Through a consideration of the dynamics within complex systems, the authors argue that the ways in which these defensive dynamics are worked with may determine the levels of learning attained – work which requires skill in adopting appropriate strategies in relation to defensive dynamics.

Van der Vegt, G.S. and Janssen, O. (2003) 'Joint impact of interdependence and group diversity on innovation', *Journal of Management*, 29 (5): 729–51.
This questionnaire study among 343 members of 41 work teams in a financial services organization examined the effects of individual team members' perceived task interdependence and perceived goal interdependence on innovative behaviour in teams characterized by different levels of group diversity. Multilevel analyses revealed that individual's perceived task and goal interdependence were not related to innovative behaviour in homogeneous teams, but were strongly and positively related in heterogeneous teams.

11

BEING DIFFERENT

In this chapter, we consider some of the ways in which people in organizations can be seen to be different from each other, and the positive and negative consequences of such differences for the person who is different, for the person who notices the difference, and for the organization. We consider the experience of being different from the norm, which everybody has to some extent and in some places. We talk about the role of language to define, demonstrate and enforce differences. We look at the very closely related concepts of attitudes and prejudices, and at the process of stereotyping. Towards the end of the chapter, we focus on a theme that is implicit in the earlier part, namely identity. People value their differences as a way of telling themselves and others who they wish to be taken to be. Differences may be important to the self, and even if this is not the case, there are plenty of situations in which differences are positively valued, for example by making the person more visible.

DIFFERENT DIFFERENCES

It is said that 'variety is the spice of life'. The differences between people, from physical characteristics to the views which they hold, are endlessly fascinating. So why are we not simply celebrating the idea that we are different from each other? Ask a group of students what they would like to do if they had enough money, and the answer is often that they would like to travel. Why? Not just for spectacular scenery or historic buildings; they want to be able to meet different people and see how they live. Ironically, sometimes students will tell you this while sitting in a seminar room in partly segregated groups, sitting next to their friends, and subtly avoiding sitting next to people from different **cultures**. Perhaps many of us are happier with talk about difference and diversity than we are with practice.

There are certain differences in which we can all take pride. Most people who read this book will at some time have been praised for being cleverer and more effective in their work than some others of their age. There are many other ways in which people are pleased to be different from their peers – they may kick a ball further, they are better looking (if only in their own eyes), they dance better, they support a better football club, they possess some characteristic or other which in their view makes them stand out from the crowd. We use differences as part of our way of understanding ourselves, of defining and declaring our **identity**; we also use sameness for this purpose – identifying some people who we see as like ourselves – 'one of us'. We see ourselves as a particular kind of person, and find ways of letting others know that this is who we wish to be taken to be. For physical characteristics, think of a time when you were meeting someone new, and had to describe yourself so that they could recognize you. The descriptions which people give under such circumstances can be very revealing about their sense of their own physical identity ('I'm short with dark curly hair, well built, and I look younger than 28'). Then when you meet that new person, another round of self-presentation may start to take place, as you selectively demonstrate to them various characteristics that you think will appeal to them: your sense of humour, your knowledge, your aggression, your cleverness, or whatever you pride yourself on and wish to display to this particular audience.

Not only do we enjoy showing the ways in which we are different, we may also delight in the ways other people are different from the norm. A new person in the office may be seen as quite different from all the others, and may be welcomed for this. 'At last we have got someone who can finish jobs off/do the accounts/reach the top shelf ' or whatever the special characteristic may be. Affectionate statements made about a colleague usually tell you about some way in which that person is different; 'she is wonderful, she is a really good listener' or 'he was always asking the difficult questions, so we really miss him'.

However, we also enjoy being similar to other people, being with people who we see as like ourselves, whom we feel we can predict and fit in with easily. This is why almost everyone has experienced the other side of being different, when you are made to feel uncomfortable about it. You may feel isolated, on the wrong side of some difference which binds others together and seems to make them dislike or misunderstand you. Many of us have found ourselves in an uncomfortably small minority at some time, where that minority does not seem to be valued by others. We may feel, for example, that we are the only member of our race, religion, sexual orientation, style of upbringing, moral persuasion, hobby group or age. Often this produces nothing more than a mild feeling of loneliness and frustration. But the universal character of that experience means that we should be able to empathize with those who are made to feel pain, or at least extreme discomfort, because of their differences. As someone we spoke to in a company put it:

> It was very obvious that I was the only Asian in the section. No one was rude, but they seemed to expect me to smell of curry the whole time, and they did not think I would be house trained – you know, I wouldn't know how to behave with customers. And the funny thing is that most of them were odd in their own way. It just wasn't so obvious to them.

We often fail to show much empathy for those who are different from us. This is easily seen at the level of international relations, where evidence of aggressive lack of empathy is evident in every newspaper. Equally, at a local level, we enjoy our status as members of the majority or of a privileged minority. It may be that not only the majority but also some minorities are given a good deal. For example, if a company is struggling to meet a government quota for its number of physically disabled employees, this group may find themselves well looked after. If it is trying to show a more equal gender balance in its board, women may find promotion is easier. But not all minorities are privileged, and when they are, they are often also placed in a complicated double bind. When members of a minority display their disaffection and **alienation**, they are then blamed for failing to make an effort to blend with the majority and abandon their difference. Invisible psychological lines are drawn. The majority seeks to disregard the plight of the minority by asking it to forget its difference and act 'like everyone else'. The minority, for its part, responds by focusing on its difference as its source of identity, since it is this difference which accounts for its subordinate status; its members are drawn to each other as fellow victims who need each other's support. This, in turn, invites further marginalization and lack of empathy from the majority. In this way, both the majority and the minority may contribute to the definition of difference. The minority is cast in the role of being different by the majority, and accepts that role as the only way to maintain its self-respect and dignity.

Privilege itself may have its drawbacks. Individuals who have great wealth or those who acquire sudden riches and fame may feel distanced from their peers. They may be excluded just as effectively as those who are disadvantaged, ending up by feeling cut off and alienated. As was said of one rich student of ours: 'The trouble is he's got so much money and he's either embarrassed about it or he thinks that everyone else wants to sponge off him, so he ends up with his only relationship being with his horse'.

LANGUAGE AND DIFFERENCES

Differences are closely associated with the way they are labelled. We may have a sense of a difference, but before we can remember how we are differentiating among things and before we can carry **attitudes** from one object to another, we have to work out what to call that difference, or in other words how to label it. But the words that people use to describe differences do not simply describe; they create and maintain the difference that they relate to. You may have a generalized dislike or suspicion for someone, but it is only when you have used the label 'cheat' for them, heard someone else use it, or seen them described that way in a newspaper or on television, that your feelings turn into hostility or contempt. Which comes first: the words or the feelings? It is impossible to say, but they seem to reinforce each other in people's minds in a vicious or a virtuous circle. Some of the words which we use to describe people have emotional overtones, positive or negative, whereas others appear to be more neutral. So the choice of word can generate a significant difference with positive or negative overtones or, alternatively, may contain or neutralize the difference. Consider, for example, the difference created by using words or phrases like 'spastic' and 'disabled', 'dyslexic' and 'can't read or write'. If I describe someone as 'lively' that may be a term of approval for me, while it might fill you with foreboding.

Discourse analysts are a group of researchers who have suggested that the words and phrases that we use do not simply reflect but actually constitute our thought. This means that words cannot be safely taken as neutral descriptors. Phrases that we use about other groups do not merely store or convey our thoughts about that group – they equally create the thoughts that we have about that group. The words are not simply how the thoughts are phrased; they should not be treated as transparent things that we can go through to see what 'lies behind' those words. They actually *are* the content of the thoughts.

This is why 'politically correct' **language** is not the triviality that it is sometimes made out to be. Some people find it very irritating to be corrected when using a phrase which may have been part of their habitual speech for years, and so they mock others' insistence on, or even preference for, non-sexist and non-racist language. But the argument has gained ground in recent years that language does not simply reflect but encourages a **sexist** and **racist** approach. Use the language and the feeling follows, as attitudes are shaped by language in the vicious circle described above. A test case of this is the use of the male noun 'man' or pronoun 'he' to indicate a person of either gender, in spoken or written work. Many have complained that the use of 'he or she' or 's/he' is stylistically clumsy and that no one need take offence at what is after all a long-standing convention. 'Man is a social animal' may sound more elegant than 'people are social animals'. Yet the argument has, rightly in our view, prevailed that constant use of the male as the representative of humanity marginalizes women, casting them in the permanent role of the unseen and unspoken 'other'.

Another important feature of the language system in organizations, by which differences are generated and maintained, is **jokes** (see Chapter 18, 'Serious Joking'). If you are a member of a group which is subject to jokes, should you laugh and join the mocking of your group and feel included in the wider group? Or should you not laugh and risk being excluded and maybe further baited? This becomes even more difficult if you find the jokes funny. After a course on 'Differences in Organizations', one of the authors was presented by a group of his female students with a book of *Stupid Men Jokes*. Many of them were very funny, while they were undoubtedly and intentionally **sexist**. Should he feel guilty about laughing at them? Does it make any difference if he laughs at them in private, in front of a group of other men, or in front of a group of women? The same dilemma faces members of minorities more starkly. Are **racist** or ethnic jokes acceptable if told by the race they are about? Is there still too much risk that people have felt pressured to make fun of their own differences? Or is this altogether too precious and restrictive? Is there a risk of outlawing one of the bonds that holds different people together, the most positive, enjoyable and uniting part of social interaction, namely the use of humour, in the pursuit of political correctness? How do we find the moral boundaries of joking relationships, and maintain good, relaxed, anxiety-free dealings with others, while also being careful not to hurt people, and not to harbour and encourage our own prejudices?

LABELS AND PREJUDICES

A first step in tackling prejudice can be to redefine the labels we use. 'Physically challenged' or 'restricted' can replace disabled or crippled; 'ethnic background' can substitute for race or colour. People can be described as 'large' rather than fat, and 'gay' now replaces queer. Even the two categories 'men' and 'women' can, according to some observers, drive a wedge between the genders. The writer Deborah Tannen (1995) illustrates this:

> A female executive at a large accounting firm was so well thought of by her firm that they sent her to a week-long executive-training seminar ... Not surprisingly, considering the small number of women at her level, she was the only woman at the seminar ... This did not surprise or faze her, since she was used to being the only woman among men.

All went well for the first three days of the seminar. But on the fourth, the leaders turned their attention to issues of gender. Suddenly, everyone who had been looking at her as 'one of us' began to look at her differently – as a woman, 'one of them'. She was repeatedly singled out and asked to relate her experiences and impressions, something she did not feel she could do honestly, since she had no reason to believe they would understand or accept what she was talking about. When they said confidently they were sure that there was no discrimination against women in their company, that if women did not get promoted it was simply because they didn't merit promotion, she did not feel she could object. (p. 129)

In this tale, being defined as different, a woman, by a male majority, ended up stifling the apparently laudable intentions of the latter part of the course. The very focus by men on the one 'woman' created an uncomfortable difference for her, placing her in a category that, hitherto, she had not been aware of within the meeting, a category she was asked to defend or explain – to men. It is also interesting that part of her discomfort came from her believing that they 'would not understand or accept what she was talking about', and this is *her* **prejudice**. Majorities do not have a monopoly on prejudice. Some labels make us very self-conscious, inhibit communication and create barriers; others can invite stereotypical responses in accord with their label: '… well, women think …'; 'I guess students are typically …' .Why should you have to express your view as a Muslim, or as a Jew, a communist, a Christian, a lesbian or indeed as a member of whatever minority you might find yourself in? At one level, the very use of a label creates a difference and distinction that may not have existed before, but how much that matters depends on the **meaning** of that label to those who use it, and to those to whom it is applied. One of our friends and mentors, Galvin Whitaker, tells how he responds when people in other countries ask him what he, as an Englishman, thinks about some issue. 'First, I tell them that I'm not an Englishman, I'm a Yorkshireman. Second, I tell them that I'm not a Yorkshireman, I'm Galvin bloody Whitaker'.

Discourse theorists have pointed out that language, rather than being a mere transmitter of opinions, actually constitutes those opinions. The discourse we use – its signs, labels, grammar and expressions – are the very substance of our thinking and attitudes. Thus, to return to our earlier discussion, if we take for granted that the use of the male pronoun is to stand for all human beings, then male automatically gets privileged over female. It is a delicate issue understanding how the use of language can create categories which are, or are not, experienced, as prejudicial. For example, as a mark of non-discrimination within an organization, management may studiously avoid direct reference to its black and Chinese staff in those terms. Yet this can sometimes backfire; lack of reference to them in racial categories can be seen by black and Chinese people as an attempt to deny important features of their identity, to pretend their ethnicity and colour are not important.

STEREOTYPING

'If students weren't so concerned about avoiding work and buying their assignments off the internet, then higher education might get us somewhere.'

'Accountants? Just about the most boring people you can imagine.'

'Big business won't take any interest in trying to make employees happy; all they care about is profit.'

'Environmentalists love talking about trees, bunnies and bullfrogs, but none of them have a clue about the real world of industry.'

These are **stereotypical** judgements. All the people belonging to a particular group are regarded as having the same characteristics. So, as a student, accountant, business leader or environmentalist, you are pre-judged, fitted into a category which is seen as summing you up. Stereotypes massively condense the amount of information we need to know about someone in order to make a judgement. They are primitive, often instant, categorizations, but they are widespread and enduring. Some stereotypes have survived for many centuries, especially those associated with nationality and religious, or ethnic, origin. People are not easily argued out of their stereotypes, a 'don't confuse me with the facts, my mind is made up' type of response.

Certain stereotypes can be self-confirming, in that people seek out and exaggerate a quirk or peculiarity in others to validate their own stereotypical views of them. Those who are stereotyped may even fit in, or play up, to others' stereotypes of them, so that they can feel more accepted, such as a 'fat' person acting 'jolly', an 'old' person being 'forgetful', or a French person being 'romantic'. Such action, when well timed, can also be used ironically, to mock the stereotyper. Indeed, mocking the use of stereotypes often makes successful comic humour, such as the 'little old lady' who turns out to be a tough street fighter, the small child with an enormous vocabulary, the philosophical policeman, the gambling priest or the villain with the heart of gold. Such events surprise and amuse us because they challenge some of our taken-for-granted perceptions.

Stereotyping is no doubt socially and psychologically functional. It is a way of coping with much variability in human behaviour by reducing it to small, manageable categories. It is also a way of making ourselves look and feel better or superior by assigning negative characteristics to groups we choose not to like or approve of, and positive characteristics to members of our own 'tribe'. Football world cups tend to be a setting where the most obviously tribal stereotypical allegiances are fomented, with some England supporters aggressively chanting *En-ger-land* to proclaim their superior affinity, while picking fights with other national groups to 'show them who's best'.

DOES STEREOTYPING MATTER?

The answer to this question is: 'it all depends'. Some stereotypes are benign, others less so. To think, for example, of all students as 'inquisitive', all scientists as 'serious' and people who live in the countryside as 'escapist' is a different order of judgement from extreme negative stereotypes, such as expressions of hate or disgust because of a person's sexual preference, race or religious belief. Many of these latter stereotypes are deeply rooted in people's belief systems and **cultural** ways, to the extent that the individuals who hold them are convinced they know what their targets (e.g. women, gays, blacks, strangers, skinheads, the old and so on) are 'really like'. While clear company policies, and even legislation, may discourage some overt stereotyping, the underlying opinions and feelings are less easily touched. They have a habit of bubbling to the surface in particular social conditions, such as during difficult economic times and in periods of high unemployment. **Scapegoats** are sought to take the blame, such as 'foreigners', 'Jews', 'Gypsies', 'Muslims' or 'asylum seekers'.

To stereotype is to pre-judge. Some stereotypes we term **prejudice**, pre-judgements at the root of discriminatory practices in society and in organizations. The prejudice may be directed at women – 'not good drivers'; older people – 'slow learners'; the disabled – 'need too much special attention'; blacks – 'good at sport' and so forth. Such beliefs are rarely explored or examined in depth by those who hold them because it serves their interests not to do so. The prejudices help buttress their own views of the world which, in the hands of powerful people, can be translated into discriminatory practices at work, such as excluding some people from promotion or recruitment. Ironically, sometimes the very hallmark of prejudice is its denial, classically expressed as: 'but of course, some of my best friends are …'. Some people are able to maintain and protect their particular prejudice about a social group, while making an exception for some members of that group. But that exception may not survive a severe test: the prejudice often wins out in the end.

Prejudice often has negative connotations, but not always so. The **attitudes** – beliefs, feelings and behaviours – that prejudice embraces can be positive. We may hold favourable prejudices towards beautiful women, towards children, film stars, tall men, people who do charitable work. We may personally discriminate positively in their favour: we like them more, seek them out, give them more attention. Some organizations may mirror such prejudices, such as offering more posts to attractive women or to publicly well-known job applicants. They may favour those who have education from a particular university, or who are family members of existing employees. Should we be concerned about this? Is this better or worse than negative prejudices? After all, by favouring some groups, others, the less-favoured, will be excluded.

What is judged as desirable or undesirable prejudice depends on the social times and place. Prejudicial remarks towards women, different racial groups, the elderly and homosexuals used to be tolerated, even encouraged, but now it is far less so in many Western organizations. Social attitudes change because of a number of processes: the greater visibility, power and voice of discriminated groups; a better understanding of the perspectives and feelings of the victims of prejudice; vigorous moral debate in the media; laws against discrimination. It can also be that prejudice simply moves to another target. As the unfairness of one set of prejudices becomes understood, so another arises to take their place. Where prejudice creates tension and division in the workplace, it can be in management's interest to reduce it, if for no other reason than to maintain organizational efficiency and effectiveness. As organizations become more multicultural and multi-gendered, there is some evidence supporting the 'contact hypothesis', that the more people mix with those they stereotype, the less they are likely to cling to their stereotypes.

However, social attitudes are not homogeneous. Prejudices seem to thrive in some organizational settings, while in others they are far less apparent. The social **norms**, **sub-culture**, **values** and traditions provide more or less oxygen for prejudices to survive. Moreover, the attitudes which form prejudices can be complex – some people will think and feel prejudice, but suppress it in their visible behaviour. Others will try to segment their prejudices, epitomized by statements of the sort: 'I have nothing against gays, but we can't have a gay priest – people are not ready for it'.

Many organizations now claim equal-opportunity, anti-discriminatory policies. Some such claims do not survive close scrutiny, and are worth little more than the paper they are written on. Others can be more substantial. For example, the British DIY company, B&Q, actively promotes a policy of recruitment which claims not to exclude older job applicants. Typically, such people find it hard to find employment. Encouraged by legislation, some firms have specifically allocated jobs to the disabled. But, as organizations representing the disabled point out, this often results in just minimal compliance. An additional complication is that the best of intentions for the disabled can become entangled in other layers of discrimination and prejudice within an organization.

The behaviour of organizational leaders gives vital clues to the rest of the members about the true priorities of an organization, its commitments and its **values**. It is important, therefore, that leaders should provide an example of understanding, honouring and managing differences. Leaders who can mix with different cultural and occupational groups, who make an effort to understand how the views and priorities of these groups differ from those of others, who are seen to take a proactive stand against **prejudice** and **discrimination**, encourage their subordinates to do the same. By contrast, leaders who regard differences as an inconvenience and seek to minimize them or ignore them are liable to fuel resentment and **conflict**.

DIFFERENCES THAT MAKE A DIFFERENCE

Why do some differences become the focus for people's **identity**, while others remain trivial matters of detail? How do differences and identities develop together? Why do some differences become the focus of enormous symbolic importance?

Differences and Identity

When people join a company or university, they often have to listen to several speeches from senior staff who tell them how proud they should feel as a new member of that organization. The speakers are trying to impress on the listeners that the status of being a member of that particular institution should become a part of their identity. However, not everything that we do becomes part of our identity. Watching television may not be part of our identity, though being a fan of a particular programme can become part of it. Wearing casual clothes may not be part of our identity, though a much loved item of clothing or a particular way of dressing can become part of who we are. Our identity is composed of numerous **meanings**, images and ideas which enable us to think of ourselves as distinct and integrated entities.

Not all features of our identity are conscious. Consider, for example, our physical size. A manager with whom we worked had always used his considerable height to portray himself as a 'big, relaxed guy'. This was both part of his identity and part of his self-presentation. He came to a new job and went in to meet one of his staff:

'I knocked on Rex's door and went in. He got up to shake my hand, and I thought he was never going to stop getting up. He is a good four inches taller than me, and suddenly my whole big, relaxed act was in tatters. I had to think of something new in this department!' It was only when he stopped being the tallest person in his department that our friend realized what an important part of his identity his height had been all along. In the same way, we may discover whether our nationality is important for us when we find ourselves in a foreign country.

The same is true of our organizational identity. How important is it for us to belong to a particular organization? When members of an organization go on temporary secondment to an overseas branch, they may find themselves surprisingly happy when they get back. They greet colleagues to whom they were previously indifferent as long-lost friends, and enquire eagerly as to what has been happening in their absence. The same thing can be seen in many expatriate working communities: people who would have found little in common in their country of origin seem to develop a herd instinct and spend a lot of time together. As a company club manager at an expatriate centre told us: 'If we said that this evening's activity was that everyone would come up to the club and walk slowly round the swimming pool behind each other, they would come. There is nothing that these people would not do so long as they are together.'

Developing Differences and Identities

We give each other clues as to the differences that are important to us. Some people literally wear their old school tie to identify themselves or keep talking about some sporting or other achievement in the distant past which is important for them. The central hero of the film *Requiem for a Heavyweight* kept reminding himself and others that he had been the '*fifth*-ranking contender for the world heavyweight title'. This is what sustained his identity throughout his years of hardship and made him somebody at least in his own eyes, if not in the eyes of those who saw him as a 'has-been'. Alternatively, our identity may be based extensively on anything from objects, people or institutions that we love, to beliefs, hobbies or behaviours that are central to our sense of self, to experiences that are part of our past or to dreams which we have for the future.

In presenting our identity to others, we normally adopt different approaches according to their interests and identities. Presenting oneself as a person with an exceptionally thorough knowledge of pop culture may go down well with one group, but not impress their parents. To suggest that it is one's nature to be a particularly tough manager might be seen by the interview panel as being the best qualification for a job, but not gain much enthusiasm among the candidate's new subordinates. Identities are neither easy to form, nor easy to change. Many people go through periods of identity crisis when they are not sure of the core features of who they are or see themselves to be, and what aspects of themselves they might be happy to change. They may then experiment with different beliefs, different lifestyles, different accents, different friends, different jobs and careers, until they discover those in which they feel most comfortable. Smoking, drinking and drugs are initially all forms of experimentation which people may try while seeking to leave behind

NOISE TO SIGNAL
Rob Cottingham

"On Facebook, 273 people know I'm a dog.
The rest can only see my limited profile."

Figure 11.1

an identity they are not happy with and construct a new one. They may try new hairstyles or fashions, they may tattoo or pierce their skin, they may affect new attitudes or ideas, they may entertain different fantasies about the future and make different plans. These are periods which psychologists call 'identity moratorium', when different and sometimes conflicting identities fight within us for predominance. Eventually, one or more coherent identities emerge, which can persist over a period of years until they get threatened again by a new identity crisis. Identity crises often accompany the major life transitions, like adolescence, parenthood and retirement or great traumatic and testing periods in our lives, like those surrounding divorce, the death of loved ones, redundancy or serious illness – these are periods when new identities must be forged out of old ones. This often involves the discovery of new differences and the obliteration of old ones.

Differences which become embedded in our identity are certainly not easy to change, even if we suffer in order to sustain them. Taking drugs may be an important act in forming an identity which rebels against the conformity of childhood or the conservatism of our parents – admonishments regarding their harmful consequences may then fall on deaf ears, or be part of the attraction. Eventually, 'having a drug problem' may itself become part of our identity. If a problem is a valued part of someone's identity, they are unlikely to welcome help, however destructive the problem; if you succeed in helping them, you are in effect also robbing them of part of their identity. If someone sees themselves as a panicky person, it is going to require much more effort to help them stop panicking than if they see it as a temporary state caused by unique circumstances. If someone regards herself as a 'macho' manager by nature, it is not going to be easy to help her find different ways of managing her subordinates.

Differences with Symbolic Importance

As an experiment, an American school teacher separated her class into those who had brown eyes and those who had eyes of any other colour. She then started treating the brown-eyed group as superior to the other, explaining that they had to carry the other group which was not as good as their own, while being quite abusive to the children whose eyes were not brown. The following day, she reversed the prejudice, with the brown-eyed group being blamed for everything that went wrong.

The object of the teacher's experiment was to show her class how easily symbolic differences could be set up and reinforced in organizations. Eye colour may not be a difference automatically loaded with **symbolism**, but it only takes a small amount of **discrimination** to set it up as one. Race, gender and physical capacity, on the other hand, are all readily recognizable as having symbolic significance, associated with privilege and supremacy over centuries.

Why are some differences seen as having greater symbolic importance than others? The answer to this is unclear. Particularly puzzling is race. Race is a social construction – a label used as a definition which is taken to have meaning within a social group or culture, rather than a description of a physically observable set of qualities. How do we determine people's race? Skin colour is very variable within races, as are the bone structures of the face and the texture of the hair. So how and why do people draw sharp lines of 'racial difference'?

Historically, the importance of race has been propped up by different arguments, depending on ideologies that were current at the time. Early European explorers in South America engaged in correspondence with the Pope to discuss whether the local inhabitants should be thought of as human beings at all, whether, in other words, they had souls and whether their souls were liable to conversion and salvation. In Germany, in the 1930s, a violently racist policy was given an economic foundation: the 'Zionist conspiracy' was presented as the explanation for the financial woes of the country. In South Africa in the time of Apartheid, the Dutch Reformed Church found ways of arguing for racist policies on the basis of the Bible. In recent years, there have been various claims to produce a 'scientific racism', as people produce one controversial scientific claim after another to suggest the superiority of one race over another, especially in areas such as intelligence or adaptability. It seems that there is a market for such ideas, and a new book to make a lot of money for its author, however weak the argument, approximately every ten years.

The number of different ideas used to justify and maintain **racist** beliefs and attitudes highlights the symbolic character of this difference. Race lives on as an important symbolic difference, even when the arguments for its importance crumble.

When racial differences are taken to be physical, it is particularly puzzling that some of the worst racial violence has been committed by people who are physically difficult to distinguish from their victims. Psychoanalysis has noted a phenomenon which helps to explain this and other kinds of prejudice against others who seem not so different from those who are prejudiced against them. It is called the 'narcissism of small differences' – groups that appear most similar may in fact perceive each other as the gravest threat to their identity and pride. In order to defend this identity, they exaggerate the importance of minuscule factors, investing them with massive symbolic significance. This may apply to rival football clubs in neighbouring parts of a city, which reserve their greatest hatred for each other. Similar exaggerations of small differences underline the hostility between rival urban gangs, competitor organizations or competing groups within organizations. What the narcissism of small differences suggests is that individuals and groups tend to exaggerate the importance of the tiniest differences which set them apart from those closest to them. We have to recognize that there are some differences which, however small and insignificant they may seem to us, produce especially powerful emotional responses in people. To the dispassionate observer, such responses can look like a severe failure in the sense of proportion or even the sense of humour of the person or group that is so angry about such small differences from themselves.

Differences can be Positively Valued

Differences and diversity do not usually make life easier, but they do make it richer, and the more we can accept and celebrate the diversity that we see in the people around us, the more creative and productive we are likely to be. Proactive organizations in this area do not merely preach equal opportunities for all employees and prospective employees, but they actively seek to promote diversity and be seen to be doing so. Equal opportunities policies and procedures involve a variety of measures aimed at enabling all members to develop their full potential and thrive within the organization. These may include recruitment policies, such as ensuring that advertisements for posts are constructed in such a way as not to discourage applicants from minority or under-represented groups; they include the elimination of artificial barriers (such as working hours which are difficult for people who are responsible for school-age children) which de facto filter out less advantaged social groups; they include the presence in promotion or appointment panels of a diverse group of people (including women, members of **ethnic** minorities and less senior employees) who will not automatically opt for appointing the candidate most like themselves.

In order for these measures to be effective (rather than lapse into meaningless ritual), organizations and individuals must constantly proclaim and demonstrate their commitment to diversity and their encouragement of difference. Awareness and sensitivity training programmes, in which members of different **groups** are brought together for the expressed purpose of identifying and sharing their concerns and worries, can make considerable contributions to the acceptance and appreciation of the unique qualities that different groups of employees can bring to the workplace. They can undermine negative stereotypes and build solidarity out of diversity and difference.

Yet lingering behind many social judgements in organizations, sometimes with dramatic consequences, are two enduring features of interpersonal perception: **stereotyping** and **prejudice**.

IN CONCLUSION

Difference is a vital aspect of organizations, especially those which operate in a complex, multicultural society and those whose operations stretch globally. Difference is an important part of group identity formation and acts both as a source of solidarity and as a source of hostility, **conflict** and **aggression**. Working with differences in organizations requires both personal skill and sensitivity. It also requires the setting up of institutional arrangements which address the concerns and interests of **groups** which have traditionally experienced **prejudice** or **discrimination**, to ensure that people have equal opportunities of reaching positions of privilege and power.

KEY POINTS

o   Most people value variety but find it harder to work with people different from themselves.

o   The meanings assumed by differences are products of different cultural traditions.

o   Differences become embedded in the identity of individuals and groups.

o   Differences which seem important to one group or individual appear unimportant to another.

o   Language is not merely a tool through which differences are expressed; it can actually construct differences and similarities, and is instrumental in whether differences are positively or negatively experienced.

o   Sexist, racist or offensive language cannot be justified on grounds of convention, convenience or amusement.

o   Ignoring differences in organizations does not make them melt away.

o   Stereotyping is a natural human activity by which over-simple judgements are made.

o   Sometimes stereotyping does not matter, but it needs watching with suspicion.

o   Leadership can be crucial to how differences and diversity are handled within organizations.

> > > > > > > > > > > > THEORETICAL SIGNPOSTS > > > > > > > > > > > >

The major themes in this chapter have been covered in the following areas of literature:

> language as an important part of how differences are seen
> prejudicing and stereotyping as natural human activities
> differences as markers of identity and distinctive contribution.

Language as an Important Part of How Differences are Seen

The role of discourse and organizational language has been mentioned a few times in this chapter. Theoretical underpinnings for this go back at least to the work of George Kelly (1955) and his work on Personal Construct Theory, as a way of understanding how all people act like scientists in their attempts to understand their world by creating theoretical constructs and testing out those constructs for themselves, and then elaborating them when they turn out not to be satisfactory. Another line of work was developed by Kelley (1972) in Attribution Theory, which considered how people attributed particular qualities to other entities, including other people. For example, if something turns out well, do you attribute this to the qualities of the colleague who did it, or if you are suspicious of that colleague, do you assume that it could not have been a result of their efforts and should be attributed to good fortune? Recent developments in Discourse Analysis (Grant et al., 1998a) have taken this further, noting that the discourse can be seen as a separate object of study, and not merely a window to what was happening (Potter and Wetherell, 1987). This should be seen alongside the ideas of cognitive dissonance (Festinger and Carlsmith, 1959) which would imply that such differences in language would affect behaviour. Cognitive dissonance suggests that people need to keep their attitudes and their behaviour aligned, but are as likely to change their attitudes to fit their behaviour as vice versa.

Prejudicing and Stereotyping as Natural Human Activities

Prejudicing and stereotyping have been studied for many years (Allport, 1959; Potter and Wetherell, 1987); it is worth noticing that Potter and Wetherell come to very different views than Allport, because they understand prejudice in terms of discourse. There is also the less negative sounding, but effectively very similar, concept of attitude (Katz and Kahn, 1978). Within this category, race in organizations has been approached from several different angles. (For an overview, see Nkomo, 1992.) Several economists have explored dual labour markets and the benefits accruing to capitalist organizations by a workforce divided along racial lines. Alderfer and colleagues (1980) sought to go beyond issues of discrimination and prejudice and identify the meaning of race for majority groups in America. Omi and Winant (1987) and Anthias (1982) have explored how the meanings of race become part of identity formation. Thomas (1993) has explored how race boundaries in American organizations may be burdened by intergenerationally transmitted emotions, rooted in the experiences of slavery and racial exploitation.

Differences as Markers of Identity and Distictive Contribution

These evoke a theoretical tradition which goes back to Erikson (1964, 1968) and which have found more recent development in several areas of work (Brockmeier and Carbaugh, 2001; Brown, 1997; Carr, 1998; Collinson, 1988; Du Gay, 1996a, 1996b;

Giddens, 1991; Harré, 2001; Pullen and Linstead, 2004; Pullen et al., 2007; Ricoeur, 1991; Wenger, 1997). A wide-ranging account of equal opportunities in organizations is offered by Legge (1995). Wilson (1995) presents the arguments of numerous researchers on gender in the workplace, and the visible and invisible barriers which inhibit women's career progression. Much of the discussion on women's careers has revolved around the metaphor of the 'glass ceiling' which stops women from reaching the top of organizations (Davidson and Cooper, 1992; Marshall, 1984, 1995).

REVIEW QUESTIONS

1. How important is the use of language, and the way people are labelled, in understanding the way that differences are handled in organizations?

2. If stereotyping is an inevitable part of the way people see each other, is it worth worrying about?

3. What is the relationship between differences in organizations and personal identity?

4. What are the costs and benefits to organizations of trying to handle the differences between people effectively?

---

companion
website
w.sagepub.co.uk/fineman

Reading On

The articles below are available for free to readers of the fourth edition of *Organizing & Organizations* via the book's companion website at www.sagepub.co.uk/fineman

Chang, S. and Tharenou, P. (2004) 'Competencies needed for managing a multicultural workgroup', *Asia Pacific Journal of Human Resources*, 42: 57–74.

This study was designed to assess the competences needed for a manager to manage a multicultural group of subordinates. Open-ended semi-structured interviews were conducted in order to derive the competences used by managers who are already managing a multicultural group, identifying five key traits for managers to effectively manage a multicultural workforce.

Chrobot-Mason, D. (2004) 'Managing racial differences: the role of majority managers' ethnic identity development on minority employee perceptions of support', *Group Organization Management*, 29: 5–31.

This article examines potential sources of variance to explain with-group differences in White managers' abilities to manage non-White employees, measuring ethnic identity development, ethnic group self-identification, education and participation in diversity training. The authors find a significant relationship between the interaction of manager and employee ethnic identity and managerial support.

Ng, E.S.W. (2008) 'Why organizations choose to manage diversity? Toward a leadership-based theoretical framework', *Human Resources Development Review*, 7: 58–78.

Research suggests that equal employment opportunity (EEO) legislation and affirmative action programmes (AAPs) have been only partially successful in promoting women and minorities in the workplace. Firms are voluntarily pursuing diversity management, but only when business objectives coincide with the needs of women and minorities. This article proposes a theoretical framework for linking CEO commitment to diversity practices.

Zane, N.C. (2002) 'The glass ceiling is the floor my boss walks on: leadership challenges in managing diversity', *Journal of Applied Behavioral Science,* 38: 334–54.

This article analyses layers of meaning that are embedded in the concept of diversity in a financial institution. By tracking the conversational patterns between a CEO and the discourse communities of his organization, this research highlights the processes by which meaning gets ascribed to the concept of organizational diversity and its impact on organizational structures and culture across time.

12

MORALS

The social responsibilities of businesses have been very much in the news in the past two decades. This chapter examines how morality and ethical conduct are defined, refined and at times perverted within social processes of organizing. We examine the texture of major corporate scandals, harassment and cheating, as well as everyday 'misdemeanours'. We see how personal standards can be eroded by organizational norms and by the exercise of formal power. And, in counterbalance, we see how some people – whistle-blowers – will risk all in order to expose an organizational wrongdoing.

REAL-LIFE EXAMPLE

Real-Life Example

In August 2001, Sheeron Watkins, Vice President of Enron, a huge energy utility, made a momentous decision. She sent a memo to Enron's Chairman, warning him that the company might implode in a wave of accounting scandals because of the financial irregularities she had spotted. The warning was ignored, with company officials pocketing millions of dollars in false stock-market gains. The company collapsed in December 2001, just before it was able to eject Watkins. Enron's 'core values' were 'RICE': Respect, Integrity, Community and Excellence.

REAL-LIFE EXAMPLE

Real-Life Example

In 2002, Scott Sullivan, the former chief financial office of WorldCom, the US telecoms giant, was indicted for a $7 billion accounting fraud and the largest bankruptcy in US corporate history. Sullivan was accused of overseeing the hiding of billions of dollars of company expenses, telling staff to mark operating costs as long-term investments thus making earnings look very much stronger than they actually were.

These stories made international news and continue to reverberate in the folklore of corporate financial corruption. However, a few years later, they were to be upstaged – by Bernard Madoff of Bernard L. Madoff Investment Securities. In December 2008, he was arrested. His company was forced into liquidation, exposing the world's biggest fraud. For many years, Madoff had run an illegal 'pyramid' investment scheme, attracting major institutional and celebrity investors across the globe, from major banks to small charities. He managed to hide the scheme from regulators as well as falsify documents to camouflage massive losses. He gave investors unusually generous returns – but from money paid in by other investors rather than real profits. It required a constant supply of new investors to maintain itself, but the supply dried up during the 2008 world recession and existing investors wanted their money back. The pyramid collapsed leaving some 50 billion dollars of debt. Those who knew Madoff described him as 'affable' and 'high-profile, but not in a loud way'. He went to great lengths to cultivate an aura of exclusivity and trust.

Elsewhere, and completely out of the limelight, a manager at a prestigious British firm of chartered accountants confidently adds an administration charge to a client's account, based on an invented item of 'work done'. In the forecasting department of a multinational cigarette company, a clerk wryly alters the sales forecasts for a fourth time, because top management 'still don't like them' (the clerk has learned that she needs to produce work which will back up management's objectives for end-of-year sales). And an engineer, on a domestic call to fix a central heating boiler, replaces a component in perfect working order and adds it, and an extra hour's fitting, to the final bill.

All these are actual events. How are we to understand them, both great and small? Are they all part of the **game** of business and organizing? (see Chapter 8, 'Politics and Deals'). Does it not matter what you do, as long as you are not found out? Is it **power** that determines what has to be done – who wields the biggest stick? What unites the incidents are questions of **value** and **morality**, the distinctions between what is right or wrong in organizational behaviour and whether, and how, such distinctions are made and acted upon.

KNOWING RIGHT FROM WRONG

We can add further examples which, in their different ways, go to the heart of moral practices and beliefs:

- The internet site that sells high-price 'rare', but actually non-existent, tickets for major sporting event and concerts.
- Company directors who award themselves generous bonuses while the rest of the company is being downsized.
- The 'charity' organizer who takes our money and then steals it for himself.
- Railway maintenance contractors who knowingly skimp on essential repairs thus risking a major rail disaster.

When we look closely at such incidents, there is a cluster of 'dubious' behaviours: lying, 'one rule for them, another for us', deceit, fraud, evasion, negligence. In most **cultures**, such behaviours generate strong feelings of indignation and disapproval. We may argue that no organization or business should be run that way. But many are, and organizational members invent terms which help them to do so, such as 'creative accounting', 'being economical with the truth', 'tidying the books', 'not rocking the boat' and 'safeguarding the interests of the shareholders'. Some are blunter in their rationalization: 'I don't care; it's simply what I do to get on here'. All are expressions of a sub-morality – to which we shall return.

But when are issues really **moral** ones? And who makes such judgements? This is problematic, both philosophically and psychologically. For example, 'I don't care; it's simply what I do to get on here' reflects a view that life is for instant gratification (the 'now' society), is fragmented and consumer-driven, a key feature of postmodern living that grips the city trader as much as the teenager at school. It is divorced from traditional moral yardsticks. The old moral certainties, the strong influence of higher authorities, such as the church, teachers, elders and parents, have crumbled. Such **attitudes** can be found in some organizations and it is common to hear comments such as 'many young employees nowadays don't care about anyone or anything, other than what's in it for them' or 'city centres are populated by gangs of feral youths'. But set against this startling picture is a less radical one, suggesting that the moral society is far from dead, although it is sometimes a bit wobbly. The reasoning runs as follows.

We all start to make moral judgements early on in our lives, as we learn to distinguish right from wrong, partly by noting our parents' approval and disapproval of different types of behaviour. Some of these judgements reflect the values of our culture, which become part of us as we grow older. Early on, we may resist the temptation to steal our sister's or brother's book or to break their favourite toy for fear of punishment. Gradually, however, we learn to tame our impulses not so much for fear of punishment, but because we accept that certain types of behaviour are intrinsically wrong. It is only when these processes are absent, inconsistent or perverted in some way that our sense of right and wrong becomes confused, anaesthetized or simply not considered.

Stealing, lying, hurting or insulting others, deceiving and destroying and killing are acts that typically offend our moral conscience, unless they are experienced as serving a still more fundamental moral principle. For instance, lying in order to save someone from unnecessary hurt may be seen as permissible – a 'white lie'. Yet, as we grow older, we find ourselves facing moral dilemmas, situations where different moral principles are at odds with each other, and where no clear right and wrong option is readily available. Is peace more important than justice? When is it right to use violence in pursuit of moral objectives? Is our duty to our parents greater than that to our children? Is it right to lie in order to protect someone's honour and dignity? Is our loyalty to our friend more important than our right to criticize and castigate him or her when they act wrongly?

Moral dilemmas can cause us much unease and **anxiety**. We each discover different ways of dealing with these unpleasant feelings. As we saw in Chapter 5, one way is to shield ourselves behind organizational rules, denying that our actions have any moral import at all – they are merely the enactment of someone else's regulations. Another way is to diminish their importance and overlook the implications of our decisions. Alternatively, we might invent plausible-sounding reasons to persuade ourselves of the rightness of our actions.

There is a psychological distinction between actions which produce feelings of shame or guilt in the individual, and those which produce embarrassment. The former relate directly to morality. So, if an engineer knowingly fails properly to service a valve on a gas line which leaks and kills a colleague, the guilt he feels relates to his feeling of culpability in harming another human being. The principle of not harming somebody through one's actions, directly or indirectly, lies at the heart of moral concepts. The person who lets down colleagues by not turning up for a key meeting which leads to the loss of a client may feel deeply embarrassed. She has transgressed the expectation of her work **group**, but it is not felt as a moral issue. The harm is neither as devastating nor as irreversible as that which followed the engineer's actions. The roots of the harm principle go deep into society's codes of conduct, but it is expressed in different ways according to the cultural and religious history of a country.

ORGANIZATIONAL MORALITY AND VESTED INTERESTS

Institutional processes can wreak havoc with our sense of right and wrong. They can subvert, even obliterate, moral judgement, producing their own counter-morality or amorality. Feelings of guilt can be rationalized away in terms such as: 'well, that sort of person deserves what they get'. Many organizations so strongly inculcate their members with their own values that people become blind to individual moral issues. In effect, the organization's **values** come to stand for what is moral and what is not. The fate of Stephen Lawrence illustrates this. In April 1993, Stephen, an 18-year-old Londoner of Jamaican parentage, was fatally stabbed by five white youths, all of whom had a history of race baiting. Three of the suspects in his case were acquitted in 1996 after a widely faulted prosecution, and could not be tried again. The result of an eight-month inquiry into how the case was handled exposed a floundering justice system and a corrupt police culture that tolerated racism: racist beliefs were part of the taken-for-granted way the police carried out their duties. It was 'institutionalized' racism, so embedded that the police were unable to see their own racist ways. The police attitude towards blacks was so negative that officers failed to seek or uncover convincing evidence for a court case.

The morality 'bubble' that organizations can produce is most horrifically demonstrated by the events in Nazi Germany. The defence offered by German officers who systematically brutalized and annihilated millions of human beings was: 'I was only obeying my orders'. Indeed, the response to organizational 'orders' says much for the frailty of human moral conduct when it is subjected to a strong organizational mould. The Nazi doctrine had an additional feature to help crush conventional moral thought: Jews, Gypsies, the mentally ill and others were to be considered as sub-human, or even as the diseased parts of society, who threatened to infect everyone else, so they merited their fate. Some 65 years on, we find some echoes of this amongst American guards in the Abu Ghraib prison in Iraq. They were revealed to be abusing, torturing and grossly humiliating prisoners in their charge and taking 'trophy' photographs of the results. When eventually called to account, one of the major protagonists claimed that he was following orders and that 'there's a war on. Bad things happen.'

Organizations present their members with various tests of loyalty, situations where they have to decide whose side they are on, which can seriously stretch ideas of right and wrong. Mirella, a temporary employee at a cosmetics multinational, was confronted with such a test. In the course of a casual conversation with her boss, Carol, Mirella discovered that Peter, a colleague, was due to be moved from the company's headquarters in Paris to an outpost in Germany. Mirella knew that Peter would be devastated (he had only recently moved his family to Paris from Australia). Should she warn him or prepare him? Or should she stay quiet?

REAL-LIFE EXAMPLE

Mirella's Story

In the space of five minutes, the destiny of a man I did not know that well had been revealed to me. I felt I had become an accomplice in this 'multinational mechanism', where an invisible hand allocates resources in the most efficient way. I knew things about him that he would probably find out about in about a year's time, by which time his family would have only just settled down. However, I could not warn him. My information came from the grapevine and was therefore not reliable. I was supposed to mind my own business and pretend I did not know.

That was what everybody else was doing; this is how you were supposed to behave if you were working in that organization. The fact that Carol was meant to be a close friend of Peter implied that she should be the one to talk to him, I thought. I realized later that loyalty to the organization came first, even before friendship; nobody would ever dream of arguing against a decision made by the 'invisible hand'. Certainly, I thought, an offer to move to another country can be refused, but that is true only in theory.

Once your destiny has been decided somewhere up in the hierarchy, the invisible hand will make sure you will find it too disadvantageous to refuse. In other words, the organization is willing to provide its employees with considerable privileges and good working conditions, but their identity is taken away from them in return. These are the rules, and once you are in the mechanism, it is very difficult to get out, almost impossible.

In this account, Mirella's sense of right and wrong is overwhelmed by an organizational code which requires her to be silent. She finds numerous rationalizations for staying silent, but cannot escape feelings of discomfort, even guilt. She does not look forward to the day when she finds herself in Peter's position:

I still cringe at the idea of having one day a comfortable office in one of these organizations. Deep down, I will be conscious of the fact that I have become like a circle-shaped object and someone I don't even know is desperately trying to find the corresponding circle-shaped hole.

When morality is replaced by organizational **norms**, or by a professional code of practice, people can defer to them as the arbiters of the rightness or wrongness of their action. They provide a short cut to moral **decision making**, relieving people of much of the burden of having to make up their own mind. This can, step by step, move people into self-justifying positions, **rationalizations**, which, by any other criteria, would be immoral. So it is 'just tough', or part of the 'realities of doing business', that Joe's job will be removed when he is away on holiday and he will not know until he gets back. And 'we'd lose the contract' if local residents were told the true noise levels of the new factory that is going to be built near their village.

Leaders in many organizations set the moral tone for their employees. In some organizations, a sense of deep social and moral responsibility is emphasized by the leader, the need for each and every member to be morally scrupulous and above reproach. They can pride themselves on their respect for human rights, for the **environment**, for the fair treatment of minorities and so forth. Such organizations may attract public attention, as journalists, politicians and academics test the strength of such claims, especially when they clash with harsh financial realities. Other leaders may encourage turning a blind eye, disregarding what they view as moral niceties (such as giving employees advance notice of redundancies, or offering them re-training). The leader in these circumstances is setting an agenda of personal self-interest and gains, whatever the cost.

Immorality and **corruption** can sometimes infect an entire organization, turning every member into a silent accomplice to shameful acts. Occasionally, cases come to light of companies which have embezzled or recklessly speculated vast amounts of shareholders' money (such as the examples at the start of this chapter), of children's care homes where children have been systematically abused, of hospitals which run roughshod over patients' health, or of firms which ruin or jeopardize the natural environment. Questions are then asked: 'why wasn't any action taken to prevent this?'; 'Why was it not made public earlier?'; 'Why did nobody say anything?' Answers to such questions are usually found in the vulnerability and corruptibility of individuals when exposed to organizations where everybody routinely flaunts the normal precepts of morality.

Some organizations have 'ethics committees' to consider the morality of adopting new programmes or procedures in their work. We find these especially in medical and research settings. **Ethical** codes of practice, like professional ethics, are meant to guide individuals when faced with moral dilemmas. However, actual decisions in most organizations are rarely subjected to such scrutiny. Most just happen, a product of the personal beliefs of the actors involved, their **roles** and professional expectations, and the **politics** and **culture** of the organization. All of these come into play when, for instance, a board of directors is deciding on which bit of their company to close down, whether to continue promoting a product with a poor safety record, or the extent of their own pay rises compared with those of their employees.

Over recent years, the directors of many large corporations have been awarded very large pay increases while their businesses have been failing. Many have insisted that their staff receive modest or zero pay rises, and that some be made redundant – 'in order for the company to survive'. 'It makes good economic sense', assert the directors. Such explanations, once accepted as a reality of the market economy, are now

Figure 12.1 Northern Rock's crisis.

challenged by vociferous shareholders of the company as morally unacceptable, fundamentally unfair and a source of shame on the company. Thus, the moral spotlight can shift with changing times. We see this in the reaction to Adam Applegarth's payout in 2008. He was chief executive of a failed UK bank, Northern Rock, which created panic among its investors (see Figure 12.1).

The Times newspaper reported as follows:

Architect of Northern Rock failure may get £ 76,000 payoff

The banker who presided over the collapse of Northern Rock is to get a pay-off of up to £760,000.

Applegarth, 45, once the second youngest chief executive of a FTSE 100 company, is seen as the main architect of Northern Rock's misfortunes. He earned £1.4m in 2006, including a bonus of £660,000. He lives in a £2.5m mansion in Northumberland and drives a £60,000 BMW X5. At least 2000 employees will lose their jobs.

The compensation package is likely to anger shareholders who lost money in Northern Rock. Vincent Cable, Treasury spokesman for the Liberal Democrats, has said that any compensation package for Applegarth would be 'an insult to the millions of Northern Rock customers, shareholders and employees who have suffered due to his incompetence'.

The Sunday Times, 30 March 2009 © NI Syndication/*The Times* 2008.

PERSONALIZING AND DEPERSONALIZING

We are most likely to feel issues as moral ones when they touch us personally – with a sense of the disquiet or guilt from feeling party to a possible injustice or harm. There are decisions which some people find hard not to experience as morally problematic, such as sacking, takeovers, not promoting, demoting. The anguish can be seen in the following comments from a senior computer analyst:

> There are parts of my job that I hate. Today I've written a report where I've almost suggested that there ought to be redundancies in certain areas. I've felt dreadful about it. It's the first time I've done anything like that, and I'm really not sure what I'm doing. I'm talking about people I know. It would be a new computer system which would replace two people with one part-timer. I never thought I'd be in a position where I would be making these recommendations. But it's just a recommendation, not a decision.

Advice on how to handle these situations is usually aimed at damage limitation, not on confronting the moral dilemma. So we find instructions to the carriers of bad tidings to 'offer help and constructive criticism along with the bad news', 'present the broader organizational and economic picture', or 'hire an external expert to do the job'. A crisp and soothing organizational **language** exists to help decision makers depersonalize and rationalize their anxieties and put them into the organization's 'moral' framework, where it is just part of the job or the rules of the game. They aim to persuade themselves, as well as others, that, for example:

On dismissing someone:

- 'Sometimes you have to be cruel to be kind; it's in their ultimate interests to work for someone more suitable.'
- 'It's your job or theirs.'
- 'The organization's efficiency is at stake.'

On promising an unlikely delivery date:

- 'Well, we must win the contract first. We'll worry about delivery later.'

On selling an environmentally damaging product:

- 'It's our job to make profits. It's the government's job to protect the environment.'
- 'It's not illegal yet. If we don't sell them, someone else will.'

And on selling weapon-potential chemicals to an unreliable military regime:

- 'As far as we are concerned, they are for agricultural purposes, and the government has not opposed an export licence.'

In the world of economic rationalizations, winning a contract, staying in business, satisfying shareholders is 'what it's about'. Lies are not lies; they are 'selective truths' which 'make good economic sense' or underpin a 'free market'. Someone has to get hurt in marketplace competition and **conflict**, goes the argument; there 'must be winners and losers'; fine altruistic values cannot survive the cut-and-thrust world of business. In these various ways, tough, and potentially harmful, decisions are transformed into blander organizational procedures or control devices (see Chapter 5, 'Rules are Rules').

Between the Cracks

But not all morally questionable actions are easy to hide or neutralize within the organization. **Harassment** is a case in point.

Verbal, sexual or physical harassment is usually felt as a moral violation. The perpetrator, however, might talk about it as 'simply a bit of fun', 'a game' or 'all part of everyday working'. Individuals are often alone with their moral conscience when they experience, or witness, harassment. Should they complain? If it is happening to them, will anyone be sympathetic? Helen recalls her first week in a major corporation:

> We were in this boardroom, three male managers and me. One pointed to the large table in the middle of the room, and said to me: 'go on, lie out on that. We'll all have a go then.' I felt dizzy, sick and horrified. I wanted to run out, but I held on. They thought it was a great joke.

Joanne describes the constant sexual taunts, disguised as humour, from male managers in the oil company in which she worked. It went on so long that she eventually summoned up the courage to turn on the men responsible. They immediately chided her for her 'over-reaction'. She ended up feeling angry, embarrassed and humiliated.

With Helen and Joanne, we enter the realm of the **sexual** politics of the organization (see Chapter 17, 'Sex'). In many companies, codes of sexual conduct and 'acceptable' sexual attitudes are dominantly male and male-dominated. This can be powerfully oppressive, leaving women vulnerable and unsupported. The male-centred ideology can also contribute to a devaluation of the worth of women when it comes to decisions on selection and promotion. The '**gender** logic' of the organization, like the commercial logic, is influenced by the values of the dominant coalition of people who hold the **power**. Other social and interpersonal matters are also affected in this manner – from AIDS, gays, blacks and the disabled, to policies on maternity leave, paternity leave, job sharing and crèches. The tension is between decisions which, at one level, may be regarded as about morally significant issues, but at another level, as a matter of **conformity** to the economic values, or convenience, of the organization.

POWER AND THE ORGANIZATIONAL IMPERATIVE

People will act with apparent moral integrity in one situation, but then with little moral concern elsewhere. The key to this paradox lies, as already hinted, in the **power** that different organizations (the 'church', the 'office', the 'business') can have over what we do (see Chapter 9, 'Influence and Power'). An early psychological experiment by Darley and Batson in 1973 (Darley and Batson, 1973) forcefully illustrates the point. Forty seminary students, who expressed particularly high standards of moral

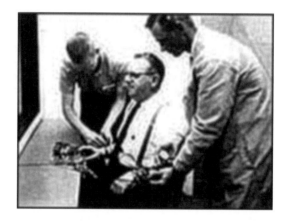

Figure 12.2   Milgram's experiment.

behavior, were told to prepare a lecture on one of two topics: the parable of the Good Samaritan or job opportunities for seminary graduates. Half the students in each group were told they had a very tight time schedule; the rest were told they had plenty of time. Then, sneakily, the experimenters made it impossible for the students not to pass an obviously 'distressed' man, moaning and coughing, on their way to the lecture room. Only 16 stopped to help him, most of them being from the group that thought they had plenty of time to get to the lecture. Those who were going to do a Good Samaritan lecture were just as likely to walk past the man as those who were not. Some literally stepped over the man in their hurry to get on.

So here we have morally aware people acting in ways quite contrary to their expressed values in order 'to get the job done'; the context or situation is very powerful. An even more startling, and famous, experiment, was conducted by social psychologist Stanley Milgram (1974) in the 1960s. Forty males, of various ages, volunteered for paid participation in an experiment on 'the effects of punishment on learning'. They were instructed to administer electric shocks to a 'learner' who was strapped to a chair in an adjoining room (see Figure 12.2). Each time the learner gave a wrong answer, or no answer, the shock had to be increased. The volunteers operated their own control switch which was marked from 'slight shock' through to 'danger: severe shock', ending with an ominous 'XXX' marking. As the shocks increased, the volunteers would hear cries from the learner, and pounding on the adjoining wall. Any hesitation to go on was met with a cool instruction from the experimenter to the effect that they had to continue in order to complete the experiment.

Milgram found that all the volunteers were prepared to administer 300 volts to the learners, and 26 of them went to the end of the shock series, despite the fact that the learner had gone silent by then. Milgram himself was taken aback:

I observed a mature and initially poised businessman enter the laboratory smiling and confident. Within 20 minutes he was reduced to a twitching, stuttering wreck. He was rapidly approaching nervous collapse. He constantly pulled on his ear lobe and twisted his hand. At one point he pushed his fist into his forehead and muttered 'Oh God, let's stop it'. And yet he continued to respond to every word of the experimenter, and obeyed to the end.

The exercise was rigged so that the learner would deliberately give wrong answers and feign distress. There were no actual electric shocks. The experiment has itself been criticized as morally questionable as it was deliberately deceptive and, under the forgiving cover of 'science', gave the realistic impression that it was acceptable to injure another person. The studies, nevertheless, leave us with two important messages: first, that we may firmly espouse a moral stance to help, or not to injure, others, but organizational life is a severe testing ground where the best of us can fail to support our beliefs with moral action; second, obedience to commands from a superior is a strong force in our society, even if it means we will hurt another human being.

Cheating – Institutionalized 'Immorality'

The revelation of massive fraud and criminality in some very large organizations leave most people with a mixed response. On the one hand, there is the sense of moral indignation that such empires can cheat and exploit in the way that they have done. On the other hand, there is the growing expectation that all businesses misbehave and have their seamy side, but some are simply seamier and more hypocritical than others.

It is likely that few organizations operate without some form of hidden economy where individual profits are made from 'fiddling': bending the rules, pilfering, short-changing or overcharging. Our moral appraisal of this depends on where we stand. If we do the fiddling ourselves, we can view it as a 'fair perk', or a 'necessary action' given the lack of other rewards. If we are the victims of fiddling, we become morally indignant. Also, who we fiddle from comes into the moral equation. We might regard the wealthy, and well-insured, superstore as fair game for a little pilfering. The same action towards the small corner shop could inflict unacceptable injury on its owners.

Fiddling has a long history. There are ancient records of theft from Egyptian storehouses which reveal a remarkably similar recipe to today's thefts (Mars, 1982). An insider supplied grain and fabrics from the storehouse to an outside ship's captain (the 'fence') who in turn bribed the temple scribes to alter the stock records so no one would notice the shortfall. Fiddling can take various forms, from organized theft to unauthorized phone calls, inflated expense claims and 'borrowed' paper, computer discs or pens.

The persistence of fiddling suggests it is intrinsic to the social organization of work, acting as a necessary adjunct to other financial and psychological rewards. Fiddling offers some people the opportunity to rectify, or compensate for, felt injustices in their working arrangements (see Chapter 9, 'Influence and Power'). It can offer an escape from stifling **bureaucracy** and arbitrary **control**. For a minority, fiddling can make the difference between a job on which they can financially survive and one on which they cannot. Such was the rationale presented for fiddling 'time sheets' in a building-repairs organization where one of us once worked:

Every Friday we had to fill in our time sheets for work done that week. Bert, the tradesman I worked with, called them 'fiddle sheets'. It was soon apparent why. At the bottom of the sheet was a space for overtime hours worked. Every week Bert put in 15 hours and told me to do the same. The first time this happened I was astonished. We hadn't worked 15 hours overtime; in fact we hadn't worked any overtime. We hadn't even worked our required 42 hours! Bert reassured me: 'listen. You do exactly what I do. Our pay is lousy and this bumps it up a bit, helps us get by. As you work with me we both put down the same hours, OK? It will be alright'. And it was alright. The foreman received our timesheets and immediately signed them without a blink. It soon became apparent that he was in the same game. I felt really torn to start with, as it was so plainly dishonest. Soon, though, I saw their point. Their take-home pay was among the lowest in the country.

Here we see a guilty conscience transformed with a rationalization of the sort: 'Well, it's fair to lie in these particular circumstances'. Usually, fiddles have a complex set of internal rules and checks: small fiddlers do not automatically turn into big ones; lone fiddlers do not necessarily progress to gang fiddlers. How much is taken, and by whom, is usually fairly well worked out within the group. For example, restaurant workers on the fiddle will work out a hierarchy of reward – the food, alcohol and other products – which each person can take. There are shop assistants in clothing stores who have bought similar clothing, on discount, outside the shop, to re-sell at a personal profit in their shop – but 'just' one or two items a month. Fiddling is taken for granted in some big corporations, by fiddlers and fiddled alike. It is built into the overall running costs, and is tacitly accepted as part of the informal organization of work. Often, preventive policing simply gives rise to more cunning fiddling, and the costs of heavy surveillance may soon outweigh the company's losses.

Blowing the Whistle

There are, as we have shown, social processes within organizations which create their own particular brands of morality. They permit, and often encourage, conduct which is self-serving, conduct dislocated from the values the organization might publicly profess, and from the principles by which, privately, organizational members try to live.

Sometimes, the uneasy balance between these different forces is dramatically upset: someone 'blows the whistle' – goes public on some practice they see as dishonest, illegal or unethical (see also Chapter 9, 'Infulence and Power'). The whistle-blower may reside within the corporate ranks, or be an outsider. Either way, the motive is the same: a deep disquiet about something that is going on in the organization that they regard as very wrong, so wrong that they are prepared to take on the organization in order to ensure that the malpractice is brought to public attention and prevented from recurring. Typically, whistle-blowers will act from an overriding sense of moral conscience, whatever the personal consequences. One whistle-blower speaks poignantly about what he saw his company doing to the natural environment:

It was amazing. Here we were dumping poison into the [environment] and nobody wanted to talk about it, as if talking about it would make it real. Well, it was real all right, but we went around pretending it wasn't. I thought I was going crazy. Like it wasn't happening. You think I'm some kind of hero 'cause I blew the whistle. The only reason I spoke up was because I didn't want to go crazy. I had to say what we were doing. (Alford, 2001: 13)

Because the personal risks are very high, there are not many whistle-blowers. Some whistle-blowers have strengthened and protected themselves by becoming organized as pressure groups. They act as watchdogs, sniffing out dubious or immoral organizational practice. In the 1960s, Ralph Nader started a consumer watch after he publicly exposed the American Ford Motor Company which was, it seemed, deliberately continuing production of a car they knew was liable to explode on impact. His style of work is reflected in the activities of many consumer associations across the world. Certain whistle-blowers focus their work in particular areas, such as Friends of the Earth, Greenpeace and Earth First! who make it their business to expose companies whose actions are harming the natural environment.

The status of whistle-blowers in broader society varies. Some are elevated to the level of hero or heroine when the cause they espouse has a strong, popular impact and the risks they take are high. Not surprisingly, they are seen rather differently by the enterprises they attack. If they are employees, they can be branded as traitors, as disloyal. Complaints based on moral grounds are often met by a wall of organizational defensiveness. The organization is keen to limit damage to its trade, regardless.

Big pressure groups, such as trade unions and consumer organizations, may be a reasonable match for large corporations in the conflict and legal slog which usually follows whistle-blowing, and there are now some specialist organizations which assist and protect individual whistle-blowers. On their own, though, individual employees are very vulnerable. Their intimate knowledge of the organization and its secrets poses an enormous threat to those who have profited from irregular practices, negligence or law breaking. Whistle-blowers are to be feared, and some corporations will go to extraordinary lengths to disable them. Robert Jackall (1988), an American anthropologist, tells the tale of Brady who worked for a major food-processing company:

REAL-LIFE EXAMPLE

Brady's Story

Brady, a conscientious Financial Officer (trained as a chartered accountant), noticed that a peer of his in marketing had overshot his budget, and had faked $75,000 of invoices to cover the discrepancy. He submitted a report on the matter to the CEO, but was dismayed to find the report blocked before it got to him. Brady was asked, several times, to drop the matter.

Gradually, he was frozen out of key decisions and his authority was cut back. Nevertheless, he stumbled across further, even larger, financial irregularities – the manipulation of pension funds which guaranteed large personal bonuses for top managers. Brady was deeply troubled and, for want of some access to the CEO, informed a friend in the company who had the CEO's ear. The information reached the CEO, without mentioning Brady's name. Immediately following a meeting between the CEO and his top aides, Brady's friend was fired and escorted from the building by armed guards.

Brady then realized that the CEO was part of the conspiracy, and took the matter to the corporation's chief lawyer who 'did not want to touch it with a barge pole'. Brady was advised by a senior manager to accept it as 'part of the game in business today.' He could not. He was summarily fired and ejected from the company building by a security guard.

This story poignantly characterizes the way an organization can evolve a 'working' morality to suit itself. Using **power** and fear, certain members can twist the professional conventions of business to serve their positions and greed. As fear and secrecy take hold, moral concerns give way to the pragmatics of 'keeping your nose clean', 'doing what you are told' and 'obeying orders'. As one manager in Jackall's study pithily asserts:

> What is right in the corporation is not what is right in a man's home or in his church. What is right in the corporation is what the guy above wants from you. That's what morality is in the corporation. (1988: 105-11)

It would be wrong to conclude that organizations inevitably sap the moral energy of those who work in them. However, we need to appreciate that in organizations as various as food processing, churches, steel manufacturing and schools, the most moral of citizens can gradually find themselves doing things that they never would have imagined they could – or should.

KEY POINTS

- Caring, upright, moral citizens can change dramatically when they arrive at work, breaking their personal moral codes.

- People's personal morality can be subverted by strong organizational norms.

- Organizations can invent their own brand of morality which may be in conflict with more conventional moral behaviour.

- Self-interest, the drive for profit and fear can induce individuals and corporations to harm others and the environment.

- Organizational humour can disguise acts such as harassment and abuse.

- Cheating, to some degree, is a part of most enterprises; it can be organizationally helpful as well as destructive.

- Whistle-blowers act as the organization's conscience and are often treated roughly for being so.

> > > > > > > > > > > > > **THEORETICAL SIGNPOSTS** > > > > > > > > > > > >

Moral issues in organizations are informed by three major conceptual areas:

> business ethics
> corporate governance
> power – its use and abuse.

Business Ethics

Morality is the subject matter of ethics, of which business ethics is a subset. Essentially, business ethics asks what is right or wrong, good or bad, in business practice. It is not without major controversies. At one extreme, there are forceful theorists such as Milton Friedman (1962), who argue that the very notion of business ethics is redundant, a distraction from the core 'ethic' of simply being left alone to make profits for shareholders. Indeed, Jackall (1988) and (MacIntyre, 1981) see managers working in a cut-and-thrust, self-serving world where the pragmatics of personal survival are all; moral concerns are left behind. Recent corporate scandals seem to fit this view, stimulating writers such as Sen (1991) to argue that businesses have to be checked and constrained by governments. But the stark portrait of the unethical manager has been countered by Watson (2003) and Fineman (1988, 1998) who reveal managers not as simple technocrats, slaves to market forces, but as actively struggling with the ethics of their actions. Even though they do not always get it right, and can get confused by the conflicting demands placed upon them, they are not 'morally mute' (Bird and Waters, 1989). Out of this debate has evolved a vibrant Corporate Social Responsibly (CSR) movement where ethical business practice is promoted, to include hiring and firing, non-discrimination, anti-bullying, anti-racist, pro-environmental and pro-community policies. CSR has been advocated by governments, academics and professional associations as ethically proper and good for business (Fisher and Lovell, 2003; HBR, 2003; Porter and Van der Linde, 1995; Room, 1997). Some firms, such as The Body Shop, Ben & Jerry's and Seventh Generation have taken to heart such values. In others, there has been a mixed response, especially in trying to reconcile conflicting stakeholder pressures (Carroll, 2004; Fineman and Clarke, 1996).

Corporate Governance

Cases of corporate maladministration in the early twenty-first century focused attention on how well, or poorly, organizations are formally governed by their senior managers. Corporate governance focuses on the rules and procedures by which those who run the organizations are accountable for their actions – in particular, on how the outside owners and shareholders (the 'principals') can ensure that managers and executives do not simply work for themselves and their own self-aggrandizement, but rather for all legitimate stakeholders (e.g. consumers, employees, communities, shareholders)

(Gourevitch and Shinn, 2005). Part of corporate governance is the establishment of ethics programmes, transparent structures on executive boards and the public disclosure of all major aspects of corporate performance. How corporate governance actually works in practice, though, is an intriguing question for organizational behavior theorists, especially in terms of the politics of board membership (Pye and Pettigrew, 2005; Solomon and Solomon, 2003), the networks of influence in and on corporate decision making (Ouchi, 1980), and how trust, affiliation, ties and transparency are 'managed' within and across organizations (Oliver, 2004).

Power – Its Use and Abuse

Power and powerlessness lie at the roots of individual and instutionalized discrimination, exploitation, harassment and greed (see Chapter 9, 'Influence and Power'). Coser (1974) wrote of 'greedy institutions' that take over more and more of an employee's commitment and values such that independent thought is relatively squashed in favour of the 'corporate line'. The organization's versions of morality are eventually received by workers uncritically, for good or ill. Alford (2001) and Rothschild and Miethe (1994) discuss how contests of power lie at the heart of whistle-blowing where the organization's practices are eventually challenged on ethical grounds. The use and abuse of power underpin gender politics and harassment in organizations (Lee, 2000; Wilson and Thompson, 2001) and are explored in some depth in Chapter 17 ('Sex').

REVIEW QUESTIONS

1. Why is it that some organizations appear to be morally mute? Does it matter?

2. How is power so central to unethical behaviour, such as harassment?

3. Would you ever blow the whistle on your organization? What, if anything, would prevent you?

---

companion
website
www.sagepub.co.uk/fineman

Reading On

The articles below are available for free to readers of the fourth edition of *Organizing & Organizations* via the book's companion website at www.sagepub.co.uk/fineman

Barker, R.A. (2002) 'An examination of organizational ethics', *Human Relations*, 55 (9): 1097–116.
This paper argues that explanations of organizational behavior that encompass conventional views of business ethics are overly simplistic and limited in their ability to provide constructive guidance for managers to understand and to manage moral problems in organizations. The guiding question is 'why do management effectiveness programmes rarely work?'

Chamberlain, L.J., Crowley, M., Tope, D. and Hodson, R. (2008) 'Sexual harassment in organizational context', *Work and Occupations*, 35 (3): 262–95.
This study sheds light on the organizational foundations of sexual harassment. The authors evaluated a theoretical model underscoring the influence of worker power, workplace culture, and gender composition using unique data derived from the population of English-language, book-length workplace ethnographies. The findings reveal that organizational attributes influence not only the presence of workplace sexual harassment but also the specific form in which it manifests.

Gini, A. (2004) 'Business, ethics, and leadership in a post Enron era', *Journal of Leadership and Organizational Studies*, 11 (1): 9–15.
Next to the Hippocratic Oath, the accounting profession claims the second oldest code of ethical standards, so how did Enron transform itself from one of America's paragons to one of its chief pariahs? This article explores what went wrong, and the implications for moral leadership and ethics as a body of knowledge.

Rothschild, J. and Miethe, T.D. (1999) 'Whistle-blower disclosures and management retaliation: the battle to control information about organization corruption', *Work and Occupations*, 26 (1): 107–28.
Based on nationwide data the authors collected on whistle-blowers and on silent observers, this article reports that whistle-blowing is more frequent in the public sector than in the private, that there are almost no sociodemographic characteristics that distinguish the whistle-blower from the silent observer, that whistle-blowers suffer severe retaliation from management, especially when their information proves significant; and that no special method of disclosure or personal characteristics can insulate the whistle-blower from such retaliation.

13

GREENING

This chapter examines the dilemmas, achievements and failures of industry in tackling the environmental damage that it causes. Industrial interests intersect with those of consumers, environmental scientists, governmental regulators and green pressure groups. Between them, the nature and extent of environmental damage and its protection are often contested. There are conflicting ideologies and perspectives leading to conflictual, politicized and now, often, negotiated responses. The power of various parties to influence environmental protection action, to block or facilitate it, is often unequal, but power can shift as environmental disputes unfold. The ingredients for cultivating greener organizational cultures are discussed.

Consider global warming, polluted seas and rivers, melting ice caps, flash floods, depleted rainforests, waste mountains, air that is difficult to breathe, loss of unique wildlife habitats. The second millennium has brought with it a bleak picture of the environmental costs of economic progress and industrialization. In satisfying our craving to produce and consume, we have, it seems, begun to erode the very basis of what sustains the planet. Are we now reaping the costs of our endless desire for the goods and services that we now regard as essential: the cars, fuels, aircraft, heating and cooling systems, lighting, plastics, chemicals, synthetic building materials and foodstuffs? Or is this all undue scaremongering, another one of history's many doom-laden, end-of-the-world prophecies that fails to come true, like nuclear Armageddon?

Somewhere in this, industrial organizations need to respond, because much of the blame, rightly or wrongly, is placed at their doorstep. Wrongly, in that environmental care is a part of a wider system of economic values, free market **ideology**, **consumption** and employment. Rightly, in that industry and its leaders invariably play some part in these processes. What, then, is it like for organizations that take environmental concerns seriously, via the green route? And how should we understand, and respond to, those who choose to ignore or evade their environmental responsibilities?

WHAT ENVIRONMENTAL DAMAGE?

There is a widespread belief that science can take us forward into new, exciting eras, as well as alerting us to emerging problems. So when hard science suggests that something is hazardous, polluting, toxic or destructive, then is the time to take immediate action. Furthermore, much damage we cannot see, so we have to trust science to alert us to its existence. That is the theory. But, by the end of the twentieth century, many of us were unsure of quite what to believe – what 'facts' were true? How much global warming is specifically due to industrial activity and what will really happen if the ice caps melt and the seas rise? *Will* they actually rise, and by how much? Losing various species of flora and fauna has been intrinsic to our planet's evolution, so why should we worry about current changes? What are the real risks? Biologists argued with other environmental scientists as well as with each other, and from time to time a consensus emerged – only to be challenged by another set of experts at a later date. We realized that scientific evidence is fast **politicized**, always filtered though the eyes of various interest groups.

Today, there are still disagreements, but now far less over the nature of the general trend: human action is very probably having an irreversible effect on the warming of the planet, especially from ever-increasing emissions of carbon dioxide. The burgeoning new economies of Asia and Eastern Europe add to the stress on the planet, while the old economies are not doing sufficient to curb their own emissions.

But sometimes it takes a crisis to define what is important, such as an explosion at a nuclear plant, a chemical fire, a massive oil spill at sea, a series of flash floods, or an uncontrollable forest fire consuming rare plants and animals. Then the **environmental** damage is clear, palpable. Public dismay is orchestrated by the media and, often, by political celebrities – such as Al Gore, Vice President of the United States under Bill Clinton. In 2006, Al Gore captured worldwide attention, and the following year a Nobel Peace Prize, with his engaging public presentations of 'An Inconvenient Truth'. It was a hard-hitting rendition on the dire effects of global warming, in which industry is complicit.

Opinion surveys continue to record our considerable concern about environmental pollution, especially climate change and the sustainability of the seas and forests. But few of us seem prepared to significantly modify our personal lifestyles to help out. Environmental degradation is still, in sociological terms, *contested terrain*. We rationalize it away, ignore the messages of Gore and his like, or make some small adjustments that feel good, but really sacrifice little of what we are accustomed to. Different interest groups – industry, green activists, governments, consumers – make their separate cases to shape perceptions of what is or is not an environmental problem. For example, it may well be to the commercial benefit of a chemical company to interpret damage or toxicity of their new fertilizer as 'not significant' while, for Friends of the Earth, just the opposite pertains. They have different partialities, or perceptual sets. Shell's attempt to sink one of its redundant oil-storage buoys, the Brent Spar, in the north Atlantic, well illustrates such differences.

In 1995, Shell UK announced publicly that, after careful technical analysis, they had decided that sinking the Brent Spar (see Figure 13.1), a huge structure, in the north Atlantic, would be a good method of disposal – and the best environmental one. They would slowly tow the buoy from its current moorings in the North Sea, to its burial

Figure 13.1   The Brent Spar storage buoy.

place at sea, off the west coast of Scotland. They had cleared it with the officially des-ignated parties, such as the British Government and Scottish Heritage, so the solution seemed decided. But it was not so. Greenpeace swung into action, claiming that Shell had no moral right to dump its unwanted rig in the sea – it set an appalling precedent. Moreover, the buoy still had a significant toxic-oil residue, which would add to any environmental damage.

Soon a media frenzy broke out, enveloping other Shell operating companies and galvanizing public protests, including boycotts of Shell filling stations. Shell UK reit-erated its technical arguments and hardened its stance. Meanwhile, various experts and scientists argued about the validity of its claims. Greenpeace suffered a temporary setback when it was revealed that they had over-estimated the amount of residue oil on the buoy. However, they insisted that their moral case was intact: the sea should not be used as a dumping ground; that is the route to environmental ruin.

Greenpeace boarded the Brent Spar and what resembled a naval battle ensued, under the full glare of the world's media. Greenpeace activists clung to the structure while an army of Shell security officials attempted, forcibly, to remove them. The David and Goliath impression proved highly damaging to Shell's image and Shell eventually capitulated. The Brent Spar would, instead, be sliced up to extend a quay in Norway and Shell entered a new era of consultation and public dialogue.

Politics

Here we see how environmental concerns are often highly **politicized**. They are beyond a simple technical fix, or single reading of what is the best solution. There are many views to reconcile, something that Shell had misjudged. Industrial environ-mental crises can reach in many directions and reverberate for communities and industry alike, many years after the event. For instance:

- In 2003, a court case opened in a small frontier town on the edge of the Amazon forest in Ecuador. Some 30,000 local people claimed that their lives and livelihoods were damaged by ChevronTexaco operations between 1964 and 1992. They argued that the company extracted 1.5 billion barrels of oil and systematically disposed of its oily waste in open, unlined pits which had leaked and contaminated water supplies. ChevronTexaco responded that they were simply doing what was acceptable at the time.

- Just after midnight on 24 March 1989, the oil tanker *Exxon Valdez* hit a reef in Alaska's Prince William Sound. Eleven million gallons of oil spewed into one of the most bountiful marine ecosystems, killing birds, marine mammals and fish. It devastated the ecosystem in the oil's path. To this day, continuing damage is observed, while local communities have yet to resolve compensation from Exxon, who were found to have been grossly negligent.

- Five years before *Exxon Valdez*, there was a lethal gas leak from the Union Carbide plant in Bhopal, India. It killed up to 8000 people within the first three days. After the disaster, Union Carbide abandoned the factory, leaving large quantities of toxic chemicals behind. To date, 20,000 people have died as a result of the disaster and exposure to a lethal cocktail of chemicals left in Bhopal. Many more are still suffering from incurable diseases. In 2001, Union Carbide merged with Dow Chemical. Dow-Carbide has refused to bear corporate liability for the gas disaster, and the event has been enshrined in the legends of corporate evasiveness and irresponsibility.

Taking Precautions

Given the long-term, often irreversible, effects of environmental damage, it is perhaps wiser to avoid the problem occurring in the first place. This is the *precautionary principle*: 'better safe than sorry'. The precautionary principle states that we should not wait for absolute proof of environmental damage before acting because it may then be too late, too costly, and anyhow absolute proof is often an unrealizable goal. So we should err on the side of caution, limiting the industrial processes that we think might cause ecological damage – even though we are not sure how much. The precautionary principle encourages changes, especially technological ones, along the whole spectrum of the design, manufacture and disposal of industrial goods and services. While it does not eliminate squabbles between different experts, it reflects a broader, pro-environment form of thinking. It moves away from crisis management and who is right or wrong in environmental debates and attempts to infuse green thinking into all our industrial processes 'from cradle to grave'.

The precautionary principle is often embraced by organizations that regard environmental responsibility as central to the **ethics** of their business. In the 1990s, especially, some of our major international corporations – oil, chemical, supermarkets, automotives, mining, fashion, power generation – appeared to take the green message very seriously. Various **stakeholders**, groups who had a special interest, or a stake, in the corporation's performance, helped them in that direction – citizens' groups, Greenpeace, Friends of the Earth, stockholders, banks, insurers, the media. As a consequence, their mission statements became reassuring, such as:

> Protecting the earth and its natural resources is indeed one of the most critical issues facing mankind. As a concerned corporate citizen and a manufacturer of automotive products that have environmental impacts, we are supportive of initiatives that have a positive effect on the environment.

Or:

> Environmental protection is a primary management responsibility as well as the responsibility of every employee here. Our concern for the environment extends beyond the fence lines of our chemical-producing facilities and into the communities in which we live and work.

These statements suggest a green organizational **culture** where the environment is part of all key organizational **decisions**, because it has become proper and ethical to do so. Such companies will conduct environmental audits of their own and, sometimes, their suppliers' activities – on production, waste, energy, recycling, land use and so forth. Some will engage in carbon offset schemes to compensate for their own carbon dioxide emissions. They create departments with special responsibility for environmental management. They will also seek national or international accreditation for their green efforts. Recent corporate leaders include Marks & Spencer who pledge a 'Plan A' – with no alternative Plan B:

ABOUT PLAN A

Plan A is our five-year, 100-point 'eco' plan to tackle some of the biggest challenges facing our business and our world. It will see us working with our customers and our suppliers to combat climate change, reduce waste, safeguard natural resources, trade ethically and build a healthier nation.
We're doing this because it's what you want us to do. It's also the right thing to do. We're calling it Plan A because we believe it's now the only way to do business.
  There is no Plan B.[1]

Running a business as green can create particular competitive advantage by attracting green consumers, hence firms such as The Body Shop, Natural Step, B&Q and the Co-operative Bank claim to make a positive environmental policy pay. Some of them subscribe to Fair Trade principles (see Chapter 8, 'Politics and Deals'). These encourage producers to engage in environmentally friendly practices which manage local resources sustainably. Typically, Fair Trade members work directly with producers to develop products based on the sustainable use of their natural resources, giving communities an incentive to preserve their natural environments for future generations.

  Such moves offer a decidedly brighter picture of industry than that associated with belching smokestacks, arid landscapes and greedy entrepreneurs. But is this the 'fix'? Unfortunately, self-proclaimed ethical corporations have still been responsible for leakages of nuclear waste, oil pollution, chemical explosions and deforestation. It is notoriously difficult to find out what a company has actually done or failed to do, except when things go dramatically wrong. Some companies do offer accounts of environmental accidents and improvements in their annual reports, but these are often brief and do not go beyond the minimum legal requirements. However, the most progressive sectors of industry realize that, in the long term, there are benefits from full transparency.

NEGOTIATING THE ENVIRONMENT

Imagine a smart, panelled boardroom. You are inside the headquarters of the truck division of a worldwide automotive corporation which boasts of its advanced environmental policy. Around the large table sit seven senior managers from different functions and an external environmental consultant. The meeting is chaired by the manager from corporate environmental affairs …

REAL-LIFE EXAMPLE

The mood of the meeting is cool; there is little sense of urgency. The agenda is a long one. The first item is about entering a national environmental award competition. The chairman says: 'we have no choice but to enter this one'. The meeting struggles for some 30 minutes. What could they offer? The new tyres? The energy saving in the plant? Nothing feels right, or is sufficiently outstanding to boast about. The item fizzles out.

A new agenda item: the consultant delivers his specially commissioned environmental audit to the group. Everyone is now faced with what to do with the long, neat list of 'actions required'. People look glum. There is a fair amount of ducking and weaving around the table before the Chairman begins mechanically to tick off the jobs and allocate them to each manager around the table. The Production Manager suddenly springs to life, slightly panicky. He rummages in his briefcase and produces various environmental action forms and other bits of paper. He had been busy, he said. We should appreciate that.

Another agenda item: plastic cups. The mood gets excited and it turns out to be the emotional high spot of the morning. How can they prevent people taking two plastic cups from the drinks machine to stop burning their hands? There are reusable cup holders provided, but people keep throwing them away. And how about recycling the cups? People clearly enjoy this item and the debate is prolonged, animated and sometimes humorous. No solution is found.

Final item: beautifying the work's grounds and physical environment. The Chairman waves a brochure from the Groundwork Action Trust, a charitable organization devoted to working with industry to improve their sites. 'They have approached us before', says the Chairman. 'Maybe the time's right to do something …' The room is silent. After a while, the Chairman fills the uncomfortable vacuum. 'Mmm … planting trees and all that; not sure we're equipped to get involved with that sort of rubbish.' The item is dropped and the meeting closed.

Real-Life Example

This is an actual event. Here, the environment is condensed into 'items' to deal with in a **bureaucratic** fashion. Other than the plastic cups issue, there is little passion or enthusiasm to the meeting. The trucks themselves hardly get a mention and protecting the planet is, seemingly, remote from people's thinking. This is a kind of 'greenwashing', looking green on the outside but rather greyer on the inside. Why? Do the managers simply not care? Maybe not. Can they not try a bit harder? Perhaps. But the most likely explanation lies in the way that technical responsibilities in organizations tend to displace wider **moral** concerns (see Chapter 12, 'Morals'). For the corporate manager, the natural environment is both everywhere and nowhere. In a busy, pressurized work life, the meaning of carbon dioxide levels in the atmosphere or even traffic pollution seem fairly irrelevant, certainly distant – unless there is an irresistible compulsion to act.

The environmental damage caused by a company's overseas operations can easily fall victim to selective **perception**, that is, not be seen. It is sometimes hard for a manager, or other worker, to connect his or her relatively self-contained position inside the organization with wider responsibilities to the environment 'outside'. The job of meeting production deadlines, sorting out sales targets and, ultimately, making profits, is all, and it is in these areas that the employee is individually judged. So environmental demands are seen, at best, as a nuisance, at worst, as a threat. In this manner, the organization can be regarded as something of a psychic prison, entrapping its members in a particular way of thinking and feeling. The environmental director of another automotive manufacturer summed it up bluntly:

> It's all about 'can we afford it?', 'What will it give us in return?', 'How long will we have to wait?', 'Any competitive advantage?' No fine moral sentiments in this.

The **ethics** of business, in this view, is primarily to compete and to make profits and the natural environment has to take its place accordingly. Pro-environmental policies are OK as long as they deliver direct profit.

SHALLOW GREEN, DEEP GREEN

Organizations such as Patagonia, Seventh Generation, Timberland and The Body Shop are often lauded as the acceptable face of capitalism, where environmental care, consumerism and profits can comfortably co-exist. And this is exactly where the problem lies, according to deep-green critics of industry. It is false, they argue, to believe that making products and services greener solves our environmental problems. At best, it slows down the *Titanic* rather than changing its course. The crucial challenge is to the belief that progress is an ever-increasing gross national product, and that happiness is the accumulation of evermore material goods. It is a view that gained prominence at the end of the first decade of the twenty-first century, but not for ethical reasons. It was a period of recession, a reality check for those who could no longer liberally consume.

Eco-**feminists** have a distinctive view here, speaking from a less controlling, more nurturing perspective on organizing. They stress that preserving nature is more than reducing industrial pollution. All natural entities deserve to be valued in their own right, not just in terms of what they deliver to us. This means respecting that all associations between the environment, nature and humans are one, in a holistic relationship. Since the

1970s, the influential physicist and environmentalist, James Lovelock, has been proclaiming this very notion in his 'Gaia Principle': that we and our planet are intimately connected. Having ignored this crucial principle, using the planet as if it is an infinite resource, the planet is now taking its revenge.

The alternatives proposed by critics of our current economic system vary from a radical re-appraisal and transformation of our **values** and lifestyles, to a reform of the instruments by which we judge economic success. This latter approach takes issue with economic indices such as gross national product (GNP). GNP is a conventional mark of a nation's prosperity – the sum of the values of all the produced goods, services and labour of a nation's economic activities, *regardless of their particular purpose or ends*. So into the GNP calculation goes the money value of the labour and materials involved in checking or repairing the effects of pollution and environmental damage (e.g. flood protection, rescue services, insurance, fire fighting, hospital treatment, re-building, policing, ecological care, pollution control). Also included is the work involved in caring for those who suffer **stress** or **unemployment** in our industrial systems. But if, instead, all such activities were regarded as the costs of industrial growth – the downside – then the curve of progress looks substantially less attractive. Some economies seem to be moving in reverse, environmentally in ever-increasing debt.

Protests

Once environmental concerns were expressed by just fringe members of society, 'awkward' critics of the establishment. Now such voices are apparent across the political and social class spectrum.

In the USA, Canada, Europe and beyond, there have been citizens' protests against road projects, airports, housing developments, nuclear power, dams and other activities that are seen to damage the environment, or to create more environmental problems than they solve. Some of these protests have been remarkable in that they represent temporary organizations of very different people, held together by a common cause. Their specific **motives** vary though. Some are NIMBYs (Not In My Back Yard). They object to local environmental changes which adversely affect their own lives, but are less fussed when it happens elsewhere. Others are more deeply committed to preventing environmental despoliation (as they see it) anywhere. They might lash themselves to trees or burrow underground, confidently face TV cameras and give press interviews. **Leadership** is often emergent, sometimes charismatic, as certain people take control of events or tasks as and when it seems appropriate.

To a casual observer, such settings can appear disorganized, even chaotic, but the shared purpose and mutual enemy often create sufficient cohesion to mobilize people's efforts in a similar direction. Other protests rely on organizations that also have a very mixed membership, but have a much clearer, more formal, core structure. Friends of the Earth and Greenpeace, for example, are now international organizations with paid officers, including experts in environmental matters and media relations. Also, like other large organizations, they have their splits and dissentions about who does what, and in particular the choice of target for the next campaign. These organizations are dependent on voluntary **labour** as well as donations, so their resources are always somewhat precarious.

How have industrial organizations responded to these pressures?

KEEPING AWAY THE GREEN FOE

> Why on earth should we be driven by a particular group that shouts the loudest? [thumps his desk] Who do they think they are? Well, they're not going to have my scalp. I'm certainly not going to make strong environmental claims for anything.

This is a corporate director of a major supermarket, and no friend of the green movement. He felt his autonomy and role profoundly compromised, and lashed out in anger. Essentially, he was deaf to their arguments and liked even less the unorthodox ways they were sometimes expressed, such as 'throwing blood over frozen fish'. Another supermarket director makes a similar point:

> I'm sure the hundreds of letters I've had in here aren't written by our customers, but campaigners from these [green] organizations. If they were our customers I'd be really impressed. We can't be seen to buckle to that sort of pressure!

Such bullish responses are becoming less common, but can be regarded as understandable in an industrial sector that is exposed to much public scrutiny. Traditionally, supermarkets have been more concerned with what sells fast rather than what ought to sell on ethical criteria. The reactions do, however, illuminate how the **emotionality** of responses can be extremely important in shaping organizational behaviour. Pressure from green activists has traditionally not been welcomed by industry, although some sectors are now accepting it, even incorporating it into their strategy deliberations. A site manager of a large chemical firm makes the point:

> They've brought to us and to the public all the problems that are out there. There's no doubt that you can't just go on digging holes in the ground and throwing stuff in it and pretending it doesn't exist. From that point of view they've done a good job.

As the various green organizations – from 'eco warriors' and local citizens' groups to national and international organizations (such as National England and World Wildlife Fund for Nature (WWF)) – have mustered their influence, they can, and do, embarrass organizations. For this reason alone, they cannot be entirely ignored by industry. They are able publicly to expose environmental performance or transgressions that some organizations would prefer to hide. Bad public relations are bad for business even if, as the target industry or organization often claims, the accusations are exaggerated or simply wrong.

Some companies have tried to head off the attention of green pressure groups by launching their own green publicity in advance. Others have attempted to discredit their efforts by demonstrating the inaccuracy of their accusations. Still others have managed to gain green kudos by bringing 'the enemy' on board: recruiting high-profile environmentalists onto their own environmental campaigns. But some powerful corporations,

Figure 13.2   Saving the planet.

Concept: Mike Adams. www.NaturalNews.com

resenting any incursion by environmental pressure groups, have chosen to fight their corner more aggressively. One approach has been to hire global public relations firms to promote anti-environmentalist images, portraying environmentalists as, for instance, religious fanatics, anti-American even (and ironically) as destroyers of civilization. One US public relations company, John Davies Communications, can undertake such work:

> John Davies helps neutralize [green protesters] on behalf of corporate clients including Mobil Oil, Hyatt Hotels, Exxon, American Express and Pacific Gas and Electric.

Davies describes himself as 'one of America's premier grassroots consultants', and once ran a full-colour advertisement designed to strike terror into the heart of the bravest CEO. It contains a photo of the 'enemy' – literally a 'little white-haired old lady', holding a hand-lettered sign that reads, 'Not In My Backyard!' A caption imprinted over the photo says, 'Don't leave your future in her hands'. 'Traditional lobbying is no longer enough … To outnumber your opponents call Davies Communications' (Stauber and Rampton, 1995: 89).

Efforts such as these underline some of the value conflicts as industry faces pressures to be greener. What is construed by environmental groups as obviously good is seen by some industries as a threat to their business, their freedom and their very being. When the ideological battle lines are so drawn, the rules of the game are not always fair and clean.

LEGISLATING GREEN CHANGE

There are other pro-environmental forces on industry, in addition to green pressure groups. When industry fails to protect the environment, the law can step in. Environmental protection is now a feature of national and international legislation. It obliges industry to take certain measures to ensure its processes do not pollute the atmosphere, land or water – a formal application of the precautionary principle. It contains directives on the storage and disposal of waste, on recycling and on packaging. It has special provisions for very toxic chemicals and nuclear waste. Environmental law is interpreted and administered by special regulators, such as the Environment Agency in the UK and the Environmental Protection Agency in the USA. These are substantial organizations. The US Environmental Protection Agency employs some 17,000 people. The Environment Agency has over 10,000 environmental specialists and managers deployed in offices throughout England and Wales. Agency inspectors visit industry and grant permits to operate processes if the company meets the required environmental standards. If they do not, the inspector has the power to prosecute the company.

Typically, most companies take the regulator seriously. If environmental groups can embarrass a company, so can the regulator. But regulators also have the power to inflict financial and reputational damage; consequently, most 'environmental' boardroom time will be devoted to handling regulation and its demands. In the UK, this turns out to be less straightforward than it might appear. Managers treat environmental regulation as a **negotiated** and **political** process: the regulator presses for more changes while the regulated try to minimize their costs. A production manager in car manufacturing describes his side of events:

> The inspector from the Agency comes in. It's obvious where she stands. She takes the view that big, multinational corporations like us have the money and she'll insist that we spend it on controlling pollution emissions from our chimneys. I say that we're probably the highest ratepayers in the county and we employ 1000 people and they need to realize what they're playing with. It might well be that this company decides it's not worth the gamble. She doesn't believe that, but I do.

From the inspector's point of view, it's a balancing act, as one explained:

> It's how can I push him to do as much as possible? You can turn the regulatory screw and make life hell for them, but that's rarely necessary. It requires sitting down and talking; chats over lunch.

Large firms, especially, employ their own experts to try and outfox or outgun the regulator. In the UK, in particular, environmental standards are contested and much re-shaped through informal discussions behind closed doors (the US approach is more open and litigious). On the whole, regulation increases pollution control, which is good news for the environment. But there is a danger that when the regulator and the regulated get too close to one another, there can be a mutual capture that dilutes the regulator's power and, ultimately, environmental protection.

ECO-CENTRED OR EGO-CENTRED?

As noted earlier, the sober reality of the present state of greening is that while we, as citizens, may express our worries about environmental degradation – ours and others' – few of us are prepared to forgo the many apparent benefits of industrialized society, or contemplate alternatives: to leave our cars at home, cycle, walk, buy less, own less, accumulate less, live more simply, be less like slaves to fashion, use local produce, conserve energy rather than burn it, use aircraft less, work more from home and so on. Many people will now pay lip service to some of these notions, but continue doing what they have always done.

This cannot be blamed simply on our moral weakness or short-sightedness. We, ourselves, are the products of societies where self-interest and materialism dominate as positive values in national and international relations. In this way, we are caged by what we have all helped to create. The influential economist, Milton Friedman, has stated that it is not for businesses to take on any responsibilities other than looking after themselves by making money and accumulating wealth, a creed that has been especially influential in the USA and Britain. In other words, making profit *is* being socially responsible and that is all a company has to consider in order to discharge its civic duty (see Chapter 12, 'Morals'). Greed is good. Critics of this view point to the near collapse of the world's banking system in 2008, requiring massive state support, as the final nail in the coffin of Freidman's free-market philosophy. But his supporters note, paradoxically, that greed can sometimes end up being good for the environment because it produces the wealth to fund environmental clean-ups. There is some truth, as well as perversity, in this perspective. Technological know-how in pollution abatement and investment in special equipment is costly and affordable only by rich countries or industries.

On the other hand, many ecologists argue that industrialization has created, and continues to create, irreversible damage and losses, sometimes far from the original source of pollution and distant from corporate headquarters. Indeed, there are many countries that have serviced foreign powers or industries, helping them get rich while shouldering the bulk of the environmental costs. Such was the accusation made to Shell in the 1990s for despoiling land in Nigeria during their oil operations. The local communities protested loudly – and continue to do so. There are persistent, often sophisticated, armed attacks against Shell installations and employees in the region, while Shell in the West makes much of its green credentials.

When the green agenda and business agenda coincide, it is money and profit that links them, not altruism. If greening pays, or can be made to pay, then it fits well with the dominant logic of business. If it provides **competitive** advantage, then that is even better for some business. Environmentalism becomes a tool to displace a competitor to gain more power and control. For this reason, some firms have welcomed regulation because they have the resources to comply, or to go beyond compliance, while their less wealthy competitors cannot do so. It is not a scenario that comforts the deep greens; it is 'more of the same', a reinforcement of the economic structures that caused the problem in the first place. But a dilemma for some environmentalists is whether to work with industry or against it. To work with industry mostly ends up with light greening or greenwashing, with industry calling much of the tune. To work against industry can invite a harsh backlash.

BUSINESS – AS USUAL?

Meanwhile, back in the boardrooms and side offices of industry, the environment is treated with more or less seriousness according to its perceived business benefit. Perhaps unsurprisingly, we find small, cash-starved enterprises claiming to have problems enough without worrying about the environment. For some of them, avoiding the costs of environmental protection makes a lot of business sense. There is a twilight zone where, for example, the illegal disposal of waste flourishes, with truckloads of garbage and industrial residue tipped into remote country lanes, ponds, canals and rivers. Indeed, as the regulation of waste disposal has become tighter and more expensive for industry – in order to encourage recycling and waste minimization – the extent of illegal dumping has increased.

Greening has also spawned its own industry of officials and services. Apart from regulatory agents, we have many environmental consultants content to ride the 'green boom', offering services ranging from environmental audits to specialist technical advice on pollution control. As the legal penalties for environmental damage have increased, some industries have taken greening predominately to be a legal challenge, to fight it in the courts. This has created a new breed of lawyers, experts in environmental law able to defend (or prosecute) industry. The company lawyer has now become a prominent person in shaping an organization's environmental strategy.

We are still a long way from radical changes in organizations towards greening and many companies are still reluctant to take environmental damage seriously, especially when it is not in their own backyard. Yet, more optimistically, much can be achieved within the current system. The recipe for success, organizationally, seems to be a combination of: firm external regulation; a sincere green champion at the top of the organization; green structures and training throughout the organization; green considerations in all major functional policies; and regular auditing of progress. As citizens and consumers we, also, have a role. What we buy (or do not buy), what we preserve, how we travel, where we invest our money, the environmental groups we join and what we protest about, can all make a difference. Living our lives according to the precautionary principle and perhaps more holistically makes sound environmental sense. Together with economic incentives that push industry down an environmental path, it is perhaps the best chance we have currently of leaving our planet in reasonable shape for our children – and theirs.

KEY POINTS

o What constitutes environmental damage is not straightforward; it is contested terrain.

o There are different stakeholders who have an interest in, or claim on, industry's environmental performance.

o Environmental protection can be viewed as a technical or ethical issue. Some firms make strong ethical claims which do not always survive close scrutiny.

o Often, corporate environmentalism amounts to relative minor shifts in work practices rather than major green cultural transformations.

o Legislation, forcing green organizational change, is often the most potent force.

o Powerful industries most threatened by green pressures have tried to undermine the efforts of environmental groups.

o Creating a green organizational culture requires commitment from the top of the organization as well as structures at all levels to promote green beliefs and practices.

> > > > > > > > > > > **THEORETICAL SIGNPOSTS** > > > > > > > > > > > >

The greening of organizations can be explored from a variety of different perspectives, but most important for this chapter are:

> the philosophy of an organization's place in environmental protection
> the politics of environmental damage and action
> greening organizational culture.

The Philosophy of an Organization's Place in Environmental Protection

At the heart of this debate is whether a capitalist culture, the raison d'être of which is to exploit natural resources for wealth creation, can possibly be truly green and sustainable. Writers such as Lovelock (1979), O'Riordan (1981) and Schumacher (1973) raise major concerns over this possibility, arguing that planetary sustainability and raw capitalism cannot co-exist. Diamond (2005) draws on historical cases to show how once stable communities sank into a vicious circle of environmental degradation and conflict as their natural resources were plundered or radically re-engineered – a picture that chimes with the damage to indigenous communities today following indiscriminate deforestation or the re-routing of seas or rivers. Key debates over the depth of greening possible in a consumerist culture, and their ethical implications, are addressed by Curry (2005) and Carroll (2004), while writers such as Welford (1995) and Shrivastava (1995) have tried to reconcile the tensions between capitalism and greening to demonstrate that, with some radical changes, sustainability in organizations is indeed possible.

The Politics of Environmental Damage and Action

The complexity of appraising environmental damage is discussed by Hannigan (2006). He draws attention to *who* makes environmental claims, how they are popularized and what authority is attributed to them, particularly claims by scientists, politicians and environmental groups. Underpinning such debates is Ulrich Beck's (1992) influential notion that we all live in a 'risk society' and we face particular challenges. How are we to define those risks? How we might mitigate them? And how, ultimately, can we live with them? The politics of organizational action involves dealing with the influence of external stakeholders. Their role and integration into organizational practice is discussed by Madsen and Ulhøi (2001). For some observers, the Brent Spar case holds special lessons for more effective stakeholder management (Löfstedt and Ortwin, 1997; Zyglidopoulos, 2002). The significant, but politically complex, way that external regulators work with and on organizations is elaborated by Fineman (2000a, b) and by Hanf (1993), including why some firms choose to go beyond minimum compliance standards while others resist (see Fineman and Clarke, 1996; Pinkse, 2007; Prakash, 2001).

Greening Organizational Culture

This feature of greening draws on a view of organizational culture as comprising different levels of meaning and practice – from surface symbols and artefacts to deeper values and beliefs (see Frost et al., 1985; Schein, 1996). The trend amongst writers on the greening of organizational culture is that 'end of pipe' ventures – such as preventing the toxins from a polluting manufacturing process from entering the atmosphere or a water course – are a start, or technical fix. However, they fail to address the deeper values of an organization's culture, essential for addressing the whole life-cycle of commerce, from 'cradle to grave', in a sustained and sustainable way (Harris and Crane, 2002; Room, 1997). It is what Shrivastava (1995) has termed ecocentric management, where ecological values and considerations are built into the very conception of a product or process, and thereafter into all aspects of its design, production, marketing, sales, consumption and recycled disposal. It requires strong green values throughout the organization (Bansal and Howard, 1997; McDonagh and Prothero, 1997). Ecocentric management aligns with a 'triple bottom line' culture which aims to balance social, economic and financial considerations (Henriques and Richardson, 2004). Achieving this ethos is not easy, but there are now exemplars in different industrial sectors – such as furniture, clothing, cosmetics, coffee and computers – that have moved significantly in this direction (see Arena, 2004; Saviz and Weber, 2006).

REVIEW QUESTIONS

1. How can a capitalist system *not* undermine the natural capital on which it ultimately depends?

2. What kind of organizational leadership can create greener organizational cultures? Is it sustainable?

3. Consider the value of the stakeholder approach to environmental management. What is *your* stake?

NOTE

1. See http://plana.marksandspencer.com/?action=PublicAboutDisplay

Reading On

The articles below are available for free to readers of the fourth edition of *Organizing & Organizations* via the book's companion website at www.sagepub.co.uk/fineman

Etzion, D. (2007) 'Research on organizations and the natural environment, 1992–present: a review', *Journal of Management*, 33 (4): 637–64.
This article reviews the literature on organizations and the natural environment published since 1992, with the purpose of determining if and what the contributions have been to strategy and organizational theory. The author performs the review at three levels – firm, industry, and organizational environment, and subsequently discusses empirical and conceptual constraints on the production of quality research.

Fineman, S. (2001) 'Fashioning the environment', *Organization*, 8 (1): 17–31.
Should we regard 'greening' as a management fashion? While green concerns are prevalent in political and industrial rhetoric, how is greening made to appear attractive and productive to organizational actors who plainly feel just the opposite? This paper explores the social and emotional architecture of greening, and its tensions and contradictions. The analysis shows that, despite a strong societal surge towards greening, it can often appear neither attractive nor rational to industry – yet it is adopted, or presented, in some form.

Hood, C. and Rothstein, H. (2001) 'Risk regulation under pressure: problem solving or blame shifting?', *Administration Society*, 33 (1): 21–53.
This article explores a style-phase model of staged organizational responses to external pressure for change against two competing hypotheses, focusing on demands for greater openness and transparency. A study of six risk regulation regimes in the United Kingdom revealed that only half were exposed to substantial pressures of this type. Response of

organizations in the 'high-pressure' regimes were varied, but the overall pattern was consistent with a mixture of an autopoietic and staged-respose hypothesis stressing blame prevention.

Roome, N. and Wijen, F. (2006) 'Stakeholder power and organizational learning in corporate environmental management', *Organization Studies*, 27 (2): 235–63.
The literatures on stakeholder engagement by companies and organizational learning give little consideration to the power (or influence) of stakeholders to affect the process or content of organizational learning. This paper seeks to address these omissions, examining how and why stakeholder power and organizational learning interact, drawing on comparative case studies of the environmental management practices found in two major companies.

14

MACHINES AND ROUTINES

We live in an era of great technological innovations. Technology, whether in the area of electronics, medicine, communications or farming is often viewed as generating unprecedented prosperity to ever-increasing numbers of people. But technology also creates risks, often failing to fulfil its promises, leading instead to all kinds of unexpected problems – unemployment, pollution, surveillance, violence, climate change and so forth. In this chapter, we examine technology and its role in organizing and organizations; we examine some of the possibilities and threats that it creates for managers and other members of organizations. Technology, we argue, is not just about tools and machines but involves recipes, techniques and know-how. Technology has been a motive force of capitalist development, but often at the expense of worker deskilling, alienating jobs and unemployment. Technology, and especially information technology, also creates strong dependency; we become unable to function without mechanical or electronic props. We examine some of the meanings that machines and technology have in our lives and some of the emotions they stir up.

Man is a tool-using animal; without tools he is nothing, with tools he is all. (Carlyle)

REAL-LIFE EXAMPLE

K woke up with a start; his alarm had not gone off. K looked at it accusingly and noticed that both hands were rigidly stuck on 12 o'clock. He jumped out of bed looking at his watch, but that too had stopped at 12 o'clock. He dressed himself in haste, remembering that he had an important work appointment that morning. He picked up the phone, thinking of suitable excuses, but it was dead. Over the next few minutes, K realized with rising frustration that his electric razor, the kettle, the radio, the TV, the fridge and all the machines in the house were not working. He slammed the front door and left his flat. As the door smashed shut, it set off the burglar alarm, whose shrill monotone pierced his skull. He woke up for real this time, the alarm buzzing noisily.

Life without machines has become inconceivable. Our age has been described as 'The Age of the Machine'. Machines dominate our physical landscape, they **control** our daily routines and affect every moment of our lives. Machines have enabled us to fulfil some of the oldest dreams of our species and have given us powers which our ancestors reserved for gods. With the help of aeroplanes, we can fly, while telephones help us to communicate across vast distances, and the internet provides huge amounts of information at our fingertips. Jupiter's thunders look rather tame in competition with the weaponry available to today's warriors and Vulcan's magic bellows are pathetic compared with the robots that fill modern factories.

Alongside these visible, physical machines, there are wider social forces heading towards mechanization and routinization. Machines bring a repetitive orderliness to physical and mechanical tasks, and procedures and systems in organizations seek to do the same for other tasks. The internal mail system in an organization tries to treat pieces of paper and objects in as predictable and orderly a fashion as the way a telephone treats speech. With its regular collection times, its rules about what will and what will not be carried, and its defined collection and delivery points, it attempts a similar level of efficiency to a machine by accepting similar limitations. In this respect, it is a machine, even though it does not involve mechanical or electronic components, and as such it is relatively easy to replace with another machine, such as electronic mail. At a personal level, organizing may be done with the aid of time management systems (a way of mechanizing time allocation). The appeal of the filofax and the PDA is that they offer some mechanization for difficult tasks that can be expected to require judgement and care.

HOW MACHINES MADE THE TWENTIETH CENTURY

There are three primary purposes that we hope machines and tools will fulfil for us: to protect us against our natural environment; to help us control it and profit from its resources; and to make our lives easier. Think of any domestic appliance: a dishwasher eliminates the tedium of washing up, a refrigerator extends the life of food, a microwave oven speeds up and simplifies cooking. Advertisers emphasize the labour-saving qualities of domestic machines, keen to portray the consumer as freed by their latest offering and able to pursue other, more pleasurable interests.

Not for nothing has our species been called 'a tool-making animal', an animal who seeks to fulfil needs not only directly by taking what nature offers, but also by using nature's own resources to control her. Control over fire gave people some measure of control over the temperature of their ambient environment and opened the way towards control over metals, clay and glass. The water mill, invented in the first century BC, made the grinding of corn immeasurably easier, offering welcome relief for women (and especially slaves) who had spent most of the day grinding with pestle and mortar to provide for their families and masters. 'Stop grinding, you women who toil at the mill', wrote Antipater of Thessalonika in a poem dating from that time.

> Sleep late, even if the crowing cocks announce the dawn. For Demeter has ordered the water Nymphs to perform the work of your hands, and they turn the axle which, with its revolving spokes turns the heavy Nisyrian millstones. We taste again the joys of primitive life, learning to feast on the products of the earth without labour.

Since the early days of humanity, however, machines have served another, less edifying purpose. This is illustrated in an early sequence of the classic film *2001: A Space Odyssey*, when the chiefs of two primitive tribes are about to attack each other. Suddenly, one of them focuses on a bleached thigh bone lying nearby, his face lights up, he grabs it and proceeds to beat his opponent senseless with it. A primitive instrument of war to be sure, but it proves to be an effective one under the circumstances.

As the ancestor of intercontinental ballistic missiles and nuclear submarines, the thigh bone sums up two important features of **technology**. First, it shows how a part of nature, something lying out there, is transformed into a tool through the power of an idea; it is the idea, eventually crystallized into know-how, which turns inert matter into technology. Second, the thigh bone underlines the fact that fighting and the domination of one's fellow human beings is a mother of invention, on a par with economic necessity and the desire to dominate nature. War has spawned many new tools, new machines and new technologies. From the primitives' poisoned arrows to Archimedes' catapults and mirrors, and from Leonardo's prototype machine gun to twentieth-century developments in explosives, poison gas, nuclear and other technologies, warfare and destruction have acted as a stimulant of human technological genius.

Machines do not just help us go about our business, in peace or war. They also define our business. They shape not only our physical but also our social and psychological world. The lift, invented in the 1880s, did not just help people get from floor to floor; it genuinely revolutionized architecture by paving the way towards 'vertical living', culminating in the skyscrapers of Manhattan. The lift created new opportunities not only for those living in vertical buildings but also for those seeking to undermine or destroy them. It was, along with the aircraft, one of the machines which enabled the attacks on Manhattan of 11 September 2001 to take place, revealing new risks and vulnerabilities. Maybe the biggest change engendered by these attacks was psychological: much of the previous understanding of security had been based on the assumption that people would not be prepared to kill themselves to achieve their goals, and breaking this assumption was crucial to the attacks.

If the lift was a major breakthrough in dominating vertical space, a machine, dating from the thirteenth century, whose central feature is a perfectly steady rotation of one or two mechanical hands around a central pivot, has revolutionized our perception of time. The clock, whose failure started off K's nightmare, arose initially from the needs for time-keeping in medieval monasteries. The clock was not merely a means of keeping time, but a means of synchronizing people's actions. The marking of hours and, from the seventeenth century, of minutes and seconds, turned people into time-keepers, time-savers and eventually time-servers (Mumford, 1934).

In the Factory

It is not accidental that the mechanical clock, and the time-keeping and time-saving consciousness which accompanied it, emerged just as the growing European cities were calling for orderly routines. Neither is it an accident that it found its place of honour as the only 'decorative' item to grace the interiors of Victorian factories. In the factory, time is money: it is against the ticking seconds on the clock that work, machines, outputs and money are counted.

Figure 14.1   Early factory in Manchester.

Not everyone liked this. In the 1810s, the Luddites, bands of workers who saw their livelihoods ruined as traditional cottage industries were swept aside by manufacture, had roamed the manufacturing areas of England breaking machines and destroying factories. A hundred years later, French railway workers bequeathed the term 'sabotage' as they removed the shoes (sabots) holding the railway lines.

Philosophers too expressed profound reservations about machines. John Stuart Mill wrote: 'it is questionable if all the mechanical inventions have lightened the day's toil for any human being'. Instead of more leisure time for all, manufacture brought forced unemployment. Moreover, workers found that their role was to serve the machine, feed it with raw material, remove its product, always at the pace set by the machine, on the terms of the machine. 'The machine unmakes the man. Now that the machine is so perfect, the engineer is nobody', wrote Ralph Waldo Emerson.

With the rise of machines, production was detached from the **skills** and ingenuity of individual workers. The intelligence and craft which had hitherto resided in the operator was now incorporated in the mechanical process. The worker found that his or her specifically human qualities and creative capacities were no longer required.

Owing to the extensive use of machinery and to division of labour, the work of the proletarians has lost all individual character, and consequently, all charm for the workman. He becomes an appendage of the machine, and it is only the most simple, most monotonous, and most easily acquired knack, that is required of him. (Marx and Engels, 1848/1972: 479)

Figure 14.2 Luddites smashing machinery.

MECHANIZING MANAGEMENT

While industrial machinery had already revolutionized production, a new manage-ment movement emerged in the early decades of the twentieth century, known as '**scientific management**'. Its chief exponent was F.W. 'Speedy' Taylor and its greatest achievement was the 'supramachine', Henry Ford's assembly line.

Taylor argued that managers had been unsystematic in their approach to produc-tion. Maximizing efficiency and rationalizing production was the proper task of man-agement, and ought to be done in a scientific way. Taylor proposed his principles of scientific management which included:

- Remove all brain work from the shop floor; managers must plan and organize production and limit the worker to the task of implementation – 'We are not paying you to think'.
- Standardize products, parts and production methods. Scientific methods should be used to determine the most efficient options.
- Fragment the production process to elementary tasks, each of which can be optimally standardized.
- Select the most appropriate individuals for each specified task, train them to work precisely according to rules and formulae and monitor them to ensure that they adhere to these.

- Offer financial incentives to the workers linked to their output. Taylor believed that workers, as well as their employers, would benefit from the results of increased efficiency.

Taylor's theory was not about machines but the mechanizing of organization. His interest lay in the detailed study and design of often simple instruments, like shovels, and the work activities themselves, in the belief that small changes in the planning and organization of production and instruments of work can lead to great changes in output.

An apt illustration is provided by one of Henry Ford's assembly lines. One man took 20 minutes to produce an electrical alternator; when the process was spread over 29 operations, assembly time was decreased to 13 minutes. Raising the height of the assembly line by eight inches reduced this to seven minutes, while further **rationalization** cut it to five minutes. But more planning by management meant less control by the worker, who is now further reduced from being a servant of the machine to being a part of it. Like parts of machines, workers are interchangeable, their jobs require little or no training, and the speed and quality of their work are easily controlled since no skill or thinking is involved. In the film *Modern Times*, Charlie Chaplin memorably captures and criticizes the spirit of Taylorist ideas and Fordist applications. The worker is seen being fed by a giant feeding machine while working on an assembly line, where his day is spent tightening pairs of bolts with two spanners. The feeding machine goes berserk, scattering bits of corn and tipping bowl after bowl of soup on the worker's face. This is a common theme of critiques of technology: what if the machine declares its independence of us, either ruling the world or functioning in unintended ways?

The history of twentieth-century industry is inextricably connected with Taylorism. Highly sophisticated technological products are produced by workers whose skills took hardly more than a couple of days to acquire, who know virtually nothing about the products they are producing and, at times, do not even know (or care) whether the parts they are making will end up in washing machines or nuclear submarines.

Assembly lines became the established mode of industrial production, dominating not only manufacturing but also service industries and office work. One ingenious application was in catering, where fast-food technology ensured the production of a consistent, standardized product and service with the help of virtually unskilled staff. The process is designed to ensure that the food will be prepared to specific standards by people who may be unable to boil an egg at home. The self-service principle transforms every customer into his or her own waiter.

The ingenuity of this technology, however, leaves the workers with few intrinsic benefits. In contrast to simple cooking technologies which allow cooks scope for initiative and experimentation, fast-food staff are handlers of materials. Their experience resembles that of production line workers, with the additional pressures that direct contact with the customers brings. 'It is not an easy job, but it's very monotonous', said one who had worked in fast food for two years. 'If there was more variety and skill, people here would be less short-tempered. The staff would stay longer too; in this place I've met two or three hundred people who came to work and only five or six of us are still here.' As work becomes more routinized (unlike the work of professionals or skilled crafts people), it becomes purely a means of earning a living, something to put up with for as long as one can.

Figure 14.3 Ford Model T – the world's first mass produced car 'You can have it any color you like, as long as it is black'.

Routinization is not necessarily a bad thing. We all look for ways of routinizing parts of our work so that we do not have to pay attention to them and can focus on the aspects of work that require creativity and skill. The difference for fast-food workers as well as every other worker whose work has become **deskilled** is that all creativity and control is removed from their work – routinization is imposed on much of what they do.

INFORMATION MACHINES

The technological revolution of our time is that of **information**. This is not the first revolution in information handling. The invention of writing in the fourth millennium BC was seminal, permitting the keeping of accurate records and the development of accounting. In the fifteenth century, the invention of typography combined with the production of cheap paper revolutionized the dissemination of information. The mechanical clock itself is an information device. The invention of the telegraph in the nineteenth century provided a cheap and instantaneous method of communicating information across vast distances; previously, with the exception of smoke signals, semaphores and drums, information had travelled at the speed of the fastest horse.

Information technology consists of many instruments apart from computers (such as pens, paper and erasing fluid), machines (such as typewriters, adding machines, telephones, computers) and systems for gathering, storing, processing

Figure 14.4   The Anticythera mechanism – the world's oldest mechanical calculator.

and communicating information. Taylorism in the office has sought to emancipate the processing of information from the personal quirks of clerks. Maximizing output and efficiency were pursued through the standard **Taylorist** recipes: fragmentation, standardization and **control**. This approach was suited to large bureaucratic organizations handling vast amounts of routine information. The issuing of passports or of electricity bills, the handling of insurance claims or of mortgage applications yielded easily to long paper-processing lines. Each individual received a set of documents in an in-tray, carried out one or two simple operations or simply signed them, and then placed them in the out-tray.

The shortcomings of this approach are familiar to all whose documents get 'lost in the system', whose special requests cannot be accommodated within the standard forms or who have to wait for ages until their cases are seen. Personal service to the customer is unknown, service of any sort rudimentary. The clerk becomes a bored 'pen pusher' or a 'paper shuffler', enjoying no discretion, variety or security, having little contact with fellow workers and almost none with the customer.

On the other hand, there are undoubted benefits to some people. The arrival of electronic office equipment has changed dramatically both the nature of information handling in organizations and also the nature of information itself. Instantaneous access to and updating of records, multiple access to them, processing and communicating

Figure 14.5   Early mechanical calculator.

Figure 14.6   Early Personal Computer.

capacities previously undreamed of, open up new possibilities both for the service offered to the customer and for the planning, forecasting and organizing of production. The desktop computer, at best, enables the clerical staff to process individual cases through from beginning to end, offering a more personal and prompt service to the customer. Errors can be rectified more effectively, and controls can be introduced discreetly. On the other hand, the simplicity and routinization which computers bring to those tasks mean that there are fewer clerical staff to undertake them; instead, the same work is often performed as an extra by the person who used to manage the (now redundant) clerical staff.

Many of the recent examples of mechanization have been about the introduction of computers into some aspect of an organization's life. The conclusion we can draw from most of this experience is a mixed one. Technology itself is neither enslaving nor liberating. It is the *management* of technology that is important. Information technology, like earlier manufacturing technologies, was used here to replace human intelligence and **skill** and to increase control over the individual. The worker, stuck in front of a terminal, sees the world shrink to a range of symbols on a screen and a sequence of voices at the end of a telephone line. Feelings of meaninglessness, boredom and **powerlessness** prevail. There are some serious dangers inherent in current information technologies. In essence, they are not so different from the dangers of technologies past, but with past technologies, we have often only seen their dangers later, whereas with information technology, we can try to handle the consequences more actively.

The personal computer also offers a more restricted view of the world. One study by Weick (1985) suggests that it is generally hard for people to make sense of what they are doing in front of terminals; there are five deficiencies, which together lead to a chaotic understanding of the world:

- Action deficiencies: the operator cannot see, hear or smell data from the outside world, but only see symbols on a screen.
- Comparison deficiencies: the operator cannot walk around and look at things from a different angle, but has to rely on one, uncontradicted data source.
- Affiliation deficiencies: people often work out what is going on by talking to other people, and working at screens discourages this.
- Deliberation deficiencies: it is hard to see the wood for the trees, to tell the important from the unimportant, on a screen.
- Consolidation deficiencies: material on a screen does not look like work in progress, and it is hard for people to go away and think about it, as they might with less imposing-looking information.

These five points apply generally to the world as mediated by a television screen. The limited world of the television viewer has been brought into the workplace.

THE MEANING OF MACHINES

But there is another side to machines. Some people like them; they even become addicted to them. Far from leading to meaninglessness, machines enhance the lives of these people, filling them with meaning and anchoring their sense of identity. For such people, machines like cars and computers can become the focus of folklore, generating stories which are full of meaning and feeling. Some people may end up treating machines with greater care and affection than their human companions. An analyst uses the following story as an opportunity to describe her own relation to computers:

> I'll never forget going to a party and there was one of the most eccentric programmers that I've ever met in my life, sitting on a sofa with a bottle of gin, and he proceeded to tell me that he preferred computers to women because they didn't answer him back and he was serious! He was totally serious. His whole life revolved around

computers. I just think it's sad. It's funny but it's sad. And I think that a lot of people become obsessed with it, I think I was, when I first started learning about computers, oh I loved it! It was exploration, there was always something you didn't know, there were always things to find out, but it was always achievable, you'd get there in the end. Whereas I don't feel like that any more!

This story expresses the feelings of many computer enthusiasts, for whom computers are a challenge, a source of satisfaction and a major part of their life. In a research project conducted by one of us, we collected a number of stories featuring computers at the workplace. More recently, we have collected data and made observations which would suggest that everything which we say here about computers can also be said about the internet. Three major types of plot were identified:

- In some stories, the computer features as a physical object, as a machine, which gets stuck in lifts, falls off trolleys or 'crashes' to the basement. In these stories (some of which are extremely funny or unpleasant), the role of the computer could be taken by some other machine, like a photocopier, without drastically changing the meaning of the story.
- In other stories, the computer is treated as a 'living being', whose strange and unpredictable behaviour puzzles, amuses, threatens and dismays. In these stories, the computer appears as a true character in the narrative, most frequently as the villain or the fool of the piece, occasionally as the innocent scapegoat, now and then as the hero.
- In the largest number of stories, the computer features as a unique resource or tool, often a priceless one, which can be used or abused, which may be mastered and whose control confers great power on its owner. In these stories, the computer functions just like the magic rings or golden keys in folk tales. The commonest presentation of computers in stories is as a valuable but dangerous tool or resource.

Consider, for example the following story, told light-heartedly, by an executive of a large computer manufacturing company:

I used to work for a company where we had regular bomb practice. The security chief would hide a package with a sign saying 'BOMB', to see how quickly people got out of the building and how quickly his boys would locate the 'bomb'. They carried out this exercise many times and were pleased with their response times. Until eventually the bomb was hidden under the mainframe computer, where it proved impossible to locate; for hours they searched all over the building, but nobody thought of looking under the machine!

It is interesting to speculate why the security staff failed to check under the mainframe. Was the machine seen as being above suspicion or was it a taboo object? Did the men perhaps fail to see the computer altogether, regarding it as a fixed part of the building, like a joist?

The story was presented as an illustration of an earlier comment to the effect that, to the non-expert, computers are mystifying and threatening. The executive telling the story was seeking to have a little fun at the expense of security men, hardened men who will go after bombs, and yet will not go near a computer. It is the computer which is the real threat in the story, rather than the fake 'bomb' of the drill. At the same time, the executive uses the story to cast himself and his expert colleagues as brave individuals at the cutting edge of a technology which mystifies lesser mortals. This view of computers as dangerous items acquired fresh meaning at the turn of the century, when most users were gripped by a blind panic concerning the 'millennium bug': throughout the late 1990s, forecasts of doom and gloom regarding the inability of software (often including some code that dated from the 1960s, even though the overall packages were up to date) to deal with the year 2000 abounded.

If in Doubt, Blame the Machine

Computer experts, in our research, often attracted negative nicknames from non-experts, like 'zombies', 'androids' or 'the zoo'. But, they were rarely the direct target of stories. In most of their stories, it was the computer itself which was ridiculed or blamed for organizational failures. The non-experts enjoy computer failures almost as much the experts are amused by the naïvety of the ordinary users. In their stories, the computer emerges as 'a dumb machine, pretending to be smarter than it is' whose humbling is similar to that of the pompous and pretentious person discussed earlier. In some of them, human wit and common sense come to save the day when the machine fails to deliver the goods. For example, in the library of a large manufacturing firm, they liked to tell the story of a director urgently requesting a copy of an article that had appeared in a newspaper. No amount of online searches could identify the article until a seasoned librarian phoned up all the newspapers and eventually tracked down the article. It had been written by a freelancer who held the copyright and did not feature in the online version. The point of this story seemed to be that old-fashioned librarian skills came to the rescue in a situation which the computer could not handle.

Similar stories of staff having to fall back on their traditional skills and use their cunning and experience every time the computer crashes or fails can be found in many organizations. Even in highly automated environments, such stories seem to proclaim that the computer does not have the last word. People cannot and must not become mere servants of the computers; they must maintain their skills and aptitudes and remain in control of the machines. One of our colleagues tells the story of water repair engineers in a town in the UK who had been told that all their records must be digitized. Many of these records were on old cigarette packets, or ancient faded scraps of paper with drawings on them. The database of digital records was duly produced. However, the engineers salvaged all the old paper records and stored them in a filing cabinet, obligingly housed by a café on the outskirts of their town. The engineers used to meet up at the café for a coffee a chat and to look at the records because they knew their way around the paper records and could also glean a lot of information that was lost in the digital version. For example, they could see the age of the piece of paper with the drawing of where the water pipes went, and in combination with seeing the site for their work, that told them something about the likelihood of having to dig under tarmac to find the relevant piece of pipe.

To sum up then, stories about the computer in organizations reveal a variety of meanings that are vested in them – a source of power and advantage, a useful but dangerous resource, a baffling and mysterious force, a convenient excuse for every failure, a cause of much frustration, irritation and boredom. At the heart of many of these stories lies an unease; this combines a recognition that computers make our lives easier, more comfortable and more fun with a feeling that computers are already too clever to be controlled by humans. We have become far too dependent on them to be able to function without them.

BEYOND MECHANIZING

The effects of new information technologies on production have been far reaching. Product differentiation and targeting of consumers (known as 'mass customization'), decentralization, the contracting out of products and services, globalization of financial services – all these were logistically impossible before, but now become possible thanks to the computer. Flexibility replaces standardization and routinization as the order of the day – flexibility of products and production methods, flexibility of working practices and labour markets, flexibility in geographic and financial terms.

For a time, Japan was hailed as the prototype of the new industrial age, in which success depended not on churning out a uniform product cheaply, but on very fast adjustments to market and other external **changes**. 'Japanization' and its developments have now been imported into virtually all advanced production systems. New computerized technologies require a new range of industrial skills and new work attitudes. The worker must have an overall understanding of **systems** and must be able to switch from one area of production to another, from production to maintenance, from maintenance to service, and from service to information processing.

It is becoming popular to argue that the age of mass production is now giving way to post-Fordism, the era of the intelligent machine. While it may be too early to judge how current developments in information technology will shape tomorrow's organizations, certain trends are already apparent. A move away from the **hierarchical** pyramids of the past towards flatter, leaner **organizational structures** is widely regarded as essential for survival. While classical **management** theory recommended that each superior should be in charge of between five and ten subordinates – the number of people he or she could 'keep an eye on' – today's managers might manage 100 or more subordinates, in different locations, with the help of computerized information processing. Henry Ford's own organization has seen its levels of management decline from more than 15 to 7, a number which has proven adequate for the Catholic Church through its history, and which would still be seen as excessive by most Japanese companies. Middle management is squeezed out, as senior executives have instant access to information that would have been processed by numerous intermediaries in the past.

The optimists view this as an opportunity to bring the human factor back to the workplace, to restore meaning and dignity to work and to do away with the drudgery and monotony of much manual **labour**. The **alienated** mass-production worker will be replaced by the expert information handler. Just as very few farmers can provide enough to feed a nation, it is argued, in future a few manufacturing workers will supply most of the material commodities required. The rest will be engaged in managerial, service and information-processing work.

Others take a more pessimistic view. The term **McDonaldization** has acquired considerable currency as a description of a phenomenon whereby 'the principles of the fast-food restaurant are coming to dominate more and more sectors of American society as well as the rest of the world' (Ritzer, 1993/1996). According to this view, far from reversing the principles of Taylorism and Fordism, our organizations raise them to new heights and extend them into new sectors. McDonaldization extends homogeneous products, standardized work routines, deskilling and homogenization of labour into every sector, from financial services to catering, from tourism to management consultancy, from health to education.

Where McDonaldization goes substantially beyond Fordism is in its total imposition of a consumption mentality in many spheres of social activity and subsequent rationalization of these activities according to the dictates of markets. Thus, universities are transformed into McUniversities, hospitals into McHospitals and even churches into McChurches. McDonaldized consumption treats consumers as sovereign, seeking to offer them choices and stimulate their fantasies and desires. At the same time, however, it seeks to control in minuscule detail every aspect of the relation between customers, employees and managers (see Chapter 21, 'Producing and Consuming'). Disneyland serves as a prototype of this sort of consumption, where fun, fantasy and artifice loom at every turn and yet the movements of crowds, their actions, interactions and even their emotions are constantly monitored and controlled. Where Fordism was dominated by ultra-efficient production machines, McDonaldization marks the sovereignty of the ultra-efficient selling machine.

Electronic spies monitor our every move, huge databases maintain records of our every credit card purchase, computers decide where and how to commit vast sums of capital which sooner or later are translated into jobs lost and gained, livelihoods created or destroyed. This, the pessimists argue, is not flexibility but perpetual insecurity and suffocating impotence.

KEY POINTS

- ○ Technology is not just tools and machines but recipes, techniques and know-how.

- ○ While many tools and machines make our lives easier, technology has for a long time been linked to the requirements of production and warfare.

- ○ The application of new technological methods in production has, under capitalism, led to some deskilling and degradation of work.

- ○ Taylorist principles and Fordist mass production subordinated the worker to the mechanical requirements of production.

- ○ This has resulted in alienation and feelings of powerlessness and meaninglessness.

- ○ Technology, and especially information technology, can create strong dependency; people become unable to function without technological supports.

- ○ Computerization may offer some relief from monotony in the workplace.

- ○ Computerization often reduces people's control over their work and severely restricts awareness and understanding of what they are doing.

- o   Developments in information technology facilitate changes in organizational structures, notably towards greater flexibility and shorter managerial hierarchies.

- o   McDonaldization represents an extension of Taylorist and Fordist principles into new sectors of the economy and, under the guise of consumer sovereignty, it further rationalizes relations between customers, employees and managers.

- o   It remains an open question whether technology offers solutions to today's social and organizational problems or whether it stands at the very root of these problems.

- o   There is abundant evidence that machines can end up becoming the masters of humans rather than their servants.

> > > > > > > > > > > > **THEORETICAL SIGNPOSTS** > > > > > > > > > > > >

The subject of technology is approached from various angles in connection with organizations and management. These include:

> the effects of technology on our lives and more specifically on working conditions
> the changes in the nature of organizations brought about by new information and other technologies
> the ways in which technology becomes incorporated in people's actual practices.

The Effects of Technology on Our Lives and More Specifically on Working Conditions

One of the enduring debates on technology concerns whether technology itself is to blame for the troubles that it brings to our lives or whether these are the results of 'abuses' that may be prevented through a more enlightened approach. This debate is regularly rehearsed in connection with different technologies, from television to hand guns. Lewis Mumford (1934) in his classic book *Technics and Civilization* takes the view that, under capitalism, technology is used to accumulate profits rather than for the benefit of humanity. Thus, F.W. Taylor's (1911) *Principles of Scientific Management* are firmly aimed to enhance productivity, no matter the costs in human alienation. The argument that mass-production technologies cause worker alienation was put forward by Blauner (1964), who argued that fully automated process production brings about a reduction of alienation. The view that Taylorism has been the dominant influence in shaping the modern corporation was first put forward by Braverman (1974), who argued that throughout the twentieth century, the working classes in industrial countries have been systematically de-skilled through the application of Taylorist ideas. Braverman viewed Taylorism as a doctrine which bolstered management control over the productive process and reduced the workers to mere extensions of the machines. The concept of de-skilling has been borne out by numerous field studies, including Beynon (1973), Nichols and Beynon (1977), Pollert (1981) and Gabriel (1988). Braverman's work generated a tradition of scholarship, referred to as 'labour process theory', which addresses issues of control over the workplace and the limits of management control. Increasingly, researchers have focused on different mechanisms of worker resistance to management's attempts to control the work process. Several accounts of the resistance–control process are offered in the collection edited by Jermier et al. (1994).

Fritz Schumacher's book *Small is Beautiful* (1973) has rightly become an emblem for advocates of sustainable development. In it, Schumacher advocated a new ethos for technology, an ethos that eschews the gargantuan proportions of contemporary technology in favour of technologies on a human scale, that support communities and their ways of life. He referred to such technologies as 'intermediate'; they are now more widely referred to as 'appropriate'. Thus, a solar-powered or winding transistor radio can bring information and entertainment to millions of people with no access to electricity; low-cost computers can bring the benefits of education and communication to those who have been disenfranchised through poverty.

The Changes in the Nature of Organizations Brought About by New Information and Other Technologies

Since the spread of desktop computing, the internet and mobile telephony, the effects of computerized information systems on management have been exhaustively debated. Early contributions by Zuboff (1985) focused on different ways in which such technology are implemented, while Weick (1985) offered fascinating insights into the shrinking world of the employee who spends increasing parts of his or her time in front of a computer screen. The incorporation of computers in organizational language and folklore has been discussed by Bloomfield (1989) and Gabriel (1992). Numerous authors have discussed the Japanese phenomenon, the causes and nature of Japan's manufacturing success, and the extent of Japanization of the industries of other countries. Womack et al. (1990) identify the origin of Japanese success as lying firmly in its pioneering of radical manufacturing systems of lean production which mark a major leap ahead of Taylorist systems. Other authors, however, notably Wilkinson (1996) and Wilkinson et al. (1995) have challenged both these views and the culturalist views (which argue that culture is the secret of Japanese success); instead, these authors believe that Japanese success is essentially due to an intensification of the same disciplines and controls as those embodied in Taylorism.

McDonaldization is a term first coined by George Ritzer (1993/1996, 1998), though it is now extensively used by many authors. The effects of McDonaldization on relations between organizations and their customers have been explored by many authors (e.g. du Gay and Salaman, 1992; Korczynski, 2003; Long, 1999; Sturdy, 1998, 2001; Sturdy et al., 2001). Several authors have explored call centres as terrains where the contradictions and conflicts of McDonaldized production are enacted (Frenkel et al., 1999; Korczynski, 2001; Sturdy and Fleming, 2003).

The Ways in Which Technology Becomes Incorporated in People's Actual Practices

The concept of technology-in-use represents an attempt to dissolve the distinction between technology as instruments, machines and recipes on the one hand and the actual uses to which it is put on the other. It represents a similar effort to Foucault's fusion of power and knowledge in a single concept of power/knowledge (Foucault, 1980) and even more to Giddens' (1984) fusion of action and structure through the concept of structuration. Thus, Orlikowski argues that 'technology is physically constructed by actors working in a given social context, and technology is socially constructed by actors through the different meaning they attach to it and the various features they emphasize and use' (Orlikowski, 1992: 406). This approach rejects the view of technology as a neutral external force that 'impacts' on social and economic activities and looks at it as an integral dimension of these activities. This is an approach that has emerged from the works of Bruno Latour (1991) and Carlo Ciborra (2002), as well as Orlikowski, Yates and their co-workers (see e.g. Orlikowski, 1992; Tyre and Orlikowski, 1996; Yates and Orlikowski, 1992).

Approaching technology in this manner suggests that different inventions and innovations are constantly adapted, modified and subverted in the course of different practices in and out of organizations. Consider the example of PowerPoint that has attracted much criticism as a technology that de-skills presenters and 'dumbs down' audiences, tyrannically reducing knowledge to lists, pictures and charts. Approaching PowerPoint as a technology-in-use suggests that different people enact it differently and with different results, often removed from the intensions of its designers and merchandisers. PowerPoint may be used in an imaginative or dull way, to support or reinvent presentations. Creative users of PowerPoint can assimilate the technology in their own presentational styles, displaying many of the qualities of bricolage and improvisation that have long been associated with more primitive forms of technology. Used in this way, PowerPoint does not necessarily simplify, codify and objectify knowledge but can become part of a multi-level engagement with organizational complexity (Gabriel, 2008a).

REVIEW QUESTIONS

1. How does technology affect social relations at the workplace?

2. Why does technological change almost invariably generate resistance? How might such resistance be addressed?

3. Why do so many promising technological solutions fail when implemented in practice?

---

companion
website
w.sagepub.co.uk/fineman

Reading On

The articles below are available for free to readers of the fourth edition of *Organizing & Organizations* via the book's companion website at www.sagepub.co.uk/fineman

Brocklehurst, M. (2001) 'Power, identity and new technology homework: implications for "new forms" of organizing', *Organization Studies*, 22 (3): 445–66.

This paper reports on research which tracked the experience of a group of professional workers as they moved from being conventional office workers to becoming homeworkers where they used new information and communication technologies, but remained as full-time salaried employees. The paper evaluates the value of Giddens' conceptualization of power, identity and time/space in explaining the consequences of this move and compares his approach to postmodern theorizations, which draw on the work of Foucault and Lash and Urry.

Gabriel, Y. (2008) '*Essai:* against the tyranny of PowerPoint – technology-in-use and technology abuse', *Organization Studies*, 29 (2): 255–76.

PowerPoint has emerged as a powerful piece of communication technology, having profound consequences on presentations (business and educational), classroom communication and, possibly, on the nature of lecturing itself. This article examines some uses to which the software is put and some of its potential shortcomings, and argues that the package can be used more creatively to build on our culture's emphasis on spectacle and image to elicit a critical, creative and active response from its audience.

Spicer, A. (2005) 'The political process of inscribing a new technology', *Human Relations*, 58 (7): 867–90.

What shapes the use of a new technology? This article argues that technology use is shaped by political processes rather than being inherent in the technology itself. A study of a case where interested groups attempt to inscribe the possible use of an Australian public broadcaster's website during a public inquiry shows that technical inscriptions are continually contested and resisted.

15

INNOVATION AND CHANGE

In this chapter, we shall consider first the nature of innovation, the process by which new products and processes come into being. We then look at why innovations succeed or fail, and the relationship between innovation and imitation. Sometimes people innovate not just products, but whole organizations, so this takes us on to the topic of entrepreneurship. Innovation is about making new things happen, and bureaucracy is about making things happen in a more efficient or fairer fashion, and these two processes are always in tension in organizations; innovation without building a bureaucratic support structure is likely to be chaotic and expensive, and bureaucracy without innovation produces an unchanging and uncompetitive organization. This takes us on to considering organizational change. We consider the ways that people may love or hate change, and the different interpretations that we can make of resistance to change, while recognizing that some people build their careers on change. We consider whether it is possible at all to manage change, and look at the difference between coping with change and leading it. We discuss the importance of considering a stakeholder approach to change, and conclude with a discussion of action research as a means of organizational change.

INNOVATION

Picture the world in the 1970s. There are no mobile phones or digital cameras, no personal computers, no computer games and no internet. There are no video recorders; credit cards are the preserve of a tiny elite. There are no personal stereos and no compact discs. Against this background, in 1979, a tiny, personal tape recorder is launched by Sony, the Walkman, a device that was destined to revolutionize people's listening habits, the music business and even possibly the leisure industry.

If Sony had not launched the Walkman, somebody else undoubtedly would have. Still, the conception, launch and marketing of the Walkman makes for an instructive example in the study of innovation. The idea for the Walkman emerged from a discussion between Masaru Ibuka and Akio Morita, Sony's founders. This is how Morita describes it:

> The idea took shape when Ibuka came into my office one day with one of our portable stereo tape recorders and a pair of our standard-size headphones. He looked unhappy

and complained about the weight of the system. I asked him what was on his mind and then he explained, 'I like to listen to music, but I don't want to disturb others. I can't sit there by my stereo all day. This is my solution – I take the music with me. But it's too heavy.' I had been mulling an idea over in my mind for a while, and now it was coming into focus as Ibuka talked ...

Ibuka's complaint set me into motion. I ordered our engineers to take one of our reliable small tape recorders we called Pressman, strip out the recording circuit and the speaker, and replace them with a stereo amplifier ... Everybody gave me a hard time. It seemed as though nobody liked the idea. At one of our product planning meetings, one of the engineers said, 'It sounds like a good idea, but will people buy it if it doesn't have recording capability? I don't think so.' (Morita, 1987: 79–80)

In spite of their reservations, Morita's engineers were up to the challenge; they adapted several different components to the task, miniaturized others, and in a relatively short period of time came up with a prototype whose sound quality, size and economy impressed Morita.

I rushed home with the first Walkman and was trying it out with different music when I noticed that my experiment was annoying my wife, who felt shut out. All right, I decided, we needed to make provisions for two sets of headphones. (Morita, 1987: 80)

Even when the final product was ready, Morita and Ibuka's passion for their 'baby' was not shared by others.

I thought we had produced a terrific item, and I was full of enthusiasm for it, but our marketing people were unenthusiastic. They said it wouldn't sell, and it embarrassed me to be so excited about a product most others thought would be a dud. But I was so confident the product was viable that I said I would take personal responsibility for the project. I never had reason to regret it. The idea took hold and from the very beginning the Walkman was a runaway success. I never really liked the name Walkman. But it seems to have caught on everywhere. I was away on a trip when the name was chosen by some young people in our company, and when I got back I ordered them to change the name to something like Walking Stereo, or anything a bit more grammatical, but they said it was too late: the advertising had already been prepared and the units were being made with that name. ... Now I'm told it is a great name. (Morita, 1987: 81)

The Walkman (see Figure 15.1) hardly needed advertising – it sold faster than the company could produce it. It enabled people to listen to music of their choice without forcing it on other people. It became one of Sony's most successful products and a key factor in its success, its profits and its reputation as an innovating company.

What does the Walkman story tell us about **innovation**? First, there is an idea that stems from a dissatisfaction or the need *of a user,* rather than an inventor. The idea is traded between two people; it gets *cross-fertilized* in the process, various possibilities and problems emerge and different solutions are offered. A new product is conceived, designed, produced and tested. The product itself involves many existing ingredients and old components but they find themselves in *new combinations* and new arrangements. The product meets *resistance* – 'No one will buy a tape recorder

Figure 15.1   Sony Walkman.

that doesn't record' – but it has *champions* prepared to take the responsibility and run with it. The product needs a *name* – something that will mark it in the minds of the consumers. The name is reached by serendipity, while the boss is away. When the product is launched, it meets new markets and new uses which its original inventors had not planned or intended.

What this story does not explain is the cause of the Walkman's triumph. Numerous innovations run along similar lines only to end up as forgotten episodes for business historians, or even as objects of ridicule. Think of Sir Clive Sinclair's C5 motorized vehicle (see Figure 15.2) or even Sony's own Betamax video tape that, in spite of its technical superiority, lost out to JVC's successful VHS format (see Figure 15.3).

There is a systematic **decision making** issue that is important here. If a potentially good innovation is rejected, most people will never be aware of this (the exception being when the innovator goes public later on who turned the idea down before someone had the courage to take it up). If a poor innovation is accepted, the loss will be plain for all to see. So there may be a bias in favour of doing nothing on innovations which is potentially quite damaging.

WHY DO INNOVATIONS FAIL?

Many new products hitting the market, from electronic gismos to cosmetics and chocolate bars, fail. Why? Some innovations have obvious design flaws (at least with hindsight) that reduce their value to potential consumers. Champions of new products can easily be blinded to such flaws by their enthusiasm. The flaws may be major, as in the case of the Sinclair C5; the public had no interest in buying a vehicle which might be very cheap, but which did not appear to protect its occupants either from the weather or from

Figure 15.2   The Sinclair C5.

Figure 15.3   Betamax vs VHS.

serious injury, or to move them around very quickly. Later motoring innovations like the GWhizz, the Smart car or the IQ have all majored on safety and have succeeded – but then the C5 may just have been too far ahead of the public imagination, and of concern about environmentally damaging transport. Equally, the flaws may be minor, for example, where a competitor entering the market with the benefit of hindsight can

"I love this room, so many happy memories of killing innovation..."

Figure 15.4

Source: http://www.cartoonstock.com

reap benefits by learning from the mistakes of early pioneers. The ease of imitation is a key factor affecting the chances of success of most innovations, something that companies seek to minimize by taking out patents that seek to defend their intellectual property.

Logistics can be another cause of innovation failure – the ability to match supply with demand for the new product, of ensuring distribution at the right place and the right time and in the right quantities. The pricing of the product can also be a cause of failure – too high and consumers are discouraged, too low and the product may be successful but fail to make any money for the company. The Mini, one of the most innovative cars ever launched, lost considerable sums of money for its original manufacturer, the British Motor Corporation, by being underpriced. By contrast, overpricing was one of the factors behind Betamax's loss in the video-cassette format wars. The technical superiority of Betamax over VHS as a recording format was undisputed, but the market turned out to be for a cheap way of recording, rather than for a way of making good recordings. Sometimes the forming of prior alliances is crucial for the success of an innovation. For example, Philips and Sony had, in cooperation, led a large number of the major players in the hifi industry in specifying and preparing the CD format, which then lasted with little challenge for a long time. Competitor formats, such as DVD Audio and SACD never had the collaborative support of enough industry players to develop the same kind of dominance.

Good timing and good luck is behind the success of many innovations, just as bad timing (and bad luck) is the cause of failure for countless others. Small details and small miscalculations can lead to the failure of essentially sound products. Innovations always entail a degree of unpredictability – they spur new habits and actions from consumers, new ideas and new products from competitors. The experience of the iPod, the Walkman of the twenty-first century, suggests that highly innovative products spawn many parasitical ones offering accessories, add-ons and other services. They may also spawn other innovations in a wide range of related products. For example, many of the reviews of the new Smartphones compare their quality and features as reproducers of sound with the iPod.

INNOVATION, IMITATION AND FASHION

Innovation does not only entail new products. It may equally be found in new processes or new applications for existing ones. A new procedure for heart by-pass operations or for producing wine may substantially reduce costs, eliminate risks and waste and generate profits for inventors and investors. There was a very successful period of innovation in Japan through much of the second half of the twentieth century where most of the innovation was in the manufacturing process, competing by producing products like those already available from Western manufacturers, but with greater reliability in both process and product, giving price and quality advantages. Likewise, a new way of marketing shampoo ('a shampoo for blondes') or a holiday destination ('create your own myth in Greece') may not involve a dramatic new product but a new way of approaching an existing one.

Joseph Schumpeter, a theorist whose work on innovation in the 1930s is now viewed as highly innovative in its own right, saw innovation as the motive force for economic growth. Schumpeter argued that innovators and **entrepreneurs** are driven to develop new products, processes and services by the 'carrot of spectacular reward' and the 'stick of destitution'. This resulted in 'gales of creative destruction' across society, a process where the new always destroys the old, often at considerable economic and social costs. Traditional **skills** such as cotton-weaving, printing and engineering are rendered obsolete by automation that cuts costs. **Consumers** are drawn to discard their perfectly functional DVD players and television sets by the arrival of high-definition and flat-screen alternatives.

Imitation is a key part of this process. Imitation drives the behaviour of consumers as they seek to 'keep up with the Joneses'. Imitation also drives entrepreneurs, businesspeople and managers to adopt products and methods that have worked elsewhere. Imitation lies at the heart of fashion. Fashions spread as more and more people seek to imitate those seen as successful and innovative, the trendsetters. But imitation also creates a need for difference. All the time, people come up with new ideas which become imitated; but with imitation, the attractiveness of the original idea diminishes, and new innovations are searched for. Thus, fashion constantly renews itself.

INNOVATION, CREATIVITY AND ENTREPRENEURSHIP

Fashion is a dynamic and capricious process. Innovations that catch the wind of fashion are liable to soar to great heights while others remain firmly earthbound. Catching the wind may require resources, will and perseverance. This is where entrepreneurship comes in. Entrepreneurship involves spotting opportunities, identifying market gaps and commercial exploitation of innovations. It also involves risk, the willingness to take a stake in the practical exploitation of an innovative idea and to sustain losses if the idea fails.

Entrepreneurship is often viewed as a quality of personality. Entrepreneurs are imaginative, dynamic, ambitious and risk-taking individuals. They are prepared to question assumptions and break rules. The line between crime and entrepreneurship can be a thin one – indeed, many would argue that some crime is a form of entrepreneurship by other means. A 14-year-old boy is brought in front of a magistrate's court in the UK accused of stealing video recorders. It turns out that he runs a well-organized gang of child thieves who can steal any particular model of video recorder or television set on demand for specific customers and will deliver them to order. A budding entrepreneur or a child criminal doomed for a lifetime in correctional institutions? Either way, both entrepreneurship and crime require the imagination to think of actions that society does not expect, and the willingness to carry these actions out.

Entrepreneurship is commonly hailed as the ultimate source of wealth creation. Many entrepreneurs become stars whose achievements are celebrated by the mass media. Governments seek to attract and nurture them as a means of renewing their economies and creating new employment opportunities. Entrepreneurship includes start-ups, but also corporate venturing, management buyouts, mergers and acquisitions. It includes both private-sector and public-sector activities. It can also include the difficult process of growing a small start-up into a larger-scale business – what is called the 'sapling to seedling' transformation.

Social entrepreneurs are individuals who recognize the creative potential of an idea to address a social problem or to bring about a social transformation. Muhammad Yunus, a Bangladeshi banker and economist, was honoured with the Nobel Prize for Peace in 2006, for his successful application of microcredit – small loans – to entrepreneurs and other individuals too poor to qualify for traditional bank loans. Again, the link between entrepreneurship and crime can be seen here – when does microcredit become loan-sharking? Michael Young, a sociologist and public campaigner, has demonstrated many different aspects of entrepreneurship through his career. He is credited with introducing the word 'meritocracy' to the English language. He also founded a number of public-service organizations in the UK, including the Open University, the Consumers' Association and, at the age of 81, the School for Social Entrepreneurs.

For the last 200 years, many business entrepreneurs, like Robert Owen, Andrew Carnegie and Bill Gates, have also sought to become social entrepreneurs, using their extensive fortunes to bring about social transformation. By the same token, social enterprises, like Fairtrade, have also emerged as sizeable business ventures in their own right. The concept of a triple bottom line (or 'TBL', '3BL', or 'People, Planet, Profit') has been proposed for measuring the success of social and other enterprises along a spectrum of criteria and values – economic, environmental and social.

INNOVATION, CHANGE AND BUREAUCRACY

Bureaucracy with its emphasis on order, predictability and routine is often seen as stifling innovation and change. In a famous book published in 1983, Rosabeth Moss Kanter lambasted organizations for their 'segmentalist approaches':

> Segmentalist approaches see problems as narrowly as possible, independently of their context, independently of their connections to any other problems. Companies with segmentalist cultures are likely to have segmentalist structures: a large number of compartments walled off from one another – department from department, level above from level below, field office from headquarters, labor from management, or men from women. (Kanter, 1983: 28)

Segmentalist companies are threatened by **change** and tend to stifle it. It threatens too many fiefdoms. They produce the kind of internal world where everyone knows where they are and how to relate to other parts of the organization, but not how to relate to a changing context in the outside world.

For the past 40 years or so, much thought has gone into how organizations may overcome the problems of change, and we shall now turn our minds to these.

CHANGE AND STABILITY

REAL-LIFE EXAMPLE

Tim was an experienced manager who had been responsible for large divisions of companies for ten years or so. Just after his 50th birthday, he was headhunted by another company to go and take over a division that had been performing satisfactorily, but which was not considered to be ready for the increasing competitiveness of its marketplace. 'I'm not sure we've got the right people there, or that we are being professional enough', said Patrick, Tim's new boss. 'Some of them have been there for years, back from the days when the customers used to come and find us. Are they up to speed on aggression and customer service for the way things are now? And what about the enquiries funnel – how can we lose less customers between enquiry and sale?'

Tim had taken on jobs like that (or worse) before, and was not fazed by the long-service records of his new team or their familiarity with their environments, nor by the easy banter and friendship they had with each other. If need be, he could soon start changing all that. But he had also been around for long enough, and had enough confidence in his own abilities, to want to make his own judgement about the team. Were they doing things the way they had always done them purely out of habit, or because they knew their situation thoroughly and found those ways of doing things to work well?

Over the first few weeks, as he got to know the team, he realized that they were actually very competent. The people who dealt with customers did not look or sound as slick as Patrick and his senior colleagues might have liked, but the customers loved them, and found them thoroughly professional and effective. Not only that, but when Tim looked at the conversion funnel of enquirers to customers and compared it with competitors, he found that his team was doing much better than the opposition. He only had to be in the office on a few occasions when the final phases of negotiation were taking place to see the commitment of his team to winning customers and closing deals – no lack of aggression there.

Tim is in the quite common situation of being expected to bring about change in a situation which does not need it. He now has the problem of explaining to his seniors that the purpose for which they brought him in was misguided, and that the situation is such that what needs managing is not change but stability. Of course, he might lose some key members of staff, the market might change or his competitors might come up with a new product, and he would have to manage change quickly and effectively. But the misdiagnosis (in his view) by the senior management would remain; this is not at present a situation that requires change.

Change is all around us, and many feel that the world is changing faster than ever before. As Isaac Asimov said, 'The only constant is change'. Whether the world is *really* changing any more quickly than it was during the Industrial Revolution in the nineteenth century is difficult to know, but in any case, many people certainly feel the pressure of rapid, unrelenting change. Donald Schon (1971) suggested that we all think that this is a temporary phenomenon, and that at some future stage of our lives, stability will reassert itself, even though we can see the evidence that this does not seem to be happening for anybody else.

Studies of change in organizations have produced a set of practices called Organization Development through which consultants try to help organizations undergoing processes of change. These practices are usually based on behavioural science (or organizational behaviour) knowledge, and they aim to help change to become a more planned or at least more plannable process. The style of change is like self-reflection. Members of the organization look at the processes that are used to carry out work, emphasizing the social processes, and consider together how those processes could be improved. Organization Development was one of the first fields to emphasize the importance of emotions and feelings in organizational life, and is one of the antecedents of the current emphasis on these aspects. It also emphasized the importance of relationships in organizations, and pioneered much of the current thinking in that area. Many of the people engaged in Organization Development activities are wearing some other label in the workplace – HR director, Chief People Officer, Special Projects Officer – we have even come across one company where this activity was being done by the Financial Controller. In Tim's case, he might well have found that Patrick had lined up some help for him with Organization Development (OD) to help him implement change before he had the opportunity to decide that change was not necessary. OD practitioners are quite accustomed to that situation, and most will then help Tim with his management while acknowledging that the change they were brought in for was not needed.

Some recent theorists have discussed a particularly dynamic form of stability in **institutional theory**, in which we see organizations imitating others in their own field of operation, and thus resisting change at the level of the organization rather than at the level of individuals resisting organizational change. For example, in a law firm, there is an incentive to have similar structures and procedures to other law firms, so that your clients can easily see what you offer in comparison, and so that your newly recruited employees know how everything works from the start. So, in any one sector, firms may be surprisingly similar to each other, and may resist changing in any way which makes them less like their competitors.

LOVING, HATING AND RESISTING CHANGE

The pressure, however, is still on Tim. If he says that no change is needed, and even if he shows the evidence, he may be accused of being 'resistant to change'. Early studies in organizational change often considered how to overcome resistance. It was suspected that many people, and especially workers and older people, hated change,

"This is the conference room; that's the international symbol for 'Don't rock the boat'."

Figure 15.5

Source: www.cartoonstock.com

and would resist it simply because they were creatures of habit and did not want to have to question their habits. Alternatively, they might have vested interests in the way things worked. They might have learned how to play the system, and might be reluctant not to capitalize on this learning.

More recent thinking has focused on asking why people are resisting change. If the people who know the situation best do not welcome a change, this *might* be because they are right – they know the situation better than anybody else, and are therefore aware of the damage and disruption that will result from the change, and the cost that this will entail. Resistors to change may be driven by good knowledge of the situation rather than personal fear. To dismiss them as just resistors who need to be overcome could miss out on important insights.

Who are these people who resist change? Perhaps 'resistance to change' is a phrase for dismissing people from the conversation when we cannot find a good argument to win them over to our point of view.

What is often overlooked is the number of people who love change. If you are getting bored at work, you may welcome change, whether or not it is a change for the better in terms of how the organization works. Equally, if your job is getting out of control, a certain amount of change may be a great way of covering your tracks. If things are changing, and everyone is a little uncertain about the direction being taken, it is much harder to make any blame stick for things that have not gone right.

BUILDING YOUR CAREER ON CHANGE

Going beyond this, there are also people in Tim's position who have been brought in to produce or to manage change. This is extremely common. Every government minister who is appointed to any government in the world feels the pressure to show that they are making a contribution and, for this to be shown clearly, they need to introduce some changes or reforms. If they are not changing anything, how can they be seen to be earning their money? It is extremely hard to say exactly what the effect of these changes is, at least until research is done long after the event. This means that it can be difficult to tie politicians to the outcomes they promise in their manifestos, or managers like Tim to the outcomes that senior management wanted from him. It is much easier to judge them by their inputs. Did they 'shake things up' by introducing a whole lot of changes? Many health systems around the world are crippled by the determination of their ministers to demonstrate that they can change them, with each set of changes arriving before the previous one has been tested out, and all the staff trying to keep up with how to conduct everyday activities in turbulent circumstances. Similarly, chief executives and other senior managers are appointed in the expectation that they will make change, and may feel pressure to be seen to be 'doing something'. The biggest risk in some senior jobs may be to be accused of doing nothing.

In Tim's case, he has to decide whether to take this risk, once he has established that the 'reforms' he was brought in for were probably a bad idea. He has been appointed to lead a change programme. Can he explain to Patrick why it might be more productive not to make the suggested changes? How much pressure might there be on Patrick too? It is possible to be quite flexible about the changes being made, that is, to make different changes, to change something else which will do no damage, in order to show that you are capable of change. So, rather than make a change that you think will be harmful, you change something else to demonstrate that you can! As Jean-Baptiste Alphonse Karr said, 'plus ça change, plus c'est la même chose' (the more things change, the more they stay the same).

This could be more difficult if Tim had sold himself at interview as being a transformational leader, and thus now needs to show consistency of character by transforming things all over the place. The pressures of selection discourse are such that it is easy for managers to get into implicit pressure to introduce change regardless; to say in an interview, 'I only change things if I find it to be necessary once I get into the role' is unlikely to help the candidate get the job.

CAN CHANGE BE MANAGED?

Implicit in bringing people in to manage change is the idea that change can be managed. This has been questioned. Does anybody ever really manage it, or is it more a matter of doing the best to adapt to change quickly as it happens to you? Is change management more a matter of selling people on the idea of change, and then letting it happen?

There is something heroic about the idea of managing change, but we are reminded of the surfboarder, who appears to be in control and to be achieving a magnificent physical performance, and yet is totally dependent on following the current and the waves. Is managing change more like surfboarding than commanding an army?

This is one of those questions in organizations that is very hard to know the answer to. There are so many people who have made their reputations on managing change, or who have earned very high consultancy fees for assisting in the change process, that they are never going to be content to let it be said that they are simply following the current. However, there are also many more modest practitioners who would say that what they are doing is helping with change, facilitating it, rather than actually managing it. Tim is going to want to be seen as a good manager of change, even though he might want to understand the situation, the currents and the waves, before he starts taking action.

COPING WITH CHANGE AND LEADING CHANGE

It would be wrong, however, to suggest that change is some big phenomenon in the face of which we are all relatively passive. Being able to cope with change is important; there may be little that anyone can achieve in their career if they are unseated by change. But coping may not be an adequate goal. If one is engaged in **leadership**, then one will not simply be coping, but also creating the change that others in turn have to cope with.

This takes us back to the theme of **innovation** at the beginning of this chapter. Innovation is very much a matter of creating change which others will then have to respond to. When the innovators at Sony came up with the Walkman, they were not responding to change or coping with it. They were creating a change in the whole market for portable audio equipment, and in the expectations that customers would have about what could be achieved by such equipment. Innovation is an attempt to lead change.

STAKEHOLDERS IN CHANGE

It is often helpful to think about the different **stakeholders** in any organizational change. Several different lists have been given of the different characters to look out for, and it is probably best to think about your own list for any change situation that you are involved in, but, for example, there may be a *sponsor*, who is behind the change without necessarily being involved in it, a *champion*, who is promoting for the change within the situation, *potential winners* and *potential losers* who may expect to gain or lose from the change taking place, *bystanders* who may act as an audience and may even applaud or boo, and so on. Thinking about all the different stakeholder groups and how their stakes might work out often helps participants to understand why a particular change is going well or badly.

Tim could consider the stakeholders in his situation. Patrick is the sponsor of the change, but if Tim now goes on and does an audit of the other stakeholders, he may be able to learn whether everybody is actually doing a good job and the organization is working satisfactorily, or whether there are some powerful potential losers from change who want him to believe that all is well. He will also need to consider how to fulfil Patrick's needs as sponsor of the change, especially if he is choosing to work differently from the way that he was initially expected to work.

ACTION RESEARCH AND CHANGE

The focus on organizational change began just after the Second World War, at about the same time as the early studies on **scapegoating** and **prejudice**. There was much interest in human systems at that time, fuelled partly by puzzlement about how people and organizations could have behaved as they did during the war. A contributor to many of these debates was Kurt Lewin, a founding figure of **action research** and of the concept of Organization Development that we discussed above; action research can be seen as one of the favourite techniques of Organization Development. Kurt Lewin (1951) argued that the best way to understand a complex system is to try changing it. To understand an animal, for example, one might try moving it or teaching it to run. That attempt at change will give a lot of information about how the animal works. Similarly, in order to understand an organization, one might try changing it and see how the organization responds. Does it push back, and prevent change? Does it change in ways that were not predicted? Does it change into something quite different?

From this, Lewin and later writers developed the notion of action research as a way of building up an understanding of how organizations change. Those who are responsible for change (sometimes referred to, perhaps optimistically, as 'change agents') will do something that could move the organization in the direction that they wish to go. They will do so in the full knowledge that their action may not have the intended consequences, but whatever the consequences, they are likely to learn more about how the organization works, and thus to go back in with another action which has a better chance of moving the organization in their desired direction. (see Figure 15.6)

This cycle can be started at any point, but let us assume it starts from diagnosing. The action researcher tries to work out what is wrong with their organization, and plans

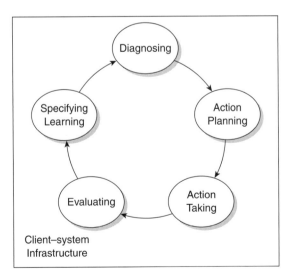

Figure 15.6   The action research cycle.

Source: http://www.cis.gsu.edu/~rbaskerv/CAIS_2_19/Image208.gif

actions which may help to improve things. They then take those actions, and evaluate carefully the results of their actions. This step and the next are two of the distinctive features of action research; in most organizational action, careful evaluation is swept aside by the pressure to get on with the next activity. Next, the action research specifies the learning that was achieved by evaluating that action. Again, this is an activity which can be pushed aside by trying to get on too rapidly with the next action. These two activities of evaluating and specifying learning are what give action research the 'research' part of its name. They are like small experiments, designed to see and measure carefully what happens when you make a particular kind of change. The reason why action research is shown as a cycle is that there is an expectation that it will not be right first time, and the presumption that further experiments will be needed is one of the liberating features of action research as a tool of organizational change.

This action research cycle has become a feature of a very large number of organizational change programmes, and helps all involved deal with the uncertain, unplannable, unpredictable nature of organizational change. If Tim wants to understand his new organization, he may wish to introduce some limited, experimental changes to see what their effect is. Not only will he learn something about the organization, but he will also have some action to point to when asked what he has been doing.

KEY POINTS

○ Innovation is a matter of serendipity.

○ Deciding which innovations to go with is difficult, with many potential innovations never coming into being and other innovations failing.

○ Innovation can be of process as well as of product.

○ Entrepreneurship is when someone innovates an organization to support an innovation that they have made in product or process.

○ Innovation needs to be balanced with stability in organizations.

○ All organizations are changing all the time.

○ Organization Development is a set of ideas and practices intended to help work with organizational change.

○ People can love or hate change, and when they resist it, this may be for good reason.

○ Some people build their careers on their reputation for making change.

○ Change may not be manageable.

○ Leading change in an industry is an important part of doing business, and goes well beyond ideas of coping.

○ To understand change, it is helpful to consider how it looks to each of the stakeholders.

○ Action research is a way of making change in an experimental fashion, so that lessons can be learned and further actions designed from the outcome.

>>>>>>>>>>>>> **THEORETICAL SIGNPOSTS** >>>>>>>>>>>>>>

The major themes in this chapter have been examined in the following very broad areas of literature:

> innovation
> organizational change
> action research.

Innovation

Innovation, often studied in connection with creativity and entrepreneurship, is increasingly seen as a quality conferring competitive advantage on individuals, firms or even nations. In his classic text *Capitalism, Socialism and Democracy*, Joseph Schumpeter examined the technological forces underpinning economic growth, arguing that entrepreneurs develop new products and services by the 'carrot of spectacular reward' and the 'stick of destitution', resulting in 'gales of creative destruction' across society (Schumpeter, 1943).

Technological innovation involves new products, new services or new processes for producing and delivering products and services. Change may be incremental or radical. Incremental innovation occurs frequently in many industries, involving the exploitation of existing know-how and is a major source of underlying profitability. Radical innovation involves a great deal of uncertainty and risk, occurs infrequently, requires an organizational setting that promotes exploration (rather than exploitation) and may destroy existing competencies (March, 1991; Tushman and Anderson, 1986).

In the recent past, a number of information and communication technologies have converged, enabling firms to innovate more rapidly, efficiently and accurately than ever before (Dodgson et al., 2005). This 'Innovation Technology' (IvT), includes eScience, virtual reality, modelling, simulation techniques and rapid prototyping (Gann and Dodgson, 2007). Using this emerging technological infrastructure requires changes in the innovation process, with consequences for strategy and management. It offers the potential to overcome some of the barriers to innovation, making things that were previously costly and difficult to risk-assess more straightforward, providing better and more comprehensible information from researchers, customers and other stakeholders. It can enable firms to develop new products and services more quickly and efficiently than in the past, allowing people to create more adventurous innovations. It can also bring new risks and uncertainty about the quality of data and nature of decision making (Dodgson et al., 2007).

Organizational Change

Change and resistance to change are important features of organizational life. Not all change is deliberate, nor can it always be safely managed and controlled. Nevertheless, some change may be necessary for the economic survival of an enterprise, and may be very much in the interests of its owners and managers. However, change is often seen by some people (including managers) as threatening their position, status, relationships, competence or security. It is for this reason that change is often accompanied by some conflict.

Theorists of organization have been preoccupied by change, both as something that happens naturally and as something that may be planned, implemented and resisted. Theorists distinguish between *first-order* change and *second-order* change (Bartunek and Moch, 1987). The former involves small adjustments to work methods, such as having more team meetings to solve a communication problem, while the latter looks more deeply at the beliefs and **assumptions** behind existing work practices.

Yet, in spite of the scholarship that has been generated by change, most organizational change attempts end in failure. According to one estimate, only a third of all change initiatives lead to any success at all (Beer and Nohria, 2000: 2). One reason is a tendency to underestimate the extent to which people need order in their lives. Change, whether advocated by politicians or business leaders, is seen as a 'good thing' and those who **resist** it are deemed to be standing in the way of progress. Yet, routine, stability and order are important to most people's lives. Every change causes disruption and is, therefore, costly and, to an extent, unpredictable.

Theorists of change differ in their views on how far change can be managed. At one extreme lie theories such as Theory E (Beer and Nohria, 2000) which believe control is both possible and desirable and that change should be directed. At the other extreme lie complexity and chaos theories (Stacey, 1992, 1995) which argue that managers are powerless to control the change process. Other approaches fall in between. Theory O (Beer and Nohria, 2000) advocates that managers build commitment and so change can only be shaped rather than directed. This is also a line taken by authors studying cultural change in organizations (Ogbonna and Harris, 2002a). Theorists of transformative **leadership** see managers' role as one of leading through interpreting or reinterpreting the world (Tichy and Devanna, 1986), while Pettigrew's processual/emergent model approaches change more as a matter of navigating than controlling (Pettigrew et al., 2001).

Action Research

Action research is a form of inquiry in which the researcher makes small or large interventions to a situation or a **system** he/she is observing and then observes the outcomes of these actions and adjusts them. These interventions can be seen as quasi-experiments or imperfect experiments, where all external conditions cannot be controlled but convincing links can be made between causes and effects. The term action research was coined by social psychologist Kurt Lewin in the 1940s, who defined it as 'a spiral of steps, each of which is composed of a circle of planning, action, and fact-finding about the result of the action' (Lewin and Lewin, 1948: 206).

The use of the term 'action research' has been broadened over the years. It has sometimes been used to refer to consulting activities, where the motivation of the 'researcher' has more to do with showing the client that an 'experiment' has succeeded, and that it is therefore worth paying the bill, than to do with any search for as yet unknown answers to questions (Eden and Huxham, 1996; French and Bell, 1999; Reason and Bradbury, 2001; Whitehead, 2000).

REVIEW QUESTIONS

1. How would you help an organization to be more innovative? Are there costs as well as benefits to this?

2. Change is an essential part of life in organizations. Why would people resist change, and what can others do if they find themselves working with people who resist?

3. Organizations are so complicated that the only way to understand them is to try to change them. How can action research help in the understanding of organizations?

---

companion
website
w.sagepub.co.uk/fineman

Reading On

The articles below are available for free to readers of the fourth edition of *Organizing & Organizations* via the book's companion website at www.sagepub.co.uk/fineman

Bartunek, J.M. and Moch, M.K. (1987) 'First-order, second-order, and third-order change and organization development interventions: a cognitive approach', *Journal of Applied Behavioral Science*, 23 (4): 483–500.
This article discusses how recent developments in the cognitive sciences can illumine the practice of organization development. On the basis of a cognitive perspective, the authors discuss the relationship between organizational change and schemata, describing several orders of change that might result from OD. To show how understanding the differences among orders of change can help clarify problems and solutions from an intervention, the authors discuss how a paternalism schema affected a particular quality of working life intervention.

Caldwell, R. (2005) 'Things fall apart? Discourses on agency and change in organizations', *Human Relations*, 58: 83–114.
This article presents a selective interdisciplinary history of competing disciplinary discourses on agency and change in organizations, classified into *rationalist, contextualist, dispersalist* and *constructionist* discourses. Although the four discourses clarify the meta-theoretical terrain of agency in relation to organizational change theories, the growing plurality of discourses challenges the social scientific ambitions of the research field to be objective, cumulative or unified

Sorge, A. and van Witteloostuijn, A. (2004) 'The (non)sense of organizational change: an essai about universal management hypes, sick consultancy metaphors, and healthy organization theories', *Organization Studies*, 25: 1205–31.

This paper argues that the global business world is infected by a virus that induces a permanent need for organizational change, fed by the management consultancy industry. The authors argue that the application of healthy organization theories offers ample guidelines for organizational change initiatives that make more sense than prominent management consultancy rhetoric and plead for the development of an evidence-based (change) consultancy practice.

Swan, J., Scarbrough, H. and Robertson, M. (2002) 'The construction of "communities of practice" in the management of innovation, *Management Learning*, 33 (4): 477–96.

This article contributes to the debates on the construction of communities of practice and their role in the innovation process through a case study of a radical innovation for the treatment of prostate cancer. While the case highlights attempts by managers to construct communities as 'social objects', it also underlines the shift in management strategies and practices associated with such a construction.

16

FEELINGS

This chapter brings feelings and emotions to the foreground. Behaviour and performance in organizations are intimately connected to what workers are feeling and how they are able, or unable, to express those feelings. Emotion theories give us some clues as to what may be happening – for instance, how emotions are learned within different national and organizational cultures and how they are bound by implicit and explicit rules. Many jobs require emotional and aesthetic labour, a fact that has been exploited in the burgeoning service industry. The role of specific emotions for enhanced performance has been much vaunted, especially those associated with job satisfaction, emotional intelligence and being positive. Do they deliver as promised? And, contrastingly, how can toxic emotions be avoided, buffered or contained?

It's hard to answer the phone when there's a customer who is screaming right from the start. It catches you off guard. You take offence. Then the customer says that they don't mean to vent on you. And you say 'I understand' (the call-centre representative is gritting her teeth as a demonstration of holding back her anger). (Pratt and Doucet, 2000: 212)

The Body Shop talks about the body, having relaxed forms of interaction. People are frisky, touch, hug, kiss. Women are so excited by their work. They have an emotional support system. They are valued. They have new ways of communicating. (Martin et al., 2000: 130)

Organizations may well portray themselves as **rational** and dispassionate, but it is clear that the human beings who operate them do not park their feelings at the reception desk or factory gate. We bring with us the difficulties, moods and **desires** from last night or the day before. We confront colleagues and customers we feel warm, neutral or decidedly uneasy about. We have 'up' days and 'down' days. We anticipate the stresses of the next production meeting and the fun of the night out with colleagues after work. Organizations are *emotional arenas* where we play out different dramas, some toned with boredom, disaffection, perhaps fear; others with joy, pride and excitement.

Figure 16.1   Emotions.

Working with our own and others' **emotions** is part of the unacknowledged, but fundamental, fabric of organizational life. Organizations have different emotion **cultures** and **sub-cultures** which shape the way feelings may or may not be expressed. The contrasting quotations above show how a call centre and The Body Shop place very different emotion expectations on their employees – what has to be controlled and what can be expressed. Few organizations are emotion-free ports where anything goes. There are always boundaries to acceptable and unacceptable emotion display, learned through organizational socialization (see Chapter 4, 'Motives and Motivating').

Many emotional encounters happen unremarkably, fleetingly. For example, Alice's boss John strides purposefully to her desk:

> 'Morning Alice. A new week ... and how are you today?'
> Alice replies quickly, with a slightly strained smile: 'Oh, I'm fine, John. It's a nice day, isn't it?'

Such interactions appear trivial. They are often ritualistic ways of mutual acknowledgement, of saying 'hello'. But they also mark out communicative territory, such as whether to close or continue an exchange. John goes for a more probing follow-up:

> 'Yes, it's nice today. Sure you're OK? You look a bit tired. Oh dear, something been happening over the weekend?'

The ways that such interactions continue depend on the emotional rules of engagement and protocols within the office sub-culture, shaped by power differences and the history relationships. For instance, what John did not know, and would not know from Alice, was that her 'tiredness' was a symptom of much deeper troubles. Her unsaid thoughts and feelings were: 'Well, John, I had a terrible time last night with my boyfriend. I think we're going to break up. I feel shattered. But that's none of your business. I feel really pissed off working here too, especially the way you pretend to be interested in my welfare when I know you really couldn't care less'.

MASTERING THE DISGUISE

In our **socialization**, from a very early age, we are rapidly taught when to disguise our feelings and how to present the 'correct' face for a particular situation or circumstance – for instance, the importance of appearing calm in workplace interactions and not looking upset, even if one feels quite distressed. We may harbour strong feelings – fears, anger, passions – but they are to be kept under control and carefully managed. Brenda, an office clerk, reveals how:

> There are good days, mostly when he [the boss] is not in ... I think things are picking up, maybe I'm starting to fit in, maybe I was imagining all the bad stuff and I don't have to look for a new job ... But then the next day is terribly bad and I just scream in my car on the way home. (Harlos and Pinder, 2000: 253)

While it is common to use the terms 'feeling' and 'emotion' interchangeably, it is helpful to separate them. Feelings are essentially private, 'internal' experiences, which often have both psychological and physical manifestations, such as the stomach churning and sense of apprehension before a job interview. They provide an essential, personal readout on how we are doing, how we are relating to the world as we try to deal with it. We also have feelings about feelings, such as being angry at feeling upset, or anxious about our infatuation with someone. Emotions can be seen as the outward presentation of our feelings through learned social codes. We may, for example, express our feelings of anger in very restrained or 'acceptable' ways during a meeting at work (such as Alice did earlier), more openly at home, 'screaming' in the car like Brenda, or heavily masked in the presence of an authority figure, such as a police officer. Our emotions may be entirely faked, such as appearing very jolly but feeling miserable at a party: jollity is the expected 'thing', the party norm.

Different ways of disguising or managing feelings are essential features of human **communication**. They distinguish national **cultures**. Travellers switching cultures, such as from emotionally constrained Northern Europe to more expressive Latin or African countries, are often acutely aware of these differences and the problems they pose. Do the smiles and nods mean pleasure, acceptance or just recognition? Is the 'angry' face serious or playful? Is the physical touching a sign of intimacy and sexual attraction or a more routine acknowledgement? Organizations, of course, are microcosms of such processes, but are overlaid with their own emotion rules and codes as the call centre and The Body Shop show. Some organizations, like theatre groups and social clubs, celebrate the open expression of feelings, especially joy or disappointment. Others, such as the military and civil service, pride themselves on their stricter control over feelings: there is a narrower band of feelings which are legitimate to express. In each case, emotion codes are firmly set within the formal hierarchical culture and its different operational settings. Soldiers, for instance, learn when and where it is appropriate or inappropriate to display fear, grief, anger or pride.

Organizational position and gender make a difference. Top managers often have to demonstrate that they are clear, decisive thinkers, not simply 'victims' of their feelings, a legacy of a long history of 'maleness' in management and leadership. Female leaders who show 'decisive' characteristics win a certain ironic praise, such as the 'iron maiden' descriptions of the UK's Prime Minister Margaret Thatcher back in the 1980s. While women may be permitted to be rather more emotionally expressive than men, they are often to contain their 'unreliable' feelings in public in the interests of logic, rationality and decorum. If they do not, they risk confirming the negative **stereotype** that people, especially men, hold of them (see Chapter 17, 'Sex'). One female principal of a school was convinced that a golden rule for her own survival was never to show her feelings of vulnerability: 'You have to be careful about the people you ask advice from … I wouldn't ask advice from another principal, especially if it was a male because I would be afraid that they would be making judgements about my not coping (Sachs and Blackmore, 1998: 275).

Typically, corporate success for women has meant learning male-type behaviours and male emotional expression: competing with men on men's terms. A female middle manager in a dominantly male, and macho, car retailing organization, described her position to us as follows:

> They call me 'dearie' or 'young lady', even those who are much younger than me. If I'm ill or a bit off colour, my manager keeps asking me whether I'm pregnant. They have reluctantly agreed to pay for me to study for a part-time MBA, but only if I sign a pay-back clause in case I leave the firm within two years. The interesting thing is that no male manager has ever been asked to do this. I need to swallow all this stuff and meet them on their terms. I have to show that I'm one of them even though I feel I'm not. So, for example, I've taken to putting on overalls, going down to the car service bay, driving onto a ramp, and saying to the boys there: 'OK, I want to learn to service it; show me'. They're amazed, and it works a treat.

Gendering influences the meaning and expression of feelings such as care, pain, love, sensitivity, aggression and anxiety – what is regarded as appropriate for a man or a woman. Women can reveal their pain and distress (but that could make them 'unsuitable' for many top management positions); men should hide it. Women can cry (only to be judged by men as 'emotional', which women often resent); men should not show tears. While these differences are not as extreme as they once were, such gendering encourages occupational stereotyping – with women's jobs and men's jobs divided according to supposed emotional and **skill** requirements. There is no biological or emotional necessity for such gender divisions; however, it may be convenient for men to believe that they are more temperamentally suited to jobs which happen to have the most **power**, pay and prestige in our society.

INTELLIGENT EMOTIONS?

There has been a long tradition of separating feeling from thinking, or *affect* from *cognition*. Feelings have been regarded as interference to the 'higher' faculties – of good thinking and wise judgement. Recently, however, this view has been turned on its head. Feelings do not interrupt or sidetrack decision processes, they help *make* them. Indeed, without feelings, we cannot sense the world, we cannot make choices or decide on what is right or wrong. Dealing with problems and organizational relationships often involves 'gut feelings', hunches and anxieties informed diffusely and often non-consciously from our past learnings and experiences, and these are key in shaping where we go and what we do. Rational decision aids, such as step-by-step guides or statistical modelling techniques cannot *make* decisions. *We* do this, guided by our feelings.

The connection between feeling and thinking has been given a particular slant in the idea of **emotional intelligence**. Emotional intelligence refers broadly to the different ways that people are able to recognize and 'read' emotions in themselves and others, and then manage them effectively. For example, we may recognize that we feel angry with a colleague. An emotionally intelligent response could be to give ourselves a period to cool down rather than risk an instant confrontation which could permanently damage the relationship.

Emotional intelligence has been much promoted in the media and popular management literature. Some promise to raise your emotional intelligence, or emotional quotient (EQ), by special training. Many claim it is the key to managerial leadership, even life success, especially in the use of positive emotions such as empathy, composure, hope and enthusiasm.

Rarely, however, have there been instant-fix solutions to complex organizational problems, and it is wise to see emotional intelligence in this light. Currently, there is confusion as to its precise conceptualization – different theorists emphasize different qualities or behaviours. There are also many different measures of emotional intelligence which tend not to correlate with each other, raising questions as to how emotional intelligence can be reliably and validly assessed.

Emotional intelligence is still struggling for academic clarity, yet its undeniable wider appeal suggests that, as a general idea, it is seen as a hitherto missing ingredient in our understanding of organizational behaviour. This attraction is significant. It rests on the belief that some emotions can be deployed better than others to productive organizational ends; it is much less to do with valuing emotions in their own right. The jury is out as to whether emotional intelligence can be learned like many other life skills, or whether it is already fixed, one way or another, in the adult personality.

PUTTING FEELINGS TO WORK

Since the 1950s, managers have been interested in the way that workers' feelings of satisfaction with their job affect their productivity. The intuitively plausible assumption has been that a satisfied worker is also a productive one. Consequently, much research has been aimed at seeking ways of enhancing job satisfaction, from playing music while you work to splitting assembly lines into 'autonomous working groups'. Jobs became 'enlarged' and 'enriched'. Volvo, for example, broke with the traditions of mass car production, permitting their assemblers to work in teams around separate workstations. Together, team members could decide on how much they would produce and in what way. Participation was seen to be central to worker satisfaction. And it was for some, for a time. For others, it was not.

It soon became clear that a satisfied worker was not necessarily a more productive one. For example, while jobs can be enriched in the manner described, this rarely touches the essential meaninglessness of the task to many operators. Other than in spe-cial cultural conditions, such as in Japan, it is unusual to find mass-production workers strongly identifying with the product. Overall design, control and supervi-sion still, typically, rest with management. What employee participation provides, however, is an opportunity for workers to come out of their social isolation (e.g. standing at a workstation on a long production line) and to enjoy emotional release and bonding through chat and sharing with colleagues. Their social satisfaction can rise, but that does not mean they work any harder or that the task is seen as any more attractive.

There is a further consideration. Satisfaction is a complex phenomenon, which can-not simply be produced, or induced, at the turn of a managerial key. Overall **job satisfaction** or dissatisfaction disguises the frequent fluctuations in satisfaction as the day passes. So a person's high satisfaction at, say, 11.15 a.m. (met a deadline), may drop to mild dissatisfaction at 12.20 p.m. (can't contact an important customer), to deep dissatisfaction at 4.00 p.m. (report rejected by boss). Satisfaction is deeply embedded in the subtleties of our relationship to our work and organization, dis-tinctly coloured by our personal desires and the different **meanings** that events have for us. Grand managerial attempts to raise job satisfaction are, at best, likely to be only partly successful.

Getting Positive

Following in the footsteps of satisfaction (and, to a degree, emotional intelligence), organizational researchers have recently explored the role of different kinds of positive emotions in the workplace, including vitality, compassion, optimism, meaningfulness, exhilaration and fulfilment at work. Take compassion. Compassion is the way people reach out to others when they are distressed or hurting. It is something most of us value receiving, but can find hard or awkward to offer in the confines of the role rela-tionships at work. But compassion can be helped along:

> When Alan was breaking up with Mary he was late to work, he was making mistakes, and the boss understood about it. He allowed him to make more mistakes than he usu-ally would have. He sort of let the rest of us know that we needed to keep an eye out to help him or whatever. He talked to everybody about it. (Frost et al., 2000: 31)

Small acts such as these can open, or refresh, communication channels, and have a positive impact on the way participants feel about the organization and each other. A positive perspective also looks at, for instance, how the experience of pride, joy and contentment at work can produce a self-reinforcing, upward spiral of well-being, and how tasks can be shaped to engage people in a positive way, producing feelings of 'flow', or total absorption in one's work (of the sort often reported by creative writers, surgeons, artists and computer programmers).

Positive approaches such as these are appealing. Who would not want a workplace where good feelings and good acts prevail, where the very best is appreciated? But, like some of the caveats we have raised about emotional intelligence and satisfaction, we need to look somewhat cautiously at the area. While genuine compassion may be welcome, a climate of forced jollity can jar. It can be especially oppressive when one actually feels little pride, joy or optimism in one's work. A positive ethos, or 'positive mental attitude', is much in tune with North American cultures, but less so with, for example, the more wary British and less demonstrative Northern Europeans. Moreover, a rounded emotional life feeds off joys and disappointments, fallibilities as well as strengths. A degree of pessimism is self-protective, helping us do our best by preparing for the worst. And a negative voice can be the realistic one, puncturing over-comfortable illusions and collusions in an upbeat organizational culture.

Cultivating positive attitudes and feelings obscures the fact that many jobs are designed with little interest in worker joy, meaningfulness or fulfillment. The rapidly expanding world of 'fast' or 'instant' customer services (e.g. fast food, telesales, call centres, theme parks) has come to epitomize the fine-tuning of technical and human operations, but where flow is a production goal not a psychological experience. The *appearance* of employee pleasure, though, is often crucial to their service and public image.

For example, one study reveals how McDonald's and Burger King's managers in New York frequently prompt migrant employees to 'leave your problems at home' and to report to work in a 'good mood'. If they do not comply, a tougher regime is imposed. A manager explains how:

> I'll go up to their faces and I go, 'What is wrong?' They look at me and they don't know what I am doing. 'What is wrong with your face?' 'I am smiling. You don't know what it is like? You have to smile right?' (Talwar, 2002: 114)

McDonald's and Burger King have taken seriously the role of displaying the 'right' emotions in promoting their wares, but they make little concession to the different cultural backgrounds and difficulties of those they employ. These companies are part of a fast-growing trend in the prescription of emotions that they regard as essential to sell their goods or services.

Engineering Emotions

British Airways once ran an advertisement for customer service agents. It portrayed a smiling employee's face with the caption: 'when you're smiling the whole world smiles with you'. The Disney theme-park 'cast' are instructed to 'always make eye contact and smile; greet and welcome each and every guest; say "thank you" to each and every guest; demonstrate patience and honesty in handling complaints'. And in a training session for financial services telesales staff, participants are told to practise an 'upbeat emotional tone by imagining good things; if all else fails you should fake it "'til you make it"'.

Here, the 'correct' emotion is an intrinsic part of the service. The smile, the 'caring' face, the optimism is intended to engage or sooth the customer and also encourages repeat business. As some emotions are contagious, the client or customer can 'catch' the sales agent's emotions and, it is hoped, warm to the service offered. Centrally, however, employees have to sustain the right emotions if they are to survive in the

Figure 16.2   Forced smiles.

job; it is by their **emotional labour** that they are judged. The rules about what to express, and how to express it, have been decided in advance by executives in a boardroom and have to be learned by heart. Of course, effective salespeople have long had an intuitive appreciation about the importance of displaying the appropriate interest, concern, understanding and warmth if they are going to clinch a sale. What has changed is the extent of corporate control over what they should or should not express or feel. It is inculcated in training sessions, and in corporate 'universities', such as McDonald's 'Hamburger University' and the 'Disney University'.

The point comes over strongly in a study by an American researcher, Arlie Hochschild. She studied what happened to flight attendants in a major American airline. The flight attendants were pushed very hard by their company to practise an 'inside-out' smile. They needed to believe the act and take it within themselves. In this way, they should feel OK about the crowded, hectic life in the cabin of the aircraft, and they really should not mind whatever a passenger throws at them – metaphorically and sometimes literally. Flight attendants were taught to perfect their emotional performance and keep it fresh through regular training. In this way, as superheroes and heroines of the aircraft cabin, adversity and abuse should be received and re-processed with a smile and a kind word.

Emotional labour is now prevalent among many mass-produced services. Some employees treat it as a challenge, with the fun of putting on an act that they can easily slip in and out of. Others, however, get caught up in the company message,

Figure 16.3   The inside-out smile.

taking it to heart to the extent that they become confused about their own feelings. Still others end up cynical and exhausted, numb from having to keep up contrived appearances for hours on end:

> A young businessman said to a flight attendant, 'Why aren't you smiling?' She put her tray back on the food cart and said, 'I'll tell you what. You smile first, then I'll smile.' The businessman smiled at her. 'Good,' she replied. 'Now freeze and hold that for fifteen hours.' (Hochschild, 1983: 127)

> Some days I just can't do it. There's only so much you can smile and put on a phony face. Sometimes I'm actually too tired or bored or pissed off at the world to pretend I am happy, but my jobs require that I am happy all the time. (Pinder, 1988: 111)

Relief in such circumstances can be hard to find. The call-centre operator, for example, on long, closely supervised shifts can feel drained by the constant 'smile down the phone' to callers who can be brusque, angry or insulting. The mask can only be safely dropped in zones where different **emotion rules** and expectations apply, such as short breaks by the water cooler or over coffee with colleagues. For flight attendants, the galley of the aircraft can be a haven, where the awkward customer or client can be mocked, cursed or reviled.

Many organizations have such 'backstage' zones where the public courtesies of emotional control can be relaxed. The school staff common room, the restaurant kitchen, the nurses' rest area, the works' cafe and the judge's 'chambers' are all nogo areas for the public. There, feelings about the student, customer, patient, accused or client can be more freely expressed. The professional mask is dropped for a while and private feelings can spill out. The switch from public mask to private and back again can occur many times in a working day. The waiter epitomizes this as he or she criss-crosses the boundary between restaurant and kitchen – calm, cool and collected at one moment; shouting for orders and being shouted at the next. Similarly, a police officer can show restrained politeness to an abusive motorist just caught for speeding, but then 'return' the abuse in the privacy of his patrol car – to the eager ear of a colleague. These examples remind us that emotional labour is not restricted to scripted customer service work; it is what managers and professional workers do too.

Yet what is emotionally presented backstage is not an emotion-free zone. It is itself regulated by the norms of the workgroup. There are *implicit* emotion rules, often carefully constructed by group members. We can see this in the following description of a US receptionist (dispatcher) responding to a call on a police emergency line:

> 'Police department. Pardon me? Okay, hold please.' Julie hung her head, slapping her forehead with frustration. 'This guy wants to know if oral sex is illegal in this state. I don't have the patience for this tonight,' she announced. [No one] appeared to be too fazed by the call. Her partner, Susanne, shouted out the question to a police officer, who happened to be walking out of the despatch room. He came back and informed the dispatchers, 'Yes, actually it is illegal. It's under sodomy.' Julie pushed the hold button to reconnect the waiting caller. [Coolly she said]: 'An officer on duty just said that it is illegal in this state' … and then [she] hung up. The officer, who was now standing next to the dispatchers, said, 'I've never broken the law,' and then started laughing. 'Shut up and get the hell out here!' replied Julie with mock indignation. (Shuler and Sypher, 2000: 51)

The dispatcher interacted with the caller with professional neutrality, displaying neither impatience nor mirth. Her emotional labour remained intact. But off-line, ironic humour was an acceptable way of dealing with the absurdity and irritation of the call. In this same setting, however, dealing with the effects of major crises was regulated in a very different manner. Many calls were about disaster, tragedy, sorrow or pain. Containing these intense feelings demanded hard, sometimes overwhelming, emotional labour. The **norm**, however, was not to share these feelings with colleagues so as to avoid overburdening the group. As 'coping **professionals**', they were expected to take these responsibilities on themselves; or failing that, to an independent counsellor.

The Gift

Emotional labourers in bureaucratic settings are often pretty much shackled by prescribed emotion rules and scripts. There is little they can give emotionally to customers other than what they are told or trained to give. Off-script conversations with customers are usually discouraged, even prohibited. But there is an unwritten rule in organizational behaviour of the sort: the more you constrain people, the more they will find ways of loosening those constraints. In other words, people will find ways of expressing themselves, regardless. For example, in one telephone banking centre, emotional labour was extreme and relentless, but this did not entirely suppress worker spontaneity:

At the weekend, on a Saturday, you get old women or men phoning and they just want to talk. It's great, I love getting these calls.

Another expressed similar sentiments, but with a sense of caution:

We get a lot of people who are on their own, they're pensioners. They ask for a balance, and they will want a chat ... 'what's the weather like?' I'm quite happy to chat to them, but it's always in the back of your mind, got to watch my average handling time. (Callaghan and Thomson, 2002: 250)

This is philanthropic emotional labour. It is giving something for free that offers the receiver pleasure or solace. Ironically, it is such spontaneous events that can endear some customers to the service, but at the same time be seen by management as an inefficient use of the operator's time as 'they should be moving on to the next caller'.

THE BRANDED BODY

Many emotional labourers are on public display. They literally embody their employer's product or brand. They exhibit it through the uniform they wear, their make-up, hairstyle or costume. Behind the hotel-chain reception desk, on the restaurant floor, at the doorway of the fashion store, on the theme park 'stage', the employee sports the product image – its colours, styles, actual merchandise. In these circumstances, emotional labour fuses with *aesthetic labour* – having to look pleasing to the observer, but pleasing according to the corporate brand.

Codes on dressing 'suitably' have long been embedded in all occupations – formal or informal, suit or casual, hair length and so forth – but the level of corporate prescription has grown considerably. 'Total branding' is now common, which includes all physical features of the product, packaging, marketing, advertising, service – and the employee. For example, Cadbury's high-street shops in the UK have the distinctive colour and logo style of their chocolate wrappers, including all shop decorations, carpets, furnishings and the assistants' clothing. Body appearance is meticulously 'designer' for flight attendants, to match the airline's image of the day, while the Disneyworld 'clean-cut' appearance is enforced through exact requirements on hair length and style, make-up, deodorant, nail polish and length of fingernails. And in some restaurant chains, the waitress's skimpy clothing is a mandatory part of the 'cool', 'sexy' image.

Aesthetic labour means working to look right in appearance, poise and general demeanour. Aesthetic labour can be felt in different ways by the worker. It can be fun, performing publicly and looking good. It can be a source of personal pride to be visibly associated with an organization that has a distinctive and respected brand in the marketplace. But there is a downside. Rarely does one aesthetic size fit all. A worker's self-image can clash with the organization's brand, creating emotional dissonance, a tension between expected appearances and feelings about oneself. In some work settings, such as fast food, the uniform can identify the worker as a member of a low-status, stigmatized occupation. Indeed, there is evidence that this can expose them to **harassment**, inside and outside of work.

In organizations where the worker is expected to appear warm, friendly and 'available' to the 'sovereign' customer, the public/private divide is often frequently tested, sometimes to breaking point. The welcome aura that the worker portrays can be taken as an invitation to make unreasonable and unwanted demands. A male hotel receptionist recalls his anxieties during one such incident:

> One guest, oh my God, he comes down and says, 'Do you have any entertainment?' And we said 'What?' 'Can you send one of your colleagues up to our room?' and I said 'Hm – no, I don't think she'll go up to your room' and he goes 'Well, you'll do anyway' and I said 'No, we don't provide that service' and walked off. (Guerrier and Adib, 2000: 689)

The receptionist draws a line that he will not cross. Many hotels take pains to inform their guests that they will be 'doing all we can to make your stay more pleasurable'. It is the individual worker who has to live the full implications or realities of the maxim, and somehow also retain his or her self-respect.

TOXIC EMOTIONS

It has long been observed that extreme stress can be contagious. People can arrive at work reasonably relaxed but, because of another person's **stress**, end up feeling stressed themselves. As stress carriers, especially those in powerful positions, move around an organization, their influence can become widespread, emotionally miasmic. The spread of toxic emotions, such as pain and fear, can paralyse people, creating a defensive and depressed workforce. This can be especially prevalent in times of uncertainty when, for instance, redundancy is in the air or when the workload peaks ('how on earth will we cope?').

Some toxins are linked to leadership. **Leaders** who rule by fear, impulse or harsh command can seed anxiety and fearfulness in the organization. It soon spreads unless it is contained in some way. 'Toxin handlers' can play this role. Toxin handlers are rather like sponges, soaking in and holding the damaging emotions, keeping the worst of the distress of pain away from others. One manager describes his approach:

> I feel very protective towards them because they are my team and I built that team and they are working for me. Some of the stupidity of the politics – it would be unfair to allow it to hit them.

Managers will often shield their team, work group or department. In hierarchical organizations, especially, diffusing or deflecting impatient or angry demands from 'above' can be part of the **skill** of keeping a work team intact. Indeed, some high-profile chief executives, known for their maverick, abrasive styles, have survived due to the efforts of their toxin handlers. The handlers translate and smooth their boss's messages into a palatable form for other members of the organization. They are often the unsung heroes of organizations, their resilience being vital to the organization's functioning.

FEELINGS – AND VIRTUAL WORK

So far, our discussion about feelings relates mostly to organizations where employees meet face to face. But what happens to feelings and emotions when the physical presence goes, when organizing is virtual – through the computer screen, webcam or mobile phone? Is teleworking an emotionally impoverished world, remote and lonely? Or are there different ways that emotions operate in a virtual context?

The considerable flexibility attributed to virtual work presents a one-sided picture. It omits the role of emotions in the making and breaking of relationships. It is normally hard to know what colleagues, customers or clients are feeling without face-to-face contact. Trust, for example, usually requires physical presence and exposure to verbal and non-verbal signs of emotion, and all their subtlety. People dealing constantly with virtual customers can lack the sense of immediacy and feeling knowledge that come from eye-to-eye encounters. Interactions can feel hollow and alienating for all parties involved.

For some global teleworkers, who work from wherever they happen to be on the planet, the virtual window never closes because of international time zones. It is a toil that can create 'e-stress', where email silence and delayed response are met with anxious anticipation and compulsive logging in. Feelings of loneliness and separateness can grip the virtual worker, tied to his or her machine with no colleagues with whom to socialize.

It is clear that working virtually can be emotionally demanding. But virtual technologies, like all forms of communication, also offer new ways of working with, and expressing, emotion. In other words, we are able to construct for ourselves different emotional possibilities, where virtuality becomes a virtue rather than a handicap. For example, emails have become emotionalized with emoticons and various font notations for indicating feeling. Email and web communications are a liberating influence for some, because they do not reveal the sender's race, sex, age, appearance or dress, by which people typically are pigeon-holed and **stereotyped**. Similarly, feeling shy or intimidated in face-to-face situations is not an obvious problem when communicating online: the medium provides an open door for the socially less confident. And while some teleworkers can feel oppressed with their load and isolation, others experience exactly the opposite. It provides them with relief from the stress and dreariness of commuting to work and from unrewarding office **politics**. It helps give flexibility to their life, to better balance the different spheres.

Virtual working is more than an ingenious application of information technology to different ways of working. It is also a radical restructuring of our social and emotional lives. While the emotional losses for some are gains for others, there is an important lesson to be drawn. The design and management of virtual forms of work are also exercises in emotion management; they are inextricably linked. Concentrating on the technology alone is insufficient (see Chapter 19, 'Virtuality').

IN CONCLUSION

Feelings are not an unfortunate by-product of organizational life. They are not sand in the organizational machinery, but key lubricants for making things happen. Feelings, while essentially private, can also become public property in the way organizations deliberately shape and use them to sell their goods and services. What we may appreciate receiving – the smile, the 'hi', the 'have a nice day', the seductive or branded uniform – can be a source of pride, toleration, discomfort or despair by those who assume them. As organizations create and confront different markets and technologies, the emotional consequences will change. Understanding, and acting on, these changes is a new challenge for management.

KEY POINTS

○ Feelings and their control are intrinsic to human organizing; organizations have rules of emotional display.

○ Many jobs involve the creation of the 'right' emotional expression for particular situations.

○ Some jobs and roles require more personal effort than others to control one's private feelings. The emotional labour involved can be stressful.

○ Some organizations systematically manipulate employees' feelings and body image for commercial gain.

○ Emotional intelligence and positive emotions have become particularly fashionable, as well as controversial, in recent years.

○ We learn the rules of emotion display according to our culture, our gender and our work organizations.

○ Many organizations develop informal rituals through which private feelings can be more easily expressed.

○ Social changes, especially from feminism, have challenged traditional assumptions about feelings and rationality in organizations – but male ways still tend to prevail.

○ Virtual organizations have brought their own particular codes and challenges to the way emotion can be expressed and shared.

>>>>>>>>>>>> THEORETICAL SIGNPOSTS >>>>>>>>>>>>

Feelings and emotions in the workplace have recently become a special interest among organizational researchers. Their theoretical backgrounds reflect a variety of disciplines, especially psychology, sociology and biology. However, historians and anthropologists have also provided important insights. Broadly, though, the field is located in two major streams of literature:

> accounts about the nature and functions of human emotion
> the application of emotion theories to the workplace.

Accounts About the Nature and Functions of Human Emotion

There are both competing and complementary theories on the role of emotion in human behaviour. They include theories that consider emotion's evolutionary role in human survival, such as in dealing with personal threats and danger ('flight or fight'); emotion as a key signalling and communicative device in social interaction; and emotion as essential to the making and creation of meaning and action choices. Oatley et al. (2006) and Fineman (2003) provide a good overview of these perspectives, particularly: how many emotions are socially constructed and learned and reflect our culture, gender assumptions and power structures; the importance of how we appraise a situation or event as a trigger to specific feelings; and the psychoanalytic/Freudian view that our early life experiences set the emotional sub-structure for later desires and anxieties, sources of which we are often unaware.

The Application of Emotion Theories to the Workplace

A very readable introduction to these areas can be found in Fineman (1993, 2003). More in-depth discussions are covered by Ashforth and Humphrey (1995). Together, these writings show how emotions can be understood as part of the culture, structures and rules of organizational life, as well as being specific to particular organizational practices. Psychoanalytic applications can be found in the analysis of dysfunctional work groups and leadership (see Gabriel, 1999b; Gabriel and Carr, 2002). The effects of 'neurotic' leadership and the fears and anxieties of change are examined by Kets de Vries and Balazs (1997) and Kets de Vries and Miller (1991).

The way gender is both emotionalized and politicized in the workplace has been reviewed by Lewis and Simpson (2007). Others have critically examined the significance of how emotion is controlled, and by whom, in organizations (see Fineman, 2007; Sturdy and Fineman, 2001). Hochschild (1983) has developed the notion of 'emotional labour', now explored in a variety of occupations (see Harris, 2002; Mann, 1999). This body of research considerably extends Hochschild's original work to reveal the very different ways that emotional labour is experienced, controlled and expressed. The allied field of aesthetic labour – the marketing and marketplace of bodily appearance – is explored by Nickson and Warhurst (2007) and Hancock and Tyler (2000). Frost (2003, 2004) has written extensively about the effects of toxic emotions at work and how compassion is an often missing, but important, antidote. The recent trend towards displaying positive emotions at work can be found in a collection edited by Cameron et al. (2003) but, for a more critical perspective, see Lazarus (2003) and Fineman (2006a).

The standard, popular work on emotional intelligence is by Goleman (1996). Emotional intelligence has, however, generated much controversy concerning its conceptualization, its measurement and its trainability. For an extensive academic review, see Mayer et al. (2008), and also the arguments proffered by Becker (2003) and Fineman (2000d, 2004). Not a lot has been written on the emotionalities of virtual work, but a helpful introduction can be found in Gackenbach (1998). More recently, a special issue of the journal *Human Relations*, edited by Fineman et al. (2007), marks out a research agenda for the field.

REVIEW QUESTIONS

1. To what extent are we culturally programmed to feel what we feel and to express certain feelings – but not others?

2. What are the pros and cons of the current fashion for 'emotion intelligence' in the workplace?

3. Is positiveness at work quite simply a 'good thing'? What is the counter-argument?

---

companion
website
www.sagepub.co.uk/fineman

Reading On

The articles below are available for free to readers of the fourth edition of *Organizing & Organizations* via the book's companion website at www.sagepub.co.uk/fineman

Boudens, C.J. (2005) 'The story of work: a narrative analysis of workplace emotion', *Organization Studies*, 26 (9): 1285–306.
This paper argues that work-related emotion is best accessed using indirect means, including figures of speech and narrative. An analysis of 452 narratives drawn from previously published works is presented to the end of addressing two research questions: Where is the emotion in work? and What is the emotion in work?

Fineman, S. (2004) 'Getting the measure of emotion – and the cautionary tale of emotional intelligence', *Human Relations*, 57 (6): 719–40.
This article critically examines the growth of emotion measurement in organizational behaviour, arguing that the epistemological and phenomenological consequences of psychometrically 'boxing' emotion are problematic and restrictive. How can emotion be 'known', other than through measurement and numbers? The article suggests some different approaches towards researching an important, but enigmatic, concept.

Taylor, S. and Tyler, M. (2000) 'Emotional labour and sexual difference in the airline industry', *Work Employment Society*, 14 (1): 77–95.
This paper examines service work within a contemporary airline industry shaped by managerial initiatives aiming to deliver 'quality service'. The authors focus on the gendered consequences of this, arguing that competitive pressures and accompanying managerial initiatives are intensifying demands upon female employees for the production of emotional labour, subjective commitment to organizational aims and sexual difference within parts of the airline industry.

17

SEX

Human beings are by nature sexual, and any account of organizations which does not take account of this is limited. In this chapter, we start by looking at the talk and banter about sex which is part of life in most Western organizations. We go on to look at office romances, which are rare compared with sex talk but which do occur, with consequences which may be significant for those involved, and sometimes for those around them. We then turn to the more conspicuously negative side, sexual harassment, and also look at the ambiguity which often surrounds it; when does banter and joking become harassment? There is discussion of the way that sex is used, either by those who can turn attractiveness to their own advantage, or by those who have the power to order others to use their sexual attractiveness to the benefit of the organization. We conclude with some discussion of the implications of and for male sexuality, which has tended to be ignored even more than the overall topic of sex.

REAL-LIFE EXAMPLE

'Well, I'll sit here to look at Vanessa's legs', announced the director of a manufacturing firm as he sat opposite the company trainee at the start of a meeting. Vanessa was not impressed. 'Before I worked at Powertech', she said later, 'I did not have much sympathy with women who complained about sexism in the workplace as I really did think it was a thing of the past. I was absolutely unprepared to deal with all the comments and attitudes I encountered in the company. Many of these attitudes are very subtle. Many of the offenders do not understand that they are being sexist, they just feel they are "having a laugh", or being friendly'.

The issue of sexual harassment has lately placed sexuality at the centre of discussions about organizations. For a long time, sexuality in organizations has been a non-topic.

Try looking at the index of any organizational behaviour text. It is as if people lock up their sexual thoughts and desires the minute they walk into their workplace. After all, workplaces are not places for pleasure, romance or sensuousness, let alone sex. Most people see sex as a private matter, not as public business (see Chapters 12, 'Morals' and 22, 'Working and Living').

SEX TALK

Looking at organizations purely as places of work is almost as naïve as looking at sex purely as sexual intercourse. Men and women are sexual beings. Our sexuality is a central part of our personality. We all have sexual desires, anxieties and **fantasies** and we spend some of our working time talking, joking and thinking about sex. The frequently quoted statistic that on average men think about **sex** every three minutes, or 40 seconds, or whatever, does not have any authority that we know of.

But the graffiti in toilets and lifts, the pin-ups in lockers and workshops, the sex gossip and casual conversations provide evidence that sex is very much on people's minds during their time at work.

In some organizations, sex talk goes on incessantly. Its variety is enormous, ranging from the subtle to the explicit, from the friendly to the hostile to the downright nasty. Consider the following two examples:

> I had been doing consultancy for the launch of a US software product called Soft-tool. With a name like this you don't stand a chance. I told the manufacturers, you have to change the brand name. No luck, it was company policy to use the same name in all its geographic divisions. My job was to come up with a logo for this product, imagine now: 'buy Soft-tool to increase your performance'. When they realized their gaffe they changed the name to ... Hard-tool! (Computer executive)

> I think it's mainly me really they tease, about the post boy. Because he's so sweet, you know, I say he is my toyboy, and the others ask me: 'Have you seen your toyboy today?' Silly things like that, it just lightens the day up ... Or the gentleman across the corridor, I notice him because he is always working, he's such a nice gentleman, such a nice character, and I always say: 'I just met him on the first floor, I think he's madly in love with me!' Silly things. We just laugh about them. (Office worker)

It may come as no surprise that the first story was told by a man and the second by a woman. In their distinct ways, both narratives could be seen as revealing sexual anxieties: the man's worry about masculinity and the woman's concern about being loved. They both suggest fantasies, the first a fantasy about sexually inadequate men, the second about an innocent post boy and a romantically inclined 'gentleman'. Both stories court embarrassment as they shake some taboos and use potentially risky words. Told in the wrong way to the wrong audience, they could lead to stony silence and embarrassed glances. Told in the right way to the right audience, they generate a unique kind of pleasure, strengthen the sense of intimacy among those present and bring **femininity** and **masculinity** into the heart of organizational life.

Wholly male and wholly female work environments spawn distinct brands of sex talk. Yet, sex talk is not confined to groups of the same **gender**. In some mixed offices, continuous sex teasing goes on between men and women. Men may tease women about their appearance while women may tease men about their virility. In two district offices of a privatized utility, sexual banter and obscene jokes were traded endlessly across the genders in apparently good humour. Not one of the 47 people interviewed by one of us admitted to being upset about them. For Andrew, fresh from university, the office had been a **culture** shock:

> *Andrew*: when I first came here, I just couldn't believe the language people used. Gossip about who's going out with whom, who fancies whom, it's just like school. The jokes! Not down to the level of whistling, but about how people look.
> *Interviewer*: do the women mind about it?
> *Andrew*: I'd say they enjoy it. I've got to be honest, the difference between here and college is huge, people could no way get away with some of the jokes. The attitude here is totally different. It's horrible saying this but most of the women seem to enjoy it. Totally sexist thing to say. But it goes on and on and on. Like the story about two people who are having an intimate situation, this is how it started, and people just constantly crack jokes about them. It's become like a serial. Probably none of it is true.

Nicky, a 21-year-old clerk who had joined the company as a trainee four years previously said:

> I don't mind sexist jokes, I make them myself. Men tease me about the size of my backside but it's all in good spirit. Mind you, I have taken down the nude calendars. I wouldn't like nude men on the walls either, in fact, I'd rather have the women!

Figure 17.1

OFFICE ROMANCES

Much of the sexual behaviour at work takes place at the level of talk and fantasy. Nevertheless, physical display and contact are far from absent. Touching, hugging or kissing may not be much in evidence in most workshops or offices, but many have apocryphal tales, such as what went on at the Christmas party, or during the residential conference, or behind the closed doors of the office. In the organization above, in the interest of better understanding between clerical and technical staff, once a year each clerical worker accompanies a service engineer on house calls. On a different day, each engineer sits in the office paired with a clerical worker. The joint house calls fed a constant stream of innuendoes. Eventually, one of the women in the office married 'her' engineer, providing a happy ending to another local soap opera. She was not alone: many people find their partners at the workplace.

Some organizations are distinctly lukewarm about workplace romances. An engineer in a multinational high-tech company reported:

> In this company, any mention of sexual harassment is fatal. Nobody dare do something that might be understood as molestation. Employees in the US were fired because they had sexual pictures in their office or on their computers, or even for making a joke with a sexual connotation.

All the same, there was one romantic story that he reported:

> They are now a married couple. He had been relocated to the US five years ago where he met the woman who had been also working there for the firm. Both reported to the Israeli branch when they met. When they both returned, they continued working for the company. We always assigned them to different team projects, but they still got married and have lived together since.

The story appears to epitomize the organization's 'cold climate' – it is presented as an exceptional event, taking place while the employees are away from their home base, while the company seeks to protect itself by keeping them apart. Other companies, however, are far more relaxed about sexual relations between their employees. Indeed, some seem positively to encourage them. The manager of a spa resort and hotel in Israel providing massage, sauna and a wide range of beauty and health services reported: 'It is nice, very nice. I think it is positive. Really positive. When people meet each other in the workplace, become friends and then get married, it is very nice'.

At this organization, romantic attachments were commonplace:

> I know of several couples that got married after working in the organization, and I know of quite a few that became [intimate] friends. In some cases, one of them was working here, and brought his spouse to work in the organization. There are all kinds. It is very common. Work in the hotel is around the clock, 24 hours, weekends, many shifts and many employees. The employees are the same age mostly, in their twenties ... There is always gossip [about romantic relationships], and I also know about them first hand. There are all kinds. Some people cheat their partners, and all kinds of things.

This employee recounted several romantic stories including the following one:

> There is a very nice story to tell you about an Assistant Chef who came from England and a girl that was a shift manager in the restaurant. They were together all the time because of their work interdependence. She was in the kitchen all the time and then they fell in love. Now they got married. He even converted to Judaism for her. They moved together to work in a hotel in Eilat (southern Israel), I think they have twins now. This was a very lovely story. He was not a Jew. A foreigner comes here and falls in love with an Israeli and they worked together and he even had a circumcision at the age of 30 to marry her. [In Israel, people cannot have a religious wedding unless both partners are Jewish. Registry office weddings exist, but are generally not approved of.]

Many organizations today emphasize image – both organizational and individual. Much emphasis is paid to appearance, which is enhanced through decoration, jewellery and other aesthetic features, which highlight that the organization's image depends crucially on its employees, its buildings and its publicity looking smart, fit and stylish. Such organizations may be related to tourism and catering as well as retail, advertising, communication and marketing services. Much of the media and entertainment industries may represent such aestheticized environments in which fantasies, including sexual ones, are never far from people's minds.

Sexual fantasies are an escape from the ordinariness of work. Sex talk breaks the monotony, introduces a playful element and brightens up what can otherwise be a rather boring day. Sex talk also reminds people that their bodies are not just labouring instruments hiding inside uniforms and suits, but are also sources and objects of pleasure and **desire**. Nor are their feelings tied exclusively to the demands of their work.

This is half the story; the other half is less agreeable. Sex in organizations goes far deeper than being a mere diversion from the monotony of work. Discrimination, AIDS and harassment remind us of some darker aspects. The rest of this chapter explores some of the ways in which sex cuts across and strengthens the power relations in organizations.

SEXUAL HARASSMENT

Increasing awareness of the dark side of sexuality within organizations has coincided with an explosion of concern about sexual harassment in the United States and Britain. Sensitivities, **attitudes** and feelings are changing. On the one hand, there is an increasing recognition that **sexual harassment** is not an exceptional occurrence but a routine phenomenon in some workplaces and that large numbers of women (and to a lesser extent, men, especially gay men) suffer in silence. On the other hand, there is a sense that forms of behaviour which used to pass as 'innocent' and 'well intentioned' involve a covert attempt to humiliate women, to bolster negative stereotypes and to preserve organizational forms in which men generally occupy superior positions to women.

The norms of permissible and abusive sexual behaviour are changing. What used to pass as 'innocent banter' is now sometimes viewed as offensive behaviour. 'Friendly' compliments are frequently resented, either because they are perceived as implied propositions or because they are seen as devaluing other qualities. Some women now feel that they tolerated such forms of behaviour in the past, pretended not to notice or feel ashamed about it, instead of recognizing the hurt that it caused and fighting back. At the same time, many women and men are debating the boundary between harassment and the inevitable and even pleasurable sexuality of much organizational life. The 'sexless' organization which was seen as the safe option to aim for in the 1980s was found to be too dull to survive in. But the problems, of sexual activity or attraction between people of unequal power that it was intended to solve, remain.

Sexual harassment comes in many forms. At its worst, it amounts to nothing less than rape, or the demand for what some call 'sexual favours' in return for promotion or other material benefits. This is sexual bullying, the abuse of **power** to exploit, humiliate or hurt and the pleasure of doing so. Sexual harassment may, equally, assume more subtle forms. Persistent compliments can be irritating as can excessive familiarity, exaggerated intimacy or physical closeness. One of the commonest forms of harassment, however, lies in sexist remarks which either reduce people to sex objects or re-affirm unpleasant **stereotypes**. This puts them, and especially women, in a rather invidious position; if they express disgust or disapproval, this tends to reinforce the stereotypes (e.g. 'women lack a sense of humour', 'they are emotional' and so on) while if they bottle up their feelings, they offer tacit encouragement for their aggressor.

One of our students reported three incidents that took place in quick succession between her and her manager in a bank:

> I came to work in a smart trouser suit and Paul greeted me with: 'did you forget to take your pyjamas off, Suzie?' (He knows I hate being called Suzie). A little later, I was trying to print some documents and said: 'this printer is so temperamental!' and Paul quipped: 'It's obviously female'. Eventually, the fault was found to be in the computer and he said: 'Have you broken it already?' Me: 'no'. Paul: 'ah, that's what happens when you let women near machines'.

Susan tolerated this type of put-down for several days. The worst thing, she explained, was not knowing whether these comments were meant as friendly teasing or as serious criticism. She put on a brave face, hid her feelings and tried to 'rise' above this baiting. One day, however, she felt especially annoyed and when Paul told her that he planned to take a three-week holiday, she quipped: 'why, visiting your Spanish sweetheart again?' before she had time to check herself. 'Don't be cheeky!', said Paul. 'I can remember experiencing mixed feelings about what had happened'. Susan said:

> Perhaps I overstepped the mark, the fine line between what an employee can and cannot say to a manager. As a result, I told myself off for not checking myself, I blamed myself. But I also felt that it didn't seem fair that I had to take his jokes in good humour, no matter how bad they were, while his position meant that I couldn't give as good as I got.

How certain can we be that this is a case of harassment? Surely this kind of unequal rights (for instance, the right to joke at someone else's expense) is common to interactions between senior and junior members of staff. But, for women, this raises extra difficulties. Are they being laughed at because they are young, because they are junior or just because they are a woman? It is sometimes hard for women to know. The suspicion of harassment remains and this shapes their experience.

THE AMBIGUITIES OF HARASSMENT

When does a well-meant joke or compliment become sexual harassment? This is a thorny issue. A joke which in one organization may cause amusement, may cause offence in a different one. During a workshop run by one of our colleagues, a participant told of his plans to tour the Far East: 'just three men, without women to complicate the party or disapprove'. Challenged to say what they intended to do, he casually remarked: 'oh, a little bit of rape and pillage!' The comment outraged many of the others and led to a heated debate in which men and women were sharply polarized. What seemed like an innocent joke to some of the men was felt to be a vicious sexist and racist comment to the women. Whether or not the teller of the joke had meant it as an abusive comment to the women present, this is exactly how they experienced it.

In most circumstances, we rely on social **norms** to guide us through what is acceptable and what is unacceptable social behaviour. Tact and sensitivity alert us to the needs and feelings of others. In the area of sex, however, norms vary enormously and leave a lot of ambiguity. They have also been changing very rapidly – and not necessarily in an obvious direction – over recent years. To make matters more complex, being on the edge of what is acceptable seems in itself to be an almost sexual pleasure for both genders, but perhaps with different views of what is pleasurable about it.

What problems does this leave us with? For men, sexist innuendoes are often presented as 'innocent jokes' with no intention to offend or hurt. All the same, the excuse 'I didn't mean to hurt you' sounds highly unconvincing in most cases. Nor does the word 'innocent' seem altogether appropriate for some of the obscene graffiti in male lavatories or some all-male conversations in bars. This suggests that hate and scorn are sometimes as much part of men's feelings towards women as are attraction and love. The jokes and the graffiti may be less prevalent than they were a few years back, but their continued existence points to a lasting anti-woman undercurrent.

Men's **emotions** towards women can be ambivalent. Their feelings are often in conflict with each other. They frequently stereotype the women they meet in one of a few basic categories, like mother figure, iron maiden, witch or defenceless 'pet'. Men idealize 'the virgin' while denying that the 'mother figure' has any sexuality at all. Women with independent sexual desires are often typecast as 'tarts' or 'whores' against whom large amounts of both male lust and aggression are directed. Unless perceived as virgins or mothers, women are often said to be bringing male violence upon themselves through provocative or flirtatious behaviour. 'She asked for it' becomes the stock defence of perpetrators of male violence against women. Instead of blaming the wrongdoer, it is the victim who gets the blame.

SEX AND ORGANIZATIONAL POLITICS

Blaming the victim by turning women into deserving targets for male violence presents sexual harassment as a purely personal matter. But sexual harassment would not have become a major issue if it amounted to nothing more than the actions of a few male chauvinists, let alone the experience of a few over-sensitive females. One of the reasons it has become a major political and management issue is that sexual politics is closely related to organizational **politics** and **conflicts**.

Sex is a feature of many organizational **games**. As Susan noted in the earlier story, men and women rarely enter these games as equals. In competing for jobs in the labour market, women have faced visible and invisible barriers, **prejudice** or **discrimination**. If direct discrimination is rare these days (women being paid less for doing the same jobs as men), many more or less subtle forms of discrimination disadvantage women from rising to positions of great power or influence (see Chapter 20, 'Career Shifts'). What are these forms of discrimination? If you are a woman, you will probably already know. If you are a man, you may know; if you do not, ask a woman who trusts you not to respond dismissively to her answer.

In most organizations, women tend to occupy subordinate positions, either directly 'servicing' male managers and bosses or coming into direct contact with the organization's customers as sales staff, telephonists, air stewardesses, waitresses and the like. **Feminists** have pointed out that women's sexuality is far from peripheral in most of these jobs. On the contrary, it is harnessed either to lure the customer, or to boost their boss's ego and image or to project a glamorous image for a company or an industry. Femininity and sex appeal are virtual prerequisites for employment in many such jobs. In many organizations, an attractive secretary is still seen as indicative of the **status** of her boss, while glamour is part of the image cultivated by industries, such as cosmetics, airlines, advertising and the mass media.

But women's sexuality is also harnessed by organizations in subtler ways. In jobs involving direct contact with customers, consumers or employees, the 'feminine touch' is deployed to defuse awkward or dangerous situations and to maintain a discreet form of social control. Female telephonists, sales staff, receptionists, cashiers, nurses, teachers and police officers are all expected to exercise their delicate interpersonal skills on behalf of their organizations, preventing things from getting out of hand. Of course, the same may be expected of their male counterparts too, but a feminine presence in most organizations is seen as a civilizing influence and a balancing counterpart to male aggression.

In some organizations, management maintains a low-level sexual 'simmer', placing great emphasis on women's appearance and demeanour, encouraging smart dressing, make-up and so on. One of our students worked for a pizza restaurant which placed high emphasis on the appearance of the waitresses; it also paid minimal wages. Result:

> Some of the waitresses would do anything to earn a tip. Some of the younger ones wore black bras which were clearly visible underneath their pink blouses. Some deliberately shortened their skirts. Some compared this to prostitution, selling yourself in order to make money. I have to agree with them.
>
> Other waitresses adopted their own tip-making strategies. For example, Elaine in her spare moments would go over to the customers and start up a conversation. She would often tell customers about any personal problems that she had. It appeared as though she was begging for a tip.
>
> I swore I would not sink to this level. However, I did and developed my own strategies. One of these was to ask customers with relatively young children whether they would like a bowl and a spoon for the children to use. This was actually quite successful and I believe that it encouraged customers to leave tips.

'USING SEX'

This astute account illustrates one of the linkages between sexuality and power in organizations. The waitresses gained money and sometimes power by adopting sexual and emotional tactics, which could then be used against them (and women in general) to **stereotype** them and disparage them (e.g. 'Women use their sexuality to gain favour'; 'successful women have only got there by devious means' and so on). It also illustrates both the distress that having to adopt such demeaning forms of behaviour causes women and the pleasure which successful use of such tactics can bring to the performer. Joanne's story illustrates this:

> I went along to the product launch with Marianne, my assistant. She's very young, and she thought she could charm her way around the directors on her own and not rely on me for her power base. But she doesn't have either the shape or the experience. I thought: 'I've been doing this for ten years longer than you matey, and I'm bloody good at it', so I put all my lights on, drew the directors into a group around me, and left her invisible. It was great. Now that's what I call girl power.

Femininity, encompassing physical allure, warmth, tenderness and subtle interpersonal skills, is part and parcel of how some of women's work in organizations gets done. But in some organizations, women are placed in a 'double-bind' or no-win situation. The same work environment which encourages femininity and even seductiveness, chastizes women for using their 'feminine charms' to gain personal advantage and influence. On the other hand, women who suppress their **sexuality** and seek to confront men as equals are often branded 'iron maidens', lesbians and so on. Women frequently feel that they are treading a dangerous ground of permissible and non-permissible displays of femininity, between being 'too sexy' and 'not sexy enough'. When Republican vice-presidential candidate Sarah Palin winked, repeatedly, during televised debates in the 2008 American presidential election, there was a huge amount of publice debate about this potentially not very important piece of non-verbal behaviour. Several commentators, of both genders, suggested that the intimacy of a wink was the kind of behaviour that was only indulged in by a candidate who was in no way qualified for the job for which they had applied.

There is little evidence that women gain personal advantage against male colleagues by using their sexuality, although they are often accused of doing so. If anything, there is some evidence of the opposite. To the extent that certain jobs emphasize attractiveness, they are seen as requiring little in the way of intellectual abilities, qualifications and motivation, although it is also the case that more attractive people are usually assumed to be more intelligent than is justified by their intellectual powers alone. Attractive women in positions of genuine power are often accused – even if they are not genuinely suspected – of having risen on the basis of their physical attributes, and become a target of male hostility and sexual harassment.

MALE SEXUALITY

While sexual harassment and discrimination have forced us to look at female sexuality in organizations, it would be wrong to imply that male sexuality is excluded from them. To be sure, the stereotypes of men in organizations tend to underplay sexuality, just as those of women emphasize it. Think of grey-suited businessmen, rational, tough, analytic, and you would be forgiven for imagining that they are pure brain and will, detached from bodies and **desires**. Yet, sexual **fantasies** and wishes frequently feed organizational sex talk.

Physical appearance is as central an ingredient of male sexuality as it is of female. A computer analyst in a large firm prided himself on his bulging muscles, the product of long sessions spent in the gymnasium. 'I had an office', he recounted not without self-irony, 'next to the girls in the legal department, and they were talking about the sexiest man in the building, and they were coming up with all these men I'd never heard of before. So I went into their office and said: 'sorry about this ladies, I thought that I was the real star, the hulk'. They cracked up laughing and said: 'we had a vote and you were voted the most boring old fart in this place'.

Sex teasing in organizations can be good-humoured and benign, but relations between men and women are unsymmetrical and unequal. A woman entering an all-male office saying: 'sorry about this lads, but I thought that I was the sex sensation here', would doubtless elicit a very different response from the witticism of the earlier story. A man who prides himself on his sexual exploits may attract a well-deserved taunt but may be secretly admired as a 'stud'. A woman doing likewise may still be derided as fast, promiscuous or worse.

While women have to tread a precarious line between 'not sexy enough' and 'too sexy', displays of masculinity come under more lenient controls. Even when it assumes the distasteful shape of sexual harassment, it often goes unpunished. There is, nevertheless, a taboo in most workplaces against **homosexuality** and, more generally, against men's displays of physical closeness or affection. Hugging and kissing among Mediterranean men give rise to great anxiety in many Anglo-Saxons, who regard them as a possible blot on their masculinity.

One of us was attending a conference in Italy with two close colleagues from our university department and remembers vividly the following incident:

There was Roberto, an old associate, who I met about once a year. He threw his arms around me and gave me an affectionate hug. I was pleased to respond to his warmth. My two British colleagues gave me 'knowing' glances. I was a little embarrassed and they teased me. I laughed it off. Throughout the day, the teasing continued: jokes, quips and innuendo about my 'relationship' with Roberto. I still smiled. After all, I could take a joke, couldn't I?

The teasing, as I recall, resumed the next day. They seemed to be having great fun at my expense, while I felt increasingly uncomfortable. It was now beyond a joke. It seemed curiously childish behaviour, insensitive, silly. Then it was one remark too many. 'I am not enjoying these remarks, could you please stop?', I snapped at Chris. He seemed surprised. Chris communicated my comment to Geoffrey. There was a slightly uncomfortable feeling between us, and then it stopped. A couple of years later, Chris and I discussed the incident. We both agreed about the 'facts'. As for the meaning of the incident, there seemed to be a gulf dividing us.

With few exceptions, Western organizations are neither kind nor permissive towards gays and lesbians, who often become victims of vicious sexual harassment. Gays and lesbians find themselves in especially invidious situations, looking for strategies of survival while constantly suppressing their sexuality. Denial, overcompensation, avoidance or straight lying are strategies which take their toll emotionally. Having to laugh at your colleagues' anti-gay jokes (or even initiating them yourself), not disclosing the gender of your partner, keeping constant vigilance over what others know of your **desires** and **fantasies**, 'splitting' your sexual self from your work self – these are all psychological ways of coping, which exact their price in anxiety, stress and guilt.

But male **sexuality** at the workplace is not limited to displays of **masculinity** and bravado. It is also revealed in very masculine styles of **management**, sometimes referred to as 'macho management'. Confrontation, ostentatious use of force and intransigence, contempt for compromise and compassion became the trademarks of this style of management. Its champions included 'hard men' 'who introduced new tough regimes in their companies which broke all other forms of power base. Talking tough and acting tough is a matter of masculine pride for those who see it as their mission to restore 'managers' right to manage'. Television and film images of tough managers present them as exploring heroes – perhaps the modern equivalent of the cowboy movie. Cowboy movies were less misleading, however, because not many of the cinema audience were going to take up careers as cowboys. Films portraying macho managers may have a disproportionate influence on audience behaviour as people look forward to trying out the strong tactics they have seen on screen. In many organizations, this is dealt with by gentle mockery (see Chapter 18, 'Serious Joking'), as they gradually mentor their young staff away from the film images to something gentler and more effective. In other organizations, particularly if the manager is the son of the boss, or if the organization is very small or under threat, behaviour learned from films is allowed to persist.

Whether macho management has become the norm or not is debatable, as is its success in restoring order and peace in many organizations. It appears, nevertheless, that macho management has now gone out of fashion, at least in its brashest manifestations. Yet the qualities of aggression, competitiveness, rigidity and hardness are not only accepted but encouraged by organizations which find them as useful as they find the feminine qualities we discussed earlier. The essential difference lies in the fact that while masculine qualities enhance **career** prospects, feminine ones, though indispensable for many organizations, are frequently an impediment to personal success.

IN CONCLUSION

Sexuality plays a large part in how people relate to each other. Whether as colleagues or as rivals, as superiors or as subordinates, as friends or as lovers, gender is everpresent. Our ways of looking at things and relating to others is shaped by our identities and our identities are sexual. It is not surprising, therefore, to find sexuality in most episodes of organizational life. In this chapter, we have argued that sexuality is not just incidental to organization, but of the very essence.

Organizations harness the sexuality of both men and women, mould it and frame it. The women's and gay movements must claim the credit for demonstrating how sexuality becomes entangled in organizational politics, revealing its ugly side in incidents of sexual harassment and intimidation. Women's femininity is more severely manipulated and controlled than masculinity, with stereotypes from wider culture conveniently invoked as excuses for discriminatory and unequal treatment.

At the same time, we have argued against the view which automatically equates sex in organizations with oppression and exploitation. We have suggested that sexual joking, banter and innuendo is welcomed by the majority as a break from the impersonal routines of organizations and as a reminder that inside every overall, suit or uniform, there is a human body, which is not just an instrument of labour, but also the source and object of pleasure and desire.

KEY POINTS

o Sexuality is expressed directly and indirectly in organizations, ranging from sex talk, innuendo and office romances to stereotyping, harassment and discrimination.

o Gender issues and sexuality often become enmeshed with organizational politics in which, almost invariably, men have greater power than women.

o Sexual harassment can take many different forms, including exaggerated compliments, offensive language, sexist jokes and sexual blackmailing.

o Sexual harassment tends to re-affirm gender stereotypes and frequently puts the victim in an invidious no-win situation.

o Men's attitudes and behaviour towards women are often conditioned by naïve stereotypes of women such as 'virgins', 'pets', 'mother figures' and 'whores'.

o Organizations mould both masculinity and femininity, though in different ways.

o On the whole, the controls placed on female sexuality and homosexuality are tighter and more inhibiting than those placed on what is seen as 'traditional masculine' traits.

>>>>>>>>>>>> **THEORETICAL SIGNPOSTS** >>>>>>>>>>>>

The major themes in this chapter have been covered in the following areas of literature:

> sexuality in organizations
> sexual harassment and stereotyping
> the treatment of sexual minorities in organizations.

Sexuality in Organizations

This has only recently become part of academic study. The work of Burrell (1984), Hearn and Parkin (1987) and Hearn et al. (1989) is especially relevant in exploring the contexts and social construction of sexuality at work. These authors criticize previous analyses of organizations (most of which are by male authors) for not acknowledging human sexuality. Where gender has been discussed, it has usually been in the context of equal opportunities and discrimination – or in other words, as gender without sex. Hearn and colleagues speak of sexuality as associated with the 'politics of the body' and the negotiated expectations between the genders. Sexuality is embedded in the pattern of emotions and language of the organization. Gardner (1995) also develops a number of similar themes, but more broadly in various social settings. There is a considerable literature on office romances (Mainiero, 1989; Pierce, 1998; Pierce et al., 1996; Pringle, 1989; Quinn and Judge, 1978; Williams et al., 1999; Yelvington, 1996) and its ramifications for organizational performance. There is also some work on the different nature of office romances in different organizational climates (Mano and Gabriel, 2006), where some climates seem to encourage office romances to emerge as a challenge to the organization. Foucault (1978), in *The History of Sexuality*, talks about how sex is transformed into discourse.

Numerous authors have noted how organizations sexualize their services and products by deploying the sexuality of their employees to attract and keep customers (Adkins, 1995; Hall, 1993). This is most evident where employees act as an organization's 'front' to the customers, such as receptionists, sales assistants, holiday reps and so forth. In certain organizations, relations between employees and customers become sexualized, part of a strategy to entrance and captivate the latter. In this way, the employees' sexuality becomes an important organizational resource for jobs where emotional and aesthetic labour are essential. The organizational deployment of human sexuality is even more direct in the sex industry and pornography.

Sexual Harassment and Stereotyping

These issues, along with their links to power and gender, have been widely discussed (Di Tomaso, 1989; Guerrier and Adib, 2000; Gutek, 1989; Pierce and Aguinis, 1997; Williams et al., 1999). Harassment can include offensive language, sexist jokes and negative stereotypes, and frequently plays on the power differences between the harasser and the harassed. It can also play on the ambiguity of whether a particular piece of language is offensive or not, thereby leaving the target doubly disabled from being able to respond. Victims of sexual harassment are often reluctant to report it because it operates by making the victim feel guilty that in some way they have 'brought it on themselves' (Pierce et al., 2004). Collins and Blodgett (1981) offer an everyday business perspective on sexual harassment, while the different national-cultural and perceptual issues are explored by Brant and Too (1994). Important here is how different cultures and sub-cultures define appropriate sexual display, reminding us of the cultural relativity of sexual, and other, organizational behaviours.

The Treatment of Sexual Minorities in Organizations

This has only recently received much attention. In a fascinating study, Ward and Winstanley (2003) report how sexual minorities, notably gay men and lesbians, resort to different strategies of silence in order to defend their social identities. There is a developing body of literature around the identities of members of sexual minorities in the workplace (Chrobot-Mason et al., 2001).

REVIEW QUESTIONS

1. Is it possible to keep sex and sexuality completely out of the workplace? Is it desirable?

2. If people fall in love with work colleagues, that is nobody else's business. Or is it?

3. Harassment and stereotyping, in a mild form such as teasing and joking, are a normal part of discussions between adults. Why should anyone try to spoil the fun of light-hearted office banter?

companion
website
sagepub.co.uk/fineman

Reading On

The articles below are available for free to readers of the fourth edition of *Organizing & Organizations* via the book's companion website at www.sagepub.co.uk/fineman

Mano, R. and Gabriel, Y. (2006) 'Workplace romances in cold and hot organizational climates: the experience of Israel and Taiwan', *Human Relations*, 59 (1): 7–35.
This study examines how organizations influence the emergence, development and discourses of workplace romances. Using qualitative fieldwork from three organizations in Israel and four in Taiwan, the authors examine if and how organizational climate – cold, temperate and hot – influences the ways workplace romances are reported and narrated.

Elsesser, Kim and Peplau, L.A. (2006) 'The glass partition: obstacles to cross-sex friendships at work', *Human Relations*, 59: 1077–100.
This study explores cross-sex friendships within the professional workplace and examines the impact of the workplace environment and heightened awareness of sexual harassment on cross-sex friendship formation. The authors label barriers to cross-sex friendship at work the 'glass partition' and discuss the potential impact of this glass partition on women's and men's careers.

Brewis, J. (2005) 'Signing my life away? Researching sex and organization', *Organization*, 12: 493–510.
In this paper, the author describes how her personal and professional lives have blurred into each other throughout her academic career, focusing on one aspect of this blurring – that certain colleagues believe she is intimate with her co-authors, and that she engages in or has experienced the sexual activities which her research has explored – and seeks to account for this interpretation of her private life through the lens of her public endeavours.

Alvesson, M. (1998) 'Gender relations and identity at work: a case study of masculinities and femininities in an advertising agency', *Human Relations*, 51: 969–1005.
This paper explores gender relations and gender identity, based upon an ethnography of a Swedish advertising agency. The organization is of special interest as it has a strong gender division of labour, where men hold all senior posts, at the same time as creative advertising work seems to have much more similarity with what gender studies describe as 'femininity' rather than with forms of 'masculinity'.

18
SERIOUS JOKING

Most organizations are serious places. People go about their business with deliberate seriousness. They fill in forms seriously, they answer phones seriously, they write letters seriously, they tap the keyboards of their computers seriously, they attend meetings seriously, they discuss strategy seriously, they bargain seriously, they operate different types of machinery seriously. An air of no-nonsense fills organizational spaces.

From time to time, humour makes a tentative appearance. A **joke** in the middle of a stuffy meeting or a cartoon on an office wall lightens the atmosphere and raises a smile. But books on management and organizations have not paid much attention to such phenomena, which were not seen as a part of the serious business of organizing, but merely as an aberration.

OUR ORGANIZATION IS NO JOKE

To the outsider, **organizations** tend to present a uniformly serious front: entering a bank, a hospital or a government department, reading company reports or sales literature, telephoning the local office of the gas or electric company, one finds little that could be described as amusing. But if, with an innocent eye, we glance backstage in these organizations, a rather different picture is revealed, a picture which may combine the ridiculous, the absurd and the funny. For example, there are people being very serious about matters which, from a distance, appear utterly trivial, such as a group of executives discussing at length the precise phrasing of a strategy document which they know will have little impact. Or people carefully filling in forms in triplicate, for no apparent reason other than that they have 'always done it that way'.

In addition, unlike the official visitor who sees the serious front of the organization, the insider in its offices may share a joke about the latest fiasco (10,000 Valentine cards delivered 'as promised' on 15 February – a day too late), start gossiping about the latest comeuppance of the brash young executive ('you should have seen the state of that BMW after he reversed into the garage wall') or recollect a practical joke played on an awkward colleague ('do you remember how angry he was when we set him up to get more and more emails from that employment agency offering him a job on the factory floor?').

While some organizations are doubtless less fun places to be in than others, it does not take long to discover that the air of seriousness in many organizations is only paper-thin.

Underneath, a continuous humorous banter goes on, providing an unofficial commentary on organizational life. People joke, laugh, play tricks on each other and generally try to have a good time. Often, the mere mention of some individual or group, like 'the Inspector', 'Human Resources' or 'the Accountants', is enough to generate a funny story. 'The computer's gone down again; it must be the Director pouring another whisky on his keyboard!'; 'no, it's the computer boys trying to wipe out the last three years' accounts!'; 'more likely, someone unplugged the server to boil the kettle'; 'or perhaps they just forgot to put another coin in the slot'.

JOKES, MEANING MAKING AND SURVIVAL

Workers who have recently joined an office may find many of the jokes unfunny or incomprehensible. For a time, they may smile to show that they too are in on the joke, but soon they will start trying to join in. Not being able to share a joke, however unfunny, makes one feel excluded. A person without a sense of humour quickly becomes the butt of many jokes, even stigmatized. St Thomas Aquinas went so far as to argue that 'a lack of mirth is sinful because someone without a sense of humour is burdensome both by failing to offer the pleasure of playful speech to others and because their dourness stops them from responding to the humour of others'.

Sharing a laugh and a joke is an important way of creating personal **meaning** and purpose in a job, especially for those people who feel stuck in mundane and repetitive jobs. Laughter and humour make light of the many injuries that we sustain in organizations, physical injuries as well as injuries to our pride and dignity. Fred, who lost part of his finger in an apple-pie-making machine, becomes the target of many good-humoured jokes a mere few days after the accident. The women checking the beans on a continuously moving conveyor belt joke about management's attempt to replace them with pigeons, trained to pick the dud beans, only to find that the Royal Society for the Prevention of Cruelty to Animals has ruled that the task is too cruelly repetitive for the pigeons. Such jokes celebrate survival against the odds; they make the unbearable more bearable.

Jokes and laughter defuse tense situations, break the monotony and let the weak turn the tables on the strong. 'You have to have a sense of humour to survive in this job' is a statement one hears often when talking to people doing jobs that are generally unpleasant and tedious, or where the **bureaucratic** frustrations can be enormous. 'You don't have to be mad to work in this place but it helps' proclaim signs in innumerable workplaces, expressing what many people must feel. The humour was taken one stage further when the Royal College of Psychiatrists used the phrase as a title for a course they were running for prospective entrants to the profession.

Above all, however, humour gives people licence to say things that could not be said otherwise. For example, criticizing superiors to their face is not, typically, a recipe for promotion or success. However, a joke about superiors with people who share similar views permits the venting of emotions, such as fear, hostility and contempt. The joke carries safely one's discontent (see Chapter 16, 'Feelings'). A joke laden with irony or sarcasm can cloak one's negative feelings. To exclaim directly: 'the

Figure 18.1

manager is a lazy so and so' may cause embarrassment, even if several people in an office recognize it as true. Saying instead: 'our boss is an extremely ambitious man; his greatest ambition is to draw a salary without doing any work', lightly camouflages the hostility and allows the teller to see if others share the same opinion. A joke, then, offers an amnesty to the teller, enabling a particular view and a range of **emotions** to evade organizational and **moral** censorship and find an expression. If the joke reaches a receptive audience, it provides a sense of togetherness and mutual support. If the joke fails, however, there is always an escape route: 'I was only joking'.

Laughter bonds people as tightly as a shared secret. One cannot tell oneself a joke or a secret, just as one cannot tickle oneself. Jokes and secrets require a social relationship, a shared understanding based on a common **language** which excludes others. Most organizational jokes are also secrets; some people are in and some people are out of these secrets: 'if only the Chairman knew what we say behind his back … '. A joke strengthens the sense of **trust** for those who share it. A shared joke, especially one that is directed against someone who is excluded from the group, can generate mutual warmth and respect. In this way, the joke unleashes two types of emotion: affection for those who share it, and **aggression** towards the target (see Chapter 10, 'Us and Them').

Some jokes test the invisible boundary between the inclusion and exclusion of others. The 'practical joke' achieves just this, playing a trick on someone at their expense. It is what the Germans call *schadenfreude* – talking pleasure in another's misfortune. For example, James, a junior manager, tells the following story:

REAL-LIFE EXAMPLE

I checked my new car in for a service at a local garage. They said they'd call me at work when it was ready for collection. It wasn't a very expensive car, but I was very proud of it – because it was my first new one – and everybody knew about it!

Around four o'clock in the afternoon, I had a call from the garage. I was stunned when they told me that they had had the car on a test run and it had been damaged! They were very apologetic and said they would, of course, repair it. If I could call them in an hour's time, they would let me know how long it would take. I put the phone down dazed and absolutely furious. The incompetency! And my beautiful new car!

I sounded off at my neighbour, George, who was in his office. He was really sympathetic and offered me any support I wished. He was a good guy.

I phoned the garage back, prepared to tell them what I really thought about them. They were puzzled by my ranting: 'What damage, sir? We have no record of any problems with your car; it's ready for collection'. I was utterly confused and lost for words. I guess I was also a bit relieved.

I knocked on George's door to tell him about the latest bizarre twist in the tale. As I walked in, I saw a smirk on his face. He then confessed that he had made the original call to me.

I'd been set up. By then, everyone in the department had heard about what had happened and they thought it was a great joke. I forced a smile, but inside felt very angry and embarrassed. I never quite trusted George in the same way after that.

Practical jokes such as this are both bonding devices for the observers, and a test of willingness for the victim to 'take it', to 'shrug it off'. James' pride in his new car also made him look different, perhaps a source of envy for George, and so someone to be brought down a peg or two. But an innocent joke, as we can see, can backfire, and be hurtful and hard to forget for the victim.

Few incidents generate as much *schadenfreude* as the humbling of a pompous person in a position of authority. Such misfortunes are invariably celebrated by their subordinates and turned into jokes, generating the same type of laughter as pies in the face and slipping on banana skins. A manager whose tie gets caught in the office shredder will provide much amusement, especially if he places great store by his appearance; likewise, an executive who insists on punctuality yet himself turns up late for a meeting.

The greater our hostility towards the victim of misfortune, the greater our enjoyment. The undeserved suffering of our fellow human beings may trigger in us feelings of sympathy and compassion. Yet no amount of suffering provides protection against ridicule, so long as we can convince ourselves that the victims brought it upon themselves with their arrogance or foolishness: they 'deserved it', or simply it was their turn to be laughed at. As Erasmus said, 'the mad laugh at the mad; each provides mutual enjoyment to the other'.

IN-GROUP HUMOUR

Individuals who persistently deviate from group **norms** may find themselves on the receiving end of disparaging humour – cutting or ironic remarks from their colleagues. Social norms guide our behaviour and shape our expectations of other people's behaviour. Much psychological research has gone into demonstrating how we become **socialized** into the norms of the society and the groups we belong to, so that the norms eventually become part of ourselves. Norms affect most aspects of our life, from relatively minor matters of etiquette to major aspects of our **personality** and life choices, like sexual preference or career choice. Our moral **values** themselves, our sense of what is good and what is evil, depend to a substantial degree on the values of the groups of which we are members (see Chapter 12, 'Morals'). Most of the time, social norms guide our behaviour without us being aware of them. Eating with a knife and fork, for example, becomes second nature to us, such that we cannot appreciate how difficult little children may find the mastery of these implements.

Within organizations, as in society at large, our behaviour is regulated not only by written rules and regulations, but also by unwritten norms. Not all groups impose their norms with the same severity, but generally deviance from group norms is discouraged. Humour is crucial both in re-affirming group norms and in enforcing **conformity**; it is a type of sanction relying on embarrassment to pressure the offending individual back into conformity.

An office worker who dresses in an unorthodox manner, a pupil who rushes to answer each of the teacher's questions, a worker who consistently works harder than the rest, a manager who fawns before his/her superiors, soon begin to attract disparaging remarks, frequently expressed as jokes. This acts as a first reminder that such behaviour threatens group cohesion and undermines the group's accepted standards of behaviour. It is surprising, at times, how tiny details of appearance or behaviour become symbolically extremely important for different groups. The college student who drinks half pints of beer while his or her friends are downing pints will soon be picked upon, as if he or she had violated an important group taboo. If sarcastic remarks are the group's first attempt to pull individuals back to the norms, exclusion, verbal abuse or physical violence may follow.

Humour, then, is often the first indicator of the line between acceptable and unacceptable behaviour. It acts as a mechanism of group **control**. People who persistently break group norms face two possibilities. They may be marginalized and ultimately rejected by the group. Alternatively, they may become accepted as 'eccentrics', exceptions who reinforce the norms. They are figures of fun whose tolerated existence is taken to show the strength and confidence of the system from which they are allowed to deviate.

JOKING RELATIONS

Anthropologists have used the term 'joking relationships' to describe relationships which are built around continuous teasing, horseplay, ridicule and jocular repartee, but without resulting in offence. Such relationships have been studied in factories, offices, department stores, hospitals and shipyards as well as in informal gatherings. Obscenity, cursing, insults and vicious pranks are part and parcel of joking relationships, yet in a curious way, the coarser the insult, the greater the affection, warmth and respect it is meant to **communicate**.

Much of the humorous banter that can be heard in offices, building sites and other workplaces takes the form of friendly teasing. Individuals are routinely teased for their appearance, their accent, their **ethnic** origin or their tastes. Such teasing can be quite

Figure 18.2

rough but is generally good-natured, a sign of trust and intimacy. Targeting an individual, in this case, can be a sign of affection and esteem – the assumption is that the target 'can take it', without offence. As we saw from the practical joke example, proving that 'you can take a joke' is often important in order to be accepted as a full group member.

New recruits in military or police academies and new boarding school pupils are often subjected to bizarre tests, known as **rites of passage** or initiation, which will later provide the material for jokes. The police recruit may be asked to go and arrest a supposed criminal hiding on an island in the middle of a lake in a park. A new computer analyst may find that their machine has been tampered with, seeming to delete precious files in front of their very eyes. The Chairman's new chauffeur may be asked to go and pick up the Chairman from an address in the red-light district in the middle of the night. The individual who successfully survives these initiation ordeals is then accepted as a full member of the group and as fit to take part in joking relationships (see Chapter 2, 'Entering and Leaving').

THE UGLY SIDE OF HUMOUR

While humour cements groups, builds trust and humanizes **impersonal** relations, the line between friendly teasing and brutal **bullying** can be very thin. What passes as an innocent joke may, to its target, amount to abusive racial or **sexual harassment**. Teasing intended to be good-natured has the potential rapidly to turn sour.

We saw earlier how the weak and exploited members of organizations use humour to symbolically turn the tables on those who dominate them. The reverse of this happens when the dominant party of a relationship forces his or her abusive humour on his or her subordinates, inviting them to laugh at grotesque wisecracks. Under the mock trust of a joking relationship, black employees may be invited to laugh at **racist** jokes and women at **sexist** jokes (see Chapters 11, 'Being Different'). Indeed, sexist and racist jokes are especially humiliating types of harassment, placing the target in a no-win situation. Laughing at the joke (while secretly despising themselves for doing so) reinforces the joke and makes it socially and morally acceptable. Refusing to laugh, on the other hand, automatically excludes the target from the group and turns them into a legitimate target of sarcasm – for 'lacking a sense of humour'. This can encourage yet further insulting jokes.

In such situations, it may be possible to respond to the joke with another joke, one that twists its meaning and turns the aggressor's innuendo on its head. In one engineering organization, we interviewed employees about their job attitudes. It was soon apparent that many disparaging jokes were targeted against central headquarters (for example: 'what is the difference between HQ and a bag of manure? The bag'). The local managers were in on most jokes, being no mean wits themselves. Much of the banter and teasing in the office was overtly sexual: people's appearance, their secret crushes, the engineers' exploits on house calls were the source of continuous joking. After Jenny, a young and outspoken office worker had been interviewed, Brian, one of the managers, asked her – tongue in cheek in the presence of several bystanders – 'did you spill the beans, sweetheart?' 'Sure', she replied, 'I told him that you are a dirty old man'. 'Me, old?', he retorted without a moment's hesitation. Everyone listening to the conversation burst out laughing. This short exchange is charged with danger and innuendo. It starts by breaking a little organizational taboo, threatening the established order. The joke then defuses the tension, leaving an atmosphere of goodwill and effervescence. Or does it?

Jokes and joking then can be liberating and subversive but they can equally be oppressive and humiliating. They can challenge assumptions and express unpalatable truths or they can reinforce **stereotypes**. They can provide a soothing ointment for the scars of organizational life or can be a prime cause of such scars; very often, they can do both simultaneously. The funniest jokes are often those that are in some way closest to the edge, whether it is the edge of social acceptability or the edge of offence.

JOKES AND CULTURE

How much do jokes differ in different cultures? It is very hard to give a definitive answer to this question, but with the growing internationalization of organizations, it has become an increasingly important issue. There are cases where national languages give us a clue to the preferred style of joking in different cultures. For example, there is no word or phrase in Greek for 'sense of humour', although there is a phrase which says that someone tells good jokes.

Jokes seem not to translate very well from one language to another and are often dependent on subtleties, puns and figures of speech. Newspaper headlines often illustrate this well, telling a clear story to those who share an idiomatic usage of the language, but remaining incomprehensible to those who do not. Intimate familiarity with the colloquialisms and local usages of language is fundamental to appreciating humour. Because of this, even different countries sharing the same mother tongue can find each other's humour baffling. For example, a comedy show that succeeds in the

USA can fail in the UK (and vice versa), underscoring George Bernard Shaw's comment that 'England and America are two countries divided by a common language'.

In these circumstances, it is easy to dismiss others as lacking a sense of humour. This is a severe form of exclusion, and a strange one because it often has more to do with the ignorance of the person dismissing than the capabilities of the person dismissed. It is a common occurrence among people whose first language is English. They will talk and joke, whether in the boardroom, the business conference room, the MBA class or the undergraduate seminar, as if everyone can understand their idiomatic expressions. Those deeply schooled in English as a second language may be able to join in and feel included, but many others may feel clumsy and incompetent. However, when they are talking in English to others for whom English is also a second language, they are able to joke with confidence.

ORGANIZING HUMOUR

Much of what we have described so far concerns the different ways that humour and joking spontaneously arise in organizations. In recent years, however, humour has been regarded as a management tool, something that can be deliberately cultivated to improve employee morale and performance. The 'fun' activities are wide-ranging in style and form. For example, British Airways has hired a corporate jester; IBM has experimented with 'playrooms'; Lands End, a US mail-order company, offers 'inside out' days where employees can wear their clothes inside out; while a UK engineering firm encourages 'silly hat days'. The lucrative potential of such activities has attracted management **consultants**, some of whom offer 'humour solutions' to companies which, in the words of one consultancy, 'help people get more smileage out of their lives and jobs'.

Organizing fun in this manner can be an antidote to stress and boredom, especially in highly routinized jobs. A playful atmosphere can help defuse tensions and conflicts and provide an acceptable relief valve for pent-up feelings. It is cathartic, therapeutic. But there is a catch. As we have shown, humour and fun gain their force and purpose by emerging from within the culture of an organization or work group. Manufactured humour can appear gimmicky, a management ploy that backfires. It is awkward or embarrassing for the person who does not want to join in. More sharply, it can fuel cynicism if it is seen as an easy way for managers to avoid tackling poor working conditions or unsatisfactory jobs.

JOKES AND THE IRON CAGE

Jokes that people tell at the workplace can reveal much about the organization, its management, its **culture** and its **conflicts**. If anything, under the moral smokescreen supplied by humour, people can express deeper feelings and views. Even more, they can express the ambiguity that they feel: simultaneous respect and frustration, oppression and freedom. Even the scarcity of humour can be extremely revealing about an organization. Joke-free zones have been said to exist, both at the level of countries and organizations, though we are not sure that we have ever found an example that stands up to examination. All the cases we have explored turned out to be places where outsiders did not understand, or were not allowed to see, insiders' humour. People's sense of humour may wane if they are brutalized to quiet resignation or if they take themselves and the organization extremely seriously. The majority of organizations, however, can neither **control** their members to such an extent, nor persuade them of the seriousness of their objectives.

Humour thrives as a way of killing boredom, creating solidarity and scoring symbolic points against internal and external oppositions. For these reasons, the different types of jokes examined here seem perfectly suited to the exigencies of organizational life. There is, however, one type of joke which best captures organizational humour: the joke against the organization itself. This is the type of joke epitomized in satire, such as that directed at military organizations or at **authoritarian** regimes. The organization, satire proclaims, is an absurd farce. Instead of trying to make sense of it, let us have a good laugh at its expense. Satire celebrates the chinks in the armour of those impressive organizations which dominate our society. It shows that behind the formidable administrative, technical and financial resources of these giants, there are people messing about and making mistakes. Behind their **rationality**, there are absurdities, foul-ups and blunders. A whole tradition of satirists, from Erasmus and Rabelais through Jonathan Swift up to the present time, have helped people to oppose pomposity, self-aggrandisement, greed and malice (Harries, 1998: 29).

Organizational satire can be seen as a protest against the 'iron cage of bureaucracy' and all those who are eager to provide their services to it. **Organizations** themselves, for the greatest part, do little to discourage it. To be sure, a practical joke that results in serious loss of production or the wiping out of the company's records will not go unpunished. However, so long as the work gets done and the orders are obeyed, most organizations are willing to tolerate humour and satire, even if they themselves become the object of ridicule. While offering no prizes to the quickest wit or the most original prankster, they recognize that even defiant humour is a protest, not a rebellion. Its victories are **symbolic**, not material.

IN CONCLUSION

Humour and jokes, far from being inconsequential, are important features of organizational life. They break the organizational routine and enable people to cope with boring or **alienating** jobs. They generate trust and affection for those sharing a laugh and a joke and permit the venting of unacceptable views and **emotions** (like aggression or contempt), by offering a moral amnesty which permits the breaking of taboos.

The targets of organizational jokes are varied, but most work groups have an individual or another group which serves as the butt of disparaging humour. When directed against superiors or outsiders, jokes strengthen the solidarity of a group and enable the group to score symbolic victories against their psychological adversaries. When directed against members of a group, jokes may be part of joking relations, highlighting the intimacy and trust between the group's members, or they may serve to re-inforce group norms and force compliance. They can also be a means of teasing or bullying some members, but with many of the common forms of language joking, the jokers may end up excluding themselves rather than those they intended to hurt. Humour may also be exploited as a management tool.

Finally, the target of jokes may be the organization itself, whose foul-ups and absurdities are celebrated because they undermine the façade of rationality and seriousness. Such jokes, for a brief moment or two, explode organizational order and restore the human factor, in its fallibility and unpredictability, at the heart of organizations.

KEY POINTS

○ Under the veneer of seriousness, jokes, irony and humour play an important part in most organizations.

○ Jokes offer a way of saying things and venting emotions which could not otherwise be expressed.

○ Humour can provide a way for the powerless to turn the tables on the powerful, having a laugh at their expense. It therefore functions as an important survival mechanism.

○ Laughter bonds people, generating feelings of solidarity, intimacy and trust.

○ In-group humour establishes the boundaries between acceptable and unacceptable behaviour and provides a way of testing group norms.

○ Jokes and mockery can act as a group sanction against those who violate group norms.

○ Jokes are very often based in a particular usage of the language, and may not translate either to other languages or to non-native users of the same language.

○ Racist and sexist jokes tend to rely on crude stereotypes; when addressed at a member of the stereotyped group, they can be seen as a form of harassment.

○ Organized humour can be used deliberately by management to lighten the working atmosphere, but this can also be received by employees as false and manipulative.

> > > > > > > > > > > THEORETICAL SIGNPOSTS > > > > > > > > > > >

The major themes in this chapter have been covered in the following areas of literature:

> the use of humour for production and subversion in organizations
> humour as a way of coping with contradiction in organizations
> humour for expressing serious concerns
> humour for acceptance.

The Use of Humour for Production and Subversion in Organizations

This is explored through an overview of the different contours of humour in organizations in the work of Collinson (1988, 2002). Rodrigues and Collinson (1995) comment on the functionalist perspective of a lot of what literature there is on humour in organizations, i.e. a lot of it argues one of the following: 'if you make people laugh, they will work harder for less money'; 'if you make people laugh, they will buy your product'; 'if you allow yourself to laugh, you will be more effective'. By contrast, their article emphasizes the more subversive use of humour in an organization where other forms of resistance are not available. Duncan and Feisal (1989) have attempted a typology of humour at the workplace, along with a set of recommendations for managers. Their approach is in many ways the converse of the Rodrigues and Collinson one, not because they disagree with each other's points but because the assumptions they make and the values they claim are so different from each other, and it would make for a good balance to read the two together.

Humour as a Way of Coping with Contradiction in Organizations

This is emphasized in the work of Hatch and Ehrlich (1993), which takes us out of the frame of one party using humour in an instrumental fashion in their relationship with another, whether motivationally or subversively. They are interested in the rather different theme that organizational life is full of contradictions and incoherence, and humour can be a way for people to handle this for themselves. The intricacies of humour arising from the fine grain of workgroup culture are excellently illustrated by Linstead (1988), while the way the 'iron cage' of bureaucracy is softened and undermined by humour is discussed by Davies (1988).

Humour for Expressing Serious Concerns

This is discussed by Yarwood (1995). Although his research is based in the American public sector, there is no reason why the points made should not apply equally to other sectors. Yarwood's analysis includes relating the topic to humour about organizations as found in novels and the like, which opens up another whole interesting discussion that we have not given space to earlier.

Humour for Acceptance

This is discussed in a very brief summary by Fisher (1996) which summarizes recent research which suggests that women are held back by not being adept at the use of humour in organizations. The suggestion from the study is that managers who use humour get rated more highly, and that the women managers in the study were seen as less humorous, possibly because they were holding themselves back from bringing humour into the serious business of managing.

A rich source for all these themes will be found in Westwood and Rhodes (2006).

REVIEW QUESTIONS

1. Discuss the different ways in which humour is used in organizations by powerful people and less powerful people.

2. Humour can be a great bond between people, and can also leave some people feeling really excluded. How can you try to encourage a use of humour which you would regard as healthy in your work group?

3. Organizational life and work are complicated, and things are bound to go wrong sometimes. How does humour help people to cope with these situations?

---

companion
website
sagepub.co.uk/fineman

Reading On

The articles below are available for free to readers of the fourth edition of *Organizing & Organizations* via the book's companion website at www.sagepub.co.uk/fineman

Cooper, C. (2008) 'Elucidating the bonds of workplace humor: a relational process model', *Human Relations*, 61: 1087–115.

A number of studies have demonstrated that humour can impact both horizontal and vertical relationships in organizations, but little is known about the interpersonal processes underlying this link. The author reviews classical theories of humour before showing how research in the fields of social psychology, communications, and leadership provides insight into the social processes in humour exchange.

Grugulis, I. (2002) 'Nothing serious? Candidates' use of humour in management training', *Human Relations*, 55: 387–406.

This article explores the use made of humour in three different private sector organizations. It draws on observations of managers working towards a management qualification and, from the jokes they exchange, argues that studying humour may offer insights into sentiments not easily articulated in 'serious' conversation. Humour's complexity makes it a particularly appropriate vehicle for conveying ambitions, subversions, triumphs and failures, and this article considers some of the 'serious' messages underlying the jokes.

Schnurr, S. (2008) 'Surviving in a man's world with a sense of humour: an analysis of women leaders' use of humour at work', *Leadership*, 4: 299–319.

This article explores some of the ways in which women leaders make use of humour in order to enhance their leadership performance while also resolving the challenges of being the 'odd girls out' in a predominantly masculine work environment. Drawing on authentic discourse data collected in two New Zealand organizations, this article illustrates that women leaders skilfully employ humour to portray themselves as effective leaders while at the same time negotiating and performing their gender identities in a masculine domain.

Taylor, P. and Bain, P. (2003) 'Subterranean worksick blues: humour as subversion in two call centres', *Organization Studies*, 24: 1487–509.

This article emphasizes the subversive character of humour in the workplace, rejecting perspectives which see humour as inevitably contributing to organizational harmony. In the authors' study of two call centres, humour contributed to the development of vigorous countercultures in both locations, which conflicted with corporate aims and priorities, including strengthening support for the trade union and weakening managerial authority.

19

VIRTUALITY

One of the big changes in organizations over recent years has been increasing virtuality. In this chapter, we talk about virtual organizations, but virtuality has gone much further than that. The rise of online trading means that many seemingly conventional companies have developed a virtuality in the way they handle their processes that would have been unimaginable 20 years ago. We also have a level of virtuality in services that would have been unimaginable to a previous generation, fuelled not only by the possibilities of the internet, but also by deregulation. So the collapse in the banking and credit system which was witnessed in 2008 is a result and an example of virtualization, where financial products have been offered that are so complicated that no one fully understands them, and where credit is extended without anyone being able to trace exactly how much is owed to whom. One of the triggers of the 2008 crisis was the large number of sub-prime mortgages in the United States, that is, the number of loans for house purchases made to buyers with a poor credit record. This triggered a panic which was made worse because no one in the banking system seemed quite sure who the ultimate owners of the debt were, because of the complicated way in which loans had been reassigned and covered. This chapter will therefore also look at some of the issues of trust that are raised by the whole nature of virtuality.

WHAT IS VIRTUALITY

Virtuality is everywhere – and nowhere. The 'virtual organization' has become of great interest to business and to academics, particularly with the development of new forms of **communication** which enable us to organize ourselves in quite different ways. A virtual organization is one in which we behave 'as if' the organization were real, while for one reason or another it is not real in our usual sense of the word; it does not have the expected sense of place, the tactile sense of being able to find it, that we associate with other organizations. To some extent, all organizations are like this. We act as members of our organization even when we cannot see any property or buildings that belong to that organization. But in this chapter we are especially interested in organizations which have gone the extra stage in detaching themselves from physical location – the bank which has no solid marble banking halls, the software company with no identifiable headquarters, even the terrorist organization which is organized as a network, with no physical head or headquarters to attack.

Traditionally, there has been some sense of place for organizations. As we said in Chapter 1, for any organization, the location may not be as clear as might traditionally be assumed. Organizations do not end at the factory gate or the office door. People are still members of their organizations when they are working at home or when they are having a meeting in an overseas airport. There is still an office even though they are not working in it today. There is still some notion of a physical **building** in a geographical space which could be described by coordinates on a map. People will refer to themselves as 'on-site' or 'off-site'. It is as if they feel there is a 'home' base at which they can locate their work, even if they are absent most of the time. Insurance salespeople, who spend most of their time out with clients, refer to times when they will be 'in the office'. They are in someone's office most of the time, but this is not what they mean; they mean 'their' office, their base, even if they spend little time there.

In contrast to this, the concept has grown up in the last few years of the **virtual organization**. This may mean an organization with no physical centre, all of whose members work at a distance from each other and from any associated assets. For example, a software company might consist of a central group of people who come with ideas that they think will sell, and then others who sit at home or in the offices of other employers and actually write the software, possibly without ever meeting others who are working on a different aspect of the same project, or the managers of the enterprise. In other cases, it means an organization pieced together from parts of different organizations. Thus, there could be a virtual pathology laboratory which hires testing ability from a pharmaceutical company, diagnostic ability from a hospital, and marketing expertise from a medical supplies firm. The people providing these services never meet together, have no shared loyalties, and their control and coordination are by contracts for service rather than by **hierarchy** and employment relationships.

Other examples of virtual organizations include drug dealers, where it is notoriously difficult for the police to find their way past the smaller functionaries to the main operators behind them. Many criminal organizations benefit enormously from not having any central location that can be policed, by being able to melt away when they wish to do so. We have seen this in recent years with the attempts of the US government to tackle al-Qaeda and other **networks**. The richest, most powerful government on earth has struck out wildly in an attempt to disable a network of people with no clear base or hierarchy. Such new forms of organization show one of the great benefits of virtuality, familiar to guerrilla warriors for a long time; powerful forces do not know how to direct themselves against virtual organizations. Worse still, their misdirected efforts may lead to strengthening the position of the organizations they sought to attack.

The two elements usually associated with virtuality are firstly a lack of a distinct physical centre, and secondly network characteristics (rather than, or alongside, a traditionally hierarchical structure). These elements may be present in different proportions in different virtual organizations. This makes them very different from, for example, 'flat organizations' where the hierarchy may have fewer levels than in the past, but is nonetheless a system of command and control, possibly all the more rigorous for being relatively pared down. At one end, virtual organizations would include network organizations, those that are put together for the purpose of cooperation around a particular task. Here, there is an emphasis on network relationships with others. For example, many retailers sell their own brands of clothing, groceries or whatever, sourcing these from manufacturers with whom they have increasingly close relationships. At one time, such relationships could be described by a contract; one company will supply another with so many shirts of a particular specification at the agreed price. With increasing consumer choice, more sophisticated branding and higher demands for quality, this has changed. Now the retailer often wishes to intervene in aspects of the production process, so that it makes less sense to speak of the retailer and producer as separate organizations, even though that is the official position. Instead of traditional, hands-off, buyer–seller relationships, they are networking in a form of virtual organization.

Consider the production of a textbook. The authors may work in different organizations. They meet the publisher very occasionally, and while the quality and timing of their work is controlled by contract, it is not easy to establish what constitutes fulfilment of that contract. There is no explicit hierarchical arrangement, though implicit hierarchies may arise. Nor is there any clear means by which anybody can discipline or dismiss anyone else. The publisher will involve other professionals whose base is in yet other organizations in giving advice about the content and style of the book. They then employ a freelance worker to read the book thoroughly for consistency of style and content, while another freelance expert designs a jacket. They contract with a printer to print the book, and another freelance worker to proofread it. Yet another freelance specialist will be responsible for putting together publicity material, under contract to the publisher's own, employed marketing department. So even the production of something so physical as a textbook is undertaken by a range of organizational arrangements, many of which are more 'virtual' than 'visible'. Organizations do not have to be one or the other; much organizational work is done in a way that is partly virtual and partly face to face. Many conventional organizations have increasingly virtual aspects to their operation.

Interestingly, sometimes companies seem to be more virtual than the industries they are part of. So while many software companies are run with a high degree of virtualization – remote home working by networked computers being the norm – the software industry still congregates, for example, in Silicon Valley in the USA or the M4 Corridor in the UK.

THE TECHNOLOGY OF VIRTUALITY

The idea of virtuality is often associated with significant usage of Information and Computing Technologies (ICT). It is widely assumed that virtual organizations are a new form that has been made possible by advances in ICT. We have been taking a rather different view, which is that virtuality is more about networking, although ICT may be an essential factor in networking. Nevertheless, ICT has a crucial part to play in enabling virtual organizations.

Virtuality has only come to prominence recently, and its prominence has certainly been fuelled by ICT and other recent technological advances. The foremost of these has been the cheap and widespread availability of computer technology, and its connection through the internet. Not far behind have been the developments in telephony and, in particular, the rapidly falling costs of video conferencing and mobile telephony. All of these factors are waiting to be exploited, and for many people, the opportunity to work with such technology, and the opportunity to learn by experience how to make good use of it, is something which they value in itself. There are several definite incentives to virtualization both for the organization and the potential worker: as well as the lower costs, organizational and personal, which we will come back to, there is also a feeling that the learning gained may have high resale value. It is good for the career prospects of the individual to be able to show experience in a virtual organization.

Flexibility is sought in many different business operations, and virtualization can often offer plenty of flexibility. If some or all, staff are working at a distance, and if many operations are being outsourced, start-up costs are likely to be radically less than for a more traditional organization. Fewer physical assets will probably be needed. It may well be possible to avoid the delays of recruiting staff by using part-timers or by **outsourcing** activities to those who are already employing suitable staff. Risks are reduced. If the product does not sell, there are no permanent staff to make redundant or physical plants to sell off at reduced prices.

DISTANCE WORKING

Much of the early usage of the idea of virtual organizations was for institutions where people might work at a distance. If employees are engaged in work that can be done as well from home as by travelling to a workplace, both employer and employee may agree that it is better for the work to be done at home. The employer does not have to supply space, light, heating and so on, thus cutting their costs. The employee does not have to travel to their place of work, thus saving time and travel costs. The employee can also design their working environment to suit them best, whether that means that they choose their own music, that they are at home to take delivery of the new television, or that they can fit their schedule to their children's school times.

There is a less positive side to this. Many of the jobs done by distance working are among the poorest paid. For example, much of the clothing industry saves money by not supplying workplaces, but requiring people to supply their own space, light and

"I DO MISS THE CHANGE OF SEASONS, BUT THANKS TO TECHNOLOGY, I'VE OFF-SHORED EVERYTHING."

Figure 19.1
Source: http://www.cartoonstock.com

power while stitching clothes for very poor pay. Similar exploitation is practised on keyboard operators who may be paid piece rates for data entry, and those rates may be such that they have no chance of earning a reasonable wage. Those who are caring for small children or elderly parents at home have become easy targets for very low-paid distance working.

The uneven power relationship between employer and employee is made even more unequal when the employees are not physically aware of each other. They have no opportunity to interact, to discuss their work or to organize any form of response to the employer's power. They can also become very lonely. New forms of technology which may be liberating and enlivening for some can also lead to ever tighter forms of **control**. The poorly paid computer data entry worker, working as a freelance from home via the internet, can be inspected and controlled at least as closely as would be possible in an office, because their number of key strokes per minute can be monitored, the time in which the machine is inactive can be measured, and even the number of words queried by a spellchecker can be inspected as a surrogate measure for quality. They also effectively lose the protection that many governments have now put in place for employed organizational members on such matters as health and safety, and maximum working time.

On the other hand, there is less that the company for whom they are working can do directly to control their work. For many who are tired of the office or factory routine, distance working sounds like an attractive taste of freedom. There is no longer the supervisor's gaze checking whether they are doing what they should be doing; they are safely away from time clocks, and from critical comments from others if they do not work long hours.

There are some particularly interesting examples where work is neither fully virtual nor fully face to face. Within the knowledge economy, many jobs now enable people to work at home one or two days a week, keeping fully in touch with others via internet connections or mobile phones, but without having to travel on those days, and still being available when the television is to be delivered. This pattern is increasingly common in many professional and managerial jobs. It offers the employee the best of both worlds, and this means that very often the people with most power and influence have the most positive view of the experience of virtual working. They can see that it gives them more freedom to arrange their lives and to make the boundaries between working and the rest of life more comfortable, while they are losing nothing in terms of security, conditions or interpersonal relationships.

THE INVISIBLE TEAM

Studies of managers in traditional organizations have shown that they spend most of their time in conversation – often 80 per cent or more of managerial time is spent in this way (Mintzberg, 1973). When people at any level of an organization talk about their work, they tend to talk about the other people there. Very often, their **talk** will be a series of **stories** about those other people and their activities. The most interesting or engaging part of work for many people, the part that is worth talking about, is to do with others. Even if this seems quite trivial, for example where it consists of taking a gossipy interest in the events of other peoples' lives, as if they were in a soap opera, it often provides entertainment and interest in an organization.

Figure 19.2

Now let us imagine the situation where they never see those others, where they may know nothing about them apart from their technical output. Work has suddenly been stripped of both its most interesting but also its most ambivalent aspect. As Jean-Paul Sartre said at the conclusion of his play *No Exit*, 'hell is other people'. We often find others infuriating and frustrating, but also lovable and entertaining. Much of the best and the worst of our working day is taken away from us if there are no others around. Virtual working may be somewhat insipid compared with the face-to-face experience. **Teamwork** is a case in point. Traditionally, work teams consist of people with different abilities making different kinds of contributions. In many workplaces, team roles are evolved through interaction. Someone in the team realizes that no one is giving the team much in the way of ideas to work on, so they undertake this role. In a different team, there seems to be a lack of any social connection between the members – they never go out for lunch together, so one of the members takes on the social organizer role. People watch the workings of their teams and fill in the gaps. In virtual teams, it is not so easy for anyone to see what is happening and, more importantly, what is not happening.

Indeed, the very word 'team' hardly seems to make sense if the members are physically separate. All our notions of 'team spirit', 'team leadership' and other features of team working are based on face-to-face teams. The word is usually first encountered by children in sports teams. The metaphor of 'team', carried from the sports field to the workplace, seems to break down for virtual teams. For example, most of us feel bad about letting down other members of our team, whether we are cooperating on a project or playing in a football match. But if we cannot see them, the feelings of guilt become much less sharp. Practical commitment to others is often enhanced by being able to see them face to face, and 'saving face' may become less important when our dealings with others are virtual. Much of management practice has been based on getting people to work together in teams, to motivate each other, control each other, and to simplify the coordination of different kinds of work. Is any of this possible within virtual working? If not, we may need to develop a range of new management practices to achieve the same ends. Virtuality may require more new thinking for managers than has yet been appreciated.

VIRTUAL TRUST

Like other forms of relationship, we are used to developing **trust** face to face. We are much less experienced in developing it at a distance: how can we trust people whom we cannot see, and whom we have possibly never seen? While some have argued that it is in the nature of trust that it requires direct interpersonal contact, other researchers have suggested that there is another kind of trust, 'swift trust', that can be developed very quickly in electronic communication (Meyerson et al., 1966). This is based, like face-to-face trust, on **non-verbal communication**, but in a different way: swift trust is based on the speed with which people communicate and respond, and on the optimism and enthusiasm which they show in those responses. The traditional non-verbal cues are not available, but we seem to be able to generate some alternative ones very quickly.

One helpful approach (Sako, 1992) divides trust into three different phenomena. The first of these is *contractual trust*, where you believe that someone will do what they say they will do, and that they will do it in an acceptable way (for example, they will deliver on time). For example, a telephone network may well state its coverage of a country by stating the proportion of places in which its subscribers can expect to be able to receive and make calls. Can they be trusted to offer the level of service they have led others to expect and that they have contracted for? The answer will usually be yes, but there are also times when such companies lose their customers' trust. Rail companies in the UK are currently not trusted to deliver a safe and reliable service. Banks have lost the trust of the public in a very big way over the last few years. Can a university be trusted to provide the course that it has promised? It will almost certainly have to vary its provision; some staff will leave, others will join, new electives will be created and others dropped. At what point do they lose their students' trust? It is not simply when they vary the contract; it seems that we have some notion of what constitutes a reasonable variation.

For example, John's director told him that he would raise the issue at the board meeting about re-housing John's department, which was currently in five different buildings with some miles in between them. 'Yes, of course, it is not acceptable for you to have to work like that in the longer term – I'll certainly get it discussed'. Should John feel reassured by this? It all depends on his level of contractual trust: is this director someone who does what he says he will do? The judgement that John makes about that will depend on considerable knowledge of the director concerned and of the context in which the director would have to make his remarks. It is much harder to know the director sufficiently, or to know enough of the context, to form trust in a virtual organization.

Sometimes such trust is broken and legal remedies are considered. This is why this is known as contractual trust. The judgement that is made will depend on knowledge of the provider concerned and may be affected by newspaper reports and contact with other customers. In any case, it may be harder to place such trust in a virtual organization because it lacks the tactile qualities that suggest solidity and dependability in some face-to-face organizations, such as the marble-lined banking hall that we mentioned earlier. There is the feeling that a virtual organization could disappear altogether before the customer can recover goods from it.

The second type of trust is labelled *competence trust*. Is the other person actually able to do what they are supposed to do? Can we trust them to do what they say without making a mistake? We may trust someone to do their best to fulfil their contract, to try to do what they have said they will do, but we do not think they have the ability to deliver. Everyone liked Alec, who was a very warm character, convincing, and so far as anyone could tell, with genuine good intentions. He could also be highly skilled in his work as a management consultant, noticing things which others failed to notice, and coming up with solutions and suggestions no one else had thought of. However, he had, it seemed, no ability to keep hold of the big picture over long periods of time. So his projects, well intentioned and in parts well executed, could never be relied on to turn out as he promised. He had plenty of competence in some areas, but many of his clients were still not able to have competence trust in him. Such trust can be based on a number of cues when you are working face to face. Is Alec looking alert? Have you seen him talking to all the people he needs to talk to? Is he around quite a lot of the time and spending time on the project? Of course, some of those cues could be faked, but with virtual working, none of those cues are available to us.

The third kind of trust is *goodwill trust*, where people have an expectation of open commitment to each other. This form of trust happens when people believe that the other person's intentions are good, that 'their heart is in the right place', even if things are not always working out just as they might have hoped. This kind of trust usually develops face to face, as we see people over time, see how they treat us, see that they are willing to be our allies, to share a joke about the CEO, and show us non-verbal cues of warmth and friendship. This is fundamentally important to other kinds of trust too. In working with others, it is often quite difficult to say whether they have delivered on their contracts or whether they have been competent. If someone we trust gets things slightly wrong on the contractual or the competence side, we are likely to forgive them so long as we have goodwill trust towards them. However, it is a much more difficult matter to develop goodwill trust in a virtual organization. How might we ever decide that someone bears goodwill towards us and is going to want to be as trustworthy as possible? Interestingly, email messages seem to be becoming less bare and functional than in their earlier days, and it may be that the more discursive conversations that now take place by email are more conducive to goodwill trust than the terse messages of a few years back.

We have seen that there are ways in which each of the three forms of trust has extra challenges in a virtual organization. For all three, the difference is that the scope for testing out what people are saying and doing by looking from several different angles is greatly reduced (Weick, 1985). If, for example, all information comes through a computer screen, there is no possibility of literally being able to go round and check it from several different points of view. There is no chance of taking information from many different sources and comparing it in the same way as could be done by someone who was physically present and could talk to other people about what the boss meant by a particular statement, or what some new element of the company's policy was intended to do. There is usually no opportunity to observe body language in a virtual organization. If someone's non-verbal cues seem to be at variance with what they are saying, we may be less likely to trust them. If someone says they are very excited about their project, while yawning and showing other signs of boredom, we have a basis for not trusting what they say. Many people who do not have this means for testing out trust will tend to be more cautious. Thus, it becomes more difficult to build and test trust in a virtual organization.

If we feel that we cannot trust people, we may well put in safety nets – ways of insuring against unreliable behaviour on their part. For example, we will check up on whether they have done what they said they would do. But this tends to start a vicious circle. If someone knows that the people she is dealing with are checking up in case she behaves in an untrustworthy way, this may make her less concerned to try to be trustworthy. Recent commentators on trust have suggested that it is harder to trust if we know too much about the other person (O'Neill, 2002), and that the current concern with being as open as possible about everything actually destroys trust. Virtual working gives us many ways of finding out more about others, but always mediated by technology, and we are only just learning how to develop the crucial element of 'goodwill trust' through electronic media.

AFTER VIRTUALITY?

So what happens next? People predicting the future of organizations have an extremely poor record. For example, for the last 100 years, organization theorists have predicted that increasing efficiencies would lead to a shorter working week, but what has actually happened is a longer working week for some and no working week for others. The pattern of virtual organizations is still emerging and we are not yet aware of the full picture. Some of the effects of virtualization on working life are still only beginning to emerge. For example, in one telecommunications company, employees are hardly ever parted (including in the evenings and at weekends) from their mobile communications devices which enable them to speak or to receive emails almost anywhere and at any time. This will change both the way that work is done and the way that life is led: you are never safely away from your workplace if you have such a mobile communications device. Top executives now have these devices switched on while in meetings and even while giving public lectures. Recently, the CEO of the biggest company in the world in his field gave out his email address in a public lecture to students. All those who were present can now contact him at any hour of the day or night on a device which was picking up messages in front of him while he was talking. The continuous availability of almost everybody through such means will make a big difference to how organizations work. Many of the privileges which went with being well placed in the communications loop are losing their scarcity value. Modern forms of communication seem to be democratizing the process of contacting others.

New forms of organization become possible with the higher connectivity between people. Being so easy to reach for so many people means that they are part of a large number of electronic conversations, and there may be pressure on them to act within all of them. They are expected to keep large numbers of plates spinning, large numbers of projects and conversations moving forward, large numbers of relationships maintained, and this has consequences for their focus and their stress levels. This experience of having to keep many different activities on the move at once is often blamed on virtualization, but we would suggest that it is a feature of all modern business life. A new way of life is being accepted, even welcomed, based on the speed with which multiple conversations can be handled and multiple relationships maintained. We can work with a larger number of people on a larger range of projects than would have been conceivable even ten years ago. This is both the joy and the threat of new forms of communication, and it is accentuated by virtuality.

We have tended to talk about virtual organizations by comparison with face-to-face organizations and that is symptomatic of the stage of development that has been reached in studying them. Virtual organizing as a process is still developing and evolving. It may be possible, in ten years' time, to talk about it as a phenomenon in its own right, rather than as if it were a variant on face-to-face organization. It is full of new possibilities, and while there are some difficulties that we have discussed about working virtually, we have not seen any sign of those who are doing so wanting to move back into more traditional, face-to-face working.

KEY POINTS

- Virtual organizations are detached from the sense of physical location or place that other organizations have.

- Virtual organizations tend to be structured as networks, making them harder to understand from outside, and harder to attack.

- Even when organizations are virtual, the industries they are part of often co-locate.

- Virtuality is often enabled by information and computing technologies.

- Virtual organizations may offer distance-working and home-working opportunities.

- Distance workers may miss the company of others, but avoid the clashes and irritations.

- Teamwork and trust operate differently in virtual organizations.

- Virtual organizations are evolving rapidly with the change in technology.

- Virtuality, networking and technology seem to be increasing the number of conversations that employees are expected to be able to sustain at any one time.

>>>>>>>>>>>> **THEORETICAL SIGNPOSTS** >>>>>>>>>>>>>

The major themes in this chapter have been covered in the following areas of literature:

> virtual organizations
> distance working
> trust.

Virtual Organizations

On, *virtual organization* the hyperbole has known no bounds, but there has also been some serious work on how working practices have been affected by greater opportunities for virtuality. Several examples of this are included in Jackson (1999) and Budd and Harris (2004). Some more fundamental questions about the theory of virtual organizations have been posed by Mowshowitz (2002). Warner and Witzel (2004) offer a pragmatic and rounded picture of current thinking on virtual organizations. The connected theme of network organizations has gained increasing interest in recent years with the prevalence, in news stories, of terrorist networks. There have been good explorations of the themes of interlinking and networks (Barabasi, 2003), which have a range of consequences for thinking about life in organizations. In particular, many argue that many other kinds of interlinkage or contact are now of at least equal importance to the traditional, and less ambiguous, linkages of the boss–subordinate relationship.

Distance Working

This was explored at length by Holti and Stern (1987), and other more recent authors have developed some of the issues around the costs and benefits to both employers and employees of such forms of work. Earlier writers used the word 'teleworking' for the same phenomenon, with the word building in rather more of the technological assumption behind the practice. There is some evidence that the willingness of organizations to countenance distance working varies across cultures (Peters and den Dulk, 2003). It has also been suggested that distance working may offer considerable flexibility, but only to a minority of workers (Wilson, 1991). Over recent years, a degree of distance working has become so normal that academic interest in it as a phenomenon has tended to decline. The arrival of the Blackberry and of mobile broadband means that distance working now happens all around us on public transport, in coffee shops and so on.

Trust

On *trust* in virtual organizations, a range of issues are discussed in Kasper-Fuehrer and Ashkanasy (2001). An interesting recent empirical study is reported by Clases et al. (2004). Trust is based on some length of acquaintance and on seeing people in a number of situations over time (Sennett, 1998). How can someone communicate trustworthiness in a virtual environment? One theory suggests that they need to show reliable Information and Communication Technology (ICT), the establishment of a common business understanding and strong business ethics (Kasper-Fuehrer and Ashkanasy, 2001). Another study confirms the importance of ability and integrity in the formation of trust, but also suggests that trust has little impact on the performance of the virtual team (Aubert and Kelsey, 2003). Another study has suggested that trust in virtual teams may not carry all the same prejudices as in face-to-face teams. For example, people of different age groups may be more inclined to distrust each other face to face, but the impact disappears in a virtual team, while birthplace dissimilarity can be positively related to trust in computer-mediated teams (Krebs et al., 2006).

REVIEW QUESTIONS

1. Some of the characteristics of virtual organizations are now being found in many face-to-face organizations. Think of an organization that you know well, and discuss the features of virtualization that it has taken on.

2. Why can it be difficult to build trust in a virtual organization, and which form of trust do you think is particularly difficult?

3. Do you think that virtualization in organizations will increase or decrease the pressure on those who work in them?

---

ompanion
website
.sagepub.co.uk/fineman

Reading On

The articles below are available for free to readers of the fourth edition of *Organizing & Organizations* via the book's companion website at www.sagepub.co.uk/fineman

Kasper-Fuehrer, E.C., Ashkanasy, N.M. (2001) 'Communicating trustworthiness and building trust in interorganizational virtual organization', *Journal of Management*, 27: 235–54.
This article proposes a theory of trust in interorganizational virtual organizations that focuses on how trustworthiness can be communicated and trust built in this environment. The theory highlights three issues that must be dealt with if the potential obstacles to the development of trust in the virtual context are to be overcome: the communication of trustworthiness facilitated by reliable Information and Communication Technology (ICT), the establishment of a common business understanding, and strong business ethics.

Aubert, B.A. and Kelsey, B.L. (2003) 'Further understanding of trust and performance in virtual teams', *Small Group Research*, 34: 575–618.
Trust has been deemed to be critical in ensuring the efficient operation of virtual teams and organizations. This study empirically verifies ability and integrity as being antecedents of trust

formation in virtual teams. However, effective team performance was found to be independent of the formation of trust. Further analysis suggests that information symmetry and good communication distinguish high performance teams from low performance teams.

Knights, D., Noble, F., Vurdubakis, T. and Willmott, H. (2001) 'Chasing shadows: control, virtuality and the production of trust', *Organization Studies*, 22: 311–36.
This paper focuses on the issue of trust as it appeared in online financial services and smart cards. Notions of trust are often opposed to concepts such as power or control, and are deployed as part of a dualistic either/or proposition. This paper attempts a more nuanced exploration by focusing on attempts to 'manage' trust, the problems such attempts encounter, the various techniques employed in their resolution, and the power relations in which they are embedded.

Gillam, C. and Oppenheim, C. (2006) 'Review article: reviewing the impact of virtual teams in the information age', *Journal of Information Science*, 32: 160–75.
This paper provides an overview of virtual teams in the information age, focusing on the definition of virtual teams, their salient characteristics, the communication issues they face (including information overload, geographic and social distance), the technical issues involved (linking this to theories of media use), the issues raised by cultural diversity in the teams (including identity, trust and conflict) and managerial implications.

20
CAREER SHIFTS

Career prospects dominate the work outlooks of many people. A career easily becomes part of our self-image or our identity; in order to enhance our careers, we often sacrifice many pleasures, pursuits and relations. Yet, for many people a career or even a job seems unattainable because of their region's chronic unemployment, because of their age, gender, ethnicity or infirmity. Career patterns themselves are fast changing: a job for life is now rare; employability is more important; flexibility and new knowledge are essential. As loyalty to self replaces loyalty to the organization, for many people, a career becomes a sequence of sideways steps, interspersed with periods of self-employment, part-time employment or unemployment. For others, a career becomes a portfolio of different jobs and activities at any one period of time. Career paths are intimately linked to organizational politics, personal connections and alliances and private networks. Women are less likely to be part of the informal (male) power networks and they can hit a 'glass ceiling', blocking their career progress. The work–life balance can be harder to achieve with the growth of dual careers, long hours of work and fragmented patterns of employment.

Try responding: 'well, nothing', or 'I watch TV a lot' to enquiries at parties about what you do. The notion of job and career reaches deep into our childhood experiences. 'And what are you going to do when you grow up?' is a challenge put to most children, long before paid work has any remote significance in their lives. But that soon changes. At school, one's parents' occupations become part of one's own social identity, and there are pressures from teachers, relatives and friends to state a future job or pathway. We soon learn that we ought to have job or career ambitions (see also Chapter 22, 'Working and Living'). This point was forcefully brought home to one of us when his nine-year-old son was enticed onto the stage of a professional theatre during a Christmas pantomime show. The little fellow was interrogated by an ebullient compere:

'And what's your name, sonny?'
'Where do you live, Daniel?'
'Now, tell me what job are you going to do when you're grown up?'

To the astonishment of his parents, Daniel grasped the microphone and firmly asserted: 'I'm going to be an archaeologist'. There were roars of approval from the audience. In a post-pantomime debrief, Daniel said he had no idea what archaeologists were, nor what a job was, but he felt he ought to say something that sounded good.

Daniel's response is part of the story-telling about careers. Despite the many advice books and supportive techniques that speak strongly about planning one's career, events often do not unfold that way. We may have hazy ideas about the future, and rarely can we predict the way a particular job, or our life and relationships surrounding that job, will work out. Often, we do not know what we want out of a job until we have tried it, testing out our beliefs and filling in our ignorance. And then we can be left with a sharp image about what we do not like, but still confused about what we want next. More often than not, our decision 'choices' are determined by expediency and chance.

This process occurs in a context where a lifelong career in the same organization, industry or even profession, is becoming rarer; where periods in and out of work and breaks for re-training or further education are acceptable, even encouraged. So why retain the notion of **career**? Maybe we should abandon the idea? This could be difficult. We often feel more comfortable about the future if we believe that our past was coherent and logical. This is nowhere more strongly symbolized than in the curriculum vitae – a document in which a careful selection of academic qualifications, prizes, jobs and civic duties are assembled to show just how planned, and glorious, our past was. Career gaps are carefully camouflaged: we need to convince others, and ourselves, that we have known, and still know, where we are going. Careers, in this form, are constructed as **narratives**. We **create meaning** and consistency by providing accounts – stories of progress, moves and decisions – that give the impression that we are in charge of events and moving onwards and up. These all reflect highly prized values in industrialized, competitive societies and become internalized as part of our individual **identity**. They are a key part of how we define ourselves, how we are seen and valued by others, and where we fit into society's pecking order. Indeed, to feel, and be perceived, as a victim of circumstances, indecisive, or simply opportunistic, is often a recipe for failure in job interviews. The fact that many people, in practice, survive and prosper in exactly this manner has not yet undermined the myth that we all are, and should be, in charge of our destinies. Only those who are secure and have 'made it' can publicly declare otherwise. Indeed, it is often worn as a badge of honour by celebrities who claim it was only because of 'good luck', being 'accidentally discovered', that they have got where they are today.

Full control over one's destiny may be a fiction, but it is one that dovetails with the image of an organizational career: a succession of challenging steps within and across organizations. With each move, there is an increase in power and status, and most rewards are reserved for those who reach the top of the pyramid and attain leadership positions. Many people have made satisfying, or at least eventful, lives in 'careers' outside formal work (e.g. a career of crime, of being a housewife, of leisure); however, careers are most typically linked to jobs and paid employment. But how does this image survive close scrutiny?

WHAT CAREER?

Firstly, we need to appreciate that the concept of an occupational career is somewhat rarefied, even elitist. There are many millions of people in the world who have little prospect of any sort of meaningful career. The majority are unskilled or semi-skilled migrant workers who pursue work, any work, simply to survive. Moreover, as global capitalism seeks out the cheapest labour markets, once securely employed people can find their jobs outsourced to different corners of the globe, such as Western banks and manufacturers employing inexpensive workers based in India or China.

Those starting their careers in the third millennium are likely to face very different types of organizations and working patterns from their parents. Once, an employee traded his or her loyalty for security and lifetime employment. Now employers tend to regard themselves as vulnerable to international market forces and unable to protect their workforce from recessions and takeovers. Ownership, and managership, of organizations can change rapidly. People get knocked off the corporate ladder in this process, which can be catastrophic for those whose career and identity has been wrapped up in a company for many years. A 56-year-old chief engineer describes what it feels like:

> I never considered I'd be out of work. I was really shocked when I learned I'd have to go. The more people sympathized with me the worse it got. I was there 14 years, and most of this period I enjoyed the job. I've been trying virtually everything to recover my self-respect and status but people just walk over me. Yes, I'm feeling bitterly disappointed. A works director, also in his mid-50s, is even sharper in his summing up: 'After 28 years in an enjoyable job, what on earth can replace it? A damn big part of your life, just gone.'

Traditionally secure, stable enterprises, such as major banks, steel and car manufacturers, can now undergo structural changes where people's jobs and careers are thrown into disarray. One employee gives a first-hand account:

> I had quite frequently heard people say: 'they have sent the axeman in' and 'have you heard about so and so, he has gone to the block'. Such jokes were told with relief that the axe had not fallen on them. Following the breakup [in the bank], many people I had known and dealt with in my job were made redundant. There was one particular day in my department when no one did any work at all. They all sat there waiting to be called to a meeting and individually told what their future would be. What I failed to realize fully at the time was the extent to which their livelihoods depended on their jobs. This sounds a bit dramatic, but in today's economic climate it is very hard to get another job in banking as all the major banks are making people redundant ... Careers become linked to the fate of an empire [in the bank]. Obviously, being good at your job is a factor in deciding promotion, but it was certainly not the only reason. Unless these people were noticed by another empire head, they could find themselves side-stepped.

This account reveals the unplanned, often idiosyncratic, twists and turns of careers. It is also consistent with studies which reveal the anchoring effects of employment in our lives. Apart from providing us with a livelihood, employment gives us something to get up for in the morning (the unemployed soon find themselves disoriented in time). It offers us people to be with, beyond friends and family. It confers social **status** (try approaching a bank manager, finance house or new employer when jobless). Most of all, perhaps, it gives us regular activity (the unemployed soon run out of ideas about how to pass the time). Employment is woven deep into our social and psychological being and is part of our self-perception. Even 'bad' jobs give us something to complain about, outside the normal worries of living. Yet, as a bubble of security and **meaning**, careers hold some odd contradictions, often evident to those close to the end of their working life. As one wit put it: 'when you're on your deathbed, will you wish you had spent more time at the office?'

The grip of jobs and careers may have loosened, but they show no signs of disappearing. However, the old formula of a job for life, or a career practising one particular kind of expertise, no longer applies. Indeed, skills can date fast so that people who start climbing the corporate ladder can soon find that their ladder rests against the wrong wall – other skills are being rewarded, not theirs. The trick now is to become sufficiently qualified and flexible to be employable, rather than just being employed.

CHANGING SCENES

In contrast to the traditional, organizational career – a series of upward moves in a single organization – we now have something approximating a 'boundaryless' career. This can be seen in people who move fairly easily and frequently across different kinds of work, in and out of different levels or functions in organizations, and who will gladly trade off time at work for more time with their family. They are independent of the constraints of a traditional organizational career. Where once high specialization was counted as a virtue, we now see a swing of the pendulum: the market favours flexibility and the willingness to try new things. Ron and Jean are cases in point:

> Ron has been a maintenance man, a barman, a bar manager. He has built his own house, and with his wife he has owned and run a small farm, a tavern, an ice cream delivery van and an ice cream parlour. Seven years ago he acquired his present job as a cigarette delivery van driver ... through a contact with an acquaintance from a job he had held 15 years previously. His present job is ideal, with regular hours and few demands. Ron uses his savings to take regular overseas holidays, and looks forward to retiring on as much as he needs around the age of 60.
>
> Jean has served in shops, worked a metal press in a factory, been a caretaker, a secretary, a cook, a delicatessen manager, and a food factory supervisor. At different stages she and her husband owned a corner store, a lunch bar, and a candy stall. Not all the jobs and ventures were successful: at one stage they were stuck with an unprofitable lunch bar for several years and eventually sold it at a loss. Now Jean has a steady job as a merchandiser, assisting supermarkets with displays on behalf of suppliers. Through her career run threads of service and an interest in the food business. (Arthur et al., 1999: 112–13)

There have, of course, always been Rons and Jeans, flexible, inventive and unfazed by the next change in their lives. The difference now is that their skills are more likely to be rewarded than those who stick to the one thing they know best. However, we are not all like Ron or Jean in **personality** or resourcefulness. How, then, do we approach boundaryless conditions? Notions of 'lifelong learning' and 'the intelligent career' – having the right kind of **knowledge** at the right time – have been proposed as possible solutions. These involve a number of related approaches, such as:

- cross-functional training and education
- cultivating opportunities to improve one's education and skills
- moving on before getting trapped by one's role or status
- knowing the industry's criteria for success
- cultivating networks and friendships within and across different organizations.

In these circumstances, the nature of loyalty changes. There is a shift in **psychological contract** – the unspoken promise of what the employee can offer and what the employer can grant in return. In the traditional psychological contract, employees gave their loyalty, conformity and commitment in exchange for career prospects, training, care and a pension. With the new contract, such mutual obligations have faded or disappeared altogether. Employees are committed more to themselves, to the moment and the project in hand, not to the long-term goals of the organization. They will also work long hours, take added responsibility, use a broader range of **skills** and tolerate change. In return, they will receive high pay – and a job.

To an extent, this model can be regarded as a way of opening parts of the organization to people who, previously, would have been blocked by existing job holders. They do not have to wait for people to serve their time, or hope for a vacancy of the right rank or status. Having the appropriate skill is the key requirement. The model also values new employees who have moved around the job market and improved their learning, qualifications and skills: mobility is not a sign of disloyalty, as it once was. The downside, though, is that it is particularly hard on those caught in the crosscurrent of changes, forced out of positions that they can no longer fill. Moreover, the social **capital** of the organization is fragmented; there are fewer familiar faces to nourish feelings of collegiality. The organization resembles more a collection of hotel rooms, housing short-term guests.

SURVIVAL AND PORTFOLIOS

The main casualties of the new economy are those who find it very difficult to acquire new skills or learning. They have had a long-term investment in the old economy and its predictability. Older workers, especially, can be less welcome in the open job market, where ageism obscures the benefits of their experience and maturity. Such workers, as a few employers have discovered, do have advantages over their younger counterparts: they tend to be more reliable and more committed. Some, however, are ostrich-like in the face of changes: 'it won't happen to me'; they hide their heads in the sand. Denial is a useful coping mechanism for a while, but ultimately fails to protect from the inevitable such as permanent **unemployment**.

New skills and experience can mitigate the risks of career failure, but they can be approached in different ways. Some commentators advise a 'portfolio career', running a number of different jobs, so if one falters or fails, there is always a backup. It is analogous to spreading the risk in a portfolio of financial investments. For example, a person may spend two days a week as a marketing consultant, one day lecturing at the local college, and the remaining time helping his partner with her decorating business. Portfolio careers lend themselves well to teleworking, where one's place and pace of work are flexible. Teleworking can involve working partly or wholly from home, offering a service that can be transmitted to a client through telecommunications technology (see also Chapter 19, 'Virtuality').

CAREER CLIMBING FRAMES

Many people still navigate careers within 'real' organizations, each with its own career logic. This is rather like facing a climbing frame, the shape of which varies from company to company. Climbing frames are not apparent to the unattuned eye. They are not to be found neatly illustrated in company brochures, nor necessarily will they match the organization chart. They are located in the reward, **power** and political arrangements of the organization. Moving across the organization's invisible lines requires an especially keen sense of the unwritten climbing-frame rules, a special kind of knowledge. For example:

'It's not what you know here, it's who you know.'

Personal expertise is essential, and the more variety the better, but it does not always get one fairly rewarded. It can often help to have a powerful friend or mentor in the organization who can speak well of you to other powerful people who make reward decisions. Winning friends and influencing people has a long tradition in public and corporate **politics**. It can be a remarkably effective way of getting on, while being equally effective at putting the wrong person in the wrong job. Most of us can spot people who are progressing rapidly in organizations, yet who seem to display extraordinary incompetence. The realpolitik of organizational life has, it seems, little to do with natural justice.

'You've got to be seen, really noticed, to get on here.'

People who perform well may not progress well because their job has low visibility; they are not noticed. A key administrative role can require much hard work and dedication, but because it is in the backroom, the results are not seen; they are taken for granted – until things go wrong. Other roles are more visible, such as those associated with company rescues or product launches. If successful, the person is remembered and becomes a recognizable face in the crowd.

'Watch out for the glass ceiling.'

It is still relatively rare for women to reach top management posts. Organizations offer a host of reasons for this, such as: they do not apply for top posts; they do not have suitable qualifications; they are not likely to want the pressures of senior positions; they are more likely to leave because of family commitments and so forth. While these statements may contain a grain of truth in particular circumstances, rarely do they survive close examination because, more often than not, they are **rationalizations** or defensive positions constructed to preserve male prerogatives and empires. Fear, **prejudice** and stereotypes are often at the root of such judgements. They are not unlike those applied to different **ethnic groups**, who can also hit glass ceilings, as well as glass walls, based on covert or overt racial prejudice. Promises of 'equal opportunities for all employees' are often severely tested in such circumstances.

For an ambitious woman, the frustration is that there are no visible barriers preventing her progress. Often, she knows she is being blocked, but is uncertain why: she hits an invisible ceiling. To break through, it usually requires exceptional courage, ability and political skill. If we look at the informal power **networks** of men – their clubs, golf courses, lunches, locker rooms and mentors – it is soon apparent what women are missing. They are not connected to the 'helpful' networks of influence, and they are excluded from entry. There is also a primitive gender prejudice, of the sort: 'would you really like to work with, or be bossed around by, a woman?' The 33-year-old male general manager of an expanding company of 500 employees put it as follows:

> Working with men is cosy. You can eff and blind, and if they don't like it, tough. Blokes are like that. One of the things that would make me uncomfortable about having a woman on the team is that if somebody picked on her, I'd feel it was bad form.

This manager did have one woman in his department who, he acknowledged, was 'indisputably better' than a man of similar status. But the manager could not bring himself to promote the woman over the man: 'I owe him a lot. If he hadn't been work-ing with me, I probably wouldn't have been able to move on. He would take great exception to working for her and I feel I would be letting him down enormously'. There are, of course, women who have made it to the top – in national politics and in corporate life. Ironically, it has been noted that these people often do not go out of their way to help other women into senior posts. It is as if they are jealously guarding their own hard-won positions and pulling up the ladder behind them.

> 'You've got to move fast, early on, if you're going to get on.'

In some Eastern parts of the globe, an employee with wisdom accumulated from many years of experience is much valued. People in their 50s and 60s upwards are regarded as key personnel. In the West, there is a reverse ageism, as we have noted. Professions such as advertising, marketing and publishing are known for their 'if you haven't made it by 30 ...' ethos. It is rare indeed to spot an advertisement for a senior industrial position aimed at the over 40s. Those on the fast track get there at an early age. Not necessarily because they have planned things that way, but more by recog-nizing and capitalizing on opportunities, with a sense of timing of when to move and when to stick. Like good poker players, their game improves fast with practice. Most make a number of rapid job changes in thier early career, maximizing their visibility and network of contacts. Because of this, they are more likely to be headhunted: approached by another company, or by a consultant employed to find talented employees for client organizations.

DUAL CAREERS

It is common to encounter dual-career relationships, where partners are trying to balance career demands with those of their relationship and family. The balance can be precarious.

Highly career-oriented people can find it difficult to manage their jobs and family in parallel; they spill emotionally into one another. In traditional marriages, the woman supported the breadwinning male, absorbing his work anxieties and managing the household and children. There has been a considerable shift away from this structure, with a significant growth in two-career families either from the outset of a partnership, or when a woman returns to work after a career break to raise children. The permutations vary from two full-time careers to combinations of part-time and full-time.

The changing balance of work roles has far-reaching consequences for the organization of one's life space. Domestically, it has left a question mark over who manages the household and children. Traditional beliefs, and stereotypes, about male and female roles overshadow the liberalization of work arrangements. Many women find themselves returning home from work, to assume most of the domestic chores and child managing – in effect, working an extra shift. Even in 'new man' families (he spends time with the kids, does the shopping, cleans the house and cooks some meals), the woman still finds herself shouldering the responsibility for planning these events, while anticipating the needs of her children. If they can afford it, some dual-career families will hire help for household and child management. In some countries, this attracts people (usually women) who, ironically, have to leave their own children unattended: it is the only kind of work they can obtain.

In the face of an increase in dual careers, organizations have had to reflect on their employment policies. People are often reluctant to relocate and desire greater flexibility to accommodate the needs of children through maternity/paternity leave, crèches, child minders and time off for sickness, school holidays and emergencies. Furthermore, the heightened profile of women in the workforce (now over 40 per cent across Europe, and more than 50 per cent in the USA) adds to the pressure for career compatibility with men. There has, however, been no rush by companies to adapt to changing career needs.

KEEPING GOING

Career motivation rarely maintains an even course or force. There are peaks, troughs and plateaux. The mid-career plateau, or crisis, is much discussed and popularized, so much so that people who do not experience it can even feel guilty or embarrassed. The 35–45-year-old, goes the argument, has to come to terms with what she or he has achieved, and the opportunities that have been missed. Or, perhaps, having made it, 'it' does not seem nearly as interesting or rewarding as it once did. What new challenges are there? Do I have the energy or ability to do something new? And if I do not, might I get stuck for the rest of my working life?

The most serious trough is **burnout**, where high initial expectations about what one can achieve are steadily eroded. Eventually, some people give up, withdraw demoralized or do just the bare minimum to get by. Some jobs are particularly prone to burnout, such as nursing, social work and school teaching. These jobs deal with constant human issues, but often in a context of limited resources and support. There are some successes, but many experience tough failures which ultimately take their toll, leaving people exhausted and disillusioned. Burnout, however, is not confined to such groups. Managers and administrators burn out too – from cumulative failures to achieve desired changes, or from the sheer volume of work. Rescuing people from burnout is harder to achieve than burnout prevention, such as by spotting the early signs of disillusionment and cynicism and addressing their causes.

In late career, pensions and savings become important in ways that many young employees find almost incomprehensible. Indeed, a combination of collapse in the traditional careers and an increase in lifespan has added insecurity to those facing retirement. Will my pension provision or savings be sufficient? What will I do without my work activity? One approach to this is to keep working. Self-employment, temporary contracts and portfolios can sometimes be extended beyond the normal retirement age of 60–65. Further paid work is possible for some professional or skilled people whose expertise is in demand, such as offering consultancy services to a network of personal contacts built up over the years. For the energetic and healthy, this can be an attractive option.

The end of a formal career opens what have been termed 'third age' opportunities. Learning and re-training can continue through special courses aimed at the retired. However, such opportunities are not for everyone. Without special preparation and contingency plans, the organizational careerist can find retirement a shock. The switch from organizational routines to domestic and 'leisure' ones can be confusing, especially if the person's status and identity have been shored up by his or her position and earnings in an organization. Outside the context of regular work, holidays, DIY activities and gardening can lack lustre. A lifetime's career, or sequence of jobs, leaves a legacy of habits, routines and social expectations which do not disappear suddenly after the final farewell to one's work colleagues (see Chapter 2, 'Entering and Leaving').

KEY POINTS

o A career, or job, becomes part of our self-image at an early age.

o There are many people for whom a career or job seems unattainable because of a region's chronic unemployment, age, gender, ethnicity or infirmity.

o Career patterns are fast changing: a job for life is now rare; employability is more important; flexibility and new knowledge are essential.

o Loyalty to self has replaced loyalty to the organization.

o Careers can be mixed, with a portfolio of different jobs and activities at any one period of time.

o Politics, personal connections and private networks influence many career paths.

o Women are less likely to be part of the informal (male) power networks and they can hit a 'glass ceiling', blocking their career progress.

o The work – life balance can be harder to achieve with the growth of dual careers, long hours of work and fragmented patterns of employment.

o Career motivation fluctuates considerably over a lifetime and retirement is now more likely to be a period of insecurity.

>>>>>>>>>>>> **THEORETICAL SIGNPOSTS** >>>>>>>>>>>>>

Careers are currently approached from a variety of angles – these include:

> the changing character and nature of careers, as organizations become less hierarchical and bureaucratic
> the ways careers become a part of personal identities and self-image
> career obstacles faced by particular disadvantaged groups in society.

For a helpful overview of the field of careers, including recent changes and developments, see Baruch's (2004) comprehensive review. In organizational studies, the concept of career can be traced to the foundational writings of Max Weber (1946) on ideal type bureaucracy. A central feature of bureaucratic organizations is a career ladder of ascending offices, with ever-increasing power, responsibility and status. However, many authors have argued that the bureaucratic machine is in decline, as organizations look for leaner and more flexible structures. As a result, the well-organized career patterns of the past are becoming much less clear-cut. Richard Sennett (Sennett, 1998) has discussed the great insecurity of identity generated by the collapse of traditional organizational and employment structures. Herriot and Pemberton (1995b) and Arthur and Rousseau (1996) talk of the change in the psychological contract between employee and employer as organizations become 'boundaryless' – personal choices that people make in search of self-fulfilment, a 'contract with one's self' rather than with an organization. Hall (1996) echoes this point, claiming that the 'protean', or fleeting, career has now come of age.

Daniels et al. (2000, 2001) discuss some of the advantages and drawbacks of teleworking, while its emotional consequences are described by Fineman (2003). Lewis and Cooper (1989) outline the challenges of two-career couples, while Hochschild (1989) gives graphic descriptions of different career arrangements among American couples. The extreme stresses and burnout in some occupations are reviewed by Maslach and Leiter (1997). Levinson (1979) gives an account of how life stages, or 'seasons', interact with career and self-identity, and the effects of retirement, forced or voluntary, are researched by Isaksson and Johansson (2000).

The 'glass ceiling' is one of a number of issues faced by women in organizations, and there is a lively debate on whether women have a unique style of managing compared with men – see Powell (1993), Rosener (1990) and Auster (1993). There are different ways that people make meaning out of their work and seek to express their own values through new career identities. It is a controversial area – see Arthur et al. (1999), Ciulla (2000) and Ibarra (2003). The dilemmas of the of work–life balance are part of this, reviewed by Crooker et al. (2002) and Tess (2003).

REVIEW QUESTIONS

1. What are the core differences between a career and a job?

2. Why has the metaphor of the 'glass ceiling' gripped the imagination of academics, journalists and others?

3. Why has it been argued that the pursuit of a career acts as a powerful disciplining mechanism over individuals? Are all people equally susceptible to this discipline?

---

ompanion
website
.sagepub.co.uk/fineman

Reading On

The articles below are available for free to readers of the fourth edition of *Organizing & Organizations* via the book's companion website at www.sagepub.co.uk/fineman

Cox, T.H. and Nkomo, S.M. (1991) 'A race and gender-group analysis of the early career experience of MBAs', *Work and Occupations*, 18(4): 431–46.
This study examined race and gender differences in four career experience variables using a sample of black and white MBAs. Results supported hypothesized race effects for job involvement, access to mentors, career satisfaction, and gender differences in job involvement and hierarchical level. However, black MBAs were not at lower hierarchical levels than white MBAs of comparable experience, and female MBAs did not report significantly less access to mentors or lower career satisfaction than did male MBAs.

Fenton, S. and Dermott, E. (2006) 'Fragmented careers? Winners and losers in young adult labour markets', *Work, Employment and Society*, 20 (2): 205–21.
It has been argued that people's engagement with work is becoming more like a series of encounters than an enduring relationship. This article addresses the question of whether this fragmentation is characteristic of people in the early stages of their working lives by drawing on a study of young adults in Bristol, which suggests that employment fragmentation is concentrated among young adults with less education, and in lower status, lower paid occupations, and does not support a generalized picture of uncertainty and discontinuity.

Fournier, V. (1997) 'Graduates' construction systems and career development', *Human Relations*, 50 (4): 363–91.
The paper draws on the Chicago School's conceptualization of career and on Personal Construct Psychology to examine the relationships between graduates' construction systems and patterns of career development during the first four years of employment, seeking to identify differences in trends of constructive revision between 'successful' and 'less successful' graduates.

Platman, K. (2004) '"Portfolio careers" and the search for flexibility in later life', *Work, Employment and Society*, 18(3): 573–99.
This article examines the experiences of older professionals as freelancers in the UK media industry where portfolio careers, freelancing and consulting have long been common. By examining this relationship from the employer's and older freelancer's perspective, this article aims to discover the true extent of choice, freedom and autonomy experienced by portfolio professionals in late career.

21

PRODUCING AND CONSUMING

Today's society is widely referred to as a 'consumer society'. Consumption plays an important part in most people's lives, not only as a means to stay alive, but also as an avenue to pleasure, meaning and social esteem. The consumer embodies many of the values of contemporary capitalism, notably the freedom of choice, the freedom to pursue happiness through material possessions and the ability to transcend class and other divisions through the power of money. Yet, the consumer has only recently been viewed as an integral part of organizations. In this chapter, we examine how the consumer has now become an insider to most organizations. Organizational success and survival are increasingly seen to rely on customer service and the ability to initiate and take advantage of consumer fads and fashions. Here, we will examine how consumers affect the work experiences of organizational members who deal with them directly or indirectly. We will also look at how we all reconcile our experiences as workers and those as consumers. We must not forget that the same people, who busily try to satisfy an organization's consumers, are themselves the consumers that other organizations seek to attract. Finally, we will examine the consumption that takes place within organizations themselves, in diverse forms, ranging from corporate hospitality and business travel to company accounts and perks at work.

'The customer comes first.'
'We pride ourselves on the close relationships we have with our clients.'
'A world-class service to consumers.'
'Quality, Quality, Quality!'

It is rare to find businesses that do not proclaim such slogans, as central ingredients of their **culture** and philosophy. The consumer reigns supreme in our time. Most organizations seem desperate to please their customers, to pander to their every demand and delight them with new choices, new products and new services. Increasingly, government organizations, from social services departments to universities and prisons, are asked to address their constituencies as customers and consumers. Many students

Figure 21.1   A 'cathedral' of consumption.

today pay considerable amounts for their education and view themselves as consumers, expecting high-quality services and a wide range of choices. Far from being seen as an outsider to the world of organizations, the consumer has, in the last 15 years, come to the core of management and organization studies.

WHO IS THE CONSUMER?

We all consume, as humans have done throughout the ages. We consume food and water, we consume electricity, we consume cigarettes, we consume services like education, we consume the air we breathe. Clearly, we could not stay alive without consuming; nor could other animal or plant species survive without consuming those natural resources that are necessary for maintaining the delicate balances of life. To consume is necessary for life – to be consumed signifies the drawing of life out of something. An old, though still current meaning of the word 'to consume' was 'to use up' or 'to destroy'.

If consumption has remained a necessity for human beings throughout the ages, the **meaning** of consumption has changed dramatically. Today, we live in a society often referred to as a 'consumer society', a society in which we do not consume in order merely to stay alive, but we consume for pleasure, for adventure and for excitement. From a very young age, we experience the power of choosing how to spend our pocket money and learn the important differences between the objects through which we may fulfil our desires. As children, most of us are exposed to alluring advertisements for toys, images and experiences which stimulate our imaginations and the demands we make on our parents' purses. From this young age, we learn to distinguish between different badges, different brands. In this way, we invest the commodities we use, those we buy ourselves and those given to us by others, with **meanings**. The meaning of a Barbie doll or an electric train may change as we grow older, but the idea that objects, commodities, carry meanings is one which we will never grow out of.

Later, we learn to identify the meanings carried by particular brands of watches, holiday destinations or pieces of designer clothing. In our consumer society, commodities become important **status symbols**. By displaying expensive clothes, glamorous cars and other trappings of wealth, individuals can earn the esteem of others. **Success** is often assessed in terms of how much money people have to spend and how they spend it. After all, commodities are there for all to see, unlike a person's family lineage, school or university. Commodities promise to infuse our lives with **meaning**, happiness and pleasure. By being the proud owners of a prestigious brand, we appropriate something of the brand's glamour and make it part of our own image of ourselves. The house we live in, the car we drive, the watch we wear thus become part of us, almost like extensions of our bodies, parts of our history and **identity**.

In Western and increasingly other **cultures**, consumption has become a prolific source of meanings and identities, meeting **needs** which in earlier times might have been fulfilled by religion or politics. Scholars are increasingly arguing that consumption has even supplanted **work** as the source of our images of ourselves. Who we are does not depend so much on the job we do, our **career** or the organization which employs us, but rather on our consumer tastes and the extent to which we can support them. In our work, we may be bossed about, frustrated and dependent; but as consumers, we can be kings, choosing what we like, experimenting with different products, services and lifestyles, controlling our bodies, our images and our destinies. While in our work many of the decisions are already made for us, in our consumption we can exercise choice. What is more, our choices and preferences as consumers matter, as indicated by the desperate efforts of advertisers and marketers to entice us to their products. Consumer choice, then, is one of the chief values of our culture; its emblem is the supermarket, or better still, the shopping mall in which we explore new fashions, compare the merits of different styles and products and make the two gestures which epitomize our sovereignty as consumers: we pay for the things we choose and offer no explanations for the things or suppliers we reject.

The social and economic **institution** which forms the basis of the consumers' sovereignty is the **market**: the market is also what most organizations keep their eyes firmly on. In the market, they compete against each other to attract the attention and the favour of the consumer. Earlier generations of entrepreneurs competed against each other for the favour of the consumer, mainly on price. Henry **Ford**'s great achievement was his ability to turn cars into a mass-produced, mass-consumed commodity, cheap enough to be within the budget of many American families. Many of today's consumers would not put up with Ford's arrogant 'they can have it any colour they like, so long as it's black' (his model T Ford was only available in black). Instead, consumers today want choice or at least the feeling of choice – they want difference. The right to choose among alternative products was one of the four fundamental consumer rights proposed by John F. Kennedy in his classic statement to the American Congress in March 1962 (the others were the rights to information, safety and representation by government regulators). What is more, today's flexible manufacturing technologies have enabled many industries, from woollen sweaters to cars, to move away from mass producing identical products to turning out short runs of highly differentiated goods. Niche marketing, where specific segments of consumers are targeted with specialist products, has replaced much of the mass marketing of old.

This necessitates a great degree of flexibility in working practices. Companies must be able to employ, lay off and re-deploy staff at very short notice in very different positions. It also necessitates constant vigilance to trends in the market, new consumer fashions and styles, new niches and new ideas. From an organization's point of view, then, the consumer does not exactly look like a king, more like an unpredictable child, whose fickle desires must not only be met but anticipated, shaped and guided towards what the organization can offer. Even more than quality, service and value for money, many companies seek to mollycoddle their customers, feeding their fantasies, their vanity and their search for individuality and **meaning**.

Consumers, for their part, have become quite suspicious of the claims made by manufacturers and advertisers. They often resist the suppliers' attempts to lure them into new products or they use products in unconventional, unusual ways, creating a distance between the meaning which products have for them and those advocated by the producers and the advertisers. Consumers' suspicions can escalate into total mistrust and rejection, as has been the case with numerous products tarnished by health scares or when products become targets of boycotts.

IN THE LINE OF FIRE

Meeting the customer face to face is what Jan Carlzon, former president of Scandinavian Airlines System, calls a 'moment of truth'. It is a company's opportunity to impress customers, to convince them that they matter and that their needs and loyalty are vitally important.

> Last year, each of our 10 million customers came in contact with approximately five SAS employees, and this contact lasted an average of 15 seconds each time. Thus, SAS is 'created' 50 million times a year, 15 seconds at a time. These 50 million 'moments of truth' are the moments that ultimately determine whether SAS will succeed or fail as a company. They are the moments when we must prove to our customers that SAS is their best alternative. (Carlzon, 1987: 3)

SAS, like many other companies, spends much time and money on selecting and training the staff responsible for handling these moments of truth. Looks, manners and, above all, 'attitude' are essential – they are not mere attributes of employees but attributes of the organization, an integral part of the service the customer obtains. An alluring and responsive employee, radiating competence and responsiveness, can create a far more satisfied customer than a harassed, bad-tempered one, even if the latter is offering an identical product or service for a fraction of the price.

To the individual employee who has found shelter in the back office, being exposed to the critical eye of the customer for the first time is an important trial. Like actors who have only performed in rehearsals, they are suddenly exposed to a whole new experience, an experience of operating without a safety net. In the following description, Sandra, a student trainee with a large accounting firm describes her feelings, as she finds herself having to explain some rather intricate tax procedures to a client.

REAL-LIFE EXAMPLE

My manager received a letter from one of the clients, a supermodel, requesting that in future her husband should do her tax return – could we explain to him the process. John (my manager) asked me to write a letter instructing him, but I suggested that it would be much quicker to run through it with him in person. John agreed. Up until this point I had not been allowed to come into contact with clients face to face, so I was looking forward to the opportunity to attend a meeting, although I believed that I would be playing rather a passive role. John began his usual jokes, this time the theme being that I was going to be thrown in the den of the lion alone. For a moment I panicked, but my other colleagues reassured me that he was only teasing me.

The day was approaching and still John continued his joking. Taking precautionary measures, I briefed myself on the whole issue, producing handouts and examples, just in case. The meeting time finally arrived, and I cannot express my relief as John put on his suit jacket, following the phone call from reception informing us of the client's arrival. I went up to the meeting room and John arrived with the client. He introduced me as his colleague who specialized in VAT, and promptly left, closing the door on exit.

It took me a few seconds to regain my composure, and I then proceeded to carry out the hour-long meeting. John arrived just as I was winding up the final details, and said that he had a few other matters to run through with the client. I shook hands with the client, and left.

I feel that I learnt more about myself and my position in the firm in that incident than perhaps I learnt throughout my placement. I felt valued especially with so many colleagues congratulating me, and John's praise when he returned from the client. John also told me that he was pleased that I had never really believed that I would be doing it on my own, or I would have panicked. It was surprising that John was so perceptive, as I thought that I was the only person in the firm to have the time to put together a set of assumptions and perceptions about the people I worked with.

Sandra's experience is not unique. Meeting the customer is a moment of truth in many organizations. After two decades of 'customer orientation' programmes and initiatives, employees in many organizations have internalized the significance of those moments. In some organizations, this has the effect of creating two categories of employees, a front line in contact with customers and a back office servicing the front line with information, materials and resources. It is not uncommon for the former to be lionized, leaving the latter with a sense of being less appreciated.

In a privatized utility, which one of us studied in some detail, 20 clerks were dealing over the telephone with customer queries, requests and complaints. The office was buzzing with activity. On a wall, an electronic panel informed everyone of how long the customers were waiting before their calls were answered. The clerks were busily trying to arrange for visits by service engineers, meter readings and appliance deliveries. They never saw the consumer and the consumer never met them, but talk about the consumer, with his/her complaints, irritation, impatience and demands, was everywhere in the office. Furtive conversations could be heard about Mrs Merton's order being delayed yet again and Mr Parsons' car being rammed by one of the company's vans. Most of the clerks appeared to have the interest of the consumer at heart, even when their organization's red tape and interest in cost-cutting made it hard for them to respond quickly and efficiently. Margaret Benton, a Senior Clerk, said:

> When you are trying to help a customer, you sometimes come up against a brick wall. The customer needs an appliance fixed, the house is freezing, you can see the problem and you do all you can to help. Then, you get the attitude from above: 'no, it can't be done, no I haven't got an engineer to send'. And I'm thinking: if only I was near the [engineering] depot, I would get an engineer and say you go and do this job right now. It makes me go mad.
>
> When all the odds are against me, you know, I'm trying to help this consumer and everybody is saying: 'no, you can't have the engineer', In the end, I won't let go – I go on and on up the line, higher and higher, and eventually somebody will listen and then the job gets done. And then the customer rings up, and she says: 'I'm happy, thank you' and then I put the phone down and I think: 'hurrah, we've done it'. But then why is it necessary to go through all this trouble? For me, it is a challenge when this happens and I get more excited; but, in the end, it shouldn't be like that.

Another clerk reported her anger about the way that customers are divided into groups – the rich ones who pay for the services and the poor ones, those living in public housing, whose problems seem not to matter.

> What makes me cross quite often is how the customers are treated, which is disgusting. The classic one is, if you are a council tenant, you are beneath the lot as far as I can see. When a job comes up, the computer tells you whether it is a council property, and whether or not there is a service contract – three-star contract is the best one. With a Three-star contract, we are supposed to send someone at once. Council tenants, on the other hand, are left to wait. 'We will endeavour to call today' – this is what we are meant to say, which doesn't give them a yes or no. In reality, their job number goes to the bottom of the pile and they may be kept waiting for days.

The division of customers into different classes mirrors the divisions of the employees themselves. The office staff who speak to the customers are subordinate to the true elite, the engineers who serve the customer directly, but superior to the other office workers, referred to as 'admin'.

> My job is very much where you are at everybody's beck and call; it is the nature of the job, Admin basically covers so many things – menial-type tasks, photocopying, stationery, equipment. When frontline staff want something, you are the one to find it for them. In that respect, my job is responsible, because people need that equipment to perform their jobs properly. But I would prefer to deal with the customers and what is actually going on out there rather than what is going on in the office.

Figure 21.2   Physical labour? Or emotional?

In this way, many organizations create 'internal' consumers, whose requirements derive from the fact that they service the external consumers. If these internal consumers require resources, information or anything else, their claims take precedence over everything else. Being in the front line of contact with customers gives employees a distinct sense of purpose and also considerable power within the organization.

'Serving the customer' can become an excuse for virtually any type of behaviour. A major computer company held a weekly early-morning meeting of its senior executives, a meeting known informally as the Holy Council. At one such meeting, one of the executives failed to arrive, something that had never happened before. He eventually got there breathless in the middle of the meeting; he might have expected a rough reception, but he told his colleagues: 'I was with a customer'. Order was at once restored. In this way, customers are increasingly viewed as integral parts of an organization rather than as outsiders. In the interest of customer service, many organizations find that they have to relax management **controls**, allowing greater discretion among their employees.

Frontline work makes different demands on individuals (both managers and workers) and groups from manufacturing or back office jobs, where they are safely insulated from the critical gaze of the customer. Instead, frontline jobs emphasize the importance of the employees' **emotional labour** (see also Chapter 16, 'Feelings'), social and verbal skills, appearance and demeanour under pressure. One would hardly use the metaphor of a theatrical performance to describe the behaviour of a metal-basher or a pen-pusher, yet this metaphor becomes quite apt in capturing some of the qualities of frontline work, with its thrills, unpredictability and audience scrutiny.

A CAST OF THOUSANDS

As industrialized countries move from manufacturing to service, an ever-increasing proportion of employees take their place in the front line. As we saw in Chapter 16, the emotional tone that these employees adopt becomes an integral part of the service which they provide. Nurses must show care and concern, sports coaches enthusiasm and drive, funeral directors dignified respect and professional wrestlers anger and hate. Managing one's emotions is a key feature of many frontline jobs. Equally important is managing the **emotions** of others. A waiter must diagnose whether a customer's anger is serious and rightful and use his own **emotional** techniques for defusing the situation. A sales assistant must sense the needs of the potential customer in order to effect a sale.

One of the central features of our consumer society is that the act of working itself is often camouflaged. The consumer does not wish to be reminded, let alone to see, the sweaty faces of the workers who produce the gleaming surfaces of the objects he/she buys; nor does he/she want to see the bored expressions of the workers who service him/her, impatient for the moment when they can pack up, go home and become consumers in their own right. A screen is brought down between work and consumption. And the workers who service the consumer at the moment of consumption must cease to appear as workers. They must appear as props, livening up the consumer's

Figure 21.3   The magic kingdom.

experience, as performers of admirable routines, smiles and emotions, as artists in their own right.

Disney, a pioneer in these matters, is a company that has managed to persuade consumers of the incredible fun they will have, notwithstanding having to wait in interminable queues or to resist their children's constant pleas for yet more purchases of memorabilia. The theatre of Disney has gone the whole way by referring to its employees as 'cast' members. In this way, road sweepers, burger tossers, machine operators and lavatory cleaners are no longer workers, but actors, artists even. While sweeping roads, tossing burgers, operating machines and cleaning lavatories, they must sustain the consumer's fantasy of being in a fabled world where dreams come true. Other companies, in the retailing, catering, travel, tourism and leisure sectors have also adopted human resource management techniques aimed at enhancing the customer orientation of their employees – it is no longer enough to provide an efficient and competent service, but one must also provide a personalized, caring and flattering one.

An interesting implication of this organizational trend concerns the employee's sense of **identity**. This has two distinct facets, as each employee is also a consumer. Many employees are also consumers of the industries that employ them. As more and more young people spend some of their time working in fast-food restaurants, it is forecast that in 20 years, the majority of customers of these restaurants will be former employees of fast-food companies. An increasing number of individuals have experiences from both sides of the counter, of serving and being served. How does this shape their expectations and their experiences of being served? Consider the importance of the company uniform that employees are requested to wear. Uniforms are now worn by an increasing number of workers, from airline staff to sales assistants and from chartered accountants to fast-food employees. They are meant to connote professionalism, uniformity and a corporate ethos: 'we are all here to serve you', they seem to proclaim to the customers. And yet, the uniformity of the uniform denies the very individuality which staff, in their capacity as consumers, have come to expect.

The ambiguities, even confusion, generated by uniforms are illustrated by a sales assistant interviewed by Paul du Gay. Much as she disliked wearing the uniform at the workplace, out of work, she felt even more resistant:

> They said we can wear this uniform on our way home and I said, 'I wouldn't be seen dead in this, man.' I tell you, one time I was late out so I thought to get home in time I'd better leave my uniform on instead of wearing my own clothes. And I get to the bus-stop and everyone starts laughing. One of my friends said 'What happened, man? You had a fight with your trousers?' And the man on the bus, he says, 'That shirt, man, it looks like someone been sick on you.' And I thought, 'Oh thanks, man.' So since then I haven't ever worn that uniform home or from home to work. (du Gay, 1996a: 172)

The **identity** of young people like this is put under constant strain: as employees, they are part of their employers' visual identity, marked by the company uniform, even though as consumers, they are constantly looking for individuality and uniqueness.

Recognizing this tension, some companies now allow their employees a degree of freedom in the way they dress or speak. Some personalize their uniforms, like when a waiter at a pizza restaurant serves customers wearing a bowler hat. Some companies, notably those flirting with a youthful, rebellious and daring image, may tolerate or even encourage such behaviours, in the belief that they increase their popularity with young customers. Most companies, however, have come to the conclusion that such individualism alienates the majority of their customers and undermines their image of professionalism and customer-centredness and increasingly insist on standard uniform.

The example of the uniform is typical of the general dilemma facing many members of organizations, in their efforts to reconcile their experiences as employees with those as consumers. Some develop virtually split selves, where their opinions, **emotions** and even personalities as employees are quite different from those as consumers. Others try to integrate the two experiences by treating one of the two spheres, mainly the work sphere, as a game: their behaviour at work is not a reflection of who they are but of how they perform in the game. Yet others may manage to identify with the consumers to such an extent that it justifies every personal sacrifice and hardship; they work uncomplainingly, delivering diligent service, believing in the deeper sense that they are doing to others, their customers, what they expect to receive themselves as consumers. Some of us seek to harmonize our experiences as producers with those as consumers, using them to forge our precarious and ever-changing **identities**.

CORPORATE CONSUMERS

We saw earlier that employees in the front line of contact with the consumers are themselves internal consumers of the services and products provided by their back office colleagues. Employees, however, engage in another very important type of consumption. This is a form of consumption which places them in a very different type of dilemma from that described earlier: the consumption which they carry out *as members of the organizations which employ them*, which includes products and services ranging from subsidized meals to company cars and corporate hospitality.

As members of their organizations, many employees get a taste of consumption considerably higher than outside the workplace. Consider, for example, the case of Harry. Harry is a 55-year-old man, the son of a Yorkshire miner, with a self-made **career** as a manager of a British food wholesaler. Harry lives in a comfortable house and drives a comfortable though unostentatious car, supplied by his firm. His clothes are modest. He chooses his holidays carefully for the best bargain in a comfortable but hardly flashy resort. Yet, twice every year, Harry lives the life of a millionaire. He travels Club Class, making ample use of the complimentary champagne on offer. Attractive stewardesses hover over him, ready to pamper his every desire. He is driven by limousine to expensive resorts guarded by special security forces. His commodious room is equipped with a Jacuzzi and an almost limitless supply of drinks. By night, Harry visits the local hotspots, by day he splits his time between the golf course and the boardroom. What accounts for Harry's metamorphosis from a

Figure 21.4   Uniforms.

member of the parsimonious middle class into a jetsetter? Simple. As a result of an accident to his superior, a few years back, Harry had to replace him at short notice on a trip to the Far East to negotiate with tea suppliers. He enjoyed his time out there and made sure that he became the man for the job. Twice a year, Harry travels to the Far East, where he finds himself to be a very popular man, with local businessmen competing for his custom and willing to offer lavish entertainment in exchange for the hope of a deal.

Harry's experience as a corporate consumer may be extreme, but it is not exceptional. Many company employees these days find themselves consuming in their capacity as members of their firm, at a far higher level than they do in their private lives. Expensive meals, opulent hotels and other hospitality services, extravagant entertainment, corporate gifts and perks, company accounts, foreign trips, conference attendances, costly taxi drives, to say nothing of the ubiquitous company cars – these are all consumption opportunities which are enjoyed as long as they serve their company. One need not be a senior executive to enjoy these privileges. Accountancy trainees are regularly flown to foreign resorts for training residentials, successful employees are rewarded with luxuries beyond their individual budgets, and even the entire workforce may be occasionally entertained in glamorous hotels. But even beyond this – many people work in buildings which are more opulently decorated, more spacious and better air-conditioned than their homes. They make use of expensive facilities and resources from stationery to computers and telecommunications. In this way, many organizations lavish resources on their employees, allowing them glimpses or more extended experiences of expensive lifestyles, while at the same time they draw them into a deal. In exchange for these, the organization expects, and sometimes gets, loyalty, hard work and, more importantly, an internalization of the company's **identity** as part of their own identity.

Corporate consumption emerges as a mechanism through which some organizations seek to generate commitment on the part of their members. As a benevolent parent who lavishes presents and affections on his/her children, the company brings itself to the centre of the emotional life of its employees. In exchange, it asks that the employee should serve it properly, presenting the right front to outsiders, keeping any unpleasantness inside the family and serving the organization's customers in any way that is required. Many employees, in such situations, tend to idealize their companies, whose power, glamour and wealth rubs off onto their own sense of identity and self. As individuals, they may be vulnerable, needy and ordinary; as members of an organization, on the other hand, they can feel important and powerful. Others may resent their company's opulence and splendour, especially when it is juxtaposed to cutbacks, redundancies and wage cuts. In such cases, they may grab the company's largesse without feeling any reciprocal obligation, becoming more cynical and disenchanted.

IN CONCLUSION

The study of organizations can no longer disregard the world of consumption and the consumer. Consumption is not something that happens at the boundary of the organization when it sells its output to some impersonal markets beyond its control; it is something that happens within every organization. In order to do their jobs properly, individuals must consume resources; workers are consumers in their own right;

finally, organizations themselves offer special opportunities for consumption to their employees, as special incentives or rewards aimed at strengthening commitment and loyalty. In our consumer society, the demands of consumers have a direct impact on how organizations are run.

We have examined the responsibility resting on the employees who come directly into contact with the customers and have argued that they, in turn, become customers for the services provided by backroom staff. We then examined the dilemmas facing individuals who, as employees, are driven to increasing uniformity, while, as customers, they are accustomed to searching for difference and individuality. Finally, we examined the experiences of employees as consumers of their own organization's wealth. These different experiences influence the way that individuals fashion their personal identities and shape the nature of their commitment to their company and its customers.

KEY POINTS

○ Consumption takes place both at the margins of organizations and at their centres.

○ Consumption is an important source of meanings and identities in contemporary society.

○ Most individuals construct identities which try to accommodate their experiences at work with those as consumers.

○ Contact with consumers creates special pressures for 'frontline' employees.

○ Direct contact with consumers is also a basis for internal divisions within organizations, typified in the 'front office' and 'back office' divisions.

○ Corporate consumption is a mechanism through which some organizations seek to generate commitment on the part of their members.

>>>>>>>>>>> THEORETICAL SIGNPOSTS >>>>>>>>>>>>

Consumer studies have emerged as a major area of academic theorizing in the past 20 years. Many disciplines, including psychology, cultural studies, economics, social anthropology and political theory, have studied contemporary consumption, its meanings and implications. Several lively debates are currently revolving around the role of consumption in today's organizations. These include:

> discussions of contemporary society and the question of whether it has moved beyond modernity to 'post-modernity'

> the impact of a strong preoccupation with the customer for organizations and the working experiences of their members
> the emotional and aesthetic aspects of the work of frontline employees in service industries.

Discussions of Contemporary Society and the Question of Whether it has Moved Beyond Modernity to 'Post-modernity'

Consumption lies at the heart of much current theorizing on contemporary society and culture; many postmodern writers, including Baudrillard (1970/1988), Bauman (1988, 1992) and Fiske (1989) view consumption as the sphere through which individuals construct meanings and identities, experimenting with different images and experiences. Towards the end of the twentieth century, it is argued, mass consumption underwent a significant transformation. New technologies, along with enhanced standards of living, permitted an increasing proliferation of alternative products and services, which allowed or even required consumers to exercise ever-increasing choice on how they spent their money. In such a culture of consumerism, individuals and groups seek to enhance their lives with meaning, experiment with and develop their identities, and discover a sense of belonging and success not through work, but through their consumption tastes or, more generally, their lifestyles. In this connection, consumers increasingly turn not to material objects but to images, spectacles and experiences. Even when they buy material objects, like cars, watches and clothes, it is the brand image of these objects that makes them desirable rather than their functional utility. Fantasy becomes the driving force behind the desires for new and different experiences, services and objects. In this way, consumption becomes the great and problematic source of meaning in many accounts of post-modernity (Baudrillard, 1970/1988; Bauman, 1992; du Gay, 1996a; Featherstone, 1991; Gabriel and Lang,1995). Gabriel and Lang (1995) offer a complex picture of the contemporary consumer and examine the views of the consumer (such as victim, rebel, identity-seeker, and so forth) adopted by a wide range of theoretical approaches. They argue that contemporary consumption has become fragmented, driven by numerous conflicting forces at the same time – the consumer becomes a 'construct' shaped by different discourses.

The Impact of a Strong Preoccupation with the Customer for Organizations and the Working Experiences of their Members

The trends noted above have had a pronounced effect on the way organizations are conceptualized and managed. The consumer is no longer seen as an 'outsider' to the world of organizations, but very much an insider, whose desires, caprices and fantasies provide an organization's lifeline towards profitability and survival. Organizations dedicate ingenuity, innovation and resources not merely to devising quicker and cheaper ways of producing standardized outputs, but to imagining original, creative and expensive ways of enticing consumers to diverse outputs (Campbell, 1989; Korczynski et al., 2000; Ritzer, 1999). Furthermore, they take the utmost care and attention in ensuring that employees who come in to direct contact with consumers project the right organizational image to ensure customer satisfaction and loyalty. Customer service becomes as important as providing reliable products at competitive prices (Sturdy et al., 2001). As a result, the demands on employees have changed. The display of an attractive personality and the right emotional attitude becomes a vital 'front' of the organization, as employees are increasingly required to perform emotional labour in addition to physical and intellectual labour (Leidner, 1993). Some organizational theorists have noted the increasing prevalence of internal organizational markets and quasi-markets, which encourage organizational participants to relate to members in other departments and units, not as colleagues but as internal consumers and providers (Ferlie et al., 1996).

The Emotional and Aesthetic Aspects of the Work of Frontline Employees in Service Industries

'Customer service' is the label that has come to stand for the incorporation of the consumer into the world of organizations. Following early contributions in this area (du Gay, 1996a; du Gay and Salaman, 1992; Knights and Morgan, 1993; Leidner, 1993), this has now gathered pace, as increasing numbers of authors in the area of organizations seek to assess how the discourse of customers and consumers is reshaping the world of organizations. One of the reasons why the consumer has been brought into the world of organizations is the increasing proportion of workers who are working directly with customers in service and other occupations. In sectors like education, health, catering, tourism, retail, finance, transport, professional services, computing and so forth, large armies of employees are involved in 'frontline work' – dealing with customers, servicing them, advising them, keeping them happy. Frontline work makes different demands on individuals (both managers and workers) and groups from manufacturing or back office jobs, where they are safely insulated from the critical gaze of the customer. Instead, frontline jobs emphasize the importance of the employees' emotional labour, social and verbal skills, appearance and demeanour under pressure (Sturdy et al., 2001). One would hardly use the metaphor of a theatrical performance to describe the behaviour of a metal-basher or a pen-pusher – yet, this metaphor becomes quite apt in capturing some of the qualities of frontline work, with its thrills, unpredictability and audience scrutiny.

The emotional and moral attachments binding employees to their organizations and their customers were explored in early works by Schein (1980, 1988) and Schwartz (1987) and, more recently, by Korczynski (2003) and others who reveal the complexities and ambiguities of service work. Much work has been dedicated to call centre employees (Korczynski, 2004; Pratt and Doucet, 2000; Sturdy and Fleming, 2003; Taylor and Bain, 2005); these workers often experience strong ambivalent feelings towards their customers and organizations – intense pleasure and dedication alternating with frustration, anger and rage. Caught between the customer and management, frontline

workers turn to each other for support, sustenance and escape – they form communities of coping (by analogy to communities of practice), where emotional labour is not
oriented only towards the customer but also towards each other. Communities of coping create informal, dense cultures among the service workforce, which cannot be
easily controlled or tamed by managers (Korczynski, 2003).

The emotional aspects of labour, when the worker comes face to face with the consumer, have been explored by Hochschild (1983) and Fineman (1993, 2000a; 2000e).
More recently, several authors have argued that aesthetic labour is a characteristic of
many service occupations where 'looking good' and 'sounding right' is every bit as
important in being hired as physical or intellectual skills (Hancock and Tyler, 2000; Tyler
and Taylor, 1998; Warhurst et al., 2000; Witz et al., 2003). Guerrier and Adib (2000)
have carried out research indicating that frontline staff in highly aestheticized
organizations, like hotels and holiday resorts, frequently find themselves bearing
the brunt of any abusive and sexual behaviour from customers.

REVIEW QUESTIONS

1. It has been argued that call centre employees are typical of today's economies
   just as Henry Ford's manufacturing workers were typical of mass-production societies. Is this comparison plausible? What are the main similarities and differences
   between manufacturing cars and answering customer calls?

2. Does it make sense to talk of hospital patients, university students and, even,
   prison inmates as customers? Do the principles of customer service apply in
   these instances?

3. What are the advantages and disadvantages of organizations relying on 'internal markets' to regulate the relations between different units and departments?
   How realistic is it for organizations to introduce such internal markets?

Reading On

The articles below are available for free to readers of the fourth edition of *Organizing &
Organizations* via the book's companion website at www.sagepub.co.uk/fineman

Korczynski, M.(2003) 'Communities of coping: collective emotional labour in service work',
    Organization, 10 (1): 55–79.
This article argues that communities of coping among frontline service workers are an important part of what Hochschild has called 'collective emotional labour' in service work. The
structure of workers' social situations means that they are likely to turn to each other to cope
with the pain caused by irate and abusive customers, forming informal communities of
coping. Drawing on extensive research in four call centres in Australia and the USA, the article
highlights this process in action.

Stein, M. (2007) 'Toxicity and the unconscious experience of the body at the employee–customer interface', *Organization Studies*, 28 (8): 1223–41.
Drawing on words used by frontline service workers, and using concepts from psychoanalysis and its application to organizational dynamics, this article proposes that frontline workers may have the unconscious fantasy that they have been polluted by toxic substances. The author argues that the theme of toxicity helps us connect the employee–customer interface with a deep reservoir of primordial human experience that links the body with emotions.

Sturdy, A. (1998) 'Customer care in a consumer society: smiling and sometimes meaning it?', *Organization*, 5 (1): 27–53.
This article proposes a focus for research by drawing on two distinct streams of literature – on service/emotion work and organizations in consumer society, in particular examining experiences of 'customer care' and related 'corporate culture' initiatives.

Taylor, P. and Bain, P. (2005) '"India calling to the far away towns": the call centre labour process and globalization', *Work Employment and Society*, 19 (2): 261–82.
This article challenges the widely-held assumption that offshoring voice services is a seamless undertaking, principally through an investigation of the Indian call centre labour process. This enquiry is informed by an analysis of the political-economic factors driving offshoring and shaping the forms of work organization to have emerged in India. The authors argue that the Indian industry reproduces in exaggerated and culturally-distinctive forms, a labour process that has proved problematical for employers and employees alike in the UK and elsewhere.

22
WORKING AND LIVING

'Home' and 'work' have long been seen as separate spheres; yet, for many people, including farmers, writers, tele-workers and many self-employed people, their home is also their workplace. Work is often associated with 'paid work'; unpaid work can be just as physically, intellectually and emotionally demanding, but it enjoys inferior status, something that has disadvantaged women for a long time. In this chapter, we examine how our attitudes and values towards work are shaped within the family, the school and the wider culture and how people's orientations to work have varied across cultures and social groups. We investigate why many of today's organizations expect a 24/7 commitment from staff, especially senior staff, who are expected to socialize as well as work for the company and assess the effects of those demands for family life. We also address how today's itinerant careers may make it difficult for people to develop a coherent story of either their working or their family life. Finally, we examine how many men's undivided commitment and loyalty to their organizations frequently rest on the sacrifice of women's career prospects and their greater commitment to the home.

I come here and work my shift; I don't trouble them, they don't trouble me. People do sometimes get into trouble; I haven't got into trouble yet. I come here to do my job. I don't need much help. My private life is my private life.

These are the words of Mrs Vickers, a hospital cleaner. Some people have no difficulty understanding what 'my private life is my private life' means. It separates the world of work and organizations, the public sphere, from the world of the family and the home. The division between work and home is second nature to many people, although it makes less sense to people like farmers, self-employed shopkeepers, sailors or soldiers, who either work 'from home' or whose **organization** *is* their home. It makes even less sense to many of the most ambitious people in society, for whom the blurring of the distinction is part of what makes them high performers. We asked Derek, who we saw as being in the above category, how many hours a week he worked.

God knows; what sort of figure would you like? Am I working when I go to a smart dinner, and I intersperse the talk about football with the talk that might get us a new contract? Am I working when I have old college friends around for a drink? They are real friends, and I really enjoy the evening, but quite a few of them are also in positions where they might be useful to me. I am not just trying to milk them, but they are people I would like to do business with. Am I working when I go out to lunch with the lovely Sarah, who is great company and who also may give me a discount? Am I working on Sunday when I cook the dinner with the family around me, answering a few emails in the quiet moments? Am I working when I have a mostly social phone call in the evening to catch up with Paul, who left us a few months ago, and may end up taking me with him? What about the company quiz night – it certainly didn't feel like work! But I was laying down my stomach and my liver for the company again, I suppose.

For Derek, there is a lot of pleasurable social activity which could be defined either side of the work–leisure boundary, and he does not seem to care which side is which. Others have a much more alienated approach. 'Work is a four-letter word' says a poster. 'Thank God it's Friday' says another. The 'Monday morning feeling' is not usually one of excitement and joy at the prospect of the start of a new week. In the world of work, our time is sometimes seen as someone else's time, the tools and machines we use someone else's, the premises we occupy someone else's, our **actions** determined by someone else's **decisions** and directions.

Some people see themselves as having a distinct private world, the world of the family and the home, in which they do not feel accountable to an employer, in which their time is their own, their business is their own. Mrs Vickers was expressing this and also saying where her personal boundaries were: 'you may ask me questions about my work. My boss gave you permission to do that. You may not ask me questions about my life outside this hospital. What I do there is my own business and does not concern you.'

IDENTITY MATTERS

It does not take much probing to make the distinction between work and private life disintegrate. **Work** does not take place exclusively in the public sphere, nor does play only take place in the private. Looking after a young child is work, whether you are doing it in your own home and the child is your own, or at a nursery and the child is someone else's. Some people play golf or drive fast cars for a living, while others mop floors, change nappies and cook lunches for nothing more than gratitude. What separates the work we do in the public sphere from that of the private is neither its quantity nor its quality. It is whether we get paid for it or not.

There is no denying that the two types of **work** – paid and unpaid – enjoy vastly different **status** in Western **cultures**. Looking after your infirm grandmother who lives with you requires effort, skill and application, but ironically is not seen as 'proper work', the way that looking after other people's grandmothers in an old people's home is. Washing up at home hardly makes you anybody; washing up in a restaurant makes you an 'employed person'. Work is part of how people see each other – part of their identity

Some people have found it helpful to distinguish between work, the activity involving physical and mental effort, and employment, the means whereby the majority earn a wage or salary. The public world can then be seen as the time which we spend in 'gainful employment', in contrast to private life, essentially the rest of our time. As we all know, people eat, sleep, go to the movies, participate in amateur dramatic societies, have children, support football teams, look after sick relatives, suffer from neurotic attacks and so on. Have these things no bearing on our behaviour in organizations?

One of the central assumptions of this book has been that the private and the public are inextricably linked, even if people sometimes try to keep them in separate compartments, as Mrs Vickers was trying to do. We take our work back home and, conversely, we take our home out to work. **Attitudes** and **values** formed within the family, the school or the wider **culture** remain part of us when we cross the boundary of an organization, as do our **sexuality**, sense of humour and **emotions**. Equally, our experiences inside organizations inevitably colour our personal and family lives. Our lives outside organizations and our lives within them cannot be studied apart from each other, even though some of us try to keep different parts of our lives in rigid compartments, while others prefer to integrate them. Very few can develop totally split personae, one for work and one for home.

NIGEL'S STORY: WHEN HOME DISRUPTS WORK

REAL-LIFE EXAMPLE

Nigel's Story

Nigel prides himself on being a 'good' father. Ever since Emily and Alex were born, he has taken an active interest, spending as much time with them as his busy job as a senior advertising executive will allow him. Nigel loves the long summer evenings, when he can spend time playing with the children in the garden. The children are both at school now, and Anne, Nigel's wife, has decided to resume her own career as a hospital administrator.

Monday 20 May was an important day for Nigel. It was the day of two crucial events: A presentation to a major customer and a meeting with the Revenue and Customs over a disputed VAT return. It was also a significant day for another reason. This had been the first weekend that Nigel had spent alone with the children; Anne was on a three-day residential course, due to end today.

The weekend had been a big success – safari park on Saturday, splashing around the garden on Sunday – the kids had loved it and Nigel was happy. Nigel had some apprehensions about Monday morning. Taking both children to school, then dashing off to the office for the 10.15 presentation was going to be tight, but it could be done and it would be done.

It's Monday morning. Nigel wakes up and cheerfully calls the children. No answer. He goes to their room, where they seem to be sleeping soundly. 'Alex, Emily, quick, time to get up', he shouts, but his voice has no effect. It takes some more calls (his voice has now developed an edge) before Nigel realizes that the children's bright red cheeks, bleary eyes and sullen expressions tell their own story. Both children are running fevers.

Now Nigel is nothing if not a man who loves a challenge. 'Problems don't exist, only opportunities' is a favourite motto of his. For once, however, Nigel has a problem. He quickly appraises the options. The children must clearly be seen by a doctor, and someone has to be found to take them and look after them during the day. But who? Anne perhaps; she could come back early from her residential; oh God, she will be so disappointed. What is more, Anne couldn't be back soon enough for him to make it to work on time.

The children are now awake; they need care, they need reassurance, they need affection. And Nigel needs someone to give them all this and take them to the doctor. The minutes are ticking away and Nigel is no nearer to fulfilling his opportunity. Nigel is getting desperate and, what's more, he is getting furious with himself for getting desperate. He, the champion of dozens of bruising campaigns, the winner of apparently lost causes, the master problem solver, is coming apart with the simple task of having two sick children looked after for say eight or ten hours at most.

He feels angry. He knows it; he should never have let Anne go to her wretched residential. Look at the mess she has left him with. Besides, what the hell did she need the residential for? Isn't it just an excuse for drinking, anyway? The children are now crying but Nigel can only think of his own chagrin, his own problem. Strange thoughts come into his head. Perhaps one of the girls from the office could come and spend the day with the children. Or, perhaps he can stuff them solid with medicine, take them to school, let the school sort it out … good God, what a thought. If only his parents lived a bit nearer! If only … Nigel thinks of the client, all the top management, getting ready at that very moment for a decisive day. He is covered in cold sweat.

Then Nigel thinks the unthinkable – he thinks a thought that makes all other taboos seem like kids' play. *He* is the 'someone' who will have to take the children to the doctor, *he* will have to look after them, to comfort them and soothe them. They are still *his* children, just as they had been his children the day before, when they were playing happily in the garden. He is still their father. His mind is made up at once. A quick nagging question: how will he present his absence to the office? Surely, he can't say that he is staying at home to look after his sick children. What will they think of him? To hell with it, *he* is a man, *he* is not a child, *he* needs no excuses.

He picks up the phone. Good old Shirley – she is already there to answer the phone, a good 20 minutes before the office opens. 'Oh, Nigel, glad you phoned', says Shirley as soon as she hears his voice, 'Mr Wilmott called just a minute ago, from United Cereal, to say that they can't make it to the presentation today – any chance of rescheduling it for next Monday?' Nigel felt a surge of elation. Had Shirley been in front of him, he would have kissed her.

For an instant, Nigel thought he might squeeze out of his resolution to devote the day to his children. Take the kids to the doctor, call Anne, make sure she's back in time for him to meet those Revenue and Customs clowns – the thought crossed his mind like a flash. But, no, Nigel had understood something and there was no going back.

'Thanks, Shirley', he said, 'that's funny, because something has cropped up here, and I was phoning to say that I can't make it to the office today'.

'I hope it's nothing serious', said Shirley.

'No, no, it's just … I need to take my children to the doctor', said Nigel. He felt vulnerable, saying this, exposed. 'Would you please phone the Revenue and Customs and ask to rearrange our meeting for another time'.

'Yes, of course, Nigel, don't worry at all about it, I'll sort it all out', said Shirley.

She too was aware that an important barrier had been crossed, and was pleased to be reassuring and business-like. 'What's going on in Nigel's life?', she wondered, 'I should try and find out discreetly'.

Nigel's story is a true story. Most working women would regard his 'problem' as boringly familiar, accustomed as they are to juggling work and family **commitments**, to be in two places and to think of four things at once. 'Who's picking up Liz from school?'; 'when can I nip to the shop to get James' scout uniform?'; 'ought to quickly phone Janet to see if she could pick up the dry-cleaning'. These are ordinary thoughts, the likes of which are rarely far below the consciousness of a large section of the population, and yet rarely trouble the minds of people like Nigel, who have been sheltered from the painful **conflict** between the demands of work and those of the family and home.

There is even an argument that these expectations may train women to be better fitted to modern working life than men. Studies have shown that women tend to be polychronous where men are monochronous (Bluedorn, 2002). Polychronous people flourish at doing several things at once, and may even do all of them better for the fact that they are doing other things at the same time, where monochronous people tend to do better if they concentrate on one activity at a time. Life in the rough and tumble of a busy, changing organization may fit better with polychronous tendencies.

What makes Nigel's story interesting is that an ordinary experience should have an extraordinary effect. Nigel is neither an insensitive nor an inconsiderate person, as a father or as a husband. Yet, his work had until that Monday morning been 'sacrosanct', untouchable. Nothing could be allowed to interfere with his important appointments. What his children's sickness forced him to confront were the double standards he had always employed in evaluating man's work and woman's work. It forced him to confront his own responsibilities as a father and to re-assess his own priorities. It also forced him to question one of his assumptions about his own colleagues and subordinates at work: people should leave their homes behind them when they go to work and should devote themselves wholeheartedly to their work and their organization. Finally, it forced him to question what he had always taken for granted: that people should not grumble when asked to work late or to take a bit of work home over the weekend.

Nigel realized that some men are able to devote themselves unreservedly to their work because of an army of women supporting them and their children, nurturing them and working for them; this even happens in dual-career couples, like Nigel and Anne. By assuming the **gender role** of 'main family breadwinner', these men have abdicated from the responsibilities created by other **roles**, leaving the painful conflicts, the messy compromises and the juggling to their partners. And yet they may have been the first to criticize women for lack of **commitment** to the organization. Nigel himself had not been above the odd comment to Shirley that she was 'abandoning him' in the office to sort it all out, long after all other secretaries and most of the executives had left for home.

ORIENTATIONS TO WORK AND WORK ETHICS

What is exceptional about taking a day off work, when whole industries run on reduced numbers of working days in the week? An American car worker was asked why he only turned up to work four days each week and his answer is legendary: 'because I can't earn enough to make a living on three days a week'. His attitude is a universe apart from those who cannot contemplate missing a single day in the office. The American worker works to live: he expects little satisfaction or fulfilment from work, only a comfortable standard of living. The **meaning** of his life, his **identity**, are not linked to his job. For others, on the other hand, work is a very important part of life. They live to work and work fills their lives and underlies their identity. Only when the demands of family life come into conflict with those as a member of an organization do they notice for the first time some of the sacrifices that they have been making and some of the consequences of their attitudes towards their work.

We came across an emerging view of this recently when talking to a senior recruitment consultant about a course we were thinking of running at weekends:

> If you do that, you will make the gender bias worse. You are talking about doing it at the weekends because people can't get away from their office in the evenings, but it tends to be men who can't get away because they can't resist the group togetherness, the group hug, which they feel when they stay late in the office. Women are much better at resisting peer pressure and walking out when they need to be somewhere else. But they are still the ones who want to make sure that they have caught up with the ironing on Saturday.

This implies that one of the reasons for staying long hours in the office is wanting to be part of a feeling of togetherness; this is not necessarily related at all to wanting to get more work done. Hochschild (1997) has suggested that the pressures of domestic life may be such that many people will choose to be at work as a way of escaping. The lack of support for knowing what to do next, and how you are performing, on the domestic front, contrasts sharply with the clarity and the colleague base to be found in the workplace. Work has become friendlier and more engaging, while home has become less secure and less fulfilling.

Attitudes towards work vary widely. In the Bible, work is God's punishment for disobedience; it must be endured with forbearance. The ancient Greeks, on the other hand, thought that work was a base activity suitable for slaves, unworthy of cultured, free men. The free Spartans did no work at all, occupying themselves with things martial, while the free Athenians preferred intellectual and aesthetic pursuits. The Trobriand islanders of the South Pacific, by contrast, worked hard on their gardens and harvested many times the amount needed to sustain them; the quantity and quality of their product was seen as a sign of their worth as members of their community.

The attitudes which we bring to the workplace are partly shaped by the wider **culture** of which we are part. In trying to understand the development of capitalism in the West, it has been suggested that a crucial role was played by the 'Protestant **work ethic**'. This was an orientation towards work which grew out of the emergence of Protestant religion and, especially, Calvinism. Hard work was seen as a sign of godliness. Wealth and profit, far from being derided, were seen as signs of God's favour. Saving money, living frugally, refraining from the pleasures of the flesh and sheer hard work are the key ingredients in this version of the Protestant ethic (Weber, 1958).

Views on the Protestant ethic differ. Most people would agree, however, that, nowadays, its meaning has been stripped of its religious association. It has come to mean 'a sense of duty to work hard', and it is by no means restricted to Protestants. A friend told one of us about his Chinese Buddhist father:

> He used to keep his shop open until 10.30 every night. No one came in after 8.30, but it is part of the Confucian culture that you should keep your shop open whether anybody wants it or not, because they always might want it. And even if they don't, you have to do your best for everybody.

One of our students told us about his upbringing in another culture:

> My dad goes to the factory every day. He does not need to – it is closed at the weekends. But he loves it there. He has built it up from nothing and it is as much his child as I am. Even if he only reads the newspaper when he gets there, he just likes being there for a little while each day.

Some people just love either their work or their place of work. They have an unfeigned delight in spending more time at their workplace. One way of thinking of this is to say that each of us has our own **story** about ourselves: who we are, where we come from, where we are going, what sort of life we are leading and what it might mean to others (all of which gets told when we go for a job interview, for example). Similarly, we have a story that we tell others and ourselves about our organizations. We are interested in their history and how they are developing. When these two stories start intertwining, when our own story and our organization's story start meshing with each other, we become really involved and interested in our working lives.

WORK AND CLASS

Work attitudes, like many other types of attitudes, are linked to social *class*. A study which established the instrumental orientation of manual workers (Furnham, 1990) also found that clerical workers were more concerned with the work itself, its **status** and chances of **career** advancement. White-collar or clerical workers have traditionally been seen as having middle-class lifestyles and attitudes, emphasizing style, status and individual effort. They speak with middle-class accents and have middle-class tastes. This seems to apply more or less globally; while different cultures find each other's class systems funny, they all have them.

Class takes us back again to identity: how people place themselves and how others place them in a class structure is to do with who those people want to be seen to be. Sennett (1998) tells the story of the work and class of a father and son he knew. The father, Enrico, was an Italian immigrant in the USA who worked all his life as a janitor. This typically working-class job, in which he was often poorly treated by middle-class people and had to do heavy work, gave him a sense of structure for his life and his identity. He saved money to give himself and his family a better life, as he saw it, and to enable his children to have more opportunities in life than he had. His son, Rico, was now an expensively dressed consultant, with a postgraduate business degree, a wife and family, and a career which had made him move from one part of the USA to another on several occasions. Rico has all the trappings of a successful middle-class life. But, in one way, his life is very impoverished compared with his father. Enrico's life story for himself was quite clear: he was saving up money and improving his home, year by year, in order to improve the conditions for his family. He remained in touch with his community even when he moved out to the suburbs, so that other people knew him and were part of his story for a long time. Rico, on the other hand, lacked his father's sense of **control** over his own life. As a consultant, the direction, location and hours of his work are unpredictable in a way that his father's janitorial hours never were. The future flow of work and the directions that he might have to take to ensure that future are also uncertain. His wife's life is equally out of control, but in her case this is because of the complexities involved in managing a team of distance workers. Friendship and location are much shorter term for them than they were for Enrico, and the demands of their work meant that they had little time, energy or conviction to help their children build their lives. The rootlessness of modern middle-class life provides no long-term audience for the development of an **ethical** life story.

Class and work often reinforce each other. Middle-class people manage, control and command working-class people. Many of the misunderstandings, breakdowns of communication or trust and conflicts at the workplace which seem bizarre or irrational to an outside observer become understandable when the class barriers which divide people are taken into account. A comment which may have gone unnoticed in most cases can make a person feel deeply hurt if it is interpreted as a class insult, just as a **joke** can go very badly wrong if it is seen as a sexist or racist jibe.

ALTERNATIVE WORK AND NON-WORK ETHICS

Work ethics change. They shift with changes in the class structure of society, with technological innovations as well as with broader economic and cultural developments. There are some who argue that the Protestant work ethic is disintegrating under the massive changes currently affecting our societies. Instead of work, individuals turn elsewhere in their search for **meaning** and **identity**; they turn to family life, leisure activities, 'style' and material possessions.

At some points, young people with limited hopes of permanent work and few opportunities for **careers** were seen as espousing a 'welfare ethic', content to live off the state and refusing to feel degraded or shamed by unemployment. Such people may do casual work in the summer and live on state benefits (where available) for the rest of the year. Others, with more prospects, may espouse a 'gap year' ethic, where it can be seen as legitimate and even socially desirable to take a year out before or after university. Braver, but increasingly acceptable, is the 'career break', where a person chooses to take time to travel, or develop a different skill, for a period.

The rich and the upwardly mobile are re-discovering a different type of ethic, a 'wealth ethic'. Wealth, according to this view, is to be attained not through hard work but through clever deals or inheritance, and is to be enjoyed rather than copiously saved and invested. The wealth ethic merges with a 'hedonistic' or 'leisure' ethic which places great emphasis on pleasure, and paradoxically unites the 'idle rich' and those with a welfare ethic. Enjoying life becomes more important than having a good job, even though those two groups enjoy very different levels of material comfort. **Success** is to be measured not through achievement, but through consumption (Gabriel and Lang, 1995; see also Chapter 21, 'Producing and Consuming').

Arguably, neither the rich nor large sections of the working class, at least in Great Britain, have ever been ruled by the Protestant work ethic. What is more surprising is the decline of this ethic among the achievement-motivated middle class. One of our friends was recently headhunted for a job which carried with it a very smart 'compensation package', as the financial terms were euphemistically referred to. He was flattered and excited to be offered the job. However, as he thought about it, he decided that the phrase 'compensation package' was all too apt. In terms of how much of his identity he was expected to hand over, and how many weekends he was expected to work, 'compensation' was exactly what he would need. He did not wish to give precious hours out of his life to something which was going to require compensation. He already had a satisfactory job. He turned down the offer.

As the Protestant work ethic is waning, it has been suggested that even the middle class is moving to different ethics. These include the 'narcissistic ethic' centred on self-admiration, the 'body ethic' based on lavish care for the physical body, and the 'spirit ethic' focused on self-development and self-actualization. What unites all these ethics is the shift away from hard work as a source of **value** and **meaning**. Yet, the importance of work as a dimension of **identity** is unlikely to be supplanted in the near future. The time has still to come when people introduce themselves as avid readers of Proust, as owners of a Golf GTI, as 'being in analysis', or as proud fathers of two delightful children rather than by referring to the work that they do.

Instead of disappearing completely, the Protestant work ethic may be about to undergo yet another radical transformation, just as it earlier shed its religious connections. And so long as work provides our main means of livelihood, most of us will have to reconcile the demands which it makes, with demands made by our homes, our families and friends, as well as our own desires.

IN CONCLUSION

In some organizations, people are expected to keep their work and their home lives separate, and in others they are expected to blend them, which usually means that their home life is likely to be invaded by work, though the converse is also sometimes countenanced. In the first category are the kinds of work where physical presence and concentration are crucial, such as manufacturing, or organizations where **emotional labour** is expected, and nothing from outside must be allowed to interfere with trying to produce a 'happy' experience for the customer. In the second category are those more total organizations that expect their members (usually the word that is preferred to 'employees' in these places) to relax, play and socialize for the organization, as well as work for it. The first of these views takes it that the conflicts and worries of people's personal lives are not *the organization's* problem or responsibility, but private concerns of the individuals involved. It creates a set of double standards, justifying or even encouraging **discrimination** against women. It fosters the curious stance that employees should, for the duration of the working day, cut themselves off from emotional and moral attachments to their families and friends and commit themselves wholly to their organization. The second view can be equally destructive as organizational members find themselves unable to defend any area of life against the domination of their work. All other relationships become secondary as their own personal story becomes more and more closely intertwined with their organization's story.

Our lives in organizations cannot and should not be studied in isolation from the rest of our existence. Organization itself, as we have studied it in the pages of this book, is not a separate, distinct universe of human activities, isolated and cushioned from the forces of disorganization and chaos. Some modern forms of working life, such as Rico's, bring the forces of disorganization and chaos that we discussed at the beginning of this book right back into the middle of the working experience, in a way which affects life outside work as much as inside.

KEY POINTS

○ 'Home' and 'work' constantly interact.

○ Work and play take place both inside and outside the home.

○ Our attitudes and values, shaped within the family, the school or the wider culture, influence our actions in the workplace, as do our family and other commitments.

○ People's orientations to work vary enormously across individuals and cultures.

○ Many current organizations expect a 24/7 commitment from staff, especially senior staff, who are expected to socialize as well as work for the company.

○ Work orientations (for example, whether work should be a means towards an end or whether it should be enjoyable in itself) differ across the social classes.

○ Modern itinerant careers may make it difficult for people to develop a coherent story of either their working or their family life.

○ Men's undivided commitment and loyalty to their organizations frequently rest on the sacrifice of women's career prospects and their greater commitment to the home.

>>>>>>>>>>> **THEORETICAL SIGNPOSTS** >>>>>>>>>>>>

The balance between work and home has been approached from a variety of per-spectives. These have generally developed from pioneering feminist discussion of the implications of a gendered division of labour and the adverse effects of child-birth and housework for women's careers. Some of the core discussions concern:

> the gendered nature of the division of labour and its effects for women's careers
> the relations between home and work experiences and the construction of individual identities
> the changing social attitudes regarding work, leisure, family life and consumption standards
> the tendency of many of today's organizations to turn their employees into workaholics and the implications of this for family life.

The Gendered Nature of the Division of Labour and its Effects for Women's Careers

Research in this area has addressed the ways in which women's responsibilities at home interfere with their work lives and inhibit their career development (Cockburn, 1991; Marshall, 1995; Sharpe, 1984; Wilson, 1995). These studies offer a theoretical account, backed up by empirical case material, of the fashioning of contemporary identities from both work and domestic experiences. More information on women's careers can be found in the Theoretical Signposts of Chapter 20.

The Relations Between Home and Work Experiences and the Construction of Individual Identities

The relationship between consumption and work, especially in connection with issues of identity and selfhood, is discussed by Gabriel and Lang (1995). The classic work on identity and identity crisis is Erikson's (1968). Willis (1990) has offered one of the most insightful accounts of identity formation among adolescents as a process that prepares them to limit their ambitions to low-paid jobs. More recently, a great deal of scholarship has been dedicated to the discussion of whether people today shape their identities predominantly through their work and career experi-ences or their experiences as 'sovereign consumers', making lifestyle choices and crafting individual selfhoods out of these choices. Du Gay's (1996a) contribution in this area has been especially influential – he argues that, in spite of the emphasis on consumption, most people continue to develop their personal identities with reference to their work experiences. Similar arguments have been developed by Ransome (2005) who, like du Gay, emphasizes the interconnected nature of work and consumption. Bauman (1996) and Baudrillard (1970/1988), on the other hand, have tended to emphasize the dominance of consumer experiences over work experiences in shaping contemporary identities.

The Changing Social Attitudes Regarding Work, Leisure, Family Life and Consumption Standards

Sociologists have long studied how social attitudes regarding work, leisure and family life are shaped and how they change over time. The classical 'affluent worker' study (Goldthorpe et al., 1969) produced extensive research material about the domestic and industrial attitudes of workers in Luton in the 1960s. While dated, the work has provided influential theories on work ethics and the relation between the work and the domestic sphere. The study's key finding was that workers in newly affluent urban settings had given up expecting genuine job satisfaction, opting instead for the pleasure of consumer society, without, however, adopting middle-class values or lifestyles. A wide-ranging discussion of the Protestant work ethic is offered by Furnham (1990), while Maccoby (1976) and Lasch (1984) have provided accounts of emerging ethics which are currently displacing the Protestant ethic.

The Tendency of Many of Today's Organizations to Turn their Employees into Workaholics and the Implications of this for Family Life

The classic studies on achievement motivation, in juxtaposition to affiliation and power motivation, were carried out by McClelland (1961, 1971). The phenomenon of addiction to work or *workaholism* has been studied by Oates (1971) and Machlowitz (1980). Statt (1994) offers a broad-ranging discussion of different sociological and psychological approaches to work. Allison Pearson's novel, *I Don't Know How She Does It* (2002), creates a vivid description of some work–life issues for a woman in a senior job in the financial services. In *The Time Bind*, Hochschild (1997) explored what she views as a major contradiction in the lives of career couples – while claiming that their families came first, in reality they acted as if work was a harbour from the stresses of family life. For many, work rather than family was seen as drawing out their best qualities and giving them the experience of appreciation and even security.

REVIEW QUESTIONS

1. When all is said and done, what do you care more about (honestly) – your family or your work? How does this affect your personal identity?

2. Do you recollect any powerful experiences as a consumer? Did these have a lasting impact on you?

3. 'For workaholics, all the eggs of self-esteem are in the basket of work.' Discuss.

Reading On

The articles below are available for free to readers of the fourth edition of *Organizing & Organizations* via the book's companion website at www.sagepub.co.uk/fineman

Lyon, D. and Woodward, A.E. (2004) 'Gender and time at the top cultural constructions of time in high-level careers and homes', *European Journal of Women's Studies*, 11 (2): 205–21.
The demand for long working hours in leading positions is seen as a primary obstacle for women entering, leading to suggestions that public policy support better compatibility between work life and home. This article explores the character of the time of women and men pursuing high-level careers in Belgium, where state support for the domestic sphere is high, and yet women's advance in management and politics has been relatively low.

Watson, T.J. (2008) 'Managing identity: identity work, personal predicaments and structural circumstances', *Organization*, 15 (1): 121–43.
Social science research can play a valuable role in enabling people to understand how their personal predicaments relate to the broader structures and historical circumstances in which they arise. This article makes a close examination of two managers' identity work and the part played in this by their involvement in one specific organization in particular structural and historical circumstances.

Furnham, A. and Rose, M. (1987) 'Alternative ethics – the relationship between the wealth, welfare, work, and leisure ethic', *Human Relations*, 40 (9): 561–74.
This study attempted to devise and evaluate four belief systems regarding how people acquire their money and spend their time: the Protestant Work Ethic (PWE) which emphasizes the positive feature of work, the leisure ethic which sees recreation rather than work as the main means to personal fulfilment, the wealth ethic which stresses the accumulation of wealth to ensure independence from others and work, and the welfare ethic which is based on the idea that one should exploit state benefits as a primary source of income.

Harpaz, I. and Snir, R. (2003) 'Workaholism: its definition and nature', *Human Relations*, 56 (3): 291–319.
The term 'workaholism' is widely used, but there is little consensus about its meaning, beyond that of its core element: a substantial investment in work. This paper examines the relationship between workaholism and possible attitudinal, demographic, and situational variables through two representative samples of the Israeli labour force, with gender found to be the strongest predictor – that is, men have a higher likelihood of being workaholics.

23
LEARNING AND ORGANIZING IN UNCERTAIN TIMES

As you reach the end of this book, it is tempting to think that you have concluded your learning on the subject of organizations. You have followed our arguments, familiarized yourself with various theories, and become aware of some of the main issues involved. You may have some good ideas of your own on how to apply this knowledge in practice. We hope that from now on, when you enter a shop, when you start a new job or when you think about the administration of your university, you will do so with more inquisitive eyes and be able to read and understand some of the processes which may have remained opaque in the past.

The deeper message of the book, however, is that learning about organizations can never end. Even if you learned all that there is to know about the subject, organizations do not stand still. In fact, many of them are undergoing important transformations, which call for different types of understanding and different management and practical skills. The organizations of tomorrow may not be like the organizations which have inspired the theories and ideas presented in this book. Neither theory nor practice stand still. New ideas, new ways of looking at things, new concepts emerge which cast new light on what now seems tired or familiar. Thirty years ago, studying organizations through their **symbols** or their **stories** may have seemed bizarre, yet today it has become routine.

Two things about the future are certain. First, organizing will continue to occupy the time and minds of people on an increasing scale. Second, learning as a lifelong process will continue to support, inform and enhance our organizing activities. Organizing and learning will absorb increasing amounts of resources, time and effort, as information proliferates and as times and distances shrink. Lifelong learning has become a political cliché, yet it captures an important idea, the idea that learning is always interim, it never stops. Or better, that when learning stops, knowledge and understanding can decay into dogma and routine. And this is the paradox which is often concealed by political cliché: old learning and old ideas can act as a hindrance to new learning and new ideas. This is especially true if the learning has been acquired with a lot of effort, pain and sacrifice – giving up or going beyond old ideas can be anxiety-provoking and even painful, especially if these ideas have served us well in the past. And yet, this is often the price we have to pay for new learning. A famous world chess champion was once asked whether it was possible to improve his game further. 'Yes', he answered, 'I only wish I could unlearn all that I know about chess and start from scratch'.

As we saw in Chapter 3 ('Lifelong Learning'), this is not quite how learning works. Our past learning is not a stack of knowledge, such that we could take things off the top and discard them when we wished. Learning is more active than that and it changes us. It is more a question of how we hold what we have learned. It is when we think we have learned all we need in an area, when we think that we have worked it out, that we make ourselves incapable of new learning. Holding our learning loosely takes courage and requires an ability to drag ourselves out of our comfort zone, the zone we create with the help of our existing stock of concepts, ideas and theories. At times, learning takes us precariously near uncertainty and chaos. 'Without "chaos", no knowledge' argued Paul Feyerabend (1975: 5) the philosopher of science, in what now seems less like iconoclasm and more like common sense. Chaos is a term that is used more and more frequently in studies of organizations. At times, the word 'complexity' is preferred, sounding more scientific and less threatening.

Chaos and complexity theories emerged in the natural sciences in the 1960s, drawing on the study of non-linear dynamic systems, such as the weather or the turbulent flow of fluids. They have found increasing applications in other fields, including the study of organizations. Complex systems are systems which do not return readily to a condition of equilibrium, nor, however, do they suddenly collapse into utter disorder. In this book, we have avoided the view that organizations are systems, because much traditional systems theory disregarded those vital meaning-creating processes that are central to our concerns. Complexity theory, on the other hand, presents a view of systems which is unpredictable, uncertain and even unmanageable. It views the future as inherently unpredictable and accepts that small causes, including accidents, can have disproportionate effects. In one famous image, a butterfly flapping its wings in China causes a hurricane in America. Managers try in vain to plan for the longer term, since the longer term for most organizations is unknown and unknowable, like the weather. A new range of metaphors for understanding organizations is now emerging: organizations as precarious entities, whose success and survival may be jeopardized at any moment by entirely unforeseeable factors.

Under such conditions of unpredictable change, successful organizations are those whose leaders and members do not seek to predict the future and control it, but rather those which can rapidly change course, re-define themselves and learn to live with uncertainty and even chaos. These organizations must be prepared at times to be wasteful, destructive and conflict-ridden in order to be creative and innovative. Looking for targets to apportion blame to or give the credit for success to may appear to be organizationally expedient, but has little justification – single individuals are not responsible either for success or for failure, these phenomena being the products of a multiplicity of chance and systemic factors. Seeking to repeat success by applying a 'winning formula' can be futile; organizational learning has little to do with learning formulas and much to do with experimentation, reasoning by analogy and an ability to question underlying assumptions and existing patterns. Learning in such organizations means essentially being prepared to operate without the safety net of received wisdom and **knowledge**, taking risks and never standing still.

At the same time, in a period of transition, it is tempting to follow fads and fashions, prematurely discarding practices and ideas which have still got life in them. This is a form of premature obsolescence of ideas: simply because they are no longer new, they are assumed to be unproductive. There are also many consultants and management gurus who stand to make money out of those who believe that new ideas will always be the best. Here we encounter another facet of the learning paradox: the need to maintain old learning in new learning, knowing how much of the old to preserve and how to modify it and use it. Learning, therefore, must both preserve the old and identify when it is time to discard it. Unfortunately, much of university education does not help us in this type of learning.

Knowledge, all too frequently, comes to be equated with who said what, with definitions and lists. The **authority** of the lecturer, both as a source of all knowledge and as a final arbiter of learning in the judgement game of examinations, is rarely questioned. The authority of the printed text, the book, is taken for granted. Students' minds are assumed to be blank pieces of paper, with no knowledge, no understanding of their own. Clarity is extolled above all other virtues in academic writing, disregarding the possibility that learning involves a movement from what is more precise to what is less clear. But the emphasis on clarity tends to close inquiry prematurely, as does the preoccupation with definitions and completeness. It is not surprising that business schools are coming under increasing criticism for producing conservative, tame and uncritical intellects, ill-suited for the challenges facing managers in the real world. The complacency which characterized the early part of the twenty-first century, assuming that growth and capitalism could roll on unimpeded, came to look very naïve when the credit crunch and recession of 2008/9 took hold. Once again, we were reminded that when we think we have understood what is going on, we are in fact vulnerable to the world changing and find that we have to learn all over again.

In this book, we have adopted a different approach. We have viewed knowledge as part of all organizations. Knowledge can be implicit or explicit, incomplete, confused or temporary. It is sometimes transferred passively from one individual to another, but then it tends to become impoverished and irrelevant. By contrast, knowledge which grows out of human action and interaction stays lively and dynamic, subject to development, criticism and correction. Ideas are continuously juxtaposed with experience, each supporting and enlightening the other. In no way do we seek to undervalue the great theories of the past to which the study of organizations owes its existence as an academic discipline. These theories must be a source of questioning and inspiration rather than a dogma in which we search for answers to the burning questions of our era.

We hope that, as you went through the pages of this book, you made connections between the concepts and ideas we presented and your own experiences of organizing or of being organized. Some of these experiences will have provided support and illustrations for our arguments; others may have qualified, modified or even contradicted what we have been saying. We have stressed throughout that **meaning** and making sense of things is personal as well as corporate. What makes sense to one person does not always make sense to another. It is not just that different people would wish to say different things about organizing; the aspects of organizing about which they think it is worth saying something are different too. One person is especially concerned with order and **control** while another is fascinated by **change** and uncertainty; one is interested in gender and power relations while another focuses on teamwork and groups.

The *meaning* of organization varies from person to person. Different individuals, working side by side in the same organization, may be working in organizations that are in effect different – one person may experience the organization as a hostile and malevolent force, while a second experiences the same organization as a model of everything that is good and right and a third 'is only doing a job' and does not care one way or the other for the organization. Likewise, different academic traditions highlight different aspects of organizations, some their impersonality, some their hierarchy, some their goals, some the preoccupation with efficiency and **rationality**. They have defined organizations accordingly. We, in this book, have accepted the plurality of views and experiences of organizations. We have not therefore tried to define them as *abstract concepts*, but have accepted them as *social constructs*, ideas which have different resonances with different people. Each one of our readers may come up with a personal statement of what organizations mean to him or her – organizations in general, and specific organizations like club, university or employer.

BEING IN THE DRIVING SEAT: ACTING WITH SENSE

In the early days of space exploration, monkeys and dogs were propelled into space in 'capsules'. Later, however, as human space travel became possible, space capsules were renamed space*ships*. Why? One reason was that astronauts were not content to play the part that animals had played in earlier trips. Nor, if they were trapped inside 'capsules', could they be presented as heroes exploring a new universe. Astronauts had to be given some control. Unlike the dogs and monkeys of the early trips who had just been physical bodies surviving extremes of speed, acceleration and gravity, astronauts were given buttons to push, instruments to read and levers to pull. This made them captains of ships whose fate seemed to be in their own hands.

Of course, astronauts had limited choices. They could hardly decide to go out for a walk or change direction and fly off to Mars. They could, however, manoeuvre their spaceships and actively participate in their missions. They could make sense of their experiences as participants in meaningful, collective expeditions. They could share these experiences with other people. They, as well as others, could learn from these experiences in ways which were not possible as long as space capsules carried passive passengers.

We are hoping that this book will enable you to accomplish a similar change in your journeys through organizations. We are hoping that you will understand more about your missions and the ways in which your organizations function, with better chances of being pilots of your ships rather than passive passengers. It would be absurd to suggest that reading the book will take you to the top of your organization or that it will free you from all the organizational pressures and constraints. We do, however, hope that the book will help you to better understand what is going on around you and better appreciate the choices which you have and the demands which you can make.

A word sometimes used to describe this relation between an individual and an organization is **stakeholder**. A stakeholder is someone who has a claim on the way an organization is run, its goals and directions; it is someone with *some* choices, *some* power and *some* responsibilities as opposed to a bystander, a pawn or a *customer*. A customer enjoys the privilege of choosing how to spend his/her money without having to offer explanations to anyone. In exchange, the customer must accept the vagaries of the market. A stakeholder, on the other hand, has a say on the meaning and goals of an organization, becomes involved in its governance and has rights as well as responsibilities. Unlike customers, stakeholders are bound to their organizations with ties of mutuality and respect. We are hoping that our readers will emerge from this book with an understanding that enables them to decide when and how they may participate as stakeholders in their organizations and when it is desirable or inevitable to sit on the sidelines. Understanding organizing and organizations does not make a person immune from occasional powerlessness or dependency. But it does reduce the chances of their needing to resort to statements such as: 'I was only obeying orders' or 'this doesn't sound right but it must be – I'm only a small cog in the machine'.

MOVING ON

We have written about the aspects of organizing, being organized, and living in organizations that seemed interesting and important to *us*. Numerous questions, themes and chapter headings, after discussions, were left out. You may emerge from this book with a whole host of different questions and themes of your own.

For those who want to continue developing their learning, a good starting point is to compare the arguments, ideas and examples which we provide with your own experiences. Thereafter, different readers will pursue different paths, crafting their own questions, addressing their own interests. Here, to conclude, are a few hints that may help:

- Criticize our ideas, qualify them, revise them, fashion them in a way that makes sense to you. How do you find **organizations**, **bureaucracy**, **leadership**, **emotions**, and so forth, work for you?
- Identify those gaps in our arguments or in our charting of the terrain of organizing and organizations which need filling. What fits and does not fit between the various topics? How, for example, are sexual and moral issues linked? Do machines dictate our life? How do we resist their influence?
- Focus on the paradoxical, the out of place, the irregular in your own experiences of organizing. Frequently, one unusual observation is worth more than large volumes of uniform data. What happens during a crisis, such as a breakdown, resignation, personality clash or redundancy programme? Often, the organization's colours are revealed when, normally, they are obscured.

- Mistrust jargon and clichés and look carefully at the use of language in general. If you think that the answers to numerous problems lie in a single concept (e.g. 'motivation', 'leadership', 'organization' and so on), test out whether that seems fair and true. Often, we like to give slick and simple labels to issues which are basically complex and can be analysed in various possible ways.
- Mistrust simple cause-and-effect explanations of human phenomena. It is unlikely to be 'all a personality problem', or 'just a matter of changing the leader' to sort out the organization. Organizations are the products of many factors, systematic and accidental; change one part and others are affected in unexpected ways.
- Try using metaphors, similes and models to make sense of your observations. If you see the organization as a machine, mad house, plate of spaghetti, brain or battlefield, does it bring some things into perspective?
- Whenever you make a generalization, look at the exceptions to check it out. Do all students, women, lecturers, civil servants and so forth do what you think they do? If not, how useful is the generalization?

And finally, there is little to be gained by prematurely closing discussions and debates in the interest of order, certainty and organization. Some of the best ideas in organizations (and in science) have resulted from accident, misunderstanding and error. Others have emerged from doing exactly the opposite of what intuition, good sense and methodology dictated. Inquiry, understanding and action will not always be in step with one another. Do not try to be *too* organized.

KEY POINTS

○ Learning about organizations never ends because organizations change as we learn.

○ Lifelong learning, and holding our knowledge tentatively, are important.

○ Chaos and complexity theories have recently been brought into organizations to help understand the indeterminacy of organizational life.

○ We should beware of fads and fashions in organizing.

○ Thinking about organizations sometimes needs to be complicated and humble; the price of clarity may be that it gives a very inadequate view of what is going on.

○ We can to some extent be drivers rather than passengers in organizational life.

> > > > > > > > > > > **THEORETICAL SIGNPOSTS** > > > > > > > > > > > >

The key theoretical ideas underlying this chapter are:

> continuous learning
> chaos and complexity
> sense-making.

Ideas of continuous learning have been explored at some length in Chapter 3, 'Lifelong Learning'. They have linked with ideas on work-based learning (Raelin, 1999). Recent work has emphasized that people in organizations need to learn not simply to learn, but to learn to learn (Argyris, 1977, 2001), with the related concept of double-loop learning.

Chaos and complexity theories acknowledge that there are limits to our understanding, particularly when it comes to understanding the details of what is going on. Seemingly minor events can have enormous and unpredictable consequences. Another property of complexity theory is that systems replicate themselves at different levels; what happens at a micro level, in an office, say, is surprisingly similar to what happens at a macro level, across the company. Summaries of this position can be found in Gabriel (1998b) and Stacey (1996).

Sense-making has in some ways been a core concept of this book. If a person cannot make sense of what is happening around them, they cannot learn from it. The processes of making sense underlie everything we have been talking about, and especially ideas such as the management of meaning. The concept has been focused through the work of Weick (1995) in recent years.

THESAURUS

absenteeism

Absenteeism is unofficial absence from work, which may be due ostensibly to illness. Illness, however, is a social as much as a medical condition, and staying away from work depends on many social and psychological factors, including people's relations with their employer and co-workers, their degree of satisfaction with their work, their conscientiousness and the interface between work and the rest of their lives. Absenteeism varies very widely across companies and sectors and is often seen as a covert manifestation of organizational **conflict** and worker **resistance**. This is especially the case in organizations with a prevailing culture of 'presenteeism', where, in other words, employees are expected to work long hours and be constantly at the beck and call of their superiors. Absenteeism is also seen as one of the more direct consequences of **stress** and **burnout** at the workplace. Finally, absence for supposed illness is seen as an entitlement (a 'fringe benefit') in poorly paid and poorly rewarded jobs where expressions like 'I have another 17 days sickness owed to me' can be heard.

(Aronnson et al., 2000; Simpson, 1998)

achievement

Achievement is deeply inscribed into the value system of many business and organizational cultures. At its most neutral, it is a synonym for 'getting something done', completing a task or activity. However, achievement has come to symbolize more than that. It is an expression of the outcome of a wider cultural belief in hard work, and success from the application of individual effort in challenging situations. The achievement ethic finds its roots in religious and cultural practices where working hard and individual achievement (examination success, sporting prowess, moving upward in the social hierarchy of occupations, earning more money) are encouraged and rewarded – and seen as a 'good thing'. In achieving societies, achievement often becomes personally internalized, part of one's self worth and self image, and something to be re-inforced in 'rewarding' work. The non-achiever, failed achiever, or anxious achiever, can be something of a misfit in a society where mainly achievement, and its trappings, are celebrated.

Achievement, and pressures to achieve, are represented in a wide range of organizational practices, especially performance measurement, personnel appraisal and pay determination. There have also been attempts to find personality qualities that drive, or motivate, people to achieve. The most notable is in the work of David McClelland on the achievement motive, or need to achieve (nAch). High-nAch people, he argues, are products of an upbringing that encourages independence and the taking of risks where there is a moderate, rather than very low or high, probability of success. So high-nAch people are not gamblers. They will take calculated risks where the outcome depends more on their own efforts than on chance. They also appreciate constructive feedback on the results of their endeavours so they can learn from their failures. McClelland and other researchers have demonstrated that managerial performance and entrepreneurial success, as well as economic development, can all be linked to levels of nAch.

(Fineman, 1977; Furnham, 1990; McClelland, 1961, 1971)

action

There are different schools of thought regarding human action. Some sociologists tend to regard all action as social, stemming from relatively fixed **norms** and **values** within any particular society; symbolic interactionists, on the other hand, view the **meanings** behind action as precarious and unstable, constantly being negotiated among the interacting parties. One school of psychologists, known as 'behaviourists', tend to disregard the meanings that people attribute to their actions altogether and focus on behaviour itself. Yet another school, known as 'depth psychology', questions some of the meanings people claim for their actions, suspecting that these are **rationalizations** or excuses. They argue that the **motives** of many actions are unconscious – in other words, we may have very strong motives for our actions (e.g. ambition, rivalry, imitation) but, for much of the time, we are not consciously aware of them.

How is action to be studied? Weber advocated that, in order to understand action, the researcher must try to enter the way of thinking and feeling of the actor. This creates a type of understanding based on empathy, sometimes referred to as *verstehen*, a knowledge from within rather than from without. In Weber's writings, we also find a distinction that has since been widely debated between action that is instrumental, driven by rational calculation of consequences and a choice among alternatives, and action that is affective, driven by emotional and often irrational desires and wishes. This distinction is now questioned, mostly by theorists who view emotion as a perfectly rational basis for certain types of action. Weber also identified another important distinction between routine or traditional action which is based on unthinking repetition and non-routine action which is triggered off by unusual circumstances.

One way of studying action that has become increasingly prevalent in the social sciences is through the use of **narratives**. By turning themselves into story characters and placing their actions within plots, individuals do often 'make sense' of already executed actions or discover plausible reasons for having carried them out. Equally, however, narratives can actively define those events that qualify as actions against others which are seen as accidental or incidental.

One especially important feature of action is the learning that it generates (Argyris and Schön, 1978). Action learning is an approach to education and training which emphasizes a 'hands-on' approach, where active participation by the learner is indispensable in generating and disseminating knowledge. Kolb's learning cycle is one variant of action learning theory, which seeks to bring together knowledge and action, theory and practice. The relationship between theory and practice is one that has long preoccupied organizational and management scholars and, in Kolb's view, it is a cyclical relationship where experience and action continuously act as triggers for reflection, which in turn generates theoretical and conceptual schemes, which in turn are tested through further action.

(Argyris and Schön, 1978; Kolb, 1985; Weber, 1946)
See also **desire, motivation**

action research
Action research is the process of finding out about a situation or organization by seeking to change it. The idea originated from Kurt Lewin who was considering how we might find out about systems that were too complicated for us simply to trace through all the individual relationships between elements. We might expect to be able to understand the way a block of metal moves when particular forces are placed upon it, but when we are faced with a number of human beings, each of unfathomable complexity, interacting in an organization, we have no chance of such an atomistic understanding. We need therefore to find other ways to explore the situation.

The action research approach was originally designed to see how a **system** reacts when we try and affect it, though more recent contributors have not necessarily taken a systems approach. In the same way as we find out the weight, elasticity and mobility of a football when we kick it, and see how it responds, we find out many things about human systems only by seeing how they respond to attempts to move or change them.

The methodology of action research has, in most descriptions, attempted to be scientific. Typical accounts include: gaining views from organization members about the nature of the problem(s) to be addressed; using this to gain a consensual view of issues; devising a testable proposition; changing something so as to collect some data to test it with; and looking back to see how those who had the problem in the first place feel about the effectiveness of the experiment.

The use of the term 'action research' has been broadened over the years. It has sometimes been used to refer to consulting activities, where the motivation of the 'researcher' has more to do with showing the client that an 'experiment' has succeeded, and that it is therefore worth paying the bill, than to do with any search for as yet unknown answers to questions.

(Eden and Huxham, 1996; French and Bell, 1999; Lewin, 1951; Reason and Bradbury, 2001; Whitehead, 2000)

actor-network theory (ANT)

Actor-network theory draws attention to the way that a network of many different things – social, material – affect the way one acts and behaves. So writing a document on a word processor involves one's previous experiences with word processing, assumptions about who one is writing for, the capacities of the machine, the way to deal with interruptions from colleagues, the lighting level and so forth. In short, there is an interlinking of a range of technical and non-technical factors that come into play. Unusually, therefore, actor-network theory suggests that it is not only humans that have agency and can 'act'; machines and matter in general can too. All are part of the understanding of organizing processes.

Callon and Latour (1981) developed the actor-network theory by following the insights of narrative theorist Algirdas Greimas who suggested that the main unit in the analysis of narratives should be 'actants', that is, units that act or are acted upon. It is only at the end of a story (that is, a study) that we can know who is a real actor and who has remained an actant; actants acquire 'character' (or identity) as they go through their programmes. Social scientists make a mistake in assuming that they know the characteristics of the actors they study at the outset. Furthermore, what the observers see as macro-actors are usually networks of actants, successfully pretending to be one actor and to speak with one voice. This is possible because they managed to translate their interests so that they are not in conflict, stabilize their connections and mobilize jointly when needed.

Actor-network theory is actually a research design, not a theory. The word 'theory' was added because a 'T' was needed to denoted the main metaphor, that of an ant. In place of a 'bird's eye view' of macro-sociologists, ANT researchers follow systematically connections between actants as they develop. ANT is especially suitable for studies of science and technology, as actants do not have to be human: they can be plants, animals, machines and any other object that can act or be acted upon.

(Callon, 1987; Callon and Latour, 1981; Latour, 1991)

aesthetics

The concept of aesthetics in organizations does not have a clear and agreed meaning even among those who write about it. The *Shorter Oxford English Dictionary* gives a definition of aesthetics as: 'the philosophy of taste, or of the perception of the beautiful'. Much of the functionalist tradition of thinking about organizations has militated against thinking about the role of taste or the perception of the beautiful, except in cases where the product may be beautiful, or be sold according to its beauty, as in the design industry. We can distinguish between judgements made on the grounds of what is beautiful (aesthetics), what is good (**ethics**) and what is useful (economics).

There can be no doubt that people get very engaged in, and agitated about, aesthetics in their organizations. For example, people may express strong feelings about the colour of their office walls or the design of the carpet. Sometimes these are comments about the quality of the aesthetics ('what a disgusting yellow!') and sometimes they are more to do with the associations that they have with the style of aesthetic choices that have been made. For example, people in one organization referred to their coffee room as 'the day room', because the décor reminded them of the sitting room in an old people's home. Such judgements will be made about many of the artefacts in an organization: the style of the furniture, the type of window hangings (if any), the use and choice of plants, the company logo and so on (Strati, 1999).

Why do aesthetic judgements take on such importance for members? In some cases, it is because they see the organization's beauty, glamour and allure as important in attracting customers; this would be true of department stores and business schools. In other cases, it is because beauty has to do with style, which symbolizes fashion and success. Our tastes say a lot about us and many of the products we consume make visible statements about us. In wealthier societies, many consumers may view purchases as an expression of identity and selfhood.

If employees view the aesthetic choices of their organization as reflecting their own identities, many organizations view the appearance of their employees as reflecting their own values and image. 'Looking right and sounding right' then become part of the employee's work. In some cases, such as Personal Assistants, retail employees and some catering staff, this is as important as the intellectual, physical or **emotional labour** that the employees do. It is then referred to as 'aesthetic labour' and it may entail spending long hours choosing clothes or working on one's appearance in front of a mirror (Hancock and Tyler, 2000; Tyler and Taylor, 1998; Warhurst et al., 2000; Witz et al., 2003).

There is another reason why aesthetics have assumed some importance in the study of organizations. Managerial work, long associated with technical efficiency, is sometimes now seen as having an aesthetic dimension. Doing things 'in style' may be as important as the things being done. Giving a talk, telling a **story** or even crafting an email can be done in many different styles, even if the actual content is very similar, yet the outcomes of these actions may differ depending on the style in which they are done as much as the content being communicated. Doing things 'in style' earns the respect of others, even when the things being done may not earn their approval.

(Cairns, 2002; Strati, 1999; Strati and Guillet de Montoux, 2002)

affirmative action

Affirmative action is a set of measures and policies aimed at reducing the cumulative effects of social exclusion, discrimination and injustice, by enhancing the chances of members of deprived social groups to reach positions of influence or power. Affirmative action has its origins in the American Civil Rights Movement in the 1960s and was initially aimed at improving the chances of young people from underprivileged backgrounds to enter higher education. Reverse discrimination was one of the measures used to this end – the adoption of lower 'objective measures' of achievement to compensate for deprivation. Additionally, quotas have been used in various organizations, stipulating that a certain proportion of recruits should represent different types of under-privileged or deprived groups in society. Affirmative action programmes prospered in academic environments (mostly in the United States) and, to a much lesser extent, state and commercial organizations in the 1970s and 1980s. Since then, however, they have been under pressure from groups defending meritocratic principles of recruitment. Such groups argue that affirmative action violates equality of opportunity and lowers overall standards of performance.

See also **discrimination**

agenda formation

While many researchers have investigated how decisions are made and how groups and teams work, some recent authors have pointed out that there is a more fundamental question, which is: how do some topics come to be talked about at all while others are ignored? In order for issues to be acted upon, someone has to be talking about them: they have to be on the 'agenda'. Similarly, people may try to manage some issues off the agenda if discussion of them does not suit their purpose. Suppose that one of their colleagues wants a re-organization and they think that this will cause fruitless disruption. In this case, they may try to ensure that there is never enough time in meetings to discuss the issue. For example, they may turn discussion to rumours of a new competitor joining the industry, in the hope that this will distract others from discussing a re-organization. Most people will have had experience during their teenage years of trying to keep issues off their parents' agenda, when discussion of those issues might have led their parents to look into areas that the teenager would rather they kept out of. Controlling the agenda is one of the standard ways of wielding **power** in an organization.

Agenda formation has had lengthy discussion in the communications and media literature, where the contribution of McCombs (McCombs and Shaw, 1972) over time has been particularly significant. This work has looked at how public agendas get set, the role of the newspapers and other media, and whether the media set the agenda or follow it. It is a topic which is very visible in political agendas: how do certain issues come to dominate political debates at one moment in time while others go undiscussed? Within management and organization, Dutton and her co-workers (Dutton, 1997) have developed a lively literature. They suggested that the role of middle managers is to 'sell' issues to top management. Others (Pitt et al., 2002) have argued that it is misleading to think of managers as selling issues to each other, because when an issue passes from one person to another, the receiving person always re-constructs it in their own understanding, so that it is not the same issue.

(Cobb and Elder, 1972; Dearing and Rogers, 1996; Dutton, 1997; Protess and McCombs, 1991; Tansley and Newell, 2007)

aggression

Aggression, as an overt physical attack on another person, is regarded as one of the most socially undesirable forms of behaviour in work organizations. There are normally strict sanctions (often dismissal) brought to bear on the perpetrator. Aggression can be embedded in practices such as **bullying** and **harassment**, sometimes viewed culturally as 'the way things happen here'. Aggression may be expressed in more acceptable forms, such as through 'aggressive' bargaining, 'tough, uncompromising' **leadership** and raw, **competitive** behaviour. The way aggression may or may not be expressed has much to do with the **culture** and **gender** balance of the organization. So, in a 'macho' production organization, it is not uncommon to hear people loudly and angrily swearing at each other. In the more genteel atmosphere of white-collar organizations, such as the civil service or academia, aggression can be disguised as sarcasm or sniping. The psychological basis of aggression can be frustration from feeling cheated, underrated, exploited or blocked, or from the desire to boost one's self-esteem through diminishing others. Some people will channel their frustrations into indirect channels – such as through political activism, and even **sabotage**.

(Gill et al., 2001; Hearn and Parkin, 2001; Hoel and Beale, 2006; Neuman and Baron, 1998)

alienation

Alienation is an important concept in sociology, following the central position of the concept in the works of the great German philosopher and revolutionary, Karl Marx (1818–93). In his early writings, Marx used the concept of alienation to describe the condition of humanity under capitalism, a condition which is summed up in Brecht's phrase: 'man can only live by forgetting that he is a human being'. The root cause of alienation for Marx is capitalist production, which separates workers from the products of their **labour**, from the activity of labour, from their fellow humans and from what Marx called man's 'species being', i.e. those features that make humans a unique species. Through the sale of their labour and through the production of commodities, workers surrender their productive capacities (which is what makes them distinctly human) to alien domination. A part of themselves is separated from them, it becomes estranged from them and confronts them as an oppressor. The alienated beings can be thought of as animals separated from their essential nature, animals which have spent their entire lives in captivity. They are discontent, oppressed and unfulfilled but, more importantly, they are not aware of the causes of their condition, as their consciousness is systematically distorted. While Marx envisaged everyone under capitalism (including the owners of capital) as alienated, he conceived of the possibility of human emancipation and freedom in a society in which the **control** of the productive process is restored to the workers. As the concept of alienation has passed into everyday use, its **meaning** has shifted and has come to mean frustration and separation. The sociologist Robert Blauner argued that alienation in the workplace comprises four emotional states: **powerlessness**, **meaninglessness**, isolation and self-estrangement. He found that increasing automation leads to increasing alienation. His theory was that as industries move from craft to mass production, alienation increases, but as they move further to fully automated process production, alienation declines. His optimistic conclusion that in the long run alienation will be resolved by the very factors which fuel it – **technology** and automation – has been criticized as reflecting the optimism of the 1950s; his arguments, however, that link **technology** to the individual's experiences in the workplace and the degree of **job satisfaction** have proven influential.

(Blauner, 1964; Marcuse, 1964; Marx, 1844/1972)

ambivalence

Ambivalence is an increasingly popular term, indicating the simultaneous existence of strong positive and negative feelings towards the same situation, person or object – for example, love and hate, attraction and repulsion, enjoyment and dissatisfaction. Psychoanalysis views ambivalence as a key feature of most important emotional relations, including those between parents and children, patients and physicians, students and teachers, managers and managed. For instance, love for a parent or a friend is rarely unadulterated with envy, rivalry or hate. Generally, mature individuals tend to control or repress one side of the ambivalent feelings (the positive or, more commonly, the negative) aiming at a consistent emotional orientation towards others. Various occasions, however, may cause the repressed or controlled feelings to resurface, by loosening the psychological defences against them or may instigate new repressions.

Numerous authors have viewed ambivalence as central to individuals' experiences in organizations, whether as members or as consumers. Some authors have studied individuals' ambivalent attachments to the organizations that employ them and to their jobs. These include simultaneous loyalty and dedication ('I owe everything to this organization') and anger and animosity ('this organization/job is killing me'). This ambivalence can lead to alternate displays of compliance and resistance to organizational leaders and organizational controls. Some authors have studied jokes and humour as outlets for the repressed parts of ambivalent feelings. Yet others have seen ambivalence at the heart of people's experiences as consumers, where they simultaneously depend on and are repulsed by the commodities and goods on which they spend their money.

Generally, the increasing recognition of ambivalence leads to a de-emphasis on rationality. People who are governed by ambivalent emotions and passions can be expected to be inconsistent, changeable, moody, impulsive and opportunistic rather than careful calculators of utility and value.

(Baum, 1987; Bauman, 1988; Casey, 2000; Collinson, 2002; Gabriel, 1999b; Grugulis, 2001; Smelser, 1998; Sturdy, 1998)

anomie

Anomie is a state of collapse of social **norms** and social **controls**. The concept was developed by Durkheim (1858–1917), one of the founding fathers of sociology, who argued that the cohesion of social groups and societies is achieved through two social mechanisms, which exist over and above the individuals making up the groups and societies: (i) social integration, the product of strong social bonds, unites groups like families, clans, military and religious groups together; (ii) social regulation **controls** the individual's needs and **desires** bringing them into line with the means available for their satisfaction. In Durkheim's view, social regulation is accomplished through the internalization of **norms**. Anomie occurs when such norms are weakened, especially during periods of rapid economic change or social transformation when aspirations and desires grow disproportionately. Their inevitable frustration leads to feelings of injustice, unfairness and disorientation. Durkheim argued that anomic societies display an increase in suicide rates and all kinds of manifestations of social deviance. Like **alienation**, anomie has had a long career in academic discourse and its **meaning** has lost some of the sharpness which Durkheim bestowed on it. Like alienation, it has assumed an increasingly psychological quality, indicating a state of being, rather than a social phenomenon coming to signify a generalized condition of **meaninglessness**, normlessness and disintegration which affects numerous social **groups** and individuals.

Does anomie afflict organizations? If organizations are viewed through the prism of Max Weber's ideal type bureaucracy, they run no risk of anomie. Written **rules** control behaviour and there is no need for social norms or social cohesion. Such a view, however, seems highly unhelpful. Real organizations are full of cohesive **groups** and they themselves can vary in the degree of cohesion and unity among their members. We have now come to view organizations increasingly as **cultures** rather than as machines; as cultures, they may have more or less integration and more or less regulation. Those organizations that have 'strong cultures' run no risk of anomie (unless for those who feel excluded and marginalized from the dominant culture) though those whose culture is highly fragmented may be more at risk. An anomic organization is one where there is little sense of collective purpose and belonging and where people's behaviour shows little sense of acknowledging the needs and aspirations of others. Organizations that have gone through a protracted trauma due to downsizing, where their members feel that they may be the next ones in line to be sacked, may well lapse into anomic states (Stein, 2001; Uchitelle, 2006). Likewise, organizations with very weak **leadership** and no sense of direction of collective purpose may lapse into anomie. In such organizations, one would expect individuals to be easily corruptible (since there are no norms or values against corruption), mobile (they would readily move elsewhere if offered better terms since they have no sense of belonging or allegiance to their employer), uncooperative and detached.

(Durkheim, 1951; Howe, 1986)

anxiety

It is frequently argued that we live in an age of anxiety, brought about by continuous change. People in Western societies are meant to be anxious about terrorism and crime, about holding on to their jobs and property, about growing ill and dying, about their physical image and bodies, about the activities of big business and big governments, about the discoveries of scientists and technologists and so forth. Anxiety is undoubtedly an unpleasant **emotion**, associated with uncertainty and exposure. It is also a very important emotion, acting as the trigger for different social and psychological processes. As the psychologist McDougall (1908/1932) pointed out, anxiety alerts the individual to the possible existence of threats and focuses our attention on how to deal with them. Anxiety can act as a signal for defensive mechanisms, although it can equally be a signal that defensive processes have failed or backfired. Neurotic anxiety, in contrast to realistic anxiety, involves feelings disproportionate to the magnitude of the threat facing an individual and may result in inhibitions (avoidance of particular people, areas or types of behaviour) or symptom formation.

Many organizational processes are rife with anxiety. **Leadership** is a process which awakens many primitive anxieties (Gabriel, 1999b). Is the leader worthy of faith and obedience? Will he/she take advantage of his/her followers? Is he/she sincere? Are his/her claims to legitimacy genuine? Teams and groups also awaken numerous anxieties. Will the group accept us? Will it respect our individuality? Will we be able to live up to our partners' expectations? Anxiety is also an important emotion associated with learning. Learning can be an anxiety-laden process: the learner is anxious about understanding what he/she has to learn, anxious about failing and anxious about making a fool of themselves in the process of learning. It is therefore important that learning institutions and teachers control such anxieties. Excessive anxiety is likely to paralyse learning. On the other hand, the total absence of anxiety is also likely to inhibit learning, since it encourages one to remain within a comfort zone of already acquired learning.

Undoubtedly, anxiety becomes exacerbated in periods of extreme organizational **change** taking place within highly unpredictable, complex or even chaotic environments. Stacey has argued that in such environments, organizations succeed and survive if they can operate in a state of 'bounded instability' or near chaos. To do so, their members must be able to accept a degree of anxiety, channelling this anxiety into learning, creativity and inventiveness.

(Antonacopoulou and Gabriel, 2001; Gabriel, 1999b; Stacey, 1992, 1995)

archetypes

Archetype is a concept developed by Carl Gustav Jung to describe inherited and deeply unconscious contents of the mind which are common to all humans; these are essential primordial images and ideas, charged with **emotion** and **symbolism**, which manifest themselves in fantasies, dreams and people's emotional responses to external stimuli which happen to be associated with archetypes. They exercise a powerful influence on the way we experience and understand the world around us and colour our perceptions. Jung viewed archetypes as part of the collective heritage of humanity and assigned them to the collective unconscious along with the instincts. Archetype theory has been used in organizational studies with some degree of success in illuminating the persistence of certain roles that people assume. These may include the warrior, the fool, the trickster, the impostor, the woman warrior, the wise old man and others. The importance of this approach lies in the primacy it accords to **fantasy** over observable behaviour. Thus, a leader may trigger off the archetype of the impostor or axeman in the minds of followers; it may then prove impossible to change an image triggered by such an archetype, no matter what he/she actually does.

(Bowles, 1989; Jung, 1968; Kets de Vries, 1990b; Moxnes, 1999)

artificial intelligence
Artificial intelligence is the use of computers to simulate human intelligence. Whether it is possible for computers to imitate human **intelligence** and achieve any genuine originality of thinking and **problem solving** is the topic of an intense debate which includes the whole notion of 'consciousness'. What is certain is that the use of computers (and their formidable 'accomplishments' in playing chess, conducting 'conversations' or proving mathematical theorems) has forced philosophers and psychologists to re-assess their notions of what it means to be intelligent. The most significant outcome of research on artificial intelligence lies in what the efforts to simulate intelligence have told us about intelligence as it is found in human beings. For example, programmes that play chess are very competent at devising winning chess strategies but very poor at picking up chess pieces. Artificial intelligence originated from attempts to understand human intelligence by asking: 'What would we have to do to simulate this?'

(Lawler and Elliot, 1996; Weizenbaum, 1976)

assumption
Assumption is taking a fact, an idea or a principle for granted. Assumptions are widely used in all human thinking and **discourse** and we can say little without making some assumptions. Assumptions are formed in **decision making** (where it is impossible to account for all the uncertainties or background factors affecting a particular decision), in model construction (as in Weber's ideal type **bureaucracy**) and in general argument and theorizing. Some assumptions are integral parts of **culture**, for example 'people marry for love', or 'people work for money'. These assumptions may be widely shared by people, enhancing their **communication**, which becomes very stilted when all assumptions have to be checked out. By contrast, members of different departments in the same organization may make different assumptions about the organization's priorities or **goals**. While assumptions are an inevitable part of thinking and knowing, they can also have dangerous consequences; and may lead to unpredictable or even catastrophic results. The assumptions that people and groups make are sometimes referred to as their 'world taken for granted'. Economists have a reputation for working from particularly massive and improbable assumptions, e.g. 'let us assume perfect competition'.

attitude
Attitude is a tendency to respond to people, objects, ideas or events in particular ways. Attitudes have traditionally been regarded as comprising components of **cognition**, **emotion** and tendencies to action. Katz and Kahn studied why all people seem to need to have attitudes and concluded that they served four functions: they help people adapt to what is around them; they enable people to feel superior to others; they are a way of expressing values; and they help people form some sort of order out of the world. **Prejudice** is an example of attitude and has inspired much of the research on attitudes and attitude change. It has been found that the effectiveness of attempts to change attitudes depends on: the perceived status and probity of the person communicating the change message; whether a conclusion is

drawn; whether both sides of the argument are put; and which is put first. One theory of atti-tude change is 'cognitive dissonance'. Recent work on attitudes has emphasized their func-tion in bracketing out threatening questions about ourselves. It has also becoming increasingly popular to argue that attitudes emerge through discourse rather than that they exist independently in the mind of the person.

(Giddens, 1991; Katz and Kahn, 1978; Potter and Wetherell, 1987)
See also prejudice

attribution

Attributions are the way that we perceive causality. An attribution is a belief about the cause or causes of an event or an action. Many events have several contributory causes. Different people will attribute causes differently, particularly when talking about complex social phenomena like those involved in organizing. If John gets angry with Jane, he may attribute his anger to Jane's unreason-able behaviour, Jane may attribute it to John's sexism, an observer may attribute it to the fact that John is always getting angry, another may attribute it to Jane winding John up, while another may attribute it to the way that John was brought up. Attribution theory (Kelley, 1972) is an attempt to bring about a systematic understanding of the way in which people attribute causes to events. Many political acts in organizations centre around attribution; how do I get my colleagues to attribute the success of this action to me, and not to attribute the failure of that project to me? To what do I attribute the fall in sales – staff incompetence, poor training or market conditions beyond our control? Attribution thus becomes one of the critical components in how people make sense of their situations, and is crucial to problem construction and decision making. It is the core process of human judgement and is thus involved in almost every topic considered in this book.

(Huczynski and Buchanan, 2004)

authenticity

To be authentic commonly signals that a person is being their true self – genuine, honest. Authenticity is the lynchpin of a humanistic perspective on organizations, where openness and honesty are encouraged. Authenticity in the workplace is, however, an ideal which often fails to square with an organization's expectations of what kind of self is to be presented. It is frequently important to be skilled at impression management, disguising 'true' feelings in order to assist social transactions, sustain a bond or trust, conduct a negotiation, sell a product, mask anger and so forth. Not showing what we genuinely feel is an essential ingredient of organizing. Organizations where 'smiling' customer service is prevalent have exploited this phenomenon, requiring emo-tional labour from their staff to ensure that that smile remains intact. It is the employer's brand of authenticity that dominates, sometimes at considerable personal cost to the employee. A postmod-ern perspective challenges the humanistic view that there is a single 'inner core'. Rather, we can have many authenticities, each attached to the different roles we play in life and the various iden-tities we assume. All are valid and all are real and all can feel authentic.

(Boltanski and Chiapello, 2005; Erickson, 1995; Morgan and Averill, 1992; Taylor, 1991)

authoritarianism and authoritarian personality

Some people are more prone than others to believe that those in authority should be obeyed unques-tioningly because of their position. Others would emphasize other bases of power, such as expertise or charisma. Research on the authoritarian personality suggests that authoritarians tend to be mild and deferential with more powerful figures and relatively imposing and inconsiderate with subor-dinates. Authoritarians tend to take structures and hierarchies very seriously, they like order and predictability and tend to be rigid and intolerant. The seminal research by Adorno and colleagues linked the authoritarian personality with prejudice, notably with anti-Semitic and racist attitudes.

After the Second World War, an understanding of obedience to authority was felt to be urgently needed so as to understand how so much tragic obedience could have taken place and to consider what could be done to prevent such a thing happening again. The concern became even greater when Milgram's experiments seemed to show just how easy it was to get American college students to obey frighteningly brutal orders.

There seem to be some conditions which are conducive to authoritarianism. For example, in times of widespread anxiety and confusion, there may be an attraction to anyone who offers 'strong **leadership**'. This has been observable at national level many times in different parts of the world several times since the Second World War. A similar phenomenon can be seen in organizations that are in trouble, where the search for a strong leader becomes paramount.

(Adorno et al., 1950; Lipman-Blumen, 2005; Milgram, 1974; Ray, 1990)

authority

Authority is a concept generally identified with legitimate **power**, or an unequal relationship in which the right of the superior party to give orders to others is recognized by the subordinate as legitimate. Weber (1864–1920) elaborated on Machiavelli's view that people obey orders either for fear or for love; he distinguished between coercion when the superior's orders are obeyed unwillingly by the subordinate because of fear, and authority (or domination) in which the orders are obeyed willingly. He then identified three sources of authority: charisma, tradition and a rational system of **rules**. Charismatic authority is based on the extraordinary qualities of the **leader** which command unconditional respect and loyalty. Traditional authority is based on the sanction of custom and practice; the leader is seen as the rightful heir of old lines of authority. In both of these, personal and emotional commitment to the leader are central to the legitimation process. Weber's third type of authority is rational–legal authority based on a system of rules which command respect because of their **rationality**. Orders are obeyed in as much as they are consistent with these rules. Unlike the previous two types, rational–legal authority is based on calculation rather than **emotion** and is **impersonal**, i.e. it does not stem from the person but from the position which the person occupies. Weber saw charismatic leadership as essentially unpredictable and turbulent and argued that there is a gradual shift towards the rational–legal type; he referred to this process as **rationalization** and identified its principal **institution** as **bureaucracy**. Most contemporary organizations involve combinations of all three types of authority as well as a variable measure of coercion and force. Authority is rarely uncontested. Even when it appears to be legitimate, it may be tested, qualified or challenged. Resistance can take active or passive forms, individual or collective forms, overt or covert forms and may range from strikes, absenteeism and sabotage to disobedience, ritualism, cynicism or sheer bloody-mindedness.

Over long periods of time, patterns of authority in society change. In traditional societies, authority associated with long-standing religious, political and civic institutions was dominant. The rise of modernity brought with it new forms of authority based on knowledge and on positions. This coincided with the rise of science and rationality, which were seen as displacing traditional beliefs and practices. More recently, the unquestioned power of science has been contested. Post-structuralists, like Michel Foucault (1980), have argued that power and knowledge form an indissoluble entity which he refers to as power/knowledge. It is not as if a set of ideas is scientific and therefore commands authority; rather, various practices and discourses at the same time assume scientific standing and command authority. More generally, post-structuralist thinking has refused to acknowledge a difference between authority and power, and has sought to identify the way that power operates through discourses, the way that words and phrases are used. For example, if the term 'dyslexic' is accepted as a scientific description of a particular condition, a person previously categorized as dull or unintelligent gets treated differently. He or she is no longer excluded from various activities, like going to university or becoming a physicist. The 'discourse of dyslexia' enables this person to claim authority that they would not have had without it. The opposite happens if a person is classified as 'mad', or, until the 1960s in many countries, as 'homosexual'. These conditions are seen as 'pathological' and a person described by them is excluded from many of the privileges and rights available to others.

Another significant development since the high point of modernity is that the authority of science and experts is itself being increasingly questioned. It is questioned on account of numerous perceived failings of science, including disastrous experiments, accidents, food scares, blunders and miscalculations. Some of the challenges to science are raised by religion; however, a different challenge to expertise comes from everyday experience. While science reigned supreme, it overrode any claims to genuine insight offered by experience. You may suffer from diabetes, but science will tell you how to deal with it; your child is at risk of contracting rubella, but science will offer you the vaccine to immunize her. Increasingly, however, the authority of science is supplanted by the authority of the person who has had a personal experience. Thus, sufferers from asthma or back pain are as likely to consult other sufferers (through the internet or patient support groups) and resort to complementary or alternative medicine, than resort to what they perceive as ineffective or toxic medication provided by their doctors. This juxtaposition between the voice of first-hand, personal experience and the voice of scientific expertise is played out today in many fields, including medicine, law, history, therapy and education.

(Foucault, 1980; Gabriel, 2004a, b; Mouzelis, 1975; Weber, 1946)
See also **power**

autopoiesis
This is a biological concept (whose inventors, Maturana and Varela, said it should only be applied to biological systems) about the way in which a system can produce itself. The way in which blood cells in an organism are produced does not seem to come from outside the organism, but rather to be something holistically generated by the cell. Autopoietic systems reproduce in the same way as they were themselves produced and thus are self-referential. Autopoietic views of organizations imply that organizations produce themselves and reproduce themselves, rather than needing or responding to mechanistic attempts to influence them in particular ways. Such views de-emphasize the **environment** and see change as being generated and controlled within the organization itself.

(Maturana and Varela, 1980)
See also **actor-network theory**

benchmarking
Benchmarking is the process of creating a norm of **achievement** and then measuring people or organizations against it. It is often difficult for people in organizations to know how well they are doing. Since most events are the results of complicated constellations of causes, and because there are so many different views of what constitutes success (profit? Share price? Long-term survival? Happiness of customers? Happiness of staff? Innovativeness of products? Contribution to society?), there are many choices to be made about what might be needed to achieve success and how one might know whether they have achieved it.

Benchmarking often consists of trying to find some organization similar to that being benchmarked and then working out one or several dimensions on which they can be compared with each other. This is the core difficulty in the process: which dimensions make different organizations similar enough to give a worthwhile benchmark, and which dimensions are different enough to be worth comparing. Each of the criteria considered for benchmarking may sound objective but the choice between them is definitely subjective. Thus, benchmarking is always subjective, however objective the results are made to look at the end. So, if we are considering a taxi company in a medium-sized town, we might consider benchmarking it against taxi companies in other, similarly sized towns. We might ask for their cooperation in comparing the organizations in terms of the size of their fleet, wage rates, profit, vehicle breakdown, average time responding to calls, average bookings per head of population and so on. Which criteria we actually choose for benchmarking will strongly affect how good the company looks, and the choice is often a matter of **politics**.

This creates particular problems when the benchmark is used as a performance criterion against which the organization and its managers are judged. Hospitals in the UK have been benchmarked on the length of time patients spend on the waiting list for operations. To many outside the sector, this sounds like a sensible way of measuring the performance and controlling the activities of hospital staff. But for managers and doctors in the hospital, this may encourage them not to put patients on the waiting list in the first place or to schedule many small operations rather than fewer big ones, regardless of clinical urgency. These are activities which affect the benchmark but not the performance. If benchmarks become oppressive, people will find ways of subverting them.

blame culture

Blame culture is a phrase for the situation in an organization when the desire to blame others for doing things which are seen as wrong dominates. When serious mistakes occur, it may be important to examine, as impartially as possible, what has happened and to ask what can be done to prevent the same thing happening again. Within a blame culture, however, rather than trying to make an assessment of all the factors that may have contributed to a problem, some people immediately try to ensure that the blame is laid at someone else's door. If they suspect that there was something they could have done to prevent the mistake, they are even more likely to try to make the blame stick to someone else.

A recent manifestation of blame culture has been the fashion for 'naming and shaming'. The rhetoric to support this has been that people should not be able to escape the consequences of their bad or ineffective behaviours. In recent years, in the name of making people take responsibility for their actions, the British government has 'named and shamed' local government departments that have performed poorly against the central government's **benchmarks**, hospitals that are regarded as having excessively long waiting lists or schools whose children perform poorly against national norms. The practical consequence of this has been that local government is blamed for not having anticipated changes in central government policy, hospitals are blamed for not undertaking cynical manipulation of waiting list statistics and schools are named and shamed for serving socially deprived areas.

People learn from reflecting on their mistakes, often in conversation with others. With some activities, such as brain surgery or piloting an aircraft, it is essential to get things right first time. For many organizational activities, however, there may well be opportunities for learning when things go wrong, and it is more productive for people to be able to acknowledge that there was a mistake from which they can learn, rather than to look for a **scapegoat**. For someone working in a blame culture, it may be dangerous to own up to mistakes. Managers in the fiercest of such cultures may find themselves re-defining the outcome of all their actions as successes, even to themselves. This is damaging both for the individual learning of the manager, and for the organizational learning within that organization. It is very difficult to achieve organizational learning when a 'right first time' approach either causes people to claim that whatever they did was right or causes blame to be substituted for a serious learning conversation about what went wrong and about what can be learned.

blaming the victim

There are two contrasting positions on the causes of personal difficulties in organizations. One is that the problem lies with the individual. For example, **stress** can be seen as resulting from a neurotic personality or lack of ability to cope with pressures; or **bullying** as a product of an aggressive and insecure childhood. The second perspective takes these explanations as misleading. They blame the victim for problems which are not of his or her making. The source of the difficulties lies in the social conditions of work. These may, for example, be over-burdensome demands, unreasonable working hours, poor pay, a macho organizational culture, oppressive leadership or an unresponsive human resource department. Often, trade unions will highlight the organizational conditions that require attention, while management tend towards individualizing the problem, blaming what the union sees as the victim. The victim may then be offered support, such as counselling, stress-management advice, sick leave or a change of job. More punitively, the victim might be deemed incurable and dismissed from the organization. He or she then also becomes a **scapegoat** for the organization's ills.

(Ryan, 1972)

body language
Body language is a crucial form of interpersonal communication, comprising the non-verbal signals we send and receive about feelings, attitudes, intentions and beliefs. They include posture and limb movement (kinesics); touch; eye contact and dilation (occulesics); facial expressions and distance (proxemics). Of facial expressions, there are extensive cues which indicate feeling, especially around the mouth region, such as the position of the tongue, grinning, yawning, sneering, tight or trembling lips.

The meaning of body language varies culturally and sub-culturally. Arab, Latin and British cultures, for example, have different physical distances between people in normal conversations. Transgressing such distances can be seen as invading the other's personal space. In Western cultures, defensiveness is often indicated by a rigid, closed posture, frowning and pursed lips. Enthusiasm is suggested by eyes wide and alert, a small inward smile and erect body posture. People vary in their skills at reading body language. Jobs requiring a high degree of sensitivity to others' behaviour, such as social work, law, policing, medicine, psychotherapy and management, often contain training on how to interpret body language. On the other side of the coin, there is advice on how to use one's body language to one's personal advantage to disguise feelings and/or enhance a message. For instance, when going to a job interview, 'lean forward to show interest, keep regular eye contact and use open-handed gestures to convey sincerity'. As most professional actors know, body language can be used to convincing effect. It is not uncommon for high-profile leaders to be coached in the fine nuances of body language to enhance their persuasiveness.

(Kharbanda and Stallworthy, 1991; Pease, 1997)

boundaries
Boundaries have always been seen as crucial qualities of human societies, groups and organizations, especially when studied as social **systems** (Katz and Kahn, 1978). One of a system's fundamental qualities is a boundary which separates it from its environment. Some organizational boundaries are physical (such as perimeter fences patrolled by guards and security cameras, the walls of a building or areas requiring security passes and keys to enter), but also legal, social, psychological, informational and moral ones. In this sense, organizations have throughputs, such as people, resources, knowledge and information, products and services, waste and by-products which continuously cross their boundaries. Some of these crossings are legitimate and controlled, while others may be clandestine or illegal, for instance when employees pilfer resources from the organization for their own private use or when intruders make their way into an organization's centre and get away with its secrets or resources. In all these respects, organizations may be thought of as walled cities, at times transacting openly with their neighbours, at others closing their gates under siege. Boundaries are patrolled, controlled, surveyed, opened carefully at times, violated at times, re-drawn and re-negotiated.

These conceptualizations of boundaries approach them essentially as defensive phenomena: boundaries protect individuals, groups and organizations from intruders and are vital in maintaining order and regularity. Recently, these views have come under some criticism. **Social constructionism** has challenged the view that separates a system from its environment for accepting unproblematically the existence of objective boundaries. Instead, social constructionist theorists argue that boundaries, along with many other social phenomena, are negotiated, maintained, dissolved and re-drawn through social interaction. According to this view, boundaries are not given or objective. Individuals have a degree of choice on how they place them or whether they place them at all. Another criticism of conventional views of boundaries comes from **complexity and chaos theory**. This approach has challenged the view of organizations as linear equilibrium systems, where small changes in the environment produce small changes in the organization and large changes in the environment produce correspondingly large changes in the organization. Instead, it proposes that most organizations operate in states of non-linear equilibrium, where small changes in a complex and unpredictable environment can have far-ranging and potentially catastrophic effects on organizations. In such an environment, organizations that fix their boundaries firmly and seek to defend them are liable to fail. Instead of having firm and well-defined boundaries, many organizations are increasingly viewed as having permeable, fuzzy or virtual boundaries, often blending with other organizations or with their wider environment which, at times, makes any distinctions between organizations and their environments meaningless.

bricolage

Bricolage is a French word meaning 'makeshift', or 'DIY' tinkering. This is a term that has found some interesting applications in describing the work of managers. Unlike an engineer, a bricoleur does not have a plan of what it is that he/she wishes to make and then go about finding the resources, tools and raw materials to make it. Instead, bricolage makes do with whatever resources are at hand, deploying them with imagination to achieve something useful, even if it is not exactly what would have been chosen. Some authors have argued that bricolage describes the work of most managers; this is ad hoc, improvisatory and makeshift. Managers survey their domains to assess what resources are available – tools, space, time, humanpower, skills, information, goodwill, raw materials and so on. They then deploy them in imaginative ways to achieve results that are good enough and make the most of the opportunities and constraints present. Such a view of management is quite different from that of **scientific management**, which sees managers proceeding with the cool and scientific efficiency of engineers, and much of strategic management, which views managers as making careful plans and deploying resources with the detached certainty of battlefield generals.

(Gabriel, 2002; Linstead and Grafton-Small, 1990; Weick, 2001a, c)
See also **improvisation**

buildings and architecture

Buildings, quite apart from facilitating or inhibiting organizational functioning, are also vital **symbols** of what organizations stand for, of what their chief corporate **values** are. At the functional level, organizational buildings allow and deter different types of interaction among organizational members. **Conflict**, collaboration and **control** within organizations are all shaped by spatial arrangements. A department split between two sites is liable to develop dual identities and cultures unless measures are taken to draw the two parts together. Two departments in adjoining parts of a building sharing some of the social spaces may work well together or, alternatively, may eye the other with suspicion lest they seek to infringe on their territory. Buildings define **boundaries** and act as controlling devices. In addition to such effects, organizational buildings create symbolic divisions and classifications. The size and siting of each office, its accessories and furnishings, act as significant **status** and **power** symbols of its occupants. Buildings themselves may come to symbolize the values of organizations, such as size, power, glamour and innovation.

Given the far-reaching functional and symbolic effects of organizational architecture and buildings, it is not surprising that physical re-location or even modest spatial re-structuring are frequently keenly contested political processes. Individuals and groups about to be relocated are liable to compare their new territory, its size, location and provisions with their previous one and with the territories of other reference groups. They may then fight for more or different resources or may seek to **resist** re-location altogether. Physical re-location is then a major dimension of organizational **change**, unleashing political forces of alliance building, conflict and resistance.

(Gagliardi, 1990a; Guillen, 1998; Gutman, 1972; Hatch, 1990)

bullying

Bullying at work has been identified as a pervasive phenomenon. It can inflict potent emotional injuries, its victims reporting insomnia, nervousness, depression, fear of social groups and **stress** diseases. Some commit suicide. The target of bullying is usually entangled in an escalating inter-personal conflict at work, where the bully's aim is to punish the victim through teasing, bad-gering and insults. Eventually, the victim feels helpless and unable to retaliate. Bullying is typically associated with differences in power and status where superiors are the main culprits. Victims appear to suffer more when exposed to bullying from their bosses than from their co-workers, but both are psychologically injurious. Group bullying, or mobbing, can be particu-larly powerful and pernicious where any feelings of guilt are diffused across the group and where group members collude to perpetuate a predatory 'game' at the victim's cost and pain.

Bullying can be understood from three different angles: the bully's, the victim's and the organizational culture's. Bullies often have been bullied themselves; their own insecurities are acted out at work by diminishing others. Some have been described as having narcissistic personalities, being deeply obsessed with themselves, wanting attention and being unable to appreciate other people's feelings. They can find an excuse to bully in any apparent difference in the target, such as in their being a novice, their skin colour, accent, gender, religion or education. Victims of bullying can, it is controversially argued, innocently contribute to the problem if they carry their own 'general anxiety disorder' and sense of guilt and worthlessness. The culture of the organization or workplace provides the social setting for bullying, where it may be quietly tolerated, ignored, even celebrated. Bullies are more likely to thrive in cultures where superiors and colleagues turn a blind eye, fearful of confrontation. In some work settings, such as the military, police and fire service, bullying and victimization can be an unofficial way of testing a new recruit, a **rite of passage**. To survive bullying makes one a worthy member of the workgroup. But, of course, not all survive.

(Adams and Crawford, 1992; Cox, 2001; Einarsen, 1999; Hoel and Beale, 2006)

bureaucracy

Bureaucracy is a form of administration conducted by appointed officials. The theory of bureau-cracy is one of the fundamental elements of the study of **organizations** and derives from the work of the German sociologist Max Weber (1864–1920). Contrary to its pejorative colloquial meaning as equivalent to red tape, slowness and inefficiency, Weber saw bureaucracy as the epitome of administrative **rationality**. He developed a model or 'ideal type' of bureaucracy based exclusively on the **assumption** of rational–legal **authority**. This type of authority is founded on a **rational** system of **rules** and regulations and is essentially **impersonal**. The ideal type of bureaucracy is a hypothetical organization involving no other type of authority or rela-tionship, no friendships or enmities, no informal cabals or cliques, no collegiate bodies or com-mittees, but merely individuals giving and receiving commands underpinned by a rational system of rules. Weber identified a number of defining characteristics of this type of bureau-cracy which include:

- a strict hierarchy of offices in which superior offices control lower ones
- the appointment of individuals to offices on the basis of their expertise, certified by written qualifications
- the conduct of each office on the basis of precise rules and regulations
- divorce of ownership from **control**, with **power** deriving entirely from the occupation of an office
- free contractual relationships between the organization and its officials
- written records of all-important transactions
- the complete separation of official activity from the private, personal and emotional life of the officials
- a system of promotion and careers based on a combination of seniority and achievement.

Weber argued that the ideal type of bureaucracy is a formidable tool of administration, its attrib-utes including precision, speed, unambiguity, discretion, subordination, no friction, economy, continuity and unity. While deploring the effects of bureaucracy on humanity, which he likened to an 'iron cage', Weber felt that organizations will inevitably move in the direction of his ideal type in search of greater efficiency. 'The decisive reason for the advance of bureaucratic organi-zation', he argued, 'has always been its purely technical superiority over any other form of orga-nization. The fully developed bureaucratic mechanism compares with other organizations exactly as does the machine with non-mechanical modes of production' (1946: 214). While Weber's bureaucracy has been criticized for a wide variety of reasons, it remains one of the foun-dations of organizational theory. Many of the criticisms have focused on his apparent disregard for the 'human factor' in organizational life. Weber would dismiss this and related criticisms for failing to appreciate the sheer magnitude of bureaucratic impersonality and for exaggerating the importance of the human factor. Another battery of criticisms have been directed at Weber's insis-tence that bureaucracy represents maximum administrative **rationality**; some of these criticisms too can be refuted by pointing out that they are directed at existing bureaucratic organizations rather than at the ideal type.

In recent times, bureaucracy has come under renewed criticism as a model of effective organization. In a highly volatile, changing world, where markets, technologies and political climates change rapidly, organizations which approximate the bureaucratic model are seen as too rigid to take advantage of opportunities and repel threats. They are doomed to be overtaken by leaner, more flexible organizations which have a greater ability to learn from experience and change their strategies and tactics accordingly. Some authors, however, have defended bureaucracy as a guarantee against management arbitrariness, narcissism and corruption.

(Boltanski and Chiapello, 2005; Courpasson and Reed, 2004; du Gay, 2000; Jaques, 1976; Kanter, 1983; Korczynski, 2004; Mayer, 1956; Mouzelis, 1975; Ritzer, 1993/1996; Walton, 2005; Weber, 1946, 1978)
See also **authority, contingency theories, environment, oligarchy**

burnout
People who have high expectations and strong ideals about what they can achieve in a job, espe-cially if it is one where they work with people in emotionally stressful circumstances, run the risk of burnout. The burned-out worker is exhausted and disillusioned by the constant frustration of failure: the social worker whose clients regress after many months of painstaking work; the doc-tor who finds he or she is unable to offer sufficient care to patients because of the unremitting workload; the new teacher whose fresh ideas quickly get rejected by pupils and colleagues; the manager whose initiatives are constantly queried. Such people can soon lose **motivation**, and their inspirational spark dies. The burned out become cynical about the very people they once cared about and will perform in a way which is only just about sufficient to get by. Burnout can be detected in many different occupations and can occur at any stage of **career**.

(Abrahamson, 2004; Maslach and Goldberg, 1998; Maslach and Leiter, 1997)

business process re-engineering
Business process re-engineering is a movement in management that began from the idea of focus-ing attention not on the workings of departments or people in an organization, but on the processes that must be achieved in order for a business transaction to be completed (Hammer and Champy, 1993). Rather than looking first at the organization and asking how it could be made to work better, it starts from asking what processes the business is trying to achieve and how, if it could start from nothing, it would best achieve them. The proponents of business process re-engineering have argued that modern control technologies mean that we can now organize much more efficiently according to the processes (or activities) that need to be achieved, rather than according to the functions that need to be contributed in order to achieve those processes.

Recent critiques of business process re-engineering suggest that it is an attempt to revive **scientific management**, without having resolved any of its problems. One of the maxims of business process re-engineering has been to remove all people and departments that do not directly contribute to the 'business process'. As one writer puts it: 'organizations dominated by images of "re-engineering" and "restructuring" are lured into reducing people and whole lives into machinery parts and mechanical functions' (Stein, 1998: 8). The objectivity implicit in the word 're-engineering' is perhaps the most misleading part of the concept, as if the human process involved in analysis was somehow irrelevant to discovering an underlying business process. Even the originators of business process re-engineering have recently admitted that they underestimated the 'people factor'.

While it is no more human in its approach, in other ways, business process re-engineering is the opposite of **scientific management**; it is seeking to put back together, as processes, what scientific management disaggregated into independent actions (Harrington, 1999). It re-integrates them through information technology, but that technology is not an innocent party. Someone has to use the information technology and make human decisions about where a process is deemed to begin or end and what other actions are relevant to it. Early demonstrations of cost saving by re-engineering now appear to have been mostly produced by defining too narrowly which staff and departments were needed to achieve the process. The costs of discarding all the other staff and departments often did not show until after the damage had been done.

(Hammer and Champy, 1993; Knights and McCabe,1998; McNulty, 2002)

capital

Capital is a pivotal term in modern economics, referring to the material wealth owned by a business enterprise, or more generally to any assets or resources that increase the wealth of an enterprise. This second definition now includes aspects of 'human' capital, that is, the wealth or potential inherent in the workers of an organization. The implication is that, like material capital, human capital should be valued and treated with care as the organization's prosperity depends on it. Human capital comprises *intellectual* and *emotional* capital. Intellectual capital is the investment that an organization has in the technical expertise, intelligence, specialist knowledge, skills and learning capacity of its employees. Ideally, these are to be nurtured through training, new learning opportunities, challenging work and promotion prospects. Emotional capital refers to the value of people's commitment to the organization, trust, loyalty, sense of satisfaction and reward. These, also, are not to be taken for granted, but fostered through honouring the **psychological contract** between employer and employed, and designing management policies that minimize alienation and uncaring leadership.

The idea of capital can be further broadened to include **cultural** and social capital. The concept of cultural capital was used extensively by French sociologist Pierre Bourdieu to account for persistent social inequalities based on tastes and lifestyles. He argued that people judge each other and create hierarchies of superiority and inferiority based on how sophisticated or 'cool' their tastes are – judging and criticizing people's tastes sustains social status distinctions (e.g. Bourdieu, 1984; Bourdieu and Johnson, 1993). Leading exponents of social capital theory have been James Coleman (1988) who viewed it as a resource facilitating individual or collective action, Nahapiet and Ghoshal (1998) who examined how it can lead to competitive advantage for organizations and, maybe most importantly, Robert Putnam (1995, 2000, 2002) who has viewed it as the central bulwark for maintaining democracy. Whether social capital is a value-neutral term or a normative one describing a desired state of affairs is strongly contested, but the term's adoption by the World Bank has offered ammunition to those who view it as an ideologically laden and theoretically barren concept that represents an attempt by economics to colonize the discourses of other social sciences (Fine, 2001).

career

Career, literally, refers to a pathway through life. Careers are the way in which people see their own story of themselves developing over time, through their understanding of who they are becoming through their working life. The notion of career may have been simpler in the past than it is now. In many companies, it used to be the case that an employee could map out their expected career in some detail from an early age. Now it is more likely that the employee will see their career not simply to do with their employment in one company. Even those who work for large companies may now work for several different employers during their working life. Interestingly, though, the prediction that we would all soon be engaged in 'itinerant' careers with rapid movement between employers and sectors was being made with confidence in the past, and has come about more slowly than anticipated.

The increased flexibility of employment of managers means that their careers are now much more like those of professionals. With less emphasis on loyalty between employer and employee, in both directions, managers are expected to be able to demonstrate their continuing employability to new employers during their working lives (Ellig, 1998; Finn, 2000). To do this, they will build up a picture of continually developing experience and skills, which may be summarized (or advertised) in their curriculum vitae. This document will often make the person's development and job moves sound far more orderly and purposeful than they felt at the time. This produces a story of one's career so that professional development and continuing learning can be clearly seen, and so that the person sounds as if they are in charge of their own life. This story can be more difficult for women who have taken a career break when their children were born. There are many models to follow when arguing that someone 'wanted a new challenge' or 'chose to broaden their experience', but there are no such **storytelling** conventions to help a woman explain that she wanted to have children without sounding less committed to her subsequent organizational career.

Not only do people now move more frequently between employers, but they are more likely than in the past to do work for more than one employer at a time. This leads to a 'portfolio career', where the person engages in a set of activities rather than in one job, and where it is recognized that they may shift their investment of time and effort between different parts of the portfolio as they go along.

The concept of 'career' has also been used extensively outside the workplace. Thus, people may speak of their careers in voluntary organizations, as criminals or as football fans. The experience of this becomes more complicated where careers intersect and some recent research has focused on the experience of dual-career couples.

(Arthur et al., 1999; Baruch, 2004; Fenton and Dermott, 2006; Grey, 1994; Han and Moen, 1999; McKinlay, 2002; Platman, 2004)

change

Change, and resistance to it, is an important part of organizational life. Not all change is deliberate, nor can it always be safely managed and controlled. Nevertheless, some change may be necessary for the economic survival of an enterprise, and very much in the interests of its owners and managers. However, others in the organization may **perceive** change as threatening their position, **status**, relationships, competence or security. It is for this reason that change is often accompanied by some **conflict**. Change within an organization may be seen to occur at two different levels. *First-order* change (the most common) concerns small adjustments to work methods, such as having more team meetings to solve a communication problem. *Second-order* change looks more deeply at the beliefs and **assumptions** behind existing work practices: why exactly are team members failing to communicate? Second-order change is about changing the way in which future changes take place. Change is often engineered by **consultants** who employ a bewildering array of techniques. They range from 'quick fix' first-order methods, such as intensive training for top **management** or the re-design of the organization's **structure**, to more profound second-order attempts to change the whole organization's **culture** through workshops, courses, counselling and employee-feedback questionnaires.

It is now common for organizations to employ specialists in change management or 'organizational development', an expertise which has developed over the past 20 years from our growing appreciation of how individuals and groups operate in organizations. Underpinning such efforts are different ways in which experts and managers construct the stimuli, or need, for change, such as something that they feel they are 'pushed towards' by 'global forces', 'competition' or 'cost reduction'. Other common reasons are for 'innovation' and 'renewal'. While some of these reasons may rest on sound economic bases, they can also disguise imposed changes which can disadvantage employees. They can favour the political ambitions of a small cadre of managers who wish to increase their power and profile in the organization. Change is not always for rational economic reasons and is often highly politicized – and emotionalized.

(Bartunek and Moch, 1987; Bent, 1999; Carr, 2001; Cummins and Worley, 2000; Townley, 2002; Watson, 2002; White, 2004)

charisma

Charisma is a term brought into social theory by Max Weber to the attraction, or social magnetism, that some people appear to exude. It originates from the Greek *kharis*, meaning 'grace'. In organizations, it is most often applied to particular, high-profile **leaders** (e.g. Alfred P. Sloan of General Motors, Lee Iacocca of Chrysler and Anita Roddick of The Body Shop). However, it could pertain equally to a small restaurant manager beloved by his staff or to a teacher who is constantly admired by her students. Charismatic leaders can create remarkable passion and loyalty among their followers and energize them to rally to the leader's cause for, supposedly, the wider benefit of the organization. They can engender devotion, love, piety and excitement. People are most willing to *attribute* charisma to a leader who voices their pains and urgent needs. In other words, charisma is likely to flourish in times of organizational crisis, when people are seeking reassurance, stability and a way out. Charisma, therefore, is context-bound, dependent upon the followers' needs as much as, if not more, on leaders' performance. For this reason, charisma rarely lasts. When needs are met, changed or betrayed, charisma can fade fast.

   Successful charismatic leaders have usually mastered the art of presenting themselves on stage and **body language**. They can perform with apparent conviction, setting out an attractive vision for their followers. Combined with skilful oratory, carefully nuanced gestures and metaphors and flattering props, they readily win converts. They are **emotional labourers**, knowing exactly what degree of enthusiasm, pathos, sincerity, joy or anger to project to win the hearts and minds of their audience. These behaviours have been 'packaged' by some management consultants who offer 'charisma training'. Some charismatics pursue a particular personal agenda, such as gaining power for a time to meet their own needs. They encourage followers' dependency, but their message rarely survives the setting that nourished them. Others are keener to **empower** their followers to take a direction that outlives the leader's tenure.

(Bryman, 1992; Conger and Kanungo, 1988; Fiol et al., 1999; Gardner and Avolio, 1998; Howell and Shamir, 2005; Lindholm, 1988)

class

Class is a foundational concept in sociology and, especially, in the theory of social stratification. Classes are large assemblies of people who share economic interests by virtue of their position in the production process and who may or may not be conscious of themselves as belonging together. Traditionally, capitalism has, according to Marx, been dominated by two large social classes: the capitalists who own the means of production and live off the profits from their investments and the working class (or proletariat) who sell their labour power in order to earn a living. Other social classes include land owners and landless peasants, independent shopkeepers and tradesmen (the 'petty-bourgeoisie'), an 'underclass' or 'lumpen proletariat' (which includes homeless people, the chronically unemployed, the sick, the criminal sections and people subsisting in the margins of society). Classes may themselves be sub-divided into fractions; thus, the working class may include both manual and non-manual workers, skilled and unskilled ones; the bourgeoisie may include both 'old money' and the nouveau riches.

   Academic discussions of social classes are extensive and include questions over the changing constitution and consciousness of social classes, the impact of alternative stratification principles (such as **status** and **power**, **gender**, **race** and sexual preference) and the extent to which class is an element of individual and group **identities**. Currently, the most important debates on class focus on whether it continues to be an important factor of social stratification or whether it has been supplanted by other factors, such as consumption and lifestyles, national, professional, organizational and other allegiances. In the past, class was meant to colour or even determine an individual's beliefs and values, political behaviour, educational achievement, choice of job and partner and so forth. This is no longer as pronounced, as social mobility generates movement across class boundaries and, possibly, as class itself becomes less and less relevant in **postmodernity**. In particular, it is argued that being working class is now more a self-perception or even a description of a lifestyle, and a fading one at that, rather than a social category of economic position. Class is seen as giving way to numerous groups and communities, sometimes referred to as 'neo-tribes' (Maffesoli, 1995), characterized by shared lifestyles and tastes, even if their economic positions are different. All the same, class has proven a remarkably resilient feature of people's self-identity and also of the judgements that they make about each other. Accents, clothes, body weight, tattoos, haircuts and so forth are easily seen as 'signifiers' of people's class or indeed as statements about individuals' class identity. It is possible that this subjective dimension of class has assumed greater importance than the Marxist 'objective' aspect.

One enduring problem concerns the class position of **managers**. These were traditionally seen as a class fraction adjunct to the bourgeoisie and representing its interests. The emergence of large-scale organizations, however, led to theories of 'divorce of ownership from control', which viewed managers as an independent social class with distinct social and economic interests from the capitalists. These theories have received new currency from views of managers as holders of exclusive professional **skills** and expertise which place them above the **controls** that owners are able to exercise. Undoubtedly, in one way, managers are employees and, therefore, workers. On the other hand, however, they enjoy considerable control and autonomy (some more than others) and their position in the process of production is often dominant rather than subordinate.

(Blackburn and Mann, 1979; Marx and Engels, 1848/1972; Sennett and Cobb, 1973; Wright, 1980)

cognition

Cognition is the activity of thinking. One way of looking at people and their actions is that there are: (a) cognitive aspects which may be thought of as the relatively cool, calculating parts of life; (b) affective or emotional aspects, which are full of feeling; and (c) connative aspects referring to the will to carry things through. In practice, the separation between different aspects of the human being is less clear and these divisions reflect poorly the thinking and being of humans as we know them. We know, from theories such as that of **cognitive dissonance**, that **emotions** can affect subsequent cognition. If you fall in love, your cognitive opinions about the person you love may be affected by this emotion, as well as your cognitions about other aspects of your world. Similarly, some writers have argued that there is a strong cognitive element in emotion, as emotion cannot be sustained without some thoughts to keep it going. 'She should not have said that to me' is the kind of sentence which a person repeats in their heads in order to stay angry, or sad. Even such activities as chess or laboratory research, which may appear purely cognitive to the outsider, are described as richly emotional by those who are really good at them. Cognitive approaches to organizations have often been characterized by an 'information processing' approach, where the computer is taken as the basic metaphor for understanding people. As with all such metaphors, this highlights some features such as **decision** processes, while placing little value on others, such as the emotion and unpredictability of organizational life.

(March, 1997)

cognitive dissonance

Cognitive dissonance is a theory about how **attitudes** change. If individuals behave in a way which is inconsistent with their attitudes, they have a feeling of dissonance between their attitudes and their behaviour. They may resolve this feeling by changing their attitudes to fit their behaviour, rather than changing their behaviour to fit their attitudes. So if someone cares deeply for the natural environment, but works for a company that they see as damaging it, they may be more likely to change their attitude and come to care less about the environment, rather than change their job or change the way their company behaves.

It is worth noting that there is nothing specifically 'cognitive' about cognitive dissonance: the sense of discomfort which goes with dissonance is a feeling, and the attitudes and behaviours that are dissonant have as much to do with emotion as they do with **cognition**.

(Festinger and Carlsmith, 1959)

commitment

Commitment is a term that has become central to thinking on human resource management to describe the attachment and loyalty of employees to their work and to their organization. Its popularization has increased the belief that high-commitment organizations are the ones most likely to survive. Management's task, therefore, is to engender employee commitment indirectly rather than use more coercive measures of control. The committed employee is expected to have greater motivation and higher performance and be less likely to go absent. Currently, the jury is out on these expectations. It is unclear whether high commitment does, in fact, work in this way, especially in circumstances where the de-skilling of jobs, surveillance and downsizing are on the increase, such as in call centres. In these settings, commitment to the actual work is likely to be low, although employers may try to offset these disadvantages with attractive fringe benefits and by creating carnivalesque diversions. Commitment to the job is more likely with professionals. However, this need not be specific to their organization. They can always take their skills elsewhere.

Commitment's sister concept is escalation of commitment. Escalation of commitment refers to the extent to which a person or group becomes tied to a course of action in the face of growing signs of failure. The investment of time, passion, money or self-esteem feel just too great to back off from. There is always the hope that just a little more commitment, just one more try, will pay off. Escalating commitment can be seen when more and more funds are invested into a failing business or project, such as London's Millennium Dome, started in 1997 and never successful, despite huge injections of public money. Key to sustaining commitment is the protection of reputations and egos: to stop the project and cut one's losses signals failure to self and others. High commitment insulates one from external criticism, a protective psychological bubble filtering out any bad or conflicting news. It is amplified in decision-making groups where group members can infect one another with their optimism and so reinforce the group's illusions. Escalated commitment has been shown to be behind major international decisions, such as the war in Iraq in 2003 and the USA's assault on Cuba in 1961.

(Boxall and Purcell, 2003; Brockner, 1992; Meyer and Allen, 1997; Walton, 1991)

communication

It has become almost a cliché in organizations to attribute all difficulties to communication. Communication may be verbal, that is, to do with the words used, or **non-verbal**. Some communication research has used an **information**-processing model, looking at inputs, outputs, 'noise' and numbers of channels. Leavitt looked at the effect of different communication networks on the performance of tasks and found that a star shape, where one central person can communicate with everybody else, is most effective for simple tasks, but the central person gets overloaded if the task is complex. All-channel communication, where anyone can talk to anyone, is slow but most effective for complex technical tasks. Should communication provide both sides of an argument to be persuasive? Should it make an appeal to people to act in a particular way if it is to affect what they do? What are the merits of one-way communication, like a lecture or a book, compared with those of two-way communication, like a discussion? Hovland and Janis, among others, have been studying these questions over the years. Much of the work is summarized by Clampitt. More recent work in communication has broadened into a whole field of 'communications studies', where the effects of different media of communication, different **cultural** contexts and so on have been considered more fully. There has also been much recent interest in electronic communication and its merits relative to face-to-face communication, as well as in the communication processes within virtual organizations (Weick, 1985).

(Clampitt, 1991; Fairhurst and Putnam, 2004; Gargiulo, 2005; Hovland et al., 1953; Janis, 1972; Leavitt, 1951; Phillips and Brown, 1993; Weick, 1985)

communities of practice

A community of practice is a **group** of people who share similar problems and have complementary skills and outlooks. They are mostly occupational groups, like airline managers, computer analysts and academics, but they can also refer to people sharing hobbies or interests, like plane spotters or amateur gardeners. Wenger (1998), one of the early adopters of the term, argues that such communities have histories and develop over time; they often work together, but their members do not have a shared task or agenda; they are not accountable to anyone outside of themselves; and they develop their own subcultures as their members learn from each other's experiences.

It is in connection to knowledge and learning that the idea of communities of practice has proven a useful concept (Cook and Yanow, 1993). Within such communities, the distinction between **knowledge** and **action** is diminished; knowledge becomes embedded in practices that are not the property of any one individual. Moreover, a great deal of this knowledge is not scientific; it cannot be codified into generalizable laws and formulas. Instead, it assumes the form of **narrative** knowledge, which includes stories, recipes and direct accounts of experience (Tsoukas, 1998). A great deal of this knowledge emerges through **bricolage** and is highly contextual (Brown and Duguid, 1991; Lave and Wenger, 1991). Two further features of this knowledge are worth pointing out. First, because members of these communities share interests and concerns, they communicate on the same wavelength and use a shared language; in this way, they are able to screen out irrelevant information or noise and can exchange ideas and experiences in a highly efficient, quick and economical manner; thus, some communities of practice can be a breeding ground for rapid **innovation** (Swan et al., 2002). The other important issue is collocation (being physically close together). While some communities of practice may operate on the internet, there are immense advantages to face-to-face exchanges. In some instances, like the rise of Silicon Valley, collocation proved the crucial factor – people's ability to communicate quickly and effectively in direct informal conversations, cutting out bureaucratic red tape and information overload. Where collocation is unrealistic or impossible, the getting together of communities of practice in conferences, symposia, workshops and festivals is vitally important for maintaining solidarity among members and also for facilitating the exchange of knowledge.

(Brown and Duguid, 1991; Handley et al., 2006; Wenger, 1998)

competences

Recent moves towards establishing whether **management** development programmes were good value for money, and towards trying to develop a qualification for the **profession** of management, led to questions about what managers actually needed to be able to do. What competences did they need to have? It seemed that in law or medicine, the competences which you would expect of the professional were clear and the same could be expected of managers. In a pioneering work, Mintzberg argued that management competences fall into three broad categories: interpersonal, informational and decisional. Others have questioned the validity of trying to establish management competences on three grounds. Firstly, management is not one activity but is different in different organizations, for different functions in the organization and under different economic and social conditions. All of these will make a difference to the competences required. Secondly, it may be that the mixture of competences, and the ability to make use of others' competences, is more important than the manager's own competence. Thirdly, management writers have not agreed sufficiently among themselves about how to describe particular activities or the competences required for them. The labels are not yet well enough developed; to speak of 'competences' sounds as if we all know what 'effective communication' or some such phrase means and this can be misleading.

The concept of 'core competence' refers to 'the collective learning in the organization, especially how to coordinate diverse production skills and integrate multiple streams of technologies … Core competence is also about the organization of work and the delivery of value' (Prahalad and Hamel, 1990). In contrast to earlier emphasis on diversification and integration, throughout the 1990s, it became fashionable for organizations to focus on their core competences and seek to outsource or subcontract other operations.

(Boyatzis et al., 2000; Cherniss, 2000; Mangham and Pye, 1991; Mintzberg, 1973)

competition

Competition is a form of conflict in which different parties are vying for the same resources or rewards, while usually agreeing to abide by a set of **rules**. Economic competition between buyers and sellers of commodities is the principal foundation of capitalist markets. Free market advocates argue that competition ensures the efficient matching of supply and demand for goods and services and acts as a stimulus for efficiency and innovation. Its critics point out that competition frequently leads to duplication of effort, disregards the wider social and environmental welfare and leads to a preoccupation with short-term profit at the expense of long-term planning. In organizational studies, competition among departments has been identified as one of the dysfunctions of **bureaucracy**, although some writers will distinguish between 'healthy' and 'unhealthy' competition, suggesting that some degrees of competition are energizing and productive while others are not. For example, Handy notes that argument, competition and conflict are types of *difference*; argument and competition which is perceived to be open and fair are beneficial for the organization, while closed competition and conflict are damaging. Kanter has observed that internal competition, such as between research teams researching the same product, can act as a stimulant to entrepreneurship.

While competition has been seen as an unquestioned **value** in capitalist economies on the grounds of spawning **innovation**, economic efficiency and improved standards of living, the **complexity** of contemporary economies and ventures often call for cooperation and partnerships among firms. **Networks** and partnerships of firms represent such cooperative business arrangements which have attracted increasing emphasis in recent years.

(Grey and Garsten, 2001; Handy, 1976; Huxham, 1996; Kanter, 1983; Porter, 1985)

competitiveness

Competitiveness is an **attitude** that predisposes to **competition**. This concept is used both organizationally and individually. For an organization, the issue may be how to gain more sales, a better reputation or higher profits than other organizations in the same sector. For individuals, competitiveness may mean trying to outshine their colleagues and catch the eye of those in authority. At both levels, it is currently generally assumed to be a good thing, reflecting a particular ideological position on how to succeed in business or even in life. But this needs to be questioned. In some industries (e.g. engineering in the UK), the competitiveness of different companies can mean that none of them generate sufficient profit to finance research or to pay sufficiently high salaries to encourage talented people to enter their profession. At the individual level, competitiveness may lead to a lack of cooperation, secrecy and even sabotage. Paradoxically, effective competition usually requires a high degree of cooperation among the participants.

(Huxham, 1996)

complexity and chaos theories

Complexity and chaos theories emerged in the natural sciences in the 1960s, drawing on the study of non-linear dynamic systems, such as the weather or turbulent flow of fluids. These are situations where there is vital randomness and unpredictability; they are situations which defy domestication within linear mathematical equations. Since its beginnings, complexity theory has found applications in the natural and biological sciences, ranging from the study of volcanoes and earthquakes to the study of the heart and the brain. More recently, it has found some applications in human sciences, in demography, geography and economics. In the last 15 years, complexity theory has started to penetrate organizational and management studies beyond the level of the fashionable cliché, generating some promising ideas.

Complex systems have a number of interesting properties. First, self-similarity across scales, illustrated by Mandelbrot's work on fractals, implies that as one 'zooms' in or out of a system, one encounters similar patterns. In organizations, one can imagine encountering the same patterns of authoritarian or paranoid **leadership** at the highest as well as at the lowest levels. A second property of complex systems is the incidence of the unexpected consequences of small changes: in Lorenz's famous 'butterfly effect', a butterfly flapping its wings in Peking today may cause a storm in New York in the future. Tiny differences in initial conditions lead to radically different outcomes for complex systems, just as two leaves blown by an autumn breeze may start from virtually the same position and end up miles apart. This accords complex systems two important characteristics: such systems are not time reversible, i.e. they do not return periodically to their original state and, within them, the same cause results in different effects, i.e. a cause–effect link observed once cannot be repeated. Complex systems are characterized by a vital unpredictability, making long-term prediction impossible, both in theory and in practice. A third property of complex systems is self-organization, a chance but not uncommon ability of complex systems to break out of a disorderly pattern into a spontaneous and unexpected order. Self-organization does not mean that the system has lapsed from complex to stable equilibrium, since it is not achieved with the help of damping feedback; instead, it generates what have been described as 'islands of order from the sea of chaos'. These islands are subject to the earlier two properties of complex systems; neither their scale nor their duration may be predicted – a butterfly flapping its wings may lead to their disappearance or re-appearance.

In recent years, complexity and chaos theories have moved in distinct ways: chaos theory looks at complex and often unpredictable patterns that emerge from the interaction of relatively simple elements or principles (like the flight of a flock of birds), whereas complexity theory has concentrated on elaborate systems (like the human mind or the global environment) which involve many interacting components and many different principles at work. Complex systems are not the same as complicated ones (e.g. a computer). The former entail a vital unpredictability and openness and cannot be reduced to an expression of relatively simple rules. Applications of complexity theory on organizations have emphasized the limited nature of managerial **control** in the absence of accurate, long-term forecasts, the precarious nature of order, the importance of self-organization (i.e. of control without anyone being in control) and the general hit-and-miss quality of most managerial interventions. It is still too early to know whether complexity theory will have a lasting impact on the study of organizations or will prove a temporary fad. All the same, it is one of the theories that is forcing scholars to re-consider what is meant by the term **organization** itself.

(Cilliers, 1998; Gleick, 1987; Griffin et al., 1998; Mandelbrot, 1982; Stacey, 1992, 1995; Thietart and Forgues, 1995)

conflict

Conflict is common to virtually all organizations and is especially acute in periods of **change**. It may be felt within oneself; it can occur between individuals; it can happen between different departments or between different levels in an organization. Conflict may be constructive or damaging, depending on whose interests are being served and the situation in which it occurs. Some features of conflict are institutionalized and routinized, such as in wage bargaining and union–management relationships. Others are less formalized and rooted in apparent differences, such as gender, status, education or ethnicity. Conflict can be productive in stimulating **change** and innovation. It can force organizations to address chronic inefficiencies and dysfunctions. Otherwise, it is likely to be damaging. The last person to mobilize in a conflict is usually at a disadvantage, so many conflicts arise because people want to 'launch' a pre-emptive strike. Schein says that during a conflict, groups close ranks against the enemy; members of the conflicting groups listen out for negative information about the other group; the winners tend to become complacent and stop working; the losers become more tense and either learn a lesson or turn on each other. Pondy suggests five stages of conflict: *latent*, where the background conditions for conflict exist; *perceived*, where the individuals or groups concerned know that there is a conflict but nothing has been publicly declared; *felt*, where one or more parties feel tense or anxious; *manifest*, where there is observable behaviour designed to frustrate others' attempts to achieve their goals; and the *aftermath*, which is the relationship between the parties after the conflict has been resolved or suppressed.

(Pondy, 1967; Schein, 1980; Waldron et al., 1993)
See also **aggression, competition, institutionalization, politics, power**

conformity

There are classic psychological experiments which powerfully demonstrate that people are prepared to disbelieve the evidence of their own eyes in order to come into line with the views or behaviours of other people. We conform to social pressures because of the discomfort and embarrassment of looking different or standing out from the crowd. We gain comfort and security from feeling we belong, so we often suppress some of our individuality in order to be accepted by the group. Through this, **group norms** and **values** grow which regulate group conduct. Paradoxically, many groups will also tolerate some non-conformists, perhaps one or two people who are allowed to be eccentric, like the traditional fool or jester. The non-conformist offers an emotional release for the group's worries and uncertainties; he or she is also given licence to criticize the group. Organizational **rules**, **hierarchies** and **bureaucracy** are features of formal, managerial **structures** designed to bring about a measure of conformity in work behaviour. However, the more restrictive these are, the greater the likelihood of loyalty and conformity to the informal **organization** with its particular freedoms and satisfactions.

(Buchanan and Huczynski, 2004)

construct and construing

While the noun 'construct' is sometimes used within organization studies to mean almost any idea, we shall consider a more technical meaning of it here. Within Kelly's 'personal construct theory', a construct is composed of a pair of psychologically opposite words or phrases which together describe a dimension in a person's thinking. Thus, 'bright/stupid', 'attractive/unattractive', 'like me/not like me' might be constructs. Kelly used repertory grids, among other methods, to discover personal constructs. The word 'personal' betokens the fact that we all have different constructs, which taken together are as personal as a fingerprint. A construct is not simply a verbal tag, according to Kelly, but goes deeper than that in our thinking. Constructs are personal not only in the words that describe the constructs, but also in the way those constructs are organized. Within one person's own construct system, 'bright/stupid' might be linked with 'employable/would not want to employ', whereas within another's, it might be linked with 'competitive/not a threat'. It is also possible for two people to have constructs with the same first word or phrase but different second words or phrases; for one person, the opposite of 'bright' might be 'stupid', while for another the opposite might be 'quiet'. As Kelly put it: the second pole of a construct is a psychological opposite, not necessarily a logical opposite. That is, it is an opposite in the thinking of a particular person, whether or not it seems sensible to someone else.

(Bannister and Fransella, 1971; Dalton and Dunnett, 1992; Kelly, 1972)

consultants and clients

In recent years, management consultancy has grown into a major industry, and at the same time, the term has changed its meaning. A consultant is a person who is contracted to work for a client company on a specific project or activity, and usually for a specified time, as opposed to an employee who may assume that his or her loyalty and **career** are with the company. Consultants are usually hired to do some specialized work which either requires a specific **skill** or expertise which is not available in the company, or requires more time than any appropriate specialist already employed can give it. Some companies which are trying to reduce the number of full-time staff, or do not want to risk the potential cost of making a specialist redundant later, hire consultants as and when needed. Some organizations employ 'internal consultants', people operating as advisers or specialists from within the organization and sometimes acting as intermediaries for external consultants. In recent years, resentment has grown towards consultants from some employees: 'they come in, borrow your watch, tell you the time, walk off with the watch, and charge you for it'. 'You know they have arrived, because their Porsches are parked in your reserved bicycle space!' However, consultancy services have grown as part of the tendency in recent years to outsource activities that are not seen as being part of the core business process. It is also the case that as companies have downsized, making many senior and middle managers redundant, they have been forced to assign their functions to those same managers, working on consulting contracts. Consultants often act as disseminators or diffusers of management **knowledge** from business schools to private and public organizations. They are sometimes accused of being responsible for the endless circulation and resuscitation of management fads and fashions, although the logic of borrowing or imitating is one that pervades much contemporary management.

(Abrahamson, 1991; Currie, 1999; Eden et al., 1983; McLean et al., 1982; Sturdy, 1997)

consumers, consumption and consumerism

Human beings (in common with other living organisms) consume: air, water and nutrients are all necessary for life. Humans also consume objects, services and ideas for pleasure, for meaning and for spiritual and emotional sustenance. Every society involves distinct types of production (hunting and gathering, agriculture, manufacturing) but also distinct types of consumption (food preparation, clothing, accommodation, artistic artefacts, music, stories and myths and so on). The twentieth century saw the emergence of 'mass consumption', the quest by ever-widening masses of population for a better life through the consumption of more and better goods and services. During that century, consumption for survival was overtaken by consumption for enjoyment, for identity and for self-growth, at least in large segments of the industrialized countries. Mass consumption emerged as the corollary of mass production: the supply of ever-more, cheaper and more novel products and services to ever-wider groups of people geared not to physical survival but to social and personal well-being.

Towards the end of the twentieth century, mass consumption underwent a further transformation. New technologies along with standards of living permitted an increasing proliferation of alternative products and services which allowed, or even required, consumers to exercise ever-increasing choice in when and how they spent their money. Thus, mass consumption was gradually replaced by a more generalized culture of consumerism. In such a culture, individuals and groups seek to enhance their lives with **meaning**, experiment with and develop their **identities**, and discover a sense of belonging and success not through **work**, but through their patterns of consumption, their tastes or, more generally, their lifestyles. Consumption becomes the great and problematic source of meaning in many accounts of postmodernity.

This has had quite a pronounced effect on the way organizations are conceptualized and managed. The consumer is no longer seen as an 'outsider' to the world of organizations, but very much an insider, whose desires, caprices and fantasies provide an organization's lifeline towards profitability and survival. Organizations dedicate ingenuity, innovation and resources not merely to devising quicker and cheaper ways of producing standardized outputs, but to imagining original, creative and expensive ways of enticing consumers to diverse outputs. Furthermore, they take the utmost care and attention in ensuring that employees who come in direct contact with consumers project the right organizational image to ensure customer satisfaction and loyalty. Customer service becomes as important as providing reliable products at competitive prices. As a result, the demands on employees have changed. The display of an attractive personality and the right emotional attitude becomes a vital 'front' of the organization, as employees are increasingly required to perform **emotional labour** in addition to physical and intellectual labour. Some organizational theorists have noted the increasing prevalence of internal organizational **markets** and quasi-markets, which encourage organizational participants to relate to members in other departments and units, not as colleagues but as internal consumers and providers.

(Baudrillard, 1970/1988; Bauman, 1992; du Gay, 1996a; Featherstone, 1991; Ferlie et al., 1996; Frenkel et al., 1999; Gabriel and Lang, 1995; Korczynski et al., 2000)

contingency theories

Two types of theories are referred to as contingency theories: theories of organizational **structure** and theories of **leadership**. Contingency theory grew out of an impatience with classical management approaches which seemed to prescribe universal solutions to all **management problems**, irrespective of different local circumstances. For example, Burns and Stalker argued that Weber's ideal type of bureaucracy does not represent an ideal structure for all types of real **organizations**. A structure which may serve one organization well may turn into a recipe for disaster when forced on another. Burns and Stalker pointed out that organizational **environment** affects the type of organizational **structure** most likely to be adopted by successful organizations. Woodward argued that optimal structures were contingent on the production **technologies** employed by different companies. Other researchers have noted that optimal organizational structure is contingent on the size of the company. Contingency theories of **leadership** argue that no single leadership style is effective in all circumstances, but that leadership styles are contingent on the organizational and situational context. Fiedler has developed a technique aimed at assisting leaders in their diagnoses of this context and enabling them to adopt a style which is likely to prove effective. Contingency theories are now often contrasted with **institutional theories**.

(Burns and Stalker, 1961; Fiedler, 1967; Woodward, 1965)

control

Control has long been seen as one of the central features of organizations and one of the main functions of **management**. Controlling resources and outputs, controlling processes and machinery, controlling information and the environment, are all part and parcel of organizational life. In particular, organizations control individuals to ensure reliable, predictable and consistent performance or organizational **roles**. This involves the monitoring of performance, its assessment against some stated standards, provision of feedback, rewards and sanctions. Examination procedures, **performance appraisals** and organizational audits are all control mechanisms aimed at ensuring that certain standards of individual and organizational performance are achieved. Physical violence was the main control mechanism of slave-drivers. In some early capitalist factories, workers were physically chained to their benches, as a way of ensuring that they put in the required number of work hours. Later, more discreet forms of control emerged. **Rules** and regulations gradually became the foundation of **bureaucratic** control, while **Taylorism** sought to incorporate control in the technical process itself. The moving assembly line or the paperwork chain set the pace and control the activities of those who work. More recently, the importance of **culture** is emphasized as a mechanism whereby control is internalized by the individual as self-control. The organization's **values** and **norms** help to ensure that its members will behave in a certain way, not because they are forced to, but because it has become second nature to them. Generally, lack of control, or **powerlessness**, is seen as a major dimension of **alienation**.

More recently, it has been argued that a wide range of organizational controls colonize the individual from within rather than from above or from outside; this is a widely held view which suggests that the controls of **postmodernity** are more invasive, pervasive and insidious than those of earlier eras. Foucault's reading of the Panopticon, a vast mechanism of surveillance in which individuals police themselves, since they can never be sure when the disciplinary gaze is focused on them, has had a considerable influence on the scholarly understanding of contemporary controls. **Language** is especially important as a discreet controlling mechanism: naming, listing, classifying and labelling can create distinctions and pigeonholes which are every bit as oppressive and controlling as direct surveillance.

The study of control is complemented by an increased interest in different types of employee recalcitrance and **resistance**. Different types of workplace resistance have been identified; these include sabotage, absenteeism, pilfering, restriction of output as well as symbolic defiance, cynicism and disparaging humour and jokes. Some resistance may assume rational forms (e.g. tactical strikes where it hurts or damages an organization), but Fineman and Sturdy have argued that **emotion** becomes a mediator between an organization's controlling practices and an individual's or group's resistance. Emotion can drive acts of overt rebellion and recalcitrance, such as whistle-blowing. In such cases, it is a sense of insult to the employee's pride or sense of justice rather than the experience of oppressive controls which precipitates opposition. Alternatively, emotion may lead to passive resistance, such as psychological withdrawal, or resistance through distance, such as the improvised departures from organizational scripts.

(Ackroyd and Thompson, 1999; Burawoy, 1979; Casey, 2000; Collinson, 1994; Fineman and Sturdy, 1999; Friedman, 1977; Gabriel, 1995, 1999a; Jermier, 1998; Knights and Vurdubakis, 1994; Thompson, 1990; Townley, 1993)

corporate culture

Corporate culture has been a popular concept in organizational studies since the 1980s. Organizations, like nations, it has been suggested, have or 'are' cultures, composed of shared **values**, **norms** and **meanings**. Some organizations have cultures which enhance efficiency, productivity, innovation and service while others have cultures which tend to fragment initiative and are less managerially efficient and productive. Corporate cultures develop incrementally through the history of the organization, often reflecting the values and prescriptions of its leaders. Some corporate cultures are deliberately engineered by leaders to promote innovation, team work and commitment, seen to be the secret behind the success of some major corporations. In their highly influential bestseller *In Search of Excellence*, Thomas J. Peters and Robert H. Waterman argue that successful companies are those which have strong cultures, i.e. *strong* commitment to a shared set of values and norms, which both unite and **motivate** organizational members. The forging of a strong culture, the strengthening of norms and values and the creation of meanings are all major functions of managers: 'good managers make meanings for people, as well as money' (1982: 29) claim Peters and Waterman. Similar conclusions are drawn by Kanter who believes that most Western organizations have developed **bureaucratic** cultures that thwart innovation and entrepreneurship by emphasizing adherence to rules and procedures. Deal and Kennedy suggest that, in future, successful organizations will have to generate cultures in which every employee has a sense of being a hero.

Such arguments have encouraged the view that managers can manipulate organizational culture at will to produce a winning cocktail, through the use of symbols, stories, myths and **metaphors**. This has proven an oversimplification. There is evidence that people will resist such manipulation when it is seen to be at odds with their own self-image and personal aims, and employees fast become cynical about new 'fashions' in organizational culture. Furthermore, **sub-cultures** and counter-cultures may spontaneously grow and prosper to complement or undermine the official values. Even the strongest-looking cultures can hide significant cracks beneath the surface and many of them have not proven to be the long-term recipe for corporate success that was initially claimed.

(Deal and Kennedy, 1999; Kanter, 1983; Ogbonna and Harris, 2002a, b; Peters and Waterman, 1982)

corporate governance
See **governance**

corruption

Corruption means doing things which violate established concepts of fairness and honesty. The view of what constitutes corrupt behaviour is influenced by cultural differences, but it is probable that in all cultures people would agree that paying a policeman not to give you a speeding ticket which would disqualify you from driving is corrupt, even if it is normal in some places. Bribing someone to give you a job that you want would also be seen as corrupt. If a company is mis-stating its profits, as happened with Enron, everyone would agree that this is corrupt. Paying a customs official privately to allow you to import goods into a country would also be widely seen as corrupt, but this is so common in some countries that large companies would argue that it is normal business practice there. If challenged, they might describe it as privatization of the customs service. Producing an agreement about what should be regarded as corrupt is one of the tasks of business **ethics**. Regulatory bodies and other forms of bureaucratic control (such as standard procedures in accountancy) form an important line of defence against corruption in organizations, even though they also restrict creative, incorrupt practice.

In any culture, there will be cases of corruption that are quite difficult to judge. In Western economies, 'creative accounting' is a term used mostly by non-accountants to describe clever practices by accountants where the outsider is never quite clear whether the practice has been corrupt or not. Perhaps most of the more skilful forms of corruption have this element of ambiguity about them, which gives anyone accused a measure of ambiguity to hide behind if necessary. Such hiding may be as much from their own inspection of their activities and their conscience as from the views of others.

(du Gay, 2000; Mars, 1982)

creativity

Creativity is the ability to think or do something novel, innovative or unexpected. The absence of creativity is often bemoaned in organizations, and yet it may be that management in many organizations might not wish to encourage it too widely. Creativity can make **control** more difficult. Most approaches to creativity encourage thinking 'outside the box' or 'outside tramlines'. In other words, they find some way of breaking out of the normal constraints on our thinking. Those techniques can range from brainstorming to lateral thinking, and even alcohol (which arguably debilitates more than it enables). If we need techniques to get past constraints, it is worth asking how those constraints have arisen in the first place. It is likely that the capacity not to think of too many possibilities, not to be continuously creative, is helpful to us in many of our activities. When giving a presentation to customers, most people do not need to be told that they should not sing their presentation, or stand on the table to deliver it.

The techniques that are offered for creativity are surprisingly similar to each other, all requiring people to relax their constraints on what they are prepared to consider. One problem is that some people think that creativity should be a substitute for hard work. Accounts from creative people suggest that creativity is actually hard work, as in Edison's famous dictum that 'genius is one per cent inspiration and ninety-nine per cent perspiration'. So long as people think that creativity is a substitute for effort, they will not see the need to work hard at any technique that is supposed to enhance it. Instead, they will assume that they have not yet discovered the 'right' technique for them, so they will search the training course brochures and the book stalls for alternatives.

Creativity techniques are often based either on separating creation from evaluation of ideas, as in brainstorming, or on transposing ideas from one field of knowledge to another, as in lateral thinking. This latter suggests that we may achieve novel ideas by taking notions from one area and applying them to another.

The view that the environment of organizations is increasingly unstable has led to the recent revival of interest in creativity in organizations. Within a pin factory in a predictable world, the need for creativity will be slight. Within an electronic business in a period of rapid change and instability, the need for creative solutions to problems, and creative definitions of problems, is urgent.

(De Bono, 1992; Handy, 1989; Henry, 2001; von Stamm, 2003)
See also **innovation**

crisis management

Managing crises is a useful point of differentiating between 'organizing' and 'managing'. While organizing aims at what is smooth, predictable and routinized, managing often entails dealing with the unpredictable, the disruptive and the urgent. It is thought that the first instance in which the expression 'crisis management' was used was by US Secretary of Defense Robert McNamara, following the Cuban missile crisis in 1962. 'There is no longer any such thing as strategy, only crisis management' is what he is meant to have said. Crisis management suggests a highly turbulent or even chaotic environment, where little can be planned in advance; it suggests an ad hoc approach which responds to changing circumstances in an opportunistic way. It is reactive rather than proactive, and treats every situation as a one-off. Crisis management is profoundly non-strategic, since it stems from the belief that no long-term forecast has any value, a belief that it shares with some variants of **complexity theory**.

If crisis management suggests limits to some of the manager's traditional functions, notably those of planning and controlling, it paradoxically also implies that crisis can be 'managed', so a certain measure of influence remains. In this sense, crisis management can be thought of as a comforting notion, since it extends the remit of **management** to every situation – everything, including crises, then is seen as manageable.

How then does one manage crises? Some crises may be handled in a relatively routine manner. The term 'fire fighting' suggests that such crises demand urgent attention and call for an interruption of anything else that goes on in an organization. The aim then is to limit the damage through the skilled deployment of different resources (fire-fighting equipment, humanpower, information and so on). Other crises, however, may refuse this type of 'regularization'. They may be unique 'one-offs', demanding improvisation and creative problem solving under conditions of extreme pressure. Events such as those that took place on 11 September 2001 in New York and Washington may fall in to this latter category.

(Mitroff, 2004, 2005; Weick and Sutcliffe, 2001)

critical theory and critical management studies

Critical theory is an influential intellectual tradition founded by a group of scholars associated with the Institute of Social Research in Frankfurt, in the 1920s and 1930s. They are sometimes known as the Frankfurt School, and include Herbert Marcuse, Max Horkheimer, Theodor Adorno, Walter Benjamin and Erich Fromm. More recently, Jürgen Habermas has been seen as the chief exponent of this tradition. Drawing their inspiration predominantly from Marx and Freud, these theorists viewed Western civilization as profoundly **alienating** and alienated. Unlike conventional social theories which reflect the conditions of alienation (and frequently serve the interests of the powerful), the Frankfurt School advocated critical theory as an emancipatory form of knowledge, which brings about an elimination of false consciousness and opens up the possibility of new forms of society free from oppression and exploitation. They viewed emancipation not only in material terms (freedom from exploitation at the workplace), but also in other spheres including sexual, aesthetic and moral.

Critical management studies represent a diverse and heterogeneous group of theoretical approaches which, generally, stand in opposition to conventional positivistic and empiricist research. They draw their inspiration from critical theory and labour process theory, but also from post-structuralist theories including those developed by Foucault, Derrida and Baudrillard. While not all scholars who associate themselves with this tradition can be described as anti-management or anti-capitalism, they generally adopt a critical approach towards the theories and ideas which claim to increase managerial efficiency, as well as towards managers who seek to increase corporate profits through the use of such ideas.

Fournier and Grey have argued that critical management studies stem from three fundamental and generally shared assumptions. First, they have a non-performative intent – in other words, they are not concerned with making the work of managers easier, more effective or even more humane. Second, they strongly oppose the 'naturalization' of managerial ideas or concepts. Instead, they seek to show that even seemingly cast-iron entities, such as 'a manager', 'stress' and 'race', depend on linguistic conventions and are socially constructed. Third, they emphasize **reflexivity**, a process whereby every act of creating knowledge alters the object of the knowledge. Representation, therefore, is never a neutral process but depends on a number of choices, implicit or explicit, made in constructing narratives.

Overall, critical management studies theorists investigate how **power** is exercised in subtle and invisible forms, for instance through linguistic categories, labels and conventions, through spatial arrangements and through organizational procedures and routines which appear to be fair or, at least, unbiased. Power is exercised not merely by applying coercive or other regulations, by drawing boundaries or by classifying and pigeon-holing different entities, but by defining reality in such a way that all of the above appear natural and sensible. Furthermore, power operates in subtle ways which block or silence alternative conceptualizations or definitions. In these respects, critical management studies have remained loyal to the common theme of both critical theory and post-structuralism (and before them, classical Marxism), namely that power involves a subtle but unshakeable shaping of consciousness.

(Alvesson and Willmott, 1992; Boje, 2001; Fournier and Grey, 2000; Grey, 2004; Hassard et al., 2001; Wallemacq and Sims, 1998)
See also **social construction**

cross-cultural management

Although considerable variation in cultures can be found within a country, this term is mostly used where managers from one country are managing people from another. Very often, they will also have managerial colleagues from that other country, but usually there is a significant power difference in favour of the country and the culture in which the organization is based. For example, in Korean companies operating in the UK or American companies operating in Singapore, the local managers often do not feel themselves fully accepted by the expatriate managers. If management can be genuinely cross-cultural, rather than subordinating one culture to another, it has a potential advantage in that it includes greater **diversity**. It will include people who are comfortable in a wider range of social situations and languages than will other organizations, and this may give access to more opportunities than would be the case with a single culture, as well as having potential for greater **creativity**. Much of the writing about cross-cultural management has been at the level of trying to ensure that expatriate managers are properly briefed for life within their new culture. Executive training programmes are run for this purpose, including instruction on how to eat in the new culture, how to meet and greet people and how to relate to people of the other gender. This tends to be the more clearly defined end of cross-cultural management. However, rather more difficult issues to deal with may arise where the cultural differences become entangled with different ways in which language is used, and especially with differences in the use of humour. Some of the ways in which language is used can be very exclusive of people from other cultures. For example, people whose second language is English may be much more comfortable speaking English to other people for whom it is a second language than speaking it to a native speaker. Work by Hofstede has given us a set of dimensions for comparing different cultures, and measures of where cultures lie on those dimensions. While some feel that cross-cultural management is too subtle to be reduced to a few dimensions, others find it useful at least as a way of discussing the issues.

More recently, a substantial body of literature has emerged dealing with issues and difficulties affecting expatriate managers, who must adapt their habits and behaviours when they take up posts in countries with whose culture they are only cursorily familiar. Some of this literature seeks to help practising managers adjust themselves to different cultural environments and stop them from experiencing culture shock.

(Eschbach et al., 2001; Hofstede, 1980; Schneider and Barsoux, 2002; Selmer, 2001)

culture and organizational culture

Culture is a concept mainly drawn from anthropology, which has acquired considerable currency in the study of organizations. Culture can be thought of as the material and spiritual heritage of a community, the stock of myths and stories, artistic and craft artefacts, buildings, tools, laws, **institutions**, rituals and customs. It is frequently argued that culture is the cement which holds communities together by establishing shared **meanings** and **values** which enable them to communicate with each other, taking many things for granted. Schein refers to these as 'basic assumptions'. For example, in many Western cultures, it is taken for granted that people marry for love, a notion which would seem alien to some other cultures. Likewise, many of our values and **attitudes** towards work, leisure, **authority**, **career**, happiness, success, death and **sexuality** are shaped by culture. Culture becomes internalized, it becomes part of us, influencing us without conscious awareness. It is only when we are confronted by an alien culture that we appreciate that values and assumptions are strong influences in our life. Harrison and Handy have argued that organizations fall into four types according to their culture: (a) *power culture*, in which orders emanate from the organizational centre and are unquestioningly observed. Political organizations, the Mafia and many small businesses have this type of culture; (b) *role culture*, dominated by **rules** and regulations, as in classic **bureaucracy**. This is common in the civil service and in large bureaucratic organizations; (c) *task culture*, in which getting a specific job done by a strict deadline is all-important. This can be found in publishing and consultancy organizations where deadlines have to be met and, in general, in organizations where project work is common; (d) *people* or *support culture*, in which the development of human potential and well-being is paramount; this may be found in some voluntary organizations, partnerships, religious or academic organizations.

(Handy, 1976; Harris and Ogbonna, 2002; Harrison, 1972; Harrison and Stokes, 1992; Hofstede, 1991; Martin, 1992; Moldoveanu and Nohria, 2002; Ogbonna and Harris, 2002b; Schein, 1985)
See also **corporate culture**

decision making

Commonly regarded as a major activity in organizational life, decision making is a rational sounding phrase for an activity which is often more multi-faceted and untidy. Much of the theoretical work on decision making has considered how it ought to be done, or how it would be done if humans were well-engineered decision machines. This has led to many 'stage' models of decision making, showing how it might be done in a sequence of rational steps. This does not necessarily fit with how human beings actually make decisions, especially in organizations. People are capable of handling complex and uncertain information or ideas, of scanning situations for anything that might be relevant, or for possible solutions that could be taken up opportunistically. Many of the decisions that are regarded as the most successful have been made by such informal means, rather than by rational processes.

Research about decision making has been divided between 'behavioural decision making', which is mostly experimental work to see what decisions are made under laboratory conditions, and 'organizational decision making', which attempts less scientific rigour in exchange for trying to research more realistically the circumstances which surround everyday decision making in organizations. There are some important differences about how decision making might take place in organizations compared with laboratories (Shapira, 1997): it is likely to be ambiguous, both in terms of the information available and in terms of what you are trying to achieve; it is longitudinal, in that the participants in a decision have also been participants in previous ones and expect to participate in future ones; there are significant incentives and penalties in organizational decision making; decisions are repeated, giving a (sometimes false) sense of confidence, coupled with uncertainty about whether this really is a repeat, or whether there is a risk of mistakenly treating something as a repeat when there is an important difference; and finally, conflict and power are involved in organizational decision making. Given all this, it is not surprising that rational choice models of decision making seem inappropriate to many people in organizations.

Many techniques have been introduced to assist decision making, such as 'brainstorming', 'quality circles', 'cognitive mapping' and 'mind mapping'. Recent years have seen the development of techniques for decision support and group decision support. Decision making has been one of the duties and rights attributed to managers for a long time, but some have pointed out that it may be a misleading label; it is very hard ever to see any direct evidence that a decision is being made, but we see actions being taken, and infer that a decision has been made. We also hear managers declaring that a decision has been made. This strengthens the need to understand decision making as an incremental process.

See also **participation**

deconstruction

Deconstruction is a popular term of postmodern theory proposed by Jacques Derrida. Derrida criticized Western philosophy for being preoccupied with discovering the essence behind appearances; instead he advocated a close study of language and texts in which words are not seen as fixed to specific objects and activities, but rather acquire their meaning in their juxtaposition to other words. Derrida argued that it is in the text itself rather than different linguistic and historical contexts that meaning resides. Deconstruction is a process which brings to the surface the tensions, contradictions, absences and silences in the text, or as Barbara Johnson has put it: 'a careful teasing out of warring forces of signification within a text'.

In organizational studies, the use of deconstruction has been the result of an increasing tendency to view organizations as texts, in other words not as concrete entities in a world 'out there', but as entities that come into being through references to them in **discourse**. Deconstruction of organization then starts with the observation that the very term 'organization' excludes elements of disorder and untidiness, which are, therefore, 'silenced' or marginalized. An organization then is seen as the dominant pole of an axis of meaning or signification whose other pole becomes invisible, along with the axis itself. Deconstruction often discovers similar dualities or dichotomies (male/female, white/black, heterosexual/homosexual), where the dominant term silences the subordinate one without ever being able to obliterate it. In a similar way, 'management' can be deconstructed as the dominant pole of a duality of control and usage. Managers control resources, processes and information; non-managers are controlled *as* resources, and are therefore informed, used and processed. Furthermore, management is the pole of an axis whose other pole is perennially obscured and under-appreciated, namely that which is unmanaged and unmanageable (Gabriel, 1995; Gabriel and Lang, 1995).

While deconstruction is most fruitful when applied to relatively small pieces of text, such as stories, euphemisms, labels and 'spin', it has been used with some success in exploring the hidden assumptions of academic texts and theories (Czarniawska, 1999; Kilduff, 1993). Its greatest success has been in demonstrating how seemingly innocent texts are full of assumptions about what is normal and abnormal, right and wrong, good and bad, and in this way supports different **power** relations. These power relations include many researchers themselves who take it upon themselves to classify, describe and represent others. Instead, as Linstead has advocated, deconstructive research emphasizes 'multiple realities, fragmentation, plurality, subjectivity, and a concern with the means by which social life is represented in accounts that create rather than transmit meaning'.

(Chia, 1996; Culler, 1981/2001, 1982; Derrida, 1976a; Feldman, 1998; Johnson, 1990; Linstead, 1993)
See also **postmodernism**

desire

Desire is a term used to explain human **motivation** which, unlike the concept of need, seeks to incorporate a social and a psycho-sexual dimension. One may need shoes for warmth and comfort, but one desires a pair of designer trainers because of what it stands for. Whether directed towards a physical object, a human being, an activity or a state of being, desire is driven not merely by instinct or need, but by the **meanings** attributed to the object of desire. Desires may be fulfilled either in practice (for example, by buying the desired pair of trainers) or in **fantasy**, by imagining that the wished-for object or state has been achieved. Alternatively, desires may by frustrated, in which case they may mutate into desires for different objects, which may be easier to fulfil, or they may be repressed into the unconscious. Three major traditions in the study of desire can be identified: (a) sociologists have argued that desires are culturally constituted, as individuals learn to desire objects and states of being valued by their **cultures**. Consumer societies, for example, are said to place enormous value on material commodities and identify happiness with escalating material possessions; (b) depth psychologists have emphasized the connection between desire and pleasure and have argued that most desires are modified residues of earlier desires, mainly stemming from childhood; these were originally repressed and later seek fulfilment in new incarnations. For example, belief in God is traced back to the child's desire to be protected by a loving father; (c) more recently, **discourse** theorists have argued that desire is an element of the discourse on sexuality – in other words, the complex and interconnected ways of thinking and talking about things sexual as against things unsexual (Foucault, 1978). The very **language** and words which dominate the sexuality discourse (**gender**, **sex**, sexual **identity**, orgasm, body and even desire itself) are historically constituted as interconnected elements, in constant interaction with other discourses, like the discourse of power and the discourse of political economy.

(Freud, 1905/1977)
See also **sexuality**

deskilling

In *Labor and Monopoly Capital*, Harry Braverman argued that, contrary to common-sense notions, throughout the twentieth century, workers have been stripped of traditional **skills** and **competences** by the onslaught of **Taylorism** and **technology**. Traditional skills of artisans like printers, potters, engineers, machinists, cooks and clerks have been eliminated, either by being absorbed into the production process itself or by being overtaken by new technological processes. The deskilled worker loses not only much of his/her bargaining power, but also **control** over his/her work, and pride and dignity in his/her work. Braverman's theory has sparked off a controversy. Especially vital has been the question of whether the computerization of work processes and clerical work leads to deskilling. Empirical studies have documented strong deskilling tendencies in numerous industries, with one (Blackburn and Mann, 1979) finding that the majority of workers use more skill in getting to work than in doing their job. Nevertheless, there is also evidence of the emergence of a new range of skills, in response to the demands of new technology. More recently, there has been much greater appreciation of the processes of employee resistance at the workplace and a recognition that deskilling is a process which is challenged and contested by those whom it affects.

(Beynon, 1973; Braverman, 1974; Jermier et al., 1994; Zuboff, 1985)

discourse

The term discourse initially described a linguistic unit longer than a sentence. Philosophers such as Descartes used it to indicate a body of closely argued philosophical text through which they developed their arguments. Currently, discourse stands at the centre of what is known as the 'linguistic turn' in the human sciences, a trend which views **language** not as a passive medium reflecting or describing the world, but as an active entity through which the world becomes meaningful to us. The study of language then assumes major importance for the study of human phenomena. Facts themselves can become 'denaturalized' – they do not just exist, waiting to be described through language. Instead, they become products or outcomes rather than the instigators of discourse. Thus, for instance, by saying that 'the crime rate has risen again', we are not simply referring to a fact called 'crime' and its increasing incidence, but we become part of a discourse which 'naturalizes' crime as an inevitable, uniform and clearly identifiable phenomenon, and forms innumerable assumptions, such as the inevitable presence of (a minority of) criminals in every society, the requirement for a police force to control them, the social obligation of governments to bring the crime rate down and their perennial failure to do so, the experience of vulnerability of decent 'non-criminal' people to the activities of criminals and so forth. As Foucault observed very well, discourse then entails different assumptions and silences, which reproduce relations of **power**.

As a very popular term in the social sciences, discourse has assumed many distinct meanings. At the simplest level, it is used to indicate any body of knowledge that claims some coherence and value for itself. In this sense, it is almost interchangeable with 'doctrine', 'theory' or even 'paradigm'. More specifically, it can be used to indicate any spoken or written text, story, conversation or narrative which is then submitted to some form of **discourse analysis**.

The use of 'discourse' in connection with organizations raises numerous issues. Least contentious is the view of organizations as terrains of discourse where conversations take place, documents are written, jokes are told, emails are sent, all of which may be analysed, interpreted or deconstructed. This view, however, presupposes that organizations exist independently of discourse, something that has been contested. Mumby and Clair, for instance, argue that 'when we speak of discourse, we do not simply mean discourse that occurs in organizations. Rather, we suggest that organizations exist only in so far as their members create them through discourse. This is not to claim that organizations are "nothing but" discourse, but rather that discourse is the principal means by which organization members create a coherent social reality that frames their sense of who they are' (1997: 181). From this perspective, organizations share the fate of other effects of modernity, the sovereign self, the body, sexuality and indeed 'facts': they are viewed as discursive constructions. Other theorists, however, have looked at discourse as constitutive of organizations but not as fully constituting them. From this perspective, 'buildings are built, products are manufactured, services are rendered beyond (and because of) all this organizational talk. Thus discourse and talk are central to organization and organizing ... but so is non-discursive action' (Hardy et al., 1998: 65). Discursive formations may appear in many forms, some of which are privileged in organizations over others, yet they do not exhaust the domain of organization. Important as it is to study discourse, it is not enough for an understanding of organizational or social practices (see Fairclough, 1992, 1995).

One feature of discourse that has become increasingly recognized is the extent to which **power** relations become embedded in it. The use of particular ways of talking privileges certain views and certain interests, while silencing or marginalizing others. Hegemonic discourses are those discourses which tend to privilege and sustain those already in power; minority or counter-discourses, on the other hand, seek to voice experiences of disenfranchisement, marginalization and oppression. On the whole, discourses are not as coherent or consistent as first thought. They entail numerous internal tensions and contradictions, which may be teased out through **deconstruction**. Furthermore, they have a tendency to fragment and disintegrate or mutate into other discourses. Finally, they are engaged in a constant interaction with other discourses. With some of them, they develop self-reinforcing or parasitic relations, with others they lapse into indifferent accommodation, while with yet others they may engage in overt or covert struggle.

(Grant et al., 1998a, 2004; Heracleous and Hendry, 2000; Mumby and Clair, 1997; Phillips and Hardy, 2002; Potter and Wetherell, 1987; Van Dijk, 1997)
See also **deconstruction, postmodernism, stories and storytelling**

discourse analysis
Analysing 'discourse' has been a recent approach to understanding organizations. It focuses on the way people talk in organizations and the texts – documents and communications – that constitute the expression of social reality. Organizational reality is said to be made tangible through discourse and the task of the discourse analyst is to explore how different discourses relate, compete and fuse to produce certain decisions or outcomes. There are, however, different approaches. For example, in making a promotion decision, a candidate may be judged around discourses such as 'competence', 'loyalty', 'time in the organization' and 'working under pressure'. Some discourse analysts would ask: 'why are these important?'; 'where do they come from?'. The critical discourse analyst will go further, seeking the power and political dynamics that constitute or inform the discourses. For instance, does 'competence' express a particularly male view of job performance in the organization? Is 'working under pressure' valued particularly by senior executives but not particularly relevant to the job in question? What is the history of the organization that reinforces and prioritizes such discourses? Other discourse analysts do not assume hidden dynamics or messages behind the text. For them, the discourse, such as the words used, are themselves the meaning, so we should not seek beyond that. Discourse has roots in social constructionist perspectives on organizations and postmodern derivatives, such as Jacques Derrida's 'deconstruction' and Michel

Foucault's views on the way discourses are used to exercise power. At its best, discourse analysis offers penetrating insights into the way language and texts both express and camouflage organizational processes and desires.

(Alvesson and Kärreman, 2000b; Derrida, 1976a; Fairclough, 1995; Foucault, 1970; Phillips and Hardy, 2002)
See also **discourse**

discrimination

Discrimination is used in different ways. It can refer to the capacity of a psychological test accurately to identify differences between groups or individuals, hence 'discriminant validity'. More generally, discrimination is giving preferential treatment, notably with respect to employment or promotion, to an individual or a group on the basis of characteristics like **gender**, age, **ethnicity**, **race** or religion. Direct discrimination, for example the hiring of a man over a better qualified woman purely on account of his gender, is illegal in both Britain and the United States. It is, however, very difficult to prove, especially if an **interview** is used as part of the recruiting procedure. More importantly, there is a wide range of discriminatory mechanisms resulting in unequal opportunities. The structure of the job market itself acts as an obstacle to equality. Childbearing and childrearing are often impediments to women's career chances, the location of jobs and educational prerequisites inhibit the chances of ethnic minority groups, and the requirement for job experience disadvantages young people. Conversely, mandatory retirement policies and limited training opportunities disadvantage the growing population of active, elderly people. The way a job advertisement is phrased can dissuade particular groups from even applying; for example, specific requirements, like long hours or foreign travel, will automatically exclude many women. Gender, racial and other **stereotypes** and sheer **prejudice** can equally fuel discrimination. Finally, harassment at work can act as a discriminatory mechanism by placing the victims on the defensive, contributing to their character assassination or forcing them out of employment.

diversity

Diversity refers to differences between people as people. Organizations are full of different roles, different levels of seniority and different geographical areas of responsibility, but diversity is about the differences that go beyond this, such as race, ethnicity, gender, sexual orientation, religion, age and physical disability. Diversity has come on to the agenda for three reasons. First, it is unfair if people are appointed, promoted and rewarded differently from each other not because of ability or performance but because of differences such as race or gender. Second, it is inefficient if organizations are not getting the best people into particular jobs because they have made biased decisions about them based on factors in their diversity. Third, increasingly there are governmental regulations demanding that equal opportunity policies should be adopted, and that others should not do business with those who fail to adopt such policies. Despite diversity awareness training and equal opportunities policies, studies in many places across the world still show women earning less than men, on average, for equivalent work, and members of ethnic minorities being similarly discriminated against.

(Christian et al., 2006; Grant et al., 1998a; Levine, 2003)

downsizing

Downsizing is reducing the size of the workforce in order to cut the direct costs of running a business. It is replete with euphemisms, such as employees being 'let go', 'helped to resign', given a 'career alternative' or 'put into the mobility pool'. It is often a last-resort initiative for a business in trouble, and/or a way of increasing competitiveness in an aggressive marketplace. Its effectiveness as an economic tool is much debated, as often the expected performance benefits do not occur. This is due in part to the negative psychological consequences of downsizing on those who still remain in the organization. The relief at having retained one's job is moderated in a number of ways, and termed 'survivor syndrome'. It includes: fear of further downsizing; increased feelings of insecurity; guilt at having survived while colleagues have not; stress from increased workloads; strained trust in, and anger towards, management; reduced risk taking and motivation. Those who have carried out the downsizing, the 'executioners', have also been shown to struggle with their feelings of guilt and betrayal. In sum, there is motivation paradox. The downsized organization demands more work, more flexibility and more creativity from people in social–emotional conditions that are contrary to these ends. Some survivors do work harder, but from the belief that it will protect them from further layoffs. Downsizing is often seen, and felt, by those affected as an abrogation of the **psychological contract**. Those who have been laid off tend to re-enter the job market more cautiously and less trustingly; they are less willing to commit themselves wholeheartedly to their jobs or new employer.

(Allen et al., 2001; Brockner, 1998; Ehrenreich, 2005; Feldman, 2000; Kets de Vries and Balazs, 1997; McKinley et al., 1998; Noer, 1993; Uchitelle, 2006; Wright, 1998)
See also **commitment**

ecology, population

In addition to its usual meaning in relation to the **environment**, ecology also represents an approach to the study of organizations known as population-ecology theory. This approach looks at populations *of* organizations, seeking to understand why and how particular types of organizational forms come into being and proliferate while others die away or disappear. The approach has dominated the outlook of some major US academic publications and has drawn its inspiration from Darwin's theory of natural selection. The core argument is that the survival of certain organizational forms is not the result of successful adaptation to their environments, but rather that they provide the best 'fit' to particular environments. Selection rather than adaptation then is the key to organizational survival. Population-ecology studies have concentrated on long time spans and used large amounts of quantitative data to support their arguments. They are of relatively limited use to practitioners, since they generally view organizational inertia as an insurmountable obstacle to adaptation and survival.

(Carroll, 1985; Hannan and Freeman, 1977)

efficiency and effectiveness

These two concepts are often distinguished from each other, and while their meaning is less precise than it might initially sound, the distinction is helpful. Efficiency refers to getting a good ratio of outputs to inputs. A process whereby all your inputs are turned into outputs is efficient, and the more by-products or unintended (or unneeded) consequences there are, the less efficient the process is. So the action that devotes the minimum energy to produce the consequence wanted is efficient. For example, it could be very efficient to send a piece of information by email, because it minimizes the effort. Effectiveness is to do with achieving desirable outcomes. However efficient an action, if it does not produce what was meant, it is not effective. Thus, if the email mentioned above was not understood properly (perhaps because it does not give very good opportunities for people to check back whether they have understood correctly), it will not have been effective. Another phrase sometimes used for the same distinction is 'doing the thing right' (efficiency) versus 'doing the right thing' (effectiveness). Effectiveness as a notion begs the question of 'effective for whom?'. Different people will be trying to achieve different ends in the organization, so an action which is effective for what one person is trying to achieve will not necessarily be seen as effective by everybody.

emotion

An emotion approach to organizations marks a departure from a traditional view – that feelings are not a proper part of organizational and management processes. It proposes that emotion is the prime medium through which people act and interact. Fear, envy, jealousy, anxiety, excitement, trust, love and hate are part and parcel of what is brought to and fomented in organizations. Who works hard, appears not to care, or resists taking the initiative, is based on emotion.

Organizations are emotional arenas where feelings shape events and events shape feelings. Different perspectives explain the way emotions operate. For example, psychoanalysts stress early life experiences, especially the unconscious wishes and fantasies that are acted out in our relationships with colleagues and leaders. Biologists and evolutionary psychologists look more to the emotional reactions that are 'hard wired' into our bodies from millions of years of adaptation to our natural and social environment. In contrast, social constructionists focus on the subtle ways that different national and organizational cultures shape the kind of ways certain feelings should and should not be expressed. In other words, we learn much of our emotional repertoire, and it is learning that can be regulated by different, powerful agencies in our life, such as parents, religious leaders, schools, professional bodies and employers. An emotion perspective has led to a wave of research into areas such as leadership, decision making, trust and negotiation, business ethics, politics, power and organizational change.

(Ashkanasy et al., 2002; Elfenbein, 2007; Fineman, 1995b, 2000a, 2003, 2008; Gabriel, 1998a)
See also **emotion rules, emotional labour**

emotion rules

Emotion rules are often tacit, learned vicariously within a culture. They govern how feelings can be displayed, especially in the face and voice, such as looking serious in job interviews, expressing sorrow at someone's misfortune, looking pleased for a friend's success, lowering one's eyes in embarrassment, appearing sad at funerals. Many such rules are culturally specific, helping to knit together the courtesies of social relationships and the protocols of an organization. Each nation has it own emotion **culture**, such as the interpersonal exuberance of Latin countries compared with the stiff restraint of Nordic ones. Unfamiliarity with these, and the subtle emotional cues of **body language**, can complicate cross-cultural negotiations. As emotion rules control the expression of feelings, they do not necessarily correspond to what is privately felt, where feeling rules play a part. Sometimes emotion rules are heavily influenced by the norms of the workplace. The physician and lawyer have to appear suitably serious to maintain their professional credibility. The effective nurse or counsellor need to appear compassionate. The police officer and security guard should exude a sense of control and authority. Emotion rules are, on occasions, corporately manipulated. This is most evident in settings where service-with-a-smile is mandatory for employees. Many supermarkets, theme parks, restaurant chains, international hotels and airlines coach their employees on the 'correct' emotions to show and will closely monitor their performance. Call centres have followed suit and customer-service employees are instructed on how to cultivate a 'telephone smile' to help win customer satisfaction and loyalty. All such procedures have come under critical scrutiny by organizational researchers. Some are worried about a potentially oppressive extension of managerial control; others about the emotional damage that can accrue when employees are continually forced to present an emotion face that is not really theirs.

(Fineman, 1995a, 2003; Hochschild, 1983; Sturdy and Fineman, 2001; Zerbe et al., 2006)
See also **emotional labour**

emotional intelligence

Emotional intelligence is a relatively recent, and popularized, concept. It refers to the way emotion can be used 'intelligently' in different situations and the relative advantage this gives to people in their social interactions and organizational performance. The emotionally intelligent, it is suggested, are adept at using their emotions appropriately. They know their emotions, they manage their emotions, and they recognize emotions in others. Emotional intelligence attempts to show how our problem solving, thinking and abilities work together with our emotions, in particular how the former can effectively steer and shape the latter. To do so, we need the skills or competences to be able to perceive and evaluate emotional information. There is controversy about whether this facility is learnable through special training or whether it is something we either have or do not have in our personalities. Huge claims have been made for emotional intelligence for business success, especially by management consultants in what has become something of a management fashion. Academics have, however, been more wary, with some disputing its validity, measurement and even the values on which it is based.

(Fineman, 2000d, 2004; Goleman, 1996; Keele and Bell, 2008; Matthews et al., 2002)

emotional labour

Emotional labour is a term coined by the American sociologist Arlie Hochschild. It refers to the labour involved in producing the emotions expected by an employer, emotions that are specific to the job. It is an appropriation of everyday *emotion work*, the effort we all put into keeping up appearances, presenting a particular emotional 'face' for the occasion. Emotional labour is most evident when employees are, in effect, instructed consistently to smile, be 'happy', 'seductive', 'tough' and so forth. Such emotions are likely to be most demanding to produce when they are not felt. Hochschild's example was flight attendants. She studied Delta Airline's flight attendants who, as part of their job, underwent rigorous training to produce the 'inside-out' smile that the airline required. She found that some did this by 'deep acting', trying to 'really feel' what they showed. Others engaged in 'surface acting', playing the emotional part but not taking it to heart. Hochschild was concerned about the psychological damage that deep acting could cause, resulting in a confused sense of identity.

Since Hochschild, emotional labour has become a major focus in the study of emotion in organizations, broadened to include many customer service jobs and other occupations, such as nurses, theme-park attendants, call centre operators, social workers, doctors, ambulance workers, police officers and debt collectors. There is controversy concerning the extent of its injuriousness. Some workers treat the demands as an enjoyable game, 'riding the role', while others distance themselves from the act, looking at it sceptically. There is little doubt, however, that emotional labour can exhaust some workers, leading to **stress** and **burnout**. Others are wary about the surveillance (sometimes secret) that some employers establish to monitor their emotional performance. There are also wider debates. One is whether jobs involving formally unacknowledged emotional labour should be specially compensated or rewarded. Another raises moral questions about the kind of '**McDonaldized**' jobs that colonize people's emotional worlds, such that they have little choice or autonomy over the how they shape their work to meet their own desires and personal characteristics.

(Ashforth and Tomiuk, 2000; Fineman, 1999, 2003, 2008; Hochschild, 1983; Humphrey et al., 2008; Syed, 2008)

empowerment

The roots of empowerment lie in providing disadvantaged communities with the resources to further their own needs, on their own terms. The concept has been adopted and translated by management and has become a popular notion in **leadership** theorizing. It is based on the idea that, given the freedom, scope and resources to achieve organizational **goals**, people will be able to contribute to leading themselves – if it is in their interests to do so. Leaders, therefore, do not tell others what to do, or attempt to sell their ideas to them. Rather, the leader's **role** is to help others achieve their own ends creatively by helping them to discover their own potential, and clearing a pathway for them. The leader, in this way, gives **power** to his or her followers. The leader is a facilitator of other people's action. Empowerment is an extension of democratization in management, and the fading of the authoritarian leader. However, it has also been seen as a paradoxical and sometimes false process. There is something strange about management taking action to 'empower' others when that is itself an exercise of power. Empowerment could also be a convenient term for managers to hide behind when they do not want to take responsibility for their own actions, and as such be seen as manipulative. Indeed, some 'empowered' workers complain that they are now expected to take on further responsibility which they do not desire, for little, or no, extra reward.

(Greasley et al., 2005; Schein 1999; Sewell and Wilkinson, 1992b; Srivasta and Cooperfield, 1986; Sturdy et al., 2001)

entrepreneurship

Entrepreneurs are often viewed by organizational theorists as leaders who can inspire others in pursuit of powerful visions and missions. These are usually commercial enterprises although the idea of entrepreneurship now extends to all-powerful and effective advocacy of innovative ideas. Entrepreneurship itself involves the application exploitation of **innovation**. Pettigrew viewed the entrepreneur as a 'person who takes primary responsibility for mobilizing people and other resources to initiate, give purpose to, build, and manage a new organization' (1979: 573). **Management** of **meaning** is vital in effective entrepreneurship, if unrealistic, untried or far-fetched ideas are to grip people and provide collective **motivation**. Czarniawska-Joerges and Wolff distinguish between entrepreneurs (who are inspirational in early parts of ventures), leaders (who can handle crises and upheavals) and managers (who are suited to managing efficiently steady states), although they acknowledge that the three may overlap. Kanter has offered some of the most powerful accounts of entrepreneurial, innovative organizations as those likely to succeed in a complex environment as against those **bureaucracies** she describes as 'segmentalist'. Segmentalist organizations kill innovation and creativity by insisting on rigid **boundaries** and **roles**. Entrepreneurial organizations, on the other hand, view new ideas as the source of competitive advantage and elevate innovators to the status of heroes and heroines.

The ethos of entrepreneurialism has now started to permeate public sector organizations, as well as commercial companies, with an emphasis on customer service, innovation, competition and quality. 'New Public Management' is often seen as the new **ideology** which views the public sector as operating under similar conditions and aiming at similar objectives as the private sector. In a stinging critique of this ideology, Paul du Gay has sought to vindicate bureaucracy with its emphasis on impartiality, equality, formality and quiet efficiency against the sweep of entrepreneurialism.

(Czarniawska-Joerges and Wolff, 1995; du Gay, 1996b, 2000; Ferlie et al., 1996; Hébert and Link, 1988; Kanter, 1983; Mitroff, 1984; Osborne and Gaebler, 1992; Pettigrew, 1979)

environment

The environment refers to the social, economic, physical, political and cultural context in which organizations operate. Closed **systems** theories have focused on organizations as time capsules or black boxes isolated from the effects of what goes on around them. While suitable for the study of a few organizations which operate in highly inert environments, such theories have severe limitations when applied to organizations where the environment is a constant source of threats and opportunities. In a pioneering study, Burns and Stalker argued that firms operating in stable environments tend to adopt *mechanistic* **structures**, with rigid **hierarchies**, **rules** and regulations. By contrast, organizations operating in changing environments tend to adopt *organic* structures enabling them to respond flexibly and rapidly to environmental threats and opportunities. This was an early example of the use of **contingency theories**.

While the organizational environment has assumed pride of place in management literature (see Peters and Waterman, 1982), it is not an unproblematic concept. In the first place, the perception of what constitutes the organization's environment may differ across different individuals. A chemical company's environment looks very different to different people in the organization. For instance, a public relations officer seeks to allay public fears about the company's record on protecting the natural environment; a production worker threatened with redundancy is concerned about the employment environment; a financial expert is concerned with the company's standing in the securities environment. Equally, in a collective way, the environment cannot be defined unless there is a shared sense of what the organization is all about. Is Ford to be seen as a car-making company (in which case the competitors' cars are a central feature of its environment) or is it a money-making organization (in which case the competitors' cars are less important as long as Ford can find new ways of making money, e.g. by trading in the currency markets). This has led to the concept of the 'enacted environment'. Instead of the 'given' environment 'out there', the enacted environment is based on the continuous trading and juxtaposing of **meaning** and interpretations about the organization and its purpose.

In recent years, in the face of increasing global warming and pollution, industry has been cast in a new role: as custodian of the natural environment. The environment, in this sense, is not an infinite 'out there' resource to be exploited, but is to be protected and conserved. This has stimulated an array of 'green' management schemes, buttressed by national and international legislation. The success, or otherwise, of these efforts has hinged upon how key leaders of organizations perceive their social responsibilities and the creation of green organizational cultures. The more enterprising have taken a 'triple bottom line' perspective, weighting equally different facets of their working environment: financial, social and natural. The less adventurous have closed ranks, anxious to protect customary ways of doing business, or find, because they are a small business under financial pressure, they have not the resources to respond. The most powerful transnational corporations have worked to undermine global treaties on environmental protection.

(Burns and Stalker, 1961; Carolan, 2007; Chen, 2008; Davis, 1991; Gore, 1992; McDonagh and Prothero, 1997; Morgan, 1986)

ethics
Ethics concern the rules and principles which shape moral (good/bad) actions, **values** and **decisions**. More generally, they investigate what is right and wrong and how people can live good, virtuous and happy lives. Some of the core questions addressed by ethics involve whether right and wrong are absolutes or relative, whether actions should be judged by their **motives** or their consequences, the nature of morality, especially in cultures which do not see it as deriving from the dictates of god, and the nature of evil.

Ethics in organizations are usually studied in three main areas. Firstly, there are the organization's social responsibilities – the harm or benefit that result from its products or services. For example, there is much debate about the ethics of producing and selling cigarettes, cars which could be safer, or using materials which deplete or damage the natural environment. The second area is the everyday decisions which affect those working in an organization: is it ethical to promote a particular friend over a more competent person? Is it ethical to fire someone without warning or good reason on 'personal grounds'? And is it ethical to exclude **ethnic** minorities from a shortlist of job applicants? The third area of ethics concerns the relationships between organizations and societies. Is it ethical to choose the cheapest third-world supplier for a product, to negotiate the lowest possible price with them and to ignore questions about their employment policies and practices? These questions involve principles of fairness and justice and standards for judging what is right or wrong. The standards will usually derive from the religious, social or professional codes that guide our lives, although moral philosophers point to two major principles: utilitarianism and formalism. Utilitarianism looks for the greatest good for the greatest number of people. A good decision is one where the aggregate benefits outweigh the aggregate costs. Formalism is less pragmatic: it measures the worth of a decision by the extent to which it meets certain fundamental liberties and privileges, such as the right of employees and customers not to have their lives or safety endangered, not to be intentionally deceived, and not to have their privacy invaded.

As dominant institutions of modernity, organizations, with their bureaucratic **rules** and regulations, have tended to supplant the moral responsibilities of individuals working for them. As Bauman has argued: 'modernity was prominent for the tendency to shift moral responsibilities away from the moral self' to an impersonal **system** (1989: 32). The result has been that many choices and decisions that we make daily as members of organizations have been stripped of their moral dimension. MacIntyre has added that in our time we have lost the ability to provide reasoned arguments about the moral qualities of our actions and rely on raw feeling to distinguish between right and wrong. Some authors have gone as far as to argue that **managers** are essentially amoral agents, concerned with efficiency, profit and ends rather than distinctions of right and wrong. Others defend managers as moral agents, at times confused, torn or uncertain, but ultimately struggling with issues of morality, justice and fairness.

(Bauman, 1989; Brady, 1990; Crane and Matten, 2006; Jackall, 1988; MacIntyre, 1981; Parker, 1998; ten Bos and Willmott, 2001; Walton, 1988; Watson, 2003)

ethnic groups

Ethnic groups are communities or collectivities usually based on a sense of shared origin, shared traditions and shared fate. Ethnic groups may be culturally, territorially or historically based. Their members have a sense of 'belonging' to the **group**, sharing many **cultural assumptions** and **values** and may derive their sense of identity and selfhood from them. Ethnicity does not necessarily imply that the group concerned has a sense of superiority over other traditions, although the term 'ethnocentrism' is generally used pejoratively to signify a group's **assumption** that its **culture** and **values** are superior to those of others. Ethnocentrism may, therefore, fuel **prejudice** and **discrimination** against members of other ethnic groups.

See also **prejudice, race**

experiential learning

Experiential learning is learning which is initiated through, and seems largely to stem from, experience. Most theories of learning involve experience, but experiential learning begins with experience which the learner then tries to make sense of, and emphasizes that the experience is core, and not just a means of testing or practising the learning. This is in contrast to propositional learning, for example, where the learner starts with an idea and then may seek to test the idea in relation to experience. Kelly pointed out that experience does not necessarily produce learning; learning is to do with how much a person is changed by experience, not simply with the number of events they collide with. The concept of experiential learning is sometimes criticized because it is difficult to verify that learning has actually taken place; it is also difficult for the person who has learned experientially to articulate precisely what they have learned. The concept has been taken further with the notion of 'self-organized learning' (Harri-Augstein and Thomas, 1991), which argues that effective learners are those who take responsibility for learning experientially how to become better learners, i.e. they learn how to learn.

(Kelly, 1955; Kolb et al., 1979; Moon, 2004)

extrinsic rewards

When used in connection with employment, this concept refers mainly to rewards unrelated to the nature of the **work** itself. Although extrinsic rewards have been used as incentives to hard work through the ages, they became a central feature of **management** philosophy deriving from **Taylorism**. According to this philosophy, the worker does not and cannot expect to derive intrinsic job satisfaction, so his/her **motivation** to work hard must be spurred by the expectation of extrinsic rewards, like pay, bonuses and performance-related benefits. Goldthorpe and colleagues, in a pioneering study in the 1960s, found that manufacturing workers working in three factories in Luton, had an instrumental orientation to work; work was seen mainly as a means to an end or rather to a range of ends related to material well-being. These workers did not expect intrinsic job satisfaction and many of them had swapped more intrinsically rewarding work for more highly paid jobs. This finding has not received unanimous support. Studies, like Beynon's investigation of workers at Ford or Gabriel's study of catering workers, have indicated that workers may adopt instrumental **attitudes** only because they feel that intrinsic satisfaction on the job is denied to them.

(Beynon, 1973; Gabriel, 1988; Goldthorpe et al., 1969)
See also **motivation**

fads and fashions

There is a huge market for new ideas and new ways of doing things in management. Companies spend considerable money on training, airport bookstalls sell large numbers of copies of management books and management consultants keep themselves in business. There is pressure to produce new ideas to replace old ones, not necessarily because the old ones did not work, but sometimes because they have never seriously been tried. There seems to be an insatiable appetite for new 'quick fixes' which trade on feelings of insecurity. Fads and fashions are often associated with a founding figure who first brought them to prominence, sometimes described as a 'management guru'. Sturdy offers six views of how management ideas and practices come to be adopted: the **rational** view – because they seem to work; the psychodynamic view – because they relieve anxiety; the dramaturgical view – because of the rhetoric of the person selling the idea; the **political** view – because someone gains power by adopting the idea; the **cultural** view – because the idea fits well with that organization; and the **institutional** view – the organization adopts the idea in order to be like other organizations in the same sector.

(Jackson, 2001; Roberts, 2005; Sturdy, 2004)

fantasy

Imagination plays an important part in our lives. People daydream, run events through in their minds, muse and imagine. This can be an involving, powerful process as if the event were actually taking place – a fantasy. Fantasizing envelops the whole person and has been shown to influence later actions. Some fantasies are surrogates for **action**, while others are rehearsals. **Skills** may be practised as fantasy, 'envisioned', to improve physical performance. There is evidence that even gymnastic and sports skills can be improved by being practised in fantasy. Many of the activities of organizing will be tried in the imagination before being acted out. For example, people will imagine how a particular meeting or telephone call might go, and practise it in fantasy. This has been shown to be a very effective form of preparation – if the fantasy is deep and involved enough, and if the fantasiser can experience some of the physical sensations that they would normally feel in the real situation. Fantasy has also been related recently to **leadership**. Some effective leaders convey a clear and attractive fantasy of how things might become; followers are then inspired to turn this fantasy into a reality.

(Bennis and Nanus, 1985; Sims, 1985, 1987)
See also **desire**, **sex**, **sexuality**

femininity

Femininity is a term used to describe equally the major components of female **sexuality** and the **role** attributes of the female **gender**. Feminist theory in the 1970s and 1980s has drawn attention to distinct features of early childhood and **socialization** which moulds the **personality** development of boys and girls and prepares them to assume different gender roles. The social construction of femininity explores how different 'agents' in society – men, magazines, storybooks, films, television, photographs, **discourses** – mould images of femininity against which women (and men) measure themselves and shape their identities. Also revealed is how patriarchal capitalist societies place greater constraints on female **sexuality** than on male, turning it against women and using it to perpetuate male privilege and domination. Psychoanalytic approaches take a different tack, focusing on early mother–child relationships. For example, Juliet Mitchell, in her book *Psychoanalysis and Feminism* argued that a girl's femininity undergoes a traumatic transformation 'from the active wanting of her mother to the passive wanting to be wanted by the father' (1975: 108). Many assumptions about the nature of femininity have proven difficult to defend across different cultural and historical contexts.

(Chodorow, 1978; Mitchell, 1975; Ross-Smith and Kornberger, 2004; Wolf, 1990)
See also **gender**, **masculinity**, **sexuality**

feminism

The feminist movement, which began in the 1960s, draws attention to the dominantly male **values** which have determined the shape of our political, institutional and organizational **structures**. Feminist writers have argued that there is a deep imbalance in societies which systematically undervalues women, relegating them to **stereotyped** roles in the home, family and work. The unequal distribution of **power** features prominently in this analysis. In organizations, the feminist case is supported by evidence of relatively few women in top positions, the disproportionate number of women in lower-**status** jobs, the poorer pay of women compared with men, and the inadequate support offered to women who wish to work and have children or to take career breaks. Feminist theorists must be credited for introducing into academic studies issues which had gone unnoticed earlier, notably relations between public and private lives and between work and sexuality. The 1990s was described as the 'post-feminist' era where many younger people have been exposed directly or indirectly to feminist thought. While some of the most rigid sex demarcations have begun to soften in the UK and the USA, most observers believe that there is still a long way to go before equal opportunities have been achieved. The shift has also been marked by some backlash from both men and women, disenchanted with more radical forms of feminism, and for whom the simple associations of 'feminist equals good' have broken down.

(Butler, 1990; Faludi, 1992; Greer, 1970, 1984; Grosz, 1994; Loe, 1999; Marshall, 1984; Miller and Metcalfe, 1998; Spencer and Podmore, 1987)
See also **femininity**, **gender**

Fordism

Fordism is a system of mass production based on the standardization of products and processes pioneered by Henry Ford (1863–1947). Stretching **Taylorist** principles to their extreme, Ford initiated the production of motor cars on assembly lines, substantially cutting production costs and improving overall quality. 'They can have it any color they like, so long as it's black', he famously said about his famous model-T, which was the first affordable car for the mass population. While paying his workers substantially more than his competitors, Ford experienced rates of labour turnover up to 400%, resulting from the **deskilling** and **alienation** of his workforce. 'We expect our men to do what they are told. The organization is so highly specialized ... that we could not for a moment consider allowing men to have their own way' (1923: 11). While Fordism dominated the world of manufacturing industries for 60 years, its domination is now virtually over. New **technologies** and new management and manufacturing techniques, notably those pioneered by the Japanese, have undermined the linking of volume, standardization and efficiency. Instead, flexibility, customer centredness, corporate **culture** and concern for quality have assumed major significance. These new production systems are sometimes referred to as post-Fordism. The thesis of **McDonaldization**, on the other hand, suggests that Fordism is alive and well, colonizing ever-expanding areas of business and social life.

(Doray, 1988; Ford, 1923; Ritzer, 1993/1996, 1998)

games

This is used in at least three senses in organizing. A style of individual and group training called transactional analysis was made popular by Berne in a book called *Games People Play*. The games he identifies have names like 'wooden leg' – a game in which a person seeks sympathy, and many other 'games' have been identified in which people treat each other in more or less inauthentic ways to achieve some undeclared end. Secondly, games refer to game theory, in which the **strategy** that a person adopts in dealing with colleagues can be understood by thinking of what they are doing as a game, with rules, moves, possibly a referee and so on. Radford has described a number of game approaches to organizational analysis. Allison pointed out that in organizations, the players are usually involved in many different games at once and the progress of one game will affect play in another. The game that is going on in the New Products Committee will affect the Chief Engineer and the Finance Director when they are both also players in the quite different game going on in the Policy Committee. To make matters more complicated, in organizational games, you may use one of your 'turns' to try to change the **rules**, rather than to play within the rules. This is called a 'hypergame', and is often indicated by phrases such as: 'I wonder if we could just check on how we are going about this task … '. Moreover, the **political** and illegitimate activities of organization members are often referred to as 'game playing'. This has something in common with both the meanings of 'game' above, but implies the similarity between much of what takes place in organizations and the school playground. Here, more or less intense, determined and possibly hurtful activities may be seen by teachers as 'just games'. But they are seen as matters of great importance by some participants, and may be very painful to them.

(Allison, 1971; Berne, 1964; Radford, 1986; Wang et al., 2001)

gender

The division of humanity into men and women has, since the sixteenth century, been assigned to the term **sex**. Sex, in other words, marks the physiological differences between the genders. Gender, however, is used to distinguish between the culturally specific patterns of behaviour or **roles** attached to the sexes (Oakley, 1972). Thus, while one is born a particular sex, one is socialized into one's gender. **Socialization** prepares individuals to perform roles consistent with their gender **identity**. Such roles may include sexual roles, family roles and work roles. In organizational settings, gender acts as a formidable divide, with women being concentrated in lower echelons of organizations, in generally low-pay, low-status industries. Even in high-pay, high-status industries, women are concentrated disproportionately in low-skill grades, mainly clerical and sales. This is partly due to old structures of **prejudice** and **discrimination**, which inhibit women's progress and **career** opportunities. More subtly, gender **stereotypes** presenting men as rational, tough, aggressive and task-oriented and women as emotional, soft, caring and process-oriented have further disadvantaged women. Women's skills, notably in clerical, sales and service jobs, are often taken for granted and lead to neither material nor **symbolic** rewards. Nevertheless, it is becoming increasingly accepted that **femininity** offers organizations a powerful though subtle mechanism of **control**; organizations like supermarkets, airlines, restaurants, media groups and banks find it desirable to maintain a low-level sexual 'simmer', the key to which is femininity, to promote their sales, enhance their image and lure customers.

(Adkins, 1995; Crompton and Jones, 1984; Lewis and Simpson, 2007; Tancred-Sheriff, 1989; Wilson, 1995)

glass ceiling

This concept has been used to explain how very able members of some groups in organizations never seem to be promoted as far as might be expected. The term was first used in talking about women in management, where there was no overt objection to them rising to the top, but they never seemed to do so. Hence the glass ceiling: they could not rise any higher because there was a ceiling in the way, but no one could see it, because it was transparent. The concept has more recently been used in the whole range of **diversity** discussions, as glass ceilings – and glass walls – can also affect many other categories of employee.

(Auster, 1993; Avery, 2008)

globalization

Globalization refers to a process where brands, capital, information, knowledge and ideas all travel freely across continents, where social, political and geographical boundaries become increasingly less meaningful. The world is increasingly influenced by global companies and global brands. People in New York, Nanjing, Nairobi and the surrounding villages of all of them want sports kit with the same logos on them. Support for football teams is no longer restricted to those in the same country or even in the same continent. Burger companies offer very similar-looking products across the world. At first, this seemed attractive; if we were all going to live in a 'global village', perhaps this would help us to live peacefully together, and perhaps the poor would benefit from living in the same global village as the rich. Then it was pointed out that global companies might be insensitive to local markets and conditions. To deal with this, global companies made gestures towards localization. For example, McDonald's in Halifax, Nova Scotia, has offered the 'McLobster', reflecting the particular tastes and availability in the area. Particular interest has been focused on global brands, which mean that marketing and production can be largely dissociated from each other, and recent commentators have mentioned the tendency to produce very cheaply in 'sweatshops' in poor countries, and then sell at high prices globally. The consumers are unaware of the poverty and harshness under which the producers of their goods have worked.

Another vital dimension of globalization is the almost instantaneous transmission of information across the world, something that makes financial markets across the globe more interdependent and more easily dominated by a handful of institutions from dominant nations. More generally, globalization refers to the increasing dominance of the **ideology** of free **markets** and free movement of goods, capitals and information (but not people) across the globe. Numerous debates are currently going on regarding globalization. Does globalization bring increasing uniformity or does it allow for local variation and diversity? Does it wipe out local traditions or does it give them a 'voice' on a global stage? Does it allow better communication and understanding across nations or does it represent a higher level in the hegemony of Western and especially American products, ideas, capital and interests over the rest of the world?

(Castells and Carnoy, 1993; Klein, 2000, 2002; Sklair, 1991; Turner, 2009)

goals

Many authors regard 'goals' as a defining feature of **organization** and speak of 'organizational goals'. At first, this appears unproblematic: the goal of a firm is to make profit, of a university to educate people, of a hospital to treat sick people. On closer inspection, however, it seems that the goals of an organization will differ in the view of different organization members. The marketing director may believe that the goal of her organization is to produce the most prestigious product in the market, and that profit will naturally follow. A lecturer may place 'research' above 'teaching' in his or her list of goals for a university, an administrator the balancing of the books, and so on. Thus, the goals of an organization appear different from different angles. Moreover, even specific goals, like 'making profit', may mean different things to different people: are we talking about long-or short-term profit, what accounting decisions have been made about the allocation of costs, and what social or personal damage may or may not have been taken into account in calculating that profit. Traditional theory, following Max Weber (1864–1920), saw organizations essentially as tools for the achievement of more or less fixed goals in a rational, business-like manner. Michels (1876–1936), however, pointed out in his *Iron Law of Oligarchy* that goals are constantly displaced in accordance with changes in the organization's environment to ensure organizational survival. A political party dedicated to a particular cause will change its objectives if they turn out to be unrealistic or unpopular. Much current management theory has sought to re-emphasize the concept of goals by subsuming it under concepts like mission or vision, which are forged by the leaders and espoused by all organizational members. Mission statements are often used as a test of goals; if your goals are inconsistent with the mission statement, you will probably keep them to yourself. Sims and Lorenzi have argued that goal setting is a crucial part of **leadership**.

(Michels, 1949; Sims and Lorenzi, 1992; Weber, 1946)

gossip

This is the act of sharing stories and snippets of information with other people. Gossip is traded in most organizations: people exchange stories with others, or tell their stories for pleasure or in order to be seen as someone in the know. Sims found that some managers will go out of their way to be in the right place to gossip with other people, believing this to be one of the most reliable ways of gaining **information** about what is going on. However, there is very little quality control on gossip, and those who engage in it may be motivated as much by their wish to entertain as by any desire to inform. The way gossip gets passed on means that there is little chance for the person being gossiped about to challenge the accuracy of the things being said about them. It is relatively easy to set a rumour going, and once someone has heard a rumour, even if they mostly do not believe it, the suspicion lurks. People will make some allowance for the reliability or the motivations of the person from whom they heard gossip, but by the time it has been through several hands, and each person has re-framed it a little to fit their interests, it may have taken on a life of its own. Gossip can sometimes be done as a virtuoso activity, for the sheer joy of spinning a good story, or to see what stories may be believed by a gullible audience. There is a related body of research, summarized by Rosnow and carried forward by Difonzo, Bordia and Rosnow, on rumours in organizations.

(Difonzo et al., 1994; Michelson et al., 2008; Rosnow, 1980; Sims, 1992)

governance
Governance is a term currently used to refer to the way organizations in the public and private sectors are ruled; it thus refers both to the **structures** through which important **decisions** are made and the processes whereby different **stakeholders** may influence these decisions. Major organizational failures, like the collapse of Enron, are often seen as resulting from failings in corporate governance. In this sense, governance refers to the ways in which a company's board of directors, shareholder bodies and executive are structured and how responsibility is shared. But governance has also another meaning, namely the processes through which **leadership** and decision making are diffused throughout an organization or even society at large, enabling citizens to participate in public affairs, develop and defend public values and promote their interests. Thus, governance allows citizens, networks, groups and community organizations to be drawn into the governing process without assuming that the government is the centre of power or the central authority for coordinating all activities (Jun, 2002: 289). In this sense, governance involves:

- de-centralized decision making
- mistrust of overtly instrumental planning
- a taming of the influence of the elite and professionals
- a furtherance of continuous organizational learning in place of ossified bodies of knowledge
- a curbing of interest-group politics by enhanced institutions of popular control and accountability.

(Castells, 1998; Deakin and Hughes, 1997; Forbes and Milliken, 1999; Rhodes, 1996; Starkey, 1995; Westphal and Zajac, 1998)

groups
Much work is undertaken by groups in some form or other. These may be formal, such as committees, project groups or teams; or informal, 'unofficial' relationships and cliques which influence the pace, quality and output of work. The study of formal groups has focused on the way different sizes, **structures** and compositions of groups affect productivity and satisfaction, and the kind of roles that people play. The dominant research in groups had been in the area of 'group dynamics': why and how groups form and how their internal workings change over time. The now classic 1930s study of workers at the Hawthorne Electric Plant in the USA first revealed that it was the groups' informal allegiances, **norms** and pressures to **conform** that could far outweigh managerial attempts to manipulate productivity. One more recent application of this type of thinking can be seen in Volvo's attempt in the 1970s and 1980s to replace the long car production line with autonomous working groups of assemblers. Informal groupings often emerge as a way of meeting social, emotional and security needs which cannot be addressed in the formal organization.

   Groups can be highly cohesive, to the extent that they will resist changes which disturb their pattern of relationships. Likewise, they can freeze out or eject members who break the informal codes of practice, such as on levels of productivity or timekeeping. Groups will often go through discernible stages of development, from an early 'sounding out' of members, through to a surfacing of differences and personal agendas (hidden desires, anxieties or aspirations), to ultimate consolidation or collapse. When groups are able to creatively combine the strengths of their members, 'synergy' is said to occur: the total product is greater than the sum of the individual efforts of the members of the group. On the other hand, groups can get trapped in their own cohesiveness. Studies of major decision-making teams have revealed the tendency to 'groupthink', where individuals feel invulnerable, rapidly dismiss opposing ideas, and take wild risks. Groupthink can be seductive – and dangerous – and has been thought to be behind some of the biggest mistakes in decision making at national and international levels, such as Britain's do-nothing policy towards Hitler prior to the Second World War and the unpreparedness of US forces at Pearl Harbor. Janis has described groupthink as the 'deterioration of mental efficiency, reality testing and moral judgment that results from in-group pressures' (1972: 9). Typically, people who try to resist the group are stereotyped as weak, stupid, even evil.

(Anzieu, 1984; Bion, 1961; Douglas, 1983; Janis, 1972; Levi, 2007)

harassment
See **bullying, sexual harassment**

Hawthorne Effect
See **human relations**

hierarchy
Hierarchy is a feature of organizational **structure**, usually referring to a **system** of **control** in which higher offices control the lower ones. Weberian **bureaucracy** forms a strict hierarchy of control, essentially like a military command structure, with no horizontal lines of **communication** across levels. While most organizations have hierarchies, they deviate considerably from Weber's model by incorporating horizontal lines of communication and appointing collegiate bodies, task forces or committees which cut across the hierarchy. Organic organizations permit individuals to communicate across levels of the hierarchy with scant regard for hierarchy. Classical **management** theory envisaged each officer as capable of controlling no more than about ten subordinates. The result was that large organizations tended to have numerous levels, i.e. their structure was tall and thin. The fashion now is to move towards short and flat hierarchies eliminating most middle levels of management. More generally, hierarchies are often seen as inhibiting innovation and creativity, locking people into relations of domination and subordination, which run counter both to the democratic ethos and to the requirements of complex organizations today. The concept of **network** organization, an organization in which individuals relate to each other in flexible, non-hierarchical ways, is then offered as an alternative to traditional hierarchies.

See also **contingency theories, environment, matrix structure, networks**

homosexuality
Homosexuality refers to a sexual preference for members of the same **sex**. While seen as a sin, a crime or a (possibly transmittable) disease by some **cultures**, it is condoned or even encouraged by others (like the ancient Greeks). Homosexuality is felt to be normal and natural for and by some men and women. It has been studied in numerous different cultures and societies, where it often merges with heterosexuality in a bisexual orientation. Psychologically, there is evidence of homosexual **desires** even among heterosexuals, even though such desires may remain repressed or may be sublimated in feelings of camaraderie and friendship. In spite of the decriminalization of homosexuality in the USA and Britain, it is still viewed with hostility by some whose sexual **norms** it undermines or threatens. Within organizations, many gays and lesbians prefer to conceal their **sexuality** rather than face the intolerance and bigotry of their superiors, peers and subordinates. Gay and lesbian liberation movements are fighting to eliminate **prejudice** and **discrimination** and to ensure that people's opportunities and freedom are not restricted by their sexual orientation.

(Hearn and Parkin, 1987; Hearn et al., 1989; King et al., 2008; Ward and Winstanley, 2003)

human relations
Human relations emerged as one of the early influential **management** theories in response to **scientific management** in the 1920s and emphasized the importance of the social and **group** factors

in explaining **motivation**. Elton Mayo (1880–1949), widely regarded as the father of this approach, argued that through work, people try to fulfil social needs (1949/1975). They generally work harder when they feel part of cohesive groups, rather than in response to financial incentives and **extrinsic rewards**. This insight was derived partly from the initially puzzling results from a series of experiments conducted by Mayo and his associates. They took place at the Hawthorne Works of the Western Electric Corporation, Chicago, in the late 1920s and early 1930s.

The investigators set out to find the optimum level of illumination for work on the assembly and inspection of relays used in telephone equipment. To their surprise, whatever level of illumination they imposed, production went up, even when the lighting was reduced to very low levels. This so-called **Hawthorne Effect** was subsequently put down to the overriding motivational effects on the workers from feeling special, part of an exclusive experiment with special attention from managers and researchers. In other observations of working practices, the investigators noted the powerful effects of group norms on how much a group produced, and the sanctions devised by the group to ensure everyone conformed. In other words, production was only partly in the control of management.

(Buchanan and Huczynski, 2006; Roethlisberger and Dickson, 1939)

human resources
This is a term now taken for granted in most organizations to suggest, in economic language, that people are a 'resource' to be used with skill and care. What was once personnel management is now, in the main, 'human resource management' (HRM), with 'human capital' following on as the next terminological change for this area, taking the language even further into the realm of economics. Such labels **symbolize** different ways in which people are seen and used in organizations. Human resources sound more objective and distant; it is easier to release human resources than it is to sack people. They also represent different philosophies of management. Personnel management, for example, reflects the notion that people have a right to proper treatment as dignified human beings, and it is the role of the personnel manager to intervene in the supervisor–subordinate relationship to ensure this occurs. Human resource management, however, places the care of employees more directly in the hands of all line managers, rather than a separate specialist. The employee's welfare and commitment is a 'resource' to manage as part of the whole resources picture (e.g. time, materials, money). HRM focuses particularly on seeking direct employee communication and involvement.

(Guest, 1987; Torrington et al., 2007)

humanistic perspective
This is a view in the behavioural sciences which says that humans are, or at least may be, different in kind from other creatures and objects, and need to be studied in a way which recognizes this. It grew out of the philosophical tradition of humanism which approached humans as free agents, capable of improving their lot through education and enlightenment. This perspective may be contrasted with the logical–positivist view of Ayer (1910–89) (see Ayer and Jules, 1959) and the behaviourist approach of Skinner (1904–90) (see Skinner, 1965). In Skinner's work, experiments were performed to deduce the kind of responses that could be associated with particular stimuli. Behaviourists regard the 'inner' working of humans (e.g. feelings and sentiments) as inaccessible to objective study. It is, therefore, more appropriate to confine one's observations to tangible and manipulable stimuli and responses.

The humanist argument has been put by Harré and Secord, among others, in, proposing an anthropomorphic model of humans. By this, they mean that we should study human beings as we actually know them to be, and not assume that we cannot access what goes on in the mind of an individual. It is not appropriate to study actions as if we were observing the behaviour of electrons. Humanist social researchers would argue that we should not be restricted in our studies by traditional scientific method, as applied to the natural sciences. Instead, we should adapt our methods to the matter being studied, such as through qualitative accounts of experience and

emotions. Among the distinctly human qualities that may be worth studying is **meaning**. Without considering meaning, and the extent to which it is produced by individual interpretation, much of what we know about organizing would be lost. This book is an example of the humanist perspective.

(Harré and Secord, 1972; Herrick, 2005; Skinner, 1966)

identity and organizational identity

Identity refers to the way a person sees him/herself, what makes him/her a unique individual and different from others. If the fact that I go windsurfing is very important to my view of what it means to be me, then we say that it is part of my identity. It is possible, but not easy, for people to change their views of themselves. On the whole, people respond quite differently to criticism when the matter in question is part of their identity. If you mock all windsurfers, and I am a windsurfer, I may not mind. But if it is really important to me that I am a windsurfer, if it is part of my identity, I may feel personally attacked and wish to defend myself. Identity is often connected with job position. If you ask people what they do, the answer will reveal something about their identity; they may answer in terms of a profession ('I am a doctor'), an organization ('I work for IBM'), a rank ('I am a lieutenant colonel'), or an activity ('I act as a sounding board for people'). In addition to the work we do, many of the objects we consume become part of our identity. Erikson argued that identity is far from easy to construct. Individuals may go through periods of identity crisis, when they are not sure exactly who or what they are meant to be. Identity crises are most common during life's major transitions, such as adolescence. Hewitt has pointed out some of the confusions surrounding identity. He distinguishes between: (a) identity, a person's sense of their place relative to others (how I see myself on my 30th birthday); (b) social identity, which is the other's cumulative sense of that person's place (how others see me on my 30th birthday); (c) situated identity, the sense of who the person is in a particular situation (how I see myself in the strategy meeting); and (d) situated social identity, which is the others' view of who the person is in that particular situation (how others see me in the strategy meeting). Recent studies in identity have looked at those whose identities are denied or devalued by their organization, and at people's own stories of themselves as ways of developing and maintaining identity.

Organizational identity and image have recently come to the fore as an analogous concept; identity is important for organizations too, especially where they are seeking **globalization** or are wanting to distinguish themselves as interesting places to work. At times, this may refer to the logo and the advertising campaign, and on other occasions it may go more deeply into the **myths** and the **management of meaning** in the organization.

(Ashforth et al., 2008; Erikson, 1968; Hatch and Schultz, 2004; Hewitt, 1984; Linstead and Linstead, 2004)
See also **alienation, resistance**

ideology

Ideology is a term that describes a dominant pattern, or patterns, of beliefs and values in a society. Typically, an ideology reinforces the control by a particular, 'representative' or governing group in society. We thus talk about the ideology of capitalism, communism or Marxism. It emerges, and is legitimized, within a culture through teaching, **socialization**, and the promotion of a specific set of values, beliefs and symbols. These condition people's thinking and feelings about their world, such that they are taken as undisputed realities about how society 'is' – the natural state of affairs. Some ideologies can become totalitarian and oppressive such as East Germany's communism and Maoism in China. Dominant ideologies in a society provide an apparently neutral, or indisputable, reason for actions in accord with the ideology. From a feminist ideology, for example, women are subordinated by men, therefore corrective action is required. Business schools tend to promote a managerialist ideology which supports the objectives of a market economy. Given this standpoint, it is possible to justify actions such as organizational restructuring, downsizing and layoffs as if there were no alternative. While the influence of dominant ideologies is ever-present, many organizations adapt to, or wrestle with, tensions between ideologies, such as consumerism versus conservation and industrial democracy versus centralized control.

(Abercrombie, 1994; Alvesson, 1991; Andrew, 2004; Edwards, 2006)

impersonality
Impersonality is a dominant feature of modern **bureaucracies**, in which many transactions and relations are stripped of their human interpersonal content and reduced to their formal dimension. Contrast the impersonal procedure of being selected for a course in higher education on the basis of your application form by people who have never met you, with the complex interpersonal relations with your friends and relatives. Arguably, impersonality confers some advantages to organizations. It limits the time spent on irrelevant chatter, it reduces arbitrariness and inconsistency and it goes some way to ensuring equal treatment. If everyone is treated as a number, everyone will be treated equally. Being treated like a number, however, is not something that most people appreciate. Impersonality is often seen as a major contributing factor to **alienation**, **meaninglessness** and **anomie**. Within modern organizations, lamented Max Weber, 'the performance of each individual is mathematically measured, each man becomes a little cog in the machine and, aware of this, his one preoccupation is whether he can become a bigger cog' (Mayer, 1956: 126–7). Also, the loss of the 'irrelevant' chatter and **gossip** can have serious negative consequences for organizational learning.

(Courpasson, 2001; du Gay, 2000; Grey and Garsten, 2001; Mayer, 1956; Reed, 1999)

implicit personality theory
In perceiving, and making judgements about, other people, we focus on a number of features or cues: their clothes, their voice quality, their size, their posture, any previous knowledge we have of their character and so forth. What do these perceptions add up to? What kind of behaviour or attitudes can we expect from the people we perceive? It is here that our implicit personality theories come into play; the kinds of actions we *believe* go with particular personal qualities. For example, one study showed that, on voice alone, 'breathiness' in men was believed to suggest a young, artistic person, whereas in a female it was regarded as indicating a pretty and shallow person. An experiment conducted by Kelley back in 1950 illustrates the point: he gave students brief written descriptions of a new guest lecturer shortly before the man performed. The description was the same for all students, except for one item which portrayed the man as 'rather cold' for half the students, and 'very warm' for the other half. After the lecture, the 'warm' group rated the lecturer as significantly more considerate, informed, sociable and popular than the 'cold' group. In other words, these qualities were seen to go with a warm, not a cold, person. We call on our implicit personality theories to make our social judgements and they can affect how we view and treat other people. They may not be accurate in an objective sense, and they may foster **stereotyping**, but they are convenient and economical.

(Hinton, 1993; Kelley, 1972; Werth and Forster, 2002)

impression formation
We form our impressions of other people by using the cues available, such as dress, voice, gait, accent, setting. We then fit them together through our 'assumptive framework': what we *expect* people to be who dress like, talk like, be in places like, to be and do. Our **implicit personality theories** are important in this process, as are our **prejudices** and **stereotypes**. Generally, these all serve to help make complex judgements manageable. The signs and **symbols** which facilitate impression formation are amenable to manipulation, to the extent that 'impression management' has become an academic field of interest in its own right. Like professional actors, we learn what 'mask' to assume for what occasion, the aim being to create the socially desired impression. So we 'need' to look jolly at parties, and 'should' look authoritative at meetings. Impression management is exploited for commercial purposes, such as the training of sales staff, waiters, receptionists and

flight attendants to appear neat, bright and positive. Some executives, like professional politicians, are coached on how to look and sound right in front of an audience or camera. Also, job applicants can receive detailed instruction on how to sharpen their self-presentation skills in order to impress an interviewer.

(Breen and Karpinski, 2008; Giacalone and Rosenfeld, 1991; Jones, 1990)
See also **interview**

improvisation

While early management writers placed much emphasis on planning and control, there has been considerable recent interest in improvisation as a way of understanding action in organizations. Like the jazz player, the skilled operator in a meeting does not know exactly how his or her performance is going to turn out beforehand. It will depend on how the other performers are behaving, on the mood of the moment, and on good ideas which occur at the time. Improvisation thus becomes a much more convincing metaphor for action in organizations than any more scripted notion that implies more detailed planning. Effective action is often opportunistic, responding to situations that had not been forseen in any great detail and making the most of them. However, it would be a mistake to think of improvisation as not being prepared. The jazz musician who has spent years of practice improving their art is easily distinguishable from the novice who really is making it all up as they go along. The skilled improvisor has practised playing skills to such an extent that they do not have to pay attention to them, and has structured in advance the framework within which they will improvise. Jazz groups usually know who is going to take the next solo, and roughly how long it will be, because they have planned it. Likewise, improvisation in organizations works well when the person improvising is skilled at what they are trying to do, and has planned how they are going to approach the task. Having done that, they can improvise successfully and make the most of the situation in front of them.

(Cornelissen, 2006; Weick, 1998)
See also **bricolage**

informal networks

Informal networks refer to the personal connections and **communications** instigated by people within and between organizations, and maintained to serve their interests. Informal networks reflect the need for **action** or influence that formal channels impede or inhibit. They are based on personal friendships, family associations or ties from shared professional, club or religious interests, as well as groups such as the smokers within an organization, whose gathering around the nearest point where they are allowed to indulge can form a good network. Informal networks often involve reciprocal favours and shared secrets and jokes, as well as a common mistrust or dislike of third parties. Studies of informal networks reveal that they can be a major, often invisible, force influencing how resources are allocated in an organization, how staff appointments are made, and how certain jobs get done. The informal network can act well as an antidote to inflexible **bureaucracy**; on the other hand, it can reinforce power elites and **oligarchies**.

(Davis and Powell, 1992; Rank 2008; Tichy and Fombrun, 1979)
See also **groups**, **politics**

informal organization
See **groups**, **informal networks**

information

Spoken words, telephone calls, emails, computer printouts, CD and video discs are all *sources* of information. Strictly speaking, we cannot meaningfully refer to them as information until they have *informed* someone, until they are selected and interpreted by the receiver. For this reason, they are better viewed more neutrally as *data*, as stimuli generated in some form of **communication**.

They become information when they begin to 'inform', reinforce or change one's thoughts, feelings, **attitudes** or **actions**. Because data are now often presented in many different ways, in enormous quantity and speed, we often encounter problems of selection and interpretation. What data produce valuable information and what are redundant? Thus, we speak of information overload when we try to assimilate and use more data than we can handle. Information is part of every **political** game, where 'intelligence' about the movements and intentions of other players is crucial in anticipating developments and taking advantage of them. In the same way, disinformation and deception ('bluffing') are features of many games. Information, accurate and inaccurate, true and false, is traded, concealed and fabricated as part of politics. The skilful handling and management of information is a key source of **power**.

Information is sometimes seen as the same as **knowledge**, since knowledge too confers power. It is misleading, however, to view all knowledge as information. A piece of information (for example, the sacking of a CEO) may be passed from person to person, without essentially changing, even though different people may read different **meanings** into it. By contrast, when knowledge is communicated from one person to another, it assumes quite different forms. The recipients of knowledge 'translate' it, refine it and develop it to fit their own needs and requirements. Thus, while the diffusion of information is sometimes likened to the diffusion of electricity across a network, the diffusion of knowledge assumes more complex and unpredictable forms. Generally, it is possible to have too much information while it is not possible to have too much knowledge.

(Boyle, 2000; Ciborra, 2002; Sturdy and Fleming, 2003)
See also **information technology**, **knowledge and knowledge management**

information technology
This phrase is often used to refer to recent electronic advances in handling information, but may also be seen more widely. Computers are an important part of information technology. So too are electronic diaries, telephones, manual card indexes, typewriters and even paper and pen. In fact, all technologies concerned with storing, processing, retrieving and communicating information can be seen as information technologies, and as such the label might well relate to **knowledge** management. Yet, the phrase 'IT' has now come to denote exclusively electronic types of information technology. The emphasis on savings and **rationalization** accomplished through the use of IT has tended to obscure some of its indirect effects on styles and quality of **work**. Weick has identified five types of deficiency resulting from working with computerized information systems: action deficiencies, because you get less feedback (sounds, smells and so on) from an information system than you do from, say, the factory that it is informing you about; comparison deficiencies, because you cannot walk round and look at it from the other side, as you would with a physical object; affiliation deficiencies, because you are less likely to form your opinions by talking through the output from an information system with others; deliberation deficiencies, as you struggle to see the wood for the trees (a particularly appropriate metaphor when thinking about the piles of printouts that can come from a computer); and consolidation deficiencies, as you may assume that the hard work of thinking through the conclusions has already been done (because it all looks so final when it comes from the computer). However, these deficiencies do not prevent us all from relying more and more on such technology and finding this an interesting and enjoyable experience.

Computerized information technologies do not merely alter the way work is done but force a re-configuration of the work that is done; tasks that would have been impossible before become possible as a result of the availability of new information technology. Thus, the availability of the internet allows for new markets (such as eBay) and new companies (like Amazon and Google) to come into existence. In hospitals or schools, the introduction of computerized information technologies does not merely lead to better and more efficient record keeping and **communication**, but can alter in a fundamental way the ways that health and education are delivered and even the meaning of the words 'health' and 'education'.

The effects of information technology on our societies have become so pronounced that some major sociologists, like Castells, refer to it as an *information age* or *informational capitalism*. In such a society, the processing and management of information determines the competitiveness and productivity of economic units, be they firms, regions or countries. Furthermore, because of the ease and speed with which information can be exchanged, many economic activities, such as the operation of markets, assume a **global** character. Finally, new information technologies allow for the emergence of new types of organizations, which assume qualities of **virtuality** or information networks.

(Castells, 1998; Fineman et al., 2007; Weick, 1985; Zuboff, 1985, 1988)

innovation

Innovation, along with the related concepts of **creativity** and **entrepreneurialism**, is increasingly seen as a quality conferring competitive advantage on individuals, firms or even nations. Innovation involves the channelling of creativity into the conceptualization of new products, new ways of doing things, new applications for existing things and new combinations of existing things. One of the important lessons of the innovation literature is that virtually none of the innovations that changed the world (for instance, Edison's electric light or Henry Ford's assembly lines) involved first principles; instead, they relied extensively on the creative and innovative deployment of existing technologies, materials and ideas. Another lesson is that many innovations arise from an ability to spot a random opportunity or an opportunity which arises out of an error. Error-free operations tend to discourage innovation. Thirdly, although often attributed to a single genius, innovation is the result of collective efforts and thrives in communities of practice which have a local character; thus, as the example of Silicon Valley suggests, innovation is the outcome, as Brown and Duguid argue, of social rather than informational **networks**, in other words, networks of people who do not merely communicate by email, but see and talk to each other from time to time. Finally, it is noted that innovation is related to variation. Uniformity and routine tend to stifle innovation; discussion, argument and criticism enhance it. While it is currently fashionable to talk of innovation excitedly in uniformly positive terms, it is worth bearing in mind that innovation has a deep dark side, suggested by Schumpeter's expression of 'creative destruction'. The new comes to dislodge and destroy the old, even where the old is perfectly serviceable. It is arguable whether the majority of innovations, including those that proved great commercial successes, have done much to enhance the overall level of human happiness and well-being.

(Abrahamson, 1991; Brown and Duguid, 2002; Burns and Stalker, 1961; Dodgson et al., 2008; Kanter, 1983; Mumford, 1934; Nonaka and Takeuchi, 1995; Schumpeter, 1943; Swan et al., 2002)

institution

Institution refers to a set of practices, a **system** of relations or an **organization** which is infused with **value** and recognized as part of the way of doing things. The monarchy in Britain, a regular television soap opera, the Superbowl, Harvard University, Rolls Royce and marriage are all institutions. Institutions sometimes acquire venerability with time as they become invested with special **meaning** and as they prove their staying power by becoming traditions. In *Leadership and Administration*, Philip Selznik argued that the task of the **leader** is to infuse **organizations** with **meaning**, thus turning inert **bureaucracies** into institutions. Institutions have a sense of permanence, consistency, clear **rules** and are objectified. Selznik's argument has re-surfaced in the recent literature of **corporate culture**, in which a primary function of leaders is the **management** of an organization's **values** and **meanings**. For example, health and safety procedures have the status of an institution in many organizations now. They are seen not merely as a set of **bureaucratic** practices, but as the right, decent and sensible way of protecting employees from risk.

(Hyman, 1989; Peters and Waterman, 1982; Scott, 2001; Selznick, 1957)

institutional theory

In contrast to the proponents of **contingency theory**, institutional theorists argue that organizations in the same field are more similar than might be expected simply from the contingent demands of their environment. Organizations in the same industry show signs of isomorphism, that is, of becoming the same shape as each other. This is because, rather than always searching for the most **rational** action they could take, organization members become used to certain practices and ways of doing things. Why do accounting firms in major financial centres end up relatively similar to each other in the way they are structured? DiMaggio and Powell argue that this is because of three factors. Firstly, there are coercive influences from government regulatory bodies, which are applied to a whole industry. For example, since the collapse of Enron and Arthur Andersen, regulations have come in the UK to prevent accounting firms offering consulting and auditing services to the same clients. Secondly, when there is considerable uncertainty, organizations cope with ambiguity by modelling themselves after other organizations that they know about. Thirdly, there are influences that come from the profession being practised by the members of the different organization. They have often trained together, they socialize with each other and they meet at continuing professional development events. This last mechanism is very much like a community of practice.

(DiMaggio and Powell, 1983; Judge et al., 2008; Morgan and Sturdy, 2000)

institutionalization

Institutionalization refers to the process of: (a) becoming dependent on an institution (e.g. patients); (b) becoming contained by an institution (e.g. political or industrial **conflict**); and (c) turning into an institution (e.g. turkey at Christmas). The second and third meanings of the term are explained under **institution**, so we restrict our comments here to the first. People who have worked or lived in an organization for a long time may find life outside frightening and confusing. This is a well-documented effect for those who have been in '**total institutions**', like prisons, secure psychiatric hospitals, ships or military organizations, for a long time. Such organizations control large areas of the lives of their members or inmates, eliminating choices about what time to get up in the morning, what to wear, where to go and so on. Life outside gradually becomes difficult to imagine and the person becomes unable to function independently. Similar processes occur among long-serving employees of some organizations, for whom working for another company becomes unimaginable. Such employees may find the transition to retirement especially taxing.

(Goffman, 1961)

intelligence

Intelligence is a controversial concept with definitions varying from 'it is whatever an intelligence test measures', to a 'profile of a range of mental abilities'. The latter includes deductive reasoning, memory, number facility and verbal comprehension. Measured intelligence is often expressed as a numerical score, an 'intelligence quotient' (IQ) in relation to the population group to which the person belongs: men, women, adults, children and adolescents. Some psychologists argue that intelligence is so important that if we measure it early enough in a child's school career, his or her educational achievement can be predicted and planned. Others see intelligence as susceptible to many of life's influences and hard to measure fairly, given people's differences in culture and socio-economic background. In response, so-called 'culture fair' paper-and-pencil tests have been devised which rely less, or not at all, on conventional language facility. These, however, often fail to account for people who have a strong practical intelligence and show their ability through doing things. Indeed, some writers, such as Howard Gardner, have argued that there are multiple intelligences. As well as the linguistic and logical ones that are valued at school, we have social and interpersonal intelligences, which contribute to our degree of emotional sensitivity – one feature of **emotional intelligence**. An argument has raged for years as to what proportion of measured intelligence is due to social environmental (nurture) factors, and what proportion we are born with (nature). On balance, one can conclude that both play a part, but often a stimulating learning environment will significantly boost intelligence scores.

(Gardner, 1993; Gould, 1996; Vernon, 1979; Wilhelm and Engle, 2004)

interpersonal skills

Interpersonal skills refer to the particular **competences** we have in relating to one another, face to face. Just as someone might be skilled at painting, lathe turning, brick laying or word processing, so we may be skilled in the way we interact socially. Typical interpersonal skills include listening, communicating, empathizing, diagnosing, negotiating, talking and assertiveness. We can become more proficient in these **skills** with training and practice. Consequently, there are training programmes available (within and outside companies) where interpersonal skills can be learned. In some occupations, such as medicine, lecturing, dentistry, social work and hairdressing, interpersonal skills are intrinsic to effective performance. Ironically, though, many of these occupations do not offer interpersonal skills training for new recruits.

(Chung and Megginson, 1981; Hayes, 2002; Kleinke, 1986)
See also **emotional intelligence, groups, informal networks, motivation**

interview

Interviews have become virtually taken for granted as a form of assessment for recruitment by employers and job candidates. They are seen to be an important way of evaluating a person's character and **competence**. Nevertheless, studies such as those of Dulewicz frequently show interviews to be questionable in their reliability and validity. In other words, the judgements made are often inconsistent and are poor predictors of later performance on the job. In addition, interviews are often conducted by specialist recruiters who may have little close knowledge of the job for which they are interviewing. The 'halo' effect is a common problem, where one quality or trait of the candidate such as attractiveness, the type of school attended, **race**, **ethnicity** or age swamps the interviewer's judgement. As Mainiero points out, this may need to be countered deliberately. Research indicates that many decisions are made within the first few minutes of an interview, and the interviewer often spends the remaining period seeking evidence to support that judgement. Well-prepared and skilled interviewers are able to reduce some of these difficulties. This involves a careful study of the job and organization question and its personal requirements, as well as a thorough familiarization with pre-interview material – application forms, references, **psychological tests**. Interviews are also used at many other points in a career, for example in **performance appraisal**, for promotion, and on leaving an organization. The same problems of reliability and validity apply to all these situations.

Job interviews have developed into a **ritual** which is easily recognizable to those who are accustomed to them. In many cases, there will be a dress code and a standard set of processes. In some places, the candidate may shake hands with all members of an appointment panel on entry, then be invited to make a presentation on what they would do if they were in the post applied for, then be asked questions that have been pre-arranged by the interview panel, and finally asked if they have any questions of their own. Those who have understood this ritual from the outset are likely to be made to feel more at ease and perform better.

(Dulewicz, 1991; Lewis, 1985; Mainiero, 1994; Muir and McFarlin, 2005)
See also **impression formation**

job satisfaction

Early theories of **management** and administration focused on ways of enhancing worker productivity and assumed that the major incentive to work was money. This assumption was challenged by a series of studies from the 1930s onwards which indicated that many people will seek job satisfaction by meeting social and emotional needs at work, as well as financial ones. Influential **motivational** theorists such as Abraham Maslow, Douglas McGregor, Frederick Herzberg and David McClelland supported this line of thought, coalescing in the 1950s and 1960s into a **human relations** perspective in organizational behaviour. This explored various ways in which job satisfaction can be achieved and how opportunities for achievement, self-actualization (realizing one's potential) and control can be designed into a job. In the 1970s, job satisfaction ideas were expanded in a wider 'Quality of Working Life' movement which placed a strong accent on the importance of worker **participation** in the decisions which affect their lives. Elements of this thinking have become standard practice in **human resource management**, often assessed though standardized measures. Job satisfaction, though, has limitations. It is restrictive in capturing the range and mobility of feelings about work and there are now approaches which aim to address the wider complexity, and emotional **meanings**, of workplace experiences.

(Arvey et al., 1991; Kusnet, 2008; Sandelands and Boudens, 2000; Smith et al., 1969)

jokes

Like myths, stories and rituals, these are ingredients of organizational **culture**, which offer insights into the feelings and **desires** of organizational members. Freud argued that jokes offer a partial amnesty, allowing repressed desire to surface and taboo ideas to be expressed. More recently, it has been argued that jokes provide a symbolic route of escape out of the iron cage of **bureaucracy**, enabling the individual to poke fun at a system which is **impersonal** and inhuman. At the same time, jokes may offer a safety valve that provides relief from boredom, stress and unhappiness, blocking any real force for change. Some jokes, especially those relying on stereotypes, may be part of ritual humiliation or bullying, re-inforcing relations of domination and subordination. Other jokes (which may also rely on stereotypes) may be part of what are known as 'joking relations', where ritual horseplay and insults serve as the basis for trust and intimacy.

(Bergson, 1980; Collinson, 1988, 2002; Douglas, 1975; Freud, 1905; Westwood and Rhodes, 2006; Zijderveld, 1983)

knowledge and knowledge management

In one sense, knowledge is the object of knowing. However, it has recently taken on an extra meaning with respect to organizations, work and the economy. With the spread and the relatively easy availability of **information**, the issue for many in organizations has become not how to gain information but how to make good use of it. When information is integrated and turned into a form where it is possible for professionals to make use of it, we describe it as knowledge. A *knowledge organization* is one in which much of the capital value of the organization is in the ability of its members to exploit knowledge or to be able to turn information into knowledge. Those who do this are described as doing *knowledge work*. Where many organizations are doing this kind of work, we have a *knowledge economy*. If knowledge is such a valuable resource, can it be managed? Many companies clearly believe that it can, because they have appointed knowledge managers to do it. Knowledge management is concerned with the question of how an organization can share as much knowledge as possible internally. As used to be said in Hewlett Packard: 'If only we knew what we know, we could be amazing'. It is not uncommon in organizations for people to make mistakes, miss opportunities or solve problems that have already been solved before, while others in the company have the knowledge that would be needed to improve matters. Knowledge management has often consisted of trying to build databases of activities, solutions, ideas and potential improvements so that others can access these as needed. This has proved difficult, partly because most people are more interested in dealing with the situation that confronts them than they are in going back after dealing with a situation and recording for the database what they did. This is partly because it is difficult to find consistent ways of describing situations so that you find what you were looking for in the database entry, partly because the search process tends to be boring, and partly because many people get their **job satisfaction** from solving problems, not from looking to see how someone else solved them. Recent work on knowledge management has emphasized more traditional, less formalized ways of sharing knowledge, such as storytelling.

(Davenport and Prusak, 2000; Denning, 2000; Swan and Scarbrough, 2001)

labour

Labour is the ability of human beings to use their creative capacities in moulding nature to their needs. Marx argued that labour is what makes humans distinctly human and that through labour, intellectual, spiritual and technical capacities develop. Capitalist production impoverishes labour, **alienating** men and women from their products, from their creative activities, and from their fellow humans. Instead of marking the proud and joyful deployment of people's creative powers, labour comes to be equated with oppression, exploitation and dehumanization. In such labour, man becomes like an animal, and only in leisure can he obtain a taste of freedom and fulfilment. Marx's uncompromising equation of labour with what makes man distinctly human has been criticized, or at least complemented by other uniquely human qualities, notably **symbolic** communication and **desire**. Nevertheless, Marx's contention that the organization of labour in a society has profound repercussions on the society's cultural, religious, legal and family **institutions** has found substantial support in the work of anthropologists. In the last 20 years, many sociologists have been moving away from work towards leisure and consumption activities as the area of life where **identities** are shaped.

Labour has traditionally been divided up into manual and intellectual – the latter has been seen as socially superior to the former. Increasingly, however, it is becoming common to talk of other types of labour, such as **emotional labour**, **aesthetic** labour or even narrative labour. Much of the **work** that people do today in industrialized countries relies on the manipulation of symbols, the tapping of keys on computers or the display of appropriate emotional or physical attributes.

See also **deskilling, emotional labour, work, work ethic**

language

Managers spend most of their time on **talk** and **discourse**, much of it in metaphor. As their activity is mediated by language, they need to be proficient at it. For visionary or charismatic leaders, language is crucial in order to convey images. The images of an 'Iron Curtain' or a 'Cold War' were central to politics after the Second World War. Studying the language people use in organizations can help us understand many of its processes. Types of address (first names, surnames, titles), jargon and so on can tell much about an organization's **culture** and **hierarchy**. Different types of word convey different kinds of **information**. For example, if one wants to look at the style in which things are done, the adverbs used to talk about it are revealing, such as 'quickly', 'impatiently' and 'sensitively'. Language is of special significance in international **communication**. Important nuances may be lost in translation, or even between different versions of the same language. People whose second language is English often find it easier to understand each other, even when speaking English, than to understand Americans or British people. The study of language has assumed extraordinary importance in the human sciences in the twentieth century.

It is now widely accepted that language is not merely a means of expression but a central faculty of the human mind, directly affecting the ways we think and feel. This suggests that far from describing an already existing world, language helps us construct a world, inventing new distinctions and observing new phenomena. It also enables us to contest particular views of the world and challenge particular **power** blocks. Language does not merely confer power on those who can use it skilfully, but it embodies and even perpetuates power relations, privileges and social injustices. The use of the term 'girl' to refer to a mature woman, for instance, may well represent an attempt to diminish her; in another context, it may represent a much appreciated attempt at inclusion and even flattery. Likewise, the use of terms like 'disabled', 'unemployed', 'homeless' and so forth establish categories of what is normal and what is abnormal that bolster social inequalities. This also reveals that language is not so different from **action** – indeed, many uses of language are actions. 'I pronounce you man and wife' are words that, in the right circumstances, effect a marriage. They also perpetuate a power relation which defines the woman ('wife') in terms of her relation to the man ('man') rather than the other way round, leaving no doubt as to who 'is meant to' be the dominant partner in this relation. Whether or not this is the case with most actual couples is a debatable point.

(Beattie, 1983; Burke, 1966; Chia and King, 2001; Fairclough, 1995; Lennie, 2001; Tannen, 1995; Thatchenkery, 2001; Westwood and Linstead, 2001)

leadership

Leadership theorizing has been prolific in organizational behaviour writings. Many different approaches have been taken. The most common-sense one has been to seek the personal ingredients for leader success – the **personality** characteristics which mark out leaders from followers, or successful leaders from unsuccessful ones. Despite a multitude of studies, this line of inquiry has been fairly sterile. In some situations, some people can be effective leaders, while in other situations, they are not. But we need to be clear about what we mean by effective. For example, high output may be achieved, but at the cost of much stress and depressed morale. Consequently, work has gone into creating 'contingency theories', mapping out the kind of personal qualities and behaviours which link with particular characteristics of situations to produce different leadership effects. The style of leader behaviour ('people' or 'task' orientation), his or her power, the structure of the task, and the particular needs of the followers, are some of the ingredients that have been put into the contingency equation. Contingency theories can be complex and difficult to translate into practice. Recent attention has moved towards a more subtle understanding of the way that followers and leaders interact and the role of the leader's face-to-face, **interpersonal skills** in moulding and directing that interaction. This can involve the leader using various **symbols** – **language**, strong images, **metaphors**, physical settings – to influence the way people see their worlds: the leader '**manages their meanings**'. Other attempts to understand leadership have considered the different arts that leaders engage in – philosophical, fine, martial and performing (Grint, 2000) – and the way that leadership may be distributed around a 'leaderful' organization, rather than concentrated in one or a few individuals (Raelin, 2003).

(Bratton et al., 2005; Bryman, 1986; Heifetz, 1994; Srivasta, 1986; Yukl, 2002)
See also **management**, **management of meaning**
See also **Chapter 7**

management

Management refers both to a set of functions and activities as well as the people carrying them out. Management functions are present whenever several people work together. Yet, management as a distinct **group**, separate from the owners of businesses, requiring specialized knowledge and training, is a late nineteenth- and twentieth-century phenomenon. The classical theory of management derives from the work of Henri Fayol (1841–1925) and Frederick Taylor (1856–1915), and approaches management essentially as 'running a business'. This involves functions like (a) coordination; (b) **communication**; (c) **control**; and (d) **planning**, aimed initially at profit making. By contrast, the term *administration* was used for the Civil Service and state organizations, and while it involved similar functions, its **goals** were not market driven. Since the 1920s and the work of the **Human Relations** School, the human side of management has been highlighted; its preferred definition would be 'getting things done through people' and its main emphasis has been on employee **motivation**.

In the 1980s, the **symbolic** function of management acquired prominence in the literature, with management being seen as 'the ability to define reality for others'. Instead of looking at managers as individuals who can run **organizations** smoothly, the emphasis now is on managers as agents of **change** and renewal. This brings the concept of management very close to that of **leadership**, and a substantial debate is going on as to whether managers and leaders are the same. Henry Mintzberg has criticized many of these approaches for focusing on what managers *should* be doing rather than on what they actually do. Based on intensive observation of actual managers, he found that much of their work involves **talking** or **communicating** and that it is conducted in short bursts of activity. Handling crises and emergencies takes a substantial part of their time; they have little time for systematic thought or **planning** and make most **decisions** on the basis of ad hoc information.

There are many enduring academic discussions on managers, management and the nature of managerial work. These include:

- the relationship between management and **leadership**
- the **moral** and **ethical** aspects and responsibilities of managerial work
- the extent to which management 'colonizes' other aspects of social, political and even personal life (e.g. the 'New Public Management' movement in public administration)
- the nature of managerial **knowledge** and learning and their acquisition development
- the limits of management and the extent to which some aspects of organizations (or life in general) are unmanaged and unmanageable.

(Alvesson and Willmott, 1992, 1996; Drucker, 1989; Gabriel, 1995; Grey, 1999; Guillen, 1994; Mintzberg, 1973; Parker, 2002; Watson, 1994)
See also **management of meaning**

management of meaning
The notion that **meaning** can be managed presupposes that the social world comprises individuals who strive to make sense, or meaning, out of their interactions and tasks. To some extent, our meanings will reflect our own backgrounds and personal desires, so they are partly self-managed. However, they can also be influenced by the actions and words of those around us, so we can talk about leaders and managers as people who manage other people's meanings. This involves the manipulation of **symbols** which convey a particular message. For example, furniture is arranged informally: the boss's door is left open; staff are trusted to manage their own budgets; secretaries do not intercept telephone calls; maternity and paternity allowances are generous and so forth. In this way, the leader is signalling how he or she would like people to think of the organization (and its leader) – as open, liberal and caring. The way meaning is managed can be political in that it can be manipulated to achieve personal ends, such as power, to control others, to capture scarce resources (budgets, equipment) or to gain status.

The management of meaning is especially important in moments of crisis, danger and uncertainty, when different meanings may compete for prevalence: is the situation to be seen as a 'crisis', a 'reversal', a 'temporary blip', 'a mortal danger', 'a challenge' or even 'business as usual'? Leaders can take the initiative in managing meaning, and occasionally they can achieve remarkable feats. Thus, a defeat (like Dunkirk) may be presented as a feat of heroic survival that prepares the way for future victory. Management of meaning often comes under the heading of 'communication'. Business, political and other leaders currently employ communications experts ('spin doctors') to help them cast each event in the best possible light, in order to maximize political advantage. This, is turn, sensitizes followers to what may amount to crude attempts at manipulation. Meaning is then contested, either by arguing for different interpretations of events or casting doubt at the motives, reputation and integrity of the 'spin doctors'. The management of meaning can be quite a difficult task of **management**. It can easily backfire or lead to contestation, cynicism and ridicule.

(Kärreman and Rylander, 2008; Kärreman et al., 2006; Morgan, 1986; Smircich and Morgan, 1982)
See also **culture and organizational culture**, **leadership**, **meaning**

market
The market is an **institution** which has become the control mechanism of choice for many organizations during the past 20 years. This started from right-wing political movements which believed that the market would be able to control greed and laziness in the public sector, where planning had failed, and has now spread almost throughout the world regardless of political persuasion. Privatization of state-owned companies was also part of the market movement, as it was believed that it would bring the discipline of the market to those companies. Within this doctrine, markets were seen as places of unbridled competition, where weak or ineffective companies – or employees – would soon be driven out. Interestingly, this market philosophy had little resemblance to the way that observable markets such as food markets in South East Asia

actually operate. There, stallholders depend on their cooperation with each other as much as their customers depend on their competition. Many organizations have also set up internal markets, where different parts of the organization bought and sold goods and services from each other; the internal market was often validated by allowing the different parts of the organization to buy and sell their services outside the company if they wished to do so. If the company's finance department has to sell its services to other departments, in competition with accounting practices and possibly with other companies' finance departments, this may prevent it becoming too unwieldy and offering too poor a service. On the other hand, such attempts to bring the market to everything can undermine cooperative efforts, and will always incur heavy transaction costs. If one department has to deal contractually with another, they have to spend much time recharging and negotiating how to recharge between them. Such internal markets can be very expensive and very inflexible in times of change.

masculinity

Masculinity is a term used to describe equally the major components of male **sexuality** and the **role** attributes of the male **gender**. The study of masculinity has lagged behind that of **femininity**. Many **stereotypes** of masculine behaviour are currently being questioned, leading to an increased interest in masculinity, notably in the United States. Books like Robert Bly's *Iron John: A Book about Men* and Sam Keen's *Fire in the Belly: On Being a Man* have argued that the attainment of real manhood is problematic for men as are **stereotypes** of macho masculinity. Such books have sought to promote a new vision of masculinity at once caring and heroic, founded not on hate or contempt for women but on strong male bonding and a reappraisal of the relation between fathers and sons. Masculinity has generally been seen as unproblematic in **organizations**; those stereotypical traits associated with the male **gender**, **rationality**, assertiveness, **competitiveness**, winning, exclusiveness and so forth have been seen as serving organizations very well. The new debate on masculinity, however, with its emphasis on a different set of male **values**, **desires** and needs, threatens to undermine the earlier cosy coexistence. Organizations, it is now argued, place almost as formidable constraints on masculinity as they do on **femininity**.

(Bly, 1990; Cheng, 1996; Hearn, 1993; Keen, 1992; Ross-Smith and Kornberger, 2004)

matrix structure

Traditional organizations have divisional or functional **structures**, typically shaped like a pyramid. They have a command structure which is narrow at the top, where the chief sits, and wide at the base where the lower management and workers can be found. There is unity of command, like a military unit. A matrix organization breaks down the single command structure and is shaped more like a flat rectangle with operating 'cells' of expertise (managers and workers) which come together in different ways at different times. The matrix organization has a dual **authority** system and is suited to organizations that change projects or products fast, in several functional areas at once, such as in manufacturing, marketing, engineering and finance. Each of the specialist functions serves a separate project or product which has its own manager and team. The project/product units share the specialized functional resources with other units, thus preventing duplication of these resources. Matrix structures can be extremely flexible, unlike traditional hierarchies. But they have their drawbacks. Without unity of command, everyone has two bosses, a functional manager and a project manager, so there is the potential for conflict and confusion in loyalties. In recent years, there has been a move away from matrix structures in large organizations, either towards simpler linear structures or looser network structures.

(Mintzberg, 1983; Sy and D'Annunzio, 2005)

McDonaldization

This term was coined by George Ritzer to describe 'the process by which the principles of the fast-food restaurant are coming to dominate more and more sectors of American society as well as the rest of the world'. McDonaldization extends the concepts of **Fordism** and represents the culmination of a **rationalization** of production and consumption that has unfolded throughout the twentieth century. This emphasizes careful planning of standardized products and work routines, **deskilling, emotional labour** and homogenization of **consumption**. Ritzer argues that McDonaldization constitutes a rejection of the thesis that we have moved on to a postmodern society in which [rational rigid structures] are quickly disappearing. Furthermore, McDonaldized systems exhibit many postmodern characteristics side by side with modern elements. In other words, the McDonaldizing world demonstrates 'both modernity and postmodernity' (Ritzer, 1993/ 1996: 159). Several authors have taken up this concept, sometimes in connection with 'Disneyization', the trend to rationalize consumption in spectacular cathedral-like places which include theme parks, shopping malls, supermarkets, casinos, tourist destinations and so forth.

(Bryman, 1999; Holbrook, 2001; Ritzer, 1993/1996, 1999; Turner, 2003)

meaning

Human beings can be seen as 'meaning-seeking' animals; words have meanings, as do stories and myths. While the precise meaning of meaning exercises philosophers, meaning can be taken as what one seeks to convey through the use of **language** or other forms of **communication**, like gestures and expressions. In this sense, meaning is the ultimate object of human **communication**. However, humans seek to discover meaning even in phenomena where no other human being is explicitly trying to communicate anything. Since time immemorial, people have looked for the meaning of dreams, of solar eclipses, of the death of their loved ones, of the position of the stars and planets at the time of their birth, or even, as Aristotle remarked, the accidental collapse of a statue. In some of these instances, people are looking for a meaning which they think a superhuman being is trying to convey to them. Meaning is linked to **symbolism**, since meaning is what the symbol stands for. Discovering the meaning of anything, like a joke, a poem or an action, requires a process of *interpretation*. Sociologists, especially those known as symbolic interactionists, argue that meaning is the product of human interaction, with people trading interpretations and inferring contrasting meanings. Depth psychologists, on the other hand, emphasize that the meanings of mental phenomena, like dreams, accidents, obsessive acts, slips of tongue or pen (the famous 'Freudian slips') and so on are linked to repressed **desires**. Existential psychologists argue that men and women strive to create meaning through decisive acts of will, because without them life is unbearable. These views are not incompatible but illustrate some of the diversity of **discourses** surrounding the concept. As far as work is concerned, all three approaches have a significant contribution to make. Sociologists have argued that the meaning of work differs across different cultures, each of which has a distinct **work ethic**. Depth psychology emphasizes that many incidents of organizational life are invested with meanings which derive from unconscious desires and wishes. Existential psychology stresses that meaningless work is unbearable work and engages in a critique of production techniques, like **Taylorism**, which deny work its meaning and purpose.

(Becker, 1962; Blauner, 1964; Schwartz, 1987)

meaninglessness

Meaninglessness is often seen as a malaise or a disease of our civilization. Trapped in Weber's 'iron cage of **bureaucracy**' and reduced to a cog by **deskilling technologies**, the individual experiences feelings of emptiness, hollowness and purposelessness. Work, instead of adding meaning to most people's lives becomes an endurance course, adding little to people's sense of **identity** and self. Blauner argued that meaninglessness is one of the four dimensions of **alienation**, brought about by mass-production techniques, which contrasts with the pride and self-esteem experienced by craft workers, whose work is a source of meaning in their lives. Other social trends which have been linked to meaninglessness are the decline of religion, the growing cynicism with politics and politicians and the rampant growth of **consumerism**. This last links **meaning** to the ownership of commodities, like cars, clothes and so on but ultimately enhances meaninglessness. As soon as the **desired** item has been purchased, its magic and its mystique disappear, and the desire for a new commodity has taken its place.

(Blauner, 1964; Gabriel and Lang, 1995; Tsahuridu, 2006)
See also **anomie**

mentor

New members of organizations are often now formally assigned a senior member to act as their mentor. Even when no such scheme is in place, they may find themselves 'adopted' by existing members who become their mentors. The role of the mentor is generally to give counselling, help, protection, career development and coaching. The relationship between mentors and their protégés has a **political** dimension, as an alliance – possibly of mutual reward. Kanter has noted that one of the barriers to women's careers is their difficulties in establishing mentor relationships with men without fuelling sexual innuendo and gossip.

(Kanter, 1977; Mullins, 2005; Murray, 2001; Ragins and Kram, 2007)

merger

A merger is the bringing together of two organizations into one new one. Sometimes this can be a hostile process, resisted by the top management of one of the companies, in which case it is called an acquisition. Most mergers and acquisitions, however, are done with the agreement of both parties. The process of merging requires the bringing together of strategic, production, delivery and human systems within the organization. For example, there will almost always be a difference of **corporate culture** between the organizations which starts to become an issue when they are one organization. Developing a new culture for the merged organization is a big task and people working in merged organizations can be found identifying each other by the parent organization they came from at least five years after the merger. Matters which might look trivial to the financial strategists, like the organizational **identity**, also turn out to be far from trivial for those whose work is threatened with **meaninglessness** by the loss of important **symbols**. Merging the **storytelling** and **myths** of two organizations may be much more difficult than merging the accounting systems. Financial analyses show that mergers are very rarely successful in strict money terms. For example, in commercial companies, an examination of the equity price very rarely shows a merger to be successful. This raises the question as to why so many mergers take place; one explanation is that, while they may not achieve much for most stakeholders, they can be valuable for managers who wish to demonstrate that they have done something important and significant, and have deserved their salaries for their heroic victories as leaders of mergers.

(Riad, 2007)

metaphors

People talk in metaphors and also do some of their thinking in metaphors. These metaphors can affect the actions that are taken. If people use military metaphors ('we won the battle but we still have to win the war') in their organizational conversation, this can signify the **meaning** of organizational life to them and indicate how they approach conflict, such as permitting 'no surrender' and 'taking no prisoners'. When we employ metaphors, we are mapping one area of life on to another as a way of capturing our feelings and the images of our experiences. We can get carried by the metaphors we use. If we say that 'organizations are machines', the metaphor allows us and others to consider the organization *as if* it were a machine. We may then see 'levers' for change and 'components' for repair, as well as taking an impersonal and functional view of the organization. Metaphorical thinking is so ingrained in us that we are not aware of doing it. Metaphors necessarily obscure as well as illuminate. If we replace the machine metaphor with 'organizations are rivers', as employed in this book, we can then see movement, flow, competing interests and storms, as well as calm, and this change of metaphor will make a practical difference to how we think and act.

(Cornelissen et al., 2008; Grant and Oswick, 1996; Morgan, 1986)

mission statement

Most organizations now have mission statements which give a brief summary of their chief **objectives**. The word is drawn from military strategy, where a unit will go on a mission to achieve a specific military objective. The term also has overtones of religious missions, where some person or group sets out to spread the message of their religious group. Mission statements are sometimes aspirational, in the expectation that the statement will make a difference to what actually takes place in the organization. This, of course, assumes that organizational members know and personally 'internalize' the mission. This may be the case in strong **culture** organizations, but in other organizations it is far less likely. It also assumes that the organization's purpose can be meaningfully summarized, and not trivialized, in a simple mission statement. There are times when a mission statement is important for charitable or tax purposes: some universities use their mission statements (which declare their educational intent) as a way of ensuring that they do not pay tax on job advertisements. While some are sceptical about the value of mission statements, they do make at least two contributions. Firstly, the process of creating a statement may be helpful in clarifying the way in which people see the organization. Secondly, the statement may be a useful test to be applied to particular new initiatives and proposals and may save the organization from losing focus.

morality
See **ethics**

motivation

Motivation typically refers to forces acting on or within an individual which initiate and direct behaviour. Motivational theories attempt to explain the source, strength and form of those forces. There are different types of theory. For example, need- deficiency theories examine the effects of unmet 'needs'. Just as hunger will direct our behaviour towards seeking food, so will our psychological hungers, such as for self-esteem, security and achievement, require satisfying. An influential, and controversial, theory by Maslow suggests that our needs are arranged in a hierarchy, starting with basic physical ones, progressing through safety and social needs, ego needs, to peak with the need to fulfil oneself – 'self actualization'. He argues that one need level has to be relatively satisfied before we are able to move on to the next. Other need theorists, such as McClelland, have focused on specific needs which seem particularly relevant to business activity, such as achievement, affiliation and power. Another form of theory is represented by the work of Herzberg and colleagues. They examined the content of jobs that motivate people. Their research suggests that people will receive positive *satisfaction* from certain factors intrinsic to the job, such as its scope for achievement, recognition and responsibility. Extrinsic factors, though, such as pay and working conditions, simply staved off *dissatisfaction*.

Some motivational theories attempt systematically to model, and measure, the specific attractiveness or otherwise of a particular **action**, and predict the motivational effort that will ensue. These have been termed *expectancy theories*. They are a close relation of *equity theories*, which examine the importance for motivation of how fairly people feel they are being treated and rewarded, compared with others. Finally, there are motivational theories which look deeply into inner psychological processes. These *psychodynamic* approaches, many rooted in the work of Freud (1856–1939), show how our particular **desires**, conflicts, anxieties and aspirations result from our relationship with family members, and our adjustment to stages of development from childhood to adult. The sources of our motivation will often be unconscious, but will still significantly influence our work conduct and preferences. These psychological theories have been broadly challenged by **discourse** theorists, interested in why the desire to attribute 'motive' has arisen, and the political effects of attaching various vocabularies of motive to people's actions. In other words, they see the creation of motivation theory as itself a curious social product, which creates its own momentum and power.

(Herzberg et al., 1959; Maslow, 1943; McClelland, 1961; Pinder, 1988; Steers et al., 2003; Watson, 2002)

myth

The word 'myth' is commonly used to signify 'popular untruths', as in 'ten myths about slimming'. As an ingredient of organizational **culture**, myths are usually based on embellished accounts of events in an organization's history, such as the overcoming of obstacles, major crises or disasters and embarrassing or amusing incidents. Myths have **meanings** and they can, therefore, be part of an organization's **management of meaning**; if different people all read the same meaning into a particular myth, for example that the appointment of a particular CEO saved a company, it can have a galvanizing effect on morale and strengthen **group** cohesion. Often, however, people may read very different meanings into the same **stories**. While myths are not necessarily accurate narratives of events, their grip over individuals stems from the powerful needs which they fulfil. For this reason, the preferred types of myths within an organization reveal some of the underlying emotional factors. In some cases, myths degenerate into self-deceptions by clouding judgement and thought, leading to delusions of invulnerability and grandeur. Some organizations have failed because of the inability of their members to detach themselves from such myths. Schwartz, for example, has argued that some major failures, such as the disaster of the American space-shuttle Challenger in 1986, occur when mythologies and **fantasies** get in the way of technical and scientific calculations.

(Bowles, 1989, 1997; Brown, 2004; Gabriel, 1991a, 2004a; Ingersoll and Adams, 1986; Schwartz, 1988)
See also **stories and storytelling**

narcissism

Narcissism is a term proposed by Freud to describe a range of phenomena in which love is directed towards oneself. Narcissism is normal and ensures that individuals have a healthy sense of self-esteem and value. However, excessive narcissism can become the source of neurosis if it means that an individual becomes self-centred, self-obsessed and unable to form meaningful relations with others. The individual may then use others as an audience that re-inforces his/her own sense of self-importance. Narcissism is of considerable importance for the psychology of organizations and especially **leadership**. A leader's excessive narcissism may then become manifested in *excessive* preoccupation with image and display at the expense of the organization's processes and products. Schwartz has argued that narcissistic decay is a common outcome for organizations whose members lapse into collective narcissism, believing themselves to be unbeatable, omniscient and beyond criticism.

(Freud, 1914/1984; Holmes, 2001; Lasch, 1980; Maccoby, 2000; Schwartz, 1990)

narratives

Narrating is a particular way of communicating about an event, organization or culture, often embedded in a history or timeline. The narrator may be an individual in direct, face-to-face communication, or voiced though another medium such as books, television, newspapers, film, the internet, dance or music. The narratives themselves may be loosely structured, such as in gossip, or more thematic, with a defined plot, such as in stories or dramas. A narrative perspective holds that our understandings and knowledge about the world are not givens; it is pieced together through the exchanging and sharing of narratives, especially tales of past events and future possibilities, brave acts involving heroes and heroines. It is through such narratives that social and moral order is negotiated and one's identity formed. In this manner, **organizational cultures** are given substance and history as members pass on tales about significant employees, crisis management, impossible production targets, the departments to avoid, celebrated Chief Executives and so forth. The power of narratives has been taken seriously by organizational researchers, who have used narratives, especially stories, as analytic tools to explore the cultural and emotional dynamics of organizations, as well as ways of facilitating change.

(Boje, 1995; Brown, 2006; Czarniawska, 1998; Gabriel, 2000; Lõmsõ and Sintonen, 2006)
See also **discourse**

negotiation

When two parties have to come to an agreement about something where they have different interests, and where neither party has the power to impose a solution, they negotiate. This is a widely recognized skill in organizational life. Many of the early studies of negotiation looked at the objective circumstances around the negotiators, using **game** theory. However, this seemed to offer little explanation of how negotiators behaved, and of the outcomes they reached. Neale and Bazerman's research showed that many of the behaviours of negotiators were quite different from what would be predicted if they were perfectly **rational**; for example, they tend to escalate commitment to previous courses of action, even when they are no longer appropriate. Recent studies have highlighted the significant role of emotions in negotiated decisions. As well as negotiating salaries, settlements, allocation of offices and so on, social scientists have talked about 'negotiating reality', 'negotiating meaning' and 'the negotiated order', where the same kind of processes are involved in coming to an agreement about what will be seen as real or meaningful, or what will be taken to be the way things should be ordered.

(Davidson and Greenhalgh, 1999; Neale and Bazerman, 1991; Strauss, 1978)

networks

Describing organizations as 'networks' contrasts markedly with the traditional image of organizations structured in free-standing, pyramidal or hierarchical form. A net comprises many independent units, all linked together for extra strength, size and flexibility. So it is with the 'network enterprise' where autonomous segments of a businesses interface simultaneously with other autonomous segments to provide each other with their particular resources and expertise. But, unlike a literal net, the links between segments can be uncoupled, to find different partners at different times. For example, where an organization would once have been in charge of all its different functions – raw materials supply, production, research and development, human resources, sales and marketing – now all these functions can be sourced as and when required. A production unit can link into different networks of suppliers as well as with other producing units in order to pool resources. Such inter-organizational networks can also apply to intra-organizational relations, where project teams and departments are structured on a matrix basis, to draw upon each other's expertise as and when required.

In addition to organizations becoming more network-like, groups of organizations are often said to become parts of networks. Such organizations are ill suited to traditional methods of management and we are only just beginning to grasp the way that trust, power and control may operate in such circumstances. They may have fuzzy **boundaries** with individuals belonging to two or more organizations at the same time. Furthermore, networks suggest a degree of sharing, cooperation and trust, rather than **competition** and **conflict** – it is for this reason that communities of practice are sometimes thought of as networks. This sharing is especially important in respect of **knowledge** and **information** which are traded either freely or in quasi-gift relations.

The prevalence of network arrangements within and across organizations has given rise to the notion of what we are witnessing as the growth of a 'network society'. Information technology has added huge impetus to this move, with the nodes of the net now spread globally. Thus, Castells has agued that industrial capitalism has evolved into 'informational capitalism' amounting to 'network society'. This has three fundamental features. Firstly, economic activity is dominated by the production, exchange and sharing of information rather than material goods. Secondly, the new economy is global: financial markets, science and technology, international trade of goods and services, advanced business services, multinational production firms and their ancillary networks, communication media and highly skilled specialty labour are all mobile and not restricted by organizational or national boundaries. Thirdly, economic activity is organized in networks which include firms of different sizes. These networks mobilize themselves on specific business projects and switch to dissolve into new networks as soon as a particular project is finished. Major corporations work to a strategy of constantly shifting alliances and partnerships, specific to a given product, process, time and space.

(Black and Edwards, 2000; Castells, 2000; Kilduff and Tsai, 2003; Knights et al., 1993; Rank, 2008)

non-verbal communication
Non-verbal communication includes all aspect of 'body language': posture, facial movements, tone of voice, how one sits, dresses and so forth. In many communications, the communicator concentrates on the verbal aspects – the words said. But the person receiving the communication will also be heavily influenced by non-verbal factors. In conversation, the communication is usually multi-channelled: verbal and non-verbal communications are taking place simultaneously. If the non-verbal communication does not seem to fit with the verbal, such as smiling while delivering bad news, then this is at least disconcerting. It is often said that it is impossible not to communicate: sitting silently can often be a powerful non-verbal communication. Various attempts have been made to codify non-verbal communication, but in most Western cultures there is considerable individual variety in the meaning of particular gestures and the enterprise becomes unreliable.

(Bond, 1993; Guerrero et al., 1999; Hall and Knapp, 2005; Kharbanda and Stallworthy, 1991)

norms
Norms are standards of behavior which result from close interaction between people over time. They are social inventions, often very powerful, which help the group to control and regulate its activities and to express its identity and values. In work organizations, norms arise as complementary, and/or in opposition, to the company **rules** and regulations. Some norms may be divulged openly to new group members: 'now you've joined us what you need to do is … '. Others will be inferred from the characteristic **behaviour** of established members. In practice, norms can determine dress code, where people sit and eat, timekeeping, productivity levels (which may be different from management expectations), appropriate **language** and the sanctions for those who deviate. In short, norms often influence and control our behaviour in subtle ways by becoming part of us, i.e. by being internalized.

(Hogg and Vaughan, 2002; Mullins, 2005)
See also **culture and organizational culture**, **groups**, **informal networks**, **socialization**, **success**

objectives
Objectives are what people or organizations are trying to achieve. The word is used of people and organizations. When we speak of a person's objectives, it is important to note that people may have several conflicting objectives rather than one clear, rational set. For example, they may wish to follow up a concept or idea in the thesaurus of a textbook, while at the same time their objective is to stop work and go out for the evening as soon as possible. It does not follow that, because the objectives conflict, one of them is less 'real' than the other. People will have conflicting objectives within organizations, often with each of them believing that it would be in the best interest of the organization to follow that person's view of the objectives. For example, a marketing person may believe that the organization's objective should be to penetrate a particular market, a production person may believe that the organization's objective should be to produce the highest quality goods, while a finance person may believe that the organization's objective should be to save money. Each of them is likely to argue for the supremacy of their own preferred objective. So agreement about an organization's objectives becomes a very **political** matter. It does not resolve the issue simply to decide that an organization's objectives are the ones set by the top management team. Firstly, they probably do not agree among themselves about the objectives and, secondly, while they might have the power to impose a statement of objectives on the organization, such imposition does not mean that these objectives are the ones that everyone else lives by and works towards.

See also **goals**

objectivity
Objectivity signifies viewing objects or events without bias, dispassionately, or in a more literal meaning, viewing something as an object – as a thing distinct from oneself. It is possible to come closer to objectivity when considering people and events about which we do not care and in which we have no interest. But even under these circumstances, objectivity is elusive. What people may mean when they say that they have been 'objective' is that they have tried to be rigorous and critical in making a subjective judgement; they did not make a snap judgement based on first impressions. It is possible to take steps to check on the quality of our subjective judgements. For example, if we think a particular manager is good, we can check our judgement by discussing it with other people, looking at the financial performance of her department, asking her about what she is doing and so on. But such a judgement remains essentially subjective – a well-tested subjective judgement. When a number of people, following discussions, come to a similar judgement, this is sometimes referred to as 'intersubjectivity'. To be objective, one would need to be able to stand outside the situation being considered, neither affecting it nor being affected by it. This may be possible when talking about measurable characteristics ('she is 1.75 metres tall'; 'he has hepatitis'), because these qualities are not affected by the person making the judgement. My presence, absence or consciousness has no impact on her height or his hepatitis. Such 'standing outside the situation' is not possible when talking about personal **meanings** and social judgements.

oligarchy
Oligarchy is the rule of the few over the many. Based on a study of the German Social Democratic Party in the early part of the twentieth century, Robert Michels (1876–1936) argued that all organizations are subject to an 'iron law of oligarchy'. Arguing against his mentor, Max Weber, Michels claimed that **organizations** are not **rational** instruments for the accomplishment of administrative **goals**; instead, he saw political systems through which small elites control the masses. Organizational survival takes precedence over the achievement of any goal, since without it the **power** and privileges of the **leaders** disappear. To this end, **goals** become displaced, **values** and doctrines are constantly compromised and organization becomes an end in itself. Michels argued that leaders have formidable mechanisms for overcoming any internal threats. They **control** information and appointments, they can reward those loyal to them and marginalize those against them. They can divide the opposition or accuse it of 'rocking the boat'. Finally, and most importantly, they build their strength on the *apathy* of the organizational members, who do not have the time, the expertise or the inclination to challenge the leaders' **decisions**. Michels' view approaches organizations as natural **systems** or biological organisms, preoccupied with survival, rather than as rational systems or tools, after the Weberian tradition. He draws attention to the organizational **environment** which was left outside Weber's ideal type **bureaucracy**. His view of bureaucracy has more in common with the common pejorative sense of self-perpetuating and unaccountable officialdom than does Max Weber's view. In spite of its power, Michels' rather cynical view has attracted criticism. Gouldner has argued that there is an 'iron law of democracy' opposing the oligarchic tendencies identified by Michels and uses as examples the numerous cases of tyrants who were eventually overthrown through popular mobilization.

(Gouldner, 1955; Michels, 1949)

organization
Most formal definitions are unclear as to which human associations should be thought of as organizations (e.g. large corporations, armies, universities, trade unions) and which should not (e.g. football crowds, theatre audiences, nuclear families, tribes, gangs). We propose a set of criteria which generally define organizations, though not all organizations fulfil all these criteria:

- Organizations are associations of several people who are aware of being members and who are generally willing to cooperate.
- Organizations are mainly long term and survive changes of personnel.

- Organizations profess some **goals** and **objectives** which they pursue in a methodical manner; these will be more or less shared or at least assented to by the members.
- Organizations involve a certain division of labour, with different people assigned to different tasks. This may amount to a **hierarchy**, a **matrix** or some other **structure.**
- Organizations involve a certain degree of formality and impersonality.

Strictly, it is problematic to say that organizations have **goals** or **objectives**, that they **act**, that they **control** individuals' behaviour. It is people, not organizations, that do these things. An organization has no mind, no consciousness, no body, no intentions. Nevertheless, these are convenient ways of describing the behaviours and actions of large numbers of people associated with each other. Furthermore, people talk and behave *as if* organizations act. The way people behave in a particular organization can be distinctive because of the **culture** and **norms** of that organization. Organizations can be thought of as more than just the sum of the individual efforts and inclinations of their members. Because people treat organizations as real, they become real in their consequences for their members.

(Thomas and Thomas, 1928)

outsourcing

Outsourcing is the current trend to sub-contract non-essential functions or tasks to other organizations. If the tendency of organizations 100 years ago was to expand, diversify and integrate their operations (Henry Ford famously produced the upholstery of his cars from material grown in company-owned farms), today most organizations seek to focus on their core **competences**, outsourcing everything else to other companies that may be able to deliver better value, more quickly and more reliably. Some outsourcing may go abroad to companies operating in countries with cheaper labour, laxer environmental and occupational health legislation or closer to raw materials. Other outsourcing may go to companies that specialize in particular services and products. One result of outsourcing has been a general downsizing of companies. Another result has been the growth of company networks which develop close cooperative relations. A third result has been an acceleration of globalization. Finally, outsourcing has placed trade unions and local employee organizations at a disadvantage, since companies can use the threat of outsourcing to tighten **control** and discipline among their workforces.

(Taylor and Bain, 2005; Uchitelle, 2006)

participation

It is a general principle in democracy that people should participate in the making of **decisions** which will affect them, either through an opportunity to openly express their views or through electing representatives to the bodies which make the decisions. Yet, participation in organizations sometimes tends to degenerate into an empty slogan behind which **oligarchy** – control by the few – reigns. Within organizational literature, participation is discussed in connection with **leadership** (seen as a feature of democratic or participatory styles) and decision making. It is often argued that the successful implementation of organizational **change** requires the participation of those affected by it in the decision-making process. Various techniques of participation have been tried ranging from consultation and suggestion boxes to quality circles (regular meetings by groups of employees in company time to discuss improvements in working practices and resolve organizational problems). In Britain, workers have been reluctant to participate in **decisions** which can be seen as compromising them or incorporating them into the process of **management**. In Germany, however, since 1952, workers' representatives have participated in the boards of directors in companies above a certain size. Socialists have frequently scoffed at participation, seeing it as an extension of **management control**, and have advocated instead 'workers' control', i.e. the management of the organization by the workers themselves. Different forms of workers' control have been devised, including elected managers, works councils and workers' cooperatives, the latter emerging in the nineteenth century, inspired by the ideas of Robert Owen in Britain and Charles Fourier in France. Workers' cooperatives can boast a number of successes, but with some notable exceptions (like the Mondragon cooperatives in Spain), they have not been able to challenge capitalist firms, nor have they matched the success of consumers' or farmers' cooperatives.

perception

Perception refers to the processes by which we create subjective **meaning** from the stimuli received by our senses. Our interpretations, the sense we make of what we receive, are our perceptions. They shape our experiences into some coherent whole. Some philosophers and psychologists argue that it is only through perception that we can know anything, so we can never know of an **objective** world beyond our perceptions. The notion of perception in organizational behaviour leads us to anticipate that people's perceived worlds may differ and that difference can explain, at least in part, what they think and do. There are factors which influence the content of perceptions. We often 'see' what we want to see: our needs, **motivations** and **emotions** will, unconsciously, start the perceptual shaping process. For example, we will more readily perceive negative characteristics in people with whom we are in conflict. Or conversely, love is blind to faults. **Ideological** stance, **stereotypes** and **prejudices** will also play their part. It is often in the interests of trade union members to perceive managers as exploitative of labour; while, in turn, managers may 'want' to perceive their workers as preoccupied with minimizing their efforts and maximizing their pay.

(Hogg and Vaughan, 2002)
See also **construct and construing, meaning**

performance

Performance is an ambiguous word in the literature on organizing. It can be used to refer to a fairly mechanistic notion of how well someone is doing, rather like talking about the performance of a car. So in some of the literature on appraisal, you will hear references to gauging a person's performance, and in some companies managers will take on performance targets. Performance is also used in the sense of 'putting on a performance' or acting. There is a 'dramaturgical' way of looking at organizations, which sees them as being stages for a performance (Mangham, 1986). This can be traced back to Shakespeare ('all the world's a stage') and beyond. Snyder has suggested that performance includes 'self-monitoring', which is the extent to which people are able to take the stance of an audience watching their own performance. High self-monitors are continuously aware of the performance they are putting on and of the impact it is having on others. Low self-monitors are not aware of performing, tend to come over as more centred and 'all of a piece', and may see high self-monitors as slippery. High self-monitors meanwhile wonder why low self-monitors are not putting more energy into their performance and may see this as a lack of commitment.

(Goffman, 1959; Mangham, 1986; Snyder, 1987)

performance appraisal

Many organizations use systems of performance appraisal to evaluate their employees' work progress. Performance appraisals are used to make decisions on salary, promotions, performance-related pay, retention or termination. They can also provide an opportunity for feedback to an employee to identify strengths, weaknesses and training needs. The format of appraisal can vary from the highly structured, using rating scales, to an open-ended counselling session. The effectiveness of performance appraisal depends on how well prepared both parties are, how serious they are about the event (i.e. is it 'for real' or an empty ritual?), the skills of the appraiser, the reliability and validity of the rating scales, its regularity, and the extent to which decisions or agreements from the appraisal are honoured.

(Audia and Tams, 2002; Townley, 1994)
See also **performance**

personality
Personality refers to the totality of a person's individuality. Personality theories, of which there are many, attempt to explain how our individuality forms, develops, changes and is structured. 'Developmental' theories look at the influence of genetically inherited characteristics compared with those which are shaped or created by key learnings, especially in our infancy and childhood. 'Structural' theories aim to locate ways of dividing up our personality into key ingredients. For example, some believe we are best described as a bundle of traits, such as friendly, warm, cold, secure, insecure, gloomy, bright and so forth. Others argue that we can reduce the almost endless list of possible traits to a small number of major factors with which any person can be described and distinguished. These may be 'types' such as extrovert or introvert, neurotic or stable, Type A or Type B. Sigmund Freud is credited with one of the most influential, and controversial, personality theories which examines the effects of early psycho-sexual periods of development on individuality, and how unconscious, primitive 'id' forces will seek expression through the control of 'ego' and 'superego' layers of personality. Tests of personality are used in personnel selection and appraisal situations to help match people to jobs, or to spot potential. They form a major element of vocational guidance. They can be easily misinterpreted or misused, therefore their availability is usually restricted to psychologists or other specially trained users.

(Pervin, 2004)
See also **implicit personality theory**, **intelligence**

planning
Planning has long been regarded as one of the core functions of management. In the past, it was sometimes assumed that planning signified the state we wish to achieve, whereas **strategy** also addressed the processes that are required to achieve the plan. Currently, planning and strategy are often subsumed under 'strategic planning'. Planning requires the ability to forecast the future, something that becomes increasingly difficult or impossible under conditions of rapid social and economic change. Influenced by developments in **complexity and chaos theories**, some theorists are now arguing that long-term planning is virtually of no strategic value, since the conditions that will prevail in five or ten years' time are highly unpredictable. All the same, even if plans have to be modified or abandoned in the light of rapidly changing circumstances, they can still offer protection from anxiety and a sense of direction and **control**. Faced with highly unpredictable futures, some companies now engage in 'scenario planning', whereby they analyse several alternative scenarios and identify the warning signs for each one of them. They then develop a variety of plans to match each potential scenario. Reality, however, often proves more unpredictable than even the most far-fetched scenarios, forcing senior management in organizations to abandon earlier plans, deal with **crises** or even learn to **improvise**. Generally, the activity of planning can be seen as helping people to think about what they are trying to do, and thus to prepare themselves for an uncertain future. The outcome of planning, however – the set of plans and scenarios – needs to be treated very flexibly. Making plans is a helpful way of thinking; following plans can be disastrous. Plans are there to be departed from.

(Mintzberg, 1993; Stacey, 1992; Weick, 2001b)
See also **strategy**

political correctness
Political correctness is a term that first appeared in *The New York Times* in 1991 to refer to a 'strain of postmarxist leftist thought in which the struggle between economic classes had been replaced, as a primary ontological framework, with the more differentiated set of oppositions based on such differences as sex, race, and sexual orientation' (Schwartz, 2001: 113). The notion is highly contested. Its advocates view it as a political intervention that aims to stop the uses of politically and ideologically offensive language which perpetuates prejudice and discrimination. Its critics view it as an attempt to limit free speech and control free expression that seeks to turn any idea or theory that might possibly upset a minority group into a taboo. Political correctness is an especially potent issue in American academia where it was seen by critics as undermining

academic freedom, compromising academic standards and playing into a victim culture. Its advocates, on the other hand, charged critics of political correctness with being reactionary bigots and defenders of a status quo that disadvantages particular groups and perpetuates social inequality.

(Schwartz, 1990)

politics
In organizations, power and influence are traded in complex, exciting and sometimes painful ways, known as organizational politics. The members of an organization form alliances, do deals with each other, anticipate one another's partialities and preferences, plot the downfall or the promotion of colleagues, or mobilize coalitions continually. Political activity can sometimes be an undesirable and destructive activity, undermining consensus and trust in an organization. But it is also true to say that it is a universal activity, and most people engage in organizational politics as a way of dealing with the tensions between different **role** demands, the partial ways in which valued resources are allocated, and conflicting career and life expectations. Organizations with proclaimed strong **ethical** systems such as hospitals and churches are, ironically, notorious for the robustness of their organizational politics. Indeed, one observer suggests that the more people believe that what they are doing is for the good of others, the dirtier the tricks they are prepared to resort to in order to get their way. The pervasiveness of politics has led to the belief that leaders and managers are ultimately more effective if they possess political skills: the capacity to anticipate and analyse the political ramifications of their own and others' actions, and to be able to steer a pathway between different people's interests and concerns.

(Bailey, 1977; Hickson, 1990; Morgan, 1986)
See also **oligarchy**, **power**

population ecology theory
See **ecology, population**

postmodernism
Postmodernism is a movement in many fields of intellectual and artistic endeavour, including the study of organizations. Postmodern philosophies describe social order as temporary, fragmented and unmanageable, unlike the regularities of modernism that we have imbued: rational thinking, organizational design and management practice. The postmodern world is also highly relativistic; there are no absolute standards and there are no fundamental reasons to privilege one type of understanding or 'fact' over another. Postmodernism in the arts has often implied a colourful, playful approach which incorporates several different styles at once, without demanding consistency or coherence. In organizing, a postmodern approach would be one that acknowledges several different ways of understanding things without trying to establish one of those as superior to the others, and without expecting to be able to make firm logical links between them. In this spirit, postmodernists will examine **discourses** and **narratives** for their unstated (Parker, 1992) assumptions and values, a process of '**deconstruction**' associated with the writing of French philosopher Jacques Derrida. It aims to 'undo' taken-for-granted meanings in particular texts to explore the way we customarily see things and raise different possibilities – for instance, how particular groups, such as managers, women, blacks and gays are presented as inherently worthy or unworthy; how firm-and-fast distinctions are made as if incontestable, such as the fine values of Western compared to those of Muslim countries; or the naïvety of environmentalists compared to those of the captains of industry.

   In the area of organizations, postmodernism has manifested itself in two complementary ways, which may be referred to broadly as ontological and epistemological. At the *ontological* level (what organizations *are*), it has been argued that postmodern organizations are likely to be more flexible and assume **network** forms, in contrast to modernist organizations which were thought to be rigid and bureaucratic. Postmodern organizations are said to rely on constant learning, **innovation** and **creativity** rather than routinized mass production for their success. At the *epistemological* level (how we can know what organizations are), postmodern theories of organizations have moved away from the positivism that characterized modernist theories. Postmodern theorizing does not seek to develop a general theory to account for all organizational phenomena; instead, it seeks to study how organizations come to exist through different **discourses** and to **deconstruct** different organizational artefacts and **narratives**. In a provocative article, Parker suggested that we may refer to post-modern (with a hyphen) organizations and postmodern (no hyphen) theory of organizations. Postmodernism itself rejects a fundamental dichotomy between ontology and epistemology.

(Boje and Dennehy, 1993; Clegg, 1992; Hatch, 1997; Johnson, 1990; Parker, 1992)
See also **reality**

power

'Power is the medium through which conflicts of interest are ultimately resolved. Power influences who gets what, when and how' (Morgan, 1986: 158). Early work on organizations took a *unitary* view, which implied that it is possible to discover common organizational **goals** towards which all members of an organization work. Anything which stood in the way of unity should be dealt with so that harmony and organizational health could prevail once again. Within this view, power does not figure very significantly. For many recent thinkers about organizations, however, power is a key concept. Some adopt a *pluralist* perspective, according to which individuals and **groups** in an organization can have diverging or even conflicting interests and goals, which they seek to promote through **politics**, drawing on a variety of sources of power to do so. This generates **conflict**, in which power is exercised and contested through confrontation and negotiation. Politics involves the forming and breaking of deals, alliances and truces, the use of force or the threat of use of force. French and Raven identified five types of power depending on their source: *reward* (being able to reward behaviour that you like with promotions, money, praise and so on); *coercive* (being able to punish behaviour that you do not like with reprimands, dismissal, sarcasm or threats); *legitimate* (being seen as having the right to a particular kind of power); *referent* (being liked and therefore influential); and *expert* (being seen as knowing best). Other thinkers on organizations have adopted a *radical* view. Radical theorists view organizations as composed of different groups and individuals with different interests, like the pluralists, but without a level playing field. Power is very unequally distributed. Some groups and individuals are seen as highly disadvantaged or disenfranchised on the basis of their **class**, **race**, or **gender**. Denied any legitimate sources of power, such groups may seek to undermine or disrupt organizational life through acts of resistance or rebellion. Lukes proposed a three-dimensional model of power, associated with the three perspectives. In the first dimension, you have power over someone else if you can force them to do something which they would not otherwise do. In the second dimension, you have power over someone if you can manage the situation so that there is no open discussion of anything which can damage you. For example, in a telephone call with your parents, you may be able to keep the conversation to safe topics. In the third dimension, you have power over someone if you can affect their view of what is in their own interests. Social and organizational factors generate power inequalities, leaving some individuals and groups with little or no power. Such individuals or groups may still work hard for the organizations which dominate them; they may have no other source of income or they may be victims of **rhetoric**, **propaganda** or manipulation. People in organizations often assume that power lies elsewhere, usually at a more senior level. Some senior managers are surprised, however, to find how constrained their **actions** seem to be.

(French and Raven, 1959; Lukes, 1975; Morgan, 1986; Pfeffer, 1992)
See also **authority**, **empowerment**, **leadership**, **politics**, **powerlessness**

powerlessness

Powerlessness is a condition of lack of **control**. The term is widely used to describe individuals' feelings within **organizations** and, coupled with **meaninglessness**, it is generally seen as leading to **alienation**. Some of the same factors which account for meaninglessness, such as Tayloristic working practices, **deskilling**, **bureaucracy** and the vast scale of some organizations, also produce powerlessness. Many low-placed members of the organization are seen as unable to control what they do, how fast they work, what they produce or a whole range of decisions which affect their lives. These decisions are made in distant boardrooms, by people they have never met and who may have little regard for their happiness or well-being. Powerlessness may lead to fatalism and resignation which may in turn translate into absenteeism from work or poor **performance**; it may, on the other hand, lead to a search for alternative forms of power through trade unionism and resistance. When the collective voicing of discontents is continuously blocked, powerlessness may lead to devious attempts at revenge through **sabotage**, fiddles, rumours and character assassinations.

prejudice

Prejudice is a form of **attitude**, literally a pre-judgement that a person is prepared to make of another. In its extreme form, it is a way of maintaining superior judgements about oneself by deprecating members of another social group. Allport has noted that pre-judgement is a normal human response; human **groups** tend to separate from each other and to look for characteristics of the other group that can be used to justify that separation. Classic studies by Sherif showed that dividing a group of boys arbitrarily into two groups, and giving each group a different name, was enough to generate prejudice between them. It is a process that echoes the ingroup/outgroup stereotyping that occurs in many organizations. Studies of neighbours have shown that most prejudice is shown when there is proximity without contact. If people of different **ethnic** backgrounds or colour live in adjoining apartments, and the doors to the apartments point in opposite directions so that those people do not meet, they are likely to form negative prejudices about each other. **Gender**, sexual preference, race, age and social class are common areas of prejudice in organizations.

(Allport, 1959; Dovidio and Gaertner, 1986; Sherif, 1966)
See also **authoritarianism and authoritarian personality**, **ethnic groups**, **race**, **sexism**, **stereotyping**

problem solving

There have been many stage models of problem solving, which suggest that it happens by: (1) recognizing the existence of a problem; (2) defining what the poblem is; (3) generating alternative solutions; (4) choosing from among these solutions; (5) implementing the solution; and (6) verifying to make sure that the problem is now solved. This has very little to do with how people go about solving problems. For example, people quite often start with a solution that they like using, and then recognize and define a problem to fit that solution. Similarly, when stage 5 is reached, it is very rare for anyone to go back to verify whether a problem was actually solved. As soon as the pressure is off, attention shifts elsewhere. It should not be assumed that problems are solved. Some problems are disposed of by forgetting about them, some are absorbed into more general problems, and some become sources of worry, where someone turns them over in their mind but never deals with them. It is not always the case that the person with the problem wants to solve it. Problems can be a source of **identity**, where people see themselves as the kind of person who has a particular kind of problem. The relationship between a person and their problems is much closer and more interesting than stage models allow for.

problems

Problems are when something is not as someone would like it to be, and the person is not sure what to do about it. Problems have the twin characteristics of a person feeling that something needs to be done or thought, and a degree of anxiety about whether they can actually deal with the problem. Puzzles tend to be tidier than problems, and with the potential for a more clearly defined solution. To set up a spreadsheet in unfamiliar software may be a puzzle, because it may take some time and thought to get it working. However, there is little doubt that it will work, and the person trying to do it will know when they have got it working. Problems are usually muckier than this. Much time in organizations is spent trying to persuade other people to see problems the same way that you do: 'the real problem is ...' is one way of introducing such an attempt at influence. The definition of problems in organizations is one of the main topics dealt with in the process of organizational **politics**. The experience of problems in organizations is influenced by how many other problems a person is facing at the same time. A problem on its own might be an intriguing puzzle, but when combined with large numbers of other problems, it may lead to **stress**.

Problems can also be socially, rather than individually, constructed. There are times when many people will see the same kinds of problems, and it does not make sense to try to attach each problem to a single owner. For example, the problem of caring for those with HIV/Aids and the problem of poverty are ones which many people would see as real, and they are defined by society and its **institutions**, rather than in the individual manner described above. Similarly, in a company, there might be general agreement that there is a problem of low morale in the despatch department. However, it is worth remembering that statements about socially defined problems are also attempts to influence others to construct problems in the same way as the person speaking.

(Bryant, 1989; Eden et al., 1983; McCall and Kaplan, 1990)

professions
Professions were traditionally those occupations which, like medicine and law, were thought to fulfil a number of criteria, like the following: (a) a systematic body of knowledge and monopoly powers over its applications; (b) a self-regulating code of ethics, emphasizing **values** such as respect for the confidentiality of the client; (c) the sanction of the community at large; (d) **control** over the profession's own qualification and entry procedures; and (e) an altruistic orientation, stressing the value of the profession's service to the community over strictly monetary rewards for the professionals. Professionals enjoy a unique source of **power** within **organizations**, which is rooted in their technical expertise and their independence. Nevertheless, doubts about the altruism and lofty motives of professionals have persisted, summed up in Bernard Shaw's mischievous definition of a profession as 'a conspiracy at the expense of laity'. This more cynical view sees professions as labour cartels, which control entry into an occupation through the erection of a variety of barriers, such as over-lengthy traineeships and examinations or the use of incomprehensible jargon to mystify and confuse the non-professionals. A number of important debates are currently unfolding on professions, including:

- What is the nature of professional **knowledge** and how is it acquired?
- Is there a natural conflict between professionals and managers in organizations that employ large numbers of the former, such as hospitals and universities?
- Is the availability of information on the internet eroding professional knowledge and privilege?
- Is there a tendency of professions to become deprofessionalized or conversely of ever-growing numbers of occupations to be professionalized?
- Is **management** a profession?

(Acker, 2006; Brock et al., 1999; Ferlie et al., 1996; Fitzgerald and Ferlie, 2000; Hirschhorn, 1989; Merton, 1968; Schein, 1988)

propaganda
Propaganda is an important mechanism for influencing others through the careful manipulation and presentation of **information**. It involves the selective presentation of facts (being 'economical' with the truth), presenting facts out of context so as to deliberately create a false impression, using emotive **language** (like 'fatherland', 'treason' and so on), powerful **symbols** (like flags, anthems and so on) or **metaphors** (like 'iron curtain'). The Nazis officially recognized propaganda as a function of the state meriting a ministry to itself, headed by the notorious Dr Josef Goebbels. Successful propaganda shares many ingredients with one kind of successful **leadership**,

notably an ability psychologically to 'read' the needs of those who will receive the message, to time and fine-tune the message exactly for the occasion and to build cumulatively on the effect of each message. The line between devious and callous manipulation, on the one hand, and good leadership, through legitimate influence, **motivation** and **information** is often a thin one; sometimes it is only a matter of different perspectives. Organizational propaganda can sometimes be dressed up in terms, such as 'public relations' and 'advertising'. Recent, less systematic attempts at propaganda have popularly been labelled as 'spin'.

See also **rhetoric**

psychological contract

Psychological contract refers to the unwritten set of expectations that exist between people in an organization, and is closely related to the concepts of **norm** and **role**. A psychological contract usually goes well beyond a legal contract of employment. It is psychological because it refers to mutual **perceptions**, expectations and informal understandings which, once transgressed, can disrupt or sever relationships. Psychological contracts are in the eye of the beholder. They imply that co-workers meet certain mutual expectations and obligations arising from the fact that they share the same organizational space and activities. These may include basic courtesies, respecting each others' dignity and worth, working to the spirit rather than the letter of the formal work contract, constructive feedback, providing work which is not demeaning, and understanding career expectations, as well as responding to non-work, personal crises. The nature of the psychological contract sets the spirit and tone of an enterprise and its development can be crucial to the organization's success and individual well-being.

(Rousseau, 1995; Singh, 1998; Turnley and Feldman, 1999)

psychological testing

Psychological testing has become a common feature of employee selection and appraisal processes, and vocational guidance. Psychological testing is based on the assumption that key features of our personality – abilities, skills, motives, attitudes, values – can be inferred from our performance in specially devised exercises or questionnaires. The best researched have been carefully structured, tried out on a lot of people in advance, and have extensive 'norms' or population scores against which to compare individual scores. They provide relative measurement and are restricted in availability to qualified users. Psychologists will judge a test by its published reliability and validity, that is, how consistent it is and how well it predicts behaviour or performance. Tests used in industry may be behavioural simulations, such as measuring performance on a set of 'real' decision-making tasks under time pressure. Also used are standardized pencil-and-paper questionnaires which tap areas such as interests, specific aptitudes and abilities, and personality qualities.

(Kline, 2000; Toplis and Dulewicz, 1997)
See also **intelligence**, **personality**

race

Race is a difficult and politically sensitive concept to define. Unlike **ethnic groups**, races are usually thought of as involving some inherited physical characteristics, most notably colour. Yet physical differences between human groups tend to be far less significant in terms of biology than in terms of the political and symbolic **meanings** attached to them. Nazis tried to develop biological 'theories' of race, mainly as a justification for racist and genocidal practices. Some psychologists have tried to link **intelligence** to race, arguing that this accounts, at least in part, for educational and social inequalities between races. Such arguments approach both race and intelligence as objective, scientific concepts, obscuring the extent to which they are both socially defined **constructs**, as well as usually constructing correlations that ignore other factors such as the **culture**-based nature of the **psychological tests** used and indeed of the variables for which they are trying to test. Race acts as a common basis for negative **stereotyping**, as well as for **prejudice** and **discrimination**. Many organizations seek to overcome these injustices through an equal opportunities policy, explicitly excluding colour, gender and so on as factors in hiring or promoting staff. In the United States, Canada and South Africa, affirmative action or 'positive discrimination' programmes go considerably further by seeking actively to encourage the hiring and promotion of members of disadvantaged communities. This is sometimes achieved through the setting of quotas or the relaxation of qualifications and standards for entry into the organization. Such programmes are at times criticized as undermining the principle of always trying to recruit the best person available, and for undermining members of previously disadvantaged communities by leading people to assume that they have achieved their role because of their race. Yet, without active encouragement, past inequalities tend to reproduce themselves. Disadvantaged communities find it difficult to break out of a vicious circle of powerlessness, prejudice and discrimination. Disadvantages in housing reinforce disadvantages in education, which, in turn, reinforce disadvantages in employment opportunities.

(Acker, 2006; Skellington, 1996)

rationality

Rationality is generally thought of as the unique property of human beings to make **decisions** on the basis of careful assessment of **information**. Economists incorporate **assumptions** of rationality into their theories of economic behaviour, employing a model sometimes referred to as 'rational economic man'; according to this view, for example, consumers will try to get the best value for money when faced with a purchasing decision. Max Weber distinguished between two kinds of rationality. Rationality of means implies that, given a certain set of goals, one adopts the optimum means for its achievement, on the basis of careful search, calculation and evaluation of the alternatives. The system of **rules** underpinning **bureaucracy** is rational in as much as it is carefully devised so as to enhance the achievement of organizational **goals**. This type of rationality is based on expert **knowledge** of the alternative courses of **action** available. It is the foundation of technical efficiency, even though it may be applied to entirely evil, insane or arbitrary goals. For example, one can go about very rationally burning down one's own house. The rationality of the ends or rationality of values is the second type of rationality, identified by Weber, though his view is that science is of little help here. Modern economists have argued that the classical criteria for rational action are too strict; if the consumer was intent to buy carrots at the lowest price, he/she would end up spending his/her entire life comparing the prices in different shops. The same goes for organizations. Instead of **decisions** based on absolute rationality, Simon has suggested that they are based on 'bounded rationality'; one makes a decision as soon as one has found a solution which is 'good enough' or 'satisficing'. Rational models of human behaviour, like those favoured by economists and Taylorist management, tend to disregard or underestimate people's impulsive, **emotional**, **desiring** and irrational qualities. These are of central importance to certain schools of thought in social psychology (like the **Human Relations** School) and depth psychology. Even supposedly rational actors, such as stockbrokers, can act under the impact of emotional forces, for example in the panic buying and selling of stock.

(March and Simon, 1958; Simon, 1957; Weber, 1946)

rationalization

This term is used to signify three different things: (a) increasing the efficiency of an organization by eliminating redundant or non-profitable elements (including departments, operations and people); (b) the provision of credible or plausible motives for one's **actions** which conceal the real motives; this includes the finding of convenient excuses; and (c) the tendency of organizations and societies to shed their traditional, emotional, supernatural, religious, aesthetic and moral qualities in favour of ever-increasing concern with economic efficiency. **Fordism** and **McDonaldization** are parts of a process of rationalization of production and consumption in this third sense. Starting with Max Weber, many theorists argued that modernity is characterized by unprecedented degrees of rationalization in every sphere of human life, which result in a process of 'disenchantment', i.e. the elimination of charm, magic and simple pleasure. Some theorists, however, are currently arguing that **postmodernity** brings about a partial re-enchantment of the world through the different mechanisms of **consumption**. Ritzer has suggested that spaces of consumption, such as shopping malls, theme parks and the internet, have become 'cathedrals'. This points up the quasi-religious, 'enchanted' nature of these new settings. They have become locales to which we make 'pilgrimages' in order to practise our consumer religion.

(Bauman, 1993; Ritzer, 1999)
See also **rationality**

reality
In philosophy and in different branches of social science, reality is a problematic concept. Is reality something absolute, constant and there to be discovered through ever more sophisticated methods of scientific inquiry? This is broadly a position taken by positivism, which has come under criticism from a wide range of perspectives, sometimes referred to as phenomenological. These pay much greater attention to the way knowledge of the world is shaped by our own psychological apparatus as well as by social, cultural and political factors. Phenomenologists contend that our world consists of many different phenomena which we come to know in many different ways, other than through scientific inquiry, such as via our feelings, superstitions, prejudices, religions and beliefs. They constitute 'common sense' that we take for granted, as well as our unique sense of reality. Hermeneutic theorists develop this further, arguing that reality consists of a process of striving to make experience meaningful. Hermeneutics is an ancient discipline, originally concerned with the interpretations of religious texts. Modern hermeneutics says that all meaning and understanding is strongly influenced by our culture and our place in it, and this 'ontological fact' is the starting point for the study of reality. Whatever we are, or now feel, is always situated in a cultural and historical context, which shapes how we come to know what is meaningful. But we also live in a world that has many social realities which are formed and re-formed though interactions between people, by different **cultural norms** and by various social **norms**. Reality here is a social construction, subject to the kind of regularities and disparities that are features of any social gathering and to tacit and open negotiation (hence the term 'negotiated reality'). These distinctions are important for practice. In organizations, what kind of realities are we operating with? Whose reality is being imposed on whom? Is the corporate strategic vision fixed on a single, objective view of its working environment, or is it one that sees a shifting, negotiated setting? Are individuals' existential realities – what they are feeling and experiencing in their work – honoured?

Two fundamental **discourses** prompted by the concept of reality are *ontology* and *epistemology*. Ontology is thought to address the nature or existence of things. It seeks to answer questions such as 'What is human nature?', 'What is an organization?', 'What is virtue?' or even 'What is being?' Epistemology, on the other hand, addresses how different types of **knowledge** can be obtained, how sure we can be about its validity and reliability and what the limits of knowledge may be. Separating ontology from epistemology is a highly problematic distinction and one totally rejected by **postmodernism**. 'What is knowledge?' is a question that clearly spans both ontology and epistemology. Unless one knows what the nature of different things is (e.g. dreams, organizations, poverty or terrorism) how is it possible to know how to study them? Postmodernist arguments would suggest that the nature of things and the truth value of different statements are products of **discourses**, there being no reality outside of discourse. Other current theories dispute this, without seeking to draw a hard and fast line between ontology and epistemology. 'Critical realism' is a current movement in philosophy and the social sciences that rejects positivism as well as naïve realism ('Things have an existence entirely independent of human beings'); but it also refutes postmodern rejections of all objective reality.

(Archer, 1998; Berger and Luckmann, 1967; Stablein, 1996)
See also **objectivity**

reflexivity

Reflexivity has now become quite a fashionable term, with the adjective 'reflexive' often used as a synonym for 'reflective', i.e. someone who is capable of taking a step back from a situation to reflect on it. Thus, the 'reflective practitioner', as defined by Argyris and Schön, is the manager or consultant who is capable of mentally withdrawing from the hurly-burly of **action** and **experience** to reflect and learn from them. 'Reflexive', however, is a term that can go beyond 'reflective'. A reflexive activity is one in which subject and object co-create each other. For instance, in telling the story of my life, I make sense of past events and create a person living in the present as a continuation of the story. In this way, I as the author of the story and the story's central character co-create each other. At every moment, the storyteller creates a protagonist, whose predicaments re-define the storyteller. Although this term was popularized by French post-structuralist philosophers, it was implicit in Marx's theory of **labour**, where the worker creates him/herself as a worker in creating an object. Social research can be viewed as a reflexive practice, one in which the presence of the researcher and the act of research creates an object of study. Reflexivity emphasizes the ability of **language** to constitute social reality and has become a trademark of **critical management studies** and approaches hostile to positivism. All the same, as Lynch has suggested, it easily disintegrates into fashionable cliché through which the self-proclaimed reflexive individual seeks to elevate him/herself above the supposedly non-reflexive others.

(Argyris and Schön, 1978, 1996; Cunliffe, 2003; Hardy et al., 2001; Lynch, 2000)
See also **critical theory and critical management studies**

resistance

Resistance refers to a wide range of activities through which members in organizations seek to oppose official or unofficial forms of **control**. Resistance may be organized or disorganized, individual or collective, conscious or unconscious, active or passive, continuous or one-off. It can take a great diversity of forms, including strikes, **sabotage**, restriction of output, go-slow, insubordination, ritualistic compliance, jokes, sarcasm, bloody-mindedness, whistle-blowing and cynicism. Resistance is part of organizational **politics**, yet it can take highly **symbolic** forms. Even small gestures, such as keeping a button undone or inscribing company property with graffiti, can be acts of resistance. Resistance can be an important part of an individual's **identity**. While resistance is often discussed in connection with the management and implementation of change programmes, it is all too easily forgotten in discussions of **management of meaning**. The decline in traditional forms of worker militance (strikes, boycotts, work-to-rule and so on) was assumed to mean that employees, in advanced capitalism, have surrendered to increasingly sophisticated mechanisms of control. This view has been consistently challenged by authors who identify and emphasize more subtle and tactical forms of employee resistance. Resistance is also discussed in connection with consumers and the extent to which they challenge attempts to entice them, seduce them and control them with a wide variety of images, products and methods.

(Ackroyd and Thompson, 1999; Ezzamel et al., 2001; Gabriel, 1995, 1999a; Jermier et al., 1994; Marx, 1995; Sturdy and Fineman, 2001)

rhetoric

Rhetoric is often seen in pejorative terms, as dealing with surface appearances and lies. However, rhetoric is the basis of a more noble art – that of persuasion. It is a fundamental part of human communication, inherent in our use of **language**, conversational and written. The skilled rhetorician learns to shape phrases and select words and **metaphors** in ways which enhance their attractiveness, or accentuate a given message or **meaning**. Politicians are often marked by how well they form their rhetoric, as are key **leaders** in organizations. Clearly, however, rhetoric may be used to meet aims that are fine and noble, or decidedly corrupt.

(Hunter and Anderson, 1992; Keiser, 1997; Nash, 1989)
See also **management of meaning, propaganda**

risk
Risk is when we do not know in advance the outcomes of our actions. This is true in almost all situations, but the experience of risk becomes more challenging when those outcomes are not trivial. If someone tells their boss that there is a serious fault in his reasoning, they may end up being promoted or dismissed; either way, they have taken a much greater risk than they would have by saying nothing. In daily working decisions, there are always many factors that we do not know about which create risk. We do not know what the weather is going to be like when we order the ice cream for the restaurant, we do not know how many people are going to buy our new product, and we do not know how a young member of staff is going to respond to rapid promotion. Some people are averse to risk while others find it exciting. Organizations may consider what would be appropriate levels of risk for them to take. If there are too many cautious people in key jobs, no exciting new developments are ever tried. Leave those who are most inclined to take risks too much room for manoeuvre, and you may find yourself bankrupted by them, as happened to Barings Bank. There are ways of reducing risk, for example by insurance. Internal auditing is often presented now as a discipline to help organizations manage risk.

risky shift
Risky shift is a widely recognized phenomenon whereby groups of people tend to make more risky **decisions** than individuals. This is believed to be due to the fact that responsibility is diluted among many. It is generally thought that risky shift affects groups faced with many different tactical and strategic choices, but not when they are faced with decisions that are perceived to be **moral**. All the same, the extent to which groups veer towards or against risky decisions is the outcome of complex and, at times, unpredictable **group** processes, depending on numerous factors (e.g. how cohesive the group is, how large, how long they have worked together, how **leadership** is handled and so on), and risky shift should not be uncritically expected in all group situations.

rite of passage
Rites of passage were first documented by anthropologists to describe the way people ritualize and celebrate key social transitions in their communities, such as birth, coming of age, marriage and death. We see, for example, the importance of the bar mitzvah in the Jewish tradition where the 13-year-old boy becomes a man after reading a specifically prepared piece of the Old Testament, a carefully orchestrated **ritual** in the synagogue. Rites of passage in organizations also mark a change of personal status. They can be informal and/or formal occasions. For example, a craft apprentice can earn full craftsman status by passing formal tests and exams; an undergraduate's move to graduate status is marked by a conferment ceremony, replete with formal garb and accolades. However, colleagues can also create their own tests such as abuse or humiliation. This latter type of rite of passage can be meted out to new recruits in the military, or to new prisoners by their cell mates. In each case, the initiate is having to earn his or her new or changed place in the organization by 'passing' or surviving the tests. More gently, there is the rite of passage out of the organization after a successful career. The leaver is expected to receive gifts and praise at a ceremony, give thanks, celebrate – and leave.

(Deal and Kennedy, 1988; Kuper, 1977; Trice and Beyer, 1984)

ritual
A ritual is a formal **action**, normally repeated in a standardized way. While people often associate the idea of rituals with religions, organizations too generate rituals. Some of the rituals, like the singing of the company anthem in Japanese corporations, are formal, while others like gathering round the coffee machine at exactly 10.30 am each day are less so. In both cases, the essence of ritual is its **meaning** and **symbolism.** Knowing how to participate in important rituals in an organization is a crucial part of being seen as a fully fledged, competent insider. Rituals are generally thought of as having a strong bonding effect, though their compulsive repetitive quality gives

them a similarity to certain neurotic traits, like the compulsive washing of hands (itself a form of ritual in several religions). Trice and Beyer have identified different types of rituals in organizations, including **rites of passage**, rites of degradation and rites of renewal.

(Deal and Kennedy, 1988; Trice and Beyer, 1984; Turner, 1969)

role

Role is a central unit of analysis in sociology and social psychology. It refers to the duties, obligations and expectations which accompany a particular position. We can visualize ourselves as a member of a 'role set', a number of significant people who influence how we should behave – they are our 'role senders'. A married woman could have her husband, children, best friend, boss, mother, previous partner and various in-laws all setting role expectations for her, which may conflict with, or complement, each other – or some mix of the two. At work, we may experience role conflict, such as being required to appraise a colleague's performance while also being her friend and mentor. Or there is ambiguity of role – unclear or confusing messages about what is expected of us. Reconciling various role demands can be a significant source of **stress**. Students, for example, will often report significant tensions in trying to satisfy the academic demands of their different lecturers and professors, while also meeting social obligations that are regarded as an essential part of being a student.

(Hogg and Vaughan, 2002; Kahn et al., 1964)

rule breaking

Rule breaking, or 'fiddling', describes an array of illegal operations going on in many organizations, at times with the tacit or active involvement of **management**. These practices include pilfering and stealing, the illicit use of company property, tampering with records (for example, for the purpose of clocking additional overtime), the making of false expense claims and the use of company accounts for private ends. Some organizations have, in effect, **institutionalized** rule breaking as a job benefit and in some cases the proceeds increase the longer an employee stays and the more loyal he or she proves. Rule breaking can be collective in which case it serves to bind together those involved, or individual, engaged in especially by those who feel powerless or excluded, and who feel that this is a way of 'getting their own back' on the employer who is causing them to feel like that. Its frequency, scale and scope vary considerably across different organizations, but in the food wholesaling industry, for example, most companies make provisions for 'shrinkage'. People rarely regard their own fiddling as a criminal, illegal or immoral activity and see it as a **norm**-guided behaviour, with its own **rules**, **ethics** and limits.

(Gabriel, 1988; Mars, 1982; Mars and Nicold, 1984)

rules

Most organizations have formal rules, governing working hours, safety practices and so on. These rules will often go unchallenged (and quite possibly unread), although on occasions, an organizational rule will be challenged as being in conflict with social or national laws; for example, rules about retirement age in some organizations have been challenged as they have come into conflict with laws banning **discrimination**. There are also informal rules; few large companies lay down what their managers should wear. But without being told, the managers do not turn up on Monday morning in the jeans and jumpers they have been wearing over the weekend. Such informal rules operate like **norms** and those who infringe them are likely to be ridiculed or ignored rather than openly punished. There are also the rules of the **game** of organizational life; in some organizations, you are allowed to advertise your individual **success**, in some you are allowed to boast of having tricked a competitor, whereas in other organizations the same behaviour would not be legitimate. It is now believed that rules by themselves do not determine behaviour or action; nearly all rules require some degree of interpretation regarding their enforcement and strictness. Narrative knowledge, i.e. the collection of stories told about breaking different rules and their consequences, is believed to function as a guide to how rules are applied in real-life situations.

(Berne, 1964; Hood, 1986; Tsoukas, 1998; Tsoukas and Hatch, 2001; Weber, 1946)
See also **bureaucracy**, **rationality**

sabotage

Although infrequently discussed in textbooks, sabotage is reported in numerous empirical studies. Sabotage is the deliberate destruction of the employer's property (including machinery) or, more generally, the hindering of the work process. In its simplest form, sabotage can be an individual act of defiance, the throwing of the proverbial spanner in the works. However, sabotage is frequently an organized activity aimed at slowing the pace of work or even at re-asserting some **control** over the productive process, especially as a last resort for the **powerless** and disenfranchised.

(Beynon, 1973; Hyman, 1989)

scapegoating

In Biblical times, the sins of the Jewish people would be collectively re-assigned to a goat who would then be allowed to wander off into the wild, **symbolically** taking their sins away. From this procedure has come the term 'scapegoating', which usually means blaming one member of a group, or one group ('administration', 'management', 'personnel') within an organization, for everything that goes wrong. It is often used as a means of not confronting, or taking ownership, for specific difficulties or problems. It can be particularly corrosive when combined with **stereotyping** and **prejudice**, where a person or group find themselves the focus of blame because of their ethnicity or gender.

(Eagle and Newton, 1981; Hirschhorn, 1988)

scientific management

This school of **management** is associated with Frederick Taylor (1856–1915), an American mechanical engineer. Taylor, struck by what he regarded as the inefficiency of many production systems, argued that there was one best way to perform any particular task, and that way could be discovered 'scientifically'. Human-machine operations should, therefore, be precisely tracked and measured using time-and-motion studies, standardized tools, individual financial incentives and close supervision. His *cause celèbre* was a detailed study of the handling of pig iron which, once exposed to the rigours of his analysis, was re-designed to increase output and decrease waste. Taylor developed a set of principles of scientific management, which included the separation of brain work from manual labour, the fragmentation of the productive process and the standardization of production. Scientific management (or Taylorism as it came to be known) provided some of the impetus behind **Fordism** and **McDonaldization**. Vestiges of scientific management can be seen in many of today's mass-production and service operations, from cars to hamburgers. Taylor's work partly mirrored the times – high unemployment and cheap, poorly organized, unskilled labour – and Taylor himself, an engineer. But he spectacularly failed to recognize the importance of **social** needs at work, non-financial incentives, informal work practices and non-directive supervision.

(Guillen, 1994, 1998; Taylor, 1911)
See also **control**, **deskilling**

self-presentation

We present ourselves differently to different audiences, partly because of the various **roles** we play in life. In other words, we try to assume the face, mannerism, dress, language and posture that are expected of us in particular settings, without deviating too much from the **norm**. This might mean disguising how we feel or how we want to be. Like the stage actor, we take on the characteristics required of the role. A 'dramaturgical' view of behaviour suggests that much of social life is a matter of consciously and unconsciously shaping our self-presentations, making them acceptable for various situations and audiences in which we find ourselves. Difficulties occur if: (a) we do not know what image is required of us; (b) we are insufficiently skilled to present the desired image; and/or (c) the required image is uncomfortably different from how we feel.

(Giacalone and Rosenfeld, 1991; Goffman, 1959; Mangham and Overington, 1987)
See also **authenticity, impression formation**

sex

If it is not identified with sexual intercourse, or used to distinguish between males and females, sex is a rather difficult concept to define. Sex is a quality of whatever arouses desire, especially physical **desire**. It can be sparked by a poster, an image, a person, an item of clothing, a sound, a smell, a word (consider words with instant sexual connotations). Different **cultures** have very different ideas on which things are meant to generate sexual feelings and which are not, as well as different ideals of physical attractiveness. What is certain is that we can learn to respond sexually to a diverse range of stimuli, something which has not escaped the attention of advertisers and marketers. For this reason, Germaine Greer has described it as the 'lubricant of consumer society', adding that 'in order to fulfil that function the very character of human **sexuality** itself must undergo special conditioning' (1984: 198). The range of consumer items whose appeal is linked to sex is bewildering – from cars to clothes, and from airlines to computer software. The sexualization of everyday objects underlines two important features of **sexuality**. First, activities, objects and states of being that appear to have little sexual content may be symbolic expressions of sexual **desires** and attempts to fulfil these desires in **fantasy**; for example, the desire to appear masculine and virile is expressed in driving a fast car. The car has come to stand for virility, it has become its **symbol**. Second, in Western cultures, fantasy, rather than passion, love or obsession, has emerged as the chief representation of sexuality. It is as a shared complex of fantasies rather than as anything else that sex stakes its public terrain.

(Foucault, 1978; Freud, 1905/1977; Greer, 1984; Mano and Gabriel, 2006; Packard, 1957)
See also **gender**

sexism

Sexism is a negative **attitude** or **prejudice** about a person on the basis of their sex. This has been considered mostly in the prejudice that men have about women, where many jobs have been kept as a male preserve. While this may not be as flagrant as it was in the past, there is still plenty of evidence of sexism at work; in many professions, women face a 'glass ceiling', an invisible barrier to how high they can go in their jobs. They are excluded from the informal friendship and **mentoring** which are crucial in organizational **politics** and they are often assumed to be less concerned about their work than men, and to be willing to subordinate their **careers** to the career of a male partner. Underlying this may be the male ego – the enormous need of many men for approval and admiration, and their fear of women who are independent enough to choose not to give them such approval and admiration. Sexism is also found in the prejudice against **homosexuals**.

(Gutek, 1985; Hearn and Parkin, 1987; Hearn et al., 1989; Marshall, 1984; Ward and Winstanley, 2003)
See also **race**

sexual harassment

Sexual harassment is a concept dating from the early 1970s, describing the experience of unwanted attention – physical, or verbal, direct or by innuendo – of a sexual nature. Harassment can range from offensive **language** and **sexist** jokes, the use of exaggerated compliments and negative **stereotypes**, to the use of moral blackmail to extort sexual favours. The victim of sexual harassment is likely to feel anxious and oppressed by what is happening. Most, although not all, reported cases are of men harassing women, and here the issue interacts with the **power** structure of organizations and society which tends to favour men. A number of studies suggest that harassment is more commonly directed towards those women who are perceived by men as threats. This supports feminist arguments that sexual harassment is not exceptional, nor just an individual's problem, but rather a wider symptom of **power** relations between the **genders**. Sexual harassment is difficult to manage institutionally because of its sensitive and personal nature, the fear on behalf of the woman that her complaint will not be taken seriously, even ridiculed, and the possibility of the accusation being contested by the harasser. **Perceptions** may well differ about what was 'only a bit of fun', and there are cultural and subcultural differences on what is regarded as acceptable sexual attention in the workplace.

(Di Tomaso, 1989; Guerrier and Adib, 2000; Gutek, 1985; Pierce and Aguinis, 1997; Williams et al., 1999)

sexuality

sexuality is the complex of physical **desires** and their expressions. The expressions of sexuality may be physical, emotional, verbal or even artistic but, in a direct or indirect way, these desires aim at *pleasure*. While the sexuality of most individuals may seem consistent and stable (most desires, for example, are directed towards pleasure through heterosexual intercourse), social and psychological research indicates that sexuality is highly complex and variable. In contrast to animal sexuality which is mechanically linked to instinctual behaviour, human sexuality is mediated by desires, a large part of which are either learned or **symbolically** constituted. Sociologists and anthropologists have observed wide variations of sexual behaviour across different cultures and societies. Malinowski, for example, studied the highly promiscuous sexual behaviour of the Trobrianders which contrasted sharply with the rigidly controlled behaviour of some of their neighbours. Western **cultures**, it is argued, spotlight one feature of sexuality, **fantasy**, as it is uniquely suitable to the demands of both consumer society and modern organization; they also create an obsessive preoccupation with penetrative sex and orgasm as the aim of all sexual activity, at the expense of other forms of pleasurable behaviour. Psychologists following a psychoanalytic approach view human sexuality as dynamic, i.e. it develops through early childhood, going through a number of important stages, where different complications may arise. Freud (1856–1939), in particular, observed four stages of development: (1) the oral, in which most desires focus around the area of the mouth; (2) the anal, when most desires revolve around the control of the bowel movement; (3) the phallic, when the penis and the clitoris come into the centre of sexual feeling; and (4) the genital, which represents the usual terminus of adult sexual development, but which incorporates features of the earlier stages. Sexuality can also be seen as complex, involving numerous **desires**, many of which may conflict, and most of which are unconscious. No line between 'normal' and 'perverse' behaviour can be drawn, since the sexuality of 'normal' people invariably contains repressed desires that could be classified as perverse.

(Burrell, 1984; Burrell and Hearn, 1989; Freud, 1905/1977; Gutek, 1989; Mitchell, 1975; Williams et al., 1999)
See also **gender**, **sex**

skill

Skill describes a competent or even virtuosic performance in almost any kind of activity. Carpentry, playing the violin, telling jokes, speaking a language all involve skills. Skills are generally acquired **competences**; they require learning, practice and application. Yet, there can be no doubt that people differ widely in their ability to develop different skills. Organizational life requires a great diversity of skills, yet there is no general agreement on the precise skills involved in organizing. Some skills required by organizations are social and interpersonal, such as communication, team-building or problem-solving skills. Other skills are of a more technical nature, for example computer programming or engineering. One of the peculiarities of skill is that many people with highly developed skills (for instance at playing a musical instrument or doing mathematical computations) are incapable of talking about them or explaining what it is they do. Perhaps this is not surprising: high levels of skill become part of oneself, operating at a subconscious level. Those who have greater difficulty with acquiring a particular skill (for instance, learning how to swim, to drive or to speak a foreign language in later life) may have to think about it more, and thus be better able to talk about it. Improving your skill in the short term may involve some **deskilling**. This is because instead of focusing on the task at hand, the novice tends to focus on the way the task is carried out. Improvement in the performance comes when the new skill has become natural ('second nature'), i.e. subconscious. High levels of skill, in sport, martial arts, and probably organizations, may depend on being able to practise and develop the skill in **fantasy**. While some individuals in organizations display highly skilled performances, under the influence of **scientific management**, many employees throughout the twentieth century were engaged to carry out highly de-skilled tasks. Deskilling brought down the costs of labour and bolstered management control over the productive processes. It also made the quality of the output independent of the skills of individual employees. However, the strategy of de-skilling is one that no longer seems to work in an increasing number of industries, where employee commitment, flexibility and learning are of paramount importance.

(Braverman, 1974; Legge, 1995; Strati, 1985)

social construction
Social constructionism is a philosophy in its own right, which puts interacting individuals at the centre of their own universe, as architects, more or less, of their own world views and **meaning systems**. According to social constructionists, when people act, they do so on the basis of inter-subjective understandings of a particular situation – they *define* the situation in interaction, or negotiation, with others. How people know what to do and how to behave in a particular social situation comes about from an exchange of many communications and performances: exchanges of voice, eye contact, body posture, facial expression, gestures, testing out old understandings and experimenting with new ones. From these, social **reality** is constructed. People weigh up interpretations of the signs and signals to make judgements about others' intentions and, where necessary, seek shared understanding for the formulation of rules of conduct. Such rules are not fixed, immutable; they are always being shaped and re-negotiated as new understandings emerge. The socially constructed world is always dynamic, but some shared meanings are more resistant to change than others because they are familiar and seem to work well most of the time. So we are not always seeking to re-define, within our culture, the courtesies of greeting a stranger, conducting ourselves in a smart restaurant, or how to behave in the presence of our boss. These norms do shift, but slowly over time. Nor, in the socially constructed world, are we completely free to re-define situations. In the hierarchies of power and status in organizations – themselves social constructions – we invest some people with more influence than others, so they can impress their definition of the situation on us. Less formally, many social interactions in organizations involve give-and-take, where we sacrifice some of our own interpretations in the interest of collaboration and cooperation.

(Berger and Luckmann, 1967; Gergen, 1999; Shotter, 1995)

socialization
Socialization is the process by which people become part of a social unit. It is the taking on of the beliefs, **values** and mores of the society or organization to which they belong. Key agents of socialization are parents, teachers, peers and possibly religious officials. Competing hard with these traditional sources are the mass media and entertainment: magazines, television, film, pop stars. From these various sources, we learn our national cultural ways, including what is appropriate behaviour for our sex, social class and educational background. Organizational socialization is a microcosm of these processes. Companies seek to mould employees to their way of thinking and doing things. They do this by stressing their values and expectations at the recruitment stage. These are then reinforced by joining **rituals**, **rites of passage**, training, promotional criteria and various forms of

organizational literature. Some companies are known for their particular vigour in such efforts, reflecting the desire to create a 'strong' organizational **culture**.

(Hogg and Vaughan, 2002; Schein, 1988)

stakeholder

This is a group or individual seen as having some special interest, or *stake*, in the outcome of an organization's activities. Most organizations have core stakeholders, such as owners and shareholders, employees, suppliers and governments. Other possible stakeholders are customers, local communities, financial institutions, environmental protection groups and political parties. Stakeholders in organizations may be drawn more or less widely, and decisions about who a company regards as its stakeholders often reflect its **values** and priorities. For example, a radical environmental pressure group may see itself as one of an oil company's stakeholders, but the company refuses to acknowledge such a relationship. A stakeholder perspective for management means that no organization can be considered as an island. Managers need to map their key stakeholders, consider their expectations and demands, their interrelationships and their power to influence the organization's outcomes and reputation. Stakeholder theory sometimes assumes the form of old-fashioned pluralism, viewing organizations as a political game in which different interest groups (or stakeholders) seek to influence the outcomes. The field on which the game is being played is rarely level and the **power** with which stakeholders enter the game is rarely evenly matched. In these circumstances, stickholder may be a better metaphor than stakeholder. The bigger stick prevails.

(Mason and Mitroff, 1985; Mitroff, 1984)

status

Like **role**, status signifies a social position. Yet status goes beyond **role**, as it embodies an evaluation of merit, prestige or honour. Age, gender, birth, education, acquaintances and lifestyles are all important sources of status, though how they affect an individual's status may differ across different **cultures**. A person's job or occupation, frequently referred to as 'socio-economic status', is an extremely important source of status in Western cultures. Within organizations, professionals and clerical workers usually enjoy superior status to manual workers. Status **symbols** are visible signs establishing an individual's or a group's status. A BMW as well as a Volkswagen Beetle can be status symbols, as are the size of an executive's office, a fashionable pair of trainers, a title such as Sir or Dr, an address in a fashionable part of town or a badge on a piece of clothing.

stereotyping

This term was introduced by the journalist Walter Lippman in 1922, who described stereotypes as 'pictures in our heads'. Stereotypes have been described by Baron and Byrne as 'clusters of pre-conceived notions' (1977: 155). Stereotyping assumes that all the objects in some category will share other similar characteristics. Often, they are crude allusions, such as 'fat people are jolly', 'the Scots are canny', 'women are emotional'. Stereotyping is a shortcut to meaning; a simplistic way of making sense of the complexities of the world. In doing so, however, it very often attributes characteristics to people unjustly, blinding the perceiver to important individual differences. Indeed, stereotyping is one of the ways in which **prejudice** operates. People may also fall victim to their own stereotypes. For example, male managers can start to behave in macho ways because they have absorbed a stereotype that this is how a 'real manager' should behave.

(Wilson and Rosenfeld, 1990; Yee, 1992)
See also **attitude**, **prejudice**, **scapegoating**

stories and storytelling

Storytelling has long been a feature of human societies, groups and organizations. Stories are pithy **narratives** with plots, characters and twists that can be full of **meaning**. While some stories may be pure fiction, others are inspired by real events. Their relation to such events, however, is tenuous – in stories, accuracy is almost always sacrificed for effect. Stories entertain, inform, advise, warn and educate. They often pass moral judgements on events, casting their characters in roles like hero, villain, fool and victim. They are capable of stimulating strong **emotions** of sympathy, anger, fear, anxiety and so forth.

Whether in or out of organizations, we often recount our experiences in story-like forms and listen to stories of others. By placing ourselves at the centre of our stories, we seek to make sense of these experiences, whether happy, trying or painful. Organizational theorists have now become aware that much learning in organizations takes place through storytelling; this is sometimes referred to as **narrative knowledge**. They have also realized that there is much we can learn by studying the stories that people tell about each other and about the organization as a whole. Stories can open windows into the cultural, political and emotional lives of organizations, allowing people to express deep and sometimes hidden or conflicting emotions. There are numerous uses to which storytelling has been put by theorists of organizations, which include:

- stories as a part of an organization's sense-making apparatus
- stories as a feature of organizational politics, attempts at **control** and **resistance**
- stories as symbolic artefacts expressing deep **mythological** archetypes
- stories as performances aimed at influencing hearts and minds
- stories as a means of disseminating **knowledge** and learning.

In recent years, numerous **consultants** have turned to stories as vehicles for enhancing organizational communication, performance and learning, as well as the management of **change**. While the success of these approaches is qualified, there can be little doubt that, in the hands of imaginative leaders, educators, gurus and prophets, stories are powerful devices for **managing meaning**.

(Boje, 1991, 2001; Czarniawska, 2004; Denning, 2000; Gabriel, 2000, 2004a; Orr, 1987, 1996; Polkinghorne, 1988; Rhodes and Brown, 2005; Sims, 2003; Tangherlini, 1998)

strategy

Strategies are major courses of **action** that an organization plans to take in order to meet **objectives**. At its simplest, and in its military origin, it means looking several steps ahead and considering what to do over the longer term, rather than looking only to the immediate term ('tactics'). Most often, strategies are formulated by the top management team as an expression of their interests, inclinations and views about the purpose of the business. The process of strategic planning has become central to the operation of many organizations. It involves decisions on the organization's mission in the light of opportunities and threats, and on the long-term outlook for the business. Strategic planning will also include the allocation of resources: money, personnel, plant, land and equipment. Within the overall strategic plan, tactical planning will take place: short-term decisions, such as how a particular department will spend its own budget and achieve its production targets. Much recent research in organizations has been devoted to the process of strategy making and to the types of strategies which seem to pay off. The word 'strategy' has become debased in recent years, as the fashion has grown for describing oneself as 'thinking strategically' or working at a 'strategic level' without the label having any particular meaning beyond that the speaker thinks they are important. Those new to reading about organizations should be warned that a number of old ideas have been re-packaged, have the label 'strategy' stuck on them and are now being offered as if they were new. Some have argued that strategy is not important, and that what matters in organizational life is opportunistic action. It may be that strategy making helps people to think through a situation, and prepares them to be effective in operating opportunistically; in effect, strategy making may be best if you do not then feel you have to follow your strategy.

(Joyce and Woods, 1996; Pearce and Robinson, 1991; Pennings, 1985)

stress

Stress normally refers to unpleasant feelings and/or physical responses that people experience when they are working, for a prolonged period, beyond their capacities and levels of coping. The signs and symptoms of stress include anxiety, irritability, fear, skin ailments, high blood pressure, gastric complaints and heart disease. Certain work situations can be potentially more stressful than others, such as where there are high levels of noise, poorly designed equipment, conflicting **role** demands, a very high workload, poor support and supervision and unpredictable changes. Responsibility for others rather than 'things' (machines, equipment) can be particularly stressful. One approach to stress management, therefore, lies in improving the design and supervision of work. But the mechanisms of stress are also peculiar to the individual. One person's source of stress can be another's exciting challenge. Stress, therefore, also, depends on a person's **perception** of how threatening a particular **problem** or situation is, and his or her capacities to cope. Long periods of unresolved stress can lead to **burnout** and play a part in disabling or fatal diseases. In recent years, it has become more acceptable to talk openly about stress problems, and stress has become something of an institutionalized problem in society. It is a source of litigation for individuals who feel that their organization has put unreasonable, overbearing demands on them. Consequently, company-based stress management programmes and counselling support have become more prevalent. This 'stress culture' has generated much debate and controversy, dividing commentators. Some regard it as, finally, recognition of the afflictions caused by modern organizations. Others take the view that stress has become fashionable, an excuse to label any organizational discontent as the fault of the employer.

(Barley and Knight, 1992; Buchanan and Huczynski, 2004; Cooper and Dewe, 2004)
See also **burnout**

structuration

The theory of structuration was developed by British sociologist Anthony Giddens as an attempt to resolve a long-lasting tension in the social sciences between structure and action. Theories that emphasized structure tended to view individual actions as deriving from these structures (class relations, kinship systems, political and legal institutions and so on), allowing little room for individual freedom and variation. Theories that emphasized action, on the other hand, showed little recognition that these actions are constrained by social forces beyond the control of individuals. Giddens argued that social structures and human agency are locked in a relationship whereby structures are sustained and reproduced by individuals' routine actions. There is a similarity in the way **language** operates: its rules and grammar only exist when we use it, but we cannot use it in any way we please. Routines establish proper and improper uses and people react strongly when linguistic conventions are disregarded. In this way, structuration theory offers a way of acknowledging human agency, rationality, emotions and motives, while at the same time not overlooking the constraining influence of social structures. There have been attempts to use and develop structuration theory within organizational theory, but it would be fair to say that these remain in the early stages.

(Giddens, 1984; Heracleous and Hendry, 2000; Weaver and Gioia, 1994)
See also **subjectivity**

structure

Structure is a concept which derives from engineering, where it is used to describe bridges, buildings, towers or other constructions made up of different interconnected components. Structure has come to signify the patterned relations of components which make up any **system**. You can think of the structure as a framework on which different interconnected components are attached; it is not generally easy to alter one component without affecting the others. Organizations have different types of structure; in formal terms, some are structured in geographical or product divisions, others in functional areas (such as marketing, finance, personnel and so on) and yet others form **matrix structures**. In more substantial terms, some have rigid mechanical structures dominated by formal **roles**, **rules** and regulations, while others have more informal and flexible structures in which people collaborate and communicate in a less highly **controlled** manner. Some organizations operating in particularly turbulent and uncertain **environments** tend to adopt an extremely fluid task-oriented structure known as adhocracy.

See also **bureaucracy**, **contingency theories**, **hierarchy**, **matrix structure**, **structuration**

sub-culture

The concept of **culture** originates with societies, as in 'European culture' or 'Amazonian culture'. However, rarely are such cultures homogeneous. In the United Kingdom, for example, all its inhabitants may be said to share certain cultural characteristics of 'Britishness', but thereafter different, distinct sub-cultures exist, marking off particular groups with separate identities and ways. There are those, for example, of different wealth and social class who live in different parts of London; there are youth *sub-cultures*; clusters of particular religious groups; Scottish Highlanders compared to Glaswegians, and so forth. Applied to organizations, one may find various sub-cultures within a single enterprise. For example, staff in a computer department may follow a different, more relaxed dress code than staff in other departments. There can be a 'management' sub-culture in which members can take more relaxed working hours than hourly paid staff. On the shop floor, tightly enforced informal **norms** can mark out the way different work groups create their own subcultural 'bubble', something not apparent to the casual observer. Sub-cultures function to provide a special sense of identity, difference, and, often, pride, which is illusive in the wider, more anonymous, culture of the whole organization.

(Brown, 1995; Fortado, 1992; Smircich, 1983)
See also **human relations**

subjectivity

Usually seen as the opposite of **objectivity**, subjectivity is what makes each person unique in their perceptions, judgements, emotions and actions. Subjectivity is a term, like **identity**, self, **personality** and ego, which suggests that individuals have certain qualities that distinguish them from others and that their actions are not simply the outcome of social forces but are initiated by themselves. In traditional philosophy, subjectivity is what makes each person a sovereign agent responsible and answerable for his/her actions. Subjectivity, however, has been the subject of a persistent critique from the Marxist, Freudian and Nitzschean traditions. These have viewed subjectivity as the product of the material conditions that prevail in contemporary societies or indeed as an illusion created by these conditions. Thus, subjectivity, far from initiating or causing events, is the result or consequence of events. More recently, **postmodern** philosophy has further critiqued the idea of a 'sovereign subject' by illustrating numerous ways in which we come to view ourselves as such through **discourse**. Organizational theorists have advanced this critique by arguing that subjectivity is itself the product of discursive practices in organizations (for example, performance appraisals, the compiling of CVs, promotion applications and so on) through which individuals are disciplined and **controlled**. Thus, individuals do not exist as managers, workers, career people, customers, loyal employees and so on but come to view themselves as such through an organization's discursive formations. In this way, social problems and organizational failures can be individualized by attributing blame to individuals. There are some theorists of organizations, however, who have sought to vindicate subjectivity not as a sovereign entity that takes off in quixotic adventures, but as the site of conflicting pressures, conflicts and emotions. Above all, it has been argued that writing subjectivity out of the study of organizations undervalues the ability of individuals and groups to resist injustice, exploitation and oppression.

(Ackroyd and Thompson, 1999; Collinson, 1982; Foucault, 1970; Gabriel, 2000; Grey, 1994; Knights, 1990; Knights and Willmott, 1989; Parker, 1999; Thompson, 1993; Thompson and Ackroyd, 1995; Willmott, 1990, 1993)

success

An integral part of the Protestant **work ethic**, success, in the form of material prosperity, fame and honour, was regarded as a sign of God's favour and a reward for hard work. Protestantism, according to Max Weber (1860–1920), encouraged a methodical and calculating attitude in the pursuit of wealth, which provided capitalism with the work ethic required for its early growth in the sixteenth century. Nowadays, success has lost its religious and moral underpinning; it is no longer seen by everybody as the product of hard work, nor is it seen as generating a set of responsibilities and duties towards the community. Instead, some people would regard success as the result of successful planning, clever deals or good luck. Maccoby has argued that the successful businessman of today is essentially one who is good at **games**. Instead of hard **work** or ruthless ambition, cunning and risk taking are seen as the requirements for success. Although different people may see success differently, it remains a powerful feature of middle-class cultures in the West as well as in the East, as part of a system of **values** which includes self-reliance, individualism and material well-being but also entrepreneurship and risk. Some individuals may gauge success in terms of visible signs and **symbols,** while others may tend to assess it through personal indicators, such as contentment, happiness or love.

(Furnham, 1992; Maccoby, 1976)
See also **achievement**

symbolism

A symbol is something that 'stands for', or signifies something beyond the literal properties of the symbol itself. So a national flag can symbolize (stand for) a nation, its freedom and independence. A small lapel badge can symbolize membership of an exclusive club or sect. Consumer products are often designed to be attractive for what they stand for as much as, if not more than, for what they actually do. To own a car of a particular make, colour and shape can give others a recognizable sign that you are the sort of person who has 'made it'. Similarly, wearing specific clothes can symbolize one's wealth, youth, **status**, occupation or identification with a **sub-culture**. The words, deeds and products of organizational managers can influence those whom they manage as much through the symbolism used as through any more direct content. The symbols may be very obvious ones, such as the frequency of managers' presence and availability; the size, shape and furnishing of their rooms; the style of their memos and announcements; the way they conduct meetings; their **language** and **rhetoric**; the kinds of cars they drive; and the salaries they take and award. All these can be taken as symbols of their own **values**, style and degree of concern for others. Less obvious symbols relate to areas such as trust and reliability, subtle features of the **psychological contract**. Do managers deliver what they promise? Are confidences respected? Is promotion seen to be fair? Are all staff listened to? Inconsistency in managerial symbols can soon undermine people's confidence and enthusiasm, such as, for example, when bank staff are told they need to live up to the company's public slogan of 'the listening, caring bank', yet these same staff receive little attention or care from their own managers.

(Czarniawska-Joerges, 1992; Gagliardi, 1990a; Pratt and Rafaeli, 2001; Wasserman et al., 2000)
See also **meaning, status**

synergy

Synergy is the ability of **groups**, teams or organizations to deliver more than the sum of the parts that make them up. Synergy suggests that a well-chosen, well-drilled and well-motivated team may comfortably outperform a team made up of stars and prima donnas who have no particular interest in working together. Synergy is often seen as dependent on variety and heterogeneity within a group – each individual complements and draws the best out of the others. Synergy can exist at the level of two individuals (e.g. Lennon and McCartney) or at the level of organizations (e.g. the **merger** of Glaxo and SmithKline Beecham was justified on the grounds of synergies between the two companies). Yet, synergy can easily disintegrate into cliché, wishful thinking or self-aggrandisement for the person claiming synergy for their merger.

system

Organizations are often studied as systems. Systems are separated from their **environment** by a **boundary** which is crossed by inputs and outputs. For example, an organization's inputs from the environment may include raw materials, expertise and money, while its outputs may include products, services and waste. Systems themselves are seen as made up of components in orderly relationships, with each component having specific functions of benefit to the system as a whole. These relations make up the system's **structure**. Biological systems, like animals or plants, are often seen as having sub-systems, such as respiratory or nervous. Generally, systems are seen as responding to changes in their environment, either by adapting or by seeking to change and **control** their environment. While the concept of a system has been used extensively to describe phenomena as diverse as the solar system, the transport and educational systems of a country, the global ecosystem or an **information** system, it has been criticized for obscuring **conflict** and disorder, and presenting too tidy and rational an image of the world. Many systems approaches to organizations tend to look at them through two core **metaphors** – either of machines or of biological organisms.

Recently, the systems approach has been re-invigorated as a result of the introduction of new ideas, notably chaos, complexity, **autopoiesis** and evolutionary theory, which have questioned many of the assumptions of traditional systems theory, notably fixed boundaries, adaptive relations to a given environment and integrated internal functioning.

This textbook has highlighted organizations as terrains in which people make **decisions**, create **meanings**, face choices and experience **emotions**; these are all features which are generally underplayed by systems theory. Instead of looking at **organizations** as fixed aspects of **reality** to be studied in an objective way, the approach taken by this book has emphasized organization as something created through people's actions and interactions, discussions and differences. Organization is the outcome of organizing, an outcome that requires much effort and work and which cannot be taken for granted.

(Ciborra, 2002; Cilliers, 1998; Katz and Kahn, 1978; Keys, 1991; Luhmann, 1995; Mingers, 1995; Weick, 1976, 2001d; Wenger, 2000)

talk

Talk is a major part of most peoples' lives and, in particular, the main part of what managers do. Studies of managerial life by Mintzberg showed that the greater part of managerial activity is conducted through talk. Managers talk for their living as much as teachers, actors or chat show hosts do, a topic that has received lively and informative coverage by Tannen. Relatively little time is spent, or **action** taken, by managers on their own. Talk has been studied as a form of behaviour (Beattie, 1983), in a process called 'conversational analysis'. In a less behaviourist fashion, recent research has focused on **language**, **rhetoric** and **discourse**. Talk is not always serious. People talk and **gossip** for pleasure as well as profit; such conversations may be conducted in the spirit of idle chatter, but can still have a considerable impact on later events, when the **information** that was passed on reaches someone who wishes to make use of it. It may be left deliberately unclear as to whether such talk is idle chatter or should be taken more seriously, as a way of testing out others' reactions before being too firm oneself. The role of talk has been grossly understated in most management theorizing, which has seen it as a transparent medium by which messages are conveyed from one person to another, rather than as a substantive activity in itself. The richness and joy of talk, the influence that can be wielded by an effective talker, the activities of the virtuoso talker (who will deliberately offer a brilliant display for the joy of showing that it can be done), the significance of telling stories well, and the role of gossip in keeping people informed about what is happening in your organization, are all under-emphasized if talk is viewed as simply a functional way of conveying intended meaning.

(Beattie, 1983; Billig, 1987; Mintzberg, 1973; Potter and Wetherell, 1987; Tannen, 1995)
See also **gossip**, **language**

Taylorism
See **scientific management**

teamwork
Organizations are full of teams, and many managers and theorists have argued for the importance of good teamwork for the achievement of complex tasks. Teams are better than individuals on tasks which require either more work than one person can give, or more knowledge or **information** than one person will have. They are also important where a task calls for different **roles** or **skills** to be brought into play. But teams can also be arenas for **conflict** and this conflict can come to be of more interest to the members than their task. Since the 1970s, there has been extensive team-development work in many organizations, usually with the intention of producing more closely knit teams, and enabling team members to be more open with each other. However, well-developed teams also manifest some difficulties. They are prone to 'risky shift' – taking more risky decisions than the members would individually. They are also at risk of 'groupthink' (Janis, 1972), of going along with the opinions of their teammates, particularly if they trust and respect them, whatever their personal doubts. Some practitioners have argued that too much work is done in teams, stifling individualism; they have then offered team destruction as an alternative to team building.

(Goold and Campbell, 1998; Lembke and Wilson, 1998; Schein, 1980)
See also **groups**, **synergy**

technology
In the first instance, technology can be thought of as the tools and machines which enable us to carry out simple or complex tasks in a more effective and economical way. A nut cracker, a computer and a car are examples of technology. It quickly becomes apparent, however, that unless one knows how to use these machines, they are useless objects. In order to use machines, we need recipes, techniques, know-how and what, in the context of **information technology**, is described as software. These are, therefore, also forms of technology. Some of these 'ways of doing things' may involve ways of using human beings, for instance, by placing them on an assembly line or by devising a system for 'lean production' – these are sometimes known as social technologies. But technologies do not have to be elaborate or complex. A bump on the road is quite a simple piece of technology forcing drivers to slow down, an effect that may alternatively be accomplished by a security camera, linked to an automated computerized register of cars and a highly sophisticated ticketing system.

Technology may relieve us of the **stress** and potential overload of trying to do various tasks unaided. Yet, technologies create difficulties and extra tasks of their own. They increase the control we have over our lives, but also take away some of this control. They enhance the quality of our life, but also create expectations of enhanced quality that are not always met. Technology also carries with it the risk of system failure: action lists get lost, the central locking on cars fails to function and computers become infected with viruses. The more technology seems able to help its users, the more likely they are to let it **control** them, and the more they feel lost when systems fail. Finally, with advances in technology, the costs of failure, the risks of misappropriation and the scope for destructive uses escalate enormously. This is why the story of Frankenstein, the human creation that acquires a life of its own that threatens its former masters remains such a potent one in relation to the risks and dangers of technology.

(Feldman, 1989; Latour, 1996; Mumford, 1934; Orr, 1996; Womack et al., 1990)
See also **actor-network theory, alienation, contingency theories, deskilling, information technology, innovation**

teleworking

Teleworking is a term applied to people who work at a distance from their customer, client, colleagues or headquarters. Typically, the physical distance is bridged by telecommunications technology. Traditionally, the telephone with a computer modem attached to a PC in the worker's home or local 'telecottage' provided the necessary link. But this has now been supplemented with sophisticated additions such as mobile phones, wireless internet, email and video. All provide opportunities for teleconferencing with colleagues or managers, and linking customers, virtually, to providers anywhere in the world. Teleworking offers flexibility over one's place of work, which can range from the corner of a kitchen to the car. Using computer links, people can rapidly transmit documents over huge distances, so reducing the need for face-to-face meetings and much travel and commuting (hence the phrase 'telecommuter'). The advantages of teleworking can be considerable to those who live in isolated communities, or who wish to avoid congested towns or cities. Large companies can save on expensive office space by encouraging teleworking. On the other hand, some teleworkers find themselves lonely working without colleagues, cramped or stressed in their home work space and less secure about their work status. Teleworking is particularly suited to some jobs such as computer software services, journalism, publishing, sales and **virtual organizations** (e.g. banking), and some types of consultancy. It has also been applied to some of the lowest paid and repetitive jobs, such as data entry.

(Daniels et al., 2000, 2001; Fineman, 2003; Jackson and Van der Weilen, 1998)
See also **information technology**

total institutions

These are organizations, such as prisons, asylums, monasteries, oil rigs at sea, military camps and so forth, in which members spend long periods under one roof without the option of leaving. Following the work of Goffman, total institutions are recognized as applying certain unique pressures on individuals, dominating their lives and outlooks and governing their behaviour. They are characterized by timetables, systems of privileges and punishments and a particular *argot* or lingo. Total institutions, however, generate their own forms of rebellion and **resistance** as eloquently portrayed by the character played by Jack Nicholson in the film *One Flew Over the Cuckoo's Nest*. As alternatives to rebellion, Goffman identified three other adaptive responses of individuals to total institutions. These include: (1) withdrawal; (2) colonization – creating pockets of 'home' within the institution; and (3) conversion – identifying with the institution and adopting the prescribed mentality.

(Collinson, 1999; Goffman, 1961)

trade unions

Trade unions are **organizations** formed by employees to promote their common interests. They emerged in the early part of the nineteenth century out of the **powerlessness** of the individual worker when confronted by the **power** of the employer. They grew out of the realization that by forming an association, workers could offer mutual protection and improve their conditions of work. Most early unions were craft associations, seeking to limit the supply of labour in skilled trades thus raising the market value of these **skills**. Gradually, however, industrial unionism shifted the emphasis towards uniform conditions of work and rates of pay through industrial action, like strikes, and collective bargaining with the employers. In this way, unions have sought to limit the powers of employers to hire and fire at will, unilaterally to impose conditions of work on a take-it-or-leave-it basis, and to guarantee only minimal standards of protection and welfare as part of the terms of employment. In most industrial countries, following periods of acute conflict and confrontation, employers accepted unions as legitimate expressions of their employees' collective interests and recognized the legitimacy of collective bargaining as an **institution** for settling **conflicts** of interest.

In recent years, unions have been on the defensive in Britain and the United States, as a result of: (a) new **technologies** which have wiped out traditional strongholds of unions in the skilled trades; (b) new **management** and political philosophies which have placed heavy emphasis on the individual employee as a bargaining agent or as a member of a corporate **culture**; (c) the emergence of new sectors in the economy, notably in services, where unionization is difficult; (d) globalization of production which allows companies to shift productive operations relatively easily to countries where costs are low; (e) **outsourcing** which enables companies to close down entire departments (for instance, those known for their militance or low productivity) and subcontract their functions to other organizations; and (f) a more individualistic culture and **ideology** that look at **success** as the product of one's individual efforts.

(Hyman, 1989; Legge, 1995; Purcell, 1993)
See also **alienation, contingency theories, deskilling, information technology, resistance**

trust

Most transactions in and between organizations are not policed or supervised to make sure they happen; they rest on trust. Trust is reliance on, and confidence in, the reliability and honesty of another person; that they will do, say or deliver on what has been agreed. Trust is held in a psychological contract, an understanding (often unspoken) of what one can expect from one another. Trust is reinforced and deepened over time as promises are kept. After a while, trust becomes an important way in which people judge each other: 'he/she is a really trustworthy person'. Curiously, trust is also a fragile quality; being let down by someone whom one has learned to trust can feel especially wounding, and, depending on the issue, broken trust can be difficult or impossible to repair.

Thus, trust becomes an important lubricant of organizational action, with high-trust organizations being known for their collaborative **culture** and relative ease of management. Where trust is low, strife and turnover tend to be higher. The style of **leadership** and closeness of supervision all affect how trusted, or otherwise, people feel. Generally, trust improves in settings where genuine **empowerment** prevails. In **virtual organizations,** many of the normal, face-to-face, cues of trust building are missing and virtual workers have had to seek other ways of assessing the trustworthiness of their virtual co-workers and customers.

(Handy, 1995; Holmes and Remple, 1989; Solomon and Flores, 2001)

unemployment

Unemployment can reveal much about the role of employment, especially the aspects of work that people take for granted. Paid employment has become a major feature of all industrialized societies and provides a major source of **meaning** for those who work, even in jobs which are dreary and **alienating**. The unemployed, many of whom have been victims of **downsizing,** often report a loss of time structure to the day, difficulties with their status and personal identity, a lack of 'place' at home and, more generally, a sense of purposelessness and **meaninglessness** in their lives. **Stress** and illness are often greater among the unemployed. Poverty, or being less credit-worthy, add considerably to these difficulties: paid work is one of the few (legal) ways of acquiring money to purchase the various commodities which have become essential to comfortable survival in modern consumerist societies. Often, the loss of work can be traumatic, particularly to people who are unable easily to re-enter the work force because of their age, redundant skills or infirmity.

In high-unemployment communities, we find school leavers expecting not to work and pools of long-term unemployed men and women. For some, unemployment can become a way of life, so widely shared in their community that it does not hold a stigma. However, the unemployed can rarely participate in the wealth, opportunity and consumption enjoyed by those who do work, therefore high levels of unemployment can be socially divisive and have been linked to social unrest and crime.

(Fineman, 1987; MacDonald, 1997; Winefield et al., 1993)
See also **meaning, work ethic**

values

What do you think is ultimately important to you? What do you really care about? These are likely to be your values. Values are a set of core beliefs about what we think is right, good and desirable. Each individual, it is suggested, operates a system of values, possibly in a hierarchy of importance. Typical ones could be honesty, loyalty, freedom, respect and obedience. Values are seen as points of non-compromise; they are stable and stay with us over time. They are clear reflections of our **culture** and **socialization**, especially parents, teachers and religious influences. Values are important for our study of organizations because individuals carry their values into their organizations, and often will select work organizations for their value congruence. Some organizations, such as The Body Shop, make a virtue out of this process, stating openly their values and specifically seeking, and attracting, employees and customers who value protection of the environment and social responsibility in business. Likewise, organizations like the military are likely to be appealing to those who value obedience and loyalty. A mismatch of values is often at the heart of the most agonizing personal conflicts in organizations. It is epitomized by the whistle-blower, an employee who feels compelled to speak out publicly about what they regard as organizational acts of dishonesty, malevolence or greed. Such individuals often have an extremely clear sense of ethical probity on which they will not compromise or bargain, unlike others who move with the flow in an organization's **politics**. The whistle-blower's rigidity can be disarming; however, they can successfully reveal some of the damaging ways that private and public sector organizations can become **corrupted**, with actions sheltered under a veil of secrecy, bureaucracy and vested interests.

(Alford, 2001; Fisher and Lovell, 2003; Glazer and Glazer, 1989; Rokeach, 1973)
See also **attitude, culture and organizational culture, meaning, norms**

virtual organization

A virtual organization is one that is treated as if it were a real organization but does not have a physical presence, and sometimes does not have a conventional employment structure. Software companies employing people in their spare time and at their own homes are one example, and terrorist networks another. The virtual organization has great advantages of flexibility and often of cost, against which are set some issues about **control** and **trust**. Virtual organizations have come to the fore with recent developments in communication technology, which have enabled effective virtual communication, and hence organization. In particular, the availability of electronic databases, the internet and cheap telephone communication means that tasks which previously required proximity can now easily be achieved by units that are spread around the world. Sometimes it is a part of an organization rather than the whole which goes virtual. For example, call centres may handle customer service for consumers of different suppliers all over the USA, all from a base in India. The virtual organization often takes this principle a little further, by outsourcing numbers of different activities so that the organization gradually becomes more of a network of contracted, geographically dispersed suppliers, rather than a reconizable, hierarchical entity.

(Clases et al., 2004; Jackson, 1999; Mowshowitz, 2002)

vision statement

If the **mission statement** tells us about what an organization is seeking to achieve, the vision statement tells us about the situation that it wishes to create. As with a mission statement, these may be created and quoted with greater or lesser seriousness by organizations. The experience is that they often function as an effective rhetorical device; the discussion which is required to create them may be of more value than the statement itself, but the vision statement too may have value as people look back at their vision as it had been at one point in time and create a new one. There can be considerable frustration when a vision statement is agreed but no action follows. To make a vision happen requires **leadership**. It also often requires one or more people to champion it within the organization, but the role of the leader is to help the champion(s) to believe that they can succeed, to encourage them and to help them make any changes necessary as the vision is realized.

voice

Some people in organizations find it much harder to be heard than others. Some voices are listened to, while others are ignored. This can be one of the issues of **diversity**, as women and members of ethnic minorities are sometimes ignored seemingly because of their voices. Some women take elocution lessons to learn how to speak in a way which is taken as authoritative by others. Part of the issue may be about modelling; people may model their voices, as well as other aspects of their team behaviour, on role models, and by definition, there are less role models available for members of minorities. Voice is sometimes used more **metaphorically**, where someone is said not to have a voice when they are not seen as a legitimate person to contribute to discussion. However, like many metaphors, the metaphoric use is quite close to the literal meaning. Part of the experience of not being able to find a voice in organizations is that the person cannot imagine sounding 'right' if they did speak. It is known that the great majority of people do not like the sound of their own voices when they hear them recorded. The voice is a matter of considerable self-criticism and is something in which people can quite easily lose their self-confidence.

Hirschman saw voice as one of three responses individual employees may display towards their employer, the other two being loyalty and exit (i.e. uncritically accepting what the employer demands or leaving the company). Hirschman argued that voice **empowers** employees to influence their working environment. More recently, the concept of voice has been used to express the ability of an individual or a group to articulate their experiences and discover a **story** or a **narrative** that enable them to form an **identity** based on the ways they see themselves rather than as others see them.

(Gabriel, 2004b; Hirschman, 1970)

work

Unlike **labour**, which is a concept drawn from political economy, work is in the main a sociological and psychological concept. It incorporates a wide range of cultural assumptions regarding what constitutes work, what the purpose and **meaning** of work are, and what its values and rewards. 'What work do you do?', for example, is a question which cannot be answered without understanding the meaning which a **culture** attributes to work, the expectation of receiving payment or the **status** and prestige of different kinds of work. Different cultures have assigned widely diverging meanings to work and its corollary, leisure. Some have approached it as a primeval curse afflicting humanity, some as the true road to holiness and **success**, and some, like the Ancient Greeks, as a lower form of occupation unworthy of free individuals. Clusters of meanings around work, especially those regarding the relations between work and the good life, are often said to constitute **work ethics**.

Another meaning of the word 'work' concerns the different types of psychological effort that is regularly dedicated to different emotional tasks. Mourning the death or departure of a dear colleague, coping with an abusive customer, presenting a cheerful and competent front when inwardly unhappy or depressed – these all require the expenditure of psychological energy, they involve work. **Emotional** work is one form of such work.

work ethic

The notion of 'work ethic' implies a moral driving force in individuals to work; it suggests that people ought personally to labour, producing goods or services. There is debate about the strength and direction of the work ethic in different populations, especially about whether it has declined among young people. The 'ought' implied in the work ethic is associated with the seventeenth-century rise in Protestantism in Europe where working was regarded as a religious imperative, a major route to spiritual salvation. The link between Protestantism and business activity was explored extensively by Max Weber (1864–1920) in his influential book *The Protestant Ethic and the Spirit of Capitalism*. (1958) The religious roots of the work ethic are today diffused with the broader influences of national and community cultures. We can see significant competing 'ethics' in peoples' lives, such as leisure and various forms of self-development. Those who lament the apparent decline in the work ethic point to a 'welfare ethic': people who are now keen to live off the social provisions of the state. Inevitably, however, discussions about the work ethic become intermingled with the availability of jobs and the extent to which non-workers are personally blamed for their predicament.

(Bauman, 1992; Furnham, 1992; Hirschman, 1977; Sennett, 1998; Weber, 1958)
See also **achievement**, **success**

BIBLIOGRAPHY

Abercrombie, N. (1994) 'Authority and consumer society', in N. Abercrombie (ed.), *The Authority of the Consumer*. London: Routledge.

Abrahamson, E. (1991) 'Managerial fads and fashions: the diffusion and rejection of innovations', *Academy of Management Review*, 16 (3): 586–612.

Abrahamson, E. (2004) *Change Without Pain: How Managers Can Overcome Initiative Overload, Organizational Chaos and Employee Burnout*. Harvard, MA: Harvard Business School Press.

Acker, J. (2006) 'Inequality regimes: gender, class, and race in organizations', *Gender Society*, 20 (4): 441–64.

Ackroyd, S. and Thompson, P. (1999) *Organizational Misbehaviour*. London: Sage.

Adams, A. and Crawford, N. (1992) *Bullying at Work: How to Confront and Overcome It.* London: Virago.

Adams, J.S., Berkowitz, L. and Hatfield, E. (1976) *Equity Theory: Toward a General Theory of Social Interaction.* New York: Academic Press.

Adkins, L. (1995) *Gendered Work: Sexuality, Family, and the Labour Market.* Bristol: Open University Press.

Adler, P.S. and Cole, R.E. (1995) 'Designed for learning: a tale of two auto plants', in Å. Sandberg (ed.), *Enriching Production: Perspectives on Volvo's Uddevalla Plant as an Alternative to Lean Production.* Aldershot: Avebury.

Adorno, T.W., Frenkel-Brunswick, E., Levinson, D. and Sandford, N. (1950) *The Authoritarian Personality.* New York: Harper.

Aktouf, O. (1996) *Traditional Management and Beyond.* Montréal: Morin.

Alcoff, L. (2006) *Identity Politics Reconsidered* (1st edn). New York: Palgrave Macmillan.

Alderfer, C., Alderfer, C., Tucker, L. and Tucker, R. (1980) 'Diagnosing race relations in management', *Journal of Applied Psychology,* 16: 135–66.

Alford, C.F. (2001) *Whistleblowers: Broken Lives and Organizational Power.* Ithaca, NY: Cornell University Press.

Allen, T., Freeman, D.M. and Russell, J.E.A. (2001) 'Survivor reaction to organizational downsizing: does time ease the pain?', *Journal of Occupational and Organizational Psychology,* 74: 145–64.

Allison, G.T. (1971) *Essence of Decision: Explaining the Cuban Missile Crisis.* Waltham: Little Brown.

Allport, G.W. (1959) *The Nature of Prejudice.* Garden City, NY: Doubleday Anchor.

Alvesson, M. (1991) 'Organizational symbolism and ideology', *Journal of Management Studies,* 28 (3): 207–25.

Alvesson, M. (1998) 'Gender relations and identity at work: a case study of masculinities and femininities in an advertising agency', *Human Relations,* 51 (8): 969–1005.

Alvesson, M. and Kärreman, D. (2000a) 'Taking the linguistic turn in organizational research: challenges, responses, consequences', *Journal of Applied Behavioral Science,* 36: 136–58.

Alvesson, M. and Kärreman, D. (2000b) 'Varieties of discourse: on the study of organizations through discourse analysis', *Human Relations,* 53 (9): 1125–49.

Alvesson, M. and Willmott, H. (eds) (1992) *Critical Management Studies.* London: Sage.

Alvesson, M. and Willmott, H. (1996) *Making Sense of Management.* London: Sage.

Andrew, H. (2004) *Political Ideologies: An Introduction.* Basingstoke: Palgrave Macmillan.

Anthias, F. (1982) 'Connecting "race" and ethnic phenomena', *Sociology,* 26 (3): 421–38.

Antonacopoulou, E.P. and Gabriel, Y. (2001) 'Emotion, learning and organizational change: towards an integration of psychoanalytic and other perspectives', *Journal of Organizational Change Management*, 14 (5): 435–51.

Anzieu, D. (1984) *The Group and the Unconscious.* London: Routledge and Kegan Paul.

Archer, M. (ed.) (1998) *Critical Realism: Essential Readings.* London: Routledge.

Arena, C. (2004) *Cause for Success.* Novato: New World Library.

Argyris, C. (1977) 'Double-loop learning in organizations', *Harvard Business Review*, 55 (5): 115–25.

Argyris, C. (2001) 'Actionable knowledge', in C. Knudsen and H. Tsoukas (eds), *Organization Theory as Science: Prospects and Limitations.* Oxford: Oxford University Press.

Argyris, C. and Schön, D.A. (1974) *Theory in Practice: Increasing Professional Effectiveness.* San Francisco: Jossey-Bass.

Argyris, C. and Schön, D.A. (1978) *Organizational Learning: A Theory of Action Perspective.* Reading, MA: Addison-Wesley.

Argyris, C. and Schön, D.A. (1996) *Organizational Learning II: Theory, Method, and Practice.* Reading, MA: Addison-Wesley.

Aronnson, G., Gustafsson, K. and Dallner, M. (2000) 'Sick but yet at work; an empirical study of sickness presenteeism', *Journal of Epidemiological and Community Health*, 54: 502–14.

Arthur, M.B. and Rousseau, D.M. (1996) *The Boundaryless Career.* New York: Oxford University Press.

Arthur, M.B., Inkson, K. and Pringle, J.K. (1999) *The New Careers: Individual Action and Economic Change.* London: Sage.

Arvey, R.D., Carter, G.W. and Buerkley, D.K. (1991) 'Job satisfaction: dispositional and situational influences', *International Review of Industrial and Organizational Psychology*, 6: 359–83.

Ashforth, B.E. and Humphrey, R.H. (1995) 'Emotion in the workplace – a reappraisal', *Human Relations*, 48 (2): 97–125.

Ashforth, B.E. and Tomiuk, M.A. (2000) 'Emotional labour and authenticity: views from service agents', in S. Fineman (ed.), *Emotion in Organizations* (2nd edn). London: Sage.

Ashforth, B.E., Kreiner, G.E. and Fugate, M. (2000) 'All in a day's work: boundaries and micro role transitions', *Academy of Management Review*, 25 (3): 472–91.

Ashforth, B.E., Harrison, S.H. and Corley, K.G. (2008) 'Identification in organizations: an examination of four fundamental questions', *Journal of Management*, 34 (3): 325–74.

Ashkanasy, N.M., Zerbe, W. and Hartel, C.E.J. (2002) *Managing Emotions in the Workplace.* Armonk, NY: M.E. Sharpe.

Aubert, B.A. and Kelsey, B.L. (2003) 'Further understanding of trust and performance in virtual teams', *Small Group Research*, 34 (5): 575–618.

Audia, P.G. and Tams, S. (2002) 'Goal setting, performance appraisal and feedback across cultures', in M.J. Gannon and K.L. Newman (eds), *Blackwell Handbook of Cross-Cultural Management.* Oxford: Blackwell. pp. 142–54.

Auster, E. (1993) 'Demystifying the glass ceiling: organizational and interpersonal dynamics of gender bias', *Business and the Contemporary World*, 5 (Summer): 47–68.

Avery, S. (2008) 'Cracks appear in the glass ceiling', *Purchasing*, 137 (2): 49–53.

Ayer, A.J. and Jules, A. (1959) *Logical Positivism.* Glencoe, Ill: Free Press.

Bailey, F.G. (1977) *Strategems and Spoils.* Oxford: Blackwell.

Bannister, D. and Fransella, F. (1971) *Inquiring Man.* Harmondsworth: Penguin.

Bansal, P. and Howard, P. (1997) *Business and the Natural Environment.* Oxford: Butterworth Heinemann.

Barabasi, A.-L. (2003) *Linked: How Everything is Connected to Everything Else and What it Means for Business, Science and Everyday Life*: New York: Plume.

Barley, S.R. and Knight, D.B. (1992) 'Towards a cultural theory of stress complaints', *Research in Organizational Behavior*, 14: 1–48.

Barnstone, D.A. (2005) *The Transparent State: Architecture and Politics in Postwar Germany*. London: Routledge.

Baron, R.A. and Byrne, D. (1977) *Social Psychology: Understanding Human Interaction* (2nd edn). Boston: Allyn & Bacon.

Bartunek, J.M. and Moch, M.K. (1987) 'First-order, second-order, and third-order change and organization development interventions: a cognitive approach', *Journal of Applied Behavioral Science*, 23 (4): 483–500.

Baruch, Y. (2004) *Managing Careers: Theory and Practice*. Harlow: FT Prentice Hall.

Bass, B.M. (1985) *Leadership and Performance Beyond Expectations*. New York: Free Press.

Bate, P. (1994) *Strategies for Cultural Change*. Oxford: Butterworth Heinemann.

Baudrillard, J. (1970/1988) 'Consumer society', in M. Poster (ed.), *Jean Baudrillard: Selected Writings*. Cambridge: Polity Press.

Baum, H.S. (1987) *The Invisible Bureaucracy*. Oxford: Oxford University Press.

Bauman, Z. (1988) *Freedom*. Milton Keynes: Open University Press.

Bauman, Z. (1989) *Modernity and the Holocaust*. Cambridge: Polity Press.

Bauman, Z. (1992) *Intimations of Postmodernity*. London: Routledge.

Bauman, Z. (1993) *Postmodern Ethics*. Oxford: Basil Blackwell.

Bauman, Z. (1996) 'From pilgrim to tourist – or a short history of identity', in S. Hall and P. du Gay (eds), *Questions of Cultural Identity*. London: Sage. pp. 18–36.

Bauman, Z. (1998) *Work, Consumerism and the New Poor*. Buckingham: Open University Press.

Beattie, G. (1983) *Talk*. Milton Keynes: Open University Press.

Beck, U. (1992) *Risk Society: Towards a New Modernity*. London and Newbury Park, CA: Sage.

Becker, E. (1962) *The Birth and Death of Meaning*. Harmondsworth: Penguin.

Becker, T. (2003) 'Is emotional intelligence a viable concept?', *Academy of Management Review*, 28 (2): 192–5.

Beer, M. and Nohria, N. (eds) (2000) *Breaking the Code of Change*. Boston: Harvard Business School Press.

Belbin, R.M. (1993) *Team-roles at Work*. Oxford: Butterworth.

Bennis, W.G. (1989) *Why Leaders Can't Lead: The Unconscious Conspiracy Continues*. San Francisco: Jossey-Bass.

Bennis, W.G. and Nanus, B. (1985) *Leaders: The Strategies for Taking Charge*. New York: Harper and Row.

Bent, E.B. (1999) 'Challenging "resistance to change"', *Journal of Applied Behavioral Science*, 35 (1): 25–41.

Berger, P.L. and Luckmann, T. (1967) *The Social Construction of Reality*. Harmondsworth: Penguin.

Berggren, C. (1993) *Alternatives to Lean Production*. Ithaca, NY: ILR Press.

Bergson, H. (1980) 'Laughter', in G. Meredith (ed.), *Comedy*. Baltimore, MD: Johns Hopkins University Press.

Berne, E. (1964) *Games People Play*. New York: Grove Press.

Beynon, H. (1973) *Working for Ford*. London: Allen Lane.

Biddle, B.J. (1986) 'Recent developments in role theory', *Annual Review of Sociology*, 12: 67–92.

Billig, M. (1987) *Arguing and Thinking: a Rhetorical Approach to Social Psychology*. Cambridge: Cambridge University Press.

Bion, W.R. (1961) *Experiences in Groups*. London: Tavistock.

Bird, F.B. and Waters, J.A. (1989) 'The moral muteness of managers', *California Management Review*, 32 (1): 73–88.

Black, J.A. and Edwards, S. (2000) 'Emergence of virtual network organizations: fad or feature', *Journal of Organizational Change Management*, 13 (6): 567–75.

Blackburn, R.M. and Mann, M. (1979) *The Working Class in the Labour Market*. London: Macmillan.

Blauner, R. (1964) *Alienation and Freedom*. Chicago: University of Chicago Press.

Bloomfield, B.P. (1989) 'On speaking about computing', *Sociology*, 23 (3): 409–23.

Bluedorn, A. (2002) *The Human Organization of Time: Temporal Realities and Experiences*. Stanford, CA: Stanford University Press.

Bly, R. (1990) *Iron John: A Book About Men*. Reading, MA: Addison-Wesley.

Boje, D.M. (1991) 'The storytelling organization: a study of story performance in an office-supply firm', *Administrative Science Quarterly*, 36: 106–26.

Boje, D.M. (1995) 'Stories of the storytelling organization: a postmodern analysis of Disney as "Tamara Land"', *Academy of Management Review*, 38 (4): 997–1035.

Boje, D.M. (2001) *Narrative Methods for Organizational and Communication Research*. London: Sage.

Boje, D.M. and Dennehy, R.F. (1993) *Managing in the Postmodern World*. Dubuque, IO: Kendall/Hunt.

Boltanski, L. and Chiapello, E. (2005) *The New Spirit of Capitalism* (G. Elliott, Trans.). London: Verso.

Bond, M.H. (1993) 'Emotions and their expression in Chinese culture', *Journal of Nonverbal Behavior*, 17: 245–62.

Bourdieu, P. (1979) *Outline of a Theory of Practice*. Cambridge: Cambridge University Press.

Bourdieu, P. (1984) *Distinction: A Social Critique of the Judgement of Taste*. London: Routledge.

Bourdieu, P. and Johnson, R. (1993) *The Field of Cultural Production: Essays on Art and Literature*. New York: Columbia University Press.

Bowen, D.E., Ledford, G.E. and Nathan, B.R. (1991) 'Hiring for the organization, not the job', *Academy of Management Review*, 5 (4): 35–50.

Bowles, M. (1989) 'Myth, meaning and work organization', *Organization Studies*, 10 (3): 405–21.

Bowles, M. (1997) 'The myth of management: direction and failure in contemporary organizations', *Human Relations*, 50: 779–803.

Boxall, P. and Purcell, J. (2003) *Strategy and Human Resource Management*. Houndsmills: Palgrave Macmillan.

Boyatzis, R.E., Goleman, D. and Rhee, K.S. (2000) 'Clustering competence in emotional intelligence', in R. Bar-On and J.D.A. Parker (eds), *The Handbook of Emotional Intelligence*. San Francisco: Jossey-Bass.

Boyle, D. (2000) *The Tyranny of Numbers: Why Counting Can't Make Us Happy*. London: HarperCollins.

Brady, F.M. (1990) *Ethical Managing*. New York: Macmillan.

Brant, C. and Too, L. (1994) *Rethinking Sexual Harassment*. London: Pluto.

Bratton, J., Grint, K. and Nelson, D.L. (2005) *Organizational Leadership*. Mason, OH: Thomson/South-Western.

Braverman, H. (1974) *Labor and Monopoly Capital*. New York: Monthly Review Press.

Breen, A.B. and Karpinski, A. (2008 'What's in a name? Two approaches to evaluating the label feminist', *Sex Roles*, 58 (5): 299–310.

Brewis, J. (2005) 'Signing my life away? Researching sex and organization', *Organization*, 12 (4): 493–510.

Brock, D., Powell, M. and Hinings, C.R. (1999) *Restructuring the Professional Organization: Accounting, Healthcare and Law*. London: Routledge.

Brockmeier, J. and Carbaugh, D. (eds) (2001) *Narrative and Identity: Studies in Autobiography, Self and Culture*. Amsterdam: John Benjamins.

Brockner, J. (1992) 'The escalation of commitment to a failing course of action: toward theoretical process', *Academy of Management Review*, 17 (1): 39–61.

Brockner, J. (1998) 'The effects of work layoffs on survivors: research, theory and practice', in L.L. Cummings (ed.), *Research in Organizational Behavior*. Greenwich, CT: JAI Press.

Brown, A. (1995) *Organisational Culture*. London: Pitman.

Brown, A.D. (1997) 'Narcissism, identity, and legitimacy', *Academy of Management Review*, 22 (3): 643–86.

Brown, A.D. (2004) 'Authoritative sensemaking in a public inquiry report', *Organization Studies*, 25 (1): 95–112.

Brown, A.D. (2006) 'A narrative approach to collective identities', *Journal of Management Studies*, 43 (4): 731–53.

Brown, J.S. and Duguid, P. (1991) 'Organizational learning and communities of practice: toward a unified view of working, learning and innovation', *Organization Science*, 2 (1): 40–57.

Brown, J.S. and Duguid, P. (2002) 'Local knowledge – innovation in the networked age', *Management Learning*, 33 (4): 427–37.

Brown, R. (2000) *Group Processes: Dynamics within and between Groups* (2nd edn). Oxford: Blackwell.

Bruner, J. (1990) *Acts of Meaning*. Cambridge, MA: Harvard University Press.

Bryant, J. (1989) *Problem Management: A Guide for Producers and Players*. Chichester: Wiley.

Bryman, A. (1986) *Leadership and Organizations*. London: Routledge.

Bryman, A. (1992) *Charisma and Leadership in Organizations*. London: Sage.

Bryman, A. (1999) 'The Disneyization of society', *Sociological Review*, 47 (1): 25–47.

Buchanan, D.A. and Huczynski, A.A. (2004) *Organizational Behaviour* (4th edn). London: Financial Times/Prentice Hall.

Buchanan, D.A. and Huczynski, A.A. (2006) *Organizational Behaviour* (6th edn). London: Financial Times/Prentice Hall.

Budd, L. and Harris, L. (eds) (2004) *E-economy: Rhetoric or Business Reality?* London: Routledge.

Burawoy, M. (1979) *Manufacturing Consent*. Chicago: University of Chicago Press.

Burke, K. (1950) *A Rhetoric of Motives*. Berkeley, CA: University of California Press.

Burke, K. (1966) *Language as Symbolic Action: Essays on Life, Literature, and Method*. Berkeley, CA: University of California Press.

Burns, J.M. (1978) *Leadership*. New York: Harper and Row.

Burns, T. and Stalker, G.M. (1961) *The Management of Innovation*. London: Tavistock.

Burrell, G. (1984) 'Sex and organizational analysis', *Organization Studies*, 5 (2): 97–118.

Burrell, G. and Hearn, J. (1989) 'The sexuality of organizations', in H.J. Sheppard, P. Tancred-Sheriff and G. Burrell (eds), *The Sexuality of Organization*. London: Sage.

Burrell, G. and Morgan, G. (1979) *Sociological Paradigms and Organizational Analysis: Elements of the Sociology of Corporate Life*. London: Heinemann.

Butler, J. (1990) *Gender Trouble: Feminism and the Subversion of Identity*. London: Routledge.

Cairns, G. (2002) 'Aesthetics, morality and power: design as espoused freedom and implicit control', *Human Relations*, 55 (7): 799–820.

Callaghan, G. and Thomson, P. (2002) '"We recruit attitude": the selection and shaping of routine call centre labour', *Journal of Management Studies*, 39 (2): 233–54.

Callon, M. (1987) 'Society in the making: the study of technology as a tool for sociological analysis', in T. Pinch (ed.), *The Social Construction of Technological Systems*. Cambridge, MA: MIT Press.

Callon, M. and Latour, B. (1981) 'Unscrewing the big Leviathan: how actors macro-structure reality and how sociologists help them to do so', in K. Knorr-Cetina and A.V. Cicourel (eds), *Advances in Social Theory and Methodology: Toward an Integration of Micro- and Macro-sociologies*: Boston: Routledge and Kegan Paul. pp. 277–303.

Cameron, K.S., Dutton, J.E. and Quinn, R.E. (eds) (2003) *Positive Organizational Scholarship*. San Francisco: Berrett-Koehler.

Campbell, C. (1989) *The Romantic Ethic and the Spirit of Modern Consumerism*. Oxford: Macmillan.

Cannon, T. (1994) *Corporate Responsibility*. London: Pitman.

Carlzon, J. (1987) *Moments of Truth*. New York: Harper and Row.

Carolan, M.S. (2007) 'The precautionary principle and traditional risk assessment: rethinking how we assess and mitigate environmental threats', *Organization and Environment*, 20: 5–24.

Carr, A. (1998) 'Identity, compliance and dissent in organisations: a psychoanalytic perspective', *Organization*, 5 (1): 81–9.

Carr, A. (2001) 'Understanding emotion and emotionality in a process of change', *Journal of Organizational Change Management*, 14 (5): 421–32.

Carroll, A. (2004) *Business and Society: Ethics and Stakeholder Management*. Mason, OH: Thomson/South-Western.

Carroll, G.R. (1985) 'Concentration and specialization: dynamics of niche width in populations of organizations', *American Journal of Sociology*, 90: 1262–83.

Casey, C. (2000) 'Sociology sensing the body: revitalizing a dissociative discourse', in J. Hassard, R. Holliday and H. Willmott (eds), *Body and Organization*: London: Sage. pp. 52–70.

Castells, M. (1996) *The Information Age: Economy, Society and Culture. Volume 1 – The Rise of the Network Society*. Oxford: Blackwell.

Castells, M. (1998) *Critical Education in the New Information Age*. Chicago: Rowman & Littlefield.

Castells, M. (2000) *The Information Age: Economy, Society and Culture. Volume 1 – The Rise of the Network Society*. Oxford: Blackwell.

Castells, M. and Carnoy, M. (1993) *The New Global Economy in the Information Age*. Philadelphia: Pennsylvania State University Press.

Chang, S. and Tharenou, P. (2004) 'Competencies needed for managing a multicultural work-group', *Asia Pacific Journal of Human Resources*, 42 (1): 57–74.

Chen, Y.-S. (2008) 'The positive effect of green intellectual capital on competitive advantages of firms', *Journal of Business Ethics*, 77 (3): 271–86.

Cheng, C. (ed.) (1996) *Masculinities in Organizations*. Thousand Oaks, CA: Sage.

Cherniss, C. (2000) 'Social and emotional competence in the workplace', in R. Bar-On and J.D.A. Parker (eds), *The Handbook of Emotional Intelligence*. San Francisco: Jossey-Bass.

Chia, R. (1996) *Organizational Knowledge as Deconstructive Practice*. Berlin: de Gruyter.

Chia, R. and King, I. (2001) 'The language of organization theory', in R. Westwood and S. Linstead (eds), *The Language of Organization*. London: Sage. pp. 310–29.

Chodorow, N. (1978) *The Reproduction of Mothering: Psychoanalysis and the Sociology of Gender*. Berkeley, CA: University of California Press.

Christian, J., Porter, L.W. and Moffitt, G. (2006) 'Workplace diversity and group relations: an overview', *Group Processes and Intergroup Relations*, 9 (4): 459–66.

Chrobot-Mason, D. (2004) 'Managing racial differences: the role of majority managers' ethnic identity development on minority employee perceptions of support', *Group Organization Management*, 29 (1): 5–31.

Chrobot-Mason, D., Button, S.B. and DiClementi, J.D. (2001) 'Sexual identity management strategies: an exploration of antecedents and consequences', *Sex Roles*, 45: 16.

Chung, K.H. and Megginson, L.C. (1981) *Organizational Behaviour: Developing Managerial Skills*. New York: Harper and Row.

Ciborra, C. (2002) *The Labyrinths of Information: Challenging the Wisdom of Systems*. Oxford: Oxford University Press.

Cilliers, P. (1998) *Complexity and Postmodernism: Understanding Complex Systems*. London: Routledge.

Ciulla, J.B. (2000) *The Working Life*. New York: Three Rivers Press.

Clampitt, P. (1991) *Communicating for Managerial Effectiveness*. Newbury Park, CA: Sage.

Clases, C., Bachman, R. and Wehner, T. (2004) 'Studying trust in virtual organizations', *International Studies of Management and Organization*, 33 (3): 7–27.

Clegg, S. (1990) *Modern Organizations: Organization Studies in the Postmodern World*. London: Sage.

Clegg, S. (1992) 'Postmodern management?', *Journal of Organizational Management*, 5 (2): 31–49.

Cobb, R. and Elder, C.D. (1972) *Participation in American Politics: The Dynamics of Agenda Building*. Boston: Allyn & Bacon.

Cockburn, C. (1991) *In the Way of Women*. Basingstoke: Macmillan.

Cohen, B. and Greenfield, J. (1999) *Ben and Jerry's Double-dip: Lead with Your Values and Make Money Too*. New York: Simon and Schuster.

Coleman, J.S. (1988) 'Social capital in the creation of human capital', *American Journal of Sociology*, 94: S95–120.

Collins, E.G.C. and Blodgett, T.B. (1981) 'Sexual harrassment: some see it, some won't', *Harvard Business Review*, 59 (March–April): 73–93.

Collinson, D. (1982) *Managing the Shopfloor: Subjectivity, Masculinity and Workplace Culture*. Berlin: de Gruyter.

Collinson, D. (1988) '"Engineering humour": masculinity, joking and conflict in shop-floor relations', *Organization Studies*, 9 (2): 181–99.

Collinson, D. (1994) 'Strategies of resistance: power, knowledge and subjectivity in the workplace', in J. Jermier, W. Nord and D. Knights (eds), *Resistance and Power in Organizations*. London: Routledge. pp. 25–68.

Collinson, D.L. (1999) '"Surviving the rigs": safety and surveillance on the North Sea oil installations', *Organization Studies*, 20 (4): 579–600.

Collinson, D.L. (2002) 'Managing humour', *Journal of Management Studies*, 39 (3): 269–88.

Conger, J.A. and Kanungo, R.N. (eds) (1988) *Charismatic Leadership: The Elusive Factor in Organizational Effectiveness*. San Francisco: Jossey-Bass.

Conrad, C. and Witte, K. (1994) 'Is emotional expression repression or oppression? Myths of organizational affective regulation', in S.A. Deetz (ed.), *Communication Yearbook 17*. Thousand Oaks, CA: Sage.

Cook, M. (2003) *Personnel Selection: Adding Value Through People*. Chichester: Wiley.

Cook, S. and Yanow, D. (1993) 'Culture and organizational learning', *Journal of Management Inquiry*, 2 (4): 373–90.

Cooper, C. and Dewe, P. (2004) *A Brief History of Stress*. Oxford: Blackwell.

Cornelissen, J.P. (2006) 'Making sense of theory construction: metaphor and disciplined imagination', *Organization Studies*, 27 (11): 1579–97.

Cornelissen, J.P., Oswick, C., Thøger Christensen, L. and Phillips, N. (2008) 'Metaphor in organizational research: context, modalities and implications for research – introduction', *Organization Studies*, 29 (1): 7–22.

Coser, L. (1974) *Greedy Institutions: Patterns of Undivided Commitment*. New York: Free Press.

Courpasson, D. (2001) 'Managerial strategies of domination: power in soft bureaucracies', *Organization Studies*, 21 (1): 141–61.

Courpasson, D. and Reed, M. (2004) 'Introduction: bureaucracy in the age of enterprise', *Organization*, 11 (1): 5–12.

Cox, C. (2001) 'Harassment and bullying at work', *Occupational Health Review*, Jan/Feb: 32–6.

Crane, A. and Matten, D. (2006) *Business Ethics: Managing Corporate Citizenship and Sustainability in the Age of Globalization*. Oxford: Oxford University Press.

Crompton, R. and Jones, B. (1984) *White Collar Proletariat*. London: Macmillan.

Crooker, K., Smith, F. and Tabak, F. (2002) 'Creating work–life balance: a model of puralism across domains', *Human Resource Development Review*, 1 (4): 387–419.

Cross, R.L., Yan, A.M. and Louis, M.R. (2000) 'Boundary activities in "boundaryless" organizations: a case study of a transformation to a team-based structure', *Human Relations*, 53 (6): 841–68.

Culler, J. (1981/2001) *The Pursuit of Signs: Semiotics, Literature, Deconstruction*. London: Routledge.

Culler, J. (1982) *On Deconstruction: Theory and Criticism After Structuralism*. Ithaca, NY: Cornell University.

Cummins, T.G. and Worley, C.G. (2000) *Organization Development and Change*. Mason, OH: South-Western College Publishing.

Cunliffe, A.L. (2003) 'Reflexive inquiry in organizational research: questions and possibilities', *Human Relations*, 56 (8): 983–1003.

Currie, W.L. (1999) 'Revisiting management innovation and change programmes: strategic vision or tunnel vision', *Omega*, 27 (6): 647–60.

Curry, P. (2005) *Ecolologic Ethics: An Introduction*. Cambridge: Polity Press.

Czarniawska, B. (1998) *A Narrative Approach to Organization Studies*. Thousand Oaks, CA: Sage.

Czarniawska, B. (1999) *Writing Management: Organization Theory as a Literary Genre*. Oxford: Oxford University Press.

Czarniawska, B. (2004) *Narratives in Social Science Research*. London: Sage.

Czarniawska-Joerges, B. (1992) *Exploring Complex Organizations*. Newbury Park, CA: Sage.

Czarniawska-Joerges, B. and Wolff, R. (1995) 'Leaders, managers, entrepreneurs, on and off the organizational stage', in L. Smircich and M. Calas (eds), *Critical Perspectives on Organizational and Management Thinking*. Aldershot: Dartmouth.

Dalton, P. and Dunnett, G. (1992) *A Psychology for Living: Personal Construct Theory for Professionals and Clients*. Chichester: Wiley.

Daniels, K., Lamond, D.A. and Standen, P. (eds) (2000) *Managing Telework: Perspective from Human Resource Management and Work Psychology*. London: Business Press.

Daniels, K., Lamond, D.A. and Standen, P. (2001) 'Teleworking: framework for organizational research', *Journal of Management Studies*, 38 (8): 1151–85.

Darley, J.M. and Batson, C.D. (1973) 'From Jerusalem to Jericho: a study of situational and dispositional variables in helping behavior', *Journal of Personality and Social Psychology*, 27: 100–8.

Davenport, T.H. and Prusak, L. (2000) *Working Knowledge: How Organizations Manage What They Know*. Cambridge, MA: Harvard Business School Press.

Davidson, M. and Cooper, C. (1992) *Shattering the Glass Ceiling: The Woman Manager*. London: Paul Chapman.

Davidson, M.N. and Greenhalgh, L. (1999) 'The role of emotion in negotiation', in R. J. Bies, R.J. Lewicki and B.H. Sheppard (eds), *Research on Negotiation in Organizations, Vol. 7*. Stamford, CT: JAI Press. pp. 3–26.

Davies, C. (1988) 'Stupidity and rationality: jokes from the iron cage', in G.E.C. Paton (ed.), *Humour in Society*. London: Macmillan.

Davis, G. and Powell, W. (1992) 'Organization–environment relations', in L. Houg (ed.), *Handbook of Industrial and Organizational Psychology*: Palo Alto, CA: Consulting Psychologists Press. pp. 316–75.

Davis, J. (1991) *Greening Business: Managing for Sustainable Development*. Oxford: Blackwell.

de Board, R. (1978) *The Psychoanalysis of Organisations: A Psychoanalytic Approach to Behaviour of Groups and Organisations*. London: Tavistock.

de Bono, E. (1992) *Serious Creativity: Using the Power of Lateral Thinking to Create New Ideas*. New York: HarperBusiness.

de Certeau, M. (1984) *The Practice of Everyday Life*. Berkeley, CA: University of California Press.

de Dreu, C.K.W. and Van Vianen, A.E.M. (2001) 'Managing relationship conflict and the effectiveness of organizational teams', *Journal of Organizational Behavior*, 22: 309–28.

de Vita, G. (2001) 'The use of group work in large and diverse business management classes: some critical issues', *International Journal of Management Education*, 1 (2): 27–35.

Deakin, S.F. and Hughes, A. (1997) *Enterprise and Community: New Directions in Corporate Governance*. Oxford: Blackwell.

Deal, T. and Kennedy, A. (1988) *Corporate Cultures: The Rites and Rituals of Corporate Life*. Harmondsworth: Penguin.

Deal, T. and Kennedy, A. (1999) *The New Corporate Cultures*. London: Textere.

Dearing, J.W. and Rogers, E.M. (1996) *Agenda-setting*. Thousand Oaks, CA: Sage.

Deetz, S. (1998) 'Discursive formations, strategized subordination and selfsurveillance', in A. McKinlay and K. Starkey (eds), *Foucault, Management and Organization Theory: From Panopticon to Technologies of Self*. London: Sage.

Deetz, S. and Mumby, D. (1990) 'Power, discourse and the workplace: reclaiming the critical tradition in communication studies in organizations', in J. Anderson (ed.), *Communication Yearbook 13*. Newbury Park, CA: Sage.

Denning, S. (2000) *The Springboard: How Storytelling Ignites Action in Knowledge-era Organizations*. Oxford: Butterworth-Heinemann.

Derrida, J. (1973) *Speech and Phenomena*. Evanston, IL: Northwestern University Press.

Derrida, J. (1976a) *Of Grammatology*. Baltimore, MD: Johns Hopkins University Press.

Di Tomaso, N. (1989) 'Sexuality in the workplace: discrimination and harassment', in J. Hearn, D.L. Sheppard, P. Tancred-Sheriff and G. Burrell (eds), *The Sexuality of Organization*. London: Sage.

Diamond, J.M. (2005) *Collapse: How Societies Choose to Fail or Succeed*. Harmondsworth: Penguin.

Difonzo, N., Bordia, P. and Rosnow, R. (1994) 'Reining in rumours', *Organizational Dynamics*, 23 (1): 47–62.

DiMaggio, P. and Powell, W. (1983) 'The iron cage revisited: institutional isomorphism and collective rationality in organizational fields', *American Sociological Review*, 48: 147–60.

Dodgson, M., Gann, D.M. and Salter, A. (2005) *Think Play Do: Technology, Organization and Innovation*. Oxford: Oxford University Press.

Dodgson, M., Gann, D.M. and Salter, A. (2007) '"In case of fire, please use the elevator": simulation technology and organization in fire engineering', *Organization Science*, 18 (5): 849–64.

Dodgson, M., Gann, D.M. and Salter, A. (2008) *The Management of Technological Innovation: Strategy and Practice*. Oxford: Oxford University Press.

Doray, B. (1988) *From Taylorism to Fordism: A Rational Madness*. London: Free Association Books.

Douglas, M. (1975) 'Jokes', in M. Douglas (ed.), *Implicit Meanings: Essays in Anthropology*. London: Routledge. pp. 179–92.

Douglas, T. (1983) *Groups*. London: Tavistock.

Dovidio, J.R. and Gaertner, S.L. (1986) *Prejudice, Discrimination and Racism*. Orlando, FL: Academic Press.

Downs, A (1995) *Corporate Executions: The Ugly Truth about Downsizing*. New York: Amaco.

Drucker, P.F. (1989) *The Practice of Management*. Oxford: Butterworth-Heinemann.

du Gay, P. (1996a) *Consumption and Identity at Work*. London: Sage.

du Gay, P. (1996b) 'Organizing identity: entrepreneurial governance and public management', in S. Hall and P. du Gay (eds), *Questions of Cultural Identity*. London: Sage. pp. 151–69.

du Gay, P. (2000) *In Praise of Bureaucracy*. London: Sage.

du Gay, P. (2008) '"Without affection or enthusiasm": problems of involvement and attachment in "responsive" public management', *Organization*, 15 (3): 335–53.

du Gay, P. and Salaman, G. (1992) 'The cult(ure) of the customer', *Journal of Management Studies*, 29 (5): 615–33.

Dulewicz, V. (1991) 'Improving assessment centres', *Personnel Management*, 23 (6): 50–61.

Duncan, H.D. (1962) *Communications and Social Order*. New York: Oxford University Press.

Duncan, W.J. and Feisal, J.P. (1989) 'No laughing matter: patterns of humor in the workplace', *Organizational Dynamics*, 17 (4): 18–30.

Dunlop, J.T. (1958) *Industrial Relations Systems*. New York: Holt.

Durkheim, E. (1951) *Suicide*. New York: Free Press.

Dutton, J. (1997) 'Strategic agenda building', in Z. Shapira (ed.), *Organizational Decision Making*. Cambridge: Cambridge University Press. pp. 81–107.

Eagle, J. and Newton, P.M. (1981) 'Scapegoating in small groups', *Human Relations*, 34: 283–301.

Eden, S. (1996) *Environmental Issues and Business*. Chichester: Wiley.

Eden, C. and Huxham, C. (1996) 'Action research for the study of organisations', in S. Clegg, C. Hardy and W. Nord (eds), *The Handbook of Organization Studies*. Beverly Hills, CA: Sage.

Eden, C., Jones, S. and Sims, D. (1983) *Messing About in Problems: An Informal Structured Approach to their Identification and Management*. Oxford: Pergamon.

Edwards, P.K. (1990) 'Understanding conflict in the labour proess: the logic and autonomy of struggle', in D. Knights and H. Willmott (eds), *Labour Process Theory*. London: Macmillan.

Edwards, P. (2006) 'Power and ideology in the workplace: going beyond even the second version of the three-dimensional view', *Work, Employment and Society*, 20 (3): 571–81.

Ehrenreich, B. (2005) *Bait and Switch: The (Futile) Pursuit of the American Dream* (1st edn). New York: Metropolitan Books.

Einarsen, S. (1999) 'The nature and cause of bullying at work', *International Journal of Manpower*, 20 (1/2): 16–27.

Elfenbein, H.A. (2007) 'Emotion in organizations: a review and theoretical integration', *The Academy of Management Annals*, 1 (Dec): 315–86.

Ellig, B.R. (1998) 'Employment and employability: foundation of the new social contract', *Human Resource Management*, 37 (2): 173–7.

Elliott, A. (2002) *Psychoanalytic Theory: An Introduction*. Houndsmills: Palgrave Macmillan.

Elmes, M. B. and Kasouf, C. J. (1995) 'Knowledge workers and organizational learning: narratives from biotechnology', *Management Learning*, 26(4): 403-422.

Elsesser, K. and Peplau, L.A. (2006) 'The glass partition: obstacles to cross-sex friendships at work', *Human Relations*, 59 (8): 1077–100.

Erickson, R.J. (1995) 'The importance of authenticity for self and society', *Symbolic Interaction*, 18: 121–44.

Erikson, E.H. (1964) 'Identity and uprootedness in our time', in E.H. Erikson (ed.), *Insight and Responsibility*. New York: Norton.

Erikson, E.H. (1968) *Identity: Youth and Crisis*. London: Faber and Faber.

Eschbach, D.M., Parker, G.E. and Stoeberl, P.A. (2001) 'American repatriate employees' retrospective assessments of the effects of cross-cultural training on their adaptation to international assignments', *International Journal of Human Resource Management*, 12 (2): 270–87.

Ezzamel, M., Willmott, H. and Worthington, F. (2001) 'Power, control and resistance in the factory that time forgot', *Journal of Management Studies*, 38 (8): 1053–79.

Fairclough, N. (1992) *Discourse and Social Change*. Cambridge: Polity Press.

Fairclough, N. (1995) *Critical Discourse Analysis: Papers in the Critical Study of Language*. London: Longman.

Fairhurst, G.T. and Putnam, L.L. (2004) 'Organizations as discursive constructions', *Communication Theory*, 14 (1): 5–26.

Faludi, S. (1992) *Backlash: The Undeclared War Against Women*. London: Chatto and Windus.

Fayard, A.L. and Weeks, J. (2007) 'Photocopiers and water-coolers: the affordances of informal interaction', *Organization Studies*, 28 (5): 605–34.

Featherstone, M. (1991) *Consumer Culture and Postmodernism*. London: Sage.

Feldman, D.C. (2000) 'Down but not out: career trajectories of middle-aged and older workers after downsizing', in C. Cooper (ed.), *Organizations in Crisis*. Oxford: Blackwell.

Feldman, S.P. (1989) 'The idealization of technology: power relations in an engineering department', *Human Relations*, 42 (7): 575–692.

Feldman, S.P. (1998) 'Playing with the pieces: deconstruction and the loss of moral culture', *Journal of Management Studies*, 35 (1): 59–79.

Fenton, S. and Dermott, E. (2006) 'Fragmented careers? Winners and losers in young adult labour markets', *Work, Employment and Society*, 20 (2): 205–21.

Ferlie, E., Ashburner, L., Fitzgerald, L. and Pettigrew, A. (1996) *The New Public Management*. Oxford: Oxford University Press.

Festinger, L. and Carlsmith, J. (1959) 'Cognitive consequences of forced compliance', *Journal of Abnormal and Social Psychology*, 58: 203–10.

Feyerabend, P. (1975) *Against Method*. London: New Left Books.

Fiedler, F. (1967) *A Theory of Leadership Effectiveness*. New York: McGraw-Hill.

Fine, B. (2001) *Social Capital Versus Social Theory: Political Economy and Social Science at the Turn of the Millennium*. London: Routledge.

Fineman, S. (1977) 'The achievement motive construct and its measurement: where are we now?', *British Journal of Psychology*, 68: 1–22.

Fineman, S. (1987) *Unemployment: Personal and Social Consequences*. London: Tavistock.

Fineman, S. (1988) 'The natural environment, organization and ethics', in M. Parker (ed.), *Ethics and Organization*. London: Sage.

Fineman, S. (ed.) (1993) *Emotion in Organizations*. London: Sage.

Fineman, S. (1995a) 'Emotion and organizing', in S. Clegg, C. Hardy and W. Nord (eds), *Handbook of Organization Studies*. London: Sage.

Fineman, S. (1995b) 'Stress, emotion and intervention', in T. Newton (ed.), *Managing Stress: Emotion and Power at Work*. London: Sage.

Fineman, S. (1996) 'Emotional subtexts in corporate greening', *Organization Studies*, 17 (3): 479–500.

Fineman, S. (1997) 'Constructing the green manager', *British Journal of Management*, 8 (1): 31–8.

Fineman, S. (1998) 'Street level bureaucrats and the social construction of environmental control', *Organization Studies*, 19 (6): 953–74.

Fineman, S. (1999) 'Emotion and organizing', in S. Clegg, C. Hardy and W. Nord (eds), *Studying Organizations*. London: Sage.

Fineman, S. (ed.) (2000a) *Emotion in Organizations*. London: Sage.

Fineman, S. (ed.) (2000b) *The Business of Greeting*. London and New York: Routledge.

Fineman, S. (2000c) 'Being a regulator', in S. Fineman (ed.), *The Business of Greening*. London: Routledge.

Fineman, S. (2000d) 'Commodifying the emotionally intelligent', in S. Fineman (ed.), *Emotion in Organizations*. London: Sage. pp. 101–15.

Fineman, S. (2000e) 'Emotional arenas revisited', in S. Fineman (ed.), *Emotion in Organizations*, London: Sage. pp. 1–24.

Fineman, S. (2000f) 'Enforcing the environment: regulatory realities', *Business Strategy and the Environment*, 9 (1): 67–72.

Fineman, S. (2003) *Understanding Emotion at Work*. London: Sage.

Fineman, S. (2004) 'Getting the measure of emotion – and the cautionary tale of emotional intelligence', *Human Relations*, 57 (6): 719–40.

Fineman, S. (2006a) 'On being positive: concerns and counterpoints', *Academy of Management Review*, 31 (2): 270–91.

Fineman, S. (2006b) 'Emotion and organizing', in S. Clegg, C. Hardy, W. Nord and T. Lawrence (eds), *The Sage Handbook of Organization Studies* (2nd edn). London: Sage.

Fineman, S. (ed.) (2007) *The Emotional Organization: Critical Voices*. Oxford: Blackwell.

Fineman, S. (ed.) (2008) *The Emotional Organization: Passions and Power*. Oxford: Blackwell.

Fineman, S. and Clarke, K. (1996) 'Green stakeholders: industry interpretations and response', *Journal of Management Studies*, 33 (6): 715–30.

Fineman, S. and Sturdy, A. (1999) 'The emotions of control: a qualitative study of environmental regulation', *Human Relations*, 52 (5): 631–63.

Fineman, S., Maitlis, S. and Panteli, N. (2007) 'Themed articles: virtuality and emotion – introduction', *Human Relations*, 60 (4): 555–60.

Finn, D. (2000) 'From full employment to employability: a new deal for Britain's unemployed?', *International Journal of Manpower*, 21 (5): 384–99.

Fiol, C.M., Harris, D. and House, R. (1999) 'Charismatic leaders: strategies for effecting social change', *Leadership Quarterly*, 10 (3): 449–82.

Fisher, A. (1996) 'What's so funny, jokeboy?', *Fortune*, 134 (11): 220.

Fisher, C. and Lovell, A. (2003) *Business Ethics and Values*. Harlow: Prentice Hall/FinancialTimes.

Fiske, J. (1989) *Understanding Popular Culture*. London: Unwin Hyman.

Fitzgerald, L. and Ferlie, E. (2000) 'Professionals: back to the future', *Human Relations*, 53 (7): 713–39.

Flax, J. (1990) *Thinking Fragments: Psychoanalysis, Feminism, and Postmodernism in the Contemporary West*. Berkeley: University of California.

Forbes, D.P. and Milliken, F.J. (1999) 'Cognition and corporate governance: understanding boards of directors as strategic decision-making groups', *Academy of Management Review*, 24 (3): 489–505.

Ford, H. (1923) *My Life and Work*. London: Heinemann.

Fortado, B. (1992) 'Subordinate views in supervisory conflict situations: peering into the subcultural chasm', *Human Relations*, 45 (11): 1141–67.

Foucault, M. (1961/1965) *Madness and Civilization: A History of Insanity in the Age of Reason*. New York: Vintage Books.

Foucault, M. (1963/1973) *The Birth of the Clinic: An Archaeology of Medical Perception*. New York: Vintage Books.

Foucault, M. (1970) *The Order of Things*. London: Tavistock.

Foucault, M. (1977) *Discipline and Punish*. London: Allen & Unwin.

Foucault, M. (1978) *The History of Sexuality: An Introduction, Vol 1*. Harmondsworth: Penguin.

Foucault, M. (1980) *Power/Knowledge: Selected Interviews and Other Writings 1972–1977*. Brighton: Harvester Books.

Fournier, V. (1997) 'Graduates' construction systems and career development', *Human Relations*, 50 (4): 363–91.

Fournier, V. and Grey, C. (2000) 'At the critical moment: conditions and prospects for critical management studies', *Human Relations*, 53 (1): 7–32.

Fox, S. (1989) 'The Panopticon: from Bentham's obsession to the revolution in management learning', *Human Relations*, 42: 717–39.

Frantzve, J. (ed.) (1983) *Behavior in Organizations: Tales from the Trenches*. Boston, MA: Allyn and Bacon.

French, J.R.P. Jr. and Raven, B.H. (1959) 'The bases of social power', in D. Cartwright (ed.), *Studies in Social Power*. Ann Arbor: University of Michigan Press.

French, R. and Vince, R. (eds) (1999) *Group Relations, Management, and Organization*. Oxford: Oxford University Press.

French, W. and Bell, C. (1999) *Organization Development: Behavioral Science Interventions for Organization Improvement*. Upper Saddle River, NJ: Prentice Hall.

Frenkel, S.J., Korczynski, M., Shire, K.A. and Tam, M. (1999) *On the Front Line: Organization of Work in the Information Economy*. Ithaca, NY: Cornell University Press.

Freud, S. (1905) *Jokes and Their Relation to the Unconscious*. London: Hogarth Press.

Freud, S. (1905/1977) 'Three essays on the theory of sexuality', in S. Freud, *On Sexuality*. Harmondsworth: Pelican Freud Library. pp. 33–169.

Freud, S. (1914/1984) 'On narcissism: an introduction', in S. Freud, *On Metapsychology: The Theory of Psychoanalysis*. Harmondsworth: Pelican Freud Library. pp. 59–97.

Freud, S. (1953) *The Complete Works of Sigmund Freud*. London: Hogarth.

Friedman, A. (1977) *Industry and Labour*. London: Macmillan.

Friedman, M. (1962) *Capitalism and Freedom*. Chicago: University of Chicago Press.

Friedman, M. (1970) 'The social responsibility of business is to increase its profits', *New York Times Magazine*, September: 13, 32–3, 122, 126.

Frost, P.J. (1999) 'Why compassion counts!', *Journal of Management Inquiry*, 8: 127–33.

Frost, P.J. (2003) *Toxic Emotions at Work*. Harvard: Harvard Business School Press.

Frost, P. (2004) 'Handling toxic emotions: new challenges for leaders and their organizations', *Organizational Dynamics*, 33 (2): 111–27.

Frost, P.J., Dutton, J.E. Worline, M.C. and Wilson, A. (2000) 'Narratives of compassion in organizations', in S. Fineman (ed.), *Emotion in Organizations* (2nd edn). London: Sage. p. 31.

Frost, P.J., Moore, L.F., Lundberg, C.C. and Martin, J. (1985) *Organizational Culture*. Beverly Hills: Sage.

Furnham, A. (1990) *The Protestant Work Ethic: The Psychology of Work-Related Beliefs and Behaviours*. London: Routledge.

Furnham, A. (1992) *The Protestant Work Ethic*. New York: Doubleday.

Gabriel, Y. (1988) *Working Lives in Catering*. London: Routledge.

Gabriel, Y. (1991a) 'On organizational stories and myths: why it is easier to slay a dragon than to kill a myth', *International Sociology*, 6 (4): 427–42.

Gabriel, Y. (1991b) 'Turning facts into stories and stories into facts: a hermeneutic exploration of organizational folklore', *Human Relations*, 44 (8): 857–75.

Gabriel, Y. (1992) 'Heroes, villains, fools and magic wands: computers in organizational folklore', *International Journal of Information Resource Management*, 3 (1): 3–12.

Gabriel, Y. (1995) 'The unmanaged organization: stories, fantasies and subjectivity', *Organization Studies*, 16 (3): 477–501.

Gabriel, Y. (1998a) 'Psychoanalytic contributions to the study of the emotional life of organizations', *Administration and Society*, 30 (3): 291–314.

Gabriel, Y. (1998b) 'The hubris of management', *Administrative Theory and Praxis*, 20 (3): 257–73. [AQ – was a but already exists]

Gabriel, Y. (1999a) 'Beyond happy families: a critical re-evaluation of the control–resistance–identity triangle', *Human Relations*, 52 (2): 179–203.

Gabriel, Y. (1999b) *Organizations in Depth: The Psychoanalysis of Organizations*. London: Sage.

Gabriel, Y. (2000) *Storytelling in Organizations: Facts, Fictions, Fantasies*. Oxford: Oxford University Press.

Gabriel, Y. (2002) 'Essai: on paragrammatic uses of organizational theory – a provocation', *Organization Studies*, 23 (1): 133–51.

Gabriel, Y. (2004a) 'The glass cage: flexible work, fragmented consumption, fragile selves', in J.C. Alexander, G.T. Marx and C.L. Williams (eds), *Self, Social Structure and Beliefs*: Berkeley, CA: University of California Press. pp. 57–76.

Gabriel, Y. (ed.) (2004b) *Myths, Stories and Organizations: Premodern Narratives for our Times*. Oxford: Oxford University Press.

Gabriel, Y. (2004c) 'Narratives, stories, texts', in D. Grant, C. Hardy, C. Oswick and L. Putnam (eds), *The Sage Handbook of Organizational Discourse*. London: Sage. pp. 61–79. [AQ – was labelled a but needs to be c]

Gabriel, Y. (2004d) 'The voice of experience and the voice of the expert: can they speak to each other?', in B. Hurwitz, T. Greenhalgh and V. Skultans (eds), *Narrative Research in Health and Illness*. Oxford: Blackwell. pp. 168–86.

Gabriel, Y. (2008a) '*Essai*: against the tyranny of PowerPoint – technology-in-use and technology abuse', *Organization Studies*, 29 (2): 255–76.

Gabriel, Y. (2008b) *Organizing Words: A Thesaurus for Social and Organizational Studies*. Oxford: Oxford University Press.

Gabriel, Y. and Lang, T. (1995) *The Unmanageable Consumer: Contemporary Consumption and its Fragmentation*. London: Sage.

Gabriel, Y. and Carr, A. (2002) 'Organizations, management and psychoanalysis: an overview', *Journal of Managerial Psychology*, 17 (5): 348–65.

Gabriel, Y. and Griffiths, D.S. (2008) 'International learning groups: synergies and dysfunctions', *Management Learning*, 39 (5): 503–18.

Gackenbach, J. (ed.) (1998) *Psychology and the Internet*. San Diego: Academic Press.

Gagliardi, P. (ed.) (1990a) *Artifacts as Pathways and Remains of Organizational Life*. Berlin: de Gruyter.

Gagliardi, P. (ed.) (1990b) *Symbols and Artefacts: Views of the Corporate Landscape*. Berlin: de Gruyter.

Gandy, O.H. (1993) *The Panoptic Sort: A Political Economy of Personal Information*. Boulder, CO: Westview.

Gann, D.M. and Dodgson, M. (2007) *Innovation Technology: How New Technologies are Changing the Way we Innovate*. London: NESTA.

Garciano, L. (1999) 'Game theory: how to make it pay', *Financial Times*, 18 October: 2.

Gardner, C. (1995) *Passing By: Gender and Public Harassment*. Berkeley, CA: University of California Press.

Gardner, H. (1993) *Multiple Intelligences*. New York: Basic Books.

Gardner, R. (1995) *Games for Business and Economics*. New York: Wiley.

Gardner, W.L and Avolio, B.J. (1998) 'The charismatic relationship: a dramaturgical perspective', *Academy of Management Review*, 23 (1): 32–59.

Gargiulo, T.L. (2005) *The Strategic Use of Stories in Organizational Communication and Learning*. Armonk, NY: M.E. Sharpe.

Gergen, K. (1999) *An Invitation to Social Construction*. London: Sage.

Giacalone, R.A. and Rosenfeld, P.R. (1991) *Applied Impression Management*. Newbury Park, CA: Sage.

Giddens, A. (1984) *The Constitution of Society: Outline of a Theory of Structuration*. Cambridge: Polity Press.

Giddens, A. (1991) *Modernity and Self-Identity: Self and Society in the Late Modern Age*. Stanford, CA: Stanford University Press.

Gill, M., Fisher, B. and Bowie, V. (eds) (2001) *Violence at Work*. Cullompton: Willan.

Glazer, M. and Glazer, P. (1989) *The Whistleblowers: Exposing Corruption in Government and Industry*. New York: Basic Books.

Gleick, J. (1987) *Chaos*. Harmondsworth: Penguin.

Goffman, E. (1959) *The Presentation of Self in Everyday Life*. Garden City, NJ: Doubleday Anchor Books.

Goffman, E. (1961) *Asylums*. Garden City, NJ: Doubleday Anchor Books.

Goffman, E. (1967) *Interaction Ritual*. Garden City, NJ: Doubleday Anchor Books.

Goldthorpe, J.H., Lockwood, D., Bechhofer, F. and Pratt, J. (1969) *The Affluent Worker: Industrial Attitudes and Behaviour*. Cambridge: Cambridge University Press.

Goleman, D. (1996) *Emotional Intelligence*. London: Bloomsbury.

Goold, M. and Campbell, A. (1998) 'Desperately seeking synergy', *Harvard Business Review*, 76 (5): 131–44.

Gore, A. (1992) *Earth in Balance*. London: Earthscan.

Gould, S.J. (1996) *The Mismeasure of Man*. London: W.W. Norton.

Gouldner, A.W. (1954) *Patterns of Industrial Bureaucracy*. Glencoe, IL: Free Press.

Gouldner, A.W. (1955) 'Metaphysical pathos and the theory of bureaucracy', *American Political Review*, 49: 469–505.

Gourevitch, P.A. and Shinn, J. (2005) *Political Power and Corporate Control: The New Global Politics of Corporate Governance*. Princeton: Princeton University Press.

Gramsci, A., Hoare, Q. and Nowell-Smith, G. (1971) *Selections from the Prison Notebooks of Antonio Gramsci (1929–1935)*. London: Lawrence and Wishart.

Grant, D. and Oswick, C. (eds) (1996) *Metaphor and Organizations*. London: Sage.

Grant, D., Keenoy, T. and Oswick, C. (eds) (1998a) *Discourse and Organization*. London: Sage.

Grant, D., Keenoy, T. and Oswick, C. (1998b) 'Introduction – organizational discourse: of diversity, dichotomy, and multidisciplinarity', in D. Grant, T. Keenoy and C. Oswick (eds), *Discourse and Organization*. London: Sage. pp. 1–13.

Grant, D., Hardy, C., Oswick, C. and Putnam, L.L. (eds) (2004) *The Sage Handbook of Organizational Discourse*. London: Sage.

Greasley, K., Bryman, A., Dainty, A., Price, A., Soetanto, R. and King, N. (2005) 'Employee perceptions of empowerment', *Journal: Employee Relations*, 27 (4): 354–68.

Green, T.B. (1992) *Performance and Motivation Strategies for Today's Workforce: A Guide to Expecatancy Theory Applications*. Westport, CT: Greenwood Press.

Greer, G. (1970) *The Female Eunuch*. London: Granada.

Greer, G. (1984) *Sex and Destiny: The Politics of Human Fertility*. London: Secker and Warburg.

Grey, C. (1994) 'Career as a project of the self and labour process discipline', *Sociology*, 28 (2): 479–97.

Grey, C. (1999) '"We are all managers now"; "we always were": on the development and demise of management', *Journal of Management Studies*, 36 (5): 561–85.

Grey, C. (2004) 'Reinventing business schools: the contribution of critical management education', *Academy of Management Learning and Education*, 3 (2): 178–86.

Grey, C. and Garsten, C. (2001) 'Trust, control and post-bureaucracy', *Organization Studies*, 22 (2): 229–50.

Griffin, D., Shaw, P. and Stacey, R. (1998) 'Speaking complexity in management theory and practice', *Organization*, 5 (3): 315–39.

Griffiths, M. (1995) *Feminism and the Self: The Web of Identity*. London: Routledge.

Grint, K. (ed.) (2000) *The Arts of Leadership*. Oxford: Oxford University Press.

Grosz, E. (1994) *Volatile Bodies: Towards a Corporeal Feminism*. Bloomington, IN: University of Indiana Press.

Grugulis, I. (2001) 'Nothing serious? Candidates' use of humour in management training: expressing and containing resistance'. Paper presented at Critical Management Studies II, Manchester.

Guerrero, L.K., Devito, J.A. and Hecht, M.L. (eds) (1999) *The Nonverbal Communication Reader: Classic and Contemporary Readings*. Longrove, IL: Waveland Press.

Guerrier, Y. and Adib, A.S. (2000) '"No, we don't provide that service": the harassment of hotel employees by customers', *Work, Employment and Society*, 14 (4): 689–705.

Guest, D. (1987) 'Human resource management and industrial relations', *Journal of Management Studies*, 24 (5): 503–21.

Guillen, M.F. (1994) *Models of Management: Work, Authority, and Organization in a Comparative Perspective*. Chicago: University of Chicago Press.

Guillen, M.F. (1998) 'Scientific management's lost aesthetic: architecture, organization and the Taylorized beauty of the mechanical', *Administrative Science Quarterly*, 42 (4): 682–715.

Gutek, B.A. (1985) *Sex and the Workplace: Impact of Sexual Behaviour and Harassment on Women, Men and Organizations*. San Francisco: Jossey-Bass.

Gutek, B.A. (1989) 'Sexuality in the workplace: key issues in social research and organizational practice', in J. Hearn, D.L. Sheppard, P. Tancred-Sheriff and G. Burrell (eds), *The Sexuality of Organization*. London: Sage.

Gutman, R. (1972) *People and Buildings*. New York: Basic Books.

Hall, D.T. (1996) *The Career is Dead: Long Live the Career!* San Francisco: Jossey-Bass.

Hall, E.J. (1993) 'Smiling, deferring and flirting: doing gender by giving good service', *Work and Occupations*, 20 (4): 452–71.

Hall, J. and Knapp, M.L. (2005) *Nonverbal Communication in Human Interaction*. Florence, KY: Wadsworth.

Hammer, M. and Champy, J. (1993) *Reengineering the Corporation: A Manifesto for Business Revolution*. London: Nicholas Brealey.

Han, S.-K. and Moen, P. (1999) 'Work and family over time: a life course approach', *Annals of the American Academy of Political and Social Science*, 562: 98–110.

Hancock, P. and Tyler, M. (2000) '"The look of love": gender and the organization of aesthetics', in J. Hassard, R. Holliday and H. Willmott (eds), *Body and Organization*. London: Sage.

Handley, K., Sturdy, A., Fincham, R. and Clark, T. (2006) 'Within and beyond communities of practice: making sense of learning through participation, identity and practice', *Journal of Management Studies*, 43 (3): 641–53.

Handy, C.B. (1976) *Understanding Organizations*. Harmondsworth: Penguin.

Handy, C.B. (1989) *The Age of Unreason*. Boston, MA: Harvard Business School Press.

Handy, C.B. (1995) 'Trust and the virtual organization', *Harvard Business Review*, 73 (3): 40–50.

Handy, C. (1996) *Beyond Certainty: The Changing Worlds of Organizations*. Harvard: Harvard Business School Press.

Hanf, K. (1993) 'Enforcing environmental laws: the social regulation of co-production', in M. Hill (ed.), *New Agendas in the Study of the Policy Process*. London: Harvester Wheatsheaf.

Hannan, M. and Freeman, J. (1977) 'The population ecology of organizations', *American Journal of Sociology*, 83: 929–84.

Hannigan, J.A. (1995) *Environmental Sociology*. London: Routledge.

Hannigan, J.A. (2006) *Environmental Sociology* (2nd edn). London: Routledge.

Hardy, C., Lawrence, T.B. and Phillips, N. (1998) 'Talk and action: conversations and narrative in interorganizational collaboration', in D. Grant, T. Keenoy and C. Oswick (eds), *Discourse and Organization*. London: Sage. pp. 65–83.

Hardy, C., Phillips, N. and Clegg, S. (2001) 'Reflexivity in organization and management theory: a study of the production of the research "subject"', *Human Relations*, 54 (5): 531–59.

Harlos, K.P. and Pinder, C.C. (2000) 'Emotion and injustice in the workplace', in S. Fineman (ed.), *Emotion in Organizations* (2nd edn). London: Sage. p. 253.

Harré, R. (2001) 'Metaphysics and narrative: singularities and multiplicities of self', in J. Brockmeier and D. Carbaugh (eds), *Narrative and Identity: Studies in Autobiography, Self and Culture*. Amsterdam: John Benjamins. pp. 59–73.

Harré, R. and Secord, P.F. (1972) *The Explanation of Social Behaviour*. Oxford: Blackwell.

Harri-Augustein, S. and Thomas, L. (1991) *Learning Conversations*. London: Routledge.

Harries, R. (1998) 'Outmocking the mockers', *Times Higher Education Supplement*, 24 April.

Harrington, A. (1999) 'The big ideas: ever since Frederick Taylor pulled out his stopwatch, big thinkers have been coming up with new – though not always better – ways to manage people and business', *Fortune*, 140: 152–4.

Harris, L.C. (2002) 'The emotional labour of barristers: an exploration of emotional labour by status professionals', *Journal of Management Studies*, 39 (4): 553–84.

Harris, L.C. and Crane, A. (2002) 'The greening of organizational culture: management views on the depth, degree and diffusion of change', *Journal of Organizational Change Management*, 15 (3): 214–34.

Harris, L.C. and Ogbonna, E. (2002) 'The unintended consequences of culture interventions: a study of unexpected outcomes', *British Journal of Management*, 13 (1): 31–49.

Harrison, R. (1972) 'How to describe your organization', *Harvard Business Review*, 50 (3): 119–280.

Harrison, R. and Stokes, H. (1992) *Diagnosing Organizational Culture*. San Francisco: Pfeiffer.

Hassard, J., Hogan, J. and Rowlinson, M. (2001) 'From labour process theory to critical management studies', *Administrative Theory and Praxis*, 23 (3): 339–62.

Hatch, M.J. (1990) 'The symbolics of office design: an empirical exploration', in P. Gagliardi (ed.), *Symbols and Artifacts: Views of the Corporate Landscape*. Berlin: de Gruyter. pp. 129–35.

Hatch, M.J. (1997) *Organization Theory: Modern, Symbolic and Postmodern Perspectives*. Oxford: Oxford University Press.

Hatch, M.J. and Ehrlich, S.B. (1993) 'Spontaneous humour as an indicator of paradox and ambiguity in organizations', *Organization Studies*, 14: 505–26.

Hatch, M.J. and Schultz, M. (eds) (2004) *Organizational Identity: A Reader*. Oxford: Oxford University Press.

Hayes, J. (2002) *Interpersonal Skills at Work*. London: Routledge.

HBR (2003) *HBR on Corporate Responsibility*. Boston, MA: Harvard Business School Press.

Hearn, J. (1993) 'Emotive subjects: organizational men, organizational masculinities and the (de)construction of "emotions"', in S. Fineman (ed.), *Emotion in Organizations*. London: Sage.

Hearn, J. and Parkin, W. (1987) *'Sex' at 'Work'*. Brighton: Wheatsheaf Books.

Hearn, J. and Parkin, W. (2001) *Gender, Sexuality and Violence in Organizations*. London: Sage.

Hearn, J., Sheppard, D.L., Tancred-Sheriff, P. and Burrell, G. (eds) (1989) *The Sexuality of Organization*. London: Sage.

Hébert, R.F. and Link, A.N. (1988) *The Entrepreneur: Mainstream Views and Radical Critiques* (2nd edn). New York: Praeger.

Heifetz, R.A. (1994) *Leadership without Easy Answers*. Cambridge, MA: Harvard University Press.

Henriques, A. and Richardson, J. (eds) (2004) *The Triple Bottom Line: Does It All Add Up?* London: Earthscan.

Henry, J. (2001) *Creativity and Perception in Management*. Thousand Oaks, CA: Sage.

Heracleous, L. and Hendry, J. (2000) 'Discourse and the study of organization: toward a structurational perspective', *Human Relations*, 53 (10): 1251–86.

Herrick, J. (2005) *Humanism: An Introduction*. New York: Prometheus Books.

Herriot, P. and Pemberton, C. (1995a) *Competitive Advantage Through Adversity: Organizational Learning from Difference*. London: Sage.

Herriot, P. and Pemberton, C. (1995b) *New Deals: The Revolution in Managerial Careers*. Chichester: Wiley.

Herzberg, F., Mausner, B. and Snyderman, B. (1959) *The Motivation to Work*. New York: Wiley.

Heugens, P. (2005) 'A neo-Weberian theory of the firm', *Organization Studies*, 26 (4): 547–67.

Hewitt, J. (1984) *Self and Society: A Symbolic Interactionist Social Psychology*. Boston, MA: Allyn and Bacon.

Hickson, D.J. (1990) 'Politics permeate', in R.H. Rosenfeld (ed.), *Managing Organizations*. London: McGraw-Hill. pp. 175–81.

Hinton, P. (1993) *The Psychology of Interpersonal Perception*. London: Routledge.

Hirschhorn, L. (1988) *The Workplace Within*. Cambridge, MA: MIT Press.

Hirschhorn, L. (1989) 'Professionals, authority and group life: a case study of a law firm', *Human Resource Management*, 28 (2): 235–52.

Hirschman, A.O. (1970) *Exit, Voice, and Loyalty: Responses to Decline in Firms, Organizations, and States*. Cambridge, MA: Harvard University Press.

Hirschman, A.O. (1977) *The Passions and the Interests: Political Arguments for Capitalism Before its Triumph*. Princeton, NJ: Princeton University Press.

Hochschild, A.R. (1983) *The Managed Heart: Commercialization of Human Feeling*. Berkeley: University of California Press.

Hochschild, A. (1989) *The Second Shift*. New York: Viking.

Hochschild, A. (1997) *The Time Bind: When Work Becomes Home and Home Becomes Work*. New York: Metropolitan Books.

Hoel, H. and Beale, D. (2006) 'Workplace bullying, psychological perspectives and industrial relations: towards a contextualized and interdisciplinary approach', *British Journal of Industrial Relations*, 44 (2): 239–62.

Hofstede, G. (1980) *Culture's Consequences*. London: Sage.

Hofstede, G. (1991) *Cultures and Organizations: Software of the Mind*. London: McGraw-Hill.

Hogg, M. and Vaughan, G. (2002) *Social Psychology*. Upper Saddle River, NJ: Prentice Hall.

Holbrook, M.B. (2001) 'Times Square, Disneyphobia, HegeMickey, the Ricky principle, and the downside of the entertainment economy: it's fun-dumb-mental', *Marketing Theory*, 1 (2): 139–63.

Holman, D., Chissick, C. and Totterdell, P. (2002) 'The effects of performance monitoring on emotional labor and well-being in call centres', *Motivation and Emotion*, 26 (1): 57–81.

Holmes, D. (2001) *Narcissism*. London: Faber.

Holmes, J.G. and Remple, J.K. (1989) 'Trust in close relationships', in C. Hendrik (ed.), *Review of Personality and Social Psychology: Close Relationships*. Beverly Hills, CA: Sage. pp. 187–220.

Holti, R. and Stern, E. (1987) *Distance Working: Origins, Diffusion, Prospects*. Paris: Futuribles.

Hood, C. (1986) *Administrative Analysis: An Introduction to Rules, Enforcement and Organization*. Brighton: Wheatsheaf.

Hovland, C., Janis, I. and Kelly, H.H. (1953) *Communication and Persuasion*. New Haven, CT: Yale University Press.

Howe, I. (1986) 'The spirit of the times: greed, nostalgia, ideology and war whoops', *Dissent*, 33 (4): 413–25.

Howell, J. M. and Shamir, B. (2005) 'The role of followers in the charismatic leadership process: relationships and their consequences', *Academy of Management Review*, 30 (1): 96–112.

Huczynski, A. and Buchanan, D. (2004) *Organizational Behaviour: An Introductory Text*. Harlow: Financial Times/Prentice Hall.

Humphrey, R.H., Pollack, J.M. and Hawver, T. (2008) 'Leading with emotional labor', *Journal of Managerial Psychology*, 23 (2): 151–69.

Hunter, A. and Anderson, D. (1992) 'The rhetoric of social research – understood and believed', *The Journal of the British Sociological Association*, 26: 149.

Huxham, C. (1996) *Creating Collaborative Advantage*. London: Sage.

Hyman, R. (1989) *Strikes*. Basingstoke: Macmillan.

Iacocca, L. (1984) *An Autobiography*. New York: Bantam.

Ibarra, H. (2003) *Working Identity*. Boston: Harvard Business School Press.

Ingersoll, V.H. and Adams, G.B. (1986) 'Beyond the organizational boundaries: exploring the managerial myth', *Administration and Society*, 18 (3): 105–36.

Isaksson, K. and Johansson, G. (2000) 'Adaptation to continued work and early retirement following downsizing: long-term effects and gender differences', *Journal of Occupational and Organizational Psychology*, 73: 241–56.

Jackall, R. (1988) *Moral Mazes: The World of Corporate Managers*. Oxford: Oxford University Press.

Jackson, B. (2001) *Management Gurus and Management Fashions*. London: Routledge.

Jackson, P. (ed.) (1999) *Virtual Working: Social and Organisational Dynamics*. London: Routledge.

Jackson, P.J. and Van der Weilen, J.M. (eds) (1998) *Teleworking: International Perspectives*. London: Routledge.

Janis, I.L. (1972) *Victims of Groupthink*. Boston, MA: Houghton Mifflin.

Jaques, E. (1976) *A General Theory of Bureaucracy*. Oxford: Heinemann.

Jermier, J. (1995) 'Labour process theory', in N. Nicholson (ed.), *Encyclopedic Dictionary of Organizational Behaviour*. Oxford: Blackwell. pp. 283–4.

Jermier, J.M. (1998) 'Introduction: critical perspectives on organizational control', *Administrative Science Quarterly*, 43: 235–56.

Jermier, J.M., Knights, D. and Nord, W.R. (1994) *Resistance and Power in Organizations*. London: Routledge.

Johnson, B. (1990) *The Critical Difference*. Baltimore, MD: Johns Hopkins University Press.

Jones, E.E. (1990) *Interpersonal Perception*. New York: Freeman.

Jones, P.R. (2006) 'The sociology of architecture and the politics of building: the discursive construction of ground zero', *Sociology: The Journal of the British Sociological Association*, 40 (3): 549–65.

Joyce, P. and Woods, A. (1996) *Essential Strategic Management: From Modernism to Pragmatism*. Oxford: Butterworth-Heinemann.

Judge, W.Q., Douglas, T.J. and Kutan, A.M. (2008) 'Institutional antecedents of corporate governance legitimacy', *Journal of Management*, 34 (4): 765–85.

Jun, J.S. (2002) 'New governance in civil society: changing responsibility of public administration', in J.S. Jun (ed.), *Rethinking Administrative Theory: The Challenge of the New Century*. Westport, CT: Praeger. pp. 289–309.

Jung, C.G. (1968) *The Archetypes and the Collective Unconscious*. London: Routledge.

Kahn, R.L., Wolfe, D.M., Quinn, R.P., Snoek, J.D. and Rosenthal, R.A. (1964) *Organizational Stress: Studies in Role Conflict and Ambiguity*. New York: Wiley.

Kanter, R.M. (1977) *Men and Women of the Corporation*. New York: Basic Books.

Kanter, R.M. (1983) *The Change Masters*. New York: Simon and Schuster.

Kärreman, D. and Rylander, A. (2008) 'Managing meaning through branding: the case of a consulting firm', *Organization Studies*, 29 (1): 103–25.

Kärreman, D., Alvesson, M. and Wenglén, R. (2006) 'The charismatization of routines: management of meaning and standardization in an educational organization', *Scandinavian Journal of Management*, 22 (4): 330–52.

Kasper-Fuehrer, E. and Ashkanasy, N. (2001) 'Communicating trustworthiness and building trust in interorganizational virtual organizations', *Journal of Management*, 27: 235–54.

Katz, D. and Kahn, R.L. (1978) *The Social Psychology of Organizations* (2nd edn). New York: Wiley.

Keele, S.M. and Bell, R.C. (2008) 'The factorial validity of emotional intelligence: an unresolved issue', *Personality and Individual Differences*, 44 (2): 487–500.

Keen, S. (1992) *Fire in the Belly: On Being a Man*. London: Piatkus.

Keiser, A. (1997) 'Rhetoric and myth in management fashion', *Organization*, 4 (1): 49–74.

Kelley, H.H. (1972) 'Attribution in social interaction', in E.E. Jones, D.E. Kanouse, H.H. Kelley, R.E. Nisbett, S. Valins and B. Weiner (eds), *Attribution: Perceiving the Causes of Behaviour*. Morristown, NJ: General Learning Press. pp. 1–26.

Kelly, G.A. (1955) *The Psychology of Personal Constructs. A Theory of Personality*. New York: Norton.

Kelly, G.A. (1972) *A Theory of Personality*. New York: Norton.

Kesey, K. (2007) *One Flew Over the Cuckoo's Nest*. London: Penguin.

Kets de Vries, M.F.R. (1990a) 'The organizational fool: balancing a leader's hubris', *Human Relations*, 43 (8): 751–70.

Kets de Vries, M.F.R. (1990b) *Prisoners of Leadership*. New York: Wiley.

Kets de Vries, M.F.R. and Balazs, K. (1997) 'The downside of downsizing', *Human Relations*, 50 (1): 11–50.

Kets de Vries, M.F.R. and Miller, D. (1984) *The Neurotic Organization*. San Francisco: Jossey-Bass.

Kets de Vries, M.F.R. and Miller, D. (1991) 'Leadership styles and organizational cultures: the shaping of neurotic organizations', in M.F.R. Kets de Vries (ed.), *Organizations on the Couch: Clinical Perspectives on Organizational Behaviour and Change*. San Francisco: Jossey-Bass.

Keys, P. (1991) *Operational Research and Systems: The Systemic Nature of Operational Research*. New York: Plenum.

Kharbanda, O.P. and Stallworthy, E.A. (1991) 'Verbal and non-verbal communication', *Journal of Managerial Psychology*, 6 (4): 10–13.

Kilduff, M. (1993) 'Deconstructing organizations', *Academy of Management Review*, 18: 13–31.

Kilduff, M. and Tsai, W. (2003) *Social Networks and Organizations*. Thousand Oaks, CA: Sage.

Kim, D. (1993) 'The link between individual and organizational learning', *Sloan Management Review*, Fall: 14.

King, E.B., Reilly, C. and Hebl, M. (2008) 'The best of times, the worst of times: exploring dual perspectives of "coming out" in the workplace', *Group and Organization Management*, 33 (5): 566–601.

Klein, N. (2000) *No Logo: Taking Aim at the Brand Bullies*. London: Flamingo.

Klein, N. (2002) *Fences and Windows: Dispatches from the Frontlines of the Globalization Debate*. London: Flamingo.

Kleinke, C.L. (1986) *Meeting and Understanding People: How to Develop Competence in Social Situations and Expand Social Skills*. New York: Freeman.

Kline, P. (2000) *The Handbook for Psychological Testing*. London: Routledge.

Knights, D. (1990) 'Subjectivity, power and the labour process', in D. Knights and H. Willmott (eds), *Labour Process Theory*. Basingstoke: Macmillan.

Knights, D. and McCabe, D. (1998) 'When "life is but a dream": obliterating politics through business process reengineering?', *Human Relations*, 51 (6): 761–98.

Knights. D. and Morgan, G. (1993) 'Organization theory and consumption in a post-modern era', *Organization Studies*, 14 (2): 211–34.

Knights, D. and Vurdubakis, T. (1994) 'Foucault, power, resistance and all that', in J. Jermier, W. Nord and D. Knights (eds), *Resistance and Power in Organizations*. London: Routledge. pp. 167–98.

Knights, D. and Willmott, H. (1989) 'Power and subjectivity at work: from degradation to subjugation', *Sociology*, 23 (4): 535–58.

Knights, D. and Willmott, H. (1990) 'Introduction', in D. Knights and H. Willmott (eds), *Labour Process Theory*. Basingstoke: Macmillan.

Knights, D., Murray, F. and Willmott, H. (1993) 'Networking as knowledge work: a study of strategic interorganizational development in the financial services industry', *Journal of Management Studies*, 16 (4): 975–95.

Kolb, D.A. (1985) *Experiential Learning: Experience as the Source of Learning and Development*. Englewood Cliffs, NJ: Prentice Hall.

Kolb, D.A., Rubin, I. and McIntyre, J. (1979) *Organizational Psychology: An Experiential Approach*. Englewood Cliffs, NJ: Prentice-Hall.

Korczynski, M. (2001) 'The contradictions of service work: call centre as customer-oriented bureaucracy', in A. Sturdy, I. Grugulis and H. Willmott (eds), *Customer Service: Empowerment and Entrapment*. Basingstoke: Palgrave. pp. 79–101.

Korczynski, M. (2003) 'Communities of coping: collective emotional labour in service work', *Organization*, 10 (1): 55–79.

Korczynski, M. (2004) 'Back-office service work: bureaucracy challenged?', *Work, Employment and Society*, 18 (1): 97–114.

Korczynski, M., Shire, K., Frenkel, S. and Tam, M. (2000) 'Service work and consumer capitalism', *Work, Employment and Society*, 14 (4): 669–87.

Kornberger, M. and Clegg, S.R. (2004) 'Bringing space back in: organizing the generative building', *Organization Studies*, 25 (7): 1095–114.

Kotter, J.P. (1979) *Power in Management*. New York: Amacon.

Kotter, J.P. (1982) *The General Managers*. New York: McGraw-Hill.

Krebs, S.A., Hobman, E.V. and Bordia, P. (2006) 'Virtual teams and group member dissimilarity: consequences for the development of trust', *Small Group Research*, 37 (6): 721–41.

Kuper, A. (1977) *Anthropology and Anthropologists*. London: Routledge and Kegan Paul.

Kusnet, D. (2008) *Love the Work, Hate the Job: Why America's Best Workers are Unhappier Than Ever*. Chichester: Wiley

Lasch, C. (1980) *The Culture of Narcissism*. London: Abacus.

Lasch, C. (1984) *The Minimal Self: Psychic Survival in Troubled Times*. London: Pan Books.

Latour, B. (1991) 'Technology is society made durable', in J. Law (ed.), *A Sociology of Monsters: Essays on Power, Technology and Domination*. London: Routledge.

Latour, B. (1996) *Aramis or the Love of Technology*. Cambridge, MA: Harvard University Press.

Lave, J. and Wenger, E. (1991) *Situated Learning: Legitimate Peripheral Participation*. Cambridge: Cambridge University Press.

Lawler, J. and Elliot, R. (1996) 'Artificial intelligence in HRM: an experimental study of an expert system', *Journal of Management*, 22 (1): 85–112.

Laws, J.L. (1978) 'Feminism and patriarchy: competing ways of doing social science.' Paper presented at the Annual Meeting of the American Sociological Association, August, New York.

Lazarus, R.S. (2003) 'Does the positive psychology movement have legs?', *Psychological Inquiry*, 14 (2): 93–109.

Leavitt, H. (1951) 'Some effects of certain communication patterns on group performance', *Journal of Abnormal and Social Psychology*, 46: 38–50.

Lee, D. (2000) 'Hegemonic masculinity and male feminisation: the sexual harassment of men at work', *Journal of Gender Studies*, 9 (2): 141–55.

Legge, K. (1995) *Human Resource Management: Rhetoric and Realities*. Basingstoke: Macmillan.

Leidner, R. (1993) 'Fast food, fast talk: service work and the routinization of everyday life', Berkeley, CA: University of California Press.

Lembke, S. and Wilson, M. (1998) 'Putting the "team" into teamwork: alternative theoretical contributions for contemporary management practice', *Human Relations*, 51 (7): 927–44.

Lennie, I. (2001) 'Language that organizes: plans and lists', in R. Westwood and S. Linstead (eds), *The Language of Organization*. London: Sage. pp. 47–66.

Levi, D. (2007) *Group Dynamics for Teams*. London: Sage.

Levine, D.P. (2003) 'The ideal of diversity in organizations', *American Review of Public Administration*, 33 (3): 278–94.

Levinson, D. (1979) *The Seasons of Man's Life*. New York: Ballantine.

Lewin, K. (1951) *Field Theory in Social Science*. New York: Harper & Row.

Lewin, K. (1958) 'Group decision and social change', in E.E. Maccoby, T. Newcomb and E. Hartley (eds), *Readings in Social Psychology*. New York: Holt, Rinehart and Winston.

Lewin, K. and Lewin, G.W. (1948) *Resolving Social Conflicts: Selected Papers on Group Dynamics*. New York: Harper & Row.

Lewis, C. (1985) *Employee Selection*. London: Hutchinson.

Lewis, P. and Simpson, R. (2007) *Gendering Emotions in Organizations*. Houndsmills: Palgrave Macmillam.

Lewis, S. and Cooper, C. (1989) *Career Couples*. London: Unwin.

Lindholm, C. (1988) 'Lovers and leaders: a comparison of social and psychological models of romance and charisma', *Social Science Information*, 27 (1): 3–45.

Linstead, A. and Linstead, S. (eds) (2004) *Organization and Identity*. London: Routledge.

Linstead, S. (1988) 'Jokers wild: humour in organizational culture', in G.E.C. Paton (ed.), *Humour in Society*. London: Macmillan. pp. 123–48.

Linstead, S. (1993) 'From postmodern anthropology to deconstructive ethnography', *Human Relations*, 46 (1): 97–120.

Linstead, S.A. and Grafton-Small, R. (1990) 'Organizational bricolage', in B.A. Turner (ed.), *Organizational Symbolism*. Berlin: de Gruyter. pp. 291–309.

Lipman-Blumen, J. (2005) *The Allure of Toxic Leaders: Why we Follow Destructive Bosses and Corrupt Politicians – and How we can Survive Them*. New York and Oxford: Oxford University Press.

Lippmann, W. (1922) *Public Opinion*. New York: Harcourt, Brace and Company.

Locke, R.R. (1996) *The Collapse of the American Management Mystique*. Oxford: Oxford University Press.

Loe, M. (1999) 'Feminism for sale: case study of a pro-sex feminist business', *Journal: Gender and Society*, 13 (6): 705–32.

Löfstedt, R.E. and Ortwin, R. (1997) 'The Brent Spar controversy: an example of risk communication gone wrong', *Risk Analysis*, 17: 131–6.

Lõmsõ, A.-M. and Sintonen, T. (2006) 'A narrative approach for organizational learning in a diverse organisation', *The Journal of Workplace Learning*, 18 (2): 106–12.

Long, S. (1999) 'The tyranny of the customer and the cost of consumerism: an analysis using systems and psychoanalytic approaches to groups and society', *Human Relations*, 52 (6): 723–43.

Lovelock, J. (1979) *Gaia: A New Look at Life on Earth*. Oxford and New York: Oxford University Press.

Luhmann, N. (1995) *Social Systems*. Stanford, CA: Stanford University Press.

Lukes, S. (1975) *Power: A Radical View*. London: Macmillan.

Lynch, M. (2000) 'Against reflexivity as an academic virtue and source of privileged knowledge', *Theory, Culture and Society*, 17 (3): 26–54.

Maccoby, M. (1976) *The Gamesman: New Corporate Leaders*. New York: Simon and Schuster.

Maccoby, M. (2000) 'Narcissistic leaders: the incredible pros, the inevitable cons', *Harvard Business Review*, 78 (1): 69–77.

MacDonald, R. (ed.) (1997) *Youth, the Underclass and Social Exclusion*. London: Routledge.

Machlowitz, M. (1980) *Workaholics*. New York: Mentor.

MacIntyre, A. (1981) *After Virtue*. London: Duckworth.

Madsen, H. and Ulhøi, J.P. (2001) 'Integrating environmental and stakeholder management', *Business Strategy and the Environment*, 10 (2): 77–88.

Maffesoli, M. (1995) *The Time of Tribes: The Decline of Individualism in Mass Society*. London: Sage.

Mainiero, L. (1989) *Office Romance: Love, Power, and Sex in the Workplace*. New York: Rawson Associates.

Mainiero, L. (1994) 'Getting anointed for advancement: the case of executive women', *Academy of Management Executive*, 8 (2): 53–67.

Majone, G. (1996) *Regulating Europe*. London: Routledge.

Mandelbrot, B.B. (1982) *Fractal Geometry of Nature*. San Franciso: Freeman.

Mangham, I.L. (1986) *Power and Performance in Organizations*. Oxford: Blackwell.

Mangham, I.L. and Overington, M.A. (1987) *Organizations as Theatre: A Social Psychology of Dramatic Appearances*. Chichester: Wiley.

Mangham, I.L. and Pye, A.J. (1991) *The Doing of Managing*. Oxford: Blackwell.

Mann, S. (1999) 'Emotion at work: to what extent are we expressing, suppressing or faking it?', *European Journal of Work and Organizational Psychology*, 8 (3): 347–69.

Mano, R. and Gabriel, Y. (2006) 'Workplace romances in cold and hot organizational climates: the experience of Israel and Taiwan', *Human Relations*, 59 (1): 7–35.

March, J.G. (1991) 'Exploitation and exploration in organizational learning', *Organization Science*, 2 (1): 71–87.

March, J.G. (1997) 'Understanding how decisions happen in organizations', in Z. Shapira (ed.), *Organizational Decision Making*. Cambridge: Cambridge University Press. pp. 9–32.

March, J.G. and Simon, H.A. (1958) *Organizations*. Oxford: Blackwell.

Marcuse, H. (1964) *One-dimensional Man: Studies in the Ideology of Advanced Industrial Society*. Boston: Beacon Press.

Mars, G. (1982) *Cheats at Work: An Anthropology of Workplace Crime*. London: Allen and Unwin.

Mars, G. and Nicold, M. (1984) *The World of Waiters*. London: Allen and Unwin.

Marshall, J. (1984) *Women Managers: Travellers in a Male World*. Chichester: Wiley.

Marshall, J. (1995) *Women Managers Moving On: Exploring Careers and Life Choices*. London: Routledge.

Martin, B. (1978) 'The selective usefulness of game theory', *Social Studies of Science*, 8: 85–110.

Martin, J. (1992) *Cultures in Organizations: Three Perspectives*. Oxford: Oxford University Press.

Martin, J. (1994) 'The organization of exclusion: institutionalization of sex inequality, gendered faculty jobs and gendered knowledge in organizational theory and research', *Organization*, 1 (2): 401–31.

Martin, J., Knopoff, K. and Beckman, C. (2000) 'Bounded emotionality at The Body Shop', in S. Fineman (ed.), *Emotion in Organizations* (2nd edn). London: Sage. p. 130.

Marx, G.T. (1995) 'The engineering of social control: the search for the silver bullet', in J. Hagan and R. Peterson (eds), *Crime and Inequality*. Stanford, CA: Stanford University Press.

Marx, G.T. (1999) 'Measuring everything that moves: the new surveillance at work', in I. Simpson and R. Simpson (eds), *The Workplace and Deviance*. Greenwich, CT: JAI Press.

Marx, K. (1844/1972) 'Economic and philosophic manuscripts of 1844', in R.C. Tucker (ed.), *Marx–Engels Reader*. New York: Norton.

Marx, K. (1975) *Early Writings*. Harmondsworth: Penguin.

Marx, K. and Engels, F. (1848/1972) 'The Communist Manifesto', in R.C. Tucker (ed.), *Marx–Engels Reader*. New York: Norton.

Maslach, C. and Goldberg, J. (1998) 'Prevention of burnout: new perspectives', *Applied and Preventative Psychology*, 7: 63–74.

Maslach, C. and Leiter, M.P. (1997) *The Truth About Burnout*. San Francisco: Jossey-Bass.

Maslow, A.H. (1943) 'A theory of human motivation', *Psychological Review*, 50: 370–96.

Maslow, A.H. (1954) *Motivation and Personality*. New York: Harper and Brothers.

Mason, R.O. and Mitroff, I.I. (1985) *Challenging Strategic Planning Assumptions*. New York: Wiley.

Matthews, G., Zeider, M. and Roberts, R.D. (2002) *Emotional Intelligence: Science and Myth*. Cambridge, MA: The MIT Press.

Maturana, H.R. and Varela, F.J. (1980) *Autopoiesis and Cognition*. Boston: Reidel.

Mayer, J.D., Roberts, R.D. and Barsade, S.G. (2008) 'Human abilities: emotional intelligence', *Annual Review of Pyschology*, 59: 507–36.

Mayer, J.P. (1956) *Max Weber and German Politics*. London: Faber.

Mayo, E. (1949/1975) *The Social Problems of an Industrial Civilization: With an Appendix on the Political Problem* (1st edn). London: Routledge and Kegan Paul.

McCall, M.W. and Kaplan, R.E. (1990) *Whatever it Takes: The Realities of Managerial Decision Making*. Englewood Cliffs, NJ: Prentice Hall.

McClelland, D.C. (1961) *The Achieving Society*. New York: Free Press.

McClelland, D. (1971) *Assessing Human Motivations*. Morristown, NJ: General Learning Press.

McCombs, M.E. and Shaw, D.L. (1972) 'The agenda-setting function of the mass media', *Public Opinion Quarterly*, 36: 176–87.

McConnon, S. and McConnon, M. (2008) *Conflict Management in the Workplace: How to Manage Diagreements and Develop Trust and Understanding*. Oxford: How To Books Ltd.

McCracken, G. (1988) *Culture and Consumption: New Approaches to the Symbolic Character of Consumer Goods and Activities*. Bloomington, IN: Indiana University Press.

McDonagh, P. and Prothero, A. (eds) (1997) *Green Management: A Reader*. London: Dryden.

McDougall, W. (1908/1932) *An Introduction to Social Psychology*. London: Methuen.

McGregor, D. (1960) *The Human Side of Enterprise*. New York: McGraw-Hill.

McKinlay, A. (2002) '"Dead selves": the birth of the modern career', *Organization*, 9 (4): 595–614.

McKinlay, A. and Starkey, K. (eds) (1998) *Foucault, Management and Organization Theory: From Panopticon to Technologies of Self*. London: Sage.

McKinley, W., Mone, M.A. and Barker, V.L. (1998) 'Some ideological foundations of organizational downsizing', *Journal of Management Inquiry*, 7 (3): 198–212.

McLean, A., Sims, D., Mangham, I. and Tuffield, D. (1982) *Organization Development in Transition: Evidence of an Evolving Profession*. Chichester: Wiley.

McNulty, T. (2002) 'Reengineering as knowledge management: a case of change in UK health-care', *Management Learning*, 33 (4): 439–58.

Menzies, I. (1960) 'A case study in functioning of social systems as a defence against anxiety', *Human Relations*, 13: 95–121.

Merton, R. (1968) 'Role of the intellectual in public bureaucracy', in R. Merton (ed.), *Social Theory and Social Structure*. New York: Free Press. pp. 261–78.

Meyer, J.P. and Allen, N.J. (1997) *Commitment in the Workplace: Theory, Research and Application*. Thousand Oaks, CA: Sage.

Meyerson, D., Weick, K.E. and Kramer, R.M. (1966) 'Swift trust and temporary groups', in R.M. Kramer and T.R. Tyler (eds), *Trust in Organizations: Frontiers of Theory and Research*. Thousand Oaks, CA: Sage.

Michels, R. (1949) *Political Parties*. New York: Free Press.

Michelson, G., van Iterson, A. and Waddington, K. (2008) Special Issue on Gossip in/around Organizations. *Group & Organization Management*, 33 (4): 485–8.

Milgram, S. (1974) *Obedience to Authority*. New York: Harper and Row.

Miller, E.J. and Rice, A.K. (1967) *Systems of Organizations: The Control of Task and Sentient Boundaries*. London: Tavistock Publications.

Miller, L.J. and Metcalfe, J. (1998) 'Strategically speaking: the problem of essentializing terms in feminist theory and feminist organizational talk', *Journal: Human Studies*, 21 (3): 235–57.

Mingers, J. (1995) *Self-reproducing Systems: Implications and Applications of Autopioesis*. New York: Plenum Press.

Mintzberg, H. (1973) *The Nature of Managerial Work*. New York: Harper and Row.

Mintzberg, H. (1983) *Structure in Fives: Designing Effective Organizations*. Englewood Cliffs, NJ: Prentice-Hall.

Mintzberg, H. (1993) 'The pitfalls of strategic planning', *California Management Review*, 36 (1): 32–47.

Mitchell, J. (1975) *Psychoanalysis and Feminism*. Harmondsworth: Penguin.

Mitroff, I.I. (1984) *Stakeholders of the Corporate Mind*. San Francisco: Jossey-Bass.

Mitroff, I.I. (2004) *Crisis Leadership: Planning for the Unthinkable* (international edn). Hoboken, NJ and Chichester: Wiley.

Mitroff, I.I. (2005) *Why Some Companies Emerge Stronger and Better From a Crisis: Seven Essential Lessons for Surviving Disaster*. New York: American Management Association.

Moingeon, B. and Edmondson, A. (eds) (1996) *Organizational Learning and Competitive Advantage*. London: Sage.

Moldoveanu, M. and Nohria, N. (2002) *Master Passions: Emotions, Narrative and the Development of Culture*. Cambridge, MA: MIT Press.

Moon, J.A. (2004) *A Handbook of Reflective and Experiential Learning: Theory and Practice*. London: Routledge.

Morgan, C. and Averill, J.R. (1992) 'True feelings, the self and authenticity: a psychosocial perspective', in V. Gecas (ed.), *Social Perspectives on Emotion*. Greenwich, CT: JAI Press. pp. 95–123.

Morgan, G. (1986) *Images of Organization*. Beverly Hills, CA: Sage.

Morgan, G. (2006) *Images of Organization* (updated edn). Thousand Oaks, CA and London: Sage.

Morgan, G. and Sturdy, A. (2000) *Beyond Organizational Change: Structure, Discourse and Power in UK Financial Services*. London: Palgrave Macmillan.

Morita, A. (1987) *Made in Japan*. London: Fontana.

Mouzelis, N. (1975) *Organisation and Bureaucracy*. London: Routledge.

Mowshowitz, A. (2002) *Virtual Organization: Toward a Theory of Societal Transformation*. Westport, CT: Quorum Books.

Moxnes, P. (1999) 'Deep roles: twelve primordial roles of mind and organization', *Human Relations*, 52 (11): 1427–44.

Muir, C. and McFarlin, D. (2005) 'Managing the initial job interview: smile, schmooze, and get hired?', *Academy of Management Executive*, 19: 156–9.

Mullins, L.J. (2002) *Management and Organisational Behaviour* (6th edn). London: Prentice Hall.

Mullins, L.J. (2005) *Management and Organisational Behaviour* (7th edn). Harlow: Financial Times/Prentice Hall.

Mullins, L.J. (2007) *Management and Organisational Behaviour* (8th edn). Harlow: FT Prentice Hall.

Mumby, D.K. and Clair, R. (1997) 'Organizational discourse', in T.A. van Dijk (ed.), *Discourse as Structure and Process*. London: Sage.

Mumford, L. (1934) *Technics and Civilization*. New York: Harcourt Brace and World.

Murray, M. (2001) *Beyond the Myths and Magic of Mentoring*. Chichester: Jossey-Bass/Wiley.

Nahapiet, J. and Ghoshal, S. (1998) 'Social capital, intellectual capital, and the organizational advantage', *Academy of Management Review*, 23 (2): 242–66.

Nash, W. (1989) *Rhetoric: The Wit of Persuasion*. Oxford: Blackwell.

Neale, M. and Bazerman, M. (1991) *Cognition and Rationality in Negotiation*. New York: Free Press.

Neuman, J. and Baron, R. (1998) 'Workplace violence and workplace aggression: evidence concerning specific forms, potential causes and preferred targets', *Journal of Management*, 24 (3): 391–419.

Ng, E.S.W. (2008) 'Why organizations choose to manage diversity? Toward a leadership-based theoretical framework', *Human Resource Development Review*, 7 (1): 58–78.

Nichols, T. and Beynon, H. (1977) *Living with Capitalism: Class Relations and the Modern Factory*. London: Routledge.

Nickson, D. and Warhurst, C. (2007) 'Opening Pandora's box: aesthetic labour and hospitality', in C. Lashley, P. Lynch and A. Morrison (eds), *Hospitality: A Social Lens*. Oxford: Elsevier.

Nkomo, S.M. (1992) 'The Emperor has no clothes: rewriting "race in organizations"', *Academy of Management Review*, 17 (3): 487–513.

Noer, D. (1993) *Healing the Wounds: Overcoming the Trauma of Layoffs and Revitalizing Downsized Organizations*. San Francisco: Jossey-Bass.

Nonaka, I. and Takeuchi, H. (1995) *The Knowledge Creating Company: How Japanese Companies Create the Dynamics of Innovation*. Oxford: Oxford University Press.

Northouse, P.G. (1997) *Leadership: Theory and Practice*. London: Sage.

Nuwer, H. (1999) *Wrongs of Passage: Fraternities, Sororities, Hazing, and Binge Drinking*. Bloomington: Indiana University Press.

O'Leary, M. (2003) 'From paternalism to cynicism: narratives of a newspaper company', *Human Relations*, 56 (6): 685–704.

O'Neill, O. (2002) *A Question of Trust: The BBC Reith Lectures*. Cambridge: Cambridge University Press.

O'Riordan, T. (1981) *Environmentalism*. London: Pion.

Oakley, A. (1972) *Sex, Gender and Society*. London: Temple Smith.

Oates, W. (1971) *Confessions of a Workaholic: The Facts About Work Addiction*. New York: World Publishing.

Oatley, K., Keltner, D. and Jenkins, J. (2006) *Understanding Emotions*. Oxford: Blackwell.

Ogbonna, E. and Harris, L. (2002a) 'Managing organizational culture: insights from the hospitality industry', *Human Resource Management Journal*, 3 (2): 42–54.

Ogbonna, E. and Harris, L.C. (2002b) 'Organizational culture: a ten-year, two-phase study of change in the UK food retailing sector', *Journal of Management Studies*, 39 (5): 673–706.

Olins, W. (1991) *Corporate Identity*. London: Thames and Hudson.

Oliver, R.W. (2004) *What is Transparency?* (1st edn). New York: McGraw-Hill.

Ollilainen, M. and Calasanti, T. (2007) 'Metaphors at work: maintaining the salience of gender in self-managing teams', *Gender Society*, 21 (1): 5–27.

Omi, M. and Winant, H. (1987) *Racial Formation in the United States*. London: Routledge.

Orlikowski, W.J. (1992) 'The duality of technology: rethinking the concept of technology in organizations', *Organization Science*, 3 (3): 398–427.

Orr, J.E. (1987) 'Narratives at work: storytelling as cooperative diagnostic activity', *Field Service Manager*, June: 47–60.

Orr, J.E. (1996) *Talking About Machines: An Ethnography of a Modern Job*. Ithaca, NY: ILR Press/Cornell.

Osborne, D. and Gaebler, T. (1992) *Reinventing Government: How the Entrepreneurial Spirit is Transforming the Public Sector*. Reading, MA: Addison-Wesley.

Osterman, P. and Arthur, M.B. (1998) 'Broken ladders: managerial careers in the new economy', *Administrative Science Quarterly*, 43 (1): 193–6.

Ouchi, W.G. (1980) 'Markets, bureaucracies, and clans', *Administrative Science Quarterly*, 25 (1): 129–41.

Packard, V. (1957) *The Hidden Persuaders*. Harmondsworth: Penguin.

Parker, M. (1992) 'Post-modern organizations or postmodern theory?', *Organization Studies*, 13 (1): 1–17.

Parker, M. (ed.) (1998) *Ethics and Organizations*. London: Sage.

Parker, M. (1999) 'Capitalism, subjectivity and ethics: debating labour process analysis', *Organization Studies*, 20 (1): 25–45.

Parker, M. (2002) *Against Management*. Cambridge: Polity Press.

Pearce, J. and Robinson, R. (1991) *Strategic Management*. Homewood, IL: Irwin.

Pearson, A. (2002) *I Don't Know How She Does It*. London: QPD.

Pease, A. (1997) *Body Language: How to Read Others' Thoughts by their Gestures*. London: Sheldon Press.

Pedler, M., Burgoyne, J. and Boydell, T. (1997) *The Learning Company: A Strategy for Sustainable Development*. Maidenhead: McGraw-Hill.

Pennings, J. (1985) *Organizational Strategy and Change*. San Francisco: Jossey-Bass.

Pervin, L.A. (2004) *Personality: Theory and Research*. Chichester: Wiley.

Peters, P. and van den Dulk, L. (2003) 'Cross-cultural differences in managers' support for home-based telework: a theoretical elaboration', *International Journal of Cross Cultural Management*, 3 (3): 329–46.

Peters, T. and Waterman, R.H. (1982) *In Search of Excellence*. New York: Warner.

Pettigrew, A. (1973) *The Politics of Organizational Decision Making*. London: Tavistock.

Pettigrew, A.M. (1979) 'On studying organizational cultures', *Administrative Science Quarterly*, 24: 570–81.

Pettigrew, A.M., Woodman, R.W. and Cameron, K.S. (2001) 'Studying organizational change and development: challenges for future research', *Academy of Management Journal*, 44 (4): 697–713.

Pfeffer, J. (1992) *Managing with Power*. Boston: Harvard Business School Press.

Phillips, N. and Brown, J. (1993) 'Analyzing communication in and around organizations: a critical hermeneutic approach', *Academy of Management Journal*, 36: 1547–77.

Phillips, N. and Hardy, C. (2002) *Discourse Analysis: Investigating Processes of Social Construction*. Thousand Oaks, CA: Sage.

Phillips, S. (1996) 'Labouring the emotions: expanding the remit of nursing work', *Journal of Advanced Nursing*, 24 (24): 139–43.

Pierce, C.A. (1998) 'Factors associated with participating in a romantic relationship in a work environment', *Journal of Applied Social Psychology*, 28 (18): 1712–30.

Pierce, C.A. and Aguinis, H. (1997) 'Bridging the gap between romantic relationships and sexual harassment in organizations', *Journal of Organizational Behavior*, 18 (3): 197–215.

Pierce, C.A., Byrne, D. and Aguinis, H. (1996) 'Attraction in organizations: a model of workplace romance', *Journal of Organizational Behavior*, 17: 5–32.

Pierce, C.A., Broberg, B.J., McClure, J.R. and Aguinis, H. (2004) 'Responding to sexual harassment complaints: effects of a dissolved workplace romance on decision-making standards', *Organizational Behavior and Human Decision Processes*, 95 (1): 66–82.

Pinder, C.C. (1988) *Work Motivation in Organizational Behavior*. Upper Saddle River, NJ: Prentice Hall.

Pinkse, J. (2007) 'Corporate intentions to participate in emission trading', *Business Strategy and the Environment*, 16 (1): 12–25.

Pitt, M., McAulay, L. and Sims, D. (2002) 'Promoting strategic change: "playmaker" roles in organizational agenda formation', *Strategic Change*, 11 (3): 155–72.

Platman, K. (2004) '"Portfolio careers" and the search for flexibility in later life', *Work, Employment and Society*, 18 (3): 573–99.

Polanyi, M. (1964) *Personal Knowledge*. New York: Harper and Row.

Polkinghorne, D.E. (1988) *Narrative Knowing and the Human Sciences*. Albany: State University of New York Press.

Pollert, A. (1981) *Girls, Wives, Factory Lives.* Oxford: Macmillan.

Pondy, L.R. (1967) 'Organizational conflict: concepts and models', *Administrative Science Quarterly*, 12: 296–320.

Porter, M.E. (1985) *Competitive Advantage.* New York: Free Press.

Porter, M. and van der Linde, C. (1995) 'Green and competitive', *Harvard Business Review*, Sept–Oct: 120–34.

Potter, J. and Wetherell, M. (1987) *Discourse and Social Psychology: Beyond Attitudes and Behaviour.* London: Sage.

Powell, G. (1993) *Women in Management.* Newbury Park, CA: Sage.

Prahalad, C.K. and Hamel, G. (1990) 'The core competence of the corporation', *Harvard Business Review*, 68 (May–June): 57–69.

Prakash, A. (2001) 'Why do firms adopt beyond-compliance environmental policies?', *Business Strategy and the Environment*, 10 (5): 286–99.

Pratt, M.G. and Doucet, L. (2000) 'Ambivalent feelings in organizational relationships', in S. Fineman (ed.), *Emotions in Organizations* (2nd edn). London: Sage. pp. 204–26.

Pratt, M.G. and Rafaeli, A. (2001) 'Symbols as a language of organizational relating work', *Research in Organizational Behaviour*, 23: 93–133.

Pringle, R. (1989) *Secretaries Talk.* London: Verso.

Probst, G. and Buchel, B. (1997) *Organizational Learning: The Competitive Advantage of the Future.* London: Prentice Hall.

Protess, D.L. and McCombs, M.E. (1991) *Agenda Setting: Readings on Media, Public Opinion, and Policymaking.* Hillsdale, NJ: Lawrence Erlbaum.

Pullen, A. and Linstead, S. (eds) (2004) *Organization and Identity.* London: Routledge.

Pullen, A., Beech, N. and Sims, D. (eds) (2007) *Exploring Identity: Concepts and Methods.* London: Palgrave Macmillan.

Purcell, J. (1993) 'The end of institutional industrial relations', *British Journal of Industrial Relations*, 31: 6–23.

Putnam, R.D. (1995) 'Tuning in, tuning out: the strange disappearance of social capital in America', *PS: Political Science and Politics*, 28 (4): 664–83.

Putnam, R.D. (2000) *Bowling Alone: The Collapse and Revival of American Community.* New York: Simon & Schuster.

Putnam, R.D. (2002) *Democracies in Flux: The Evolution of Social Capital in Contemporary Society.* Oxford: Oxford University Press.

Pye, A.J. and Pettigrew, A. (2005) 'Studying board context, process and dynamics: some challenges for the future', *British Journal of Management*, 16: 27–38.

Quinn, R. and Judge, N.A. (1978) 'The office romance: no bliss for the boss', *Management Review*, 67 (7): 43–9.

Radford, K. (1986) *Strategic and Tactical Decisions.* Toronto: Holt McTavish.

Raelin, J.A. (1999) *Work-based Learning: The New Frontier of Management.* Reading, MA: Addison-Wesley.

Raelin, J.A. (2003) *Creating Leaderful Organizations: How to Bring Out Leadership in Everyone.* San Francisco: Berrett-Koehler.

Ragins, B.R. and Kram, K.E. (eds) (2007) *The Handbook of Mentoring at Work: Theory, Research, and Practice* London: Sage.

Rank, O.N. (2008) 'Formal structures and informal networks: structural analysis in organizations', *Scandinavian Journal of Management*, 24 (2): 145–61.

Ransome, P. (2005) *Work, Consumption and Culture: Affluence and Social Change in the Twenty-first Century.* London: Sage.

Ratner, C. and Lumei, H. (2003) 'Theroretical and methodological problems in cross-cultural psychology', *Journal for the Theory of Social Behavior*, 33 (33): 67–94.

Ray, J. (1990) 'The old fashioned personality', *Human Relations*, 43: 997–1013.

Reason, P. and Bradbury, H. (eds) (2001) *Handbook of Action Research: Participative Inquiry and Practice*. London: Sage.

Reed, M. (1999) 'From cage to gaze? The dynamics of organizational control in late modernity', in G. Morgan and L. Engwall (eds), *Regulation and Organization*. London: Routledge. pp. 17–49.

Rees, N. (2008) *A Man about a Dog: Euphemisms and Other Examples of Verbal Squeamishness*. Glasgow: HarperCollins.

Rhodes, C. and Brown, A. (2005) 'Narrative, organizations and research', *International Journal of Management Review*, 7 (3): 167–88.

Rhodes, R.A.W. (1996) 'The new governance: governing without government', *Political Studies*, 44 (4): 652–67.

Riad, S. (2007) 'Of mergers and cultures: "what happened to shared values and joint assumptions?"', *Journal of Organizational Change Management*, 20 (1): 26–43.

Ricoeur, P. (1991) 'Narrative identity', *Philosophy Today*, Spring: 73–81.

Ritzer, G. (1993/1996) *The McDonaldization of Society*. London: Sage.

Ritzer, G. (1998) *The McDonaldization Thesis*. London: Sage.

Ritzer, G. (1999) *Enchanting a Disenchanted World: Revolutionizing the Means of Consumption*. Thousand Oaks, CA: Pine Forge Press.

Ritzer, G. (2001) *Explorations in the Sociology of Consumption*. London: Sage.

Robbins, S.P. (2001) *Organizational Behaviour* (9th edn). Upper Saddle River, NJ: Prentice Hall.

Roberts, J. (2005) 'Management and myths: challenging business fads, fallacies and fashions', *Journal: International Journal of Public Sector Management*, 18 (1): 96–8.

Roddick, A. (1991) *Body and Soul*. London: Edbury Press.

Rodrigues, S.B. and Collinson, D.L. (1995) '"Having fun?": humor as resistance in Brazil', *Organization Studies*, 16: 739–68.

Roethlisberger, F.J. and Dickson, W.J. (1939) *Management and the Worker*. New York: Wiley.

Roethlisberger, F.J., Dickson, W.J. and Wright, H.A. (1939) *Management and the Worker: An Account of a Research Program Conducted by the Western Electric Company, Hawthorne Works, Chicago*. Cambridge, MA: Harvard University Press.

Rokeach, M. (1973) *The Nature of Human Values*. New York: Free Press.

Room, N. (1997) 'Corporate social responsibility', in P. Bansal and P. Howard (eds), *Business and the Natural Environment*. Oxford: Butterworth-Heinemann.

Rorty, R. (1967) *The Linguistic Turn: Recent Essays in Philosophical Method*. Chicago: University of Chicago Press.

Rosen, M. (1985) 'Breakfast at Spiro's: dramaturgy and dominance', *Journal of Management*, 11 (2): 31–48.

Rosener, J.B. (1990) 'Ways women lead', *Harvard Business Review*, 68 (6): 119.

Rosnow, R. (1980) 'Psychology in rumour reconsidered', *Psychological Bulletin*, 87: 578–91.

Ross-Smith, A. and Kornberger, M. (2004) 'Gendered rationality? A genealogical exploration of the philosophical and sociological conceptions of rationality, masculinity and organization', *Gender, Work and Organization*, 11 (3): 280–305.

Rothschild, J. and Miethe, T.D. (1994) 'Whistleblowing as resistance in modern work organizations: the politics of revealing organizational deception and abuse', in J. Jermier, W. Nord and D. Knights (eds), *Resistance and Power in Organizations*. London: Routledge. pp. 252–73.

Rousseau, D. (1995) *Psychological Contracts in Organizations*. Thousand Oaks, CA: Sage.

Russell, B. (1946) *The Philosophy of Bertrand Russell*. Evanston, IL: Library of Living Philosophers.

Ryan, W. (1972) *Blaming the Victim*. New York: Vintage Books.

Sachs, J. and Blackmore, J. (1998) 'You never show you can't cope: women in school leadership roles managing their emotions', *Gender and Education*, 10 (3): 265–79.

Sako, M. (1992) *Prices, Quality and Trust: Inter-firm Relations in Britain and Japan*. Cambridge: Cambridge University Press.

Salaman, G. (1981) *Class and Corporation*. London: Fontana.

Sandelands, L.E. and Boudens, C.J. (2000) 'Feeling at work', in S. Fineman (ed.), *Emotion in Organizations*. London: Sage.

Sartre, J.-P. (1989) *No Exit, and Three Other Plays* (3rd edn). New York: Vintage Books.

Saviz, A.W. and Weber, K. (2006) *The Triple Bottom Line: How Today's Best-Run Companies Are Achieving Economic, Social and Environmental Success – And How You Can Do It Too*. Hoboken, NJ: Jossey-Bass.

Schein, E.H. (1968) 'Organizational socialization and the profession of management', *Industrial Management Review*, 9: 1–15.

Schein, E. (1980) *Organizational Psychology*. Englewood Cliffs, NJ: Prentice Hall.

Schein, E.H. (1985) *Organizational Culture and Leadership*. San Francisco: Jossey-Bass.

Schein, E.H. (1988) 'Organizational socialization and the profession of management', *Sloan Management Review*, Fall: 53–65.

Schein, E.H. (1992) *Organizational Culture and Leadership*. San Francisco: Jossey-Bass.

Schein, E. (1996) 'Culture: the missing concept in organization studies', *Administrative Science Quarterly*, 41: 229–40.

Schein, E.H. (1999) 'Empowerment, coercive persuasion and organizational learning: do they connect?', *The Learning Organization*, 6 (4): 163–72.

Schneider, S.C. and Barsoux, J.-L. (2002) *Managing Across Cultures*. Harlow: Financial Times/ Prentice Hall.

Schon, D. (1971) *Beyond the Stable State*. New York: Random House.

Schor, J.B. (1998) *The Overspent American: Upscaling, Downshifting and the New Consumer*. New York: HarperCollins.

Schumacher, E.F. (1973) *Small is Beautiful: A Study of Economics as if People Mattered*. London: Abacus.

Schumpeter, J.A. (1943) *Capitalism, Socialism and Democracy*. London: Allen and Unwin.

Schwartz, H.S. (1987) 'Anti-social actions of committed organizational participants: an existential psychoanalytic perspective', *Organization Studies*, 8 (4): 327–40.

Schwartz, H.S. (1988) 'The symbol of the space shuttle and the degeneration of the American dream', *Journal of Organizational Change Management*, 1 (2): 5–20.

Schwartz, H.S. (1990) *Narcissistic Process and Corporate Decay*. New York: New York University Press.

Schwartz, H.S. (2001) *The Revolt of the Primitive: An Inquiry into the Roots of Political Correctness*. Westport, CT: Praeger.

Scott, W.R. (2001) *Institutions and Organizations* (2nd edn). London: Sage.

Selmer, J. (2001) 'Adjustment of western European vs north American expatriate managers in China', *Personnel Review*, 30 (1–2): 6–21.

Selznick, P. (1957) *Leadership and Administration*. New York: Harper and Row.

Sen, A.K. (with Harvard Institute of Economic Research) (1991) *Markets and Freedoms*. Cambridge, MA: Harvard Institute of Economic Research, Harvard University.

Senge, P. (1990) *The Fifth Discipline: The Art and Practice of the Learning Organization*. New York: Doubleday.

Sennett, R. (1998) *The Corrosion of Character: The Personal Consequences of Work in the New Capitalism*. New York: Norton.

Sennett, R. and Cobb, J. (1973) *The Hidden Injuries of Class*. New York: Random House.

Sewell, G. and Wilkinson, B. (1992a) 'Empowerment or emasculation: shopfloor surveillance in a total quality organization', in P. Turnbull (ed.), *Reassessing Human Resource Management*. London: Sage.

Sewell, G. and Wilkinson, B. (1992b) 'Someone to watch over me: surveillance, discipline and the just-in-time labour process', *Sociology*, 26 (2): 271–89.

Seymour, D. (2000) 'Emotional labour: a comparison between fast food and traditional service work', *Hospitality Management*, 19: 159–71.

Shapira, Z. (ed.) (1997) *Organizational Decision Making*. Cambridge: Cambridge University Press.

Sharpe, E. (1984) *Double Identity: The Lives of Working Mothers*. Harmondsworth: Penguin.

Shaw, J.D., Duffy, M.K. and Stark, E.M. (2000) 'Interdependence and preference for group work: main and congruence effects on the satisfaction and performance of group members', *Journal of Management*, 26 (2): 259–79.

Sherif, M. (1966) *In Common Predicament: Social Psychology of Intergroup Conflict and Cooperation*. Boston: Houghton Mifflin.

Shotter, J. (1995) 'The manager as practical author: a rhetorical–responsive, social constructionist approach to social organizational problems', in K. Gergen (ed.), *Management and Organizations: Relationship Alternatives to Individualism*. Aldershot: Avebury.

Shrivastava, P. (1995) 'Ecocentric management for a risk society', *The Academy of Management Review*, 20 (1): 118–37.

Shuler, S. and Sypher, B.D. (2000) 'Seeking emotional labor. When managing the heart enhances the work experience', *Management Communication Quarterly*, 14 (1): 50–89.

Simon, H. (1957) *Administrative Behavior*. New York: Macmillan.

Simpson, R. (1998) 'Presenteeism, power and organizational change: long hours as a career barrier and the impact on the working lives of women managers', *British Journal of Management*, 9 (3): 37–51.

Simpson, R., French, R. and Vince, R. (2000) 'The upside of the downside: how utilizing defensive dynamics can support learning in groups', *Management Learning*, 31 (4): 457–70.

Sims, D. (1985) 'Fantasies and the location of skill.' Paper presented at the Standing Conference on Organizational Symbolism, Trento, Italy.

Sims, D. (1987) 'Mental simulation: an effective technique for adult learning', *International Journal of Innovative Higher Education*, 3 (1): 33–5.

Sims, D. (1992) 'Information systems and constructing problems', *Management Decision*, 30 (5): 21–7.

Sims, D. (2003) 'Between the millstones: a narrative account of the vulnerability of middle managers' storying', *Human Relations*, 56 (10): 1195–211.

Sims, H.P. and Lorenzi, P. (1992) *The New Leadership Paradigm: Social Learning and Cognition in Organizations*. Newbury Park, CA: Sage.

Singh, R. (1998) 'Redefining psychological contracts with the US work force: a critical task for strategic human resource planners in the 1990s', *Human Resource Management*, 37 (1): 61–70.

Skellington, R. (1996) *'Race' in Britain Today*. London: Sage.

Skinner, B. F. (1965) *Science and Human Behavior*. Glencoe, IL: Free Press.

Skinner, B.F. (1966) 'An operant analysis of problem solving', in B. Kleinmuntz (ed.), *Problem Solving: Research, Method and Theory*. New York: Wiley. pp. 225–58.

Sklair, L. (1991) *Sociology of the Global System*. London: Harvester Wheatsheaf.

Smelser, N.J. (1998) 'The rational and the ambivalent in the social sciences', in N.J. Smelser (ed.), *The Social Edges of Psychoanalysis*. Berkeley, CA: University of California Press. pp. 168–94.

Smircich, L. (1983) 'Concepts of culture and organizational analysis', *Administrative Science Quarterly*, 28 (3): 339–58.

Smircich, L. and Morgan, G. (1982) 'Leadership: the management of meaning', *Journal of Applied Behavioural Science*, 18 (3): 257–73.

Smith, A. (1997) *Integrated Pollution Control*. Aldershot: Ashgate.

Smith, P.C., Kendall, L.M. and Hulin, C.L. (1969) *The Measurement of Satisfaction in Work and Retirement*. Chicago: Rand McNally.

Smith, R. (1996) 'Business as a war game: a report from the battlefront', *Fortune* (September): 190–2.

Snyder, M. (1987) *Public Appearances, Private Realities: The Psychology of Self-monitoring*. New York: Freeman.

Solomon, J. and Solomon, A. (2003) *Corporate Governance and Accountability*. Chichester: Wiley.

Solomon, R.C. and Flores, F. (2001) *Building Trust*. Oxford: Oxford University Press.

Sorrell, T. and Hendry, J. (1994) *Business Ethics*. Oxford: Butterworth Heinemann.

Speer, S.A. (2005) *Gender Talk: Feminism, Discourse and Conversation Analysis*. Hove: Routledge.

Spencer, A. and Podmore, D. (1987) *In a Man's World*. London: Tavistock.

Sprouse, M. (1992) *Sabotage in the American Workplace: Anecdotes of Dissatisfaction, Revenge and Mischief*. San Francisco, CA: Pressure Drop Press.

Srivasta, S. (1986) *Executive Power*. San Francisco: Jossey-Bass.

Srivasta, S. and Cooperfield, D.L. (1986) 'The emergence of the egalitarian organization', *Human Relations*, 39 (8): 683–724.

Stablein, R. (1996) 'Data in organization studies', in S. Clegg, C. Hardy and W. Nord (eds), *Handbook of Organization Studies*. London: Sage.

Stacey, R.D. (1992) *Managing Chaos: Dynamic Business Strategies in an Unpredictable World*. London: Kogan Page.

Stacey, R.D. (1995) 'The science of complexity: an alternative perspective for strategic change processes', *Strategic Management Journal*, 16: 477–95.

Stacey, R.D. (1996) *Strategic Management and Organizational Dynamics* (2nd edn). London: Pitman.

Starkey, K. (1995) 'Opening up corporate governance', *Human Relations*, 48 (8): 837–44.

Statt, D.A. (1994) *Psychology and the World of Work*. Basingstoke: Macmillan.

Stauber, J. and Rampton, S. (1995) *Toxic Sludge is Good for You!* Monroe, ME: Common Courage Press.

Steers, R.M., Porter, L.W. and Bigley, G.A. (2003) *Motivation and Leadership at Work* (7th edn). New York: McGraw-Hill.

Stein, H.F. (1998) *Euphemism, Spin, and the Crisis in Organizational Life*. Westport, CT: Quorum.

Stein, H.F. (2001) *Nothing Personal, Just Business: A Guided Journey into Organizational Darkness*. Westport, CT: Quorum.

Stott, C. and Reicher, S. (1998) 'How conflict escalates: the inter-group dynamics of collective football crowd "violence"', *Sociology: The Journal of the British Sociological Association*, 32 (2): 353–77.

Strati, A. (1985) *The Symbolics of Skill*. Trento: University of Trento Press.

Strati, A. (1999) *Organization and Aesthetics*. London: Sage.

Strati, A. and Guillet de Montoux, P. (2002) 'Introduction: organizing aesthetics', *Human Relations*, 55 (7): 755–66.

Strauss, A. (1978) *Negotiations: Varieties, Contexts, Processes and Social Order*. San Francisco: Jossey-Bass.

Sturdy, A. (1997) 'The consultancy process – an insecure business', *Journal of Management Studies*, 34 (3): 389–413.

Sturdy, A. (1998) 'Customer care in a consumer society: smiling and sometimes meaning it?', *Organization*, 5 (1): 27–53.

Sturdy, A. (2001) 'Servicing societies? Colonization, control, contradiction and contestation', in A. Sturdy, I. Grugulis and H. Willmott (eds), *Customer Service: Empowerment and Entrapment*. Basingstoke: Palgrave. pp. 1–17.

Sturdy, A. (2004) 'The adoption of management ideas and practices: theoretical perspectives and possibilities', *Management Learning*, 35 (2): 155–79.

Sturdy, A. and Fineman, S. (2001) 'Struggles for the control of affect – resistance as politics and emotion', in A. Sturdy, I. Grugulis and H. Willmott (eds), *Customer Service: Empowerment and Entrapment*. Basingstoke: Palgrave. Pp.135-56.

Sturdy, A. and Fleming, P. (2003) 'Talk as technique – a critique of the words and deeds distinction in the diffusion of customer service cultures in call centres', *Journal of Management Studies*, 40 (4): 753–73.

Sturdy, A., Grugulis, I. and Willmott, H. (eds) (2001) *Customer Service: Empowerment and Entrapment*. Basingstoke: Palgrave.

Swan, J., Scarbrough, H. and Robertson, M. (2002) 'The construction of "communities of prac-tice" in the management of innovation', *Management Learning*, 33 (4): 477–96.

Swan, J. and Scarbrough, H. (2001) *Knowledge Management: Concepts and Controversies*. Oxford: Blackwell.

Sy, T. and D'Annunzio, L.S. (2005) 'Challenges and strategies of matrix organizations: top-level and mid-level managers' perspectives', *Journal: Human Resource Planning*, 28 (1): 39–49.

Syed, J. (2008) 'From transgression to suppression: implications of moral values and societal norms on emotional labour', *Gender, Work & Organization*, 15 (2): 182–202.

Talwar, J.T. (2002) *Fast Food, Fast Track*. Boulder, CO: Westview Press.

Tancred-Sheriff, P. (1989) 'Gender, sexuality and the labour process', in J. Hearn (ed.), *The Sexuality of Organization*. London: Sage.

Tangherlini, T. (1998) *Talking Trauma: Paramedics and their Stories*. Jackson, MS: University Press of Mississippi.

Tannen, D. (1995) *Talking from 9 to 5*. New York: Morrow.

Tansley, C. and Newell, S. (2007) 'A knowledge-based view of agenda-formation in the develop-ment of human resource information systems', *Management Learning*, 38 (1): 95–119.

Taylor, C. (1991) *The Ethics of Authenticity*. Cambridge, MA: Harvard University Press.

Taylor, F.W. (1911) *Principles of Scientific Management*. New York: Harper.

Taylor, P. and Bain, P. (2005) '"India calling to the far away towns": the call centre labour process and globalization', *Work, Employment and Society*, 19 (2): 261–82.

ten Bos, R. and Willmott, H. (2001) 'Towards a post-dualistic business ethics: interweaving rea-son and emotion in working life', *Journal of Management Studies*, 38 (6): 769–93.

Tess, K. (2003) 'The work–life balance in social practice', *Social Policy and Society*, 2 (3): 231–9.

Thatchenkery, T.J. (2001) 'Mining for meaning: reading organizations using hermeneutic philos-ophy', in R. Westwood and S. Linstead (eds), *The Language of Organization*. London: Sage. pp. 112–31.

Thietart, R.A. and Forgues, B. (1995) 'Chaos theory and organization', *Organization Science,* 6 (1): 19–31.

Thomas, A.B. (1993) *Controversies in Management*. London: Routledge.

Thomas, K.W. (1976) 'Conflict and conflict management', in M.D. Dunette (ed.), *Handbook of Industrial and Organizational Psychology*. Chicago: Rand McNally. pp. 889–935.

Thomas, K. (1977) 'Towards multidimensional values in teaching: the example of conflict behav-iours', *Academy of Management Review*, 12: 484–90.

Thomas, W.I. and Thomas, D.S. (1928) *The Child in America: Behaviour Problems and Programs*. New York: Knopf.

Thompson, P. (1990) 'Crawling from the wreckage: the labour process and the politics of produc-tion', in D. Knights and H. Willmott (eds), *Labour Process Theory*. London: Macmillan. pp. 95–124.

Thompson, P. (1993) 'Postmodernism: fatal distraction', in J. Hassard and M. Parker (eds), *Postmodernism and Organizations*. London: Sage. pp. 183–203.

Thompson, P. and Ackroyd, S. (1995) 'All quiet on the workplace front? A critique of recent trends in British industrial sociology', *Sociology*, 29 (4): 615–33.

Thompson, P. and McHugh, D. (2002) *Work Organizations: A Critical Introduction* (3rd edn). Houndsmill: Palgrave.

Tichy, N.M. and Devanna, M.A. (1986) *The Transformational Leader*. New York: Wiley.

Tichy, N.M. and Fombrun, C. (1979) 'Network analysis in organizational settings', *Human Relations*, 32 (9): 923–64.

Toffler, A. (1990) *Powershift: Knowledge. Wealth, and Violence at the Edge of the 21st Century*. New York: Bantam Books.

Toplis, J. and Dulewicz, V. (1997) *Psychological Testing: A Manager's Guide*. London: Institute of Personnel and Development.

Torrington, D. and Hall, L. (1998) *Human Resource Management*. London: Prentice Hall.

Torrington, D., Taylor, S. and Hall, L. (2007) *Human Resource Management.* London: Financial Times/Prentice Hall.

Tourish, D. and Pinnington, A. (2002) 'Transformational leadership, corporate cultism and the spirituality paradigm: an unholy trinity in the workplace?', *Human Relations,* 55 (2): 147–72.

Townley, B. (1993) 'Foucault, power/knowledge and its relevance for human resource management', *Academy of Management Review,* 18 (3): 518–45.

Townley, B. (1994) *Reframing Human Resource Management: Power, Ethics and the Subject at Work.* London: Sage.

Townley, B. (2002) 'The role of competing rationalities in institutional change', *Academy of Management Journal,* 45 (1): 163–79.

Trice, H.M. and Beyer, J.M. (1984) 'Studying organizational cultures through rites and ceremonials', *American Management Review,* 9: 653–69.

Tsahuridu, E.E. (2006) 'Anomie and ethics at work', *Journal of Business Ethics,* 69 (2): 163–74.

Tsoukas, H. (1998) 'Forms of knowledge and forms of life in organized contexts', in R.C.H. Chia (ed.), *In the Realm of Organization: Essays for Robert Cooper.* London: Routledge.

Tsoukas, H. and Hatch, M.J. (2001) 'Complex thinking, complex practice: the case for a narrative approach to organizational complexity', *Human Relations,* 54 (8): 979–1013.

Tuckman, B. (1965) 'Developmental sequence in small groups', *Psychological Bulletin,* 63: 384–99.

Turner, B.S. (2003) 'McDonaldization: linearity and liquidity in consumer cultures', *American Behavioral Scientist,* 47 (2): 137–54.

Turner, B. (ed.) (2009) *Handbook of Globalization Studies.* London: Routledge.

Turner, V. (1969) *The Ritual Process.* Chicago: Aldine.

Turnley, W.H. and Feldman, D.C. (1999) 'The impact of psychological contract violations on exit, voice, loyalty, and neglect', *Human Relations,* 52 (7): 895–922.

Tushman, M.L. and Anderson, P. (1986) 'Technological discontinuities and organizational environments', *Administrative Science Quarterly,* 31 (3): 439–65.

Tyler, M. and Taylor, S. (1998) 'The exchange of aesthetics: women's work and "the gift"', *Gender, Work and Organization,* 5 (3): 165–71.

Tyre, M.J. and Orlikowski, W.J. (1996) 'The episodic process of learning by using', *International Journal of Technology Management,* 11 (7–8): 790–8.

Uchitelle, L. (2006) *The Disposable American: Layoffs and their Consequences.* New York: Knopf.

Van der Vegt, G.S. and Janssen, O. (2003) 'Joint impact of interdependence and group diversity on innovation', *Journal of Management,* 29 (5): 729–51.

Van Dijk, T.A. (ed.) (1997) *Discourse as Structure and Process.* London: Sage.

Van Gennep, A. (2004) *The Rites of Passage* (trans by M. Vizedom and G. L. Caffee). London: Routledge.

Van Maanen, J. and Kunda, G. (1989) '"Real feelings": emotional expression and organizational culture', *Research in Organizational Behaviour,* 11: 43–103.

Vernon, P.E. (1979) *Intelligence: Heredity and Environment.* San Francisco: Freeman.

von Neumann, J. and Morgenstern, O. (1943) *Theory of Games and Economic Behavior.* Princeton, NJ: Princeton University Press.

von Stamm, B. (2003) *Managing Innovation, Design and Creativity.* Chichester: Wiley.

Vroom, V. (1964) *Work and Motivation.* New York: Wiley.

Waldron, V.R., Foreman, C. and Miller, R. (1993) 'Managing gender conflicts in the supervisory relationship: relationship-definition tactics used by women and men', in G. Kreps (ed.), *Sexual Harassment: Communication Implications.* Cresskill, NJ: Hampton Press. pp. 234–55.

Wallemacq, A. and Sims, D. (1998) 'The struggle with sense', in D. Grant, T. Keenoy and O. Cliff (eds), *Discourse and Organization.* London: Sage. pp. 119–33.

Walter, N. (ed.) (1999) *On the Move: Feminism for the Next Generation.* London: Virago.

Walton, C.W. (1988) *The Moral Manager*. New York: Harper.

Walton, E.J. (2005) 'The persistence of bureaucracy: a meta-analysis of Weber's model of bureaucratic control', *Organization Studies*, 26 (4): 569–600.

Walton, R.E. (1991) 'From control to commitment in the workplace', in L.W. Porter (ed.), *Motivation and Work Behavior*. New York: McGraw-Hill.

Wang, M., Liu, R. and Wang, Y. (2001) 'Negotiations with incomplete information', *International Transactions in Operational Research*, 8 (6): 693–705.

Ward, J. and Winstanley, D. (2003) 'The absent presence: negative space within discourse and the construction of minority sexual identity in the workplace', *Human Relations*, 56 (10): 1255–80.

Warhurst, C., Nickson, D., Witz, A. and Cullen, A.M. (2000) 'Aesthetic labour in interactive service work: some case study evidence from the "new" Glasgow', *Service Industries Journal*, 20 (3): 1–18.

Warner, M. and Witzel, M. (2004) *Managing in Virtual Organizations*. London: International Thomson Business Press.

Wasserman, V., Rafaeli, A. and Kluger, A.N. (2000) 'Aesthetic symbols as emotional cues', in S. Fineman (ed.), *Emotion in Organizations*. London: Sage. pp. 141–65.

Watson, T.J. (1994) *In Search of Management: Culture, Chaos and Control in Managerial Work*. London: Routledge.

Watson, T.J. (1996) 'Motivation: that's Maslow, isn't it?', *Management Learning*, 27 (4): 447–64.

Watson, T.J. (2002) *Organising and Managing Work*. Harlow: Pearson Education.

Watson, T.J. (2003) 'Ethical choice in managerial work: the scope for moral choices in an ethically irrational world', *Human Relations*, 56 (2): 167–85.

Watson, T.J. (2008) *Sociology, Work and Industry* (5th edn). London: Routledge.

Weaver, G. and Gioia, D. (1994) 'Paradigms lost: incommensurability vs structurationist inquiry', *Organization Studies*, 15 (4): 565–89.

Weber, M. (1946) *From Max Weber: Essays in Sociology*. London: Routledge and Kegan Paul.

Weber, M. (1947) *The Theory of Social and Economic Organization*. New York: Free Press.

Weber, M. (1958) *The Protestant Ethic and the Spirit of Capitalism*. New York: Charles Scribner's and Sons.

Weber, M. (1978) *Economy and Society*. Berkeley, CA: University of California Press.

Weber, M. (1981) 'Bureaucracy', in O. Grusky and G.A. Miller (eds), *The Sociology of Organizations: Basic Studies*. New York: Free Press. pp. 7–36.

Weick, K.E. (1976) 'Educational organizations as loosely coupled systems', *Administrative Science Quarterly*, 21 (2): 1–19.

Weick, K.E. (1979) *The Social Psychology of Organizing*. Reading, MA: Addison-Wesley.

Weick, K.E. (1985) 'Cosmos vs chaos: sense and nonsense in electronic contexts', *Organizational Dynamics*, Autumn: 50–64.

Weick, K.E. (1995) *Sensemaking in Organizations*. London: Sage.

Weick, K.E. (1998) 'Improvisation as a mindset for organizational analysis', *Organization Science*, 9 (5): 543–56.

Weick, K.E. (2001a) 'Improvisation as a mindset for organizational analysis', in K.E. Weick (ed.), *Making Sense of the Organizations*. Oxford: Blackwell. pp. 284–304.

Weick, K.E. (ed.) (2001b) *Making Sense of the Organizations*. Oxford: Blackwell.

Weick, K.E. (2001c) 'Organizational culture as a source of high reliability', in K.E. Weick (ed.), *Making Sense of the Organizations*. Oxford: Blackwell. pp. 33–44.

Weick, K.E. (2001d) 'Sources of order in underorganized systems', in K.E. Weick (ed.), *Making Sense of the Organizations*. Oxford: Blackwell.

Weick, K.E. and Sutcliffe, K.M. (2001) *Managing the Unexpected: Assuring High Performance in an Age of Complexity* (1st edn). San Francisco: Jossey-Bass.

Weizenbaum, J. (1976) *Computer Power and Human Reason: From Judgement to Calculation*. New York: Freeman.

Welford, R. (1995) *Environmental Strategy and Sustainable Development*. Cambridge, MA: MIT Press.

Welford, R. (1996) *Corporate Environmental Management*. London: Earthscan.

Welford, R. (1997) *Hijacking Environmentalism*. London: Earthscan.

Wenger, E. (1997) 'Practice, learning, meaning, identity', *Training*, 34 (2): 38.

Wenger, E. (1998) *Communities of Practice: Learning, Meaning and Identity*. Cambridge: Cambridge University Press.

Wenger, E. (2000) 'Communities of practice and social learning systems', *Organization*, 7 (2): 225–46.

Werth, L. and Forster, J. (2002) 'Implicit person theories influence memory judgments: the circumstances under which metacognitive knowledge is used', *European Journal of Social Psychology*, 32 (3): 353–62.

Westphal, J.D. and Zajac, E.J. (1998) 'The symbolic management of stockholders: corporate governance reforms and shareholder reactions', *Administrative Science Quarterly*, 43 (1): 127–53.

Westwood, R. and Linstead, S. (eds) (2001) *The Language of Organization*. London: Sage.

Westwood, R. and Rhodes, C. (eds) (2006) *Humour, Work and Organization*. London: Routledge.

White, M.R.M. (2004) *Managing to Change? British Workplaces and the Future of Work*. Houndmills: Palgrave Macmillan.

Whitehead, J. (2000) 'How do I improve my practice? Creating and legitimating an epistemology of practice', *Reflective Practice*, 1 (1): 91–104.

Wilhelm, O. and Engle, R.W. (2004) *Handbook of Understanding and Measuring Intelligence*. London: Sage.

Wilkinson, B. (1996) 'Culture, institutions and business in East Asia', *Organization Studies*, 17 (3): 421–47.

Wilkinson, B., Morris, J. and Munday, M. (1995). 'The iron fist in the velvet glove: management and organization in Japanese manufacturing transplants in Wales', *Journal of Management Studies*, 32 (6): 819–30.

Williams, C.L., Giuffré, P.A. and Dellinger, K. (1999) 'Sexuality in the workplace: organizational control, sexual harassment, and the pursuit of pleasure', *Annual Review of Sociology*, 25 (1): 73–93.

Willis, P. (1990) *Common Culture: Symbolic Work at Play in the Everyday Culture of the Young*. Milton Keynes: Open University Press.

Willmott, H. (1990) 'Subjectivity and the dialectics of praxis: opening up the core of labour process analysis', in D. Knights and H. Willmott (eds), *Labour Process Theory*. Basingstoke: Macmillan. pp. 336–78.

Willmott, H. (1993) 'Strength is ignorance; slavery is freedom: managing culture in modern organizations', *Journal of Management Studies*, 30: 515–52.

Wilson, A. (1991) *Teleworking: Flexibility for a Few*. London: Institute for Employment Studies.

Wilson, D.C. and Rosenfeld, R.H. (1990) *Managing Organizations*. London: McGraw-Hill.

Wilson, F.M. (1995) *Organizational Behaviour and Gender*. London: McGraw-Hill.

Wilson, F.M. (2003) *Organizational Behaviour and Gender* (2nd edn). Aldershot: Ashgate.

Wilson, F. and Thompson, P. (2001) 'Sexual harassment as an exercise of power', *Gender, Work and Organization*, 8 (1): 61–83.

Winefield, A.H., Tiggermann, M., Winefield, H.R. and Goldney, R.D. (1993) *Growing up with Unemployment: A Longitudinal Study of its Psychological Impact*. London: Routledge.

Witz, A., Warhurst, C. and Nickson, D. (2003) 'The labour of aesthetics and the aesthetics of labour', *Organization*, 10 (1): 33–54.

Wolf, N. (1990) *The Beauty Myth*. London: Chatto and Windus.

Womack, J.P., Jones, D.T. and Roos, D. (1990) *The Machine That Changed the World*. London: Macmillan.

Woodward, J. (1965) *Industrial Organization: Theory and Practice*. Oxford: Oxford University Press.

Wright, B. (1998) '"The executioners' song": listening to downsizers reflect on their experiences', *Canadian Journal of Administrative Sciences*, 15 (4): 339–57.

Wright, O. (1980) 'Class and occupation', *Theory and Society*, 9 (1): 177–214.

Yarwood, D.L. (1995) 'Humor and administration: a serious inquiry into unofficial organizational communication', *Public Administration Review*, 55: 81–90.

Yates, J. and Orlikowski, W.J. (1992) 'Genres of organizational communication: a structurational approach to studying communication and media', *The Academy of Management Review*, 17 (2): 299–326.

Yee, A.H. (1992) 'Asians as stereotypes and students: misperceptions that persist', *Educational Psychology Review*, 4: 95–132.

Yelvington, K.A. (1996) 'Flirting in the factory', *Journal of Royal Anthropological Institute*, 2: 313–33.

Yukl, G. (2002) *Leadership in Organizations*. London: Prentice Hall.

Zaleznik, A. (1970) 'Power and politics in organizational life', *Harvard Business Review*, 48: 47–60.

Zaleznik, A. (1977) 'Managers and leaders: are they different?', *Harvard Business Review*, 55: 47–60.

Zane, N.C. (2002) 'The glass ceiling is the floor my boss walks on: leadership challenges in managing diversity', *Journal of Applied Behavioral Science*, 38 (3): 334–54.

Zerbe, W.J, Ashkanasy, N.M. and Härtel, C.E.J. (2006) *Individual and Organizational Perspectives on Emotion Management and Display*. Amsterdam: Elsevier JAI.

Zijderveld, A.C. (1983) 'The sociology of humour and laughter', *Current Sociology*, 31 (1): 1–100.

Zuboff, S. (1985) 'Automate/informate: the two faces of intelligent technology', *Organizational Dynamics*, 14 (2): 5–18.

Zuboff, S. (1988) *In the Age of the Smart Machine*. Oxford: Heinemann.

Zyglidopoulos, S.C. (2002) 'The social and environmental responsibilities of multinationals: evidence from the Brent Spar case', *Journal of Business Ethics*, 36: 141–51.

AUTHOR INDEX

SUBJECT INDEX